COMPREHENSIVE CPA BUSINESS LAW REVIEW

COMPREHENSIVE CPA BUSINESS LAW REVIEW

Edmund F. Ficek, B.A., J.D.
Professor of Business Law
Illinois State University

McGRAW-HILL BOOK COMPANY

New York   St. Louis   San Francisco   Auckland
Bogotá   Hamburg   Johannesburg   London   Madrid   Mexico
Montreal   New Delhi   Panama   Paris   São Paulo   Singapore
Sydney   Tokyo   Toronto

COMPREHENSIVE
CPA BUSINESS
LAW REVIEW

1 2 3 4 5 6 7 8 9 0 DOCDOC 8 9 8 7 6 5 4 3

ISBN 0-07-020671-6

See Acknowledgments on page xvi.
Copyrights included on this page by reference.

This book was set in Caledonia by Better Graphics.
The editor was Kathi A. Benson;
the designer was Jo Jones;
the production supervisor was Phil Galea.
The drawings were done by Danmark & Michaels, Inc.
R. R. Donnelley & Sons Company was printer and binder.

Library of Congress Cataloging in Publication Data

Ficek, Edmund F.
Comprehensive CPA business law review.

Includes index.
1. Commercial law—United States—Outlines, syllabi,
etc. 2. Commercial law—United States—Examinations,
questions, etc. I. Title. II. Title: Comprehensive
C.P.A. business law review.
KF889.3.F48 1983   346.73'07'076   82-17212
  ISBN 0-07-020671-6   347.3067076

*A very special thanks to
my wife,
Teen,
and
my daughters,
Lynn and Kathy,
for their personal support*

CONTENTS

(Nonpublic) Information / Foreign Corrupt Practices Act / Other Important
Sections of the 1934 Act / Sanctions and Remedies under the 1934 Act /
Self-Quiz / Selected Questions and Unofficial Answers

PART EIGHT: THE CPA AND THE LAW

PREFACE

This book is the product of the author's twelve years of experience in preparing candidates to pass the business law section of the Uniform CPA Examination and the extremely useful input from over a thousand students who successfully completed the Illinois State University CPA Business Law Review course during these years. Its purpose is to provide a current, accurate, comprehensive, in-depth, and educationally sound single source of business law subjects to help candidates pass the business law section of the Uniform CPA Examination. The lack of such a comprehensive in-depth *single source* of business law material was recognized by the Board of Governors of the American Institute of Certified Public Accountants (AICPA) when it stated that "Many of the subjects on the examination are normally covered in standard textbooks on business law . . . . However, some subjects either are not included in such texts or are not covered in adequate depth."*

COVERAGE AND SPECIAL FEATURES

Each chapter, excluding the introductory chapter, provides a clear and concise sentence and paragraph outline (review) of rules of law pertaining to each business law topic that can be the subject of a CPA examination question. The common law, federal statutory law, and the Uniform Commercial Code provisions, including the 1972 amendments, applicable to each business law topic are stated and explained in a clear, concise, and well-organized manner. More than a thousand examples, 139 diagrams and flowcharts, and nine tables are used to help candidates see the "big picture" or "overview" as well as the specifics of the subject matter, to draw comparisons between

---

* AICPA, *Business Law—Content Specification Outline*, approved by the AICPA Board of Examiners on August 31, 1981.

related subject matters, and to understand the application of the rules of law to business problems.

The following new and/or expanded material are presented:

1. The 1972 amendments to the Uniform Commercial Code (Chapters 2, 3, and 6)
2. The Federal Bankruptcy Act of 1978 (Chapter 8)
3. The Foreign Corrupt Practice Act (Chapter 19)
4. Products liability of sellers of goods under the Uniform Commercial Code and the common law (Chapter 3)
5. Magnuson-Moss Warranty-Federal Trade Commission Improvement Act (Chapter 9)
6. Bulk transfers (Chapter 9)
7. Issuance, transfer, and registration of investment securities (Chapter 4)
8. Massachusetts (Business) Trusts, associations, Real Estate Investment Trusts (REIT), Subchapter S corporations, individual proprietorships, and joint ventures (Chapter 15)
9. Antitrust (Chapter 17)
10. Federal consumer protection laws (Chapter 9)
11. Accountants' liability under the Internal Revenue Code (Chapter 20)
12. Equal employment opportunity laws (Chapter 18)
13. Casualty insurance, including fire, automobile, and accident, and health insurance (Chapter 12)
14. Documents of title (Chapter 4)
15. Uniform Principal and Income Act (Chapter 11)
16. Administrative law (Chapter 16)
17. Securities Exchange Commission (SEC) Regulation D (Chapter 19)

On August 31, 1981, the AICPA Board of Examiners adopted a new content specification outline for the business law section of the Uniform CPA Examination, to be effective with the November 1983 examination. The outline lists the areas, groups, and topics of business law to be tested as well as the approximate percentage of the total business law examination to be allocated to each area. Until the November 1983 examination, the AICPA will use for examination purposes the generalized listing of business law subjects in its *Information for CPA Candidates* booklet. *Note:* The author clearly indicates at the beginning of each chapter of this book all business law subjects to be taught by the instructor and studied by the candidate before and beginning with the November 1983 Uniform CPA Examination.

ORGANIZATION OF THE BOOK

The subjects in this book are classified into eight major parts and twenty chapters that contain interrelated groups and topics of business law. The parts and chapters within them are arranged in a carefully preselected sequence designed to enable CPA candidates to review and cumulate their knowledge of the subjects in the most efficient and effective way. For example, knowledge of the law of contracts in Part Two facilitates mastery of the law of sales in Part Three; cumulative knowledge of the laws of contracts and sales facilitates mastery of commercial paper in Part Three; and so forth.

The introductory chapter, "How to Write CPA Business Law Examination Questions," provides important information concerning subject-matter coverage, types of questions to be expected, techniques of analyzing and answering business law questions on the Uniform CPA Examination and a summary of the AICPA grading process. Each subsequent chapter of the book consists of the following segments:

1. A sentence and paragraph outline of each business law subject.
2. A self-quiz containing key words and concepts, and questions, each of which is referenced by page number to appropriate coverage in the text.
3. Selected objective questions from previous *Uniform CPA Examinations and Unofficial Answers* or the author's objective questions.
4. Answers to objective questions from previous *Uniform CPA Examinations and Unofficial Answers* or the author's answers to original objective questions.
5. Explanations of answers to objective questions from previous *CPA Examination Critique Manuals* or the author's explanations of answers to original objective questions.
6. Selected essay questions and answers from previous *Uniform CPA Examinations and Unofficial Answers* or the author's essay questions and answers.

SIX METHODS OF EFFECTIVE STUDY AND REVIEW

Because the business law section of the Uniform CPA Examination is almost totally analytical in nature, *memorization* of vocabulary and rules of law alone *will not be sufficient preparation* for the examination. This book provides within each chapter, excluding the introductory chapter, six distinctly different yet extremely important methods by which candidates may obtain the required knowledge base of subject matter and key words and concepts and also develop necessary analytical, problem-solving skills. These methods and their objectives are as follows:

1. *Sentence and paragraph outline interspersed with numerous examples, hypotheticals, tables, and flowcharts.* A careful study of this material will enable candidates to acquire and understand the necessary vocabulary, rules of law, and their application.
2. *Self-quiz.* By reviewing the key words and concepts and the questions in the self-quiz, candidates will perform a second review of the subject matter found in each chapter outline, reaffirm their understanding of key words and concepts, and verify their knowledge of rules of law. Understanding of the key words and concepts will help candidates not only to answer definitional objective questions correctly but also to write precise and accurate answers to problem-essay questions.
3. *Objective questions.* The actual practice of answering the selected objective questions will subject candidates to a third review of the subject matter found in each chapter outline, test their ability to analyze business-legal problems, and reaffirm their ability to apply rules of law to business-legal problems. Answers to objective questions are provided in each chapter.
4. *Explanation of answers to objective questions.* These explanations provide a fourth review of the subject matter found in each chapter, help candidates realize why their analysis of an objective question may have been incorrect, and reaffirm the candidates' knowledge of the rules of law and their application to business-legal problems.
5. *Essay questions and answers.* The actual practice of writing answers to problem-essay questions and comparing them with the reprinted unofficial answers will give candidates practice in analyzing, organizing, and writing answers to selected CPA problem-essay examinations. This also causes the candidates to review the subject matter in each chapter for the fifth time and allows them to practice the correct and effective use of key words and concepts.
6. *Flowcharts and tables.* Nearly 150 flowcharts, tables, and other illustrations are included in this book. These not only aid candidates during their study of the rules of law in each chapter but also provide a sixth and final review of the subject matter.

SUPPLEMENTARY MATERIAL

A detailed and comprehensive Instructor's Manual has been developed to accompany the *Comprehensive CPA Business Law Review* book. It contains suggested additional references, a detailed outline of content, an instructor's checklist for each chapter, suggested lecture-discussion topics for each chapter, transparency masters of many flowcharts and tables appearing in the book, as well as objective and problem-essay questions and answers to be used for testing purposes.

ACKNOWLEDGMENTS

Material from *Uniform CPA Examination—Questions and Unofficial Answers*, copyright © 1972, 1973, 1974, 1976, 1977, 1978, 1979, 1980, and 1981, by the American Institute of Certified Public Accountants, Inc., is reprinted (or adapted) with permission. Material from the *CPA Examination Critique Manual*, copyright © 1977, 1978, 1979, 1980, and 1981, by John Wiley and Sons, Inc., is reprinted with permission. Figures 10-2, 10-4, 10-5, 10-6, and 10-8 in Chapter 10 are reprinted with permission from Edmund F. Ficek, *Real Estate Principles and Practices*, 2d ed., Charles E. Merrill Publishing Company, Columbus, Ohio, 1980, pp. 46, 47, 48, 52, and 99.

I am especially indebted to my colleagues and co-instructors in the CPA Business Law Review course at Illinois State University: Terry Engle, Gary L. Fish, Max Rexroad, Gene Rozanski, and Herbert Seig. Their advice, encouragement, and cooperation have been greatly appreciated.

I would also like to express my thanks for the many useful comments and suggestions provided by colleagues who reviewed this text during the course of its development, especially Professor Simeon Horvitz, Bentley College; Professor Frederick R. Jacobs, University of Minnesota; Professor Elliot Klayman, The Ohio State University; Professor Michael Oldsberg, St. Cloud State University; Professor Bill Shaw, The University of Texas at Austin; Professor Milan M. Smiljanic, Ithaca College; and Professor Jeremy Wiesen, New York University.

For typing, and other assistance with the form of the manuscript, I am indebted to Thelma Wickenhauser, Janet Kuhns, Jill Warren, Mary Beth Favorite, Janet Brandt, Rita Rimac, Margie Wolfe, Jeff Wolz, and Steve Schlueter.

Edmund F. Ficek

COMPREHENSIVE CPA BUSINESS LAW REVIEW

PART
ONE

Introduction

Chapter 1
How to Write CPA Business Law
Examination Questions

CHAPTER

1

How to Write CPA Business Law Examination Questions

The Uniform CPA Examination is one means used by boards of accountancy to measure the technical competence of its CPA candidates. The business law section is one of four areas tested on the examination, and in recent years has become one of the most difficult to pass.

The American Institute of CPAs (AICPA) prescribes the scope of the CPA exam and the level of competence expected of the candidates as follows:[1]

AICPA CONTENT SPECIFICATION OUTLINE: BUSINESS LAW (COMMERCIAL LAW) SECTION

Effective beginning with the November 1983 Uniform CPA Examination:

The Business Law section tests the candidates' knowledge of the legal implications inherent in business transactions particularly as they may relate to accounting and auditing. The scope of the Business Law section includes the CPA and the law, business organizations, contracts, debtor-creditor relationships and consumer protection, government regulation of business, Uniform Commercial Code, and property, estates, and trusts. Many of the subjects on the examination are normally covered in standard textbooks on business law, auditing, taxation, and accounting. However, some subjects either are not included in such texts or are not covered in adequate depth. Important recent developments with which candidates are expected to be familiar may not yet be reflected in some texts. Candidates are expected to recognize the existence of legal implications and the applicable basic legal principles, and they are usually asked to indicate the probable result of the application of such basic principles.

The Business Law section is chiefly conceptual in nature and broad in scope. It is not intended to test competence to practice law nor expertise in legal matters, but to determine that the candidates' knowledge is sufficient to recognize relevant legal issues, recognize the legal implications of business situations, apply the underlying principles of law to accounting

---

[1] Approved by the AICPA Board of Examiners on August 31, 1981, *to become effective with the November 1983 Uniform CPA Examination.*

and auditing situations, and seek legal counsel, or recommend that it be sought, when appropriate.

This section deals with federal and widely adopted uniform laws. Where there is no federal or appropriate uniform law on a subject, the questions are intended principally to test knowledge of the majority rules. Federal tax elements (income, estate or gift) may be covered where appropriate in the overall context of a question.

Business Law—Content Specification Outline

I. The CPA and the Law (10%)
   A. Common Law Liability to Clients and Third Persons
   B. Federal Statutory Liability
      1. Securities Acts
      2. Internal Revenue Code
   C. Workpapers, Privileged Communication, and Confidentiality

II. Business Organizations (15%)
   A. Agency
      1. Formation and Termination
      2. Liabilities of Principal for Tort and Contract
      3. Disclosed and Undisclosed Principals
      4. Agency Authority and Liability
   B. Partnerships
      1. Formation and Existence of Partnerships
      2. Liabilities and Authority of Partners
      3. Transfer of Partnership Interest
      4. Dissolution and Winding Up
   C. Corporations
      1. Formation
      2. Purposes and Powers
      3. Stockholders, Directors, and Officers
      4. Financial Structure, Capital, and Dividends
      5. Merger, Consolidation, and Dissolution
   D. Other Forms
      1. Individual Proprietorships
      2. Trusts and Estates
      3. Joint Ventures
      4. Associations

III. Contracts (15%)
   A. Nature and Classification of Contracts
   B. Offer and Acceptance
   C. Consideration
   D. Capacity, Legality, and Public Policy
   E. Other Defenses
      1. Statute of Frauds
      2. Statute of Limitations
      3. Fraud
      4. Duress
      5. Misrepresentation
      6. Mistake
      7. Undue Influence
   F. Parol Evidence Rule
   G. Third Party Rights
   H. Assignments
   I. Discharge, Breach, and Remedies

IV. Debtor-Creditor Relationships and Consumer Protection (10%)
   A. Bankruptcy
      1. Voluntary and Involuntary Bankruptcy
      2. Effects of Bankruptcy on Debtor and Creditors
      3. Reorganizations

B. Suretyship
  1. Liabilities of Sureties and Cosureties
  2. Release of Sureties
  3. Subrogation and Contribution
C. Bulk Transfers
  1. Publication, Notification, and Other Requirements
  2. Rights of Pre-Sale Creditors
  3. Rights of Post-Sale Creditors
  4. Effects of Security Interests
D. Federal Consumer Protection Legislation
  1. Consumer Credit Protection Act
  2. Magnuson-Moss Federal Warranty Act
  3. Regulation of Deceptive Practices Pursuant to Section 5, Federal Trade Commission Act

V. Government Regulation of Business (15%)
  A. Administrative Law
    1. Activities Subject to Regulation
    2. Functions of Regulatory Agencies
    3. Judicial Review of Agency Decisions
  B. Antitrust Law
    1. Price-Fixing and Other Concerted Activities
    2. Mergers and Acquisitions
    3. Unfair Methods of Competition
    4. Price Discrimination
    5. Sanctions
  C. Regulation of Employment
    1. Equal Employment Opportunity Laws
    2. Federal Unemployment Tax Act
    3. Workmen's Compensation
    4. Federal Insurance Contributions Act
    5. Fair Labor Standards Act
  D. Federal Securities Acts
    1. Securities Registration and Reporting Requirements
    2. Exempt Securities and Transactions
    3. Insider Information and Antifraud Provisions
    4. Short-Swing Profits
    5. Civil and Criminal Liabilities
    6. Corrupt Practices
    7. Proxy Solicitations and Tender Offers

VI. Uniform Commercial Code (25%)
  A. Commercial Paper
    1. Types of Negotiable Instruments
    2. Requisites for Negotiability
    3. Transfer and Negotiation
    4. Holders and Holders in Due Course
    5. Liabilities, Defenses, and Rights
    6. Discharge
  B. Documents of Title and Investment Securities
    1. Warehouse Receipts
    2. Bills of Lading
    3. Issuance, Transfer, and Registration of Securities
  C. Sales
    1. Contracts Covering Goods
    2. Warranties
    3. Product Liability
    4. Risk of Loss
    5. Performance and Obligations

   6. Remedies and Defenses
  D. Secured Transactions
   1. Attachment of Security Agreements
   2. Perfection of Security Interests
   3. Priorities
   4. Rights of Debtors, Creditors, and Third Parties
VII. Property, Estates, and Trusts (10%)
  A. Real and Personal Property
   1. Distinctions Between Realty and Personalty
   2. Easements and Other Nonpossessory Interests
   3. Types of Ownership
   4. Landlord-Tenant
   5. Deeds, Recording, Title Defects, and Title Insurance
  B. Mortgages
   1. Characteristics
   2. Recording Requirements
   3. Priorities
   4. Foreclosure
  C. Administration of Estates and Trusts
  D. Fire and Casualty Insurance
   1. Coinsurance
   2. Multiple Insurance Coverage
   3. Insurable Interest

AICPA EXPLANATION OF THE BUSINESS LAW CONTENT SPECIFICATION OUTLINE

The Board of Examiners of the AICPA explained the intended meaning and use of the business law content specification outline as follows:[2]

The content specification outlines are divided into three levels—areas, groups, and topics, with the following outline notations:
 —Areas by Roman numerals (I. Area),
 —Groups by capital letters (A. Group),
 —Topics by Arabic numbers (1. Topic).
The content specification outlines list the areas, groups, and topics to be tested, and also indicate the approximate percentage of the total test score devoted to each area. Some of the uses of the outlines will be to:
 —Assure consistent subject matter coverage from one examination to the next.
 —Assist candidates in preparing for the examination by indicating subjects which may be covered by the examination.
 —Provide guidance to those who are responsible for preparing the examination in order to assure a balanced examination.
 —Alert accounting educators as to the subject matter considered necessary to prepare for the examination.
The relative weight given to each area is indicated by its approximate percentage allocation. The examination will sample from the groups and topics listed within each area in order to meet the approximate percentage allocation. Generally, the group title should be sufficient to indicate the subject matter to be covered. However, in certain instances, topics have been explicitly listed in order to clarify or limit the subject matter covered within a group.
No weight allocation is given for groups or topics. For example, if there are several groups within an area or several topics within a group, no inference should be drawn about the relative importance or weight to be given to these groups or topics on an examination.
Candidates should realize that clear-cut distinctions as to subject matter do not always exist. Thus, there may be overlapping of subjects in the four sections of the examination. For

---

[2] Approved by the AICPA Board of Examiners on August 31, 1980, *to become effective with the November 1983 Uniform CPA Examination.*

example, Auditing questions often require a knowledge of accounting theory and practice, as well as of auditing procedures. Also, Business Law questions may be set in an accounting or auditing environment, and answers may involve integration with financial accounting and auditing knowledge.

The content specification outlines are considered to be complete as to the subjects to be tested on an examination, including recent professional developments as they affect these subjects. Candidates should answer examination questions, developed from these outlines, in terms of the most recent developments, pronouncements, and standards in the accounting profession. When new subject matters are identified the outlines will be amended to include them and this will be communicated to the profession.

Special note: The subjects to be included in the business law section of the Uniform CPA Examination are now classified into seven major areas of business law; i.e., the CPA and the law, business organizations, contracts, debtor-creditor relationships and consumer protection, government regulation of business, Uniform Commercial Code, and property, estates, and trusts.

To assist the candidate to prepare more effectively for the Uniform CPA Business Law Examination, the AICPA has specified the amount of emphasis on each major area of law that the candidate should expect on the examination. The AICPA has done so by specifying the percentage emphasis to be applied to each major area of business law on each examination; e.g., "The CPA and the Law (10%)," "Business Organizations (15%)," "Contracts (15%)," and so forth. The AICPA has also clearly indicated the specific subjects within each major area of law upon which the candidate may be examined. *The new AICPA content specification outlines are not effective until the November 1983 Uniform Certified Public Accountant Examination.* Candidates should prepare, plan, and conduct their (subject) review accordingly.

ORDER AND FREQUENCY OF SUBJECT-MATTER COVERAGE

In the past, there was no particular order in which the business law subjects were covered on the examination. This was true for the multiple-choice as well as the problem-essay questions. A contracts question may have been followed by antitrust questions, which in turn were followed by several corporations questions, and so on. A particular subject may be covered in a problem-essay question on one examination and in several multiple-choice questions on a subsequent examination. Other subjects have only been examined upon in multiple-choice questions. This author has no reason to believe that this practice will be discontinued.

Table 1-1 illustrates the frequency of coverage of areas of business law on examinations from 1976 to 1982. The subjects have been arranged according to the new AICPA Content Specification Outline. The data provided show the number as well as the type of questions previously used to cover business law subjects on the Uniform CPA Examinations during 1976–1982. The table also lists new subjects added by the AICPA and the new percentage emphasis to be expected for subject-matter coverage of the seven business law areas on CPA examinations beginning November 1983. A review of the table will allow the candidate to make a reasonably accurate determination of the minimum and maximum number of questions (i.e., multiple choice or problem-essay) that would have to be utilized by the AICPA to comply with its percentage requirements for each of the seven major areas of business law. See below for number and types of questions and weight attached to each question for grading purposes.

NUMBER AND TYPES OF QUESTIONS AND VALUE FOR GRADING PURPOSES

The Uniform CPA Business Law Examination consists of multiple-choice and problem-type essay questions. The trend has been to expand the use of multiple-choice questions. In past years, 60 percent of the examination was in the form of multiple-choice questions and the balance was composed of problem-type essay questions. For example, recent examinations have included sixty multiple-choice questions, each with an assigned value of one point and four problem-type essay questions (two-part) each with an assigned value of ten points or a total value of one hundred points for grading purposes.

Objective Questions

The candidate is required to answer three types of multiple-choice questions. The first type presents statements of fact in relation to a specific business situation. The candidate must analyze the facts given, apply basic principles of law to the legal issues presented, and choose the correct solution from the alternatives listed.

The second type of objective question is a combination analytical–true or false question. As in the first type, the candidate must analyze the facts given and apply basic principles of law to the legal issues presented. In addition, the candidate must choose the correct legal conclusion applicable to the facts. In any given question of this type, the legal conclusions may be incorrect, correct and applicable to the facts, or correct and inapplicable to the facts. This type of question permits increased coverage of several different principles of law within a single question.

The third type is a definition question that requires the candidate to choose the appropriate response to complete a statement of a basic principle of law. Ordinary true or false questions have not been included in recent CPA business law examinations, nor are they expected to be included in the future.

The examiners do not specify the subject area of law that is to be used in answering the objective questions. Candidates are expected to analyze the question, determine the applicable area of law, and apply their knowledge of that area of law in answering the questions. Their grades for this part are based on the number of correct answers. If they do not know the answer, they should guess. *It is important that every question be answered.*

Sample questions and answers in this chapter and throughout this book are reprinted from the *Uniform CPA Examination: Questions and Unofficial Answers*, published by the American Institute of Certified Public Accountants.

ANALYTICAL QUESTION

10. Nebor Industries, Inc., manufactures toys which it sells throughout the United States and Europe. Europe accounts for 25 percent of sales. Among its 5,000 employees in 1972 were 490 young males aged 14 and 15 who are paid at a rate of $2.50 per hour. Under the general rules of the Fair Labor Standards Act, Nebor:
a. Was exempt from regulation because less than 10 percent of its employees were children.
b. Did *not* violate the law since it was paying more than minimum wage.
c. Violated the law by employing children under 16 years of age.
d. Is exempt from regulation because more than 20 percent of its sales are in direct competition with foreign goods.
Answer: c

ANALYTICAL–TRUE OR FALSE QUESTION

33. Wanamaker, Inc., engaged Anderson as its agent to purchase original oil paintings for resale by Wanamaker. Anderson's express authority was specifically limited to a maximum purchase price of $25,000 for any collection provided it contained a minimum of five oil paintings. Anderson purchased a seven-picture collection on Wanamaker's behalf for $30,000. Based upon these facts, which of the following is a *correct* legal conclusion?
a. The express limitation on Anderson's authority negates any apparent authority.
b. Wanamaker *cannot* ratify the contract since Anderson's actions were clearly in violation of his contract.
c. If Wanamaker rightfully disaffirms the unauthorized contract, Anderson is personally liable to the seller.

TABLE 1-1 SUBJECT COVERAGE AND FREQUENCY CHART, CPA BUSINESS LAW EXAMINATIONS, 1976–1982

	1982	1981		1980		1979		1978		1977		1976	
	May	Nov	May	Nov	May	Nov	May	Nov	May	Nov	May	Nov	May
I. The CPA and the law (10%, effective November 1983) (entitled accountants' legal responsibility prior to November 1983)	E	E	6MC	E	½E	E	E	5MC	E	5MC	E	5MC	½E
II. Business organizations (15%, effective November 1983)													
Agency	3MC	5MC	6MC	5MC	½E	3MC	2MC	⅔E	6MC	E	4MC	5MC	4MC
Corporations	6MC	1MC ½E	8MC	1MC ½E	8MC	E	E	6MC	E	½E	4MC	E	6MC
Partnerships	4MC	7MC	E	6MC	½E	7MC	E	5MC	E	5MC	E	7MC	E
Other forms (new subject to be added, effective November 1983)													
Individual proprietorships													
Trusts and estates													
Joint ventures													
Associations													
III. Contracts (15%, effective November 1983)	4MC E	11MC	7MC	2MC E	E	5MC	7MC	4MC ½E	9MC	E	4MC	6MC	11MC
IV. Debtor and creditor relationship (10%, effective November 1983)													
Bankruptcy	6MC	½E	5MC	½E	4MC		6MC	½E	4MC	5MC	½E	3MC	4MC
Suretyship	3MC	6MC	5MC	½E	5MC	E	4MC	4MC	2MC	4MC	3MC	6MC	4MC
Federal consumer protection legislation (new subject to be added, effective November 1983)													
Bulk transfers (examined under sales prior to November 1983)	1M	½E											

V. Government regulation of business (15%, effective November 1983)

Topic													
Administrative law (new subject to be added, effective November 1983)													
Antitrust law	7MC	4MC $\frac{1}{2}$E	3MC	1MC $\frac{1}{2}$E	4MC	7MC	3MC	4MC	4MC	E	2MC	2MC	
Regulation of employment													
Equal opportunity laws (new subject added, effective November 1983)													
Workmen's compensation			1MC	1MC		1MC	1MC	$\frac{1}{3}$E	1MC		1MC	1MC	
Federal Insurance Contributions Act (FICA) (Social Security) including the Federal Unemployment Tax Act		1MC	1MC	1MC	2MC	1MC				2MC		1MC	
Fair Labor Standards Act (FLSA)	1MC		1MC	1MC					1MC	1MC	2MC		
Federal Securities Regulations Acts													
Securities Act of 1933	E	$\frac{1}{2}$E	$\frac{1}{2}$E	2MC	$\frac{1}{2}$E	2MC	1MC	$\frac{1}{2}$E	2MC	2MC $\frac{1}{4}$E	2MC	$\frac{1}{3}$E	2MC
Securities Exchange Act of 1934		$\frac{1}{2}$E	$\frac{1}{2}$E	4MC		2MC	2MC	1MC $\frac{1}{2}$E		2MC	2MC	$\frac{2}{3}$E	

Symbols: Fraction = portion of essay; Number = number of questions; MC = multiple choice; E = essay.

TABLE 1-1 (Continued)

	1982	1981		1980		1979		1978		1977		1976	
	May	Nov	May	Nov	May	Nov	May	Nov	May	Nov	May	Nov	May
VI. Uniform Commercial Code (25%, effective November 1983)													
Commercial Paper	9MC	9MC	E	10MC	8MC	E	8MC	7MC	E	9MC	7MC	E	8MC
Documents of title and investment securities (new subject to be added, effective November 1983)													
Sales	3MC E	$\frac{1}{2}$E	7MC	6MC	7MC	5MC	8MC	3MC $\frac{1}{2}$E	8MC	1MC E	6MC	6MC	E
Secured transactions	3MC	6MC	E	8MC	$\frac{2}{3}$E	5MC	5MC	$\frac{1}{2}$E	2MC	4MC	$\frac{1}{2}$E	$\frac{1}{3}$E	E
VII. Property, estates, and trusts (10%, effective November 1983)													
Real and personal property	4MC	$\frac{1}{2}$E	3MC	2MC	3MC $\frac{1}{3}$E	5MC	E	3MC	4MC	2MC	7MC	5MC	4MC
Mortgages (examined under "real and personal property" prior to November 1983)													
Administration of estates or trusts	3MC	4MC	3MC	5MC	4MC	4MC		5MC	4MC	1MC	1MC	1MC	$\frac{1}{2}$E
Fire and casualty insurance	3MC	5MC	1MC	2MC	3MC	3MC	1MC	2MC	3MC	1MC	2MC	$\frac{1}{3}$E	2MC
Life insurance (will be deleted, effective November 1983)		1MC	3MC	3MC	2MC		2MC	1MC		2MC	3MC	$\frac{1}{3}$E	1MC

Symbols: Fraction = portion of essay; Number = number of questions; MC = multiple choice; E = essay.

d. Neither Wanamaker *nor* Anderson is liable on the contract since the seller was obligated to ascertain Anderson's authority.

Answer: c

43. If an employer carried workmen's compensation coverage on his employees, an injured employee would:

a. Probably be covered even if injury was caused by a coworker.

b. *Not* be covered if the injury was caused by grossly negligent maintenance by the employer.

c. Probably not be covered if the injury was due to a violation of plant rules in operating the machine.

d. Be covered if the employee was driving to work from his home.

Answer: a

Problem-solving technique for objective questions Decide upon a problem-solving technique ("a plan of attack") for objective questions far in advance of the examination date, and practice the technique on objective questions from past examinations. For your reference, numerous objective questions from past examinations are reprinted at the end of each of the remaining chapters in this book.

There is no perfect problem-solving technique! Choose one that is most effective for you. The following technique is provided as an illustration:

1. Answer the questions in the order that they appear on the examination.
2. Read the choices *before* reading the question.
3. Read the question carefully. Ascertain and note the legal identity of all parties, subject matter, transactions, and communications.
4. Resolve the legal issue or issues presented by the facts in the question and reach a conclusion.
5. Reread the choices and compare each one with your conclusion.
6. Decide on the best answer.
7. If you are absolutely certain of the best answer to a question, mark your answer on the answer sheet. If you are not, do not mark your answer on the answer sheet but proceed to the next question and repeat steps 2 to 6 above. Continue the process throughout all of the multiple-choice questions. Return to your first unanswered question and repeat the entire process. For your final effort, reread all unanswered questions again utilizing steps 2 to 6 above, make an "educated guess" for each question, and mark your answer on the answer sheet.
8. Check your answer sheet carefully to make sure that you have marked an answer for every question.

Problem-Essay Questions

The multipart problem-essay questions pertain to designated business situations. They involve various types of legal controversies and each requires a decision. The primary objective of these questions is to determine whether candidates have acquired sufficient knowledge and understanding of required business law subjects, whether they can identify a general legal problem in a given business situation, and whether they recognize the specific legal issues involved. Candidates must demonstrate in essay form their ability to apply the applicable rules of law to the legal issues presented and thereby decide the controversy. Each answer must contain a statement of reasoning the candidate has used.

Reading the problem-essay question Be absolutely certain that you *understand the facts: who the parties are, what they did, and what happened to them.* It is very important that you pay attention to the question that is asked. You must understand it to know what you are required to decide. Almost always you will be required to decide the rights and/or liabilities of one or more of the parties to the transaction. It is sometimes helpful to make a diagram that explains the transaction and identifies the parties.

Read the whole problem through at least twice. Be sure you have not misread the facts or misunderstood the question. Never assume details that are neither stated nor inferable from the stated facts.

What the examiner will be looking for in your answer to the problem-essay question No two individual examiners are in absolute agreement as to what constitutes a perfect answer to a problem-essay question. Nevertheless, there are certain basic aspects of a "good" answer that all law examiners look for when they grade a paper.

Your answer is expected to be an *answer*. You will be given a set of facts and a question about these facts. You must answer the question that is asked. A "yes" or "no" response alone, however, is not sufficient. The examiner expects you to support your conclusions with rules and principles as they apply to the issues.

In the first instance, the examiner will probably look to see whether you have recognized and discussed all the issues involved in the problem. Next, he or she will ascertain whether or not you have stated the rules on which you are basing your decision. Lastly, the examiner looks for your application of the applicable rules to the facts as stated in the problem.

In summary, a "good" answer to a problem-essay question should include:

1. A proper reference to the applicable question, e.g., "5, part a"
2. A statement of conclusion or conclusions and ultimate decision to the legal issues in the problem
3. Evidence of recognition of one or all of the legal issues raised in the problem
4. Statement of the laws applicable to the legal issues
5. Evidence of the application of laws to the legal issues; i.e., the candidate's reasoning during analysis of the legal issues

Any one part of a problem-essay question may contain one or more legal issues. A *legal issue* is a legal question presented by the facts of the problem that must be resolved in order to determine the rights and/or duties of parties and/or to establish the character and extent of their liabilities. In many instances, the "requirements" after the statement of facts reveal the legal issue or issues to be decided. For example:

1. "What are the potential liabilities of a CPA tax return preparer under the Internal Revenue Code?"
2. "Are Arco Products, Inc., and Havalon Company in violation of the provisions of the Sherman Act? Explain."
3. "Is Ramirez liable as a surety?"
4. "If Ramirez was required as a surety to pay the debtor, what is her recourse against Alvira and Laurenz, the cosureties?"
5. "Does a contract exist? Explain."
6. "Did title and risk of loss pass to Bazik at the time of the 'sale'?"

In other instances, the legal issues are not discernible from the requirements. For example:

1. "Is Claron liable to the bank?"
2. "Discuss the rights and liabilities of Aerospace Corp., Bruno, Saporo, and Atheon."
3. "Do Fanslow and Angelo have any liability under the above-stated facts?"
4. "Can the creditors of Farro recover without establishing Farro's actual knowledge of the falsity?"

5. "What are the legal implications of the above facts? Set forth your reasons for any conclusions stated."

Problem-solving techniques for problem-essay questions   Even though one or more of the legal issues may be revealed in the "requirements," it is important to have available and utilize an effective problem-solving technique for problem-essay questions. When analyzing a problem-essay question, always start by first reading the requirements, i.e., the question asked or the statement of what you are to decide. You must then systematically determine what the answer depends upon in light of the facts given, the legal issues raised by the facts, and the applicable principles of law you have studied. In other words, resolve all subordinate issues of law and fact that must be decided in order to reach and support your conclusion on the major legal issue or issues. The following problem-solving technique for problem-essay questions is suggested:

1. Read the requirements carefully. Ascertain and keep in mind what you are asked to decide.
2. Understand the facts. Ascertain the legal identity of the following facts in the question. This should clearly identify the business law subject involved and the legal issue or issues in the problem.
   a. Parties: e.g., agent, surety, offeror, acceptor, mortgagor
   b. Subject matter: e.g., goods, real estate, services, mortgage
   c. Transactions: e.g., sale, gift, secured transaction, assignment, negotiation, lease fraud
   d. Communications: e.g., offer, acceptance, revocation, counteroffer
3. Write the legal name of the parties, subject matter, transactions, and communications immediately above each of them in the problem itself or on either side of the problem in the margin. This procedure will provide "key words and concepts" for use in your answer. *Note:* This can be done in conjunction with the performance of step 2.
4. Recall and review the applicable business law subject.
5. Identify each legal issue that must be resolved in order for you to respond to what you are required to decide.
6. Organize (outline) your answer on a piece of scrap paper.
7. Write your answer in sentence and paragraph form.

Ordinarily, each problem-essay question will involve only one subject area of the law. However, a question or any part of a question may involve several related or unrelated subject areas. For example, the law of contracts may be included with the law of sale of goods in one factual situation. Likewise, the law in relation to deeds, real estate mortgages, and accountant's legal responsibility may be applicable to a single factual situation. On the other hand, one part of a two-part question may involve partnerships and the other corporations. To help illustrate the form, composition, and requirements of a problem-essay question, the following AICPA question and unofficial answer are provided.

MAY 1981 (Estimated time: 15 to 20 minutes)

Part a.   Davis and Clay are licensed real estate brokers. They entered into a contract with Wilkins, a licensed building contractor, to construct and market residential housing. Under the terms of the contract, Davis and Clay were to secure suitable building sites, furnish prospective purchasers with plans and specifications, pay for appliances and venetian blinds and drapes, obtain purchasers, and assist in arranging for financing. Wilkins was to furnish the labor, material, and supervision necessary to construct the houses. In accordance with the agreement, Davis and Clay were to be reimbursed for their expenditures. Net profits from the sale of each house were to be divided 80% to Wilkins, 10% to Davis, and 10% to Clay. The parties also agreed that each was to be free to carry on his own business simultaneously and that such action would not be considered a conflict of interest. In addition, the agreement provided that their relationship was as independent contractors, pooling their interests for the limited purposes described above.

Ace Lumber Company sold lumber to Wilkins on credit from mid-1980 until February 1981. Ace did not learn of the agreement between Davis, Clay and Wilkins until April 1981, when an involuntary bankruptcy petition was filed against Wilkins and an order for relief entered. Ace Lumber has demanded payment from Davis and Clay. The lumber was used in the construction of a house pursuant to the agreement between the parties.

Required Answer the following, setting forth reasons for any conclusions stated.

In the event Ace sues Davis and Clay as well as Wilkins, will Ace prevail? Discuss the legal basis upon which Ace will rely in asserting liability.

Unofficial answer Yes, Ace will prevail. A partnership did exist and the parties are jointly liable. The legal basis upon which Ace will seek recovery is that a partnership exists among Wilkins, Davis, and Clay. If the parties are deemed partners among themselves, then Ace can assert liability against such partnership and against the individual partners as members thereof, since they are jointly liable for such partnership obligations.

The Uniform Partnership Act, section 7, provides rules for determining the existence of a partnership. Although it is frequently stated that the intent of the parties is important in determining the existence of a partnership relationship, this statement must be significantly qualified: It is not the subjective intent of the parties that is important when they categorically state that they do not wish to be considered as partners. If much effect were given to such statements, partnership liability could easily be shed. Further, the party dealing with the partnership need not in fact rely upon the existence of a partnership. Thus, the fact that Ace did not learn of the Davis, Clay, Wilkins agreement until after he had extended credit does not preclude him from asserting partnership liability.

The bearing of section 7 of the Uniform Partner-ship Act on this case can be examined as follows. First, joint, common, or part ownership of property of any type does not of itself establish a partnership. It is only one factor to be considered and it was present to a limited extent in this case. Second, the sharing in gross returns does not of itself establish a partnership, but its importance is rendered moot as a result of the profit-sharing arrangement between the parties. Finally, and the key factor in partner-ship determination, is the receipt of profits: The act states "the receipt by a person of a share of the profits of a business is prima facie evidence that he is a partner in the business. . . ."

Sharing in profits is prima facie evidence of the existence of a partnership. The defendants (Davis and Clay) must affirmatively rebut this prima facie case against them or lose. There do not appear to be facts sufficient to accomplish this.

Part b. Lawler is a retired film producer. She had a reputation in the film industry for aggressiveness and shrewdness; she was also considered somewhat overbearing. Cyclone Artistic Film Productions, a growing independent producer, obtained the film rights to "Claws," a recent best seller. Cyclone has decided to syndicate the production of "Claws." Therefore, it created a limited partnership, Claws Productions, with Harper, Von Hinden, and Graham, the three ranking executives of Cyclone, serving as general partners. The three general partners each contributed $50,000 to the partner-ship capital. One hundred limited partnership interests were offered to the public at $50,000 each. Lawler was offered the opportunity to invest in the venture. Intrigued by the book and restless in her retirement, she decided to purchase 10 limited partnership interests for $500,000. She was the largest purchaser of the limited partnership inter-ests of Claws Productions. All went well initially for the venture, but midway through production, some major problems arose. Lawler, having nothing else to do and having invested a considerable amount of money in the venture, began to take an increasingly active interest in the film's production.

She frequently began to appear on the set and made numerous suggestions on handling the vari-ous problems that were encountered. When the production still seemed to be proceeding with diffi-culty, Lawler volunteered her services to the gen-eral partners who as a result of her reputation and financial commitment to "Claws" decided to invite her to join them in their executive deliberations.

This she did and her personality insured an active participation.

"Claws" turned out to be a box office disaster and its production costs were considered to be somewhat extraordinary even by Hollywood standards. The limited partnership is bankrupt and the creditors have sued Claws Productions, Harper, Von Hinden, Graham, and Lawler.

Required Answer the following, setting forth reasons for any conclusions stated.

What are the legal implications and liabilities of *each* of the parties as a result of the above facts?

Unofficial answer The limited partnership, the general partners, and Lawler are all jointly liable for the debts of Claws Productions.

Claws Productions limited partnership is liable and must satisfy the judgment to the extent it has assets. Harper, Von Hinden, and Graham are liable for the unpaid debts of the limited partnership. An interesting problem posed by the fact situation is Lawler's liability. The general rule, in fact the very basis for the existence of the limited partnership, is that the limited partner is not liable beyond its capital contribution. However, a notable exception contained in section 7 of the Uniform Limited Partnership Act applies to the facts presented here: "A limited partner shall not become liable as a general partner unless, in addition to the exercise of his rights and powers as a limited partner, he takes part in the control of the business."

The statutory language covers the facts stated. Lawler assumed a managerial role vis a vis the partnership and in the process became liable as a general partner.

Planning your answer Before writing, take a few minutes to outline and establish the order in which you will present your answer. It is not a good idea to write in a disorganized manner, with unconnected sentences and paragraphs, and then attempt to organize them later by crossing out, rewriting, or inserting arrows. This procedure is almost certain to have a negative effect on the examiner. A few minutes spent in organization will save the many minutes you would otherwise need for rewriting your answer.

Determine the logical sequence of the issues presented in the problem and be prepared to discuss them in that order. Remember, actual writing should take much less time than thinking.

Writing your answer Do not fall prey to the urge to start writing immediately without a thorough examination of the factual situation presented. The examination instructions indicate the estimated time for each question. Try to stay on schedule and avoid spending more than the allotted time for any one question. Discipline yourself to follow a definite procedure in analyzing and writing your answer. You should spend approximately half of the allotted time thinking about the problem and planning your answer before you begin writing.

Remember, the examiner is not a mind reader. You must demonstrate that you have properly classified the legal problem involved in the business transaction, that you have decided the main question asked, and that you have resolved all subordinate legal issues.

Discuss each legal issue, indicating briefly what it is and why it has to be considered. Set forth the general rules of law that apply to the issue or issues. In short, tell the examiner what the issue or issues are, what the applicable rules are, and why they apply. Do not waste time restating the facts in the given problem.

The following answer-writing plan and procedure illustrates the process involved in writing a "good" answer to a legal problem-type essay question:

1. Reference the question number to which your answer applies (1, part a; 4, part b; etc.).
2. State the conclusion that you have reached; e.g., "A contract exists"; "The issuer is liable for damages under Rule 10b of the Securities Exchange Act of 1934"; "Jones

is a surety"; or "The agreement is in violation of the Sherman Act as a conspiracy in restraint of trade."

3. State the law that you applied to the facts in order to reach your conclusion; e.g., a surety is any person who makes a promise to answer for the debt or default of another.

4. Indicate how you applied the law to the facts; e.g., Jones, a partner, having agreed to personally "back up" the debts of the partnership if its creditors granted an extension of time, became a surety.

5. Use key words and concepts correctly when stating the law you applied to resolve the legal issue.

6. Use short, simple sentences in brief paragraph form; e.g., "Ludwig is not entitled to compensation for services rendered as a director from the ABC Corporation. Unless expressly agreed upon, a director is not entitled to be paid for her services. The facts do not indicate any agreement between Ludwig and ABC Corporation for compensation for services rendered and therefore Ludwig is not entitled to any compensation."

7. Analyze all legal issues presented in the problem. *Do not* state any law that *is not* applicable to the problem. You *are* required to solve the problem! You *are not* to write an essay on a broad area of law!

Make your answer readable. It is your task to make your ideas clear to the examiner. Remember, you are trying to show that you understood the problem and are aware of the principles of law that apply to it.

If you "draw a blank" or are not certain of the "correct" answer, analyze the problem-essay to the best of your ability, decide which legal issues you believe are involved, and write a clear, concise, and organized answer to the problem. Writing *something* down as an answer may make the difference between a passing and failing grade on the examination.

KEY TO EXAMINATION SUCCESS

It is recommended that the candidate carefully prepare a good subject review schedule. The schedule should allocate an appropriate amount of study time for every business law subject that may be included on the examination. Candidates should provide for and include within their schedules an adequate time-period of study and review prior to the examination. The amount of study time to be scheduled for each business law subject should be influenced by the following factors:

1. For CPA business law examinations prior to November 1983, the conclusions reached by the candidate from a careful review of Table 1-1.

2. For CPA business law examinations in November 1983 and thereafter, the American Institute of Certified Public Accountants (AICPA) Business Law Content Specification Outline that indicates the subject matter content and the relative percentage of coverage of each major business law area on the business law examination that the candidate should expect on the AICPA Uniform CPA Examination beginning in November of 1983. Refer to the AICPA Business Law Content Specification Outline reprinted earlier in this chapter.

3. The number, content, and types of courses in the legal environment of business, government regulation of business, and business law taken by candidates during their school, college, or university career.

4. The conclusions reached from the candidates' very careful and objective review of their competency in any one or all relevant business law subjects.

"Cramming" for the CPA business law examination is strongly discouraged because it usually involves only the process of memorization. Rather than rely on memorization alone, the candidates should strive to gain an understanding of the subject matter and develop the ability to accurately analyze the questions and correctly apply the relevant business law to the legal issues presented.

The subject-review schedule mentioned above may provide for a course of self-study to include the completion of a formal, professionally developed college, university, or privately sponsored CPA business law review course.

It is important that candidates exert maximum effort to study effectively according to the time frame established by their subject-review schedules. An adequate, accurate knowledge and understanding of business law subjects and vocabulary is one of the most important "keys" to examination success. Without such knowledge, confidence, problem-solving techniques, and writing skills are of very little or no value. The following list of factors provides a guide to examination success:

1. A subject-review schedule that establishes an adequate period of time for study and review. A period of three to six months would not be excessive.
2. Maximum possible effective study and review according to the subject-review schedule.
3. Confidence (obtained by adequate preparation).
4. Understanding the requirements of each question.
5. Understanding the facts of the problem.
6. Adequate knowledge and understanding of the business law subjects.
7. Knowledge and application of problem-solving techniques:
    a. Recognition of all legal issues raised by the facts of the problem
    b. Use of law to solve these legal issues
8. A good answer format and sequence for the problem-essay questions:
    a. The answer referenced to the question
    b. Legal conclusion or conclusions
    c. Law that is applicable to the legal issue or issues
    d. Statement of how law was applied to the facts to resolve the legal issues
9. Clarity, accuracy, conciseness of expression in sentence and paragraph form.
10. Careful proofreading and editing of answer.

AICPA INSTRUCTIONS TO CANDIDATES

The specific instructions to the candidate found on the examination booklet include the required method of arranging the answer pages and the following statement:

> A CPA is continually confronted with the necessity of expressing opinions and conclusions in written reports in clear, unequivocal language. Although the primary purpose of the examination is to test the candidates knowledge and application of the subject matter, the ability to organize and present such knowledge in acceptable written language will be considered by the examiners.

The examiners also clearly indicate that a failure to follow instructions will be considered as indicating inefficiency in accounting work.

Three and one-half hours are allotted for completion of the business law examination. The AICPA lists suggested times for completing each question, and the candidate must pay particular attention to these recommendations. Estimated times range from the suggested minimum to the suggested maximum that a candidate should allocate to that specific question (e.g., 110 to 130 minutes for the multiple-choice or 15 to 20 minutes for each problem-essay question). Avoid using more than the allotted time for each question.

VALUE OF A FORMAL BUSINESS LAW REVIEW COURSE

It is important that you enroll in a formal business law CPA review course. Doing so will force you to engage in a systematic and rigorous course of study in preparation for the examination. It is the author's opinion that lack of proper review is the primary cause of failure of the business law portion of the CPA examination.

THE GRADING PROCESS

Candidates should be familiar with the grading process involved in evaluating their answers to questions on the Uniform CPA Examination. The following description of the grading process is contained in the AICPA's *Information for CPA Candidates*.[3]

When the grading bases are in final form, the four-stage grading process begins. Candidates should remember that throughout the grading process their anonymity is preserved. The only information about a candidate available to the graders is the candidate number, which appears on the examination papers to identify him and the jurisdiction. No information is available to the graders about the candidate's education, experience, age, number of sittings, or other personal characteristics. As a result, the candidate's performance on the CPA examination is measured solely by the papers submitted. Candidates must receive a grade of 75 or more on each section to receive a "pass" on the entire examination.

First grading   The first grading is done by graders assigned to grade individual questions. For example, each essay question . . . will be graded by a different grader . . . .

A grader assigned to a single question, which will be graded during the full grading session of six or seven weeks, becomes an expert in the subject matter of the question and in the evaluation of the candidates' answers. Thus, grading is objective and uniform.

The purpose of the first grading is to separate the candidates' papers into three groups: obvious passes, marginal, and obvious failures.

Second grading   Upon completion of the first grading, a second grading is made by reviewers. Obvious passes and failures are subjected to cursory reviews as part of the grading controls. Marginal papers, however, receive an extensive review.

The graders who make the extensive reviews have had years of experience grading the CPA examination. They have also participated in the development of the grading bases and have access to item analysis for multiple-choice questions identifying concepts as discriminating or as rudimentary. An important indicator of the competence of the candidate is whether grade points were earned chiefly from discriminating concepts or from rudimentary concepts. During this review of the overall paper, significance is attached to the form and presentation of the paper, use of English, logic, and other factors which must be judged with an element of subjectivity.

Third grading   After the papers have been through the second grading for all parts of the examination, the resultant grades are listed by candidate number and compared for consistency among subjects. For example, if a candidate passes two subjects and receives a 69 in a third, the 69 paper will receive a third grading in the hope that the candidate, now identified as possessing considerable competence, can have the paper raised to a grade of 75 by finding additional points for which to grant positive credit. This third grading is done by the section head or a reviewer who did not do the second grading of the paper.

Fourth grading   The Director of Examinations applies a fourth grading to papers that received the third grading but have grades that are inconsistent. The Director knows that the papers have already been subjected to three gradings, and that it would be difficult to find additional points for which the candidates should be given credit. Therefore, the paper is reviewed with this question in mind: "Considering the overall presentation in this paper, does

---

[3] Copyright © 1975, 1979 by the American Institute of Certified Public Accountants, Inc.

this candidate have the technical competence to function effectively as a CPA?" If the answer appears to be "Yes," the candidate is passed. Obviously, very few candidates are passed in this manner, but this fourth grading assures that marginal candidates receive every possible consideration.

HOW TO USE THIS BOOK EFFECTIVELY

The business law subjects are classified in this book into eight major parts, which include chapters containing interrelated subject matter essentially as prescribed by the Board of Examiners of the AICPA in its "Business Law Content Specification Outline." The parts and chapters within them are arranged in a carefully preselected sequence designed to enable CPA candidates to review and cumulate their knowledge of the subjects presented in the most efficient and effective way. For example, a CPA candidate's knowledge of the law of "contracts" in Chapter 2 facilitates a mastery of the law of "sales" in Chapter 3; a cumulative knowledge of the law of "contracts" and "sales" facilitates the mastery of "documents of title and investment securities" in Chapter 4.

Because the business law section of the Uniform CPA Examination is almost totally analytical in nature, *just memorizing* vocabulary and rules of law *will not be sufficient preparation* for the examination. This edition provides within each chapter, excluding this one, six distinctly different, yet extremely important, methods for a candidate to obtain not only the required knowledge base of subject matter and vocabulary but also the necessary analytical, problem-solving skills. These methods and their objectives are as follows:

1. *Sentence and paragraph outline* interspersed with numerous examples, hypotheticals, tables, and flowcharts. A careful review of this material will enable candidates to acquire and understand the necessary vocabulary (i.e., key words and concepts), rules of law, and their application.
2. *Self-quiz.* By reviewing the key words and concepts and the questions in the self-quiz, candidates will perform a second review of the subject matter found in each chapter outline, enhance their vocabulary, reaffirm their understanding of key words and concepts, and verify their knowledge and understanding of the basic rules of law. If candidates cannot recall the meaning of a key word or concept or are unable to answer any question in the self-quiz, they can easily obtain the meaning or answer by utilizing the page references to the text provided for each key word or concept and each question.
3. *Objective questions.* The actual practice of answering the selected objective questions will subject candidates to a third review of the subject matter found in each chapter outline, test their ability to analyze business-legal problems, and reaffirm their ability to apply rules of law to legal issues. Answers to each objective question are provided in each chapter.
4. *Explanation of answers to objective questions.* These explanations provide a fourth review of the subject matter found in each chapter, help the candidates realize why their analysis of the legal issues raised in the objective question may have been incorrect, as well as reaffirm the candidates' knowledge of the rules of law and their application to legal issues.
5. *Essay questions and answers.* The *actual practice of writing answers* to the problem-essay questions and comparing them to the reprinted unofficial answers will give candidates practice in analyzing, organizing, and writing answers to selected CPA problem-essay questions. This also forces candidates to review the subject matter in each chapter for the fifth time and allows them to practice the correct and effective use of key words and concepts.

6. *Flowcharts and tables.* One hundred and forty-eight flowcharts and tables are included in the book. These not only aid candidates during the course of their study of each individual chapter but also provide a sixth and final review of the subject matter. These flowcharts and tables can be used within a week of the date of the exam to give the candidates a complete overview of each subject matter. Perhaps their most valuable purpose is to help candidates avoid a most common problem associated with the study of business law; that is, the "inability to see the forest because of the trees."

PART TWO

Formation of Contractual Relationships (15%)*

Chapter 2
Contracts

---

* This percentage allocation represents the relative weight to be given to this *area* of business law on the Uniform CPA Examinations beginning in November 1983. It also indicates the approximate percentage of the total achievable test score to be assigned to this *area* of business law for each Uniform CPA Examination beginning in November 1983.

CHAPTER

2

Contracts

The following is a generalized listing of subjects to be tested through the May 1983 Uniform CPA Examination.

This topic is concerned with the fundamental legal elements necessary for a contract to be enforceable in a court of law. The subject matter includes the following: offer, acceptance, consideration, legality, capacity to contract, unfairness in the bargaining process (e.g., fraud), the Statute of Frauds, third-party rights, performance, breach, and remedies.[1]

The AICPA Board of Examiners has adopted a new content specification outline for the business law section of the Uniform CPA Examination, *to be effective with the November 1983 examination*. The new outline lists the following business law groups and topics to be tested under the area of business law entitled "Contracts."

Contracts
- **A.** Nature and Classification of Contracts
- **B.** Offer and Acceptance
- **C.** Consideration
- **D.** Capacity, Legality, and Public Policy
- **E.** Other Defenses
    - **1.** Statute of Frauds
    - **2.** Statute of Limitations
    - **3.** Fraud
    - **4.** Duress
    - **5.** Misrepresentation
    - **6.** Mistake
    - **7.** Undue Influence
- **F.** Parol Evidence Rule

---

[1] AICPA, *Information for CPA Candidates*, Copyright © 1975, 1979, by the American Institute of Certified Public Accountants, Inc.

G. Third Party Rights
H. Assignments
I. Discharge, Breach, and Remedies[2]

The law of contracts deals with legal questions concerning promises or agreements between two or more parties that may become legally enforceable in a court of law. The CPA candidate must be familiar with the common law as well as the statutory rules that apply to all types of contracts. Types of contracts include the sale of real estate, sale of goods, employment contracts, sale of intangibles, and construction contracts. Some of the most significant changes in the common law rules are made by statute and are found in the Uniform Commercial Code (referred to as the UCC). The UCC applies to contracts for the sale of goods. The candidate must not only understand the common law pertaining to contracts, but also a special set of rules under the UCC that apply only to the sale of goods in which a merchant is involved. Some of the more important changes made by the UCC are discussed in this chapter and in Chapter 3.

CLASSIFICATION OF CONTRACTS

I. Contracts are classified in terms of their formation, enforceability, and the extent that they have been performed.
  A. In terms of their formation.
    1. *Express contract.* This is a contract the elements and terms of which are stated orally or in writing.
    2. *Implied in fact contract.* Elements of the contract are implied from the acts or other conduct of the parties. The elements of the contract are not stated in words, but are inferred from the circumstances, conversations, or conduct of the parties. The following are examples of implied in fact contracts:
      a. Cash purchase at retail establishment where money and goods are exchanged without conversation.
      b. Where a homeowner requests a carpenter to fix a door without discussion of payment. Under these circumstances, an implied contract to pay a reasonable fee for the service would result.
      c. Previously expired "output" or "requirements" contract, but goods continue to be shipped and accepted by the parties.
    3. *Quasi-contract.* A quasi-contract is one which is implied in law. It is *not a true contract* because there is no mutual assent between parties either express or implied. The courts will not add to or alter the terms of a valid contract; hence, there is no recovery under quasi-contracts where there is already an express or an implied contract. The law imposes such an agreement when necessary to prevent unjust enrichment, irrespective of the intention of the parties; i.e., "no person should be allowed to enrich himself unjustly at another's expense."
      a. The elements of a quasi-contract are:
        (1) An expectation of pay;
        (2) Benefit conferred or expense saved; and
        (3) Where in all honesty and good conscience, the goods and/or services should be paid for.
      b. Examples of situations which give rise to the application of a quasi-contract are:
        (1) Money or property received by mistake;

---

[2] AICPA, *Business Law—Content Specification Outline,* approved by the AICPA Board of Examiners on August 31, 1981.

FIGURE 2-1 BILATERAL CONTRACT

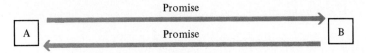

           (2) Receipt and use of necessaries by a minor or a mentally deficient person; or

           (3) Money or property obtained by fraud.

      c. Recovery.

           (1) One cannot recover in a quasi-contract for benefits voluntarily conferred on another party without his or her knowledge or consent, or under conditions which justify the belief that the benefits are a gift. For example, X had been taking care of Y in her home for several years without charge, and Y often remarked, "If you didn't care for me, X, I would have depleted my entire savings." When Y died, X made a claim against Y's estate for the fair value of the services rendered to Y over the years under the theory of a quasi-contract. In this case X would be unable to recover because the services were performed gratuitously by X, and Y never expected to pay for them despite the fact that a benefit was conferred upon Y.

           (2) The amount of recovery is based solely on the extent of the unjust enrichment; i.e., the reasonable value of material and/or services furnished to the other person.

B. In terms of the nature of the promises made in the contract.

    1. *Bilateral contract.* A bilateral contract contains a promise by one party given in exchange for the promise of another; e.g., A promised to pay B $5 in exchange for B's promise to mow A's lawn. (See Figure 2-1.)

    2. *Unilateral contract.* This is a promise in exchange for an act or a forbearance. A contractual relationship is not established until the actual performance of the act or the forbearance; e.g., A promises to pay $20 if B returns A's lost wallet. (See Figure 2-2.)

C. In terms of their enforceability or validity.

    1. *Valid contracts* contain all the essential elements of a contract. A valid contract is absolutely binding and enforceable by the courts.

    2. *Voidable contracts* are binding and enforceable. But due to the circumstances surrounding its execution, or the capacity of one or both of its parties, a voidable contract may be avoided (i.e., rescinded) by one or more of the parties.

      a. The "injured" party has the election to have the contract rescinded or may choose to perform his or her duties under the contract and sue the other party for damages.

      b. Until the contract is rescinded, a valid contract exists.

      c. The following are among the circumstances that render a contract voidable: duress, infancy, fraud, undue influence, misrepresentation, or insanity.

FIGURE 2-2 UNILATERAL CONTRACT

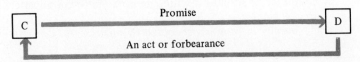

3. *Void agreements* are agreements whose subject matter or performance is against public policy.

   a. Such agreements or promises produce no legal effect or obligation upon either party; e.g., an agreement to commit a crime.

   b. As a general rule, neither party can recover any value previously conferred upon the other party by virtue of the void agreement. For example, Sam, a nightclub owner, entered into a contract with Jackson for the purchase of "white lightning," an illegal whiskey. Sam made a downpayment of $100,000. Jackson did not deliver the whiskey. Sam does not have any recourse against Jackson. As a general rule, the law will not aid a party to an illegal contract.

4. *Unenforceable agreements* are agreements that are neither void nor voidable but are still unenforceable because of the existence of a condition; e.g., an oral contract that is unenforceable because it is not in writing as required by the Statute of Frauds or a contract that cannot be enforced because of the running of the Statute of Limitations, which requires actions to be brought within prescribed time limits after a breach of contract occurs. The Statute of Frauds and the Statute of Limitations are discussed later in this chapter.

D. In terms of extent to which they have been performed.

1. *Executed contract* is a contract that becomes fully executed when all parties to that contract have fulfilled their legal obligations created by the contract.

2. *Executory contract* is a contract in which one or more of the promises are yet to be performed; e.g., a credit sale where goods have been delivered according to the terms of the contract, but payment has yet to be made. The contract is executed on the part of the seller; however, the contract remains executory to the purchaser. (See Figure 2-3.)

FIGURE 2-3   CLASSIFICATIONS OF CONTRACTS

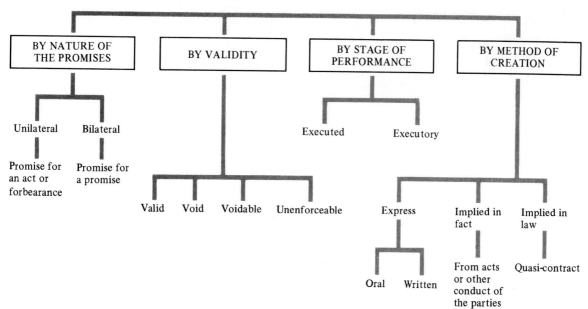

ELEMENTS OF AN ENFORCEABLE CONTRACT

II. The following elements are necessary for an enforceable contract: an *agreement* (offer and acceptance); the *genuine assent* of the parties; *consideration*; *lawful objective* and *subject matter*; *legally competent parties*; and *in writing, if required by statute*.

A. Offer (see Figure 2-4).

    1. Definitions:

        a. *Offeror.* A person who makes an offer.

        b. *Offeree.* The person to whom an offer is made.

        c. *Promise.* An expression leading another person *(promisee)* justifiably to expect certain conduct on the part of the person making the promise *(promisor)*.

        d. *Offer.* A promise on the part of one person whereby he or she *gives another the legal power of creating* an obligation called a *contract*. It may be oral or written.

        e. *Acceptance.* An express or implied manifestation of willingness to be bound to the terms of an offer by the person *(offeree)* to whom the offer was made.

    2. Elements of an offer. In order for an offer to be valid, the offeror must exhibit contractual intent, the offer must be definite (i.e., contain all of its essential terms), and it must be communicated to the intended offeree. (See Figure 2-5.)

        a. *Contractual intent.* The offeror must *intend* or *appear to intend* to enter into a legal obligation. *Test:* Should the offeree, as a reasonable person, under all the circumstances, have interpreted the statement or promise as an offer? The test is an objective one rather than subjective.

            (1) Social invitations. Ordinary invitations to social affairs are not considered to be offers. A reasonable person should realize that only a gift was intended; e.g., a promise to take someone to a dance or a promise to cook someone a dinner.

            (2) Promises made in obvious jest or excitement. A reasonable person should realize no contract is intended.

            (3) Invitations to negotiate. Preliminary discussions or inquiries as to price or terms are not offers. They are invitations to submit offers. For example:

                (*a*) Circulars or catalogs listing prices.

                (*b*) Advertisements. *Exception:* Those in which specific items are advertised on a first-come, first-served basis, and a limited quantity is available.

                (*c*) Price tags in stores or in store windows.

                (*d*) Quotations of price sent on request are not offers unless prior business dealings or custom and usage have established them to be offers.

                (*e*) Solicitation of bids for a construction project is clearly an invitation for offers. Each bid submitted is an offer.

                (*f*) Auctions. Unless specifically stated in the terms of the auction advertisement, the bidder will be considered the offeror and the seller the offeree who is free to accept or reject any bid. If the auction is "without reserve," the seller is required to sell his or her property to the highest bidder. The contract for sale is not complete until the fall of the hammer, or in other customary manner when the seller then accepts the offer to make a contract.

FIGURE 2-4   OFFER

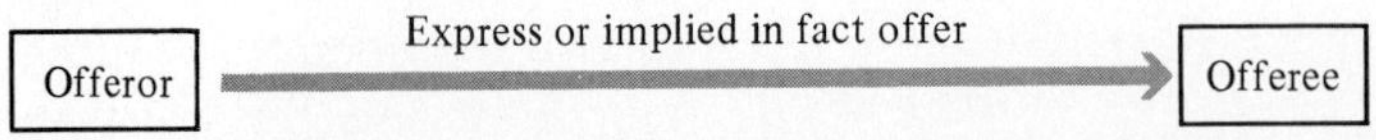

FIGURE 2-5   ELEMENTS OF AN OFFER

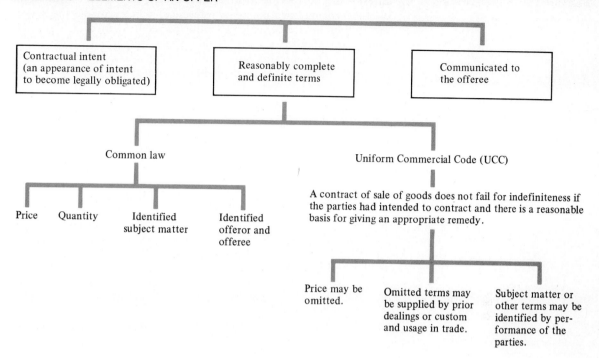

(g) Janez writes a letter to Peters in which she states: "I am interested in buying your house for $50,000. Would you be willing to sell?" This is not an offer. It is an invitation to submit an offer.

(4) Offer of reward. This is an offer to enter into a unilateral contract. It is accepted upon performance of the act or forbearance requested. There can be only one acceptance and only one contract.

(5) Agreements to make a contract in the future are merely invitations to enter into future negotiations. They are not offers. The parties do not intend to be presently bound to a contract.

b. *Definiteness of terms.*

(1) Common law. The terms of an offer must be *complete*, *definite*, and *certain*. A court will not make a contract for the parties by supplying missing or uncertain terms, and therefore an offer whose terms are incomplete or vague *cannot* serve as a basis for a contract.

(a) Under the common law, *for contracts other than the sale of goods*, the essential terms of a valid offer are:

    i. Quantity;

    ii. Price;

    iii. Identification of the subject matter;

    iv. Identification of the parties.

(b) The offeror need not state the terms of the offer with absolute certainty, but must make them sufficiently definite to allow the court to determine the intention of the parties and assign the legal obligations therefrom.

(c) If the offer states a formula or other basis whereby the terms can be ascertained and made certain, the offer is definite. Examples include an offer to pay $50 for an identified watch; an offer referring to an existing writing (incorporate by reference) which provides the necessary definiteness; an offer to sell either a specific radio or an identified stereo; an offer to sell any 10,000 apple trees from a designated acreage in a tree nursery; and an offer to pay a salary equal to 10 percent of "gross profits from a specified business venture."

(2) Uniform Commercial Code (UCC). Even though one or more of the necessary terms of a contract are absent, the contract will not fail for indefiniteness if the parties clearly intended to make a contract and there is a reasonably certain basis for giving an appropriate remedy. Indefinite offers may be made definite by subsequent words, acts, conduct, agreements, customs, prior dealings, or usage of trade.

(a) *Usage of trade.* "A usage of trade is any practice or method of dealing having such regularity of observance in a place, vocation, or trade to justify an expectation that it will be observed with respect to the transaction in question. The existence and scope of such a usage are to be proved as fact" [UCC Sec. 1-205(2)].

(b) *Open price arrangement* is a situation where the parties intend to be bound to a contract even though the price is not settled (UCC Sec. 2-305). The contract is binding even though:

  i. Nothing is said as to price;

  ii. The price is left to be agreed by parties; or

  iii. The price is to be fixed in terms of some agreed market or other standard as set or recorded by a third person or agency and is not set or recorded.

(c) *Requirement and output contracts.* A *requirement contract* arises where the buyer agrees to purchase all the material or supplies needed in a given office or factory during a specified period of time. An *output contract* arises where the seller agrees to sell all of the production from a specified production unit during a specified period of time. (See Figures 2-6 and 2-7.)

  i. The quantity term for the contract is set by the *good faith* requirement, or output of the parties. If a dispute arises, the court will look to the actual requirements or outputs of the parties in prior years to determine whether they are currently acting in good faith.

    a. The party who will determine the quantity must operate or conduct business in good faith according to the commercial standards of fair dealing in the trade.

    b. The parties are obligated to stay in business unless to do so would be economically unjustified.

    c. A decision to cease operation of a business does not excuse performance.

FIGURE 2-6   REQUIREMENTS CONTRACT

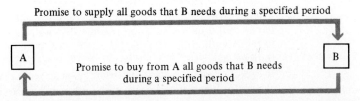

Promise to supply all goods that B needs during a specified period

A   B

Promise to buy from A all goods that B needs during a specified period

FIGURE 2-7   OUTPUT CONTRACT

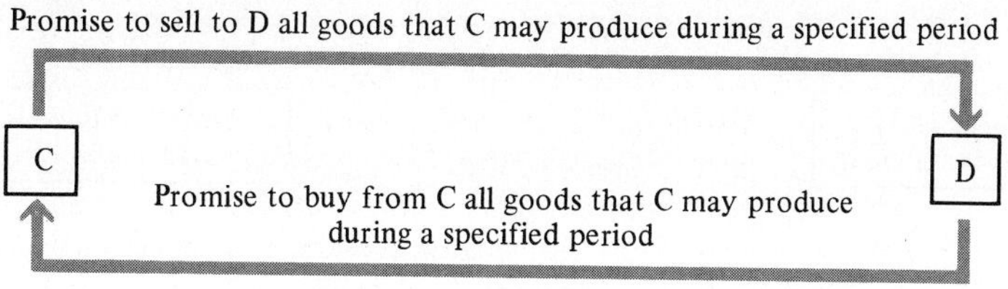

Promise to sell to D all goods that C may produce during a specified period

C   D

Promise to buy from C all goods that C may produce
during a specified period

(d) *Exclusive dealings.* Unless otherwise agreed, this agreement creates an obligation by the seller to use *best efforts* to supply the goods and by the buyer to use *best efforts* to promote their sale.

c. *Communication of offer to the intended offeree.* An offer is not legally operative until it is communicated to its intended offeree. An "offer" cannot be accepted by an intended offeree who is not aware of it.

(1) *Private offer* is an offer directed and communicated to a specific offeree by the offeror, his or her agent, or employee (communication here means actual "receipt" by the offeree).

(2) *Public offer* is an offer directed to any member of a specific group where anyone who learns of the offer becomes an intended offeree. Examples include:

(a) Members of a club—offer to sell your 1958 Edsel posted on the bulletin board of an Elks Club;

(b) Any member of the public generally. For example, an offer of reward for information leading to the arrest and conviction of a perpetrator of a crime printed in a newspaper or broadcast on radio.

d. *Duration of an offer.* An ordinary offer may be terminated *at any time prior to acceptance* even though the offeror states that the offer will be held open for a specified length of time. (*Exceptions:* Firm offers and options to be discussed subsequently.) (See Figure 2-8.)

(1) *Termination according to terms stated within an offer.* The offeror states that the offer must be accepted within a designated time period, e.g., within ten days.

(2) *Lapse of time.* If not specifically stated in the terms of the offer, the offer will remain open for a reasonable time. What is a reasonable time depends on the circumstances:

(a) Nature of the subject matter—perishable or nonperishable goods;

(b) Nature of the market—rapidly fluctuating prices; e.g., common stocks listed on an exchange;

(c) Time of year—harvested crops versus those not yet harvested;

(d) Means of communication used by offeror—e.g., more time is allowed for communication by mail than by telephone.

(3) *Revocation.* The offeror may either expressly or impliedly revoke the offer at any time prior to acceptance by communicating intention to do so to the offeree. Exceptions: a firm offer or an option.

(a) Private offer. The revocation must be communicated to the offeree, his or her agent, or anyone having authority to "receive" such messages: for example,

    i. The offeror calls the offeree and states the offer is hereby revoked;

    ii. The offeror has offered to sell a certain property to P; and thereafter, before the offer has terminated by lapse of time, the offeror

FIGURE 2-8 METHODS OF TERMINATION OF OFFERS

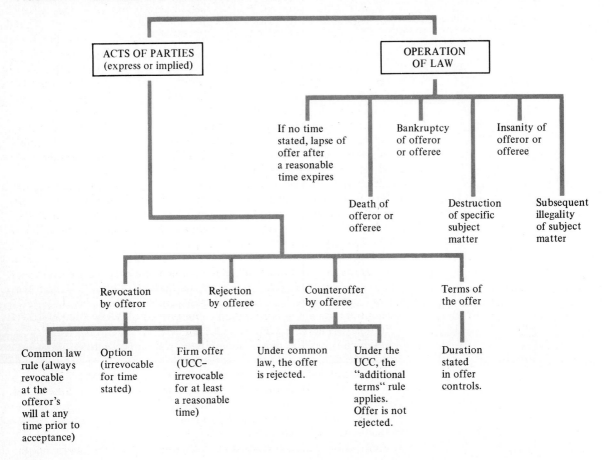

     sold the certain property to another. The offer to P is terminated when this becomes known to P through a *reliable source.*

    (*b*) Public offer. It must be revoked in substantially the same manner as made. For instance, a public offer made in a newspaper ad can be revoked by a subsequent newspaper ad. The revocation, to be effective, need not actually be communicated to all those persons who originally learned of the offer.

(4) *Irrevocable offers.* Options and firm offers.

    (*a*) *Option contract* is an offer that creates a valid contract if it is supported by sufficient consideration.

       i. It cannot be revoked, annulled, or withdrawn at the discretion of the offeror.

       ii. The optionee has no obligation under the option contract after the option is created.

    (*b*) *Firm offer* is an offer made by a *merchant* for a sale of *goods*, in *writing*, which may or may not state that it is open for a stated period of time, and is *signed* by the offeror.

       i. If no duration is stated, the firm offer must remain open at least a reasonable time.

       ii. Where the duration is stated in the firm offer, it is irrevocable during the time stated with a maximum limitation of three months provided by law.

(5) *Rejection* is an express or implied manifestation by the offeree that he or she does not wish to become bound to some or all of the terms of an offer.

    (*a*) An inquiry regarding terms of the offer is not considered a rejection of the original offer, nor a counteroffer. For example, the offeree sends a letter in response to an offer and states "Received your offer to sell Blackacre for $40,000. Would you take $38,000?"

    (*b*) A statement by an offeree stating that the offer is being held under advisement is not of itself a rejection. As an example, "Favorably received your offer of February 2, 1980, today and we are holding it for our serious consideration."

(6) *Counteroffer* is an expression of a willingness to contract with reference to the subject matter of an offer, but only under different terms or conditions. It is not an acceptance; rather it is a rejection of the original offer. The original offer is no longer in existence, and could only be accepted if it is revived by the original offeror.

    (*a*) Any purported acceptance that does not conform to the terms of an offer is a counteroffer. For example: Lynn offered to sell her automobile to Marc for $1,000. Marc replied, "I'll buy it for $750." As another example: Rex offered to sell his home to Mary with closing on the sale and delivery of the deed to be on December 1, 1981. Mary replied, "I accept your offer, but I cannot close on December 1, 1981. January 15, 1982, is open." In both examples, a counteroffer was made and no contract resulted.

    (*b*) It terminates the original offer, and the counteroffer itself becomes an offer which must be accepted prior to the formation of a contract (see Figure 2-9).

    (*c*) Under the UCC, however, additional or different terms do not necessarily prevent a contract from being created.

        i. Section 2-207 provides that, if the seller and buyer are *both* merchants, these additional terms automatically become part of the contract *unless:*

           a. The offeror expressly limits acceptance only to the terms of the offer; or

           b. They materially alter it; or

           c. Notification of objection to them has already been given or is given within a reasonable time.

        ii. Where only one party to the sale of goods is a merchant, a contract is formed only as to the terms of the offer. The additional terms do

FIGURE 2-9   NEGOTIATION FOR CONTRACT

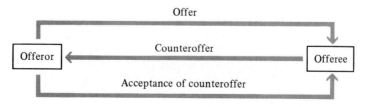

not become a part of the contract unless agreed to by the nonmerchant party.

    iii. A and B are merchants (i.e., they buy or sell goods in the regular course of business). A sends to B a written offer to purchase goods. B replies by letter clearly indicating its acceptance of A's offer, but indicates that B makes no express or implied warranties in regard to the quality of the goods. Assuming that B's additional terms are not "material" and A does not object to them within a reasonable time, A is bound to all the terms of the contract.

    iv. If in the example above A was not a merchant, A and B would be bound only to the terms stated in A's offer. A, a nonmerchant, could only become bound to the additional terms if it agreed to them.

(7) *Termination by operation of law.* An offer terminates automatically upon the occurrence of the following events:

    (*a*) Death or insanity of either offeror or offeree;

    (*b*) Bankruptcy or insolvency of either the offeror or offeree;

    (*c*) Destruction of the specific, existing, identified subject matter of the offer. For example, Z offered to sell a 1981 Citation, four-door sedan serial number F96347 to F. The offer was stated to be open for ten days. Two days later, the Citation was destroyed by a fire. The offer terminated. Contrast the offer made in the previous example with an offer to sell "a 1981 Citation, four-door sedan." Neither the serial number, location of the auto, nor any other means of identifying the specific Citation intended to be sold is mentioned. The destruction of a 1981 Citation, four-door sedan owned by Z would not terminate the offer as it was not specifically identified as the intended subject matter of the offer.

(8) *Subsequent illegality.* Where the subject matter or the performance in a proposed offer subsequently becomes illegal, the offer is terminated; e.g., sale of DDT insecticide is banned by statute after an offer to sell DDT was made.

  e. *Time when a communication between parties takes effect.* A revocation, rejection, or counteroffer is effective at the moment it is received. *Received* is defined to include:

(1) Actual receipt;

(2) Actual receipt by an agent of a party to whom the communication is meant; or

(3) Arrival at a place such messages are usually deposited. For a merchant, it is at his or her place of business. For a nonmerchant such messages are usually received at home.

B. *Acceptance* is the unqualified and unconditional manifestation of express or implied assent by the offeree to the terms of the offer (see Figure 2-10).

  1. The acceptance must be *absolute* or *unconditional*.

    a. A provision in an acceptance relating to routine or mechanical details of execution of a written contract will not impair the effect of acceptance.

    b. An additional matter requested as a favor will not be held to alter or make an acceptance conditional; e.g., a buyer accepts but asks for additional time to complete the transaction.

  2. An offer can only be accepted by the intended offeree.

    a. If a person intends to contract with A, B cannot give himself any right by virtue of his own acceptance. For instance, B's order was addressed to S, who

FIGURE 2-10   ELEMENTS OF A VALID ACCEPTANCE

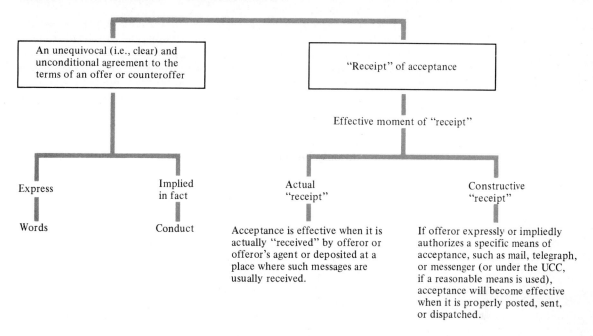

on the previous day sold his business to X. X sought to and did ship goods to B. B can refuse the goods.

   b. Anyone who reads or hears about an offer made to the public has the power to accept it and bind the offeror.
3. Manner of acceptance. The offeror or prior dealings or custom and usage dictates the terms, means, and time that the acceptance will take place.
   a. *Offeror.* Perez sent a telegram to Reilly in which she stated: "Your acceptance must be by personal messenger and received by me prior to June 8, 1980." Reilly cannot accept this offer except by his personal messenger prior to June 8, 1980, and the acceptance will not be effective until it is actually received by Perez.
   b. *Prior dealings.* See 4-a immediately below.
   c. *Custom and usage.* Slotko, a merchant, offered to buy certain china from Lu, a merchant, at a specified price. Lu accepted the offer. Lu notified Slotko that he would ship the china packed in wooden crates. Slotko insisted that the china be packed in corrugated paper boxes. The custom followed by merchants in the trade is to ship by corrugated paper box. Slotko's position would prevail.
4. Silence as acceptance. Silence of the offeree or failure to act is not generally regarded as an acceptance, unless:
   a. The parties to the agreement have expressly or impliedly, through prior dealings or custom of trade or usage, considered silence as a means of acceptance. For example:
      (1) An offer states "If I do not receive your rejection within ten days, I shall consider my offer accepted." Even though the offeree makes no response, no contract will result.
      (2) Same facts as above, except that the offeror and offeree had previously

considered themselves bound under those circumstances. A contract will result if the offeree remains silent.

    b. *Exception.* An exception to the rule occurs when the offeree, with reasonable opportunity to reject the services or goods, accepts the benefit of them although he or she knows or should know that they are offered with the expectation of pay. For example, B terminates his newspaper subscription. B continues to accept delivery of newspaper; B is liable on a contract to pay for the newspapers. B has entered into an *implied in fact contract*.

5. As a general rule, an acceptance also takes place when it is *"received."* An important exception to this rule is the doctrine of *"constructive receipt,"* which renders the acceptance effective at the time it is properly posted, dispatched, or sent. (See Figure 2-10.)

    a. This exception arises under the following circumstances:

      (1) Where the offeror expressly or impliedly authorized a particular means of acceptance; or

      (2) Under the UCC (2-206), unless the offeror specifically requires a certain means of communication of the acceptance, the offeree is authorized to use "any reasonable means."

    b. The acceptance in either circumstance (i.e., if the authorized or "reasonable" means of acceptance is issued) will take place *at the time that the acceptance is properly posted, dispatched, or sent.* The acceptance is effective even though the offeror never actually receives it.

      (1) Non-UCC contracts require an "authorized means" of communication to be effective. The authorized means can be express or implied; i.e., it may be sanctioned or directed by the offeror; or because of prior dealings or custom of trade or usage, the offeror should have reasonably expected the offeree to use the means chosen. For example:

        (*a*) Express directions of offeror, such as "return by mail." Contract exists when reply is properly mailed.

        (*b*) Prior dealings. Means of prior communication between the parties has been consistently by mail. No means of communication of acceptance is stated in offer. Contract exists when acceptance is properly mailed.

        (*c*) Custom of trade or usage. Where communication to a wine distributor is customarily a reply mailed on customer order forms provided by offeror. Contract exists when properly mailed.

        (*d*) Implied from terms of offer or conduct of offeror. Offer is sent by telegram; reply should be by telegram. A reply by telephone, mail, or messenger would not be impliedly authorized. Contract exists when the message is handed to clerk at telegram office.

      (2) UCC contracts allow "any reasonable means" of communication to be used by the offeree (2-206).

        (*a*) Unless unambiguously indicated by the language or circumstances, an offer to make a *sales* contract is construed as inviting acceptance *in any manner* and by *any medium reasonable* under the circumstances.

        (*b*) The "reasonable" means can be ascertained from prior dealings or custom of trade or usage in that particular area of business activity.

      (3) *Note:* If a reply is not communicated with "authorized" or "reasonable means," it becomes effective only when it is "received by the offeror."

      (4) Where the offeror expressly states that acceptance must be only by a certain means:

        (*a*) Any purported acceptance by another medium even though "received" is not effective.

(b) The improper acceptance is treated as a counteroffer; e.g., B states that reply to her offer must be by "telephone"; C sends acceptance by mail. Even though B has "received" the acceptance, no contract exists. C's acceptance by mail is merely a counteroffer. However, the original offeror B, can cause a contract to come into existence by accepting C's counteroffer.

C. *Legally sufficient consideration.* As a general rule, legally sufficient consideration must be present for a promise to be legally enforceable and thereby form a contract. It consists of two elements: a *legal detriment* must be incurred by the promisee, and the legal detriment must be *presently bargained for* and incurred in exchange for a promise (see Figure 2-11). Every promise in an agreement (with the important exceptions subsequently discussed in this chapter) must be supported by legally sufficient consideration in order to be binding.

1. Legal detriment on the part of the *promisee.* A legal detriment is incurred by:

   a. Either *doing or promising to do something one is not legally bound to do;* or

   b. *Refraining from or promising to refrain from doing something one has a legal right to do.*

   (1) A legal detriment *is* present in the following circumstances:

   (a) *Sale of goods contract.* A promises to sell and deliver title to his car to B, and B promises to pay a stated price. The legal detriment to A is the promise to deliver title to the car, and the legal detriment to B is promising to pay the purchase price. These are things that A and B are not legally bound to do. Consequently, the promise of B to pay money is sufficient consideration to support A's promise to deliver title to the car; and conversely, A's promise to deliver title to the car is sufficient consideration to support B's promise to pay money.

   (b) *Surety transaction.* S agrees to act as a surety and to be responsible for the debt if L will loan a certain sum of money to D. L would incur a legal detriment by lending the money to D, because she is doing something she is not legally bound to do.

   (c) *Refraining from filing a lawsuit in good faith.* P has been injured in an automobile accident caused solely by the negligence of D. P agrees, in return for D's promise to pay a certain amount of money, not to bring a lawsuit. In promising not to sue, P is promising to refrain from doing something he has a legal right to do.

   (d) *Settlement of a disputed claim or an unliquidated (not fixed amount) debt.*

   i. Good faith dispute over *amount* owed, for example:

   a. A, a retailer, has been purchasing goods from B, a wholesaler, over a period of time. A has returned some goods, and A has also made claims that other goods were faulty. A's and B's records do not agree on the amount owed. To avoid the expense of review-

FIGURE 2-11   LEGALLY SUFFICIENT CONSIDERATION

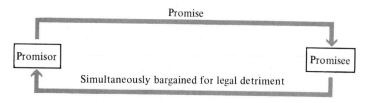

ing their records and causing hard feelings, both parties agree to settle their accounts for a certain sum. Consideration is present to support each promise. Neither was under a preexisting duty to compromise.

  b. C hired D, a plumber, to fix a leak in a water pipe. No agreement was made as to how much D was to receive for his services. D completed the job and sent C a bill in the amount of $500. C was shocked and angered by the large amount of the bill. He sent his check in the amount of $150. The check was marked "Paid in full." D cashed C's check.

  ii. Good faith dispute over *existence* of a debt. For example, E borrowed $100 from F. F demands repayment from E, but E, in good faith, claims that the debt was previously paid. Since neither could produce any written proof, they decided to settle the claim upon payment of $50 by E to F.

  (*e*) *Creditors' composition agreement.* A, B, and C, who are creditors of D, agree among themselves and D to discharge D of all her debts owing to them in exchange for D's payment of one-half her debt owing to each of them.

  (*f*) *A nonequal exchange.* S enters into an agreement with B whereby S agrees to sell his home, which has a market value of $50,000, to B for $35,000. Sufficient consideration exists. The law does not require that the consideration exchanged be equal or adequate in value.

(2) A legal detriment is *not* present under the following circumstances:

  (*a*) *Performance or promise to perform a preexisting duty or obligation.*

  i. Prior duty owed to the public. A promised $25 to a police officer to check A's house during rounds while A is away on vacation. The promise is unenforceable.

  ii. Preexisting duty owed to the promisor. D owes C $1,000. C agrees to release D of obligation to pay the entire $1,000 in exchange for D's payment of $500 in cash to C. Or A contracts to construct a two-story house for B in exchange for $50,000 upon completion of the job. Because of inflation, A realizes that her profit, if any, is going to be much smaller than anticipated. A advises B of her predicament, and B tells A, "Don't worry, go ahead and finish the house and I'll pay you an extra $3,000." A completes the house. B's promise to pay the additional $3,000 is not supported by sufficient consideration.

  iii. Prior duty imposed by law. B promised A not to harm C in return for A's promise to pay B a given sum of money. A's promise is unenforceable.

  (*b*) *Exchanges of money or identified fungible goods.* B promises to give four twenty-dollar bills for a hundred-dollar bill; or, C promises to give D twenty bushels of #2 yellow corn in exchange for fifteen bushels of #2 yellow corn. Sufficient consideration does not exist.

  (*c*) *A promise not to file a lawsuit by one who does not honestly believe he has a valid claim.* C died leaving a valid will disinheriting his daughter, D. D threatens to bring legal action to contest the will even though D believes she has no valid grounds. A promise by the executor to pay $1,000 to D in exchange for her promise not to sue is not enforceable because the promise was in bad faith.

2. A legal detriment must be presently bargained for.

a. The legal detriment must actually be bargained for as the exchange for the promise. Consideration given intentionally without being bargained for is a gift.

b. The consideration must be *presently* bargained for as the exchange for the promise. Therefore, *past consideration* is not sufficient consideration. For example: D lived with her mother and took care of her for some twenty years. Just before her mother died, she promised to pay D $10,000 for having cared for her during the twenty years. The mother's promise is not supported by sufficient consideration.

3. *Moral obligation* is not generally held to be sufficient consideration. For example, X had been taking care of Y's child while Y worked. X refused to take payment for the service, so feeling a deep moral obligation Y offered to pay X's income taxes for the year. When Y failed to do so, X would have no right of action against Y, since most courts would hold that Y's moral obligation was not sufficient consideration to support Y's promise.

4. *Accord and satisfaction.* This is a subsequent agreement to substitute a different performance than that provided for in an existing contract between the parties. The *accord* is the agreement to discharge the previous obligation. The *satisfaction* is the performance of the agreement. Upon completion of performance, the original contract is discharged, even though the accord alone would not have been enforceable because of lack of sufficient consideration.

5. Promises *under the common law* which require no consideration:

a. *Promissory estoppel* is applied to make a promise binding when the following requirements are met:

(1) The promisor must expect actual reliance to occur when he or she makes the promise or must, at least, be able to foresee that the promisee might make such a reliance.

(2) The promise must actually have induced the promisee's reliance.

(3) The act of forbearance of the promisee must constitute a substantial change of position.

(4) An injustice can be avoided only by enforcement of the promise.

(5) For example, a landowner gave a neighbor permission to take water from his land by building an aqueduct. The permission was permanent. A few years later, after the aqueduct was built, the landowner cut off the water supply. The court permitted the user to continue taking water for the remaining life of the aqueduct. As another example, S promised to insure the neighbor's property against fire loss. S neglected to do so, and a fire loss occurred. S was liable for the loss. Finally, H made a charitable pledge and subsequently the charity entered into a building contract in reliance upon it. The pledge is enforceable.

b. A written promise to pay or written acknowledgment of a debt barred by the Statute of Limitations.

c. A written promise to pay a debt discharged in bankruptcy.

6. Promises *under the UCC* which require no consideration (see Figure 2-12):

a. *Firm offer* is a written offer to sell or buy goods signed by a merchant.

b. A *signed, written waiver or renunciation* of a claim or right arising out of a breach of contract. For example, D contracts with F to have furniture delivered by June 10. The furniture is delivered on June 20. If D waives her right for legal action against F by promising in writing not to sue F, D cannot later change her mind and sue F for breach.

c. An *agreement modifying a previous contract* for sale of goods. For example, Raphael entered into a contract with Cardoza wherein she agreed to manufac-

FIGURE 2-12   LEGALLY SUFFICIENT CONSIDERATION REQUIREMENT AND EXCEPTIONS

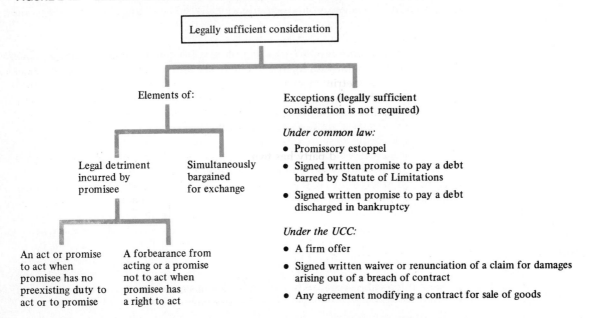

ture and sell to Cardoza 3,000 plastic bottles under a fixed price of $5 for each bottle. Because of severe inflation that caused the price of raw materials to rise drastically, Raphael realized that he would actually lose money if he fulfilled his contract with Cardoza. They subsequently agreed to a selling price of $10 for each plastic bottle to adjust to inflation.

(1) As a general rule, the modification may be oral. *Exceptions:*

    (*a*) If the contract modified was required to be in writing by the Statute of Frauds, the modification must be also in writing; e.g., a contract for the sale of goods for $500 or more, or a contract which by its terms cannot possibly be performed within a year of its date. However, if a modification of a contract for the sale of goods results in a price lower than $500, the modification need not be in writing.

    (*b*) If the original contract contained a no-modification-unless-in-writing clause, the modification must be in writing.

    (*c*) If a merchant supplies a form that contains such a clause, the consumer must sign this form.

D. *Reality of consent.* Although there may be an apparent manifestation of assent, the contract may be subject to avoidance (rescission) (voidable) by one or more of the parties because of the lack of "real consent." A court may find that a party's assent to a contract was not "real" on the basis that agreement was obtained by innocent misrepresentation, fraud, mutual mistake, duress, or undue influence. In order to avoid (rescind) the contract, the rescinding party must tender (offer to) or return any value received previously from the other party to the contract (make restitution). (See Figure 2-13.)

1. *Innocent misrepresentation* (deception) is an *innocent* misrepresentation of a material fact upon which a party justifiably relied as an inducement to enter a contract to his or her detriment or injury.

a. A contract induced by an innocent misrepresentation is voidable by the party who was deceived ("injured" party).

b. Innocent misrepresentation is not a tort; therefore, the "injured" party does not have an alternative remedy for damages.

2. *Fraud* (deception).

a. *Fraud in the inducement* is an *intentional* misrepresentation of a material fact upon which a party justifiably relied as an inducement to enter into a contract to his or her detriment or injury. In this type of fraud, the defrauded party is aware of the nature of the transaction entered into, but is deceived as to a collateral fact and thereby induced to enter into the contract.

　(1) Fraud in the inducement renders the contract *voidable* by the defrauded party only.

　(2) The defrauded party has two alternative remedies: to sue in tort (deceit) for damages *or* rescind the contract.

b. *Fraud in execution* is the intentional misrepresentation as to the very nature of the transaction whereby the defrauded party is justifiably led to believe he

FIGURE 2-13　REALITY OF CONSENT (I.E., FREE WILL)

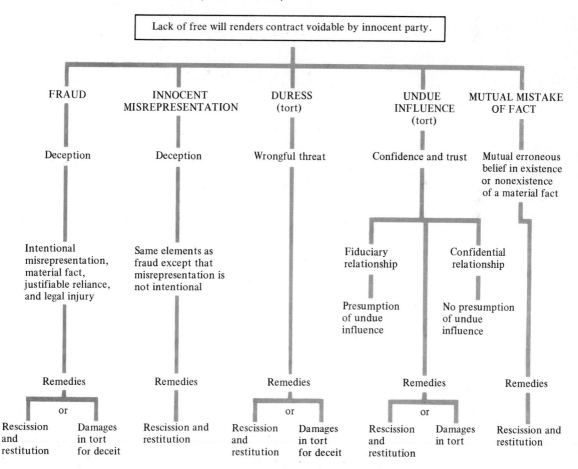

or she is entering something other than a contract. For example, X asks Y, a baseball star, for an autograph, when in reality the paper signed is a contract.

  (1) This type of fraud renders the contract *void*.
  (2) The defrauded party also has a remedy for damages based on the tort of deceit.

3. *Mistake* occurs in the formation of a contract where the party or parties to the contract believe that a person or past fact which is material to their transaction exists when it in fact does not, or believe it does not exist when it in fact does.

  a. A *mutual mistake* may occur when both parties are mistaken about any of the following facts:
    (1) Terms of the contract;
    (2) Identity of the parties;
    (3) Existence, nature, quantity or identity of the subject matter; or
    (4) Other material facts assumed by the parties as the basis for entering into the transaction.
  b. A mutual mistake renders a contract voidable by either party.
  c. A *unilateral mistake* occurs where only one party to the contract is mistaken as to a material fact.
    (1) A unilateral mistake does not render a contract voidable unless the mistake was induced by fraud.
    (2) Ignorance of the meaning of terms or the failure to read the terms of a contract does not render a contract voidable, unless the meaning was fraudulently misrepresented or the failure to read was induced by fraud.

4. *Duress* (fear) is any wrongful threat made toward a person whereby that person is forced to enter a contract against his or her will.

  a. The threat must be wrongful.
  b. The threat may be against the party to the contract, the party's property, spouse, other close relatives, or nonrelated persons.
  c. The threat may be initiated by the other party to the contract or by another person where the other party had knowledge of or consented to the action.
  d. The following are examples of wrongful threats held to be sufficient to cause duress:
    (1) Threat of bodily harm;
    (2) Threat of criminal prosecution;
    (3) Threat of destruction of property;
    (4) Wrongful withholding of goods.
  e. The party who entered into the contract under duress has two alternative remedies: sue in tort for damages or rescind the contract.

5. *Undue influence* (trust and confidence) occurs when the dominant party in a *confidential or fiduciary relationship* secures an unfair advantage in a contract with the dominated party.

  a. Undue influence is presumed whenever a contract is entered into between parties that stand in the following fiduciary relationships:
    (1) Attorney-client;
    (2) Accountant-client;
    (3) Guardian-ward;
    (4) Conservator-ward;
    (5) Doctor-patient;
    (6) Trustee-beneficiary.
  b. Undue influence can arise out of a confidential relationship even though a fiduciary relationship does not exist. The test is again whether the dominating party secured an unfair advantage in a contract with the dominated party.

Typical examples of relationships where trust and confidence are reposed in a party are:
(1) Parent-child;
(2) Husband-wife;
(3) Wife-husband;
(4) Child-aged and ill parent;
(5) Nonknowledgeable investor–investment counselor.

   c. A party who entered into a contract under undue influence has two alternative remedies: sue in tort for damages or rescind the contract.

6. *Unconscionable clause or contract under the UCC* is where one party, being in a superior bargaining position, takes unfair advantage of this position to bargain for a contract for the sale of goods. Unconscionable clauses or contracts are voidable (2-302). As an example, Farmer contracted to commit all of his current carrot crop to Canned Soup Company. Under the contract Canned Soup Company was not bound to take all of Farmer's crop. If it did take any portion of the crop, the remainder could not be sold by Farmer to others. Canned Soup Company was only obligated to pay for the carrots it accepted from Farmer. The court held the contract to be unconscionable (i.e., grossly unfair). As another example, a clause in a sale-of-goods contract fixing an unreasonably small or large amount of liquidated damages to be paid by a party upon breach of contract is unconscionable.

E. *Legality of subject matter or performance.* (Lawful objective and subject matter). An agreement is illegal and unenforceable if either its formation or its performance is detrimental to the general public interest. (See Figure 2-14.)

1. Effect of illegality. The agreement is void from its inception. The courts will neither enforce the agreement nor assist any party in recovering consideration exchanged with the other party.

2. An agreement is illegal if it is in violation of the common law, made void by statute, or is contrary to public policy.

FIGURE 2-14   ILLEGALITY OF SUBJECT MATTER OR PERFORMANCE

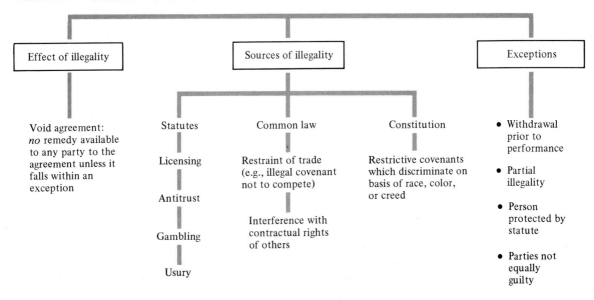

a. *Violation of common law.* The common law is a body of legal rules and principles developed by the courts. Examples of agreements held to be illegal under the common law are as follows:

(1) An agreement to commit a crime;

(2) Agreements not to compete which impose an *unreasonable* restraint of trade; e.g., after selling his grocery store to C, A promises not to operate another grocery store within 250 miles of C for twenty-five years;

(3) An agreement to commit a tort;

(4) An agreement to interfere with the contractual rights of a third person; e.g., A agrees with C to breach her present contract of employment with B in exchange for a new contract with C.

b. *Void by statute.* The following are examples of agreements declared void by statute:

(1) Agreements to fix prices in violation of the federal antitrust laws;

(2) Gambling agreements;

(3) Agreements to perform services in which one of the parties does not have the required license in violation of a regulatory statute or ordinance; e.g., attorneys, doctors, accountants, or real estate brokers. Violations of a revenue-producing statute do not affect the contracts of the unlicensed person.

c. *Contrary to public policy.* The following are examples of agreements held contrary to public policy:

(1) Exculpatory clauses. Agreements relieving a party from all liability for his or her own negligence; for example, a clause in a lease that attempts to exonerate a landlord from liability for damages resulting from the landlord's own negligence.

(2) Unconscionable agreements;

(3) Agreements to induce a breach of a fiduciary's duty; e.g., X corporation induces the president of Y corporation to breach her employment agreement in order to accept a higher paying position with X corporation.

(4) Immoral agreements;

(5) Agreements to interfere with marriage or divorce proceedings or parental relations; or

(6) Agreements to bribe a public official.

3. The following are exceptions to the general rule which denies recovery of consideration by parties to an illegal agreement (in these cases the court will allow recovery of consideration given in an action to rescind the agreement):

a. *Repentance rule.* Recovery of consideration is allowed to a party who withdraws from an illegal agreement prior to the performance of the illegal act.

b. *Partial illegality.* Where a contract contains legal as well as illegal provisions which are "severable," the court will void the illegal provision and enforce the remainder of the contract; e.g., an unreasonable restraint of trade provision in a contract of employment or in a contract for the sale of a business.

c. *Parties are not equally guilty.* Where one of the parties is induced to enter into an illegal agreement by fraud, duress, or undue influence, the court does not regard the parties as being equally guilty and will allow the innocent party to rescind and recover his consideration.

d. *The purpose of a statute is to protect the very party in the agreement.* Where a statute that makes certain types of agreements illegal and void was passed to protect a certain class of individuals, the general rule does not apply to a party to an illegal contract who is a member of the class of persons sought to be protected; for example:

(1) A purchaser of common stock which was not registered as required under a state Blue Sky Law or the Federal Securities Act of 1933;

(2) A purchaser of meat sold in violation of a state food inspection law;

(3) A borrower suing on a usurious loan agreement;

(4) A client in a contract with a professional person who has not obtained the required license under a regulatory statute or ordinance; e.g., attorney-client or real estate broker–client.

F. *Legally incompetent parties.* A contract is not binding against a party who lacked legal capacity at the time of its inception (see Figure 2-15).

1. *Infants (minors).* At common law, all persons under the age of 21 years are considered infants. The age limit has been reduced in most states to age 18.

a. All infants' contracts are voidable, but only by the infant. The adult party is bound to the contract.

(1) In general, an infant may disaffirm (rescind) a contract at any time during his or her infancy and within a reasonable time after reaching majority. *Exception:* An infant's conveyance of land cannot be disaffirmed until after majority is reached.

(2) In order to disaffirm, the infant must return the consideration received

FIGURE 2-15 LACK OF LEGAL CAPACITY

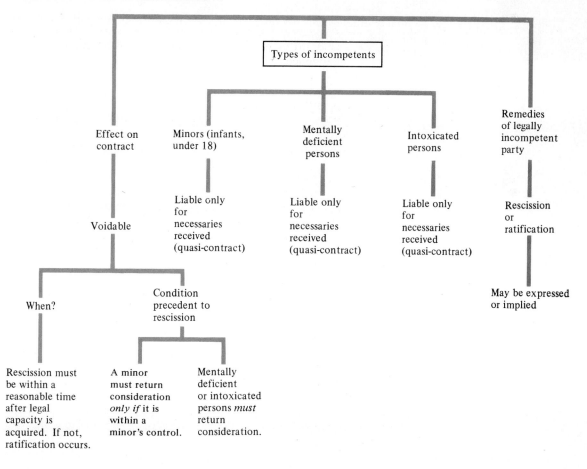

from the other party to the contract *only if* he or she possesses it and only in whatever condition it now exists.

    (3) Upon disaffirmance, the infant is entitled to a return of consideration in specie or the value thereof at the time of the contract.

    (4) For most states, an infant's misrepresentation of his or her true age will not cause the loss of the right of disaffirmance. However, in some states, the infant may be liable in tort for fraud.

  b. *Emancipation* of an infant from parental control does not enlarge his or her contractual capacity, although it may expand the types of things which may be necessaries.

  c. *Necessaries.* Although all infants' contracts are voidable, the infant is liable for the reasonable value (not the contract price) of all necessaries furnished him or her (quasi-contract). A minor (infant) has no liability for necessaries not received by him or her. For example, an emancipated 17-year-old entered into a lease of a very modest two-room efficiency apartment. Before taking possession of the apartment, the minor rescinded the lease. The minor has no liability.

    (1) Necessaries include whatever is reasonably necessary for the infant's subsistence, health, or education, taking into consideration the infant's age, existing economic status, and condition in life.

    (2) Money borrowed by the infant is a necessary only if it is used for the purchase of necessaries by the infant.

  d. Contracts entered into by an infant under authority of special statutes are enforceable. For example:

    (1) Marriage;

    (2) Contract of enlistment into the armed services;

    (3) Life and health insurance;

    (4) Educational loan;

    (5) Checking and savings accounts.

  e. *Ratification.* Upon attaining majority, an infant may become irrevocably bound by a ratification of a previously voidable contract.

    (1) A ratification may be expressed by a new promise or implied from conduct which clearly indicates a willingness to be bound.

      (*a*) Mere silence after attaining majority is not sufficient to result in a ratification.

      (*b*) Failure to disaffirm within a reasonable time after majority is a ratification.

      (*c*) Continued exercise of dominion and control of the property purchased after majority is an implied ratification.

      (*d*) Continued payment of installments on the purchase price of a good after majority is an implied ratification.

    (2) An attempted ratification while a person is still an infant is totally without legal effect.

2. *Insane (mentally deficient) persons.* A person lacks sufficient mental capacity to enter into a binding contract when unable to understand the effect and nature of the contract at its inception.

  a. A legally adjudged mental incompetent's contracts are *void*.

  b. Prior to adjudication of mental incompetency, a mentally incompetent's contracts are merely *voidable*.

    (1) An adjudicated or nonadjudicated mentally incompetent person is liable for the reasonable value of necessaries furnished him or her under a contract (quasi-contract).

(2) The mentally incompetent can only disaffirm their contracts after they become "sane" and *only if they return the consideration they received* from the other party.

(3) Upon proper disaffirmance, the mentally incompetent person is entitled to a return of his or her consideration in specie or its value at the time of the contract.

   c. Ratification. A mentally incompetent's voidable contract can be ratified by him or her after becoming "sane" by his or her express or implied indication of willingness to be bound.

3. *Intoxicated persons.* A person is without legal capacity when so intoxicated at the time of entering into a contract as not to be able to understand the nature and effect of the transaction.

   a. At his or her option, the contract may be disaffirmed or ratified after the intoxicated person sobers and learns of the contract.

   b. In order to disaffirm, *the intoxicated person must return any consideration received* from the other party to the contract.

   c. The intoxicated person is liable for the reasonable value of necessaries furnished him or her under the contract.

4. *Aliens.* As a general rule, aliens have full legal capacity to contract. *Exception:* Enemy aliens at time of war and aliens illegally in the United States are not able to enforce their contracts in court.

5. *Convicts.* Convicts have full capacity to contract.

6. *Corporations.* A private corporation, through its agents, has full capacity to contract limited only by its charter and state law.

7. *Married women.* Married women have full contractual rights.

G. *Statute of Frauds.* The Statute of Frauds applies only to executory contracts. It requires that certain executory (totally unperformed) contracts must be evidenced by a writing and signed by the party who is sought to be held liable. If a legally sufficient writing does not evidence the contract, it is voidable by one or more of its parties. (See Figure 2-16.)

1. Types of contracts within the Statute of Frauds.

   a. *A contract for the sale of goods for a price of $500 or more.* Any contract for the sale of goods for the price of $500 or more is not enforceable unless there is sufficient writing signed by the party against whom enforcement is sought or by his authorized agent. The following are *exceptions* to this provision:

      (1) *Specially manufactured goods.* When a seller has made contractual commitments to start manufacture or has substantially started the manufacture of goods he or she cannot easily sell to anyone other than the buyer, the contract is enforceable without a signed writing if it is valid in all other respects.

      (2) *Admissions by a party.* If a party against whom enforcement is sought admits in court that a contract exists, the contract is enforceable.

      (3) *Part payment or acceptance of commercial units pursuant to an oral contract.* The contract is enforceable only to the extent of those goods accepted or paid for.

   b. *A contract which by its terms cannot possibly be performed within one year from the date of the contract. Exception:* Where a bilateral oral contract is fully performed by one of the parties, the oral promise of the other party is enforceable.

   c. *Contracts for sale of any interest in real property. Exception:* An oral contract for the sale of real estate becomes binding when the buyer, with the permission of the seller, either:

FIGURE 2-16   STATUTE OF FRAUDS

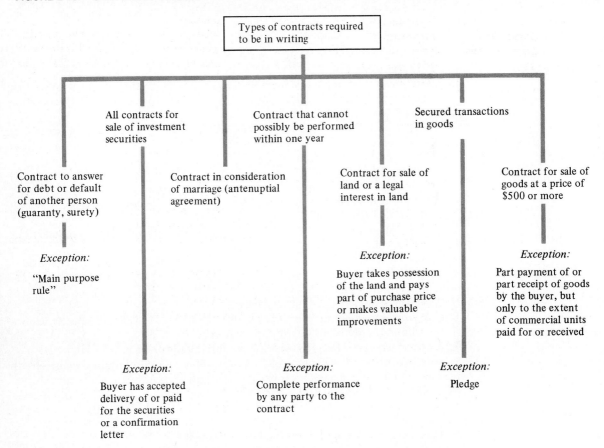

(1) Makes valuable improvement to the land; or

(2) Takes possession *and* makes a partial or full payment on the purchase price.

d. *Promises to answer for the debt, default, or miscarriage of another.* This provision only applies to a collateral (secondary) promise. It does not apply to original (primary) promises. For example, A tells B that if B will give C goods, she, A, will pay the bill. This constitutes an original (primary) promise and removes the contract from under the Statute of Frauds. *Exception: Primary purpose rule* (leading object rule)—Where the primary purpose for a promise is to further a financial interest of the promisor rather than the interests of the debtor, the oral promise is enforceable. For instance, the personal creditors of a partner threaten to attempt to reach the indebted partner's interest in the partnership. The copartners, to prevent an involuntary dissolution and liquidation of the partnership, promise to pay the indebted partner's debts if he or she does not pay them within a year.

e. *Promises by an executor or administrator to pay the obligations of an estate out of his or her own personal funds.*

f. *Promises in consideration of marriage* (antenuptial agreements). A promise in consideration of marriage occurs whenever an engagement (contract) to marry contains any promise which is additional to the mutual promises to marry; e.g., the parties to an engagement agree to a property settlement or to child support should they legally separate after marriage.

    g. *Contracts for the sale of investment securities.* Every contract for the sale of investment securities must be in writing regardless of the amount of the price involved (UCC 8-319). The following circumstances are exceptions to this provision:

        (1) The party against whom the enforcement of an oral contract is sought receives within a reasonable time a confirmation letter, but fails to send a written objection within ten days thereafter. This provision is similar to the "confirmation letter" exception under the UCC, which governs the sale of goods, except that the transaction here need not be between merchants.

        (2) The party against whom enforcement is sought admits the contract in court.

        (3) Part payment or acceptance of investment securities under an oral contract causes the contract to be enforceable only to the extent of those securities accepted or paid for.

    h. *Secured transactions involving goods;* e.g., "installment sales contracts," "chattel mortgages" (UCC 9-307-8). *Exception:* A pledge of the goods to the creditor as security for the repayment of a debt or other obligation.

    i. *Contracts for the sale of intangible personal property other than goods, investment securities, or security agreements, having a value greater than $5,000;* e.g., patents, copyrights, or contract rights (UCC 1-206).

2. Essential elements of the required *"writing"*:

    a. The writing may be executed before or after the agreement is entered into.

    b. The writing may be contained in a formal contract or a signed memo, or in several separate writings, as long as each can be incorporated by reference and the essential terms can be ascertained from all the writings.

    c. *Sufficiency of the "writing" under the common law.* The writing must contain the following terms:

        (1) Identification of subject matter;

        (2) Identification of the parties;

        (3) The price to be paid for the property or service;

        (4) The quantity; and

        (5) Signatures of the party to be held liable. Only the parties that sign the writing are liable. For example, if one party signs, only that person is liable. If no one signs the writing, no one is liable on the contract.

    d. *Sufficiency of the "writing" under the UCC.* Any writing which indicates that a contract for the sale of goods was intended by the parties is sufficient.

        (1) A writing is not insufficient because it omits or states incorrectly a material term of the contract *if* it at least states the quantity of goods sold; e.g., open price, output, and requirements contracts (see H-2 immediately below).

        (2) *Confirmation letter.* As between merchants, a letter signed by a merchant confirming a previous oral agreement for the sale of goods, makes the contract binding *on both parties* unless its recipient objects within ten days.

H. *Parol evidence rule.* An unambiguous and complete written contract binds the parties to its terms. Proof of prior written or oral negotiations and agreements (extrinsic evidence) changing or adding to the terms of the writing *may not* be introduced as evidence in court.

1. *At common law,* extrinsic evidence can only be presented to prove that the

contract is nonexistent, voidable, or void. As an example, extrinsic evidence is admissible in the following circumstances:

- **a.** To contest the validity of a contract; e.g., oral proof of fraud, illegality, duress, undue influence;
- **b.** To establish that a condition precedent necessary for the contract to become binding has not been performed;
- **c.** To explain an ambiguity or omission of the contract; or
- **d.** To prove a subsequent valid modification in the terms of the contract.

2. *Under the UCC*, which is more liberal, terms of a contract may be supplemented, added, or clarified by:

- **a.** Performance by the parties in previous similar contracts;
- **b.** Custom or usage in the trade; or
- **c.** Evidence of additional terms which are not contradictory to the written terms.

ASSIGNMENT OF CONTRACT RIGHTS

III. *Assignment of rights* (see Figures 2-17 and 2-18).

    A. *Definitions.*

        1. *Assignment.* A voluntary transfer of an *existing* contractual right to a person other than a party to the contract which gave rise to the right.

        2. *Obligor.* A person who owes a contractual duty.

        3. *Obligee.* A person who owns the right to enforce a contractual duty.

        4. *Assignor.* A transferor of a contractual right.

        5. *Assignee.* A transferee of a contractual right.

    B. *Formalities for assignment:*

        1. There must be an *intent* to make a *present transfer* of the right.

        2. Consideration is not necessary; i.e., a gift assignment is valid.

        3. The assignment may be oral or written. *Exceptions:* Under the Statute of Frauds, an assignment of contract rights, other than securities, for a value of $5,000 or more must be in writing; an assignment of investment securities intended as a sale must be in writing regardless of price or value; and an assignment which creates a security interest in the rights assigned must be in writing (secured transaction).

    C. *Assignability of contract rights.* As a general rule, contract rights are freely assignable with the exception of the following:

        1. A contract right involving personal skill and judgment; e.g., right to personal services (employment contracts).

        2. Where the contract from which the rights originated contains an express provision declaring an attempted assignment "void." *Exception:* The UCC [9-318(4)] provides that any agreement to restrict or prevent the assignment of *accounts receivable* is void.

FIGURE 2-17   ASSIGNMENT OF RIGHTS

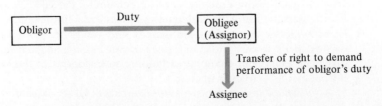

FIGURE 2-18   ASSIGNMENTS

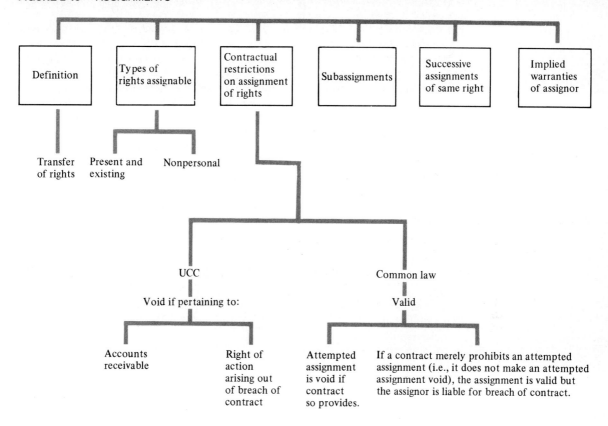

3. An assignment which materially increases or varies the obligor's duty is ineffective. For example, S contracted to sell and deliver goods to B at his retail store in Normal, Illinois. B terminated his business and assigned his right to receive the goods to his brother who owns a retail store in Alaska. The assignment is not valid.

4. Future rights are not assignable. *Exception:* (UCC 9-204). Future rights are assignable whether based on existing or nonexisting contract for the *sale of goods*.

D. *Consent to assignment.* A contract right that is usually not assignable may become assignable if the obligor consents either before or after the assignment is made. *Exception:* Contract rights made partially or totally nonassignable by statute; e.g., assignment of wages of public employees.

   1. The words "or his assigns" in the original contract signify the consent to assign by the obligor.

   2. The consent to assign may be oral or in writing.

E. *Examples of valid assignments:*

   1. S has a claim against B for the price of goods sold and delivered. S may assign his claim to C, and C may recover from B (assignment of the rights to receive money).

   2. D mortgages her property to E as security for the payment of money. E may assign the mortgage to F, and F may recover principal and interest from D (assignment of a security interest [lien] on real estate).

    3. G employs H. H may assign wages already earned to I (assignment of right to receive wages).

    4. J dies, leaving a will in which he bequeaths money or property to K. K may assign her interest in the estate to L (assignment of a right to receive money by inheritance).

    5. M has acquired an option to purchase real estate from N. M may assign her option to O (assignment of the right to accept an irrevocable offer).

    6. S sold goods to B. B may assign his right to receive the goods from S (assignment of the right to receive goods).

F. *Rights of an assignee against the obligor.* An assignee acquires only that quantity and quality of rights that his or her assignor possessed. If the right owned by the assignor is void, voidable, or subject to a counterclaim or set-off by the obligor, it possesses the same status in the "hands" of the assignee.

G. *Notice of an assignment.* Notice of an assignment is not required to be given by the assignee. In order to protect his or her rights, an assignee must give notice of the assignment to the obligor.

    1. Upon receipt of notice of an assignment, the obligor must fulfill his or her duty *only* to the assignee.

    2. Failure to give notice to the obligor does not invalidate the assignment.

    3. Where notice of an assignment is not given to the obligor and the obligor renders performance to the obligee (assignor), he or she is discharged of any duty.

    4. An assignee takes subject to all set-offs or counterclaims which may arise between the obligor and the assignor prior to the obligor's receipt of notice of the assignment.

H. *Implied warranties of an assignor.*

    1. Only an assignor *for value* makes implied warranties. In a gift assignment the assignee does not receive the benefit of implied warranties from the assignor.

    2. The warranties made by an assignor do not accrue to the benefit of subassignees.

    3. The assignor does not guarantee or warrant that the obligor will or is able to perform his or her duty.

    4. The assignor for value makes the following implied warranties unless otherwise agreed:

        a. The assignor will do nothing to destroy or impair the assigned right.

        b. The right exists and is not subject to any defense of counterclaim by the obligor.

        c. Any token or writing the assignor delivers as evidence of the assigned right is genuine.

    5. The assignor *does not* warrant that the obligor will perform or pay or that the obligor is solvent.

I. *Successive assignments* (see Figure 2-19).

    1. *Majority rule.* Regardless of which assignee gives prior notice, the *first* good faith assignee in time is entitled to the right as against subsequent good faith assignees of the same right, unless:

        a. The subsequent assignee gives value in exchange for the assignment and receives payment from the obligor;

        b. The subsequent assignee obtains a judgment against the obligor;

        c. The subsequent assignee receives some token or writing customarily accepted as evidence of an assigned right, e.g., savings bankbook or negotiable document; or

        d. The subsequent assignee enters into a novation with the obligor.

    2. *Minority rule* and that under the UCC is that the first assignee to give notice to the obligor of the assignment of an account receivable is entitled to performance.

FIGURE 2-19   SUCCESSIVE ASSIGNMENTS

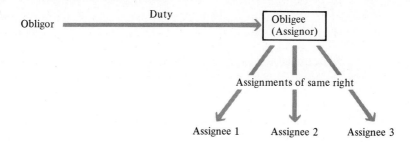

3. *Note:* Special rule for accounts receivable. An assignee of a significant amount of an assignor's outstanding accounts receivable as security for a debt can file a financing statement and thereby protect his or her security interest (take priority) against subsequent assignees of the same accounts [9-302(1)(e)]. See Chapter 6.
J. *Partial assignments.* An obligor is not bound to honor a partial assignment of any contract right unless the original contract provides for performance in installments.
K. *Revocability of assignments.*
  1. When consideration is given in exchange for an assignment, it is irrevocable.
  2. As a general rule, a gratuitous (gift) assignment is revocable unless it is:
    a. Evidenced by a writing signed by the assignor;
    b. Accomplished by delivery of a writing customarily used as evidence of the right; e.g., savings bankbook; certificate of deposit; negotiable document of title, such as a warehouse receipt or a bill of lading; an insurance policy; a certificate of stock; or a negotiable note or draft; or
    c. Executed.

DELEGATION OF CONTRACTUAL DUTIES

IV. *Delegation of contractual duties.* Rights are assigned; duties are delegated.
  A. *Definitions:*
    1. *Delegation* is a mere *authorization* to perform an existing duty given by an obligor to a third person (see Figures 2-20 and 2-21). The original obligor remains bound to perform the duty. For example, a general contractor, hired by X Corporation to construct an office building, delegated (subcontracted) the elec-

FIGURE 2-20   FORMULA COMPARISON OF ELEMENTS OF DELEGATION, ASSUMPTION, AND NOVATION

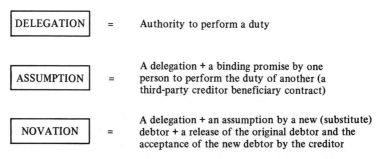

FIGURE 2-21 DELEGATION OF DUTY

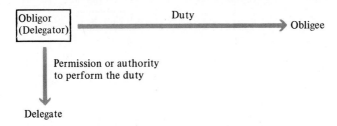

trical work to an electrician (nonemployee). The electrician negligently failed to perform the electrical work according to specifications. The general contractor is liable to X Corporation for breach of contract.

2. *Assumption.* A delegation of an existing duty to a third person which *includes a contractual promise by the third person* that he or she will perform the duty. The original obligor remains bound to perform the duty (see Figures 2-20 and 2-22). For example; Jack owned a farm that was mortgaged with 1st National Bank. Nelson, a prospective purchaser of Jack's farm, was unable to borrow enough money to meet Jack's price. Jack and Nelson entered into a contract of sale wherein Nelson agreed to pay Jack a specified amount as a down payment and assumed and agreed to pay Jack's mortgage. The legal consequences of this contract are as follows: Jack remains liable to 1st National Bank on his personal debt. Under the terms of the contract of sale, Nelson is under a duty to Jack to pay the outstanding balance of the mortgage debt. 1st National Bank must accept payments on the mortgage debt unless the mortgage made Jack's duty to pay nondelegable. 1st National Bank retains its mortgage lien and because of the assumption, it can enforce payment against Nelson by virtue of its rights as a third-party creditor beneficiary. See V below.

3. *Novation.* A three-party contract between the obligor, obligee, and a third person, whereby an existing obligor is discharged from his or her duty and a new obligor (the third person) is substituted in the obligor's place. *A novation includes a delegation and an assumption of the duty.* (See Figures 2-20 and 2-23.)

4. *Delegator.* An obligor who authorizes a third person to perform his or her duty.

5. *Delegate.* A third person who accepts authorization to perform an obligor's duty. The third person may be the delegator's agent, employee, assignee, or any other third party.

B. *Formalities for delegation:*

1. It may be oral or written.

FIGURE 2-22 ASSUMPTION OF DUTY

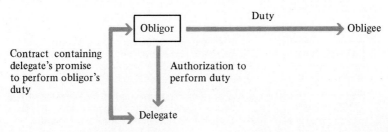

FIGURE 2-23 NOVATION

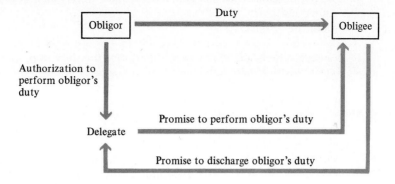

2. Consideration is not necessary.
3. The parties must clearly indicate that a delegation of duties is intended.
C. *Delegable duties.* As a general rule, all contractual duties are delegable with the exception of the following:
   1. A duty involving personal skill and judgment;
   2. Where the contract from which the duty originated contains an express provision declaring an attempted delegation to be "void";
   3. A delegation which materially changes the duty to be performed; or
   4. A duty made nondelegable by statute or the common law.
D. *Consent to delegation.* A contractual duty which is nondelegable may become delegable if the obligee consents either before or after the delegation is made. For example, a mortgage that provides that the mortgaged premises can be sold under an assumption.
E. *Effect of a valid delegation* (see Figure 2-24).
   1. The obligee must accept the proper performance of the duty by the delegate.

FIGURE 2-24 DELEGATION OF DUTIES

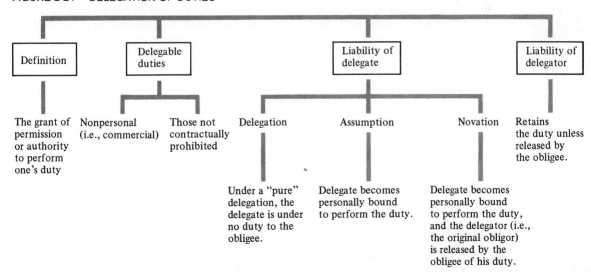

2. The original *obligor remains legally liable* on the contract to the obligee.
3. The performance by a delegate has the same legal effect as performance by the original obligor.

F. *Rights of the obligee:*
   1. Against the original obligor. The obligee has the right to sue the obligor if the delegate either fails to perform or performs the duty improperly.
   2. Against the delegate. A delegate is not personally liable to the obligee unless the obligee is a third-party intended beneficiary of a contract between the delegator and the delegate (assumption).

G. *Rights of the original obligor against the delegate.* The original obligor has no recourse against the delegate unless the delegation was part of a binding contract (assumption or novation). (See Figure 2-24.)

H. *Effect of "assignment of the contract."* Under the common law an assignment of rights does not automatically carry with it a delegation of duties. However, under the UCC an assignment of the contract or of "all my rights in the contract" raises a rebuttable presumption that a delegation of duties was also intended by the parties. The presumption can be rebutted by the following evidence:
   1. That the assignment was made as a security for a debt; or
   2. That the assignee reasonably believed that the assignor had already performed his or her duties; or
   3. That the consideration paid by the assignee was equal to the value of the rights; or
   4. That the original contract called for personal performance by only the assignor.

THIRD-PARTY BENEFICIARY CONTRACTS

V. *Third-party beneficiaries* (see Figure 2-25).
   A. Definition: A third-party beneficiary is a person other than a party to a contract who is intended to be directly benefited from the performance of a promise made in that contract.
   B. Types of third-party beneficiaries:
      1. *Donee beneficiary.* A third party named in a contract who is intended to receive a contractual right as a gift; e.g., beneficiary of a life insurance policy.
      2. *Creditor beneficiary.* A third party named in a contract who is intended to receive a contractual right in order to satisfy a duty owed by the promisee; e.g., X, in a contract with Y assumes and agrees to pay Y's mortgage debt to the ABC Savings & Loan. ABC Savings & Loan is the third-party creditor beneficiary of Y's promise to pay.

FIGURE 2-25 THIRD-PARTY BENEFICIARY CONTRACT

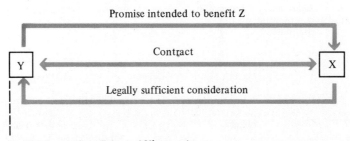

C. Rights of a third-party beneficiary:

    1. The right to enforce the promise made for his or her benefit.

    2. The rights are subject to the terms of the contract from which they were acquired.

    3. Any defenses a promisor possesses against the promisee, which relate to the formation of the original contract, may be also asserted against the third-party beneficiary.

    4. The promisor and promisee may defeat the beneficiary's rights by mutual agreement at any time before he or she materially changes position in reliance upon the promise.

D. Examples of third-party beneficiary contracts:

    1. Life insurance policy. The beneficiary designated may be a donee or creditor beneficiary.

    2. A contract to execute joint wills providing gifts to third parties.

    3. An agreement to pay a mortgage debt made in conjunction with the purchase of mortgaged real estate, i.e., an assumption of the mortgage.

    4. A contract for the sale of a business wherein:

        a. The purchaser agrees to continue the employment of certain specified employees;

        b. The purchaser assumes the seller's duty to pay debts owing to existing business creditors.

E. *Incidental beneficiary* is a third party who is *not* intended to be benefited by a contract, but yet receives some collateral benefit from its performance. He or she acquires *no* rights under the contract. For example, the city of Bloomington, Illinois, contracted with a general contractor to apply asphalt covering on the roads within a subdivision. The general contractor negligently failed to perform. A homeowner within the subdivision is merely an incidental beneficiary and did not acquire rights under the city's contract.

DISCHARGE OF CONTRACTUAL DUTIES

VI. *Discharge of contracts.* The term *discharge* refers to the termination of a contractual obligation. The obligations under contract can be discharged in the following ways:

A. *By breach of condition. A condition* is a provision in a contract which makes the enforceability of a promise conditional upon an event which may or may not occur in the future. Conditions may be precedent or subsequent. (See Figures 2-26 and 2-27.)

    1. *Condition precedent* is an event which must or must not occur *before* an obligation becomes enforceable; e.g., a contract to purchase real estate made conditional upon the buyer securing adequate financing.

    2. *Condition subsequent* is an event that will terminate an obligation if it does or does not occur; e.g., a contract providing that one party is to perform his or her obligation to the "satisfaction" of the other party before any payment is to be made.

    3. Effect of *breach of condition* prevents an obligation under contract from coming into existence or empowers a party to terminate his or her contractual obligation.

B. *Performance by a party to the contract* (see Figure 2-27).

    1. *Complete performance* occurs when a party performs his or her obligations exactly as called for by the contract. Complete performance entitles a party to recover the full price agreed upon in the contract; i.e., performance by the other party if she or he has not already performed.

FIGURE 2-26   CONTRACTUAL CONDITIONS

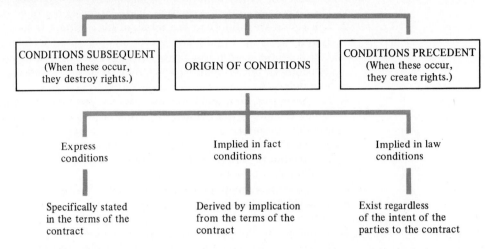

2. *Substantial performance* results in a nonmaterial breach of contract. It is a less than perfect performance but not so imperfect that its result is to destroy the value of the contract to the innocent party. For example, a person who contracts for the construction of a home expects the home to be suitable as a residence. If the defects in the home caused by the building contractor are so serious that the home is not habitable, the value of the contract has been destroyed and substantial performance has not occurred.

   a. Substantial performance (i.e., a nonmaterial breach) entitles a party to be paid the agreed-upon contract price minus any damages caused by the failure to render complete performance. For example, Don contracted to construct a house for Janis according to written specifications that required the bedrooms to be painted with soft colors of beige and pink. By mistake, Don

FIGURE 2-27   DISCHARGE OF CONTRACTUAL DUTIES

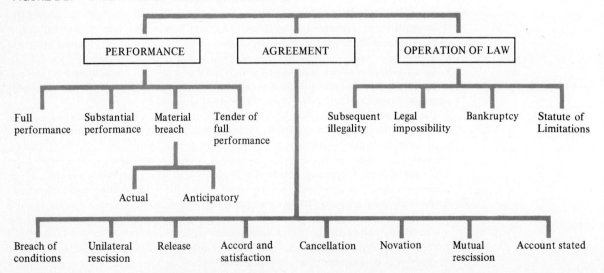

painted the bedrooms purple, dark green, and bright orange. Don can recover the contract price minus the reasonable cost of labor and materials necessary to remedy the defects, i.e., to paint the bedrooms as previously agreed upon.

    b. Nonsubstantial performance (i.e., a material breach) by one party discharges the other party to the contract from his or her obligation to perform. For example, Stan contracted to build a motor and pulley system powerful enough to operate Laura's grain mill. The motor and pulley system delivered by Stan was not mechanically defective, but it did not have the capacity to operate the mill. Laura is discharged from her obligations under the contract.

  3. *Tender of performance* is the offer to perform an obligation under an existing contract.

    a. In order to be a proper tender of performance, it must be unconditional and conform to the terms of the contract.

    b. A tender of payment of money owed does not discharge the obligation to pay, even though it is refused. The tender merely has the effect of terminating any obligation for interest after tender is made.

    c. Where the obligation is to perform an act *other than the payment of money, a proper tender* of performance discharges the obligation. For example, A contracts to sell B goods or land or to render services; A makes a proper tender of such goods, land, or services; and B refuses to accept. A is discharged from his obligation to perform.

C. *Payment.*

  1. Full payment in cash discharges a debt.

  2. Payment by check is a conditional payment. The debt is not discharged if the check is dishonored.

  3. Part payment is not complete performance.

  4. The effect of part payment where debtor maintains several open accounts is as follows:

    a. If the debtor has designated the debt he or she intends to discharge, the creditor is obligated to follow the debtor's instructions.

    b. If the debtor does not designate the payment to be applied to a specified account, the creditor may apply it to any one of the debtor's accounts.

    c. If neither party has designated a specific application, the courts will usually order that the payment apply as follows:

      (1) To the older rather than a more recent debt;

      (2) To an unsecured debt if there exist both secured and unsecured debts;

      (3) To any interest-bearing debt where there exist both interest-bearing and non-interest-bearing debts. The payment will discharge the interest first and then the principal.

D. *Merger* is the process by which one contract is extinguished by being absorbed by another. For example:

  1. An oral agreement is merged in a written contract concerning the same subject matter.

  2. A written option to sell is merged in a formal contract of sale.

E. *Novation* is a contract between a debtor, creditor, and a third person whereby the third person is substituted as debtor and the original debtor is discharged from his obligation (see Figures 2-20 and 2-21).

F. *Accord and satisfaction* is an agreement between parties in dispute to accept a substitute performance in place of a previous obligation.

  1. No new consideration is given or is necessary.

  2. There must be an offer by the debtor of new terms and an acceptance of such by the creditor (accord).

3. If performance by the debtor under the new agreement is accepted by the creditor, the original obligation is discharged (satisfaction).

G. *Substitute contract.* A substitute contract differs from an accord and satisfaction in that it is an agreement that replaces an existing obligation by an *executory contract*.

H. *Mutual rescission* is the exchange of mutual promises to rescind a totally *executory* contract.

I. *Release* is an abandonment of a right under a contract.

J. *Waiver* is a voluntary relinquishment of an existing right.

K. *Cancellation* is the defacing, tearing, or mutilating of a *written* contract with the intent to destroy its legal effect.

L. *Covenant not to sue* is a binding promise by the creditor not to enforce an existing right against the debtor.

M. *Release of joint debtor.* If a release is given to one joint debtor, the other joint debtors are also released from their obligations. A covenant not to sue is not a release, and therefore will not operate to release other joint debtors.

N. *Legal impossibility of performance:*

1. *Disability or death of the obligor* terminates an obligation to perform services which are *personal* in nature. Commercial obligations are not discharged by death or disability of the party obligated to perform them. For example, a booking agency had contracted to furnish the services of a certain famous entertainer. Subsequently, the entertainer became ill and was unable to perform. The court held that the booking agency was discharged of its obligation.

2. *Subsequent illegality.* Performance declared illegal subsequent to a contract but before actual performance is due discharges the obligations under contract, e.g., the passage of a statute forbidding sale of Laetril.

3. *Destruction of specifically identified and bargained for subject matter.* When the subject matter is *a specified and identified* item and the parties entered into the contract on the implied condition of its continued existence, the destruction of the subject matter discharges the contract. For example, A and B enter into a contract whereby B is to reroof a warehouse. Before the performance is due, the building burns down. *Exception:* When the subject matter is destroyed because of the fault of one of the parties.

4. UCC Rule 2-615 provides for discharge on the basis of *commercial frustration* or *impossibility*; e.g., a severe shortage of raw materials due to war, or as another example, an unforeseen shutdown of major sources of supply.

O. *Impossibility created by the other party to the contract:*

1. Nonperformance is excused if performance is prevented by the conduct of the other party.

2. The party prevented from performing may also bring action to recover damages. For instance, C contracts to build a machine shed for D in her factory. When C attempts to begin construction, D's security guards continually prohibit C from entering the grounds. C may sue for damages for breach of contract or consider the contract rescinded.

P. *Material alteration* is any change in the wording of a contract which alters its meaning, a party's duties, or its legal effect.

1. As a general rule, a fraudulent material alteration of the terms of a written contract by one of the parties discharges the contract. The innocent party may also elect to hold the guilty party to either the terms of the original contract or the terms of the altered contract.

2. Where the alteration is made by one of the contracting parties with the consent of the other party or if the other party learns of the alteration and consents to it, the consenting party will not be discharged from his or her obligation.

Q. *Operation of law.*

    1. *Statute of Limitations.* The failure to sue for breach of contract prior to the expiration of a legally prescribed period of time after a breach occurs discharges the party who is in breach.

    2. *Bankruptcy of a party.* When an individual debtor has been adjudicated bankrupt and has complied with all the requirements of the Federal Bankruptcy Act, most of his or her contractual obligations are discharged.

R. *Breach of contract* occurs when one of the parties to the contract refuses or fails to perform some or all his or her contractual duties when they are due.

    1. *Partial breach* (i.e., nonmaterial breach or substantial performance) does not discharge the injured party from performing his or her duties. However, once the injured party performs these duties under the contract, that party is entitled to bring an action for damages due to the partial breach.

    2. *Total breach* (i.e., a material breach or nonsubstantial performance) discharges the injured party from performance. The injured party may rescind the contract or bring an action for damages. Two types of total breach are:

        a. *Anticipatory breach* is a clear indication before the required date of performance by one party of the intention not to perform. The refusal may be stated expressly or implied from the party's actions. For example, a seller who has contracted to sell *specified* goods to a certain party and then sells them to another before the date of performance is guilty of an anticipatory breach.

        b. *Breach of contract in course of performance* occurs by an announcement during performance of the contract by one party of an intention not to fulfill his or her obligations under the contract. The other party is discharged from fulfillment of any obligations and may sue for breach of contract.

    3. *Violation of the terms of the contract.* A failure to perform according to the terms of the contract may:

        a. Discharge the other party if the promises were conditional upon each other;

        b. Not affect the performance by the nonperforming party, if the performance of the contract was wholly unconditional upon the performance of the other party. That is, if the intention of the parties was to have independent promises, each party must perform his or her duties under the contract regardless of the nonperformance of the other. For example, unless expressly stated in a lease, the tenant's promise to pay rent is not conditional upon the landlord's promise to pay taxes or make repairs. *Exception:* Anticipatory breach or renunciation of the contract during performance.

    4. *Unilateral rescission* is the rightful disaffirmance of a voidable contract by one party. (For fraud, duress, undue influence, etc.)

S. *Account stated* (debtor-creditor relationships). When creditor sends a statement to debtor who retains it for an unreasonably long time without objection, an acceptance (assent) of the amount stated is implied by law. For example, C (creditor) and D (debtor) previously entered into numerous different contracts resulting in varying amounts of individual debts owed by D to C. C subsequently sent to D his statement indicating a figure and represented it to be the total of the debts owed. D failed to object. D is bound to the amount stated by C.

REMEDIES FOR BREACH OF CONTRACT

    VII. *Remedies for breach of contract.* When one party fails to perform his or her obligations under a contract and the other party to the contract has suffered a resulting financial injury, the injured party is entitled to be placed, as nearly as is practical, in the same financial position as would have been occupied had the contract been performed.

FIGURE 2-28 REMEDIES FOR BREACH OF CONTRACT

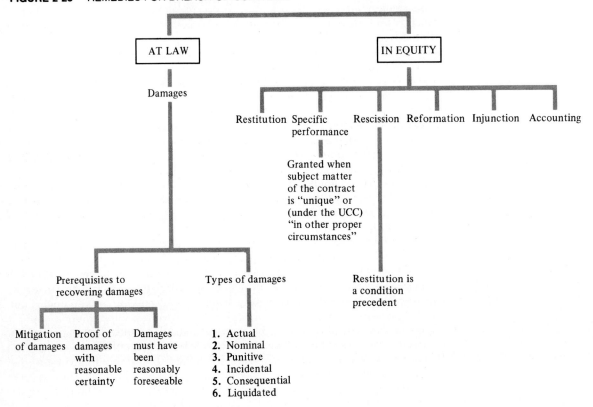

A. *Remedy at law:* damages. The following conditions must be met prior to a *recovery of damages* for breach of contract (see Figure 2-28):

    1. *Mitigation.* A party against whom a breach of contract has been committed must use reasonable efforts to minimize the resulting loss and to avoid additional expense. For example, if P is hired as an instructor at the state university and is wrongfully discharged, he is not permitted to take a vacation at the university's expense. He must make reasonable efforts to find *similar* employment. He is not obligated to change his profession or roam the country looking for a job. As another example, B contracts with C to buy ten barrels of pork, and C warrants that the barrels will not leak. After receiving the goods, B discovers that the barrels do in fact leak. She does nothing to save the pork from spoiling. B is liable to C for the value of the pork thus lost.

    2. *Foreseeability.* The damages must have been *reasonably foreseeable* as resulting from a possible breach.

        a. A nonperforming party is liable only for reasonably foreseeable damages.

        b. Reasonably foreseeable damages are those that a normally prudent person, standing in the position of a contracting party and possessing the same information, would have foreseen as probable consequences of future breach. For example, D installs a defective roof on X's dwelling, and the resulting leaks damage the walls. X is entitled to recover money spent on repairing both the walls and the roof. Or B contracts with A for unskilled factory labor. A leaves the job. B cannot recover damages incurred from the losses resulting from inability to replace A. Unavailability of unskilled factory labor is not foreseeable.

   3. *Reasonable certainty.* The damages must be proved and with *reasonable* certainty.
      a. The injured party bears the burden of proving the following:
         (1) The breach caused the loss; and
         (2) The amount or extent of the loss, with reasonable certainty.
      b. The injured party is not required to prove the losses with mathematical exactness.
      c. Past profit experience of an established business is a reasonable basis for establishing damages with reasonable certainty.
      d. Loss of profits from untried and new business ventures are usually denied as being speculative. For instance, C and D entered into a franchise contract in which D was given the right to sell a newly patented safety device. The next day, C breached the contract. D sued C, claiming as damages the profits D would have earned had C not breached the agreement. No recovery. The estimation of these profits rests on speculation.

B. *Types of damages* (see Figure 2-28).
   1. *Actual or compensatory damages* are damages which amount to the actual financial loss *caused by* the breach of contract. For example, S breached his contract to deliver certain goods to B. B purchased the same type of goods from X and paid $40 more per good than he would have paid to S. B's actual damages are equal to $40 per good.
   2. *Nominal damages* are awarded for breach of contract whenever a party has suffered no actual damages or is unable to prove the amount of damages.
      a. A judgment of nominal damages usually ranges from a cent to a dollar.
      b. For example, A contracts to sell a boat to B for $6,000. B breaches the contract. A then sells the boat to C for $8,000. A is entitled to nominal damages only. A breach did occur, but no actual damages were incurred.
   3. *Incidental damages* are expenses incurred by an injured party in mitigation of damages or in exercising his or her rights after a breach has occurred. For example, X was employed for a five-year term by Y. At the end of the third year, Y wrongfully discharged X. X, in mitigation, incurred expenses for transportation and advertisement for employment. X is entitled to recover loss of wages as actual damages and expenses as incidental damages.
   4. *Consequential damages* are damages which do not flow directly or immediately from the breach of the contract. For instance, X sells Z an apparatus for testing air pressure for $1,000. The apparatus is defective and explodes in operation, injuring Z's employee C. C sues Z and recovers $5,000 under a state workers' compensation law. Z is entitled to recover $5,000 from X as consequential damages plus the court costs and counsel fees involved in the judgments.
   5. *Liquidated damages* are damages agreed upon in a contract to be paid by the party, should a breach occur in the future.
      a. The amount agreed upon must be reasonably related to the amount of damages which probably would result from a particular breach.
      b. If the amount is unreasonable, it is a penalty and the liquidated damages clause is illegal and void. For example, a builder's promise to pay $100 a day for failure to complete a $1,000,000 stadium would be enforceable as reasonable, but a $100 a day damage clause for nonperformance of a $300 roof job would be considered unreasonable and a penalty.
      c. UCC Rule 2-718. The amount of liquidated damages need only be reasonable in the light of the anticipated or actual harm caused by the breach.

6. *Punitive damages* are damages which bear no relationship to actual damages. They are imposed to punish the party against whom they are assessed and also to serve as a deterrent to others in same or similar cases.

   a. For instance, a telegraph company was grossly negligent in handling a message entrusted to it.

   b. The Sherman Antitrust Act allows treble damages and recovery of attorney's fees for violations of the act.

   c. A nationally franchised dance studio utilized fraudulent practices to obtain contracts with older persons for exorbitant hours of dancing lessons. The evidence also revealed that some of the lessons were for dances that even professional dancers experienced difficulty in mastering. The court awarded punitive damages.

C. *Remedies in equity* (see Figure 2-28).

   1. Equitable remedies are available only if a party's remedy at law for damages is nonexistent or inadequate.

   2. Equitable decrees or orders are always directed toward the person rather than the person's property.

   3. The following types of remedies are available in equity:

      a. *Specific performance* is a decree ordering a party to a contract to perform the exact promise made by him or her in the contract. This remedy is available only where the contract of sale involves a *unique* subject matter, such as land, antiques, stock in a close corporation, race horses, a patent or a copyright, etc.

      b. *Restitution* is a decree ordering the return to an injured party of any consideration, or its value, previously transferred under a voidable, void, or unenforceable contract. An injured party is not usually entitled to receive both restitution and damages.

      c. *Injunction* is a decree ordering a party to do some act (mandatory injunction) or to refrain from doing some act (negative injunction).

      d. *Reformation* is a decree ordering the correction of a written instrument when it fails to express the actual intent of both parties because of fraud or mistake.

      e. *Accounting* is a decree ordering a formal account of a fiduciary's financial affairs; e.g., a decree of accounting directed to a partner in relationship to partnership affairs.

      f. *Rescission* is the annulment of a contract whereby the parties are restored to the relative financial and legal position that they would have occupied had the contract not been entered into. For example, the rescission of a contract on the basis of either fraud, innocent misrepresentation, duress, undue influence, or minority.

SELF-QUIZ

To check your understanding of the key words and concepts and the accuracy of your answers to the questions, refer to the text material as referenced by page number.

KEY WORDS AND CONCEPTS

QUESTIONS

1. List the elements necessary to form a contract. **(26)**
2. List the elements necessary for an *enforceable* contract. **(26)**
3. What three elements constitute a valid offer? **(26)**
4. Are all offers revocable? Which offers are not revocable? **(29)**
5. In what ways can an offer be terminated? **(30)**
6. When does an offer, rejection, revocation, or counteroffer become effective? **(32)** An acceptance? **(34)**
7. Is *consideration* synonymous with *value*? **(35)**
8. List the circumstances that do not require consideration to make a promise legally binding. **(37)**
9. Under what circumstances will a court declare a contract voidable? Void? **(38)**
10. Can a voidable contract become a valid and enforceable contract? Explain. **(44)**
11. In what ways can a person acquire rights and duties under a contract to which he or she is not a party? Explain. **(48)**
12. Under what circumstances will an attempted assignment of contract rights be legally ineffective? **(48)** List several examples of legally ineffective assignments. **(48)**
13. What is the difference between an assignment of rights and a delegation of duties? **(51)** What is the legal effect of each on the parties involved? **(51)**
14. List several ways a delegator can be released from his or her duty. **(57)**
15. List and explain the various methods by which contractual obligations may be discharged. **(55)**
16. What conditions must be present prior to recovery of damages for breach of contract? **(60)**
17. List and explain the remedies available for breach of contract. **(59)**

SELECTED QUESTIONS AND UNOFFICIAL ANSWERS

OBJECTIVE QUESTIONS

Select the best answer for each of the following items. Mark only one answer for each item. Answer all items.

MAY 1981

7. Smith contracted to perform for $500 certain services for Jones. Jones claimed that the services had been performed poorly. Because of this, Jones sent Smith a check for only $425. Marked clearly on the check was "payment in full". Smith crossed out the words "payment in full" and cashed the check. Assuming that there was a bona fide dispute as to whether Smith had in fact performed the services poorly, the majority of courts would hold that

a. The debt is liquidated, and Smith can collect the remaining $75.

b. The debt is liquidated, but Jones by adding the words "payment in full" cancelled the balance of the debt owed.

c. The debt is unliquidated and the cashing of the check by Smith completely discharged the debt.

d. The debt is unliquidated, but the crossing out of the words "payment in full" by Smith revives the balance of $75 owed.

8. Harper is opening a small retailing business in Hometown, U.S.A. To announce her grand opening, Harper places an advertisement in the newspaper quoting sales prices on certain items in stock. Many local residents come in and make purchases. Harper's grand opening is such a huge success that she is unable to totally satisfy the demand of the customers. Which of the following correctly applies to the situation?

a. Harper has made an offer to the people reading the advertisement.

b. Harper has made a contract with the people reading the advertisement.

c. Harper has made an invitation seeking offers.

d. Any customer who demands the goods advertised and tenders the money is entitled to them.

9. Martin sent Dobbs the following offer by mail:

I offer you 150 fantastic television sets, model J-1, at $65 per set, F.O.B. your truck at my warehouse, terms 2/10, net/30. I am closing out this model, hence the substantial discount. Accept all or none. (signed) Martin

Foster immediately wired back:

I accept your offer for the fantastic television sets, but will use Blue Express Company for the pickup, at my expense of course. In addition, if possible, could you have the shipment ready by Tuesday at 10:00 AM because of the holidays? (signed) Dobbs

Based on the above correspondence, what is the status of Dobbs' acceptance?

a. It is valid upon dispatch despite the fact it states both additional and different terms than those contained in the offer.

b. It is valid but will *not* be effective until received by Martin.

c. It represents a counteroffer which will become a valid acceptance if *not* negated by Martin within ten days.

d. It is *not* a valid acceptance because it states both additional and different terms than those contained in the offer.

10. On March 1, Wilkins wrote Conner a letter and offered to sell him his factory for $150,000. The offer stated that the acceptance must be received by him by April 1. Under the circumstances, Wilkins' offer

a. Will be validly accepted if Conner posts an acceptance on April 1.

b. May be withdrawn at any time prior to acceptance.

c. May *not* be withdrawn prior to April 1.

d. Could *not* be validly accepted since Wilkins could assert the Statute of Frauds.

11. Maurice sent Schmit Company a telegram offering to sell him a one-acre tract of commercial property located adjacent to Schmit's warehouse for $8,000. Maurice stated that Schmit had three days to consider the offer and in the meantime the offer would be irrevocable. The next day Maurice received a better offer from another party, and he telephoned Schmit informing him that he was revoking the offer. The offer was

a. Irrevocable for three days upon receipt by Schmit.

b. Effectively revoked by telephone.

c. Never valid, since the Statute of Frauds applies.

d. Not effectively revoked because Maurice did *not* use the same means of communication.

12. Martin agreed to purchase a two-acre home site from Foxworth. The contract was drafted with great care and meticulously set forth the alleged agreement between the parties. It was signed by both parties. Subsequently, Martin claimed that the contract did not embody all of the agreements that the parties had reached in the course of their negotiations. Foxworth has asserted that the parol evidence rule applies. As such, the rule

a. Applies to both written and oral agreements relating to the contract made prior to the signing of the contract.

b. Does *not* apply to oral agreements made at the time of the signing of the contract.

c. Applies exclusively to written contracts signed by both parties.

d. Is *not* applicable if the Statute of Frauds applies.

13. Wilcox mailed Norriss an unsigned contract for the purchase of a tract of real property. The contract represented the oral understanding of the parties as to the purchase price, closing date, type of deed, and other details. It called for payment in full in cash or certified check at the closing. Norriss signed the contract, but added above his signature the following:

> This contract is subject to my (Norriss) being able to obtain conventional mortgage financing of $100,000 at 13% or less interest for a period of not less than 25 years.

Which of the following is correct?

a. The parties had already made an enforceable contract prior to Wilcox's mailing of the formalized contract.

b. Norriss would *not* be liable on the contract under the circumstances even if he had *not* added the "conventional mortgage" language since Wilcox had *not* signed it.

c. By adding the "conventional mortgage" language above his signature, Norriss created a condition precedent to his contractual obligation and made a counteroffer.

d. The addition of the "conventional mortgage" language has *no* legal effect upon the contractual relationship of the parties since it was an implied condition in any event.

NOVEMBER 1980

14. Fernandez is planning to attend an auction of the assets of Cross & Black, one of his major competitors who is liquidating. In the conduct of the auction, which of the following rules applies?

a. Such a sale is without reserve unless the goods are explicitly put up with reserve.

b. A bidder may retract his bid at any time until the falling of the hammer.

c. The retraction of a bid by a bidder revives the previous bid.

d. If the auction is without reserve, the auctioneer can withdraw the article at any time prior to the fall of the hammer.

25. Wallers and Company has decided to expand the scope of its business. In this connection, it contemplates engaging several agents. Which of the following agency relationships is within the Statute of Frauds and thus should be contained in a signed writing?

a. An irrevocable agency.

b. A sales agency where the agent normally will sell goods which have a value in excess of $500.

c. An agency for the forthcoming calendar year which is entered into in mid-December of the prior year.

d. An agency which is of indefinite duration but which is terminable upon one month's notice.

NOVEMBER 1979

2. In the process of negotiating the sale of his manufacturing business to Grand, Sterling made certain untrue statements which Grand relied upon. Grand was induced to purchase the business for $10,000 more than its true value. Grand is *not* sure whether he should seek relief based upon misrepresentation or fraud. Which of the following is a correct statement?

a. If Grand merely wishes to rescind the contract and get his money back, misrepresentation is his *best* recourse.

b. In order to prevail under the fraud theory, Grand must show that Sterling intended for him to rely on the untrue statements; whereas he need *not* do so if he bases his action on misrepresentation.

c. Both fraud and misrepresentation require Grand to prove that Sterling knew the statements were false.

d. If Grand chooses fraud as his basis for relief, the statute of fraud applies.

3. Which of the following will *not* be sufficient to satisfy the consideration requirement for a contract?
a. The offeree expends both time and money in studying and analyzing the offer.
b. The offeree makes a promise which is a legal detriment to him.
c. The offeree performs the act requested by the offeror.
d. The offeree makes a promise which benefits the offeror.

4. Marsh and Lennon entered into an all inclusive written contract involving the purchase of a tract of land. Lennon claims that there was a contemporaneous oral agreement between the parties which called for the removal by Marsh of several large rocks on the land. Marsh relies upon the parol evidence rule to avoid having to remove the rocks. Which of the following is correct?
a. The parol evidence rule does *not* apply to contemporaneous oral agreements.
b. Since the statute of frauds was satisfied in respect to the contract for the purchase of the land, the parol evidence rule does *not* apply.
c. Since the oral agreement does not contradict the terms of the written contract, the oral agreement is valid despite the parol evidence rule.
d. The parol evidence rule applies and Lennon will be precluded from proving the oral promise in the absence of fraud.

5. Which of the following represents the basic distinction between a bilateral contract and a unilateral contract?
a. Specific performance is available if the contract is unilateral whereas it is *not* if the contract is bilateral.
b. There is only one promise involved if the contract is unilateral whereas there are two promises if the contract is bilateral.
c. The statute of frauds applies to a bilateral contract but *not* to a unilateral contract.
d. The rights under a bilateral contract are assignable whereas rights under a unilateral contract are *not* assignable.

7. Master Corporation, a radio and television manufacturer, invited Darling Discount Chain to examine several odd lots of discontinued models and make an offer for the entire lot. The odd lots were segregated from the regular inventory but inadvertently included 15 current models. Darling was unaware that Master did not intend to include the 15 current models in the group. Darling made Master an offer of $9,000 for the entire lot, which represented a large discount from the normal sales price. Unaware of the error, Master accepted the offer. Master would *not* have accepted had it known of the inclusion of the 15 current models. Upon learning of the error, Master alleged mistake as a defense and refused to perform. Darling sued for breach of contract. Under the circumstances, what is the status of the contract?
a. There is *no* contract since Master did not intend to include the 15 current models in the group of radios to be sold.
b. The contract is voidable because of a unilateral mistake.
c. The contract is voidable because of a mutual mistake.
d. There is a valid and binding contract which includes the 15 current-model radios.

MAY 1979

8. Arthur sold his house to Michael. Michael agreed to pay the existing mortgage on the house. The Safety Bank, which held the mortgage, released Arthur from liability on the debt. The above declared transaction (relating to the mortgage debt) is
a. A delegation.
b. A novation.
c. Invalid in that the bank did *not* receive any additional consideration from Arthur.
d. *Not* a release of Arthur if Michael defaults, and the proceeds from the sale of the mortgaged house are insufficient to satisfy the debt.

9. Williams purchased a heating system from Radiant Heating, Inc., for his factory. Williams insisted that a clause be included in the contract calling for service on the heating system to begin *not* later than the next business day after Williams informed Radiant of a problem. This service was to be rendered free of charge during the first year of the contract and for a flat fee of $200 per year for the next two years thereafter. During the winter of the second year, the heating system broke down and Williams promptly notified Radiant of the situation.

Due to other commitments, Radiant did *not* send a man over the next day. Williams phoned Radiant and was told that the $200 per year service charge was uneconomical and they could *not* get a man over there for several days. Williams in desperation promised to pay an additional $100 if Radiant would send a man over that day. Radiant did so and sent a bill for $100 to Williams. Is Williams legally required to pay this bill and why?

a. No, because the pre-existing legal duty rule applies to this situation.

b. No, because the statute of frauds will defeat Radiant's claim.

c. Yes, because Williams made the offer to pay the additional amount.

d. Yes, because the fact that it was uneconomical for Radiant to perform constitutes economic duress which freed Radiant from its obligation to provide the agreed-upon service.

10. Austin is attempting to introduce oral evidence in court to explain or modify a written contract he made with Wade. Wade has pleaded the parol evidence rule. In which of the following circumstances will Austin *not* be able to introduce the oral evidence?

a. The contract contains an obvious ambiguity on the point at issue.

b. There was a mutual mistake of fact by the parties regarding the subject matter of the contract.

c. The modification asserted was made several days after the written contract had been executed.

d. The contract indicates that it was intended as the "entire contract" between the parties and the point is covered in detail.

11. Montbanks' son, Charles, was seeking an account executive position with Dobbs, Smith, and Fogarty, Inc., the largest brokerage firm in the United States. Charles was very independent and wished *no* interference by his father. The firm, after several weeks deliberation, decided to hire Charles. They made him an offer on April 12, 1979, and Charles readily accepted. Montbanks feared that his son would *not* be hired. Being unaware of the fact that his son had been hired, Montbanks mailed a letter to Dobbs on April 13 in which he promised to give the brokerage firm $50,000 in commission business if the firm would hire his son. The letter was duly received by Dobbs and they wish to enforce it

against Montbanks. Which of the following statements is correct?

a. Past consideration is *no* consideration, hence there is *no* contract.

b. The pre-existing legal duty rule applies and makes the promise unenforceable.

c. Dobbs will prevail since the promise is contained in a signed writing.

d. Dobbs will prevail based upon promissory estoppel.

12. Philpot purchased the King Pharmacy from Golden. The contract contained a promise by Golden that he would *not* engage in the practice of pharmacy for one year from the date of the sale within one mile of the location of King Pharmacy. Six months later Golden opened the Queen Pharmacy within less than a mile of King Pharmacy. Which of the following is a correct statement?

a. Golden has *not* breached the above covenant since he did not use his own name or the name King in connection with the new pharmacy.

b. The covenant is reasonable and enforceable.

c. The contract is an illegal restraint of trade and illegal under federal antitrust laws.

d. The covenant is contrary to public policy and is illegal and void.

13. Keats Publishing Company shipped textbooks and other books for sale at retail to Campus Bookstore. An honest dispute arose over Campus's right to return certain books. Keats maintained that the books in question could *not* be returned and demanded payment of the full amount. Campus relied upon trade custom which indicated that many publishers accepted the return of such books. Campus returned the books in question and paid for the balance with a check marked "Account Paid in Full to Date." Keats cashed the check. Which of the following is a correct statement?

a. Keats is entitled to recover damages.

b. Keats' cashing of the check constituted an accord and satisfaction.

c. The pre-existing legal duty rule applies and Keats is entitled to full payment for all the books.

d. The custom of the industry argument would have *no* merit in a court of law.

17. Abacus Corporation sent Frame Company an offer by a telegram to buy its patent on a calculator. The Abacus telegram indicated that the offer would expire in ten days. The telegram was sent on February 1, 1979, and received on February 2, 1979, by Frame. On February 8, 1979, Abacus telephoned Frame and indicated they were withdrawing the offer. Frame telegraphed an acceptance on the 11th of February. Which of the following is correct?

a. The offer was an irrevocable offer, but Frame's acceptance was too late.
b. Abacus' withdrawal of the offer was ineffective because it was *not* in writing.
c. Since Frame used the same means of communication, acceptance was both timely and effective.
d. *No* contract arose since Abacus effectively revoked the offer on February 8, 1979.

NOVEMBER 1978

27. Martin Stores, Inc., decided to sell a portion of its eight-acre property. Consequently, the president of Martin wrote several prospective buyers the following letter:

> Dear Sir: We are sending this notice to several prospective buyers because we are interested in selling four acres of our property located in downtown Metropolis. If you are interested, please communicate with me at the above address. Don't bother to reply unless you are thinking in terms of at least $100,000.
>
> James Martin, President

Under the circumstances, which of the following is correct?

a. The statute of frauds does *not* apply because the real property being sold is the division of an existing tract which had been properly recorded.
b. Markus, a prospective buyer, who telegraphed Martin that he would buy at $100,000 and forwarded a $100,000 surety bond to guarantee his performance, has validly accepted.
c. Martin must sell to the highest bidder.
d. Martin's communication did *not* constitute an offer to sell.

28. Fashion Swimming Pools, Inc., mailed a letter to Direct Distributors offering a three-year franchise dealership. The offer stated the terms in detail and at the bottom stated that "the offer would *not* be withdrawn prior to October 1, 1978." Under the circumstances, which of the following is correct?

a. The offer is an irrevocable option which can *not* be withdrawn prior to October 1, 1978.
b. A letter of acceptance from Direct to Fashion

sent on October 1, 1978, but *not* received until October 2, 1978, would *not* create a valid contract.
c. The statute of frauds would *not* apply to the proposed contract.
d. The offer can *not* be assigned to another party if Direct chooses *not* to accept.

29. Mayer wrote Jackson and offered to sell Jackson a building for $50,000. The offer stated it would expire 30 days from July 1, 1978. Mayer changed his mind and does *not* wish to be bound by his offer. If a legal dispute arises between the parties regarding whether there has been a valid acceptance of the offer, which of the following is correct?

a. The offer can *not* be legally withdrawn for the stated period of time.
b. The offer will *not* expire prior to the 30 days even if Mayer sells the property to a third person and notifies Jackson.
c. If Jackson phoned Mayer on August 1 and unequivocally accepted the offer, it would create a contract, provided he had *no* notice of withdrawal of the offer.
d. If Jackson categorically rejects the offer on July 10th, Jackson can *not* validly accept within the remaining stated period of time.

30. Exeter Industries, Inc., orally engaged Werglow as one of its district sales managers for an 18-month period commencing April 1, 1978. Werglow commenced work on that date and performed his duties in a highly competent manner for several months. On October 1, 1978, the company gave Werglow a notice of termination as of November 1, 1978, citing a downturn in the market for its products. Werglow sues seeking either specific performance or damages for breach of contract. Exeter pleads the statute of frauds and/or a justified dismissal due to the economic situation. What is the probable outcome of the lawsuit?

a. Werglow will prevail because the statute of frauds does *not* apply to contracts such as his.
b. Werglow will prevail because he has partially performed under the terms of the contract.
c. Werglow will lose because the reason for his termination was caused by economic factors beyond Exeter's control.
d. Werglow will lose because such a contract must be in writing and signed by a proper agent of Exeter.

Answers to Objective Questions

Explanation of Answers to Objective Questions

MAY 1981

7. (c) At the time the contract was made, the debt was liquidated since the amount was certain ($500). However, the bona fide dispute changed the debt to an unliquidated debt. Payment of a lesser sum to discharge an unliquidated debt will be effective if accepted as payment in full since each party gives consideration in the form of forfeiting a claim to dispute the amount of the debt. Smith's cashing of the check was acceptance of a settlement for the full amount of the debt. Answers (a) and (b) are incorrect since they refer to liquidated debts and this debt is unliquidated. Answer (d) is incorrect since the fact that Smith crossed out the words "paid in full" has no effect. The check must be accepted in the manner offered and Smith's cashing of the check discharges the entire unliquidated debt.

8. (c) Advertisements or other offers to trade such as price lists are usually considered proposals for negotiation or invitations seeking offers. In some cases, such an advertisement could be considered to be an offer if its terms were so specific as to single out a particular person or group as offerees (e.g., an ad offers a sale price to the first person to arrive at the store the next day). Usually, however, as in this case, such promotions are not considered to be offers. Since Harper's advertisement merely quotes prices on items in stock, it would not be construed as an offer (a), and if no offer is made, there can be no valid acceptance or contract formed as a result of such an ad [(b) and (d)].

9. (a) Dobbs' acceptance is valid upon dispatch under the rules of constructive communication, even though it stated both additional and different terms than those contained in the offer. Overall, Dobbs' communication manifested an intent to accept and enter into a contract. The additional and different terms are neither material nor contrary to the terms of the original offer. Answer (b) is incorrect because Dobbs' acceptance was effective when sent. It was a reasonable means of acceptance and placed in an independent agency's control. Answer (c) is incorrect because the subject communication should be understood to be an acceptance and not a counteroffer. Additionally no UCC rule provides that a counteroffer becomes valid if not negated or rejected by the party receiving it. Answer (d) is incorrect because additional or different terms in offers between merchants will not destroy the nature of the communication as being an acceptance per the UCC.

10. (b) This question deals with an offer to sell real property, thus the UCC, hence, the firm offer rule, does not apply. Since this offer does not fall under the UCC or contain a provision for consideration to be paid to hold open the offer (an option), the offer may be withdrawn anytime prior to acceptance. Answer (a) is untrue since a valid acceptance would have to be received, not posted, by April 1 in order to comply with the offer. Answer (c) is incorrect because an offer not supported by consideration and not subject to UCC rules may be withdrawn at any time. Answer (d) is incorrect since the Statute of Frauds requires only the contract for the sale of real property (not the offer) to be in writing.

11. (b) This question deals with an offer to sell real property; the UCC—and thus, the firm offer rule—do not apply. Since Schmit gave no consideration for the option to buy the property, Maurice may revoke the offer any time before Schmit accepts. Answer (a) is incorrect since only a merchant offeror making an offer for the sale of goods under the UCC would be bound to hold open an offer without consideration for a stated period of time. Answer (c) is incorrect since the Statute of Frauds applies only to the *contract* for sale of real property, and not an *offer* to buy; thus, the offer need not be in writing. Answer (d) is incorrect, since a nonmerchant may revoke an offer not supported by consideration any time before acceptance by the offeree.

There is no restriction on how this revocation may be communicated.

12. (a) The parol evidence rule applies to all written contracts and states that once an agreement is reduced to writing, the parties may not introduce oral or written agreements made prior to the written agreement in an attempt to alter or contradict the terms of the written agreement. This is true when the parties intended that the writing constitute their complete contract. Answer (b) is incorrect because the parol evidence rule would apply to all oral agreements made contemporaneously with the written contract. Answer (c) is incorrect since there is no requirement that both parties sign the contract in order for this rule to apply. Answer (d) is incorrect because the parol evidence rule is applied whether or not the Statute of Frauds requires a particular contract to be in writing.

13. (c) The acceptance of an offer must conform exactly to the terms of the offer. If a party intends to accept an offer, but includes additional or different terms which are intended to become part of the contract, this constitutes a counteroffer and not an acceptance (a possible exception to this exists with contracts made between two merchants concerning the sale of goods). Norriss' additional term is a condition precedent and constitutes a counteroffer. Answer (a) is incorrect because a contract for the sale of real property must be in writing (under the Statute of Frauds) to be enforceable unless the doctrine of partial performance applies. Answer (b) is incorrect since a valid contract need only be signed by the party to be charged with performance. Answer (d) is untrue because the addition of a condition precedent has a significant effect on the contractual relationship since it prevents a contract from being formed unless Wilcox accepts the new term.

NOVEMBER 1980

14. (b) The correct answer is (b). In an auction, the offer is accepted when the hammer goes down and the bidder can retract his bid until this time. The law presumes the sale is with reserve unless the owner announces the auction is without reserve, making answer (a) incorrect. Answer (d) is incorrect because an auction without reserve implies that the owner must sell to the highest bidder. Answer (d) describes an auction with reserve. Answer (c) is in-

correct since the retraction of a bid does not revive the previous bid.

25. (c) Answer (c) is correct in that it describes the only agency relationship that falls within the Statute of Frauds, one not capable of being performed within one year. The agency relationship described is for one year but to be an enforceable relationship as an oral agreement it must be capable of being performed within one year of the date of formation of the relationship. Since the date of formation and the date of the beginning of performance differ, the contract is not capable of being performed in one year and must be in writing to be enforceable. Since the relationship described in answer (d) could be performed in one month it is enforceable as an oral agreement. The relationships described in answers (a) and (b) do not fall within the Statute of Frauds and are enforceable as oral agreements.

NOVEMBER 1979

2. (a) A party to a contract who wishes to rescind the agreement and obtain a refund should seek the refund on the basis of misrepresentation rather than fraud. Misrepresentation does not require the plaintiff to prove actual intent on the part of the defendant but fraud does. Answer (b) is incorrect because the fraud theory requires that the defendant knowingly intended to commit fraud. Showing the defendant intended for the plaintiff to rely on a statement which later proved untrue is insufficient to establish an action in fraud. Answer (c) is incorrect because only in a fraud case would the plaintiff be required to prove the defendant knew the statements were false. In misrepresentation, proof is limited to establishing the statements were false. Answer (d) is incorrect since the statute of frauds applies to the written requirements of contracts and has nothing to do with the tort of fraud.

3. (a) The recipient of an offer who expends his time and money in studying and analyzing an offer would not satisfy the requirements of consideration to form a contract, because such efforts are not at the request of the offeror. Answer (b) is incorrect because where the offeree makes a promise which is a legal detriment to him or a benefit to the offeror, such promise is legal consideration. Answer (c) is also incorrect because if the offeree performs an act requested by the offeror, the consideration requirement has been satisfied. Similarly, answer (d) is incorrect because it is an example of the offeree making a promise which benefits the offeror, and again the requirement of consideration is satisfied. Note that answers (b) and (d) each assume that the act or promise was solicited by the offeror.

4. (d) The parol evidence rule does not apply to the stated facts because the evidence introduced is a contemporaneous oral agreement in the face of a comprehensive written agreement. Answer (a) is incorrect because the parol evidence rule does apply to contemporaneous oral agreements. The rule is based on the presumption that the parties have incorporated every material item into the written agreement. However, the parol evidence rule does not exclude subsequent agreements although an "entirety" clause will. An "entirety" clause allows only written changes to be enforced. Answer (b) is incorrect because the parol evidence rule is designed to protect a written contract from change or contradiction. Complying with the statute of frauds in no way affects whether the parol evidence rule applies or not in a written contract. Answer (c) is incorrect because in substance, the oral agreement does contradict the written contract. As the contract is written, the seller's obligation would be to deliver a title along with proof of marketable title. Under the oral agreement an additional legal duty of the seller, Marsh, would be to remove several large rocks on the land which is in conflict with the written contract.

5. (b) The basic distinction between a bilateral contract and a unilateral contract is there are 2 promises in bilateral agreements and only 1 promise in unilateral agreements. Answer (a) is incorrect because specific performance is available in appropriate circumstances whether the contract is unilateral or bilateral. Answer (c) is incorrect because the statute of frauds applies on the basis of the subject of the agreement and makes no distinction between bilateral and unilateral contracts. Answer (d) is incorrect because rights which are otherwise properly assignable under a contract are not affected by whether the rights arise out of a unilateral or bilateral agreement.

7. (d) There is a valid and binding contract which includes the 15 current model radios. The mistake alleged by Masters is a unilateral mistake and the

general rule is that one party to a contract cannot avoid the agreement on the grounds that a mistake was made when the other party has no notice of the mistake and acts in good faith. This seems to be the case here. Answers (a) and (b) are incorrect because of the general rule stated above that agreements are not voidable on the basis of a unilateral mistake. Answer (c) is incorrect because the contract was not entered into as a result of a mutual mistake but rather as a result of a unilateral mistake. Darling Discount did not make a mistake, and they made a good faith bid based on the entire lot of radios that they were shown by Master.

8. (b) When the creditor agrees to substitute a new debtor for the original debtor, a novation has occurred. Answer (a) is incorrect because in a delegation the original debtor remains liable to the creditor. Answer (c) is incorrect because the bank did receive consideration: Michael agreed to pay the mortgage in exchange for Arthur's being released. Answer (d) is incorrect since Arthur was released.

9. (a) As part of the original contract Radiant agreed to service the heating system purchased by Williams for a flat rate of $200 per year. Thus, Radiant was under a pre-existing legal duty to perform the maintenance work and any subsequent promise to pay for such services is without consideration and unenforceable. Answer (b) is incorrect because the Statute of Frauds is not applicable to this problem. The dispute is over a service arrangement and not the sale of goods. Answer (c) is incorrect because the offer to pay the additional amount makes no difference with respect to the requirement of consideration. Answer (d) is incorrect because an uneconomical contract does not free a party from a contract unless significant unforeseen difficulties are encountered.

10. (d) A clause in a contract indicating that the contract was intended as the "entire contract" will preclude oral evidence to explain or modify any contractual terms covered in the contract. Answers (a) and (b) are incorrect because if a written contract contains an obvious ambiguity or mutual mistake of fact, the court will allow the introduction of oral evidence to explain the true nature of the contract. Answer (c) is incorrect because parol evidence rule does not prevent the introduction of oral evidence that a written contract was modified following execution. The parol evidence rule merely prohibits the introduction of oral evidence concerning agreements or statements made prior to or at the time the agreement was reduced to writing.

11. (a) Montbanks promised to give Dobbs $50,000 in commission business if the firm would hire Charles. However, Dobbs already had hired him. Therefore a promise by Dobbs to hire Charles is past consideration which does not create a contract. Answer (b) is incorrect because Dobbs already hired Charles. Therefore the legal duty to hire him was complete. Answer (c) is incorrect because a signed writing will not cure a lack of consideration. Answer (d) is incorrect because Dobbs did not hire Charles while relying on Montbanks' promise.

12. (b) A covenant by a party selling a business not to compete for a reasonable time within a reasonable geographical area of the business sold is enforceable. Answer (a) is incorrect because Golden contracted not to practice pharmacy (whether or not in his own name). Answers (c) and (d) are incorrect because only where the restraint is considered to be excessive does it violate public policy or federal antitrust law.

13. (b) Where a debt is honestly disputed, and the debtor sends the creditor a check marked "account paid in full" or similar language, the cashing or the holding of the check for a reasonable period of time will constitute an accord and satisfaction. Answer (a) is incorrect because there had been an accord and satisfaction. Therefore, the debt is discharged, and Keith is not entitled to recover damages. Answer (c) is incorrect because there is no pre-existing legal duty, as the debt is honestly disputed. Answer (d) is incorrect because courts do place great weight on industry customs.

17. (d) No contract arose since Abacus effectively revoked its offer on 2/8/79 prior to Frame's acceptance by telephoning Frame and withdrawing the offer. Although the original offer indicated that it would expire in ten days, it did not contain a promise that it would not be withdrawn or was irrevocable. Answer (a) is incorrect since it was not an irrevocable offer and in any event, Frame's acceptance would have been timely had the offer not been revoked. Answer (b) is incorrect because the withdrawal of an offer need not be in writing to be effec-

tive. It may be communicated in any manner. Answer (c) is incorrect because the offer was revoked before Frame sent its acceptance. However, had the offer not been revoked, Frame's acceptance would have been effective when sent.

NOVEMBER 1978

27. (d) The communication by James Martin, President of Martin Stores, Inc., did not constitute an offer to sell, but instead was an invitation to negotiate. The Statute of Frauds applies to the sales of interests in real property whether or not recorded, and thus answer (a) is incorrect. Answer (b) is incorrect because Markus has only made an offer and not an acceptance since no offer had been made to Markus. Answer (c) is incorrect because Martin need not sell to anyone. Martin has simply made an invitation to negotiate and may accept or reject any offers.

28. (d) Offers to contract may only be accepted by the person to whom they were made. They are not assignable to another party unless the offeror chooses to accept the assignment. Answer (a) is incorrect because no option is created since no consideration was paid. Also it is not a firm offer under the UCC because the subject matter is a service arrangement and not goods. Answer (b) is incorrect because under the facts, if an acceptance from Direct to Fashion had been sent on October 1, 1978, it would create a valid acceptance, and thus a contract. The acceptance is deemed made on the day transmitted. Answer (c) is incorrect because the Statute of Frauds would apply to the subject arrangement as it involves a contract that cannot be performed by its terms within one year.

29. (d) A rejection effectively terminates an offer, and thus the offeree cannot validly accept later, even though he purports to do so within the remaining stated period of the offer. Answer (a) is incorrect because the offer as stated can be withdrawn at any time prior to acceptance. Answer (b) is incorrect because the offer would be terminated if the offeror sells the property to a third person and notifies a prior offeree. Answer (c) is incorrect because the subject matter is real estate and an oral acceptance would be unenforceable due to the lack of a writing.

30. (d) The Statute of Frauds requires contracts that cannot be performed within a period of one year to be in writing to be enforceable. This contract of employment is for 18 months, and thus Werglow will not prevail because such a contract must be in writing and signed by an agent of the employer corporation. Thus, answer (a) is incorrect because the Statute of Frauds does apply to employment contracts such as Werglow's. The fact that partial performance has occurred as in answer (b) does not displace the Statute of Frauds. Answer (c) is incorrect because economic factors are not accepted as cause for terminating an otherwise valid contract. The general rule is that impossibility or hardship do not justify breach of an otherwise valid contract.

ESSAY QUESTIONS AND ANSWERS

NOVEMBER 1980 (Estimated time: 15 to 20 minutes)

5. Part a. Fennimore owned a ranch which was encumbered by a seven percent (7%) mortgage held by the Orange County Bank. As of July 31, 1980, the outstanding mortgage amount was $83,694. Fennimore decided to sell the ranch and engage in the grain storage business. During the time that he was negotiating the sale of the ranch, the bank sent out an offer to several mortgagors indicating a five percent (5%) discount on the mortgage if the mortgagors would pay the entire mortgage in cash or by certified check by July 31, 1980. The bank was doing this in order to liquidate older unprofitable mortgages which it had on the books. Anyone seeking to avail himself of the offer was required to present his payment at the Second Street branch on July 31, 1980. Fennimore, having obtained a buyer for his property, decided to take advantage of the offer since his buyer was arranging his own financing and was not interested in assuming the mortgage. Therefore, on July 15th he wrote the bank a letter which stated: "I accept your offer on my mortgage, see you on July 31, 1980, I'll have a certified check." Fennimore did not indicate that he was selling the ranch and would have to pay off the full amount in any event. On July 28, the bank sent Fennimore a letter by certified mail which was received by Fennimore on the 30th of July which stated: "We withdraw our offer. We are over subscribed. Furthermore, we have learned that you are selling your property and the mortgage is not being assumed." Nevertheless, on July 31 at 9:05 in the morning when Fennimore walked in the door of the bank holding his certified check, Vogelspiel, a bank mortgage officer, approached him and stated firmly and clearly that the bank's offer had been revoked and that the bank would refuse to accept tender of payment. Dumbfounded by all this, Fennimore nevertheless tendered the check, which was refused.

Required Answer the following, setting forth reasons for any conclusions stated.

In the eventual lawsuit that ensued, who will prevail?

Answer Orange County Bank will prevail. The fact situation poses a classic illustration of a withdrawal of an offer to enter into a unilateral contract. The bank's offer to Fennimore called for the performance of an act (the actual paying of the mortgage), not a promise to pay it, as the means of acceptance. The language in the offer is clear and unambiguous, providing a 5 percent discount on a mortgage if the mortgagor would pay the entire mortgage in cash or by certified check by July 31, 1980, at the Second Street branch of the bank. Thus, the bank's letter was an offer to enter into a unilateral contract that required the performance of the act as the authorized and exclusive means of acceptance. Fennimore's promise to perform the act was ineffectual in creating a contract. Contract law generally provides that offers may be revoked at any time prior to acceptance; even if the bank revoked its offer the instant before the purported acceptance, it was a timely revocation and the acceptance was too late. The tender of performance would also be of no avail since notice of revocation had been received on the 30th.

In this situation, strict common law rules would deny the creation of a contract. Some states, in recognition of the hardship of such results, have adopted what is known as the *restatement of contracts* rule. This modification of the common law rule in respect to the unilateral contract rule holds that the unilateral promise in an offer calling for an act becomes binding as soon as part of the requested performance actually has been rendered or a proper tender of performance has been made. The courts have required substantial action on the part of the offeree, which does not appear to be present here.

The fact that Fennimore was selling his property and did not disclose the fact that he would have to pay the mortgage off in any event is immaterial. There was no material misrepresentation of fact made by him, hence his action was not fraudulent nor did he misrepresent. He was silent. Additionally, the fact that the bank was using the sale as a reason for terminating the offer was immaterial.

5. Part b. Austin wrote a letter and mailed it to Hernandez offering to sell Hernandez his tuna canning business for $125,000. Hernandez promptly mailed a reply acknowledging receipt of Austin's letter and expressing an interest in purchasing the cannery. However, Hernandez offered Austin only $110,000. Later Hernandez decided that the business was in fact worth at least the $125,000 that Austin was asking. He therefore decided to accept the original offer tendered to him at $125,000 and telegraphed Austin an unconditional acceptance at $125,000. The telegram reached Austin before Hernandez' prior letter, although the letter arrived later that day. Austin upon receipt of the telegram telegraphed Hernandez that as a result of further analysis as to the worth of the business, he was not willing to sell at less than $150,000. Hernandez claims a contract at $125,000 resulted from his telegram. Austin asserts either that there is no contract or that the purchase price is $150,000.

Required Answer the following, setting forth reasons for any conclusions stated.

If the dispute goes to court, who will prevail?

Answer Hernandez will prevail. An offer is not effective until communicated to the offeree. The same rule applies to counteroffers including a change in the price, as occurred here. Therefore, a counteroffer is not effective until received by Austin, the original offeror. Hernandez's counteroffer does not destroy the offer until it is received. Thus, Hernandez's telegram, which accepted Austin's offer and arrived ahead of Hernandez's letter containing the counteroffer, is effective in creating a binding contract.

This rule applies even if Hernandez had mailed a letter that unequivocally accepted Austin's offer and that would have been effective upon dispatch. The general rule that an acceptance is effective when dispatched is subject to an exception that is designed to prevent entrapment of an offeror who is misled to his disadvantage by an offeree who attempts to take two inconsistent positions. Thus, when an offeree first rejects an offer, then subsequently accepts it, the subsequent acceptance will be considered effective upon dispatch by an authorized means only if it arrives prior to the offeror's receipt of the rejection. If the rejection arrives first, the original offeror may treat the attempted acceptance as a counteroffer which he is free to accept or not. Were this not the rule, an offeror who,

upon receipt of a rejection, in good faith changed his position (that is, sold the goods to another customer), could find himself having sold the same goods twice.

MAY 1980 (Estimated time: 20 to 25 minutes)

3. Part a. Smithers contracted with the Silverwater Construction Corporation to build a home. The contract contained a detailed set of specifications including the type, quality, and manufacturers' names of the building materials that were to be used. After construction was completed, a rigid inspection was made of the house and the following defects were discovered:

1. Some of the roofing shingles were improperly laid.
2. The ceramic tile in the kitchen and three bathrooms was not manufactured by Disco Tile Company as called for in the specifications. The price of the alternate tile was $325 less than the Disco but was of approximately equal quality.
3. The sewerage pipes that were imbedded in concrete in the basement were also not manufactured by the specified manufacturer. It could not be shown that there was any difference in quality and the price was the same.
4. Various minor defects such as improperly hung doors.

Silverwater has corrected defects (1) and (4) but has refused to correct defects (2) and (3) because the cost would be substantial. Silverwater claims it is entitled to recover under the contract and demands full payment. Smithers is adamant and is demanding literal performance of the contract or he will not pay.

Required Answer the following, setting forth reasons for any conclusions stated.

1. If the dispute goes to court, who will prevail, assuming Silverwater's breach of contract was intentional?
2. If the dispute goes to court, who will prevail, assuming Silverwater's breach of contract was unintentional?

Answer The general common-law rules require literal performance by a party to a contract. Failure to literally perform constitutes a breach. Since promises are construed to be dependent upon each other, the failure by one party to perform releases the other. However, a strict and literal application of this type of implied condition often results in unfairness and hardship, particularly in cases such as this. Therefore, the courts developed some important exceptions to the literal performance doctrine. The applicable rule is known as the substantial performance doctrine, which applies to construction contracts and is a more specific statement of the material performance rule that applies to contracts other than construction contracts. The general rule holds that if the breach is immaterial, the party who breached may nevertheless recover under the contract, less damages caused by the breach. The substantial performance doctrine requires the builder (party breaching) to prove the following facts.

1. The defect was not a structural defect.
2. The breach was relatively minor in relation to the overall performance of the contract. The courts and texts sometimes talk in terms of a 95 percent or better performance.
3. The breach must be unintentional or, to state it another way, the party breaching must have been acting in good faith.

It would appear that requirements *a* and *b* are clearly satisfied on the basis of the facts. Requirement *c* cannot be determined on the facts given. If Silverwater deliberately (with knowledge) substituted the improper and cheaper tile or sewerage pipes, then it may not be entitled to the benefit of the substantial performance exception. On the other hand, if these breaches were the result of an innocent oversight or mere negligence on its part, recovery should be granted. The recovery must be decreased by the amount of the damages caused by the breach. The substitution of sewer pipe of like quality and value would be considered substantial performance.

3. Part b. Jane Anderson offered to sell Richard Heinz a ten acre tract of commercial property. Anderson's letter indicated the offer would expire on March 1, 1980, at 3:00 p.m. and that any acceptance must be received in her office by that time. On February 29, 1980, Heinz decided to accept the offer and posted an acceptance at 4:00 p.m. Heinz indicated that in the event the acceptance did not arrive on time, he would assume there was a contract if he did not hear anything from Anderson in five days. The letter arrived on March 2, 1980. Anderson never responded to Heinz's letter. Heinz claims a contract was entered into and is suing thereon.

Required Answer the following, setting forth reasons for any conclusions stated.

Is there a contract?

Answer No. The offer for the sale of real property is governed by the common law of contracts.

Anderson's letter constituted an offer that stated it would expire at a given time. In addition to stating the time, the letter indicated that acceptance "must be received in her (Anderson's) office" by said time. This language is clear and unambiguous and effectively negated the rule whereby acceptance may take place upon dispatch. Thus, despite use of the same means of communication, acceptance was not effective until receipt by Anderson on March 2, 1980. This was too late. Thus, the purported acceptance was a mere counteroffer by Heinz and had to be accepted in order to create a contract. Silence does not usually constitute acceptance. In fact, the common-law exceptions to this rule are limited in nature and narrowly construed. The law clearly will not permit a party to unilaterally impose silence upon the other as acceptance. The narrow exceptions are the following:

1. The parties intended silence as acceptance.
2. Prior dealing indicates that silence is an acceptable method of acceptance.
3. The custom of the trade or industry recognizes silence as acceptance.

It is clear that our case is not within any of the exceptions; hence, silence does not constitute acceptance, and there is no contract.

3. Part c. Betty Monash was doing business as Victory Stamp Company. She sold the business as a going concern. The assets of the business consist of an inventory of stamps, various trade fixtures which are an inherent part of the business, a building which houses the retail operation, goodwill, and miscellaneous office equipment. On the liability side, there are numerous trade accounts payable and a first mortgage on the building.

Joe Franklin purchased the business. In addition to a cash payment, he assumed all outstanding debts and promised to hold Monash harmless from any and all liability on the scheduled debts listed in the contract of sale.

Required Answer the following, setting forth reasons for any conclusions stated.

What is the legal relationship of Monash,

Franklin, and the creditors to each other after the consummation of the sale with respect to the outstanding debts of the business?

Answer The sale of the business to Franklin was both an assignment (sale) of all rights and a delegation (assumption) of the duties connected with the business. Consequently, Monash assumes the role of a surety and remains liable to pay the existing debts immediately (for example, the mortgage) upon default by Franklin. The creditors' rights are unaffected. Franklin becomes the principal debtor and in the relationship between Monash and him, he should pay as he promised her. Although his promise was made to Monash only, the creditors are third-party creditor beneficiaries of that promise. Therefore, they have the standing to sue Franklin on that promise despite the lack of privity and even though they have given no consideration for Franklin's promise. They may also proceed on the original promise made by Monash upon which she remains liable.

NOVEMBER 1978 (Estimated time: 10 to 13 minutes)

5. Part c. Novack, an industrial designer, accepted an offer from Superior Design Corporation to become one of its designers. The contract was for three years and expressly provided that it was irrevocable by either party except for cause during that period of time. The contract was in writing and signed by both parties. After a year, Novack became dissatisfied with the agreed compensation which he was receiving. He had done a brilliant job and several larger corporations were attempting to lure him away.

Novack, therefore, demanded a substantial raise, and Superior agreed in writing to pay him an additional amount as a bonus at the end of the third year. Novack remained with Superior and performed the same duties he had agreed to perform at the time he initially accepted the position. At the end of the three years, Novack sought to collect the additional amount of money promised. Superior denied liability beyond the amount agreed to in the original contract.

Required Answer the following, setting forth reasons for any conclusions stated.

Can Novack recover the additional compensation from Superior?

Answer No. The pre-existing legal duty rule applies. Novack has not given any consideration for Superior's promise of additional compensation. The common law rules apply to contracts for services, and modifications of such contracts must be supported by consideration. In essence, Novack was already bound by a valid contract to perform exactly what he did perform under the modified contract. Hence, he did nothing more than he was legally obligated to do. As a result, there is no consideration to support Superior's promise to pay the bonus.

Section 2-209 of the Uniform Commercial Code, which provides that an agreement modifying a contract needs no consideration to be binding, is not applicable to an employment contract because section 2-209 covers only the sale of goods.

5. Part d. The basic facts are the same as stated in Part c except that one of Superior's competitors, Dixon Corporation, successfully lured Novack away from Superior by offering a substantially higher salary. Dixon did this with full knowledge of the terms of the original three-year contract between Novack and Superior.

Required Answer the following, setting forth reasons for any conclusions stated.

1. Does Superior have any legal redress against Dixon?
2. Would Superior be successful if it seeks the equitable relief of specific performance (an order by the court compelling Novack to perform his contractual undertaking) for the remaining two years of the contract?

Answer

1. Yes. A cause of action based upon Dixon's intentional interference with a contractual relationship would be available. All the requirements necessary to state such a cause of action are present, particularly the knowledge of the existing contractual relationship between Novack and Superior. The law treats Dixon's conduct as tortious and allows a recovery for damages against Dixon.
2. No. A court exercising its equity powers will not force a person to fulfill a contract for personal services. To do so smacks of involuntary servitude.

PART THREE

Uniform Commercial Code
(25%)*

---

* This percentage allocation represents the relative weight to be given to this *area* of business law on the Uniform CPA Examinations beginning in November 1983. It also indicates the approximate percentage of the total achievable test score to be assigned to this *area* of business law for each Uniform CPA Examination beginning in November 1983.

CHAPTER

3

Sales

The following is a generalized listing of subjects to be tested through the May 1983 Uniform CPA Examination.

This topic is largely concerned with Article 2 (Sales) of the Uniform Commercial Code (as amended in 1972) which includes contracts for the purchase or sale of goods, warranty protection of the buyer, privity of warranty, product liability of the seller (including federal law applicable thereto), allocation of risk of loss, and the buyer's and seller's rights, duties, and remedies.[1]

The AICPA Board of Examiners has adopted a new content specification outline for the business law section of the Uniform CPA Examination, *to be effective with the November 1983 examination*. The outline lists the following topics to be tested under the title "Sales."

   C. Sales
      1. Contracts Covering Goods
      2. Warranties
      3. Product Liability
      4. Risk of Loss
      5. Performance and Obligations
      6. Remedies and Defenses[2]

---

[1] AICPA, *Information for CPA Candidates*, Copyright © 1975, 1979, by the American Institute of Certified Public Accountants, Inc.

[2] AICPA, *Business Law—Content Specification Outline*, approved by the AICPA Board of Examiners on August 31, 1981.

I. Definitions.

A. *Sale* is a contract in which the seller transfers the ownership of goods to the buyer at the time the contract is made in return for a consideration called *price* [2-106(1), 2-401]. (See Figures 3-1 and 3-2.)

B. *Contract to sell* is a transaction in which the seller agrees to transfer ownership of goods that are not in existence or not identified to the contract to the buyer at some future time, for a consideration called *price* [2-106(1), 2-401]. (See Figure 3-1.)

C. *Special property interest.* At the moment that the goods are identified to the contract, the buyer obtains a special property interest in the goods. This interest gives the buyer the following rights:

1. To obtain casualty insurance covering the goods;

2. To sue the seller for damages in case of the seller's breach;

3. To inspect the goods; and

4. To obtain possession of the goods from the seller if the seller became insolvent within ten days of receipt of the first installment of the purchase price.

D. *Fungible goods* are goods of which any unit is the equivalent of any other unit by reason of its nature or commercial usage [1-201(17)].

E. *Merchants* are persons who deal in goods of the kind involved or who otherwise by occupation hold themselves out as having knowledge or skill peculiar to the practice or goods involved in the transaction (2-104).

F. *Title* is an interest in property which entitles the owner to the rights of possession, enjoyment, use, and disposition of the property.

G. *Risk of loss* is the burden of suffering an economic loss as a result of the damage or destruction of goods.

H. *Warranty* is any affirmation of fact, express or implied, made by the seller of goods to the buyer as a part of the contract of sale (2-312 to 2-315).

I. *Cover* is the buyer's discretionary right to buy goods elsewhere when the seller wrongfully fails to deliver the goods as required under the contract (2-712).

FIGURE 3-1 SALE AND CONTRACT TO SELL COMPARED

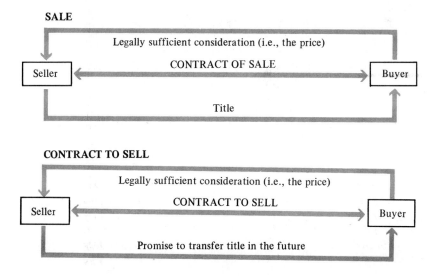

FIGURE 3-2 DEFINITION OF GOODS

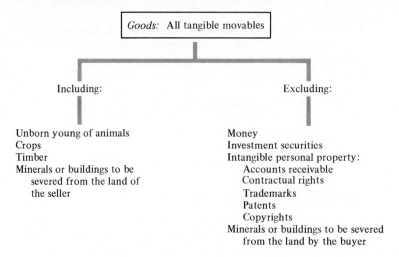

Goods: All tangible movables	
Including:	**Excluding:**
Unborn young of animals	Money
Crops	Investment securities
Timber	Intangible personal property:
Minerals or buildings to be	Accounts receivable
severed from the land of	Contractual rights
the seller	Trademarks
	Patents
	Copyrights
	Minerals or buildings to be severed
	from the land by the buyer

J. *Cure* is the seller's right to remedy nonconforming goods shipped to the buyer prior to the date final performance of the contract is to take place (2-508).

K. *C.O.D. (collect on delivery)* is a shipping term in a contract which allows the seller to retain possession of the goods until payment is made [2-513(3)(a)].

L. *Consignment* is a transfer of possession, not title, of goods to another for purposes of shipment or sale. The transferee is usually the agent of the transferor.

M. *Security interest* is any legal interest in the property which secures payment or performance of a debt or other obligation [9-102(1)(a)].

N. *Nonconforming goods* are goods which are not in accordance with the obligations under a contract to sell [2-106(2)].

O. *Identification to the contract* is an act or series of acts by a seller that clearly indicates the exact goods intended to fulfill the terms of a particular contract of sale.

NATURE OF THE SALES TRANSACTION

II. Other commercial transactions distinguished from sales.

    A. *Gift* is a present transfer of title and possession *without consideration*.

        1. To be effective, a gift requires a "delivery" of the property to the donee with intent to make a gift.

        2. "Delivery" of the property is not necessary to pass title by way of sale.

        3. The donee neither bargains for nor receives anything in exchange for the goods.

    B. *Bailment* is a transfer of temporary possession of personal property *without a transfer of the title.*

    C. *Secured transaction.* Under the UCC, a chattel mortgage, conditional sale, pledge, or any other agreement which creates or provides for a security interest (lien) in goods is called a "secured transaction" (9-102). (See Figure 3-3.)

        1. The transfer or location of title or possession is unimportant to the existence or enforceability of the security interest (lien).

        2. The owner of a security interest (lien) is protected against claims of third parties by public filing of a financing statement or by possession of the goods by the secured creditor in the case of a pledge.

80 *Part 3: Uniform Commercial Code*

FIGURE 3-3 SALE AND PURCHASE-MONEY SECURED TRANSACTION COMPARED

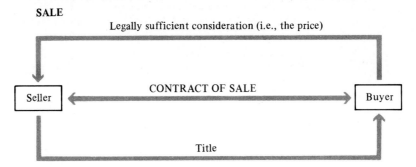

SALE

Legally sufficient consideration (i.e., the price)

Seller ⟷ CONTRACT OF SALE ⟷ Buyer

Title

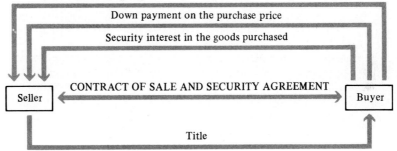

PURCHASE MONEY SECURED TRANSACTION

Debt evidenced by buyer's note for the balance of the purchase price

Down payment on the purchase price

Security interest in the goods purchased

Seller ⟷ CONTRACT OF SALE AND SECURITY AGREEMENT ⟷ Buyer

Title

3. In a secured transaction, both the creditor and the debtor have rights in the goods.
   a. The right of the secured creditor in the goods is to exercise a lien against the goods upon default of the debtor.
   b. The right of the debtor is to use, possess, and enjoy the goods and, where specifically provided, to sell them in the ordinary course of business and to account for the proceeds.
4. In contrast, a sale transfers to the buyer all of the ownership rights of the seller in the goods.

FORMATION OF THE SALES CONTRACT

III. The formation of a contract for the sale of goods is governed by the same common law rules as those governing the formation of other types of contracts. In addition, the UCC has adopted special rules made applicable *only* to contracts for the sale of goods. The chart on pages 82 to 85 provides a comparison of rules which apply to non-UCC contracts with those which apply to UCC contracts.

LETTERS OF CREDIT (Article 5 of the UCC)

IV. Letters of credit are frequently used in conjunction with sales of goods, sales of investment securities, transfers of commercial paper, and transfers of documents of title (e.g., warehouse receipts and bills of lading). The following discussion is limited to the letter of credit as it is used to facilitate a sale of goods.

Non-UCC contracts	UCC contracts
(Transactions *not* concerning contracts for the sale of goods, e.g., contract of employment, contract to sell real estate, contract to sell intangible personal property.)	(Transactions concerning *only* contracts for the sale of goods.)

A. Offer

1. An offer must be sufficiently definite in order to be valid; i.e., it must identify, at a minimum, the price, quantity, subject matter, and parties.	The UCC provides a more liberal rule so that a contract will not fail for indefiniteness if it is shown that the parties intend to make a contract and there is a reasonably certain basis for granting remedy (2-204). "Open price" agreements, "output," "requirement contracts," "exclusive dealings," open delivery arrangements, open assortments, open shipping arrangements are valid (2-305 to 311).
2. An offer unsupported by consideration may be revoked at any time prior to acceptance, even though the offeror states that it will be left open for a specified period of time.	A *"firm offer"* by a merchant may *not* be revoked until the expiration of the period of time stated by the offeror, or a reasonable time if none is stated, where the offer is made in writing and signed by the merchant and the period stated does not exceed three months (2-205).

B. Acceptance

1. *Additional terms.* Acceptance must conform to all the terms of the offer, and any additional terms will have the effect of rejecting the offer and making the communication a counteroffer.	Unless both parties are merchants, an acceptance of an offer that contains *additional terms* is a valid acceptance *but only* to the offeror's terms, and the additional terms are treated only as proposals to the contract which themselves must be approved (2-207). Between merchants the additional terms become a part of the contract unless (1) the new terms materially alter the terms of the offer, (2) the offeror gives notification of objection to the offeree within a reasonable time, or (3) the offer expressly prohibits additional terms (2-207). If the offeror is a non-merchant, the additional terms are not binding unless assented to by the nonmerchant.
2. *Manner and time of acceptance.*	Acceptance will be effective at the time it is sent or dispatched if the acceptance is made in any manner and by any medium *reasonable* under the circumstances, provided that the offeror does not expressly state the means of acceptance to be used (2-206).
3. *Actual and constructive acceptance.* The general rule is that an acceptance is not effective until it is "received" by the offeror. *Exception:* If the offeror *expressly or impliedly authorizes a specific means* by which the acceptance is to be communicated and the offeree utilizes the authorized means, the acceptance is effective at the moment it is properly posted, sent, or dispatched. If no means of communicating the acceptance is stated in the offer, it is implied that the same means used to transmit the offer is the means authorized by the offeror.	If the offeree does not use a reasonable means of communication of acceptance or does not use the means designated by the offeror, the general rule applies and the acceptance will not be effective until "received" by the offeror.

Non-UCC contracts	UCC contracts
4. *Offer for unilateral contract.* An offer to enter into a unilateral contract can be accepted only by completion of the act or forbearance requested in the offer.	When prompt or current shipment is requested, the (buyer) offeror is inviting acceptance either by the prompt promise to ship or by the prompt shipment of conforming or nonconforming goods. Such a shipment of nonconforming goods will constitute an acceptance unless the seller (offeree) reasonably notifies the buyer (offeror) that the shipment is offered only as an accommodation to the buyer (2-206).
5. *Offer for bilateral contract.* Where an offer calls for a promise as an acceptance, the offeree cannot accept the offer by performance of an act. Where an offeror calls for acceptance by shipment of goods, the offeree's shipment of *nonconforming* goods is not an acceptance.	

C. Consideration

Non-UCC contracts	UCC contracts
1. An agreement modifying a previous contract that involves a promise to perform or the performance of what one is already under a legal obligation to do is not supported by sufficient consideration and therefore is not binding.	A subsequent agreement modifying an existing contract needs no consideration to be binding (2-209). Any claim or right to damages arising out of a breach of contract can be discharged by a signed and delivered written waiver or renunciation of the claim or right by the aggrieved party (1-107).
2. A written contract which expressly states that there may be no oral modification can nevertheless be modified if the agreement to modify is supported by sufficient consideration.	A written contract which excludes modification or rescission except by a signed writing cannot otherwise be modified or rescinded. However, if a nonmerchant is to be held to such a clause on a form provided by the merchant, it must be signed separately by the nonmerchant (2-209).
3. *Seal.* In a few jurisdictions, the affixing of a seal to a written contract raises the presumption of consideration.	The legal effect of a seal has been abolished insofar as contracts for the sale of goods are concerned (2-203).

D. Defenses

Non-UCC contracts	UCC contracts
Unconscionable contracts. This defense is available only in equity.	This defense has been extended by the UCC to include cases at law as well as in equity (2-302).

E. Statute of Frauds

Non-UCC contracts	UCC contracts
1. Any contract for the sale of *personal property* for a price of $500 or more must be in writing.	Any contract for the sale of *goods* for a price of $500 or more must be in writing (2-201).
2. The writing, in order to be legally sufficient, must identify the subject matter, parties, price, and quantity.	The requirement is only of "some writing" indicating that a contract for the sale of goods exists (2-201). The terms required to be set forth in the writing under the common law are not required under the UCC.
3. Only those parties who sign the writing are bound.	The writing must be signed by each party to be charged. *Exceptions* [2-201(3)]: **1.** *Confirmation letter.* As between merchants a written confirmation of an oral contract not responded to within ten days and signed by only one of the parties is sufficient to bind both parties.

Non-UCC contracts	UCC contracts
	2. *Specially manufactured goods.* Oral contracts for specially manufactured goods are binding if the seller has made a substantial beginning of their manufacture or made commitments for their procurement.
	3. *Admission in court.* An admission in court as to the existence of an oral contract is enforceable to the extent of the quantity of goods admitted.
4. Part payment or acceptance causes the *entire oral* contract to be enforceable.	Part payment or acceptance of part of the goods binds the buyer, but *only to the extent* of the commercial units paid for or accepted under the oral contract [2-201(3)(c)].

F. Parol evidence rule

This rule prevents the introduction of *any* prior contradictory oral or written statements of the parties which would alter or add to the written terms of the contract.	Supporting oral or written evidence concerning prior courses of dealings, the usages of the trade, or the course of performance of the contract may be introduced to help clarify or explain the terms of the contract (2-202). *Also*, any oral or written evidence *consistent* with the terms of the written contract may be introduced.

G. Performance

1. *Threatened anticipatory breach.* Circumstances which are not sufficient to constitute an anticipatory breach do not entitle a party to any remedy prior to the agreed-upon date of performance.	*Assurance.* The opposing party can demand assurance of performance in writing if he or she feels "insecure" that performance will not be forthcoming on the agreed-upon date. Failure to provide assurance within a reasonable length of time constitutes repudiation (2-609).
2. *Retraction of repudiation* is allowed unless the innocent party has already relied on the repudiation and has taken some action to change his or her position.	Retraction is allowed unless the innocent party has (1) changed positions, (2) given notice of cancellation of the contract, or (3) given notice that he or she considers the breach final (2-611).
3. *Goods to be delivered by installments.* Default on one installment of a multiinstallment contract merely gives the buyer a right to sue for damages as each default occurs. No matter how "serious" the breach, the buyer is not entitled to treat it as a breach of the entire contract.	In the case of default on part of an installment contract, the buyer may treat it as a breach of the entire contract, if the default is so substantial that it impairs the value of the entire contract [2-612(3)].
4. *Impossibility and commercial hardship.* As a general rule, impracticality, commercial hardship, and unforeseen difficulties are not sufficient to free a party to a contract from obligations. Substitute performance is not valid.	*Commercial frustration.* If performance of a contract has been made commercially impractical because of a contingency *(when the nonoccurrence of this contingency was the basis of the contract)*, failure to deliver or delay in delivery will not constitute a breach [2-615(a)], for example, a disruption of the agreed-upon method of transportation, or noncompliance with an applicable government regulation.

Non-UCC contracts	UCC contracts

H. Rights of third parties

1. *Assignment of contract rights.* Consent of the other party is not necessary for an assignment of rights unless there exists special trust and confidence in the assignor; i.e., the contract calls for the performance of *personal* services.	An assignment is valid unless it would (1) materially alter the duty of the other party; (2) materially increase the burden of risk imposed on that party by the contract; or (3) materially impair that party's chances of obtaining return performance [2-210(2)].
A nonassignment clause in a contract is valid, and any attempt to assign the rights under the contract is void.	A provision prohibiting assignment of accounts receivable or contract rights is ineffectual [9-318(4)].

If the assignor has performed the required duties under the contract, any nonassignment clause is not effective (2-210). |
| Future rights are *not* assignable. | Rights arising out of future contracts for the sale of goods *are* assignable. |
| **2.** *Delegation of duties.* Assignment of rights does not impliedly carry with it the delegation of duties. An express assumption of duties is necessary. | An assignment of "the contract" or "all of my rights under the contract" includes an implied delegation of duties by the assignor and an implied promise (assumption) by the assignee to perform the duties. An express assumption of the duties is not required (2-210). |

I. Discharge, damages, and remedies

1. *Statute of Limitations.* The Statute of Limitations time period varies with state law. Common provisions are five years after a breach of an oral contract and ten years after a breach of a written contract.	The Statute of Limitations barring an action for breach of a sales contract is established at four years after a breach occurs [2-725(1)].
2. *Damages.* As damages for breach of contract, the plaintiff is entitled to receive the difference between the market price and the contract price. The market price is not established by the price paid for substitutes. Rescission or damages are alternative remedies. An injured party cannot rescind a contract and also receive damages.	By purchasing substitute goods ("cover") in good faith without unreasonable delay, the buyer is deemed to have fixed the market price at the time of cover for purposes of computing damages [2-712(2)].

An injured party may cancel a contract and *in addition* receive damages [2-106(4)]. |
| **3.** *Liquidated damages.* A contract clause providing for liquidated damages is valid as long as it is not a penalty. If the clause is a penalty, it is void. A valid liquidated damage clause states an agreement between the parties, fixing *a reasonable* amount of damages to be paid by a party in the event of that party's breach. | If a breach of contract by the buyer occurs after there has been a previous deposit or part payment, the buyer is entitled to restitution of (1) excess of the amount established in a *valid* liquidated damage clause, or (2) in the absence of a liquidated damages clause, the buyer can recover the excess of 20 percent of the total purchase price *or* $500, whichever is smaller [2-718(2)(b)]. |
| **4.** *Specific performance.* Equity will decree specific performance where the personal property involved in the contract is "unique." | Specific performance may be decreed when the goods are unique and "in other proper circumstances" [2-716(1)]. |

FIGURE 3-4 LETTER OF CREDIT

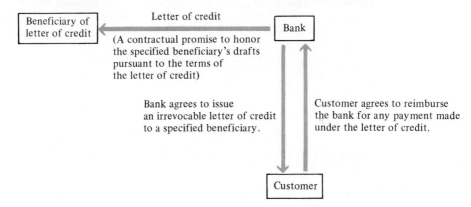

A. *Definition.* A *letter of credit* is a written, binding, legal commitment made by a bank at the request of its customer to honor (pay) drafts drawn upon it by the person specified in the letter of credit. Once issued, it is irrevocable. (See Figure 3-4.)

B. *Purpose.* The purpose of the issuance of a letter of credit is to give a seller legal assurance before the seller ships or delivers goods to a buyer that the seller will be paid for them.

C. *Nature of the transaction.* The sale of goods in conjunction with a letter of credit can be divided into three separate yet related contracts.

    1. *Contract for the sale of goods.* A buyer and seller enter into a contract for the sale of goods wherein the buyer agrees to establish with a bank a letter of credit for the benefit of the seller in an amount equal to the purchase price.

    2. *Letter of credit agreement.* Under this agreement, the buyer's bank agrees to issue an irrevocable letter of credit to the seller, and in exchange therefor, the buyer agrees to indemnify the bank immediately for any payment it may make under the letter of credit. The bank also obligates itself not to honor any draft issued by the seller unless the seller has complied with all the terms and conditions of the letter of credit. The terms and conditions usually require the seller to provide to the bank a bill of lading, an invoice, evidence of insurance on the goods, a certificate of inspection, and other documents.

    3. *Irrevocable letter of credit.* Upon issuance of the letter of credit to the seller, the bank is under a duty to honor any draft drawn upon it by the seller if the latter has complied with the terms and conditions of the letter of credit.

SALE OF GOODS BY NONOWNERS

    V. In general.

        A. A fundamental rule of common law is that people cannot transfer what they do not own.

        B. However, bona fide purchasers (good faith purchasers) for value, under certain circumstances, can acquire valid title even though the transferor possessed no title (void) or possessed only voidable title.

        C. *Bona fide purchaser for value* is a person who gives value in good faith and takes goods by way of sale, discount, negotiation, pledge, lien, or other voluntary transaction, creating an interest in the property without notice or knowledge of any defect or infirmity in the title of the transferor.

VI. *Void title* is no title.

    A. Valid title will not pass even to a bona fide purchaser under these circumstances:

        1. The transferor is a thief or a finder of the property.

        2. The transferor is a possessor of property under a forged signature on bill of sale, bill of lading, warehouse receipt, etc.

        3. The transferor had acquired the property by commission of fraud in the execution.

    B. Valid title will pass to a bona fide purchaser even though the transferor has a void title under the following circumstances.

        1. *Entrusting* occurs when an owner of goods transfers possession of the goods to a person who sells those types of goods in the regular course of that person's business [2-403(2)(3)].

            a. If the person to whom the goods are entrusted sells the goods in the regular course of business to a bona fide purchaser for value, the purchaser acquires valid title.

            b. The remedy of the prior owner is to sue for damages against the party who wrongfully sold the goods.

            c. For example, A allowed B, a used car dealer, to use his automobile. B, in the regular course of business, sold A's auto to C, who acted in good faith and without any knowledge of A's ownership.

        2. *Estoppel* occurs where the true owner of certain goods, by words or conduct, represents that the person in possession of the goods has title to the goods.

            a. A third party, acting in reliance upon the representation in good faith, who purchases the goods for value (a bona fide purchaser for value) acquires valid title to the goods.

            b. The true owner of the goods is precluded (estopped) by his or her conduct from denying the seller's authority to transfer title to a bona fide purchaser for value.

            c. For example, Junoz lent his pickup truck to Riley for use in Riley's plumbing business. Junoz did not object when Riley stenciled her business name, address, and telephone number on the door of the truck. Two months later Riley "sold" the truck to Arkos for $6,500. At the time of the "sale," Riley told Arkos that she had lost the title registration certificate to the truck. As a bona fide purchaser for value of the truck, acting in reliance of Junoz's actions, Arkos is now the owner of the truck. Junoz's only remedy is to sue Riley for the tort of conversion and recover damages.

        3. *Diversion or reconsignment of goods in transit under a nonnegotiable bill of lading* occurs where the bailee (carrier) has possession of the goods and has not received notice of any transfer and has delivered the goods and the document in the ordinary course of business to a bona fide purchaser for value [7-504(2)(b)]. For example, S sold goods to B. S then shipped the goods to B by railroad. The railroad issued to S a nonnegotiable bill of lading payable to B. Before the goods were delivered to B, S "sold" the goods to Z, who paid double the price that B had agreed to pay. S immediately notified the railroad to deliver the goods to Z. B claimed ownership of the goods. The court held Z to be the owner. B's only remedy is to sue S for breach of contract and recover damages.

VII. *Voidable title* is title acquired under circumstances which permit the former owner to rescind the transfer and be revested with valid title.

    A. A person possesses voidable title when he or she acquires title under the following circumstances:

        1. From an infant;

        2. Through use of duress;

3. Through use of undue influence;
4. By exercising fraud in the inducement;
5. By deception of the transferor as to identity of the purchaser [2-403(1)(a)];
6. In a sale of goods wherein a check given for the purchase price is dishonored [2-403(1)(b)]. For example, Retailer sold a stereo to Consumer. Consumer's check for the purchase price was returned to Retailer on the basis of "not sufficient funds," or "NSF." Before Retailer was able to rescind the sale and recover the stereo, Consumer sold the stereo to James for $1,800. James did not know that Consumer had issued the "bad" check. As a bona fide purchaser for value, James has a claim of ownership of the stereo that will prevail. Retailer's remedy is to sue Consumer for breach of contract and recover damages.
7. In a purchase of goods whereby the security interest in the goods was not perfected by filing (9-307);
8. As a purchaser at a legally defective bulk transfer (sale) by an owner (6-111).
B. A person who has voidable title has the power to pass valid title to a bona fide purchaser for value [2-403(1)]. For example, Alma purchased $50,000 worth of furniture at a bulk sale. The seller did not comply with the provisions of the Bulk Sales Act. Before the seller's creditors could proceed legally against Alma or the furniture in her possession, she sold the furniture to Evans. Evans did not know that the bulk sale was improper. Evans, a bona fide purchaser for value, has title to the furniture free from all claims of the seller's creditors. As another example, X, a 17-year-old, purchased a new automobile from Dealer. X gave Dealer $1,000 cash and a 1980 Buick as a trade-in. The next day, Dealer sold the 1980 Buick to Laslo, who was unaware of the transaction between X and Dealer. Before X reached 18 years of age, he rescinded the purchase contract entered into with Dealer and demanded of Laslo that she return the Buick to X. Although Dealer possessed only voidable title, he passed absolute title to Laslo, a bona fide purchaser for value.

PERFORMANCE OF SALES CONTRACTS AND RIGHTS AND DUTIES OF SELLER AND BUYER (Article 2 of the UCC)

VIII. Mercantile terms.
   A. *F.O.B. place of shipment.* The term *F.O.B.* (free on board) *place of shipment* requires the seller to ship the goods and bear the expense of placing them into the possession of the carrier (2-319).
   B. *F.O.B. place of destination.* The term *"F.O.B. place of destination"* requires the seller not only to ship the goods and bear the expense of placing them into the possession of the carrier but also to bear the expense and risk during transport [2-319(1)(b)].
   C. *C.I.F.* The term *"C.I.F."* (cost, insurance, and freight) means that the price of the goods includes the cost of the goods and the insurance and freight to a named destination (2-320).
   D. *C&F.* The term *"C&F"* (cost and freight) means that the price of the goods includes only the cost of the goods and the freight but does not require that the seller obtain and pay for insurance on the goods (2-320).
   E. *F.A.S.* (free alongside vessel). This term requires the seller to deliver the goods alongside a designated vessel and obtain and tender to the buyer a receipt for the goods, in exchange for which the carrier is under a duty to issue a bill of lading [2-319(2)].
   F. *C.O.D.* (collect on delivery). The term *"C.O.D."* is a shipping term which denies the buyer the right to possession of the good until payment of the price is made.

IX. In absence of an agreement to the contrary in a sales contract, the UCC prescribes rules that determine the intention of the parties as to their rights and duties.

X. *Seller's duty to tender delivery of goods.* The seller normally discharges the duty to deliver goods by a proper "tender" of conforming goods to the buyer at the time, place, and manner provided in the agreement or, if the agreement is silent, according to UCC rules.

    A. *Tender* is the act of placing conforming goods at the buyer's disposition and giving the buyer any notice reasonably necessary to enable the buyer to take delivery [2-503(1)].

    B. *Conforming goods.* Goods conform to the contract when they are in accordance with the obligations under the contract [2-106(2)].

    C. *Place for delivery* is the seller's place of business if the seller has one. Otherwise, the place of delivery is the seller's residence unless agreed otherwise in the contract (2-308).

    D. *Time for delivery* is a reasonable time unless otherwise specified in the contract [2-309(1)].

    E. *Manner of delivery.* The goods must be delivered as specified in the contract.

        1. Unless otherwise agreed upon in the contract, the following rules apply:

            a. The goods must be delivered in a single lot (2-307).

            b. A substitute performance must be tendered if the manner of delivery agreed upon becomes commercially impracticable. Examples of when a manner of delivery may become commercially impracticable are (2-614):

                (1) Destruction of loading or unloading facilities;

                (2) Lack of availability of an agreed-upon carrier.

        2. Installment contracts.

            a. The parties may agree that the goods be delivered in installments (2-612).

                (1) Every breach in regard to any installment entitles the buyer to recover damages.

                (2) Only a material breach of an installment contract entitles the buyer to cancel the entire contract and refuse to perform.

                (3) A buyer loses the right to cancel an installment contract on the grounds of a material breach if:

                    (*a*) The buyer accepts a nonconforming installment without notifying the seller of intent to cancel;

                    (*b*) The buyer files a lawsuit to recover damages *only for past installments*; or

                    (*c*) The buyer demands performance of future installments.

            b. If the contract does not specify that the goods are to be delivered in installments, they must all be delivered at the same time. Otherwise, the seller is in breach of contract.

    F. *Shipment contracts* (2-503, 2-504). The seller has the following duties:

        1. To place conforming goods in the possession of the carrier at the seller's own expense and risk of loss and obtain a proper contract for their shipment;

        2. To obtain from the carrier and promptly deliver in due form any document required by the agreement or by usage of trade to enable the buyer to obtain possession of the goods; and

        3. To promptly notify the buyer of the shipment.

    G. *Destination contracts* (2-503, 2-504). The seller has the following duties:

        1. To ship the goods and deliver them at a particular destination at the seller's own expense and risk of loss;

        2. To hold conforming goods at the buyer's disposition at the specified destination;

      3. To obtain from the carrier and promptly deliver in due form any document required by the agreement or by usage of trade to enable the buyer to obtain possession of the goods; and

      4. To give the buyer notice reasonably necessary to enable the buyer to take possession of the goods.

XI. *Seller's right to "cure."* The seller has the right to cure (i.e., to remedy or correct) an improper tender or delivery of goods under the following circumstances (2-508):

    A. The buyer rightfully and in good faith refused to accept a tender or delivery of nonconforming goods;

    B. The buyer gave the seller notice of reasons for refusing to accept the goods; and

    C. The seller made a proper tender or delivery of conforming goods *within the time allowed for performance.*

XII. *Buyer's duty to pay the price.* The buyer is obligated to pay the price if the seller has performed his or her own obligations [2-507(b)].

    A. Time and place of payment.

      1. In noncredit (cash) transactions, unless otherwise agreed, tender of payment is due at the time and place at which the buyer is to receive the goods *even though the place of shipment is the place of delivery.*

      2. Where credit is extended, the time for payment is postponed according to the agreed-upon terms. Unless otherwise agreed, payment is due at the place of the seller's business, if any. Otherwise it is due at the seller's residence.

    B. Unless otherwise agreed (e.g., a credit sale), payment of the price and delivery of the goods are concurrent conditions [2-507(b)].

    C. Where goods are to be delivered by installments, unless otherwise agreed, the buyer must pay for each installment as it is tendered or delivered.

    D. Manner of payment. Payment is sufficient when made in any manner and by any means used currently in the ordinary course of business unless the agreement calls for payment in legal tender, e.g., cash, check, or other draft [2-511(2)].

XIII. *Right of inspection by the buyer* (2-513). The buyer's right of inspection cannot accrue until the goods are identified to the contract, or tendered, or delivered.

    A. The buyer has the right to inspect the goods *before* payment or acceptance if:

      1. The inspection is at a reasonable time and place and in a reasonable manner; and

      2. The buyer bears the expense of the inspection.

    B. The buyer does not have the right to inspect the goods before payment under the following circumstances:

      1. There is an agreement otherwise (2-512);

      2. The contract provides for a C.O.D. delivery [2-513(3)(a)]; or

      3. The contract provides for payment upon delivery of documents of title (unless a prior inspection is agreed upon) [2-513(3)(b)].

XIV. *Rights of a buyer upon tender or delivery of nonconforming goods* (2-601). If the goods fail to conform to the contract, the buyer has the right to:

    A. Reject all of the goods;

    B. Accept all of the goods; or

    C. Accept any conforming commercial unit and reject the remainder.

XV. *Acceptance of the goods by the buyer.* "Acceptance" means the manifestation of express or implied assent to become the owner of specific goods. It obligates the buyer to pay the agreed-upon contract price for the commercial units accepted.

    A. Acceptance is independent of possession, delivery, or payment for the goods.

    B. Acceptance of goods occurs when the buyer (2-606):

      1. After a reasonable opportunity to inspect the goods signifies to the seller that the goods are conforming or that the buyer will take or retain them in spite of their nonconformity;

   2. Fails to make an effective rejection but such acceptance does not occur until after the buyer has had a reasonable opportunity to inspect them; or

   3. Does any act inconsistent with the seller's ownership. For example, goods are defective and the buyer attempts to reject, yet uses the goods for his or her purposes.

C. An acceptance of a part of any commercial unit is acceptance of that entire unit. For example, M sold twenty table tennis sets, including accessories, to R. R accepted the sets and upon inspection noticed that the accessories were not as specified in the contract. R, on the same day, sold twelve of the table tennis tables to Zack and attempted to reject the accessories. M refused. R can reject only eight table tennis sets. His sale of twelve tables was an implied acceptance of all twelve sets.

D. The effect of an acceptance of goods by a buyer is as follows:

   1. It obligates the buyer to pay the contract price subject to the buyer's remedies for nonconforming goods accepted.

   2. Unless entitled to revoke acceptance, the buyer is precluded from rejecting the nonconforming goods.

   3. Even though a buyer accepts nonconforming goods, the buyer does not lose the right to recover damages from the seller for breach of contract.

E. *Revocation of acceptance* (2-608). A buyer who rightfully revokes acceptance has the same rights and duties as if he or she had rejected them.

   1. The buyer may rightfully revoke acceptance under the following circumstances:

   a. The buyer accepted obviously nonconforming goods on the reasonable assumption that the nonconformity would be cured, but it had not been cured within a reasonable time. For example, Buyer received and installed fifteen heavy-duty clothes washers from Seller. Buyer noticed that the washers did not function properly and immediately notified Seller of the defects. Seller assured Buyer that the defects would be repaired. Several weeks elapsed. Not having heard from Seller, Buyer attempted to reject the washers. Seller must accept Buyer's revocation of acceptance and rejection of the washers.

   b. The buyer accepted nonconforming goods in circumstances under which a reasonable inspection would not have revealed the defects. For example, Buyer received shipment of 200 pounds of vegetable seeds from Seller. Buyer visually inspected the seeds immediately, and they appeared to be conforming to the contract. Buyer planted the seeds. Only 50 percent of the seeds germinated. Buyer has the right to revoke acceptance, cancel the contract, and recover damages from Seller.

   2. The revocation must be made within a reasonable time after the buyer discovers or should have discovered the defects.

   3. The revocation is not effective until the buyer notifies the seller of intent to revoke.

   4. The revocation cannot occur after the goods have substantially changed in condition if such change was not caused by their own defects. For example, Buyer received 250 tons of obviously spoiled cabbage. Upon inspection of the cabbage, Buyer realized that they were of poor quality and did not conform to the contract. Buyer was very busy and decided to notify Seller of the defects on the following day. The cabbage was left outside overnight and was ruined because of a very unusual autumn cold wave. Buyer may not revoke acceptance and reject the cabbage. Buyer is liable for the contract price of the cabbage.

XVI. *Rights and duties of the buyer as to rightfully rejected goods in his or her possession and control.*

    A. Rights of a buyer who has a security interest (lien) in the goods (i.e., the buyer has paid part or all of the price and/or has incurred expenses in the receipt, transportation, or storage of the goods).

        1. The buyer may possess and resell the goods in good faith and in a commercially reasonable manner.

        2. The buyer is liable to the seller for all proceeds from the resale in excess of the amount of the security interest (lien).

    B. Rights and duties of a buyer who *does not* have a security interest (lien) in the goods (2-602).

        1. The buyer has a duty after rejection to hold the goods for a reasonable time to allow the seller to remove them.

        2. If the seller does not remove the goods or give instructions to the buyer within a reasonable time after the seller is notified of the rejection, the buyer has the following *options*:

            a. To store the goods for the seller's account;

            b. To reship the goods to the seller;

            c. To resell the goods for the seller's account.

        3. Any such action by the buyer is not an acceptance or conversion of the goods.

        4. *Special rule* (2-603, 2-604): When the seller has no agent or place of business in the area where the rejection occurs, *a merchant buyer*, in possession or control of rejected goods, *has a duty*:

            a. To follow any reasonable instructions from the seller in respect to the goods; and

            b. In the absence of such instructions, to make reasonable efforts to resell the goods if they:

                (1) Are perishable; or

                (2) Are of a kind which decline in value rapidly.

XVII. *Right to assurance* of performance (2-609). When reasonable grounds for insecurity (i.e., a reasonable belief that the contract will not be performed on the date performance is due) arise with respect to the performance by either party to a sales contract, the other party has the following rights.

    A. The insecure party may, in writing, demand adequate assurance of due performance.

    B. Until such assurance is received, the insecure party may, if commercially reasonable, suspend his or her own performance.

    C. If the assurance is not provided within a reasonable time not exceeding thirty days, the insecure party may treat the contract as repudiated (anticipatory breach).

    D. What constitutes "adequate" assurance depends on the facts of the situation wherein the insecurity arose. "Adequate" assurance could be as little as a letter advising that the contract will be performed, or as much as the deposit of collateral as security or the purchase of an indemnity bond.

PASSAGE OF TITLE AND RISK OF LOSS

XVIII. In absence of an agreement by the seller and buyer to the contrary, the UCC prescribes rules that determine when title and risk of loss (i.e., by damage, destruction, or theft) pass to the buyer [2-509(4)].

    A. Merchantile terms.

1. *Sale on approval* is a transaction whereby goods are delivered to a buyer *primarily for use*. The buyer may return the goods even though they conform to the contract if they do not meet with the buyer's approval [2-326(1)(a)].
2. *Sale or return* is a transaction whereby goods are delivered to a buyer *primarily for resale*. The buyer may return the goods even though they conform to the contract [2-326(1)(b)].
3. *Ex-ship* is a shipping term which requires delivery from a ship that has reached a place at a named port of destination at which goods of the kind are usually discharged (2-322).

B. Neither title nor risk of loss to goods can pass to a buyer prior to their coming into existence and identification to the contract.

C. The UCC allows title and/or risk of loss to identified goods to pass from the seller to the buyer in any manner and on any conditions expressly agreed upon by the parties in their contract [2-509(4)].

D. Absent an express agreement to the contrary, the UCC prescribes rules to determine when title and/or risk of loss to goods passes to the buyer. The following illustrate the operation of the UCC rules in various commercial transactions *in the absence of a breach of contract* (2-509). (See Figure 3-5.)

1. Where the contract requires or authorizes the seller to deliver goods but the goods are not to be shipped or are not held by a bailee to be delivered without being moved [2-509(3)].
   a. Regardless of whether the seller is a merchant, *title* passes to the buyer at the time of the contract.
   b. If the seller is a merchant, the risk of loss passes to the buyer upon the buyer's taking *possession* of the goods.
   c. If the seller is a nonmerchant, the risk of loss passes to the buyer on *tender* of delivery.
2. Where the contract requires or authorizes the seller to ship the goods by carrier [2-509(1)(a)(b)].
   a. Shipping contract, e.g., C.O.D., F.O.B. seller's city, F.O.B. vessel, C.I.F., and C&F. *Title and risk of loss* pass to the buyer at the time and place of the shipment (transfer of possession to the carrier).
   b. Destination contract, e.g., F.O.B. buyer's city, "ex-ship," and "no arrival, no sale." *Title and risk of loss* pass to the buyer at the time and place that the goods are duly tendered to the buyer at destination.
3. Where goods are held by a bailee (warehouseman) to be delivered without being moved [2-509(2)].
   a. Title to the goods passes as follows:
      (1) If the seller is to deliver a document of title, title passes at the time and place of delivery of the document (warehouse receipt).
      (2) If goods are identified to the contract and no document of title is to be delivered, title passes at the time of the contract.
   b. Risk of loss to the goods passes as follows:
      (1) At the time and place that the buyer receives a *negotiable* document of title (warehouse receipt);
      (2) Upon the expiration of a reasonable time after the buyer receives a *nonnegotiable* document of title (warehouse receipt); or
      (3) If there is no outstanding document of title representing the goods, risk of loss passes upon the bailee's *acknowledgment* of the buyer's rights to possess the goods.

FIGURE 3-5 PASSAGE OF TITLE AND RISK OF LOSS: UCC RULES IN ABSENCE OF AGREEMENT OF PARTIES

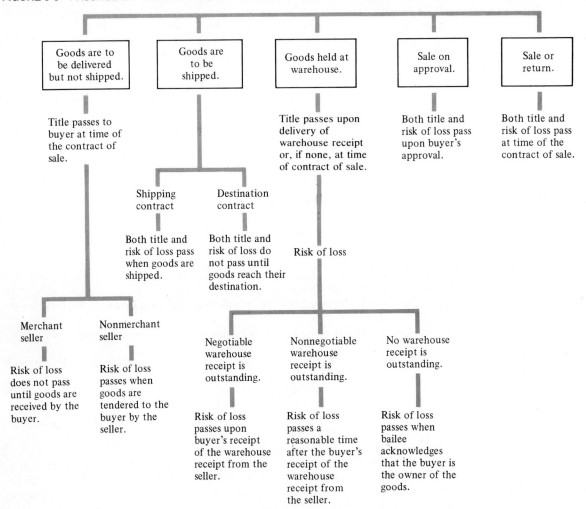

4. Sale on approval. *Title and risk of loss* do not pass to the buyer until the buyer's approval [2-327(1)(c)]. The approval may be express or implied from the conduct of the buyer.

5. Sale or return. *Title and risk of loss* pass to the buyer at the time and place of contract [2-327(2)(b)].

E. Effect of breach by the seller on risk of loss. Where a tender or delivery of goods so fails to conform to the contract as to give the buyer the right of rejection, the risk of loss remains on the seller until cure or acceptance (2-510).

F. Effect of breach by the buyer on risk of loss. Where the buyer repudiates or is otherwise in breach as to conforming goods, the seller may, to the extent of any deficiency in the seller's effective insurance coverage, treat the risk of loss as resting on the buyer for a commercially reasonable time (2-510).

G. Effect of rejection or revocation of acceptance of goods by the buyer on title. Title to goods revests in the seller automatically upon the buyer's rejection or revocation of acceptance of the goods [2-402(4)].

REMEDIES OF A SELLER AND A BUYER

XIX. *Remedies of the seller.* The seller has the following remedies against the buyer (2-703). (See Table 3-1.)

  A. The seller may *withhold delivery* of the goods (seller's lien) if:
    1. The buyer wrongfully rejects the goods;
    2. The buyer wrongfully revokes acceptance of goods tendered or delivered;
    3. The buyer fails to make a payment on or before delivery;
    4. The buyer repudiates the sale with respect to a part or the whole of the sale; or
    5. The buyer is insolvent, unless he or she tenders cash in payment of the purchase price.
  B. The seller may *identify goods to the contract* notwithstanding the buyer's breach under the following circumstances (2-704):
    1. The goods are finished and conform to the sales contract; or
    2. Where unfinished goods are demonstrably intended for fulfillment of the particular contract, the seller, in exercise of reasonable commercial judgment, for purposes of mitigating loss, may either:
      a. Complete the manufacture of the unfinished goods and identify them to the contract; or
      b. Cease manufacture and resell the unfinished goods for scrap or salvage value.
  C. The seller may *stop delivery* of the goods by carrier or other bailee (2-705).
    1. The right to stop delivery (seller's lien) accrues to the seller:
      a. Upon the buyer's insolvency; or
      b. Upon the buyer's repudiation or breach of the sales contract.

TABLE 3-1   RIGHTS AND REMEDIES OF SELLER AND BUYER

Rights and remedies	Seller	Buyer
1. Damages for breach of contract	X	X
2. Cover		X
3. Replevin		X
4. Demand assurance	X	X
5. Liquidated damages, if agreed upon	X	X
6. Recover the price	X	
7. Cancel the contract	X	X
8. Withhold delivery of the goods	X	
9. Identify goods to the contract	X	
10. Resell the goods	X	X
11. Stop goods in transit	X	X
12. Recover goods from an insolvent buyer	X	
13. Specific performance		X
14. Security interest (lien) in the goods	X	X
15. Rejection of some or all of nonconforming goods		X
16. Revocation of acceptance		X
17. Damages for breach of warranty		X
18. Cure	X	

2. The right of the seller to stop delivery ceases when:

    a. The buyer receives the goods;

    b. The bailee of the goods, *except a carrier*, acknowledges to the buyer that the bailee holds them for the buyer;

    c. The carrier acknowledges to the buyer that the carrier holds them for the buyer by reshipment or as warehouseman; or

    d. A negotiable document of title covering the goods is negotiated to the buyer.

3. A seller must properly notify the carrier or bailee so that by reasonable diligence the carrier or bailee may prevent delivery of the goods to the buyer. If a negotiable document has been issued for the goods, the carrier or bailee is not obligated to obey notice to stop delivery until the surrender of the document.

D. The seller may *resell the goods* upon the buyer's repudiation or breach of the sales contract (2-706).

    1. The sale must be made in good faith and in a commercially reasonable manner.

    2. It may be made at either public or private sale.

    3. The seller is required to give proper notice of sale to the buyer.

    4. The seller is not accountable to the buyer for any profit made on any resale of the goods.

E. The seller may *recover compensatory (actual) and incidental damages* for the buyer's repudiation or breach of the sales contract [2-706(1)].

F. The seller may *recover the price and incidental damages* [2-709(1)] where:

    1. The buyer has accepted the goods;

    2. Conforming goods have been lost or damaged after the risk of loss has passed to the buyer; or

    3. The goods have been identified to the contract and there is no ready market available for their resale at a reasonable price. That is, they are specially manufactured goods.

G. The seller may *recover the goods* from the buyer *upon the buyer's insolvency* [2-701(2)].

    1. The seller may recover the goods within ten days after the buyer has received them.

    2. The seller may recover the goods *at any time* if the buyer had misrepresented solvency in writing within three months prior to the delivery of the goods. For example, Janus offered to buy plumbing materials from Whitcomb for a price of $250,000. Whitcomb investigated Janus's credit rating and discovered that it was not good. Whitcomb expressed her concern to Janus. Janus wrote a letter to Whitcomb wherein he advised her not to worry and informed her that his (Janus's) financial situation was excellent. The plumbing materials were delivered pursuant to a sales contract entered into two months later. Four months later, the purchase price had not yet been paid and Whitcomb discovered that Janus had lied about his financial status. Whitcomb is legally entitled to repossess the plumbing material from Janus.

    3. The seller loses the right to recover goods if the buyer had resold them to a *bona fide purchaser for value* or a creditor's lien had attached to them.

    4. Upon reclaiming the goods from an insolvent buyer, the seller obtains a preference over other creditors of the buyer. For this reason, the seller is denied all other remedies with respect to the goods (2-702).

H. The seller may *cancel the contract* if the buyer repudiates or breaches the sales contract [2-703(f)].

    1. The seller must give the buyer notice of cancellation.

2. Cancellation of the contract does not destroy the seller's remedy for damages against the buyer.

3. If the buyer wrongfully fails to make a payment due or repudiates the contract in whole or part, the seller may:

    a. Cancel the contract with respect to the goods directly involved; or

    b. If the breach is a material one, cancel the entire contract.

XX. *Remedies of the buyer.* The buyer has the following remedies against the seller (see Table 3-1).

A. Upon receipt of nonconforming goods, the buyer may (2-601):

    1. Reject all of the goods;

    2. Accept all of the goods; or

    3. Accept any *commercial unit or units* and reject the remainder.

B. The buyer has the right to *cover* (2-712), i.e., the right to purchase the goods elsewhere upon the seller's breach.

    1. The buyer's right to cover may be exercised under any of the following circumstances:

        a. The seller repudiates sale;

        b. The seller fails to deliver goods;

        c. The buyer *rightfully* rejects goods; or

        d. The buyer *justifiably* revokes an acceptance.

    2. The buyer is not required to cover. Failure to do so does not bar any other remedy available under the UCC.

    3. An attempt to cover fixes the market price for purposes of computing damages.

    4. The *measure of damages* is the difference between the cost of cover and the contract price, if the cost of cover is higher.

C. The buyer *may recover damages for nondelivery of goods or a repudiation* of the sales contract by the seller. The measure of damages is the difference between the market price at the time the buyer learned of the breach and the contract price *plus* any incidental and consequential damages minus expenses saved in consequence of seller's breach (2-713).

D. The buyer *may recover damages for breach in regard to accepted goods* (2-714).

    1. A buyer who has accepted nonconforming goods must give notice within a reasonable time to the seller that the goods are nonconforming. For example, Buyer received and accepted defective television sets from Seller. Buyer had intended to notify Seller immediately. Owing to Buyer's preoccupation with labor negotiations, Buyer did not notify Seller until four days had expired. In the letter of notification, Buyer merely stated that the TV sets were defective. Buyer did not indicate the nature of the defect. Buyer lost the right to reject for two reasons: first because Buyer did not give notice within a reasonable time, and second because Buyer did not identify the defects in the notification.

    2. A buyer who has accepted nonconforming goods and has given the seller proper notice may assert the following remedies:

        a. Action for damages resulting from seller's *breach of contract*, i.e., those damages which have resulted in the ordinary course of events from seller's breach; or

        b. Action for damages on the grounds of *breach of warranty*. The measure of damages is the difference at the time and place of acceptance between value of goods accepted and value they would have had if they had been as warranted.

E. The buyer *may recover goods identified to the contract* in possession or control of the seller upon the seller's insolvency if the seller (2-502):

1. *Becomes insolvent* within ten days *after receipt* of the *first installment* of the price; and
2. The buyer *tenders* and pays the seller any *unpaid portion* of the price.

F. The buyer may *sue for specific performance* in equity when the subject matter of the contract is "unique" and in "other proper circumstances" [2-716(1)]. For example:
1. A specially manufactured good;
2. A work of art;
3. A famous racehorse;
4. An heirloom;
5. An output contract involving a particular source of the goods;
6. A requirement contract involving a particular market for the goods.

G. The buyer has the *right of replevin* [2-716(3)]. Replevin is a form of legal action to recover specific goods in the possession of a seller which are being wrongfully withheld from the buyer. The buyer may maintain an action of replevin in the following situations.
1. The goods have been *identified to the contract*, the seller has repudiated or breached the contract, *and the buyer*, after a reasonable effort, *is unable to effect cover*; or
2. The goods have been shipped under a reservation of a security interest in the seller, and satisfaction of this security has been made or tendered (2-716).

H. The buyer *has a security interest (lien) in the goods* after the seller's breach [2-711(3)].
1. A buyer who has rightfully rejected or justifiably revoked acceptance of goods has a security interest in goods in his or her possession and control to the extent of:
   a. Any payment of the price which the buyer has made; and
   b. Compensatory (actual) and any incidental damages such as reasonable expenses incurred in their inspection, receipt, transportation, care, and custody.
2. The buyer may hold such goods as security for the payment of damages.
3. If the buyer learns of the seller's insolvency *after the buyer has reshipped* them to the seller or has placed them in the possession of a bailee for shipment to the seller, the buyer may stop or withhold delivery of the goods in transit, retake possession of them, and exercise any other remedies available.

I. To *exercise the security interest (lien)*, the buyer acts as "a person in the position of the seller" [2-711(3), 2-706].
1. The buyer must immediately resell them if they are perishable, even without notice to the seller.
2. Upon giving proper notice to the seller, the buyer may sell nonperishables consistent with those same rights available to an unpaid seller.
3. The buyer must account to the seller for any excess of the net proceeds of the resale over the amount of the buyer's security interest.

J. *Cancellation of the contract.* The buyer's rights and duties are essentially the same as those of a seller upon cancellation [2-711(1)].

K. *Liquidated damages or limitation of damages* in the sales contract (2-718).
1. The sales contract may validly limit the remedy of the buyer to:
   a. Return of the goods and a refunding of the price;
   b. Replacement of nonconforming goods or parts; or
   c. Recovery of a specified amount of damages (liquidated damages).
2. The sales contract cannot limit or deny a remedy to a buyer for personal injuries resulting from a breach of warranty. Such a provision is unconscionable and void.

WARRANTIES

XXI. *In general.* The principal laws affecting warranties in the sale of goods are the Uniform Commercial Code and the Magnuson-Moss Warranty-Federal Trade Commission Improvement Act (the Magnuson Act), commonly known as the Consumer Protection Warranties Law.

    A. The UCC classifies warranties into two categories (see Figure 3-6).

        1. *Express warranties* (2-313):

            a. Affirmation of fact or promise;

            b. Sale by description;

            c. Sale by sample or model.

        2. *Implied warranties:*

            a. The implied warranty of merchantability (2-314).

            b. The implied warranty of fitness for a particular purpose (2-315).

            c. The implied warranties of title and against infringement (2-312).

    B. The Magnuson Act regulates the content and nature of disclosures in *written warranties* relating to *consumer products.* The act is discussed in Chapter 9.

XXII. Implied *warranty of title* [2-312(1)].

    A. In every contract for the sale of goods, the seller makes the following warranties of title:

        1. That the seller is conveying good title to the buyer;

        2. That the seller has the right to transfer the goods; and

        3. That the goods are free from any security interest or other lien or encumbrance.

    B. Disclaimer, exclusion, or modification [2-312(2)]. A warranty of title can be excluded or modified only under the following two circumstances:

FIGURE 3-6 WARRANTIES MADE BY A SELLER OF GOODS

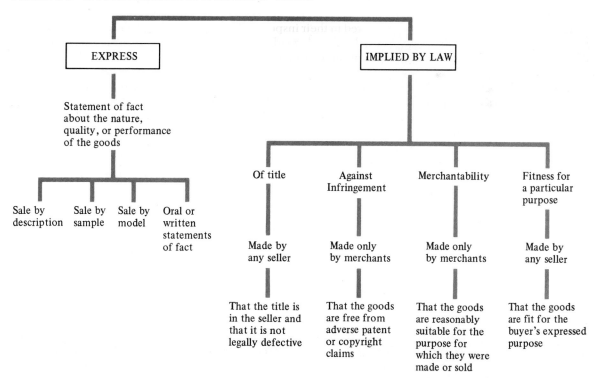

1. By specific language in the contract for sale, e.g., "all my right, title, and interest." A general disclaimer against all warranties, express or implied, or a sale of goods "as is" does not negate the warranty of title.
2. By circumstances which place the buyer on notice that the seller does not claim title in himself or herself, e.g., sales by a trustee in bankruptcy, or by an executor or administrator of a decedent's estate or by a sheriff, or by a foreclosing lienor (i.e., secured creditor).

XXIII. Implied *warranty against infringement* [2-312(3)].

    A. Every merchant seller warrants that the goods the seller deals in will be delivered to the buyer free from any adverse claims to title or claims of patent or trademark infringement.

    B. No warranty against infringement arises when the buyer provides specifications for the goods.

XXIV. Express warranties (2-313).

    A. In general. The UCC does not require that the seller actually intend to create an express warranty, nor does it require that the buyer rely upon the seller's words or conduct.

      1. *Test:* Did the parties intend the affirmations of fact, promises, or the description or sample to become a "part of the basis of the bargain"? If so, an express warranty is created.
      2. An express warranty may be made prior to, at the time of, or after the contract for the sale of goods.
      3. An express warranty need not be supported by legally sufficient consideration.
      4. An express warranty is an expression of the seller with respect to the quality, description, condition, or performability of the goods.

    B. *Affirmation of fact or promise* [2-313(1)(a)].

      1. Affirmations of fact or promises may be oral or in writing.
      2. They may be made by a seller or the seller's authorized agent.
      3. Formal language is *not* necessary to create the warranty, e.g., "warrant" or "guarantee."
      4. The affirmations of fact or promises may be made in advertisements or found in labels relating to the goods.
      5. The following affirmations do not create a warranty:
        a. Statements of opinions or commendations, i.e., "puffing" or "sales talk." For example, "This dress will wear like iron."
        b. Statements of value of goods. For example, "This automobile is worth $6,800."
      6. Statements by an expert may be a fact even though stated as an opinion. For example, a jeweler states, "In my opinion, this ring is worth $675."

    C. *Sale by description.* A sale of goods by description creates an express warranty that the goods to be delivered to the buyer will conform to the description [2-313(1)(b)].

      1. The description may be in words, oral or written, e.g., "number 2 yellow" corn, "Bermuda" onions, or "Idaho russet" potatoes.
      2. No words are necessary where technical specifications or blueprints are made part of the basis of the bargain.
      3. Prior dealings and trade usages may establish the description of quality intended when the words of the seller are unclear.

    D. *Sale by sample or model.* A sale by sample or model creates an express warranty that the goods delivered to the buyer will conform to the sample or model [2-313(1)(c)].

      1. A "sample" is a good actually removed from the bulk of goods which are the subject matter of the sale.

2. A "model" is a replica or representation of goods offered for inspection when the goods which are the subject matter of the sale are not available. A "model" is not a good actually removed from a bulk of goods intended for sale.

E. Disclaimer, exclusion, or modification. An express warranty may be excluded or modified *by clear, detailed, and unambiguous language in the contract* to that effect [2-316(1)].

XXV. Implied *warranty of merchantability* (2-314).

A. If the seller is a merchant with respect to the goods sold, it is implied in the contract for sale that the goods are merchantable *unless* the warranty is excluded or modified [2-314(1)].

B. The sale of food or drink by a merchant is considered to be a sale of goods for the purposes of the implied warranty of merchantability [2-314(1)].

C. The term *"merchantable"* means that the goods are *reasonably suitable* for the purpose for which they were made and sold and also that they are of fair and average quality established by the market.

D. The UCC provides that goods are merchantable if they meet the following minimum criteria [2-314(2)]:

   1. They pass without objection in the trade under the contract description;

   2. In the case of fungible goods, they are of fair average quality within the description;

   3. They are fit for the ordinary purposes for which such goods are used;

   4. They run, within the variations permitted by the agreement, of even kind, quality, and quantity within each unit and among all units involved;

   5. They are adequately contained, packaged, and labeled as the agreement may require; and

   6. They conform to the promises or affirmations of fact made on the container or label, if any.

E. Disclaimer, exclusion, or modification. Unless limited by the Magnuson Act, an implied warranty of merchantability may be excluded or modified as follows:

   1. By oral or written exclusionary language which *specifically* mentions the word "merchantability." In the case of a writing, the word "merchantability" must be *conspicuous*. Language which is in bolder type or of a different color than the other written provisions of the contract is "conspicuous" [2-316(2)].

   2. Unless the circumstances indicate otherwise, the warranty is excluded by expressions in the contract such as "as is" or "with all faults" or by other language clearly placing the buyer on notice of the exclusion [2-316(3)(a)].

   3. *By the buyer's examination or refusal to examine the goods or sample or model.* The buyer takes possession subject to all defects which a reasonable inspection under the circumstances would have revealed [2-316(3)(b)].

   a. A mere failure to inspect the goods is not a refusal under the UCC.

   b. In order to be a refusal, the seller must have first made a demand upon the buyer that the buyer inspect the goods.

   4. By course of dealing, performance, or trade usage [2-316(3)(c)].

XXVI. Implied *warranty of fitness for a particular purpose* (2-315).

A. An implied warranty of fitness for a particular purpose is created whenever:

   1. The seller (merchant or nonmerchant) knows or has reason to know the buyer's particular purpose for which the goods are required; and

   2. The seller knows that the buyer is relying on the seller's skill or judgment to select or furnish suitable goods.

B. Fitness for the buyer's particular purpose may or may not be equivalent to the standard of merchantability. For example, shoes for the purpose of walking are merchantable, yet they would not be fit for a particular purpose of mountain climbing; food sold at a grocery store is required to meet the same standard for both merchantability and fitness for a particular purpose, i.e., fit for human consumption.

    C. As a general rule, no implied warranty for fitness of a particular purpose will result where:

        1. The buyer asks for or insists on purchasing the goods by patent or trade name; or

        2. The contract calls for the goods to be manufactured to the buyer's specifications.

    D. Disclaimer, exclusion, and modification. Unless limited by the Magnuson Act, an implied warranty of fitness for a particular purpose may be excluded or modified in the following ways.

        1. Unlike the warranty of merchantability, the implied warranty for fitness for a particular purpose may be excluded only if such exclusion is in writing. The exclusionary language need not use the specific words "fitness for a particular purpose" [2-316(2)].

        2. As in the case of the implied warranty of merchantability, the implied warranty of fitness for a particular purpose is excluded:

            a. By the buyer's examination or refusal to examine the goods or the sample or model [2-316(3)(b)]; or

            b. By prior dealings, performance, or trade usage [2-316(3)(c)].

XXVII. Cumulation and conflict of warranties (2-317).

    A. Under the UCC, all warranties, express or implied, "shall be construed as consistent with each other and as cumulative."

    B. The UCC further provides that if such interpretation is unreasonable, the intention of the parties is to control. To ascertain the intention of the parties, the UCC provides the following rules:

        1. Exact or technical specifications displace inconsistent sample or model or general language of description.

        2. A sample from an existing bulk displaces inconsistent general language of description.

        3. Express warranties displace inconsistent implied warranties other than the implied warranty of fitness for a particular purpose.

XXVIII. Liquidated damages and limitations of remedies for breach of warranty (2-718, 2-719).

    A. *Liquidated damage clause* is a clause in a contract for sale of goods which provides a fixed amount of damages in place of actual damages (2-718).

        1. The amount agreed upon must be reasonable in light of the anticipated or actual harm caused by the breach. (Actual harm includes actual, incidental, and consequential damages.)

        2. If the provision establishes an *unreasonably large* amount of liquidated damages, it is void as a penalty.

        3. A liquidated damages clause can also be held unconscionable as being *unreasonably small* in amount.

    B. *Limitation of remedies.* As a general rule, a contract for the sale of goods may provide for remedies in addition to or in substitution for those provided in the UCC [2-719(1)(a)], e.g., a limitation of the buyer's remedies to return of the goods and recovery of the price or to the repair and replacement of defective goods or parts.

    C. The *doctrine of unconscionability* (2-302).

        1. A contract or any clause of a contract which is oppressive or unfair so as to deprive either party of the substantial value of the bargain is unconscionable.

        2. Upon finding a contract or a clause of a contract to be unconscionable, the courts have the following alternatives:

            a. To refuse to enforce the contract;

            b. To enforce the remainder of the contract without the unconscionable clause;

    b. the user or consumer has not bought the product from or entered into any contractual relation with the seller."

1. Who is liable? Any seller engaged in the business of selling the product.
2. Who can recover? Any user or consumer or other person injured by the product.
3. Test of liability. The test of liability is the defective and unreasonably dangerous condition of the product.
   - **a.** The term *"unreasonably dangerous"* means that a product is so materially defective as to be likely to cause injury.
   - **b.** Negligence or intent to harm is not a requirement for recovery.
4. Causation is required.
5. Privity of contract between the injured party and the seller being sued is not required.
6. Proof of the sale of a product in a defective and unreasonably dangerous condition is required.
7. Assumption of the risk by the injured party is a defense available to a seller.
8. Disclaimer of liability. A seller's liability cannot be disclaimed, excluded, or modified in the contract for the sale of the product.

SELF-QUIZ

To check your understanding of the key words and concepts and the accuracy of your answers to the questions, refer to the text material as referenced by page number.

KEY WORDS AND CONCEPTS

QUESTIONS

1. Distinguish between a sale and a gift, a bailment, and a secured transaction. **(80)**
2. Review the common law rules governing the formation of contracts discussed in Chapter 2. **(26)**
3. Contrast the changes made by the UCC in the common law of contracts in the following areas:
   a. Offer **(82)**
      1. Definiteness requirement
      2. Irrevocable offer
   b. Acceptance **(82)**
      1. Effect of additional terms in an acceptance
      2. Manner of acceptance
      3. Acceptance of offer to enter into a unilateral contract
   c. Consideration **(83)**
      1. Modification of a previous contract
      2. Requirement and legal effect of a seal
   d. Defenses **(83)**
      1. Unconscionable contracts
   e. Statute of Frauds **(83)**
      1. Oral contract for sale of personal property
      2. Minimum terms required in a sufficient writing
      3. Confirmation letter
      4. Exceptions to the Statute of Frauds
   f. Parol evidence rule **(84)**
   g. Performance **(84)**
      1. A threatened anticipatory breach
      2. Assurance
      3. Retraction of repudiation (anticipatory breach)
      4. Goods to be delivered in installments
   h. Rights of third parties **(85)**
      1. Assignments
      2. Nonassignment clause in a sales contract
      3. Delegation of duties
   i. Discharge and damages **(85)**
      1. Statute of Limitations
      2. Measure of damages for breach

3. Liquidated damages clause
4. Specific performance

4. Explain void title. **(87)**
5. Under what circumstances can a person who possesses void title pass a valid title to a transferee? **(87)**
6. In what circumstances will no title be passed even to a bona fide purchaser for value? **(87)**
7. Explain voidable title. Under what circumstances does it arise? **(87)**
8. What is the legal effect of a transfer of voidable title to a bona fide purchaser for value? **(88)**
9. Explain the seller's duties in regard to tender and delivery of goods. **(89)**
10. At what time and in what manner must the buyer pay the price? **(90)**
11. Explain the buyer's right of inspection. **(90)**
12. What legal consequences flow from the buyer's acceptance of goods? **(90)**
13. Under what circumstances may a buyer rightfully revoke acceptance of goods? **(91)**
14. What are the rights and duties of a buyer who has rightfully rejected nonconforming goods? **(92)**
15. Under what circumstances is a party to a contract to sell goods entitled to demand "assurance" from the other party? **(92)**
16. Can title to goods pass to the buyer before they are "identified" to the contract? **(93)**
17. Does the UCC allow parties to a contract to sell goods to determine at what time title and/or risk of loss pass to the buyer? **(92)**
18. What are the rules under the UCC which determine when title and/or risk of loss pass to the buyer? **(93)**
19. What is the effect of a breach of contract on title and risk of loss? **(94)**
20. List and explain the remedies available to a seller upon the buyer's breach. **(95)**
21. List and explain the remedies available to a buyer upon the seller's breach. **(97)**
22. What are various types of warranties that may accompany a sale? By a merchant? By a nonmerchant? **(99)**
23. How are express and implied warranties created? **(99)**
24. Explain the various types of express and implied warranties. **(99)**
25. Can warranties be limited or excluded (disclaimed)? If so, how? **(99, 101, 102)**
26. What must a buyer do to preserve the buyer's remedies for breach of warranty? **(103)**

27. What defenses may a seller assert against the buyer in an action for breach of warranty? **(103)**
28. List the elements of the tort of negligence. **(104)**
29. Why is it "easier" for an injured party to recover damages based on strict liability in tort rather than on the basis of negligence, fraud, or breach of warranty? **(104)**
30. Explain the doctrine of strict liability in tort. **(104)**

SELECTED QUESTIONS AND UNOFFICIAL ANSWERS

OBJECTIVE QUESTIONS

Select the best answer for each of the following items. Mark only one answer for each item. Answer all items.

MAY 1981

14. The Uniform Commercial Code provides for a warranty against infringement. Its primary purpose is to protect the buyer of goods from infringement of the rights of third parties. This warranty
a. Only applies if the sale is between merchants.
b. Must be expressly stated in the contract or the Statute of Frauds will prevent its enforceability.
c. Protects the seller if the buyer furnishes specifications which result in an infringement.
d. Can *not* be disclaimed.

15. Brown ordered 100 cases of Delicious Brand peas at list price from Smith Wholesaler. Immediately upon receipt of Brown's order, Smith sent Brown an acceptance which was received by Brown. The acceptance indicated that shipment would be made within ten days. On the tenth day Smith discovered that all of its supply of Delicious Brand peas had been sold. Instead it shipped 100 cases of Lovely Brand peas, stating clearly on the invoice that the shipment was sent only as an accommodation. Which of the following is correct?
a. Smith's shipment of Lovely Brand peas is a counteroffer, thus *no* contract exists between Brown and Smith.
b. Smith's note of accommodation cancels the contract between Smith and Brown.
c. Brown's order is a unilateral offer, and can only be accepted by Smith's shipment of the goods ordered.
d. Smith's shipment of Lovely Brand peas constitutes a breach of contract.

16. Ace Auto Sales, Inc., sold Williams a second-hand car for $9,000. One day Williams parked the car in a shopping center parking lot. When Williams returned to the car, Montrose and several policemen were waiting. It turned out that the car had been stolen from Montrose who was rightfully claiming ownership. Subsequently, the car was returned by Williams to Montrose. Williams seeks recourse against Ace Auto Sales who had sold him the car with the usual disclaimer of warranty. Which of the following is correct?
a. Since Ace Auto Sales' contract of sale disclaimed "any and all warranties" arising in connection with its sale to Williams, Williams must bear the loss.
b. Since Ace Auto and Williams were both innocent of any wrongdoing in connection with the theft of the auto, the loss will rest upon the party ultimately in possession.
c. Had Williams litigated the question of Montrose's ownership to the auto, he would have won since possession is nine-tenths of the law.
d. Ace Auto will bear the loss since a warranty of title in Williams' favor arose upon the sale of the auto.

17. A dispute has arisen between two merchants over the question of who has the risk of loss in a given sales transaction. The contract does not specifically cover the point. The goods were shipped to the buyer who rightfully rejected them. Which of the following factors will be the most important factor in resolving their dispute?
a. Who has title to the goods.
b. The shipping terms.
c. The credit terms.
d. The fact that a breach has occurred.

18. Doral Inc., wished to obtain an adequate supply of lumber for its factory extension which was to be constructed in the spring. It contacted Ace Lumber Company and obtained a 75-day written option (firm offer) to buy its estimated needs for the building. Doral supplied a form contract which included the option. Ace Lumber signed at the physical end of the contract but did not sign elsewhere. The price of lumber has risen drastically and Ace wishes to avoid its obligation. Which of the following is Ace's best defense against Doral's assertion that Ace is legally bound by the option?

a. Such an option is invalid if its duration is for more than two months.

b. The option is *not* supported by any consideration on Doral's part.

c. Doral is *not* a merchant.

d. The promise of irrevocability was contained in a form supplied by Doral and was *not* separately signed by Ace.

19. Ambrose telephoned Miller Adding Machine Company and ordered 1,000 pocket calculators at $4.05 each. Ambrose agreed to pay 10% immediately and the balance within ten days after receipt of the entire shipment. Ambrose forwarded a check for $405.00 and Miller shipped 500 calculators the next day, intending to ship the balance by the end of the week. Ambrose decided that the contract was a bad bargain and repudiated it, asserting the Statute of Frauds. Miller sued Ambrose. Which of the following will allow Miller to prevail despite the Statute of Frauds?

a. The contract is *not* within the requirements of the statute.

b. Ambrose paid 10% down.

c. Miller shipped 500 of the calculators.

d. Ambrose admitted in court that it made the contract in question.

20. Darrow purchased 100 sets of bookends from Benson Manufacturing, Inc. Darrow made substantial prepayments of the purchase price. Benson is insolvent and the goods have not been delivered as promised. Darrow wants the bookends. Under the circumstances, which of the following will prevent Darrow from obtaining the bookends?

a. The fact that he did *not* pay the full price at the time of the purchase even though he has made a tender of the balance and holds it available to Benson upon delivery.

b. The fact that he can obtain a judgment for damages.

c. The fact that he was *not* aware of Benson's insolvency at the time he purchased the bookends.

d. The fact that the goods have *not* been identified to his contract.

11. Base Electric Co. has entered an agreement to buy its actual requirements of copper wiring for six months from the Seymour Metal Wire Company and Seymour Metal has agreed to sell all the copper wiring Base will require for six months. The agreement between the two companies is

a. Unenforceable because it is too indefinite.

b. Unenforceable because it lacks mutuality of obligation.

c. Unenforceable because of lack of consideration.

d. Valid and enforceable.

12. Gibbeon Manufacturing shipped 300 designer navy blue blazers to Custom Clothing Emporeum. The blazers arrived on Friday, earlier than Custom had anticipated and on an exceptionally busy day for its receiving department. They were perfunctorily examined and sent to a nearby warehouse for storage until needed. On Monday of the following week, upon closer examination, it was discovered that the quality of the linings of the blazers was inferior to that specified in the sales contract. Which of the following is correct insofar as Custom's rights are concerned?

a. Custom can reject the blazers upon subsequent discovery of the defects.

b. Custom must retain the blazers since it accepted them and had an opportunity to inspect them upon delivery.

c. Custom's only course of action is rescission.

d. Custom had no rights if the linings were of merchantable quality.

13. The Balboa Custom Furniture Company sells fine custom furniture. It has been encountering difficulties lately with some customers who have breached their contracts after the furniture they have selected has been customized to their order or the fabric they have selected has been cut or actually installed on the piece of furniture purchased. The company therefore wishes to resort to a liquidated damages clause in its sales contract to encourage performance or provide an acceptable amount of damages. Regarding Balboa's contemplated resort to a liquidated damages clause, which of the following is correct?

a. Balboa may not use a liquidated damages clause since it is a merchant and is the preparer of the contract.

b. Balboa can simply take a very large deposit which will be forfeited if performance by a customer is not made for any reason.

c. The amount of the liquidated damages stipulated in the contract must be reasonable in light of the anticipated or actual harm caused by the breach.

d. Even if Balboa uses a liquidated damages clause in its sales contract, it will nevertheless have to establish that the liquidated damages claimed did not exceed actual damages by more than 10%.

15. Joseph Manufacturing, Inc., received an order from Raulings Supply Company for certain valves it manufactured. The order called for prompt shipment. In respect to Joseph's options as to the manner of acceptance, which of the following is *incorrect*?

a. Joseph can accept only by prompt shipment since this was the manner indicated in the order.

b. The order is construed as an offer to enter into either a unilateral or bilateral contract and Joseph may accept by a promise of or prompt shipment.

c. If Joseph promptly ships the goods, Raulings must be notified within a reasonable time.

d. Joseph may accept by mail, but he must make prompt shipment.

16. Which of the following requirements must be met for modification of a sales contract under the Uniform Commercial Code?

a. There must be consideration present if the contract is between merchants.

b. There must be a writing if the original sales contract is in writing.

c. The modification must satisfy the Statute of Frauds if the contract as modified is within its provisions.

d. The parol evidence rule applies and thus a writing is required.

17. Barstow Hardware Company received an order for $850 of assorted hardware from Flanagan & Company. The shipping terms were F.O.B. Mannix Freight Line, seller's place of business, 2/10, net/30. Barstow packed and crated the hardware for shipment and it was loaded upon Mannix Freight's truck. While the goods were in transit to Flanagan, Barstow learned that Flanagan was insolvent in the

equity sense (unable to pay its debts in the ordinary course of business). Barstow promptly wired Mannix Freight's office in Pueblo, Colorado, and instructed them to stop shipment of the goods to Flanagan and to store them until further instructions. Mannix complied with these instructions. Regarding the rights, duties, and liabilities of the parties, which of the following is correct?

a. Barstow's stoppage in transit was improper if Flanagan's assets exceeded its liabilities.

b. Flanagan is entitled to the hardware if it pays cash.

c. Once Barstow correctly learned of Flanagan's insolvency, it had no further duty or obligation to Flanagan.

d. The fact that Flanagan became insolvent in no way affects the rights, duties, and obligations of the parties.

27. Ford bought a used typewriter for $625 from Jem Typewriters. The contract provided that the typewriter was sold "with all faults, as is, and at the buyer's risk." The typewriter broke down within a month. Ford took it back to Jem, and after prolonged arguing and negotiating, Jem orally agreed to reduce the price by $50 and refund that amount. Jem has reconsidered his rights and duties and decided *not* to refund the money. Under the circumstances, which of the following is correct?

a. The disclaimer of the implied warranties of merchantability and fitness is invalid.

b. The agreement to reduce the price is valid and binding.

c. Jem's promise is unenforceable since Ford gave *no* new consideration.

d. Since the contract as modified is subject to the statute of frauds, the modification must be in writing.

29. Marblehead Manufacturing, Inc., contracted with Wellfleet Oil Company in June to provide its regular supply of fuel oil from November 1 through March 31. The written contract required Marblehead to take all of its oil requirements exclusively from Wellfleet at a fixed price subject to an additional amount *not* to exceed 10% of the contract price and only if the market price increases during the term of the contract. By the time performance was due on the contract, the market price had already risen 20%. Wellfleet seeks to avoid performance. Which of the following will be Wellfleet's *best* argument?

a. There is *no* contract since Marblehead was *not* required to take any oil.

b. The contract fails because of lack of definiteness and certainty.

c. The contract is unconscionable.

d. Marblehead has ordered amounts of oil unreasonably disproportionate to its normal requirements.

32. Target Company, Inc., ordered a generator from Maximum Voltage Corporation. A dispute has arisen over the effect of a provision in the specifications that the generator have a 5,000 kilowatt capacity. The specifications were attached to the contract and were incorporated by reference in the main body of the contract. The generator did *not* have this capacity but instead had a maximum capacity of 4,800 kilowatts. The contract had a disclaimer clause which effectively negated both of the implied warranties of quality. Target is seeking to avoid the contract based upon breach of warranty and Maximum is relying on its disclaimer. Which of the following is a correct statement?

a. The 5,000 kilowatt term contained in the specifications does *not* constitute a warranty.

b. The disclaimer effectively negated any and all warranty protection claimed by Target.

c. The description language (5,000 kilowatt) contained in the specifications is an express warranty and has *not* been effectively disclaimed.

d. The parol evidence rule will prevent Target from asserting the 5,000 kilowatt term as a warranty.

33. Buyer ordered goods from Seller. The contract required Seller to deliver them f.o.b. Buyer's place of business. Buyer inspected the goods, discovered they failed to conform to the contract, and rightfully rejected them. In the event of loss of the goods, which of the following is a correct statement?

a. Seller initially had the risk of loss and it remains with him after delivery.

b. Risk of loss passes to Buyer upon tender of the goods f.o.b. Buyer's place of business.

c. Buyer initially had the risk of loss, but it is shifted to Seller upon rightful rejection.

d. If Seller used a public carrier to transport the goods to Buyer, risk of loss is on Buyer during transit.

34. Milgore, the vice president of Deluxe Restaurants, telephoned Specialty Restaurant Suppliers and ordered a made-to-order dishwashing unit for one of its restaurants. Due to the specifications, the machine was *not* adaptable for use by other restauranteurs. The agreed price was $2,500. The machine was constructed as agreed but Deluxe has refused to pay for it. Which of the following is correct?

a. Milgore obviously lacked the authority to make such a contract.

b. The statute of frauds applies and will bar recovery by Specialty.

c. Specialty can successfully maintain an action for the price.

d. Specialty must resell the machine and recover damages based upon the resale price.

37. Pure Food Company packed and sold quality food products to wholesalers and fancy food retailers. One of its most popular items was "southern style" baked beans. Charleston purchased a large can of the beans from the Superior Quality Grocery. Charleston's mother bit into a heaping spoonful of the beans at a family outing and fractured her jaw. The evidence revealed that the beans contained a brown stone, the size of a marble. In a subsequent lawsuit by Mrs. Charleston, which of the following is correct?

a. Mrs. Charleston can collect against Superior Quality for negligence.

b. Privity will *not* be a bar in a lawsuit against either Pure Food or Superior Quality.

c. The various sellers involved could have effectively excluded or limited the rights of third parties to sue them.

d. Privity is a bar to recovery by Mrs. Charleston, although her son may sue Superior Quality.

38. Martha Supermarkets ordered 1,000 cases of giant pitted olives from Grove Packers and Wholesalers. The olives were to be packed, labelled and shipped in 30 days. The payment terms were 2/10, net/30 upon delivery. After the order was nearly ready for shipment, Grove learned that Martha was *not* paying its debts as they became due. Martha insisted on delivery according to the terms of the contract. Which of the following is correct?

a. Upon discovery of Martha's financial condition, Grove was relieved from any duty under the contract.

b. Martha has the right of performance since it was *not* insolvent in the bankruptcy sense.

c. Grove must perform but it is entitled to demand cash.

d. The terms of the contract provided credit to Martha and Grove is bound by it.

46. Dupree buys and sells merchandise at whole-sale. She is concerned with her insurance coverage on her purchases. Her desire is to insure the property at the earliest possible time legally permitted. Which of the following times or circumstances correctly indicates the earliest time permissible?

a. At the time the goods are identified to the contract.

b. When title to the goods has passed to her.

c. When she has received possession of the goods.

d. At the time the contract is made whether or not the goods are identified.

Answers to Objective Questions

May 1981		May 1980	
14. c	**18.** d	**27.** d	**34.** c
15. d	**19.** d	**29.** d	**37.** b
16. d	**20.** d	**32.** c	**38.** c
17. d		**33.** a	**46.** a

November 1980	
11. d	**15.** a
12. a	**16.** c
13. c	**17.** b

Explanation of Answers to Objective Questions

14. (c) In a sale by a merchant, the merchant warrants that the goods are free from a rightful claim of infringement of patent or trademark by third parties. (A seller will be protected against liability under a warranty against infringement if the buyer furnishes the specifications used to manufacture the product that infringes upon another party's patent or trademark rights.) Answer (a) is incorrect because only the seller need be a merchant. Answer (b) is incorrect because a warranty against infringement is granted along with the warranty of title and thus, does not need to be expressly stated in the contract to be enforceable. Like the warranty of title, a warranty against infringement can be disclaimed by specific language or circumstances that indicate that this warranty is not extended. Therefore, answer (d) is incorrect.

15. (d) Shipment of a different brand of peas, even as an accommodation, constitutes a breach of contract because the terms of the contract have not been complied with. Answer (a) is incorrect because the shipment cannot be considered a counteroffer since there was already a contract in existence between Brown and Smith. Answer (b) is untrue because only the promised performance will discharge Smith, unless Brown accepts the accommodation. Answer (c) is incorrect since Brown's offer to Smith constitutes a bilateral offer which was accepted by Smith's communication to Brown. This bilateral offer could have been accepted by delivery of the specified goods as well.

16. (d) In any contract for the sale of goods, unless specifically disclaimed, the seller extends a warranty of title to the buyer. Such a warranty is neither express nor implied but warrants that the seller has good title to the goods, that the transfer of said title is rightful, and that the buyer will have knowledge of all liens against the property at the time of transfer. Williams, the buyer, was not informed of all liens against the property, thus, Ace Auto must bear the loss since it violated the provisions of the title warranty. Answer (a) is incorrect because even if Ace disclaimed "any and all warranties," this would not discharge a warranty of title since specific reference to this warranty must be made in any disclaimer thereof. Answer (b) is incorrect because the seller will bear the loss in the event of defective title unless he properly disclaims that warranty. Answer (c) is also incorrect because possession of an item does not automatically result in the presumption of good title or ownership.

17. (d) Generally, risk of loss is determined by the following sequence of tests. First, if the parties have included provision for the allocation of loss as part of the contract, then that provision controls. If the contract is silent on this point, risk of loss is then assumed to be borne by any party who has breached the terms of the contract. Answer (a) is untrue since risk of loss under the UCC does not depend on which party has title at the time of loss. Answer (b) is incorrect since shipping terms (FOB shipping point/destination) are used only if there is no contract provision or breaching party. Answer (c) is untrue since credit terms have no relevance to risk of loss.

18. (d) In order for a firm offer to be effective, it

must be contained in writing signed by a merchant offeror. If the offeree supplies the form which contains a firm offer clause, the merchant offeror must separately sign that clause, otherwise it will be ineffective against the offeror. Answer (a) is incorrect since a firm offer is irrevocable for the stated period of time or, if none is stated, a reasonable period of time. However, this period of irrevocability can never exceed 3 months (90 days). Answer (b) is untrue since a firm offer made by a merchant (Ace) needs no consideration as long as the agreement is in a writing signed by merchant offeror. Answer (c) is incorrect since it is not necessary that the buyer be a merchant.

19. (d) One of the provisions of the Statute of Frauds is that a contract for the sale of goods for $500 or more must be in writing. Since this contract was oral, one of the several exceptions under the Statute must exist if this contract is to be enforceable. If the party who seeks to avoid performance makes an admission of the contract's existence in a court of law or court document, the oral contract is enforceable to the extent of the admission. Answer (a) is incorrect since the sale in question involves the sale of goods for $4,050 so the Statute applies. Answer (b) is incorrect since partial payment ($405 for 500 calculators) will only allow enforcement of the contract to the extent of the part performance. Partial performance would also require a shipment and acceptance of the goods. Answer (c) is untrue because it only involves shipment and therefore, will not even result in enforceability of half the contract unless the goods are accepted.

20. (d) Upon identification of the goods that relate to a contract, several specific rights are granted to the buyer of these goods. Among these is the right to take delivery of goods upon insolvency of the seller if full or partial payment was made at the time of the purchase and any balance due is tendered to the seller. Since the question asks which condition will prevent recovery of the goods, lack of identification is correct because identification must occur before any rights of repossession accrue to the buyer. It is not necessary that the full price be paid at the time of purchase (a) as long as tender of the balance due is made to the seller. Answers (b) and (c) are incorrect since the fact that a buyer may obtain a judgment for damages to the goods by third parties or that a buyer is not aware of a seller's insolvency will

not prevent the buyer from gaining possession of the goods.

NOVEMBER 1980

11. (d) This agreement is a requirements contract and is both valid and enforceable if executed in good faith. Answers (a), (b), and (c) are therefore incorrect.

12. (a) Answer (a) is correct since the buyer has a reasonable time in which to reject defective goods. Discovering the defect on Monday would be considered within a reasonable time, considering the goods had been delivered on Friday. Answer (d) is incorrect since the specification concerning the linings in the sales contract would be an express warranty which was breached when the linings were found to be inferior to what had been stated. Thus, the merchantable quality of the linings would be irrelevant.

13. (c) A liquidated damage provision is a contractual provision which states the amount of damages that will occur if either party breaches the contract. If the amount is reasonable in light of the anticipated or actual harm caused by the breach, it is enforceable. Answer (c) is correct. Answer (a) is incorrect because the fact that the preparer of the contract is a merchant has no bearing on the use of a liquidated damage clause. Answer (b) is incorrect because retaining a large deposit could be considered unconscionable and unenforceable. The reasonableness of a liquidated damage clause is judged in light of anticipated harm, not by a set percentage by which the liquidated damages exceed the actual damages.

15. (a) When possible an offer is interpreted to permit acceptance by either an act or a promise to perform the act. Answer (a) is correct because the offer in question can be interpreted to permit either prompt shipment of the goods or the promise to do so. However, if Joseph accepts by a promise, shortly thereafter he must make prompt shipment.

16. (c) Under the U.C.C. the Statute of Frauds is applicable if the contract as modified is within the Statute. An example of this would be an oral contract for the sale of a car for $450 which is subsequently modified by the parties to a purchase price of $500. Such a modification must be in writing to be enforceable since it is within the Statute of Frauds. Answer (a) is incorrect since under the UCC modification of a pre-existing contract for the sale of goods needs no new consideration to be binding. The modification may be oral or written, depending on whether it involves an amount of $500 or more, so answer (b) is incorrect. Answer (d) is incorrect because the parol evidence rule does not apply to subsequent modifications of a written agreement, e.g. oral changes made after the original written agreement.

17. (b) When a seller discovers that the buyer is insolvent (this includes insolvency in the equity sense) the seller may stop the goods in transit and refuse delivery except for cash. If Flanagan pays cash he is entitled to the hardware. Thus answer (b) is correct.

MAY 1980

27. (d) Even as modified, the contract would involve the sale of goods for $500 or more, thus the Statute of Frauds would require that such agreement be in writing. Answer (a) is incorrect because "with all faults, as is" does disclaim all implied warranties. Answer (c) is incorrect because a modification of a pre-existing contract for the sale of goods needs no new consideration.

29. (d) The agreement involved is a requirements contract; thus Marblehead's ordering of unreasonably disproportionate amounts of oil would be a breach by them. A requirements contract is considered definite and both parties are viewed as having provided consideration, thus answers (a), (b), and (c) are incorrect.

32. (c) The "5000 kilowatt" term is a statement of fact made as part of the basis of the bargain; thus it qualifies as an express warranty. Only the implied warranties were disclaimed, thus answer (c) is correct and answers (a) and (b) are incorrect. Answer (d) is incorrect because the parol evidence rule excludes oral statements from evidence when the agreement is in writing. The "5000 kilowatt" term was part of the written agreement, therefore the parol evidence rule would not exclude this term from the agreement.

33. (a) In an f.o.b. point of destination contract the risk of loss transfers from seller to buyer upon tender of conforming goods. However, the seller did not deliver conforming goods and the risk of loss remains upon seller even after delivery. Thus answers (b), (c), and (d) are incorrect.

34. (c) Since there are no prospective buyers of this unit due to its uniqueness of design, the seller can sue for the full contract price. Answer (a) is incorrect because the vice president would normally have authority to make such contracts. Answer (b) is incorrect because the Statute of Frauds allows enforcement of an oral contract for the sale of specially manufactured goods if substantial performance occurs before repudiation. Answer (d) is incorrect because Specialty may recover the full contract price for specially manufactured goods since there is no prospective market for this unit.

37. (b) Both Pure Food and Superior Quality would be liable under the strict liability theory of product liability. If the product leaves the hands of the seller with a defect present that causes injury, the seller is liable for injury. Under strict liability there is no requirement of privity of contract between the seller and injured party. Even though Superior was not negligent they are still liable under strict liability. This liability cannot be excluded. If Mrs. Charleston were suing on the basis of breach of warranty she would have to show privity of contract. Answer (a) is incorrect because there is no negligence on the part of the seller, Superior Quality, but only on the manufacturer, Pure Food Company.

38. (c) When the seller discovers that the buyer is insolvent, the seller may refuse delivery except for cash. Answer (c) is correct because Martha was insolvent in the "equity" sense. Answer (a) is incorrect because a buyer's insolvency does not discharge the seller's duty to perform. Answers (b) and (d) are incorrect because insolvency of the buyer in the "equity sense" is sufficient to permit the seller to demand cash before delivering the goods.

46. (a) Identification occurs when the seller designates what goods he is going to use to perform the contract. Once identification occurs the buyer has an insurable interest in the goods and can insure against any losses he might suffer if goods are damaged or destroyed.

ESSAY QUESTIONS AND ANSWERS

5. Part a. Clauson Enterprises, Inc., was considering adding a new product line to its existing lines. The decision was contingent upon its being assured of a supply of an electronic component for the product at a certain price and a positive market study which clearly justified the investment in the venture.

Clauson's president approached Migrane Electronics and explained the situation to Migrane's president. After much negotiation, Migrane agreed to grant Clauson an option to purchase 12,000 of the necessary electronic components at $1.75 each or at the prevailing market price, whichever was lower. Clauson prepared the option below incorporating their understanding.

Option Agreement
Clauson Enterprises/Migrane Electronics

Migrane Electronics hereby offers to sell Clauson Enterprises 12,000 miniature solid state electronic breakers at $1.75 each or at the existing market price at the time of delivery, whichever is lower, delivery to be made in 12 equal monthly installments beginning one month after the exercise of this option. This option is irrevocable for six months from January 1, 1978.

    Clauson Enterprises agrees to deliver to Migrane its market survey for the product line in which the component would be used if it elects not to exercise the option.

Both parties signed the option agreement and Migrane's president signed Migrane's corporate name alongside the last sentence of the first paragraph. On May 1, 1978, Migrane notified Clauson that it was revoking its offer. The market price for the component had increased to $1.85. On May 15, 1978, Clauson notified Migrane that it accepted the offer and that if Migrane did not perform, it would be sued and held liable for damages. Migrane replied that the offer was not binding and was revoked before Clauson accepted. Furthermore, even if it were binding, it was good for only three months as a matter of law.

Upon receipt of Migrane's reply, Clauson instituted suit for damages.

Required Answer the following, setting forth reasons for any conclusions stated.

Who will prevail? Discuss all the issues and arguments raised by the fact situation.

Answer Clauson Enterprises will prevail. The option in question is supported by consideration and consequently is a binding contract. The offer is definite and certain despite the fact that the pricing terms are not presently determinable. The Uniform Commercial Code is extremely liberal regarding satisfaction of the pricing terms.

Except for the presence of consideration in the form of the promise by Clauson to deliver the market survey to Migrane, the option would not have been binding beyond three months and Migrane would have prevailed. Section 2-205 of the Uniform Commercial Code provides as follows:

> An offer by a merchant to buy or sell goods in a signed writing which by its terms gives assurance that it will be held open is not revocable, for lack of consideration, during the time stated or if no time is stated for a reasonable time, but in no event may such period of irrevocability exceed three months; but any such term of assurance on a form supplied by the offeree must be separately signed by the offeror.

It is apparent from the wording of this section that the option was valid without consideration, but only for three months. It was an offer by a merchant contained in a signed writing and clearly stated its irrevocability. Furthermore, the separately signed requirement where the form is supplied by the offeree was satisfied. But the section is inapplicable to the facts of this case since bargained-for consideration was present. The Uniform Commercial Code's three-month limitation does not apply to options where consideration is present. Hence, Clauson's acceptance was valid, and if Migrane refuses to perform, Clauson will be entitled to damages.

5. Part b. On May 30, 1978, Hargrove ordered 1,000 spools of nylon yarn from Flowers, Inc., of Norfolk, Virginia. The shipping terms were "F.O.B., Norfolk & Western RR at Norfolk." The transaction was to be a cash sale with payment to be simultaneously exchanged for the negotiable bill of lading covering the goods. Title to the goods was expressly reserved in Flowers. The yarn ordered by Hargrove was delivered to the railroad and loaded in a boxcar on June 1, 1978. Flowers obtained a negotiable bill of lading made out to its own order. The boxcar was destroyed the next day while the goods were in transit. Hargrove refused to pay for the yarn and Flowers sued Hargrove for the purchase price.

Required Answer the following, setting forth reasons for any conclusions stated.

Who will prevail?

Answer Flowers will prevail because Hargrove has the risk of loss. The shipping terms determine who had the risk of loss. Section 2-509(1) of the Uniform Commercial Code provides that "Where the contract requires or authorizes the seller to ship the goods by carrier, (*a*) if it does not require him to deliver at a particular destination, the risk of loss passes to the buyer when the goods are duly delivered to the carrier, even though the shipment is under reservation. . . ."

The facts that title was reserved by Flowers and that Flowers retained the negotiable bill of lading do not affect the determination of who is to bear the risk of loss. The code makes it clear that title is irrelevant in determining the risk of loss.

NOVEMBER 1977 (Estimated time: 25 to 30 minutes)

7. Part a. Max Motors, Inc., sold a 1973 used station wagon to Sarah Constance for $3,350. Constance has corresponded with Max Motors on several occasions and has alleged that Fogarty, an experienced salesman for Max Motors, made several express oral warranties in connection with her purchase of the car. Constance alleges that there has been a breach of warranty and as a result she has suffered damages to the extent of $1,025 for expenses incurred to repair the car. Constance also indicated that in the event she does not receive a refund of $1,025, she will take appropriate legal action to obtain satisfaction.

In various letters, Constance stated that she went to Max Motors and contacted Fogarty. Before she finally made a deal for the car, she asked many questions about the car. Fogarty assured her that the car was in good condition and that he had driven the car several times. In addition, Fogarty stated that "This is a car I can recommend and it is in A-1 shape."

Constance informed Fogarty that her husband had been transferred to another state, that her child was only two years old, and that she needed the car so she could join her husband. She stated that Fogarty assured her that he knew the car and knew

the person who traded it in and it was "mechanically perfect." He also told her that, "it would get her any place she wanted to go and not to worry." Constance indicated she knew nothing about cars but would like to drive it. Fogarty replied this was not possible because he was the only man on duty at the lot that day and he could not leave to accompany her as required by company policy.

Constance stated she purchased the car in reliance on the statements made by Fogarty. Unfortunately, these statements proved to be incorrect. The car began knocking and finally broke down after being driven about 300 miles. The car was repaired by Master Mechanics and a copy of a receipted bill for $1,025 accompanied one of her letters to Max Motors.

Fogarty indicated that he believed what he stated was true, as far as he knew the car wasn't in bad condition, and he knew of no important defects in the car. He also indicated he told Constance that he could not warrant the car because it was over two years old and had in excess of 50,000 miles.

Required Answer the following, setting forth reasons for any conclusions stated.

1. Is it likely that Constance will prevail in a legal action against Max Motors? Discuss all relevant issues.
2. Identify, but do not discuss, other warranties that Constance might rely upon in addition to the oral express warranties.

Answer

1. Yes. The main issue is whether Fogarty's statements constitute an affirmation of fact as contrasted with mere opinion.

This issue has been resolved in many cases in favor of purchasers, such as Constance. It often is difficult to draw the line between an affirmation of fact, which when relied upon constitutes a warranty, and mere sales talk, which is a statement of the seller's opinion. However, the combination of the various statements made by Fogarty and perhaps the language "mechanically perfect" constituted a warranty under the circumstances.

Furthermore, the relative expertise of the parties is validly taken into account under such circumstances. Fogarty was a used car salesman with long experience and was familiar with the mechanical aspects of automobiles. It would be only natural for Constance to take his statements as being something more than idle chatter. Her total lack of knowledge of automobiles and their engines would lead her to rely on Fogarty's representations.

In addition, all the other elements necessary to establish an oral express warranty are present. Fogarty's good faith or honest belief in the truth of his statements is irrelevant. Knowledge of falsity has nothing to do with warranty. The Uniform Commercial Code reads as follows: "Any affirmation of fact or promise made by the seller to the buyer which relates to the goods and becomes part of the basis of the bargain creates an express warranty that the goods shall conform to the affirmation or promise." Additionally, the code states, "It is not necessary to the creation of an express warranty that the seller use familiar words, such as warrants or guarantees or that . . . a specific intention to make a warranty be present."

The facts clearly indicate that the affirmation or promise was a basis of the bargain; that is, that the language was intended to be relied upon by the buyer and it was. Finally, the buyer relied upon it to her detriment and suffered damages as a result. Although the Uniform Commercial Code includes cautionary language that an affirmation merely of the value of the goods or a statement purporting to be merely the seller's opinion or commendation of the goods does not create a warranty, it appears that the facts clearly establish an oral express warranty.

Another issue is the legal effect of Fogarty's statement that he could not give a warranty on the auto sold. Does this validly disclaim the oral express warranty protection? There is a general hostility manifested by the Uniform Commercial Code and the courts to allowing broad uninformative disclaimers to legally negate warranty protection. Warranties are not to be disclaimed without due notice and fairness shown to the purchaser under the circumstances. Where there are words tending to negate an oral express warranty, the purported disclaimer shall be constructed wherever reasonable as consistent with the warranty. Hence, a purported negation or limitation is inoperative to the extent that such a construction is unreasonable. Thus, it appears that the warranty has not been disclaimed.

2. Constance might rely upon the implied warranties of merchantability and fitness for a particular purpose.

7. Part b. A claim has been asserted against Ajax Motors for $7,000 arising out of the sale of a used 1975 automobile. Knox purchased the automobile in February 1977 and subsequently learned that it was a stolen car. The serial numbers had been changed, but it has been conclusively determined that the car belongs to Watts who has duly repossessed it. The contract contained a disclaimer which read as follows: "Ajax Motors hereby disclaims any and all warranties, express or implied, which are not contained in the contract." Knox has brought a legal action against Ajax Motors alleging breach of warranty.

Required Answer the following, setting forth reasons for any conclusions stated.

What is the probable outcome of such a legal action? Discuss fully the legal basis upon which Knox is relying and any defense that Ajax Motors may assert.

Answer The case should be decided in favor of Knox. The basis for recovery would be the title warranties provided under the Uniform Commercial Code which states that the title conveyed should be good and its transfer rightful, but here Watts was the rightful owner and entitled to repossess the car. The code does not indicate whether such a warranty is to be construed as an express or implied warranty. However, it can only be excluded by specific language or circumstances that give the buyer reason to know that the person selling does not claim title in himself. From this it would appear that a seller would have to clearly indicate that he does not purport to own the item in question and that the buyer is assuming the risk that the title is defective. Such was not the case. However, Ajax Motors will undoubtedly claim that the disclaimer is legally operative.

7. Part c. Fashion Footwear Company received an order on June 15, 1977, from Footloose Shoes, Inc., for 300 pairs of shoes at a price of $6.85 per pair. Footloose is the predecessor corporation to Nemo Exclusives, Inc., which acquired Footloose by statutory merger on October 12, 1977. Fashion is seeking to recover the contract price from Nemo.

The evidence shows that Footloose placed a written order with Fashion for 300 pairs of shoes at $6.85 per pair to be delivered September 1, 1977. Fashion's acceptance was dated June 17, 1977. The order incorporated a form letter which contained a stipulation that it would not be possible to consider cancellations after shoes had been cut. On June 30, 1977, all of the shoes ordered by Footloose had been cut. On that same day Footloose advised Fashion to cancel the entire order. On July 1, 1977, Fashion wrote Footloose the following letter: "In accordance with our previous correspondence, we proceeded with your order for fall shoes. We are unable to cancel your order since cutting is completed."

On September 1, 1977, Footloose refused to accept delivery of the shoes whereupon Fashion then made several unsuccessful attempts to resell the shoes elsewhere at a reasonable price.

Nemo states it was not a party to the above transaction and that in any event, Fashion can only recover its damages and not the full price for the shoes delivered and refused.

Required Answer the following, setting forth reasons for any conclusions stated.

Who will prevail? Discuss all issues and problems raised by the above facts.

Answer Fashion will prevail against Nemo. The fact that Fashion's contract was with Footloose is no defense because the surviving corporation in a statutory merger assumes the contract obligations of the absorbed corporation.

An action to recover the price of the finished shoes is clearly recognized by the Uniform Commercial Code. Although as a general proposition a seller must stop work when ordered to do so by the buyer to mitigate damages and prevent economic waste, the proposition is clearly inapplicable here. The code provides in the section dealing with the seller's remedies that where the goods are unfinished an aggrieved seller may in the exercise of reasonable commercial judgment for the purpose of avoiding loss and of effective realization either complete the manufacture and wholly identify the goods to the contract or cease manufacture and resell for scrap or salvage value or proceed in any other reasonable manner. An action to recover the price of the shoes will be successful if the goods are those identified in the contract and if the seller is unable, after reasonable effort, to resell them at a reasonable price or the circumstances reasonably indicate that such an effort will be unavailing. The situation between Fashion and Nemo (Footloose) is clearly within these rules.

CHAPTER

4

Documents of Title and Investment Securities

Beginning with the November 1983 Uniform CPA Examination, the following business law subjects can be covered in the business law section of the examination.

B. Documents of Title and Investment Securities
   1. Warehouse Receipts
   2. Bills of Lading
   3. Issuance, Transfer, and Registration of Securities[1]

DOCUMENTS OF TITLE: WAREHOUSE RECEIPTS AND BILLS OF LADING (Article 7 of the UCC)

I. The primary purpose served by warehouse receipts and bills of lading is to facilitate the sale and delivery of goods. The rules provided in article 7 of the UCC involve the application of principles and concepts found in the law of contracts, sale of goods, bailments, and negotiable instruments.

DEFINITIONS

II. Article 7 of the UCC provides the following important definitions:
   A. *Document of title* is any document which, in the regular course of business or financing, is treated as adequate evidence that the person in possession of it is entitled to receive, hold, and dispose of the document and the goods it covers [7-102(1)(e), 1-201(15)]. Examples are a bill of lading and a warehouse receipt. (See Figure 4-1.)

---

[1]AICPA, *Business Law–Content Specification Outline*, approved by the AICPA Board of Examiners on August 31, 1981, to become effective with the November 1983 Uniform CPA Examination.

FIGURE 4-1 DOCUMENTS OF TITLE

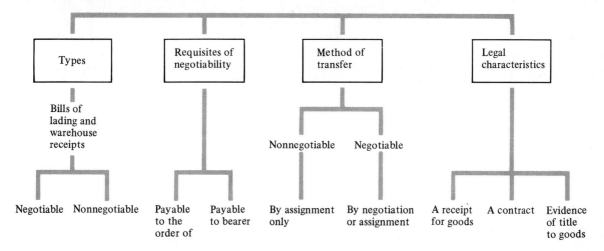

1. *Requirements.* It must purport to be issued by a bailee (i.e., a carrier or warehouseman) or addressed to a bailee (i.e., a delivery order) and purport to cover goods in the bailee's possession which either are identified or are fungible portions of an identified mass (1-201).
2. *Characteristics.* Every document of title possesses the following characteristics:
   a. It is a receipt for goods;
   b. It is a contract; and
   c. It is evidence of title.
B. *Bill of lading* is a document of title issued by a private or common carrier in exchange for goods delivered to it for shipment. It may be issued "negotiable" or "nonnegotiable" [1-201(6)].
C. *Warehouse receipt* is a document of title issued by a person engaged in the business of storing goods for hire (warehouseman) that acknowledges receipt of the goods, describes the goods stored, and contains the terms of the storage contract. It may be issued "negotiable" or "nonnegotiable" [1-201(45), 7-202].
D. *Delivery order* is a written order to deliver goods that is directed to a warehouseman, carrier, or other person who issues warehouse receipts or bills of lading in the ordinary course of business [7-102(1)(d)].
E. *Consignee* is the person named in a bill of lading to whom or to whose order the goods are to be delivered [7-102(1)(b)].
F. *Consignor* is the person named in the bill of lading as the person who had contracted with the carrier to ship and deliver the goods [7-102(1)(c)].
G. *Bailee.* For purposes of this chapter, a bailee is a person who acknowledges possession of goods and contracts to deliver them under the terms of a warehouse receipt, bill of lading, delivery order, or other document of title [7-102(1)(a)].
H. *Warehouseman* is a person who is engaged in the business of storing goods owned by others for a price.
I. *Carrier* is a person who is engaged in the business of transporting or forwarding goods owned by others for a price.
J. *Negotiable and nonnegotiable documents of title.* A negotiable document of title is a warehouse receipt, bill of lading, or other document by whose terms goods are to be delivered "to bearer" *or* "to the order of" a named person. Any other document is nonnegotiable [7-104(1)(a)(b)].

K. *Bailment* is a transfer of possession of goods without title from one person to another for a temporary period of time. The transferor is called a bailor. The transferee is the bailee.

L. *Common carrier* is a person or entity who is in the business of transporting goods for the public on a regular basis for a price.

M. *Private carrier* is a person or entity who is in the business of transporting goods on a contract basis with individual shippers for a price. A private carrier does not hold itself out as a transporter of goods for the public.

N. *Freight forwarder* is a bailee who receives goods from more than one seller, consolidates such goods into carloads, and then ships the goods to buyers by common carrier.

O. *Issuer* is a bailee who issues a document of title. The term applies to any person for whom an agent or employee purports to act in issuing a document of title if the agent or employee has real or apparent authority to issue documents of title, notwithstanding that the issuer received no goods or that the goods were misdescribed or that the agent or employee violated instructions [7-102(1)(g)].

P. *Field warehousing* is a secured transaction whereby a manufacturer or dealer that wishes to finance its inventory leases a segregated part of its premises to an independent warehouseman and then places the inventory in the segregated area under the exclusive possession and control of the warehouseman under an agreement that it be held there as security for a business loan. The inventory cannot be released without the permission of the secured creditors.

Q. *Straight bill of lading* is a nonnegotiable bill of lading.

DELIVERY OF GOODS TO A "PERSON ENTITLED UNDER THE DOCUMENT"

III. As stated previously, a document of title is a contract, a receipt for goods, and also evidence of title to goods for which it was issued. A bailee-warehouseman or carrier *must* deliver the goods it holds as a bailee to a "person entitled under the document" that represents such goods.

A. *"Person entitled under the document."* Such a person is identified as follows:

   1. *Under a negotiable document.* To qualify as a "person entitled under the document," a person must be a "holder" [7-403(4)]. A *holder* is a person in possession of a document of title which has been:

   a. Issued to bearer by its original terms, e.g., "deliver to bearer";

   b. Issued to the holder's order by its original terms. For example, Sam Jones ships goods on Erie Railroad, and the latter issues a bill of lading by whose terms the goods are to be delivered "to the order of Sam Jones";

   c. Indorsed in blank (e.g., /S/ "Sam Jones") or to bearer (e.g., "deliver goods to bearer," /S/ "Sam Jones");

   d. Indorsed to the holder's order. For example, "Deliver to General Miles," /S/ "Sam Jones".

   2. *Under a nonnegotiable document.* The "person entitled under the document" is the person to whom delivery of the goods is to be made under either one of the following circumstances:

   a. By the terms of a nonnegotiable document, e.g., "to Jon Ball"; or

   b. Pursuant to a delivery order [7-104, 7-403(4), 1-201(20)].

B. *Justifications for nondelivery to a "person entitled under the document"* [7-403(1)].

   1. *Delivery to a person with superior title* (i.e., the "true owner") [7-403(1)(a)]. For example, a thief, an unauthorized person, or a finder in possession of goods owned by another person does not have title to such goods. Consequently, such persons cannot create title to goods by delivering them to a bailee-warehouseman or carrier in exchange for a warehouse receipt or bill of lading. The documents are null and void. A bailee would incur no liability if it delivered the goods to the true owner even though another claimant could establish that it was a "person entitled under the document."

2. *Damage, loss, delay, or destruction of goods.*

    a. *Private carriers and warehousemen.* They have a duty to exercise ordinary care toward goods in their possession, i.e., to refrain from negligence. If they exercise ordinary care, they are excused from liability for their inability to deliver the goods pursuant to the terms of a document of title.

    b. *Common carrier.* A common carrier's responsibility for goods in its possession differs before and after the goods are in transit.

        (1) *In transit.* Goods are in transit when the common carrier is in possession of them, the shipper has relinquished all control over them, and the carrier has not yet notified the consignee that the goods have arrived and that the latter can have possession of them. A carrier has absolute liability (i.e., liability without fault) for *any* damage, loss, delay, or destruction of the goods (however caused) during transit *unless* the common carrier can prove that such damage, loss, delay, or destruction occurred as a result of:

            (*a*) *Act of God*, e.g., tornado, lightning, flood, or earthquake. To fall within this exception, the act of God must be a sudden, violent, and natural occurrence and not contributed to by the negligence of the carrier.

            (*b*) *Act of war*, e.g., attack by military forces of a nation at war.

            (*c*) *Act of shipper*, e.g., defective packing or loading.

            (*d*) *Inherent nature of goods carried*, e.g., normal, natural spoilage.

            (*e*) *Act of public authority*, e.g., spoilage or damage caused by delay resulting from inspection or confiscation by public health official. For example, Florida officials confiscated California fruit infested with fruit fly larvae.

        (2) *Before and after transit.* A common carrier has a duty to exercise ordinary care toward the goods while they are in its possession before and after transit, i.e., to refrain from negligence. If it is not negligent, it is excused from liability for its inability to deliver the goods pursuant to the terms of a document of title.

3. *Prior sale or other disposition of goods by an issuer in lawful enforcement of a lien* [7-403(1)(c)]. A warehouseman or carrier has a possessory lien on goods stored or shipped under a warehouse receipt or a bill of lading (7-209, 7-210, 7-307).

    a. *Extent of lien.* The lien is for all charges and expenses for storage, handling, preservation, or transportation of the goods.

    b. *Enforcement of lien.* To enforce the lien, the warehouseman or carrier may sell or otherwise dispose of the goods at any time or place and on any terms which are *commercially reasonable* after notice to all parties known to have a legal interest in them and their failure to pay the charges and remove the goods.

        (1) Proceeds from sale or other disposition must be used to satisfy the lien.

        (2) Any excess must be turned over to parties known to have had a legal interest in the goods.

    c. *Limitation on the extent of lien.* As against a bona fide purchaser for value of a negotiable warehouse receipt or bill of lading, the amount of the lien is limited to charges specified in the document of title, and if none are specified, to reasonable charges.

4. *Sale of goods upon lawful termination of storage.* A warehouseman may lawfully terminate storage and sell the goods in the following circumstances:
   a. The warehouseman has given proper notice of the termination date of the storage to the person on whose account the goods are held, and the goods are not removed on or prior to such date [7-206(1)];
   b. When a warehouseman in good faith believes that the goods are about to decline in value to less than the amount of the lien [7-206(2)]; or
   c. Upon learning that the goods accepted for storage are hazardous to people, the warehouse, or other property. The warehouseman must first give reasonable notice of termination of storage to all persons known to claim a legal interest in the goods [7-206(3)].
5. *Conflicting claims to goods.* If more than one person claims title or possession to goods, a warehouseman or carrier is excused from delivery until it has had a reasonable time to determine the validity of the adverse claims or file a lawsuit against the claimants to compel them to prove their claims (7-603).
6. *Refusal to surrender an outstanding negotiable document of title.* A person entitled under the document must surrender the *outstanding negotiable document* of title to the bailee for cancellation or notation of partial deliveries as a condition precedent to receiving delivery of the goods.
7. *Seller's stoppage of delivery.* A seller has the right under certain circumstances to stop delivery of goods in possession of a carrier or other bailee when the seller discovers the buyer to be insolvent. Upon proper exercise of such right, the bailee cannot deliver the goods to anyone other than the seller (2-705). See Chapter 3.
8. *Diversion, reconsignment, or change of instructions* excuses delivery to the person entitled under the document (7-303).
   a. *Negotiable bill of lading.* A carrier may follow instructions received from a holder of a negotiable bill of lading.
   b. *Nonnegotiable bill of lading* (i.e., a straight bill of lading). A carrier may follow instructions:
      (1) By the consignor notwithstanding instructions from the consignee;
      (2) By the consignee in the absence of contrary instructions from the consignor; or
      (3) By the consignee if the consignee is entitled as against the consignor to dispose of the goods (i.e., possesses better title).

TRANSFER OR NEGOTIATION OF DOCUMENTS OF TITLE

IV. Title, represented by a document of title, may be transferred either by assignment or by negotiation if the transferor does in fact possess title. Whether a document of title is assigned or negotiated is extremely important whenever a transferor does not possess title, or if the transferor does possess title, it is voidable or subject to adverse claims or defenses. An assignee can never acquire better title than that possessed by the assignor. On the other hand, "due negotiation" of a document of title can result in a transfer of greater rights to a bona fide purchaser for value of the document than those possessed by its transferor. A holder who receives a document of title by "due negotiation" receives title that is not defeated by a seller's stoppage of goods, a surrender of the goods to a third party by a bailee, the fact that the "due negotiation" or any prior negotiation was unauthorized or that any person had previously been deprived of possession of the document by misrepresentation, fraud, accident, mistake, duress, undue influence, loss, theft, or conversion, and even though the goods or document had been previously sold to a third person [7-502(2)]. (See Figure 4-2.)

FIGURE 4-2 TRANSFER OF TITLE TO GOODS REPRESENTED BY A DOCUMENT OF TITLE

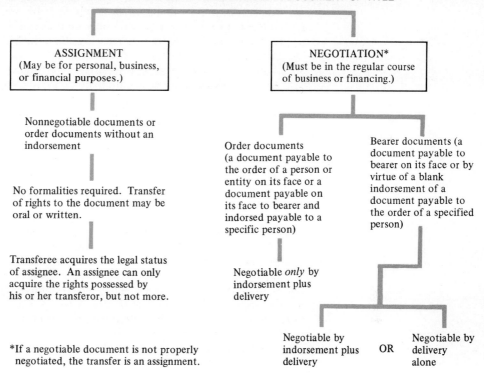

A. The requirements for a *"due negotiation"* are as follows (7-501):
1. *Negotiable on its "face."* A document of title is negotiable on its "face" at the time it is executed and issued if by its terms the goods it represents are to be delivered "to bearer" or "to the order of" a named person [7-104(a)]. *All* other documents of title are nonnegotiable.
2. *Negotiation to a holder.*
   a. Holder. A *holder* is a person in possession of a document that is:
   (1) Issued to the holder in bearer form;
   (2) Issued to the holder, and by its terms the goods are to be delivered to the holder's order, i.e., in order form;
   (3) Indorsed in blank or to bearer; or
   (4) Indorsed to the holder's order after its issuance.
   b. Methods of negotiation.
   (1) At time of issuance.
      (*a*) *Bearer document on its "face."* This type of document is negotiated when it is voluntarily delivered to any person by the bailee-warehouseman or carrier.
      (*b*) *Order document on its "face."* This type of document is negotiated at the time that the bailee-warehouseman or carrier voluntarily delivers it to the person who is named by the terms of the document as the person to whose order the goods are to be delivered. For example, by the terms of a document, the goods are to be delivered "to the order of Kracker Oats, Inc." The document can be negotiated only by delivery of the document by the bailee to Kracker Oats, Inc.

(2) After issuance.
   (a) *Order document.* An order document can be negotiated only by indorsement and delivery to the intended transferee by an appropriate person. The appropriate person is either the person named by the original terms of the document as the one to whose order the goods are to be delivered *or* the person designated by an indorsement as being the one to whom the goods are to be delivered. An order document is one which:
      i. By its terms at issuance provides that the goods are to be delivered to the order of a named person; or
      ii. After its issuance is indorsed to a specified person, i.e., a special indorsement.
   (b) *Bearer document.* A bearer document can be negotiated either by indorsement and delivery *or* by delivery alone. Any person, even a thief or a finder, has the power to negotiate a bearer document. A bearer document is one that:
      i. By its terms at issuance provides that the goods are to be delivered "to bearer"; or
      ii. After its issuance is indorsed in blank or "to bearer." A *blank indorsement* is merely the signature of the holder without any designation as to whom the goods are to be delivered to in the future, e.g., /S/ "Edmund Franks."
   (c) An order document may be changed to a bearer document by blank indorsement. A bearer document may be changed to an order document by special indorsement. Review 2-a, b above. A *special indorsement* designates the person who is to receive delivery of the goods *and* contains the signature of the transferor.
   (d) If an order document is transferred without the requisite indorsement, the transferee can compel his or her transferor to supply any indorsement necessary to the transferee's title. "Due negotiation" takes place only when the necessary indorsement is supplied.
   (e) An indorsement of a nonnegotiable document neither makes the document negotiable nor adds to the transferee's rights [7-501(5)].
3. *In good faith without notice of any defense or adverse claim.* For "due negotiation" to occur, the holder must take the document in good faith without notice of any defense or adverse claim.
4. *Value.* The holder must have paid value for the negotiable document. [7-501(4)]. Value includes money, property, security for a preexisting debt, a promissory note, or any act or promise that is considered to be legally sufficient consideration under contract law. *Exception:* Value is not given when the holder receives the document in settlement or payment of an antecedent money obligation [7-501(4)].
5. *In the regular course of business or financing.* Documents negotiated for value to a banker or a businessperson would be transferred "in the regular course of business or financing." On the other hand, a document purchased for an investment purpose by an attorney or accountant would not be so transferred.
B. *Rights acquired by a holder through "due negotiation."* Rights acquired through due negotiation are as follows (7-502):
1. Title to the document;
2. Title to the goods;

3. The right to have the bailee-issuer (i.e., warehouseman or carrier) hold and deliver the goods to the holder according to the terms of the document free of any defense or claim by the issuer or by any other person. *Exceptions:*

    a. *An adverse claimant is a person with superior title.* See III-B-1 above. Some examples of circumstances in which an adverse claimant has a superior title are as follows:

        (1) Forgery. The issuer's signature is forged. The issuer is neither a bailee (i.e., not having received goods) nor an issuer;

        (2) Good faith issuance of a negotiable document to a thief, finder, or other unauthorized person.

        (3) Duplicate negotiable documents. A bailee may issue duplicate negotiable documents representing title to the same goods. A holder by due negotiation of the first document has superior title. The holder of the second document does not acquire any rights to the goods even though the goods were acquired through due negotiation.

        (4) Sale of fungible goods by an issuer in the regular course of business. A buyer in the ordinary course of business of fungible goods sold and delivered by a warehouseman who is also in the business of buying and selling such goods takes free of any claim under a warehouse receipt even though it had been duly negotiated (7-205).

    b. *Damage, loss, delay, or destruction of the goods for which the bailee-issuer is not liable.* See III-B-2 above.

    c. *Prior sale or other disposition of the issuer in lawful enforcement of a lien.* See III-B-3 above.

    d. *Sale of goods by issuer upon lawful termination of storage.* See III-B-4 above.

C. An *assignment* is a transfer of rights represented by a document of title other than through "due negotiation."

    1. A nonnegotiable document of title can never be "duly negotiated." It can only be transferred by assignment. (See Figure 4-2.)

    2. A negotiable document may be transferred in two ways: by assignment or by "due negotiation." As stated previously, a "due negotiation" does not occur unless all of the following requirements exist:

        a. Document is issued negotiable;

        b. It is negotiated;

        c. The holder takes it in good faith and without notice of any adverse claim or defense;

        d. The holder paid value for it; and

        e. The holder took it in the regular course of business or financing [7-104(1), 7-501(4)].

    3. A transferee of a document to whom a document has been delivered but not duly negotiated (i.e., assigned) acquires *only* that title or those rights which the transferor had or had actual authority to transfer [7-504(1)].

LIABILITY OF INDORSERS

V. The indorsement of a document of title does not make the indorser liable for any default by the issuer-bailee or by previous indorsers. Compare the liability of an indorser of a document of title with that of an indorser of commercial paper. See Chapter 5.

IMPLIED WARRANTIES ON NEGOTIATION OR TRANSFER

VI. Certain *warranties* (promises) are impliedly made by a transferor *on negotiation or assignment* of a document of title (7-507).

    A. The implied warranties are made only to purchasers for value.

    B. The benefits of implied warranties extend *only* to a transferor's immediate transferee.

    C. The implied warranties are as follows:

        1. The document is genuine;

        2. The transferor has no knowledge of any fact that would impair the validity or worth of the document; and

        3. The transferor's transfer is rightful and fully effective with respect to title to the document.

    D. The implied warranties are in addition to any express or implied warranties as to the quality, character, or performance of the goods made by the transferor as a seller of goods.

    E. Collecting banks or other intermediaries who transfer documents of title for purposes of collection on a draft (e.g., trade acceptance) warrant only their own good faith and authority to transfer (7-508).

FORGERIES AND UNAUTHORIZED ALTERATIONS OF DOCUMENTS

VII. Documents of title may be forged, issued in blank, or altered subsequent to issuance.

    A. *Forgery.* A bailee whose signature on a document of title is forged is not an issuer. Consequently, the bailee does not have any liability under the document.

    B. *Blank or altered documents.*

        1. *Bill of lading.* An unauthorized alteration or filling in of a blank in a bill of lading leaves the bill enforceable only according to its original tenor (7-306). *"According to its original tenor"* means according to the terms of the document as it was in blank or in its unaltered state.

        2. *Warehouse receipt.*

            a. *Blank negotiable document.* A bona fide purchaser for value without notice that the document was filled in without authority can treat the insertion as authorized and enforce the document as completed (7-208).

            b. *Other types of alterations.* Any other type of unauthorized alteration leaves the document enforceable against the issuer only according to its original tenor, for example, a change of the name of the person to whom the goods are to be delivered or a change of the number or type of goods stated in the document (7-208).

WAREHOUSEMAN'S LIABILITY FOR COMMINGLING OF GOODS

VIII. Unless the warehouse receipt provides otherwise or the goods are fungible, the warehouseman has a duty to keep separate (i.e., not to *commingle*) the goods covered by each warehouse receipt [7-207(1)].

    A. The warehouseman is liable to the person entitled under the document or to the person with superior title for any loss caused by the commingling of nonfungible goods.

    B. Commingled *fungible goods* are owned in tenancy in common by the persons entitled to them. The warehouseman is severally liable to each owner for that owner's share of goods that are lost, destroyed, or stolen [7-207(2)].

LIABILITY FOR NONRECEIPT OR MISDESCRIPTION OF GOODS

IX. An issuer of a document of title may be liable for acknowledging possession of goods never received or for misdescription of goods that were actually received.

   A. *Warehouse receipt.* A purchaser for value in good faith of a warehouse receipt may recover from an issuer damages caused by the nonreceipt or misdescription of goods *unless* the document conspicuously indicates that the issuer does not know whether any part or all of the goods in fact were received or conform to the description *and such indication is true*; e.g., "contents, condition, and quality unknown" "said to contain," or the like (7-203).

   B. *Bill of lading.* A consignee of a nonnegotiable bill of lading who gave value in good faith or a holder to whom a negotiable bill of lading was duly negotiated who relied on the description of the goods can recover from the issuer (carrier) damages caused by the nonreceipt or misdescription of goods unless the document indicates lack of knowledge of nonreceipt or misdescription and *such indication is true*; e.g., "contents or condition of contents of packages unknown," "said to contain," "Shipper's weight, load and count," or the like [7-301(1)].

LOST OR MISSING DOCUMENTS

X. If a *document has been lost, stolen, or destroyed*, a claimant can petition a court for an order, directed to the bailee (warehouseman or carrier), ordering the latter to deliver the goods or to issue a substitute document to the claimant.

   A. If the missing document is negotiable, the claimant *must* post *security* (i.e., something of value) approved by the court in a sufficient amount to indemnify the bailee and any other person who may suffer a loss as a result of the nonsurrender of the document. If the document is nonnegotiable, posting security is in the court's discretion [7-601(1)].

   B. A bailee has no liability to any person when it delivers goods or issues a substitute document pursuant to court order.

   C. A bailee who without court order delivers goods to a claimant under a missing *negotiable* document is liable to any person injured thereby [7-601(2)].

ISSUANCE, TRANSFER, AND REGISTRATION OF INVESTMENT SECURITIES (Article 8 of the UCC)

XI. Article 8 of the UCC deals with *"investment securities"* such as bearer bonds, registered bonds, and certificates of stock. As was true in regard to commercial paper (Chapter 5) and documents of title, the rules governing investment securities attempt to promote the policies of free transferability and protection to good faith purchasers. For example, a bona fide purchaser of an investment security is treated almost in the same manner as a holder in due course of negotiable commercial paper and a "person entitled under the document." All three parties take free of almost all defenses and adverse claims of ownership made by third parties. One outstanding difference is that the law governing investment securities does not require all of the numerous formal prerequisites of negotiability as mandated by the law pertaining to negotiable commercial paper. *Note:* In 1977, article 8 of the UCC was amended to make provision for the issuance, transfer, and registration of uncertificated investment securities as an alternative to investment securities evidenced by certificates. Since very few states have adopted this amendment, the discussion below excludes coverage of uncertificated securities.

DEFINITIONS

XII. The following definitions are important to the study of investment securities:

    A. A *security* is a stock, bond, or other evidence of a legal interest in or obligation of an issuer which is issued in bearer or registered form and is issued or dealt in on securities exchanges or markets as a medium for investment [8-102(1)]. (See Figure 4-3.)

    B. A security is in *registered form* when it specifies the person entitled to the security or the rights that it represents [8-103(1)(c)].

    C. A security is in *bearer form* when its terms specify a "bearer" to be entitled to the security or the rights it represents [8-103(1)(d)].

    D. A *purchaser* is any transferee of a security.

    E. A *purchaser for value* is any transferee who gives value for a security, bona fide or otherwise.

    F. A *"bona fide purchaser"* is a purchaser for value in good faith without notice of any adverse claim who takes delivery of a security in bearer form or in registered form, issued to the purchaser or indorsed to the purchaser or in blank [8-302(1)].

    G. A *subsequent purchaser* is a purchaser who takes a security other than by original issue [8-103(2)].

    H. An *issuer* is any person who places or authorizes the placing of his or her name on a security to evidence a debt, an ownership interest, or any other legal interest in a business [8-201(1)].

    I. *Overissue* means the issue of securities in excess of the amount the issuer has corporate power to issue [8-104(2)].

    J. A *stock power* is an indorsement and assignment of rights to a security made on a document separate from the security itself.

    K. *Blank indorsement.* The signature of either a person who is specified on a security as entitled to it or the possessor of a bearer security.

    L. *Special indorsement.* The signature of either a person who is specified as entitled to it or the possessor of a bearer security that is accompanied by a designation of the person to whom the security is to be transferred or the person who has the power to transfer it next [8-308(1)(2)]. For example, "to Paul Faber, /S/ Paul Revere."

FIGURE 4-3   INVESTMENT SECURITIES

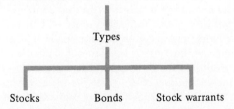

Written evidence of debt, ownership, or other legal interests in a business (an issuer)

Issued to bearer or in registered form and dealt in (traded) upon securities exchanges or markets as a medium for investment

Types

Stocks   Bonds   Stock warrants

Note: An instrument may be a "security" for purposes of regulation under the Securities Act of 1933 but may not be a "security" under the UCC, Article 8, if it is not commonly traded on the securities exchanges or markets.

APPLICATION OF CONTRACT LAW

XIII. The formation of a contract for the sale of investment securities is governed by the same rules that govern the formation of other types of contracts (other than the sale of goods). See Chapter 2. In addition, article 8 of the UCC provides special rules that are applicable only to the sale of investment securities.

    A. *Statute of Frauds* (8-319). A contract for the sale of securities must be in writing in order to be enforceable. *Exceptions:*

        1. The buyer has accepted delivery of the security or paid for it; or

        2. One party sent to the other a written confirmation of the oral contract and no objection to its contents was made within ten days; or

        3. A party to the oral contract admitted the existence of the contract in court.

    B. *Securities as fungible property.* A person contractually obligated to deliver securities may deliver any security of a specific issue. Securities are fungible [8-107(1)].

    C. *Remedies for breach.* Upon breach of contract by the buyer of a security, the seller may recover the price in the following situations [8-107(2)]:

        1. The buyer accepted the security; or

        2. The buyer has not accepted the security, and there is no readily available market for the security.

TRANSFER OF INVESTMENT SECURITIES

XIV. A security may be transferred by either negotiation or assignment (see Figure 4-4).

    A. *By negotiation.* The effect of negotiation is to allow a bona fide purchaser for value of a security to take free of most adverse claims and defenses of third parties. *Note:* In a transfer by assignment, the assignee acquires the security subject to *all* valid adverse claims and defenses of third parties.

        1. *Elements of negotiability.* Every "security" as defined in article 8 of the UCC is negotiable. See XII-A above.

            a. A security by definition must have been issued in registered or bearer form. See XII-B, C above.

FIGURE 4-4   TRANSFER OF INVESTMENT SECURITIES

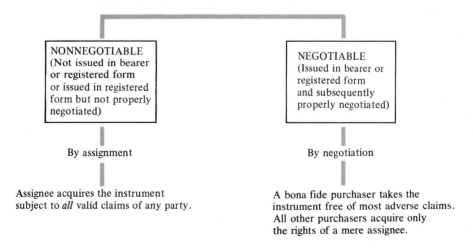

FIGURE 4-5   NEGOTIATION OF INVESTMENT SECURITIES

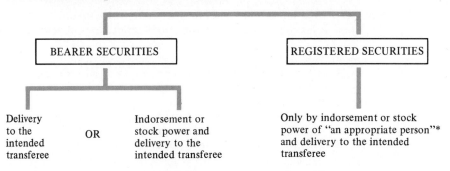

*"An appropriate person" is the registered owner, his or her authorized agent or legal representative (executor, administrator, or guardian), and a person to whom an instrument is specially indorsed.

    b. If an instrument does not qualify as a "security" as defined under the UCC, it cannot be negotiated. However, it can be transferred by assignment.

  2. *Requirements for a valid negotiation* (8-308, 8-309). (See Figure 4-5.)

    a. *Registered or bearer form at issuance.* The security must be in registered or bearer form at issuance. See XII-B, C above.

    b. *Negotiation.* The method of negotiation is dictated by the form of security at the time of issuance and subsequent thereto.

      (1) *Negotiation by indorsement and delivery.*

        (*a*) The indorsement can be made on the security itself or on a separate signed document of transfer that accompanies the security and is called a *stock power*.

        (*b*) The necessary indorsements must be made by "an appropriate person." "*An appropriate person*" includes any one of the following persons: [8-308(3)]:

          i. The person specified in a security in registered form;

          ii. The person specified in a special indorsement as entitled to the security;

          iii. If the person specified lacks legal capacity, that person's legal representative, e.g., executor, administrator, or guardian;

          iv. An authorized agent of the persons specified in parts *i* to *iii* above.

        (*c*) A security can be negotiated by indorsement and delivery only if:

          i. It is in registered form when issued; or

          ii. After issuance in bearer form, it is specially indorsed. A *special indorsement* specifies the person to whom a security is intended to be transferred or the person who has the power to transfer it [8-308(1)(2)]. The effect of delivery of a security without the necessary indorsement is as follows:

            a. A transferee cannot become a bona fide purchaser for value until the indorsement is supplied; and

            b. The transferee has a right to have any necessary indorsement supplied by the transferor (i.e., the right to obtain a decree in equity of specific performance against the transferor).

      (2) *Negotiation by delivery alone.* A security can be negotiated by delivery alone or by indorsement and delivery when it is:

        (*a*) In bearer form when issued, or

        (*b*) Indorsed (i.e., signed) in blank by an "appropriate person." See transfer of investment securities in XIV-A-2 above. A *blank indorsement* (includes an indorsement to bearer) does not specify the person to whom the security is to be transferred or who has the power to transfer it [8-308(2)].

B. *By assignment* (i.e., a transfer other than by negotiation) (see Figure 4-4).

    1. If a nonnegotiable "security" is transferred or a negotiable security is not properly negotiated, the transferee takes subject to all adverse claims and defenses of other persons.

    2. The transferee (assignee) cannot acquire more or better rights than those possessed by the transferor (assignor).

    3. The transferee (assignee) cannot be a bona fide purchaser for value.

BONA FIDE PURCHASER FOR VALUE

XVI. A *"bona fide purchaser"* is any transferee (i.e., purchaser) for value in good faith without notice of any adverse claim and to whom a security is properly negotiated [8-302(1)]. (See Figures 4-4 and 4-5.)

    A. *Rights of a bona fide purchaser for value.* Rights acquired by a bona fide purchaser for value are (8-301):

        1. Those possessed by the transferor;

        2. Those which the transferor had authority to transfer;

        3. To own the security free from all adverse claims. An *"adverse claim"* includes the following:

            a. That the transfer was wrongful; or

            b. That the adverse person is the owner of the security or has a legal interest in it [8-301(1)].

        4. To take free of restrictions on transfer of the security not conspicuously noted on the security (8-204).

    B. *Transferee from a bona fide purchaser for value.* A transferee from a bona fide purchaser for value receives the same rights that the transferor possessed *unless* the transferor had been a party to any fraud or illegality affecting the security [8-301(1)].

    C. *Special rules* (see Figure 4-6):

        1. *Forgery of a necessary (authentication) signature on the "face" of a security,* e.g., a forged signature of an authorized employee of the issuer, trustee, registrar, transfer agent, or other authorized person (8-205).

FIGURE 4-6   RIGHTS OF PURCHASERS OF INVESTMENT SECURITIES

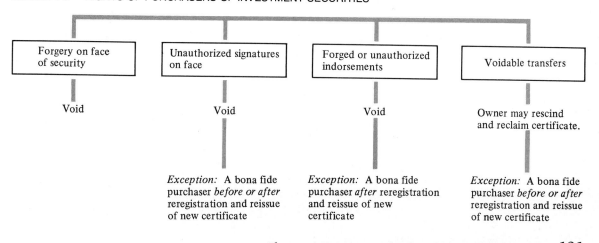

a. The security is void.

   b. Not even a bona fide purchaser for value can acquire any rights in the security.

   2. *Unauthorized signature of an authenticating person on the "face" of the security*, e.g., the unauthorized signature of a trustee, registrar, transfer agent, or employee of the issuer or of any of the foregoing who were entrusted with the duty to handle the security (8-205).

   a. The security is void as against all persons *except* a bona fide purchaser for value who took the security without notice of the unauthorized signature.

   b. The person who unauthorizedly authenticated and issued the security is liable to the issuer for any loss suffered as a result thereof (8-406).

   3. *Transfer under a forged or unauthorized indorsement on the "back" of the security* (8-311).

   a. The transfer is ineffective against everyone except a bona fide purchaser for value.

   b. It is ineffective even against a bona fide purchaser for value *up until the time* that the bona fide purchaser for value obtains a new, reissued, or reregistered security.

   4. *Incomplete security that contains the signatures necessary for its issue or transfer* (8-206).

   a. A bona fide purchaser for value may enforce the security as completed even though the blanks are filled in incorrectly.

   5. *A complete security which has been improperly altered.*

   a. The security is enforceable by all persons *but only* according to its original terms, (i.e., its original tenor).

D. *Resort to warranties.* If any person is deprived of ownership of a security because of the rules mentioned above, (i.e., negotiation, bona fide purchaser for value, or the special rules), that person may be able to recover damages (i.e., losses) from others on the basis of breach of implied warranties made by guarantee of signatures, authentication, presentment, or transfer. Implied warranties are discussed below.

IMPLIED WARRANTIES

XVII. Implied warranties are made by persons who guarantee signatures or indorsements as well as those who authenticate, present for registration, or transfer securities.

A. *Guarantee of signatures of indorsers or indorsements* [8-312(1), 8-312(5)].

   1. *Guarantee of signatures of indorsers.* Any person guaranteeing a signature of an indorser of a security warrants that at the time of the signing:

   a. The signature was genuine;

   b. The signer was an appropriate person to indorse (8-308); and

   c. The signer had legal capacity to sign. *Note:* The guarantor does not warrant the rightfulness of any particular transfer.

   2. *Guarantee of an indorsement.* Any person guaranteeing an indorsement on a security not only makes the warranties of a signature guarantor mentioned above *but also* warrants the rightfulness of the particular transfer.

   3. *Beneficiaries of a guarantor's warranties.* These warranties are made to all persons who take or deal with a security in reliance on the guarantee. The guarantor is liable to such persons for any loss resulting from breach of the warranty [8-312(8)].

B. *Warranties on authentication.* Any person who authenticates a security by placing his or her signature thereon (i.e., on its "face") warrants to a *purchaser for value* who is without notice of the alleged defect that:

1. The security is genuine;
2. That person's participation in the issue of the security is within his or her corporate power and authority;
3. That person's signature is authorized by the issuer; and
4. That person reasonably believes that the security is in the form and amount the issuer is authorized to issue [8-208(1)]. (See Figure 4-7.)

C. *Warranties on presentment for registration.* The following implied warranties are made to an issuer whenever a security is presented for registration, payment, or exchange (8-306):

1. Every person, other than a bona fide purchaser for value, warrants to the issuer that he or she has the right to registration, payment, or exchange.
2. A bona fide purchaser for value without knowledge of adverse claims who receives a new, reissued, or reregistered security warrants to the issuer *only* that *the purchaser has no knowledge* of any unauthorized signature in a necessary indorsement [8-306(1)]. (See Figure 4-7.)

D. *Warranties on transfer.* Implied warranties on transfer of securities are made *only* to purchasers for value who take the securities without notice of adverse claims. A person who transfers a security for value warrants that:

1. That person's transfer is effective and rightful (i.e., valid);

FIGURE 4-7   IMPLIED WARRANTIES ON AUTHENTICATION, TRANSFER, OR PRESENTMENT

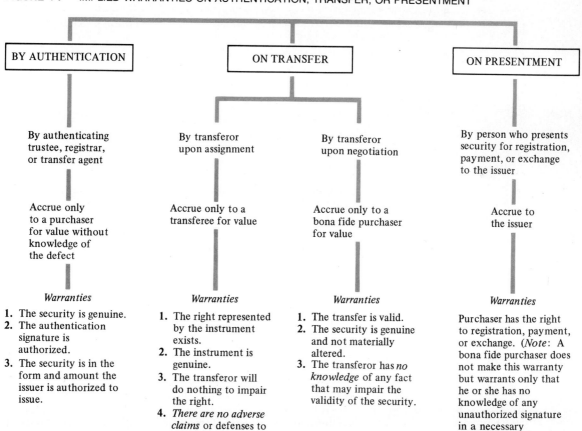

BY AUTHENTICATION

By authenticating trustee, registrar, or transfer agent

Accrue only to a purchaser for value without knowledge of the defect

Warranties

1. The security is genuine.
2. The authentication signature is authorized.
3. The security is in the form and amount the issuer is authorized to issue.

ON TRANSFER

By transferor upon assignment

Accrue only to a transferee for value

Warranties

1. The right represented by the instrument exists.
2. The instrument is genuine.
3. The transferor will do nothing to impair the right.
4. *There are no adverse claims* or defenses to the instrument.

By transferor upon negotiation

Accrue only to a bona fide purchaser for value

Warranties

1. The transfer is valid.
2. The security is genuine and not materially altered.
3. The transferor has *no knowledge* of any fact that may impair the validity of the security.

ON PRESENTMENT

By person who presents security for registration, payment, or exchange to the issuer

Accrue to the issuer

Warranties

Purchaser has the right to registration, payment, or exchange. (*Note:* A bona fide purchaser does not make this warranty but warrants only that he or she has no knowledge of any unauthorized signature in a necessary indorsement.)

2. The security is genuine and has not been materially altered; and

3. That person *has no knowledge* of any fact which might impair the validity of the security [8-306(2)]. (See Figure 4-7.)

DUTY OF ISSUER TO REGISTER TRANSFER OF A SECURITY

XVIII. If a security in registered form is presented to the issuer with a request to register a transfer, the issuer *must* register the transfer as requested if [8-401(1)]:

  A. *The security is indorsed by the "appropriate person or persons."* An "appropriate person" means [8-308(6)(7)(8)]:

    1. The person specified by the security (i.e., in bearer or registered form) *or* by special indorsement to be entitled to the security; or

    2. If the person so specified is described as a fiduciary, either that person or that person's successor; or

    3. If the person so specified is without legal capacity by virtue of death, incompetence, infancy, or otherwise, that person's executor, administrator, guardian, conservator, or like fiduciary; or

    4. To the extent that the person specified or any of the other persons mentioned above may act through an agent, the authorized agents.

  B. *Reasonable assurance is given that the indorsements are genuine and effective.* The issuer may require a guarantee of signatures, appropriate assurances of authority of an agent to indorse, or evidence of an indorsing fiduciary's (trustee, guardian, administrator, conservator, or executor) appointment by a court or otherwise. An issuer cannot require a *guarantee of indorsement* as a condition precedent to registration of a transfer [8-312(7)];

  C. *The issuer had no duty to inquire as to adverse claims or, having had the duty, the issuer made a proper inquiry* (see XIX-B below); and

  D. *The transfer is in fact rightful or is to a bona fide purchaser for value.*

NONLIABILITY FOR REGISTRATION

XIX. An issuer is not liable to the owner or any other person suffering a loss as a result of the registration of transfer of a security if [8-404(1)]:

  A. There were on or with (i.e., a stock power) the security the necessary indorsements; and

  B. The issuer had no duty to inquire into adverse claims, or if it did have such a duty, it discharged it by making a proper inquiry. The issuer *is* under a duty to inquire into adverse claims when:

    1. A written notification of an adverse claim is received that affords the issuer a reasonable opportunity to act upon it prior to the issuance of a new, reissued, or reregistered security [8-403(1)(a)]; or

    2. The issuer elects to demand, in addition to reasonable assurance, a copy of a controlling instrument, e.g., a will, trust indenture (i.e., a bond), articles of copartnership, bylaws, or other controlling instrument that affects the transfer [8-402(4)].

LIABILITY FOR IMPROPER REGISTRATION

XX. If an issuer has registered a transfer of a security to a person not entitled to it, the issuer, on demand by the true owner, must deliver a like security to the true owner *unless* [8-404(2)]:

  A. The security contained or was accompanied with all necessary, authorized, and genuine indorsements (8-308);

B. The issuer had no duty to inquire as to adverse claims or, having had the duty, discharged it by making a proper inquiry (8-403). See XIX-B above.

C. The true owner is precluded from asserting a claim because of the true owner's failure to notify the issuer that the security was lost, stolen, or apparently destroyed within a reasonable time after the owner had notice of it and the issuer registered a transfer of the security before receiving such a notification [8-405(1)]; or

D. The delivery of a like security would result in an overissue [8-404(2)(c)]. If an over-issue precludes issuance of a like security, the liability of the issuer is as follows:

    1. If a like security is reasonably available for purchase, the issuer can be compelled to purchase and deliver such a security; or

    2. If a like security is not available for purchase, the issuer must pay to the true owner an amount equal to the price a last purchaser for value paid for it with interest (8-104).

LOST, DESTROYED, OR STOLEN SECURITIES

XXI. Where an owner of a security claims that the *security is lost, destroyed, or stolen*, the issuer must issue a new security if the owner:

A. Requests the new security before the issuer receives notice that the "old" security has been acquired by a bona fide purchaser for value;

B. Provides to the issuer a sufficient indemnity bond; and

C. Satisfies any other reasonable requirements imposed by the issuer [8-405(2)], for example, a guarantee of signatures.

Note: If, after the issue of the new security to the owner, a bona fide purchaser for value presents a lost or stolen security for registration of transfer, the issuer must register the transfer unless registration would result in overissue. In such event, the issuer must either purchase a replacement security on the market or, if unable to do so, pay to the bona fide purchaser an amount equal to the price a last purchaser paid for it with interest. In addition to any rights on the indemnity bond, the issuer may recover the new security from the person to whom it was issued or any person taking under him or her except a bona fide purchaser for value [8-405(3)].

TRUE OWNER'S RIGHT TO RECLAIM A SECURITY

XXII. As a general rule, the owner of a security who has been wrongfully deprived of its possession has a *right to reclaim* it from anyone except a bona fide purchaser for value.

A. Any person against whom the transfer of a security is wrongful for any reason may reclaim it from anyone, except the following:

    1. A bona fide purchaser for value if the wrongful transfer was not due to a forged authentication (8-301, 8-205); or

    2. A bona fide purchaser for value (even if the wrongful transfer was due to a forged or unauthorized indorsement) who has in good faith received a new, reissued, or reregistered security upon registration of the transfer with the issuer [8-311(a), 8-315(2), 8-405(3)].

B. The right to reclaim extends to a new, reissued, or reregistered security received upon registration of transfer (i.e., to a person other than a bona fide purchaser for value [8-315(1)].

C. The owner can assert the following remedies in exercising the right to reclaim:

    1. Specific performance;

    2. Injunction to prevent further transfer; or

    3. Impoundment of the security pending outcome of a lawsuit filed to reclaim it [8-315(3)].

ATTACHMENT OF SECURITIES

XXIII. A security is subject to *attachment* or levy by a creditor of an owner of the security (8-317).

    A. An attachment or levy is not valid unless the outstanding security is actually seized by the officer of the court making the attachment or levy [8-317(1)].

    B. A security that is not outstanding (i.e., has been surrendered to the issuer) may be attached or levied upon while it is in the hands of the issuer.

BROKER'S LIABILITY

XXIV. A securities *broker-dealer* who in good faith receives and delivers securities pursuant to his or her principal's (seller's) instructions is not liable for conversion or for participation in a breach of fiduciary duty even though the principal (seller) had no right to transfer the securities (8-318).

SELF-QUIZ

To check your understanding of the key words and concepts and the accuracy of your answers to the questions, refer to the text material as referenced by page number.

1. What are the legal characteristics of a document of title? **(119)**

2. What distinguishes a negotiable document of title from a nonnegotiable document of title? Why is it important to so distinguish? **(119)**

3. What are the duties of a warehouseman and a common carrier? What rights accrue to a warehouseman or common carrier as a result of a lien? **(120, 122)**

4. How is a negotiable document of title "duly negotiated"? **(123)**

5. Can a person be a "holder" of a document of title without being a "person entitled under the document"? Explain. **(120)**

6. Of what legal significance is it to be a "person entitled under the document"? **(120)**

7. Under what circumstances is a bailee-issuer excused from delivery of goods represented by a document of title to a "person entitled under the document"? **(120)**

8. What legal consequences follow from an assignment of a document of title? **(123)**

9. Compare the liabilities of indorsers of documents of title with those of indorsers of commercial paper. See Chapter 5. **(125, 164)**

10. Compare the potential liability of the warehouseman and carrier for issuance of a blank negotiable document of title. **(126)**

11. Under what circumstances can an issuer of a document of title be held liable for acknowledging possession of goods never received or for a misdescription of the goods actually received? **(127)**

12. Under what circumstances can an issuer release goods to a claimant without requiring and receiving the surrender of an outstanding document of title? **(127)**

13. Compare the prerequisites for negotiability and negotiation of a security under article 8 of the UCC with those for commercial paper in article 3 of the UCC. See Chapter 5. **(129, 149)**

14. Under what circumstances can an oral contract for the sale of securities be enforceable? **(129)**

15. What is the legal significance of having the legal status of "an appropriate person"? **(130)**

16. What are the rights of a bona fide purchaser for value of a security in the following circumstances?
    a. There are no forgeries or unauthorized signatures on the security. **(131)**
    b. One of the authentication signatures is forged. **(131)**
    c. The security contains an unauthorized signature of an authenticating person. **(132)**
    d. The security was transferred under a forged or unauthorized indorsement. **(132)**
    e. The security was issued incomplete but did contain the necessary signatures of authenticating persons. **(132)**
    f. A completed security was improperly altered after it was issued. **(132)**

17. List and explain the warranties made upon guarantee of signature or indorsement, authentication, presentment, or transfer of a security. **(132)**

18. Discuss the duties and liabilities of an issuer. **(134)**

19. Under what circumstances may an owner of a security legally reclaim it from a purchaser? **(135)** From a bona fide purchaser for value? **(135)**

SELECTED QUESTIONS AND UNOFFICIAL ANSWERS

AUTHOR'S OBJECTIVE QUESTIONS

Select the best answer for each of the following items. Mark only one answer for each item. Answer all items.

1. Gant Co., a warehouseman, received goods from Lazlo for storage. Gant Co. issued a warehouse receipt whose terms state that certain goods are to be delivered "to the order of Lazlo." Lazlo signed his name and address on the back of the warehouse receipt and placed it in his billfold. He subsequently lost his billfold. Lars found the billfold, removed the warehouse receipt, and turned the receipt over to Bank as security for a business loan. Lazlo and Bank now claim ownership of the warehouse receipt and the goods it represents. Which of the following statements is incorrect?

a. The warehouse receipt was issued in negotiable form.

b. Lazlo's signature on the warehouse receipt is a blank indorsement.

c. The warehouse receipt was not duly negotiated to Bank.

d. Bank is a "person entitled under the document" and consequently is the owner of the warehouse receipt.

2. Farmer delivered a load of number 2 yellow corn to Padua for storage. Padua, being extremely busy, issued a negotiable warehouse receipt in order form which omitted the amount of corn delivered. Padua told Farmer to weigh the corn and fill in the blank. Farmer filled in "100 tons" when actually the corn weighed only 80 tons. Farmer indorsed the receipt in blank and sold and delivered it to Falcon for $50,000. Falcon, without indorsing the receipt, delivered it to Sanders in exchange for the latter's promissory note in the amount of $52,000. Which of the following statements is correct?

a. Sanders is entitled to only eighty tons of corn as that is the amount that was delivered for storage.

b. The receipt was not duly negotiated to Sanders.

c. Padua is liable only to Farmer because by the terms of the document, the corn was to be delivered to the order of Farmer.

d. Sanders is entitled to 100 tons of number 2 yellow corn.

3. X stole 200 office desks from Y. X then sold the desks to Z. The terms of sale required that X ship the desks to Z's offices in Los Angeles. X shipped the desks by common carrier and received a bill of lading by whose terms the desks were to be delivered to "bearer." X, without signing the bill, sold and delivered it to Bank for $22,000. Y, Z, and Bank each claim that the carrier must deliver the desks to them. Which of the following statements is correct?

a. The carrier would not be liable for misdelivery of the desks if it delivered them to Y knowing that its bill of lading is in possession of Bank.

b. The carrier would be liable to Y if it delivered the desks in good faith to Bank.

c. The carrier must deliver the desks immediately to either Y, Z, or Bank or be liable for damages to each of them.

d. X has no potential liability to Bank.

4. Under which of the following circumstances would a bailee (warehouseman or carrier) *not* be justified in refusing delivery of goods to a claimant who is in possession of a document of title that represents such goods?

a. The document is in bearer form, and the claimant refuses to surrender it to the bailee.

b. Dana sold and shipped goods to Josh. Dana obtained a bill of lading by whose terms the goods were to be delivered "to Josh." While the goods were in transit, Dana sold the same goods to Pam. Upon instructions from Dana, the carrier rerouted the goods and delivered them to Pam.

c. Storage, Inc., was in possession of goods valued at $1,500 that were represented by a warehouse receipt by whose terms the goods were to be delivered "to the order of Sam." Storage, Inc., notified Sam that the period of storage had ended and demanded payment of storage charges. Not hearing from Sam for some fifty days, it sold the goods at public sale.

d. Goods were shipped by common carrier. In transit the goods, through no fault of the carrier, were stolen. Jackson, "a person entitled under the document" (i.e., a bill of lading), is the claimant.

5. Which of the following statements is incorrect?

a. A warehouseman may commingle different lots of fungible goods without any liability to the owners of each lot.

b. A nonnegotiable document of title is as effective as a negotiable document of title to transfer title to goods.

c. A warehouseman may terminate storage at its option upon learning that the goods are hazardous to persons or to its warehouse.

d. For "due negotiation" to occur, a purchaser of a document of title must be a merchant.

6. Dubois delivered fifty sealed boxes for shipment to a common carrier. Dubois advised the carrier that each of the boxes contained two color television sets. In reality, some boxes contained only one TV set while others were empty. This was not known to the carrier. The carrier issued a negotiable bill of lading by whose terms 100 color TV sets were to be delivered "to the order of Eric." The bill of lading contained a standard provision printed in bold print and in a different color from other print that recited "contents or condition of contents of packages unknown." Dubois delivered the bill of lading to Eric upon the latter's payment of the purchase price. On delivery of the boxes, Eric discovered that they did not contain 100 TV sets. Eric sued the common carrier. Which of the following is incorrect?

a. Eric can recover against the common carrier because the carrier did not effectively disclaim liability in the bill of lading for its nonreceipt of the missing goods.

b. A bill of lading is a contract for shipment of goods, a receipt for goods, and evidence of title to goods.

c. Eric cannot recover because a common carrier has no duty to inspect the contents of all containers it accepts for shipment before it issues a bill of lading.

d. Eric cannot recover damages from the common carrier for breach of contract.

7. Goldfield is in business as both a warehouseman and a common carrier. During the course of several weeks, the following events and transactions occurred:

a. A thief stole Goldfield's warehouse receipts and bills of lading, forged Goldfield's signature on them, and sold them to Myers for $10,000. Myers was totally unaware of the theft or forgery.

b. Goldfield issued several warehouse receipts and bills of lading in various amounts of goods to Mack. Mack, without authority, carefully erased the numbers (i.e., amounts) of goods stated on the documents and sold them to Corinne, who had no knowledge that the numbers were changed.

c. Goldfield issued a bill of lading to Lee, leaving it blank as to the amount of goods that the document represented. Actually, the document represented the receipt of twelve tons of coal. Lee, without authority, filled in the blank with the words and numbers "twelve thousand (12,000) tons" and sold the document to Zelda. Zelda did not know or have any reason to know that the document had been issued with a blank.

d. Goldfield issued a negotiable warehouse receipt to Jackel, leaving it blank as to the amount of goods it represented. Jackel, without authority, filled in the blank with the number 10,000 and negotiated the document to Bank for $300,000. Bank did not know that the warehouse receipt had been issued with a blank.

Myers, Corinne, Bank, and Zelda sued Goldfield. Which of the following statements is incorrect?

a. Goldfield has no liability to Myers.

b. Goldfield has no liability to Corinne.

c. Zelda can enforce the bill of lading only to the extent of twelve tons of coal.

d. Bank can enforce the warehouse receipt in its completed form, i.e., 10,000.

8. Dantley was fraudulently induced to issue a nonnegotiable document of title to Marge. Marge indorsed and delivered it to Staub. Without indorsement, Staub gave the document as a marriage present to his daughter, Allisha. Allisha indorsed and delivered it to Bank in exchange for $6,500. Which of the following statements is correct?

a. If Dantley defaults on the document, Bank can enforce the document against Marge either on the basis of her indorsement or on the basis of breach of implied warranties on transfer.

b. Allisha is not liable to Bank because she had received the document as a gift.

c. Allisha can recover damages from Staub.

d. Bank cannot enforce the document against Dantley.

9. Keeper, Inc., a warehouseman, issued a negotiable warehouse receipt to Kelch, the owner of wine stored in the warehouse. The receipt clearly indicated the types and amounts of storage charges and indicated that Keeper claimed a lien on the wine for the amount of charges. Keeper's creditors filed an involuntary petition in bankruptcy against Keeper. Keeper was subsequently adjudicated a bankrupt. The trustee in bankruptcy sold Keeper's warehouse and storage business to Martin and distributed the proceeds from the sale to Keeper's creditors. Which of the following statements is correct?

a. Keeper's bankruptcy and the subsequent sale of its warehouse and business destroyed the rights of any holder of the warehouse receipt.

b. The trustee received title to the wine at the moment that he or she was appointed trustee for Keeper, the bankrupt.

c. A negotiable warehouse receipt is evidence of ownership, and as a general rule the owner of the receipt is the owner of the goods it represents.

d. The purchaser of Keeper's warehouse and business is not entitled to exercise a warehouseman's lien to collect unpaid storage charges.

10. Dennis owned a stock certificate issued by Du Mont Corporation and registered in his name. It was not indorsed. One evening Dennis's home was burglarized, and the certificate was stolen by Tolle. Tolle wrote Dennis's name on the back of the certificate and sold it through Rolla, a securities broker-dealer, to Eugene, who paid value. Neither Rolla nor Eugene knew of any wrongdoing. After Dennis discovered the theft, he immediately gave written notice to Du Mont. Eugene sent his certificate to Du Mont and requested that Du Mont issue a new certificate registered in his name. Du Mont issued the new certificate to Eugene. Subsequently, Dennis demanded that Du Mont replace his stolen certificate with a new certificate registered in his name. Du Mont refused on two grounds: (1) It had already issued a new certificate to Eugene, and (2) even if it didn't, it could not presently issue another certificate because all of its authorized shares had been issued. Which of the following statements is incorrect?

a. Rolla is not liable to Eugene for damages for breach of the implied warranty that her transfer was rightful.
b. Eugene is the owner of the new certificate registered in his name.
c. Du Mont must issue a new certificate to Dennis.
d. Du Mont is liable to Dennis.

11. Herb, as secretary of X Corporation, and Max, as its president without corporate authority to authenticate securities, signed and issued a stock certificate to Mona, Herb's girl friend. The certificate was intended to be a birthday gift. It was issued in registered form. Without indorsing the certificate, Mona sold it to Gadby for $10,000. Gadby was unaware of any wrongdoing. Gadby sent the certificate to X and requested that X issue a new certificate registered in his name. X refused. Which of the following statements is correct?

a. X must issue a new stock certificate registered in Gadby's name.
b. Herb and Max have no liability.
c. X need not issue a new stock certificate to Gadby.
d. Gadby has no legal recourse against Mona.

12. Watts, the registered owner of common stock, indorsed his security in blank and sold it to Debra. Debra paid for the security with a check that was dishonored by Debra's bank. Before Watts could reclaim the security, Debra sold and delivered it to Banks for cash. Banks had no knowledge of the bad check. Banks made a gift of the security to his son, Jimmie. Jimmie, a friend of Debra, knew that Debra had previously purchased the security from Watts

and that she had paid for it with a bad check. Watts discovered that Jimmie possessed the security and sued Jimmie to reclaim it. Which of the following statements is incorrect?

a. Debra's transfer of the security to Banks is a negotiation.
b. Banks is a bona fide purchaser for value.
c. Jimmie must surrender the security to Watts.
d. Jimmie is not a bona fide purchaser for value.

13. Alma received a security (a $10,000 bond) issued in bearer form by Gen Mo, Inc., as a Christmas gift from her father. On December 27, 1982, the security was stolen from her apartment. Alma discovered the theft on December 29, 1982. She immediately sent written notice of the theft to Gen Mo, Inc., and requested issuance of a new security registered in her name. Gen Mo, Inc., demanded that Alma post a $10,000 indemnity bond that named Gen Mo, Inc., as beneficiary. Almo posted the requested bond the next day, and Gen Mo, Inc., issued the new security to her. On January 6, 1983, Kevin presented the original security to Gen Mo, Inc., and demanded issuance of a new security registered in his name. Kevin purchased the original security for $9,950 from the thief in good faith without knowledge of the theft. Gen Mo, Inc., refused to issue the new security to Kevin. Kevin sued Gen Mo, Inc., and asked the court to compel Gen Mo, Inc., to issue a new security to him. Which of the following statements is correct?

a. Gen Mo, Inc., must issue a new security to Kevin.
b. Gen Mo, Inc., had no right to demand an indemnity bond from Alma.
c. A thief cannot acquire title to a security by theft and consequently is incapable of transferring title to such security to another.
d. If the issuance of a new security to Kevin would result in an overissue, Gen Mo, Inc., is released from all liability.

14. Which of the following statements is incorrect?

a. A bona fide purchaser for value takes title to a security free of a corporate restriction on its transfer unless such restriction is conspicuously noted on the security.
b. Implied warranties by a transferor of a security are made to all subsequent transferees.

c. A valid indorsement can be made on a separate document that accompanies a stock certificate.

d. A contract for the sale of securities must be in writing.

15. Jean James subscribed to 1,000 shares of Alpha Co. stock. The security, numbered 9893, recited that "Jean James" was the person entitled to the security. Jean James signed a piece of paper in which she stated that security number 9893 "is hereby assigned to Ralph Deranga." Jean James delivered the security and the paper containing her signature to Deranga in exchange for $300,000. Several weeks later Deranga signed his name on the back of the security and delivered it to Martin in exchange for $325,000. Martin delivered the security to Van Guard as collateral for a $250,000 loan. Van Guard lost the security while on her way to deposit it in her safe-deposit box. Offerguild found the security in an alley the next day. Which of the following statements is incorrect?

a. Offerguild is the owner of the security.

b. Deranga's signature on the security was a blank indorsement.

c. The stock was issued in registered form.

d. Jean James's signature and writing was a special indorsement.

Answers to Author's Objective Questions

1. c	**4.** d	**7.** b	**10.** c	**13.** a
2. d	**5.** d	**8.** d	**11.** c	**14.** b
3. a	**6.** a	**9.** c	**12.** c	**15.** a

Explanation of Author's Answers to Objective Questions

1. (c) The warehouse receipt was "duly negotiated" to Bank. Although the document was issued as a negotiable order document (i.e., "to the order of Lazlo"), it was changed into a bearer document by Lazlo's blank indorsement. A bearer document can be negotiated by delivery alone by anyone who has it in his or her possession, even a thief. "Due negotiation" occurs when a negotiable document of title is negotiated to a person who gives value for it in good faith. A loan of money constitutes giving value. Bank, without notice of the wrongdoing, gave value and received the document through negotiation. Bank is the "person entitled under the document." Answer (a) is correct because

a document of title by whose terms the goods are to be delivered "to the order of" a designated person is a negotiable order document. Answer (b) is correct because a blank indorsement is the signature of any person who has the power to negotiate a document, placed on the back of the document without any designation of any person to whom the goods are to be delivered. Answer (d) is correct because Bank is a "person entitled under the document." A person to whom a document of title has been "duly negotiated" is a "person entitled under the document."

2. (d) A bona fide purchaser for value without notice that a warehouse receipt was issued in blank and subsequently filled in without authority can treat the insertion as authorized and enforce the document as completed. Sanders is entitled to 100 tons of number 2 yellow corn. Answer (a) is incorrect for the reason stated above. Answer (b) is incorrect. A "due negotiation" occurs when a negotiable document of title is negotiated to a bona fide purchaser for value. A document issued in order form is negotiable and can be negotiated by indorsement and delivery by the person to whose order it was issued. Farmer, being the person to whose order the goods were to be delivered, had the power to negotiate the document. He did so by indorsement and delivery to Falcon. Farmer's blank indorsement changed the form of the document from "order" to "bearer." Since a bearer document can be negotiated by delivery alone, Falcon's delivery of it to Sanders was a negotiation. Falcon's indorsement was unnecessary. Answer (c) is incorrect. A document of title issued to the order of a specified person is a contract that contains a promise to deliver the goods to the person designated or to whomsoever that person orders the bailee-warehouseman to deliver the goods to. The negotiation of an order document is an order to a bailee to deliver the goods to the designated transferee, i.e., a specified person or bearer.

3. (a) As a general rule, a bailee-carrier must deliver the goods to the "person entitled under the document" unless it has an excuse not to do so. Such excuse exists when it receives notice of a person who has superior title to the goods (i.e., the true owner). Y could not be deprived of title to the desks by theft. A thief cannot create title by shipping stolen goods under a document of title. The document is void. Here, the common carrier could safely deliver the goods to Y, the person who owns superior title. Answer (b) is incorrect. A bailee-carrier incurs no liability if it delivers goods to a "person entitled under the document" if it does so in good faith without notice of any adverse claim. Answer (c) is incorrect. If more than one person claims title or possession of the goods, a bailee-carrier is excused from delivery until it has a reasonable time to investigate the validity of the adverse claims or file a lawsuit to resolve the dispute. Answer (d) is incorrect. A person who negotiates a document of title impliedly warrants, among other things, that the document is genuine. Bank is entitled to recover damages from X for breach of implied warranty.

4. (d) A common carrier is liable without fault for the damage, loss, or destruction of goods *during transit* unless it can prove that the damage, loss, or destruction was caused by (1) an act of God, (2) the inherent nature of the goods, (3) the act of the shipper or the act of a public enemy, or (4) the act of a public authority. Answer (a) is inapplicable because a bailee-warehouseman or carrier is excused from delivery of the goods if the claimant refuses to surrender a document of title that was originally issued in *negotiable form*. A document issued in bearer form is negotiable. Answer (b) is inapplicable because a carrier, under a *nonnegotiable document*, can follow the instructions of a consignor without liability even where it has received contrary instructions from a consignee. Here, the document recited that the goods were to be delivered "to Josh." A document of title is nonnegotiable unless by its terms the goods are to be delivered "to bearer" or "to the order of" a specified person. Answer (c) is inapplicable because a bailee-warehouseman, in exercise of its lien for storage charges, is justified in disposing of goods after (1) it has given all interested parties proper notification of the termination date of the storage, (2) demanded that the goods be removed and the storage charges be paid, and (3) the goods had not been removed and the storage charges had not been paid.

5. (d) A person need not be a merchant to receive a document of title by "due negotiation." Documents of title may be acquired by "due negotiation" by any person, association, trust, partnership, or entity. Answer (a) is correct because a warehouse can commingle *fungible* goods. The owners of each lot

commingled own the goods as tenants in common. A warehouseman has a duty to keep separate only nonfungible goods. Answer (b) is correct because any type of document is effective to transfer rights actually possessed by a transferor. It is only when the transferor has no rights or the transferor's rights in the document are voidable that the negotiability of the document is of great importance. A person through "due negotiation" can acquire more and better rights than those possessed by the transferor. Answer (c) is correct because a warehouseman can terminate storage at its option upon giving proper notice to interested parties when it discovers that the goods are hazardous to persons, other property in storage, or its warehouse.

6. (a) A bailee-carrier can disclaim liability for nonreceipt of goods by truthfully indicating in a bill of lading in a conspicuous way that it does not know whether any part or all of the goods were in fact received. Words such as "contents or condition of contents of packages unknown," "said to contain," "shipper's weight, load, and count," or the like are sufficient to disclaim a common carrier's liability. Answer (b) is correct because a bill of lading, as a document of title, is a contract for shipment of goods, a receipt for goods, and evidence of title. Answer (c) is correct because a carrier is under no duty to inspect goods prior to their shipment. Its duty is to deliver the goods that it acknowledges in its bill of lading as having been received for shipment. Answer (d) is correct. The carrier contracted to deliver and did deliver only the goods shipped. The carrier clearly indicated it did not know the types and number of goods contained in the boxes.

7. (b) An unauthorized alteration of a warehouse receipt or bill of lading leaves it enforceable according to its original tenor (i.e., as it was prior to alteration). Corinne, a purchaser for value without knowledge of the alterations, is entitled to the amount of goods stated prior to the alteration. Answer (a) is correct because a bailee whose signature on a document of title is forged is not an issuer and consequently has no liability on the document. Answer (c) is correct because an unauthorized filling in of a blank in a bill of lading leaves it enforceable according to its original tenor. The bill was originally issued by Goldfield for twelve tons. Answer (d) is correct because a bona fide purchaser for value without notice that a warehouse receipt was filled in without authority can enforce the document as completed. Bank is entitled to receive delivery of 10,000 units of the goods.

8. (d) The facts indicate that the document of title was issued nonnegotiable. A nonnegotiable document cannot be "duly negotiated." It can be transfered only by assignment. Consequently, every transferee takes the document subject to the adverse claims and defenses of other parties. The issuance of the document to Marge was induced by the latter's fraud. Dantley can assert the defense of fraud against Bank. Answer (a) is incorrect because (1) the indorsement of a document of title does not make the indorser liable for any default by the issuer, and (2) implied warranties on transfer of documents of title extend only to a transferor's immediate transferee. Bank is a subsequent transferee. Answer (b) is incorrect because Allisha, as a transferor of a document of title to a transferee for value (Bank), impliedly warranted that her transfer was rightful and fully effective. It was not. Answer (c) is incorrect because implied warranties on transfer of a document of title are made only to transferees for value. Allisha received the document as a gift from Staub.

9. (c) A warehouseman is a bailee of goods. A bailee does not receive title to goods, only possession. A negotiable warehouse receipt represents title to goods. As a general rule the "person entitled under the document" is the owner of the goods. Answer (a) is incorrect. Keeper's bankruptcy and the subsequent sale of its warehouse and business did not transfer title to stored goods. The goods are owned by the owner of the warehouse receipt. Answer (b) is incorrect because a trustee in bankruptcy acquires title only to property owned by a bankrupt. Keeper was not the owner of the wine. Answer (d) is incorrect because the purchaser of Keeper's business acquired Keeper's right to assert its lien for unpaid storage charges upon termination of storage.

10. (c) Dennis could not be deprived of his ownership of the stock certificate by theft. Since the certificate was in registered form, Dennis's indorsement was necessary for negotiation. Tolle's forgery of Dennis's name was not a genuine indorsement. Dennis is the true owner of the certificate. Because the requisite genuine indorsement was missing, Eugene was not a bona fide purchaser for value. Eugene acquired no rights in the certifi-

cate. The issuer is liable to Dennis for two reasons: (1) It registered a transfer of a security that did not contain necessary indorsement, and (2) it registered a transfer without fulfilling its duty to inquire after it had received notice of Dennis's claim. Ordinarily, Dennis, as the true owner, would be entitled to a like security. However, an issuer cannot legally issue a like security if it would result in an overissue. Answer (a) is correct. Broker-dealers are not liable in tort for conversion if they in good faith receive and deliver securities pursuant to their principals' (i.e., sellers') instructions even though their principals had no rights in the security or had no right to make the transfer. Answer (b) is correct because Du Mont, having issued the security to Eugene, is now estopped from claiming that he is not the owner. Answer (d) is correct. As explained above, Dennis cannot force Du Mont to issue a like security to him if such issuance would result in an overissue. However, Dennis, as the true owner, is not without a remedy. If a like security is reasonably available for purchase in the marketplace, the issuer must purchase such security and deliver it to Dennis. If such security is not available for purchase, the issuer must pay Dennis, the true owner, an amount equal to the price a last purchaser for value paid for it.

11. (c) An unauthorized signature of an authenticating person on the "face" of a security causes the security to be void against all transferees except a bona fide purchaser for value. Gadby is not a bona fide purchaser for value. A bona fide purchaser for value is one who takes a security by negotiation in good faith and gives value without notice of any adverse claims. The security was not negotiated to Gadby because it lacked the necessary indorsement of Mona. Answer (a) is incorrect for the reason stated above. Answer (b) is incorrect because Herb and Max are liable to Gadby for breach of warranty on authentication. Every person who authenticates a security warrants to a purchaser for value who is without knowledge of the defect that among other things (1) the security is genuine, and (2) his or her signature is authorized. Answer (d) is incorrect because Mona is liable to Gadby for breach of implied warranty made on transfer of a security. Every transferor of a security warrants to a purchaser for value who takes the security without notice of adverse claims that among other things, his or her transfer is effective and rightful. Mona's transfer of a void security was not effective to transfer any rights to Gadby, a non-bona fide purchaser for value.

12. (c) Jimmie need not surrender the certificate to Watts. Although Jimmie is not a bona fide purchaser for value, he is entitled to the rights of a bona fide purchaser for value. Purchasers (i.e., transferees) of a security acquire the same rights as those possessed by their transferors unless the purchasers themselves had been a party to any fraud or illegality affecting the security. Jimmie, although he knew of the bad check, was not a party to the wrongdoing. Answer (a) is correct. Debra did negotiate the security. A blank indorsement changes a registered security into a security in bearer form. A security in bearer form is negotiated by delivery alone even though it may be in fraud of the transferee. Answer (b) is correct because Banks is a bona fide purchaser for value. He took the security by negotiation from Debra, for value in good faith and without notice of adverse claims. Answer (d) is correct because Jimmie, as explained above, is not a bona fide purchaser for value.

13. (a) Gen Mo, Inc., must issue a new security to Kevin, a bona fide purchaser for value. The security was issued in bearer form and consequently was negotiable by delivery alone. Although a thief cannot acquire any rights to a stolen security, the thief does have the *power* to negotiate it by delivery alone. Kevin, who purchased the security through negotiation, for value and in good faith without knowledge of any wrongdoing, is a bona fide purchaser for value. An issuer must issue a like security and register the transfer in the name of a bona fide purchaser for value unless such issue would result in an overissue. Answer (b) is incorrect because an issuer, before it issues a like security, has a right to demand and receive a sufficient indemnity bond from an owner who claims that the security has been lost, destroyed, or stolen. Answer (c) is incorrect for the reason stated above. Answer (d) is incorrect because an issuer is not released from all liability in such case. If the issuance of a new issue would result in an overissue, the issuer must either purchase a replacement security on the open market or pay to the bona fide purchaser for value an amount equal to the price paid for it by a last purchaser with interest.

14. (b) Implied warranties on transfer are made only to the transferor's immediate transferee and only if it was purchased for value. Subsequent purchasers do not receive the benefits of these warranties. Answer (a) is correct. Unless the restriction on transfer is conspicuously noted on the security, a bona fide purchaser takes free of it. This is true even though the restriction was provided for in the articles of incorporation or elsewhere. Answer (c) is correct because an indorsement can be made either on the security itself or on a separate document, called a stock power. The stock power must accompany the delivery of the security in order to be a valid indorsement. Answer (d) is correct because as a general rule, a contract to sell securities must be in writing unless (1) the buyer has accepted delivery or paid the price for the security, (2) a party to the oral contract sent a confirmation letter to the other and no objection to its contents is made within ten days, or (3) the seller or buyer admits the oral contract in court.

15. (a) A finder of property does not take title to it. A finder is merely a bailee who is entitled to possession of the property as against everyone except its owner. Van Guard has the right to reclaim the security from Offerguild. Answer (b) is correct because Deranga did indorse the security in blank. A blank indorsement is the signature of either the person who is specified on a security as entitled to it or the possessor of a security in bearer form without any designation of the person to whom it is transferred or who may have the power to transfer it. Answer (c) is correct because the security was issued in registered form. A registered security is one that is issued and by its terms designates the person entitled to it. Answer (d) is correct because Jean James did specially indorse the security. A special indorsement is one that designates the person to whom the security is to be transferred or the person who has the power to transfer it next. To be an effective indorsement, it must contain the signature of either the person entitled to it or the possessor of a bearer security, i.e., the signature of an "appropriate person."

AUTHOR'S ESSAY QUESTIONS AND ANSWERS
(Estimated time: 10 to 15 minutes)

1. Livestock, Inc., pursuant to a contract to sell dated October 15, 1982, shipped by rail a carload of steers to Cattle and Hides, Inc. The shipment was

F.O.B. at the point of delivery to the carrier. The purchase price was due and payable three days after receipt of the shipment by the buyer. The carrier issued a straight (nonnegotiable) bill of lading made payable to Cattle and Hides, Inc., as consignee. While the shipment was en route, the seller learned that the buyer was insolvent and had filed a voluntary petition in bankruptcy. Before the shipment reached its destination, the carrier, upon directions of the seller, delivered the carload of steers back to the seller. In an appropriate lawsuit, the trustee in bankruptcy claimed that he was entitled to take possession of the steers and to sell them and apply the proceeds of the sale ratably among the general creditors of Cattle and Hides, Inc. In addition, he claimed that the railroad was liable because it did not deliver the goods to the designated consignee, Cattle and Hides, Inc.

Required Is the trustee correct? Explain.

Answer

a. Trustee's rights versus Livestock, Inc. When goods are shipped under a straight (nonnegotiable) bill of lading, the seller, upon learning of buyer's insolvency, may stop delivery prior to receipt of the goods by the buyer or acknowledgment to the buyer by the carrier as warehouseman that the carrier holds for the buyer, or reshipment by the carrier on behalf of the buyer. Since neither of these limiting events occurred here, the seller had a right to stop the goods and have them returned to him. The facts that the F.O.B. point was the seller's place of business and that the seller had already completed his delivery obligations under the contract do not change the result. Once a shipment has been properly stopped, the result is the same as if no delivery had ever been made. Under article 2 of the UCC, the insolvency of the buyer relieves the seller of obligation to deliver, except in exchange for cash. The trustee in bankruptcy is not entitled to the cattle unless the trustee tenders the purchase price in cash.

b. Trustee's rights versus the carrier. Unless legally excused, a carrier has a duty to deliver the goods to the "person entitled under the document." Under a straight (nonnegotiable) bill of lading, such person is the designated consignee. The UCC provides to a carrier an excuse for nondelivery when, under a straight (nonnegotiable) bill of lading, it stopped delivery upon instructions of the consignor

received prior to the consignee's acquisition of superior rights.

(Estimated time: 15 to 20 minutes)

2. Apple, Inc., a business corporation, was incorporated on January 13, 1982, by A and B. The certificate of incorporation authorized 2,000 shares of common stock of the par value of $100 each and provided for three directors. On January 14, 1982, at the meeting of the incorporators, A and B adopted bylaws containing a provision for their amendment by a majority of the board of directors. No shares of Apple, Inc., stock were issued until February 1982, when Apple, Inc., issued 800 shares, 200 each to A and B and 400 to C, upon payment of $100 a share. A is the president and treasurer of Apple, Inc.; B is vice president and secretary; and A, B, and C are its directors.

In October 1982, at a duly called meeting of the directors attended by A, B, and C, the board adopted a new bylaw providing that "any shareholder desiring to sell his or her shares at any price must first give Apple, Inc., the option for ten days to purchase said shares at such price." Apple, Inc., sent a letter to all shareholders informing them of the new bylaw but took no other action with respect thereto.

On April 11, 1983, C borrowed $5,000 from S, a stockbroker, on a negotiable note due in one year. C indorsed in blank her certificate for 400 shares of Apple, Inc., stock and delivered it to S as collateral for the loan. On May 1, S needed money and, knowing that Z was interested in buying Apple, Inc., stock, offered to sell the 400 shares to Z for $85 a share, the fair value at that time. Z, in good faith, paid S $34,000 for C's shares, which S delivered to Z. S then absconded. Z delivered the certificate for 400 shares to Apple, Inc., requesting that it register the transfer of shares to him. Apple, Inc., refused upon the grounds that S had no right to transfer the certificate and that the shares had not been first offered to Apple, Inc., as required by its bylaws.

Required Is Z entitled to have the shares purchased by him registered in his name? Explain.

Answer Z is entitled to have the shares registered and a new certificate issued in his name. Whether S had a right to transfer the certificate is immaterial to Z's claim of ownership. Common stock of a business corporation is clearly a security as defined in the UCC. Although C did not have the right to transfer title of the security to S, she did have the power to do so under the concept of negotiation. A bona fide purchaser for value of a security takes title free from the adverse claims of third parties. A person designated as entitled to a security or the person in possession of a security in bearer form can negotiate it even though such negotiation is in violation of authority or a right to do so. C's blank indorsement of the security and its delivery to S was a negotiation. A blank indorsement changes an order security to one in bearer form that can be negotiated by delivery alone. S's delivery of the security to Z without indorsement was also a negotiation.

A bona fide purchaser for value is a purchaser who takes a security by negotiation for value, in good faith and without notice of any adverse claim or defense to the security. As stated above, the security was negotiated to Z. The facts indicate that Z paid to S $34,000 in good faith without notice of the restriction. The UCC provides that a restriction on the transfer of a security is ineffective against a bona fide purchaser for value unless it is noted conspicuously on the security.

CHAPTER

5

Commercial Paper

The following is a generalized listing of subjects to be tested through the May 1983 Uniform CPA Examination.

The major provisions of Article 3 (Commercial Paper) and Article 4 (Banking) of the Uniform Commercial Code (as amended in 1972) are included within this topic, which is traditionally referred to as Negotiable Instruments. It includes the types of negotiable instruments, the concept and importance of negotiability, the requisites for negotiability, negotiation, holding in due course, defenses, and the rights of the parties to the instrument.[1]

The AICPA Board of Examiners has adopted a new content specification outline for the business law section of the Uniform CPA Examination, *to be effective with the November 1983 examination*. The outline lists the following topics to be tested under the title "Commercial Paper."

- **A.** Commercial Paper
  - **1.** Types of Negotiable Instruments
  - **2.** Requisites for Negotiability
  - **3.** Transfer and Negotiation
  - **4.** Holders and Holders in Due Course
  - **5.** Liabilities, Defenses, and Rights
  - **6.** Discharge[2]

In place of money, sellers and buyers require a simple instrument which is current in trade and facilitates use of credit. *Commercial paper* fulfills these requirements. The laws governing commercial paper and bank deposits and collections are provided for in articles 3 and 4, respectively, of the Uniform Commercial Code.

---

[1] AICPA, *Information for CPA Candidates*, Copyright © 1975, 1979, by the American Institute of Certified Public Accountants, Inc.

[2] AICPA, *Business Law—Content Specification Outline*, approved by the AICPA Board of Examiners on August 31, 1981.

FIGURE 5-1 TYPES OF COMMERCIAL PAPER

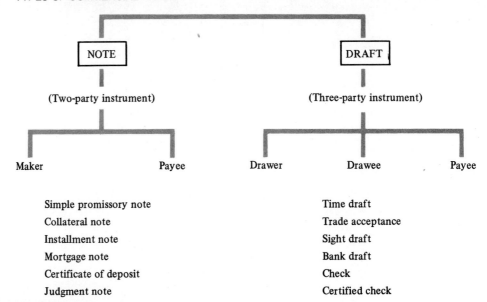

TYPES OF COMMERCIAL PAPER

I. Types of instruments (3-104) (see Figure 5-1).

    A. *Drafts* are instruments whereby one party, called the *drawer*, orders a second party, called the *drawee*, to pay a stated sum of money to a third party, called the *payee*. [3-104(2)(a)].

        1. *Time draft* is a draft payable at a specified future date.

        2. *Sight draft* is a draft payable immediately upon presentation to the drawee.

        3. *Bank draft* is a draft drawn by one bank against another.

        4. *Trade acceptance* is a draft drawn by the seller-drawer upon the buyer-drawee, payable to the seller at some future time. It is used primarily by manufacturers and wholesalers to secure the payment of the purchase price in the sale of goods.

        5. *Check* is a draft drawn on a bank and payable on demand. A check is the most common form of draft [3-104(2)(b)].

            a. *Cashier's check* is a check drawn by a bank upon itself to the order of a named payee.

            b. *Certified check* is a depositor's check accepted by the depositor's bank with a warranty that sufficient funds are on deposit and have been set aside to pay the amount stated when due.

    B. *Notes* are instruments whereby one party, called the *maker*, promises to pay to the order of a second party, called the *payee*, or to the bearer of the note a stated sum of money, either on demand or at a stated future date [2-104(2)(d)].

        1. *Simple promissory note* is one in which one party promises to pay a second party a certain sum of money on demand or at a specified future date.

        2. *Collateral note* is a note secured by a pledge of personal property.

        3. *Installment note* is a note in which the principal amount and any interest thereon is payable in specified installments at specified times until the note is paid in full.

        4. *Real estate mortgage note* is a note secured by a mortgage on specific real property belonging to the maker.

5. *Judgment (cognovit) note* is a note by which the payee can confess judgment against the maker in court without a formal trial if the note is not paid when due.

C. *Certificate of deposit* is a specialized note issued by a bank acknowledging receipt of money with an engagement to repay it upon the terms stated [3-104(2)(c)].

D. *Other instruments* that may be negotiable are provided for in other sections of the UCC. They have legal consequences very similar to issuance and negotiation of notes and drafts. These instruments were discussed in Chapters 3 and 4. They are:
   1. Letters of credit.
   2. Bills of lading.
   3. Warehouse receipts.
   4. Investment securities (certificates of stock and bonds).

ELEMENTS OF NEGOTIABILITY

II. In order for commercial paper to perform its function, it must be negotiable and readily transferable. Commercial paper can be transferred in two ways: assignment and negotiation. *Nonnegotiability does not mean invalidity.* Negotiability is a matter of form, and the UCC prescribes the standard form that a *negotiable instrument* must possess. In order for an instrument payable in money to be negotiable, it must meet the following requirements: It must be a writing signed by the maker or drawer; contain an unconditional promise or order to pay a sum certain in money and no other promise, order, obligation, or power given by the maker or drawer; be payable on demand or at a definite time; and be payable to order or bearer [3-104(1)]. These requirements must be present on the face of the instrument. An instrument not complying with these standards will be nonnegotiable, and consequently, any transferee thereof will be a mere assignee. (See Figure 5-2.)

A. *The instrument must be a writing.* The instrument must, of course, have physical existence, although there are no restrictions as to what it is written on or with what the writing is done.

B. *The instrument must be signed.* Symbols can be used as a signature, as long as the intent was to create a negotiable instrument. For example, signature by initials,

FIGURE 5-2   METHODS OF TRANSFER OF COMMERCIAL PAPER

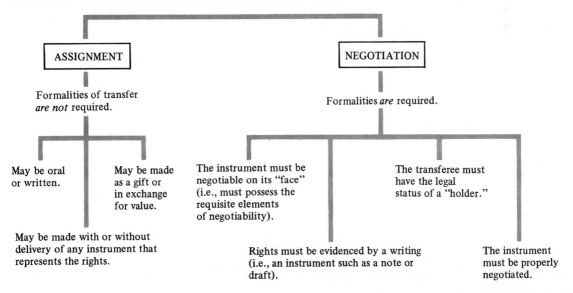

thumbprint, or "X" has been held sufficient; a rubber stamp or a letterhead printed on corporate correspondence can also be used [3-401(2)].

C. *The instrument must contain either a promise to pay (note) or an order to pay (draft)* [3-104(1)(b)]. The instrument, in order to be deemed negotiable, must show that there is an actual intention that money be paid to someone. Mere acknowledgment of a debt does not provide negotiability. That is, an I.O.U. is nonnegotiable.

1. The note need not include the word "promise," but intent to pay must be shown; e.g., "I will pay."
2. The draft must be expressed in the form of a demand upon the drawee.
3. In all cases, the language used, although polite, must show that a promise to pay or a demand to pay is being made. For example, Riker executed a note payable to Juanita in the amount of $5,000. The note stated as follows: "I, Riker, would be pleased very much to pay Juanita $5,000 on March 3, 1981." This statement is neither a promise nor an order to pay.

D. *The order or promise to pay must be unconditional* [3-104(1)(b)]. A negotiable instrument must show that money is to be paid, regardless of any other circumstances. For example, a promise to pay *if* my husband is elected to Congress is conditional and therefore nonnegotiable. The instrument is nonnegotiable even if the stated condition has already occurred, e.g., a promise in a note to pay when the Vietnam war is over. A promise or order also becomes conditional under certain special circumstances:

1. Where the instrument states that it is subject to or governed by the terms of any other agreement. Mere reference to another agreement however, does not cause the promise or order to become conditional. For example, "Pursuant to the terms of a mortgage of this date executed with First National Bank, I promise to pay _____."
2. Where the instrument states that it is to be *paid only* from a particular fund or source. This statement would make the instrument conditional because it creates a condition precedent that a fund exist and that it contain sufficient money to pay the amount promised or ordered. When the instrument merely states what account should be debited with the amount paid or indicates from which fund reimbursement is to be made, it has been held that an obligation to pay is still intended and the references to funds are merely for bookkeeping purposes. "Pay to the order of John Smith on demand $100 from the proceeds of the spring sale" is nonnegotiable, while "Pay to the order of John Smith on demand $100 and charge it to the proceeds from the spring sale" is negotiable. *Exceptions:*
   a. Where the instrument is limited to payment from a particular fund, it is negotiable as long as the instrument is issued by the government or a government agency [3-105(1)(g)];
   b. The instrument is negotiable even though limited to payment out of the entire assets of a partnership, unincorporated association, trust, or estate [3-105(1)(h)].

E. *The payment required must be of a sum certain in money* (3-106). The holder must be able to determine the amount to be received from the instrument at any specific time by the terms on the face of the instrument.

1. *Money* is defined in the code as "a medium of exchange authorized or adopted by a domestic or foreign government as a part of its currency." For example, an instrument payable in German marks is negotiable (3-107).
2. A sum payable is still a *sum certain* even though it is payable in installments, or at fixed discount if paid before maturity, or a fixed additional amount if paid after

maturity. In all such cases, the holder still knows the minimum amount he or she can expect to receive from the note [3-106(1)].

F. *The instrument may contain no other promise or order.* Where an instrument contains a promise to pay money and an additional promise other than to pay money, the instrument is not negotiable. An example is an instrument which promises to pay $50 and also to deliver five tons of grain.

G. *The instrument must be payable on demand or at some future date.* This is necessary so that the ultimate owner of the instrument will know when the maker or drawer will be compelled to pay and at what time a holder can legally demand payment.

 1. *Demand paper* is an instrument payable "on sight" or "on presentation"; it is payable at a future date. The holder of the instrument will establish the time for payment simply by presenting the note or draft for payment (3-108).

 2. *Time paper* is an instrument payable at a definite time (3-109).

  a. *On or before.* The maker or drawer has the legal right to pay the note or draft, respectively, on or before a stated date in the future, e.g., "on or before July 1, 1980."

  b. *At a fixed period after a stated date.* The instrument is payable after a certain period of time beginning with its date. For example, "Thirty days from date of this note, I promise to pay. . . ."

  c. *At a fixed period after sight.* This is frequently used in trade acceptances as a means of extending credit to a purchaser of goods; e.g., "payable ninety days after sight" or "payable six months after my death."

  d. *At a definite time subject to any acceleration.* The holder knows the definite time period beyond which the instrument may not run; however, the holder has the option to move that due date forward upon default by the promisor or for some other reason. (The code states that the holder shall accelerate only if the holder is insecure financially or if the holder, in good faith, believes the maker or drawer will not be able to pay the note in the future.)

  e. *At a definite time, subject to extension.* The maker or drawer may make an instrument payable at a future determinable time with the right to extend the due date for a specified additional time. However, an instrument with an indefinite extension clause is not payable at a specific time and is, therefore, nonnegotiable. For example, "Payable on May 1, 1982, subject to extension by the maker."

 3. An instrument payable only upon an act or event that is uncertain as to time of occurrence is not payable at a definite time [3-109(2)]. Even if subsequently the act occurs or has already occurred, the time stated is not definite; therefore, the instrument is nonnegotiable. Examples are "thirty days after my divorce," "upon the sale of my automobile," or "six weeks after Aunt Martha dies."

H. *The instrument must be payable to order or bearer* (3-110, 3-111). This provision indicates that the maker or drawer intended for the note to be negotiable. (See Figure 5-3.)

 1. *Order paper* [3-110(1)] is an instrument payable to the order or to the assigns of any specified payee. Order paper is negotiable only by *both* indorsement and delivery. An instrument may be payable to the order of either:

  a. The maker or drawer;

  b. The drawee;

  c. Two or more payees;

  d. An office, officer, partnership, or unincorporated association;

  e. An estate, trust, or fund; or

  f. A partnership or unincorporated association.

FIGURE 5-3   CLASSIFICATION OF NEGOTIABLE COMMERCIAL PAPER

ORDER PAPER PAYABLE:	BEARER PAPER PAYABLE:
"To order of XYZ Corporation"	"To bearer"
"To Ralph Zorn or his order"	"To the order of bearer"
"To Lydia Lane or her assigns"	"To cash"
"To the order of maker"	"To the order of 'John Jones' or bearer"
"To the order of Lynn Ellen and her attorney, Kathleen Ann"	"To the goodwill of the community"
"To the order of the Secretary of State, Illinois"	

    2. *Bearer paper* (3-111) is an instrument in which payment is ordered or promised to be made to the person who bears the instrument and presents it for payment. Bearer paper is negotiable by delivery alone. An instrument is payable to bearer if it is payable:

    a. To bearer;

    b. To the order of bearer;

    c. To a specified person or bearer, e.g., "to XYZ Corporation or bearer"; or

    d. To "cash" or any other indication so long as a specific payee is not named.

OMISSIONS OR PECULIARITIES ON THE FACE OF AN INSTRUMENT

  III. The negotiability of an instrument may be questioned because the instrument seems to be incomplete on its face (3-112).

    A. The following omissions or inclusions on the face of an instrument will *not* affect its negotiability:

      1. *Absence of a statement that consideration was given* in exchange for the instrument [3-112(1)(a)].

      2. *Omission of the place where the instrument is drawn and payable* [3-112(1)(a)].

      3. *The instrument is undated, postdated, or antedated* [3-114(1)]. An undated instrument will be payable upon demand. The instrument will be payable according to the date stated, regardless of the fact that it is postdated or antedated. *Exception:* The *undated* instrument, payable at a fixed time after date, is not certain as to time of payment and is, therefore, nonnegotiable.

      4. *A statement is included to the effect that collateral has been given* to secure obligations or that collateral has been authorized to be sold upon default of the instrument [3-112(1)(b)].

      5. *Inclusion of a confession of judgment clause*, i.e., an agreement of a person permitting judgment to be entered of record against that person for a stated amount upon that person's default in payment without the right to defend himself or herself in a court proceeding [3-112(1)(2)]. However, where the clause is *not* limited to situations occurring at the due date of the instrument, the instrument will be nonnegotiable.

    B. When a *required element on the face of the instrument is missing* (such as the date or signature), the instrument will be ineffective until completed. Upon completion of the instrument, it becomes fully effective and negotiable [3-115(1)].

    C. There are certain rules established by the code to resolve problems caused by *conflicting or ambiguous terms in commercial paper* (3-118).

1. When there is a question as to whether an instrument is a note or a draft, the holder may treat it as either and present it to the maker or drawer for payment.
2. Handwritten terms take precedence over typed terms and printed terms, and typed terms take precedence over printed terms.
3. Unambiguous words take precedence over figures. If words are ambiguous, figures will control. For example, "two twenty five dollars" could be either $225 or $2.25. Figures will control.
4. When a note is signed by two makers and they do not indicate in what capacity they sign, both parties are jointly and severally liable.
5. If a provision for interest is made in the note but no rate is given, the rate used is the statutory judgment rate at the place of payment, and interest accrues from the date of the instrument.

   D. The fact that the instrument is under seal has no bearing on its negotiability.

TRANSFER AND NEGOTIATION

IV. Transfer and negotiation (3-201, 3-202). "*Negotiation*" is the word used to describe the transfer of a negotiable instrument whereby the transferee becomes either a "holder" or a "holder in due course." An *instrument is negotiable* when it can be transferred by indorsement and delivery by the holder (order paper) or by delivery only (bearer paper) [3-202(1)]. The face of the instrument determines in what manner the instrument can first be negotiated. Thereafter, each indorsement will be determinate of the method necessary for negotiation. *Special note:* If an instrument is in bearer form, it may be negotiated by anyone, even a thief or finder. All negotiations (i.e., indorsement and delivery or delivery alone if proper) are effective to pass title to the instrument *to a holder in due course* even though they are voidable or void because of minority or other legal incapacity, because of illegality, or because they were obtained by fraud, duress, undue influence, or for any other reason. (See Figure 5-4.)

   A. *Types of indorsements.* The type of indorsement used in negotiating an instrument will establish the method to be used in making the next negotiation. All indorsements disclose three things: (1) the method to be used in making subsequent negotiations, (2) the type of interest being transferred, and (3) the liability of the indorser. The indorsement must be written on the back of the instrument itself unless the instrument is full, in which case it may be written on a piece of paper that is firmly affixed to the instrument (an allonge). Once an instrument is negotiable, it

FIGURE 5-4 METHODS OF NEGOTIATION

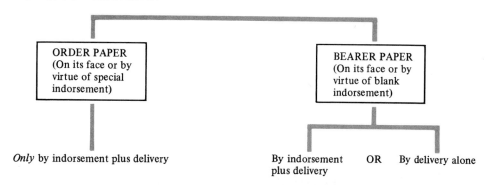

Note: If not properly negotiated, the transfer is an assignment.

is always negotiable. *No indorsement destroys negotiability.* (See Figures 5-5 and 5-6.)

1. *Special indorsement* specifies the person to whom or to whose order the instrument is payable. The instrument can be further negotiated only with the indorsement of the person to whom the instrument was specially indorsed; e.g., "pay to the order of John Jones, Ralph Smith" or "pay to the First National Bank of Normal, Illinois" [3-204(1)].

2. *Blank indorsement* is an indorsement specifying no specific indorsee. It is usually just the signature of the holder. A blank indorsement can be used to change an order instrument to a bearer instrument. Once an instrument of this type is indorsed by the original payee, it becomes a bearer instrument and is negotiable by delivery alone [3-204(2)(3)].

3. *Restrictive indorsement* (3-205) restricts the rights of the indorsee in some manner but does not prohibit the transfer or negotiation of the instrument in any way [3-206(1)].

   a. *Conditional indorsement.* The indorser, by his or her indorsement, makes the rights of the indorsee subject to the happening of a certain event; e.g., "pay A only if my ship arrives in Chicago."

   b. *Indorsements which attempt to prohibit further transfer.* Any indorsement which attempts to prohibit further transfer (e.g., "pay C" or "pay C only") will not prevent negotiation or further transfer of the instrument. The indorsement will be viewed in the same manner as the indorsement "pay to the order of C."

   c. *Indorsements for deposit or collection.* This indorsement attempts to restrict an instrument to the banking system for deposit or collection. If the instrument were to go outside the banking system, the holder would have to be sure that the money given up to purchase the instrument is used in accordance with the indorsement; that is, it is deposited in a bank. The purchaser of an instrument with a restrictive indorsement for deposit or collection could be held liable to the restrictive indorsee if the indorsee could prove that the purchaser did not adhere to the indorsement by seeing that the amount he or she purchased the note for was deposited in a bank (or collected).

   d. *Indorsements in trust.* Only the immediate transferee must comply with this restriction. These indorsements ("pay S in trust of D," "pay S for account of D") are treated similarly to those for deposit and collection except that the restriction applies only to the first taker.

FIGURE 5-5   LEGAL EFFECT OF BLANK AND SPECIAL INDORSEMENTS

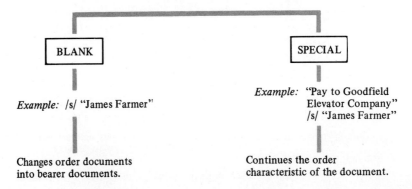

FIGURE 5-6 TYPES OF INDORSEMENTS

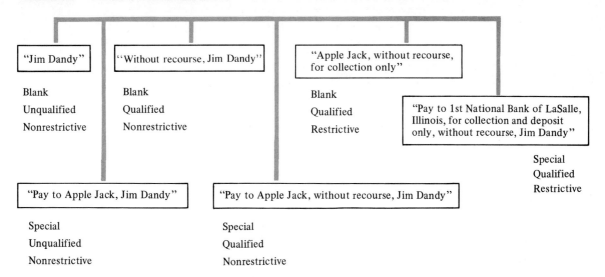

4. *Qualified indorsements* (3-414). A qualified indorsement eliminates an indorser's *secondary liability* (i.e., to pay the face amount if the person primarily liable does not pay) on an instrument, but it does not destroy any possible liability on the part of the indorser for breach of warranty. The most common form of a qualified indorsement is "without recourse, John Smith." This type of indorsement will *not* affect the instrument's negotiability.

B. *Legal effectiveness of transfers of order or bearer instruments.* Instruments may be order or bearer instruments on their face or made order or bearer instruments by indorsement. Review II-H above.

1. *Order instruments.*
   a. A proper indorsement and delivery is necessary for negotiation. An order instrument cannot be negotiated by delivery alone.
   b. Absent a negotiation, the transferee is a mere assignee who acquires no better rights to the instrument than those possessed by the transferor.
   c. A thief or a finder of an order instrument does not acquire any rights and consequently cannot in any way transfer any rights (i.e., title) to it.
   d. A forged or unauthorized indorsement is totally ineffective, and consequently, no rights to an order instrument can be transferred thereunder.

2. *Bearer instruments.*
   a. A bearer instrument can be negotiated by anyone who possesses it, either by indorsement and delivery or by delivery alone.
   b. As in the case of an order instrument, a thief or a finder of a bearer instrument does not acquire any rights to it against anyone. However, a thief or finder has the *power* to negotiate the bearer instrument to a holder in due course and thereby deprive the true owner of title to the instrument. The owner's recourse is to sue the thief or finder for damages caused by the tort of conversion.

3. *Effect of negotiation.* A negotiation is effective to transfer rights to the transferee even though it is:
   a. Made by a person without legal capacity, e.g., an infant or mentally infirm person;
   b. Made by a thief, finder, or other unauthorized person;

c. Obtained by fraud, duress, undue influence, or mistake; or

d. A part of an illegal transaction (3-207).

e. *Note:* In these situations, the transferor has the right to rescind the transfer; i.e., the transferee has voidable title. However, the transferee has the power to deprive the transferor of the right to rescind and consequently of title by negotiating the instrument to a holder in due course.

HOLDER IN DUE COURSE

V. A *holder* is any person who has possession of an instrument that was either drawn, issued, or indorsed to that person, to that person's order, or to bearer or in blank [1-201(20)]. However, in order to be deemed *a holder in due course*, the holder must take the instrument for value in good faith, without notice that it is overdue or has been dishonored or that any person has a defense against it or a claim to it (3-302) (See Figure 5-7.) A holder in due course takes an instrument free from any personal defenses (3-305).

A. *For value.* Value relates to the actual giving of consideration. A promise to give consideration in the future is not sufficient to constitute "a giving of value." A holder takes an instrument for value when the holder (3-303):

1. Performs the agreed upon consideration. For example:

a. S agrees to pay D $400 for a $500 note due in two years. S will not satisfy the requirement to be a holder in due course until she actually pays D the $400.

b. Jim agreed to pay $1,000 for a promissory note in the amount of $1,500 negotiated to him by Lois. Jim paid $750 at the time he purchased the note and agreed to pay the balance in two weeks. One week later, Jim learned that the maker on the note had a defense to it based on fraud in the inducement. Jim is a holder in due course only to the extent of the value he gave, i.e., $750. He can never be a holder in due course for the full face value of the note, i.e., $1,500.

c. Use the same facts as stated in 1-b above except that Jim paid the full $1,000 to Lois before he learned of the maker's defense. Jim is a holder in due course for the face value of the note ($1,500) because he had given full value for the note, i.e., $1,000.

2. Acquires a security interest in the instrument. For example, the holder of a note takes out a loan from the bank and gives the note as collateral for a loan. The bank is a holder in due course to the extent of the loan.

FIGURE 5-7 REQUIREMENTS FOR HOLDER-IN-DUE-COURSE STATUS

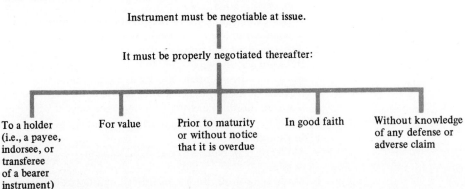

3. Takes the instrument in payment of an antecedent claim against anyone. For example, S owes F $100. Y gives S a note for $100. S negotiates this note to F. F, by discharging S's debt when she obtains the note, is considered to have given value for the note.

4. Gives a negotiable instrument in exchange for a negotiable instrument or makes an irrevocable commitment to a third person. For example, Y gives a check to bank Z, which sends an irrevocable letter of credit to customer X. Bank Z is a holder for value.

B. *No notice that an instrument is overdue, dishonored, or has claims against it* [3-304(3)]. A person is considered to have "notice" when that person has actual knowledge of the circumstances, has received a notice or notification of the circumstances, or should have reason to know that a certain situation exists from all the facts available.

1. In some instances it is apparent from the instrument itself that it is overdue. An instrument in circulation after its due date is overdue.

    a. An instrument payable on a fixed date is not overdue until the following day.

    b. An instrument is payable on demand and the holder knows or has reason to know that a demand for payment has been made. The holder cannot become a holder in due course.

    c. If a purchaser takes a demand instrument after it has been outstanding an unreasonable length of time, the purchaser will not obtain a holder-in-due course status, e.g., a check outstanding thirty-five days after the date stated on its face.

    d. The presence of an acceleration clause in an installment note does not give notice that the instrument is overdue because of a default.

    e. When notes are issued in a series or are payable in installments, a holder will not be a holder in due course if he or she has reason to know that payment had not been made on one of the notes in the series or that any installment payment had not been made. However, knowledge of a default in interest payments will not prevent a holder from becoming a holder in due course.

2. An instrument is dishonored when it is presented for payment or acceptance and the payment or acceptance is refused [3-507(1)]. Without notice of a dishonor, a holder can have the status of a holder in due course.

3. If a holder has notice of a claim or defense against the instrument, the holder cannot be a holder in due course [3-304(1)].

    a. Incomplete paper. A holder will still be a holder in due course if the holder has knowledge that an incomplete instrument has been completed, unless the holder knows that the completion was improperly made or made without authorization.

    b. Any *obvious* material alterations on the face of an instrument, such as the payee's name, the amount, the due date, or the interest rate, would constitute an irregular instrument; the holder could not be a holder in due course.

    c. A holder is charged with notice of a claim or defense if the holder knows that the obligation of any party is voidable or that all parties have been discharged. This would be the case where a note was made under fraud, duress, or undue influence or other circumstance which rendered the instrument void or voidable. If the holder has notice that only *some* of the parties have been discharged, the holder can still be a holder in due course.

    d. An instrument issued to a payee in exchange for an executory promise (a promise to perform in the future) will not affect the holder-in-due-course status unless the holder has reason to know that this promise was not performed.

C. *In good faith. Good faith* is defined by the UCC as "honesty in fact in the conduct or transaction concerned" [1-201(19)]. The term "good faith" implies honest intention. However, where a holder takes an instrument under such circumstances that should create an inference that an instrument was defective, the holder will be held to have taken the instrument in bad faith.

MISCELLANEOUS HOLDERS

VI. Miscellaneous holders.

A. *A payee may be a holder in due course* [3-302(2)]. This is possible when the payee is not an actual party to the issuance of the instrument. For example, a purchaser takes out a draft on a bank and forwards it to the named payee. As another example, a maker gave to her agent a check, complete except for the amount, for delivery to a seller (the named payee) in payment for goods. The agent filled in an incorrect amount and delivered the check to the seller, who was unaware of the error. The seller is a holder in due course.

B. *A holder cannot become a holder in due course* [3-302(3)]:

1. By purchasing an instrument at a judicial sale;

2. By taking it under legal process;

3. By acquiring an instrument in taking over an estate;

4. By purchasing an instrument as part of a bulk transaction that is not in the regular course of business of the transferor.

C. *Holder from a holder in due course.* A holder who is not a holder in due course may acquire the rights of a holder in due course if he or she receives the instrument from a holder in due course and is not a party to any prior fraud or illegality affecting the instrument [3-201(1)]. For example, Siege fraudulently induced Engal to execute a note payable to his order. Siege negotiated the note to Rexrode, a holder in due course; Rexrode sold the note to Rosanski, who had knowledge of the fraud. Although Rosanski is not a holder in due course, she acquired the rights of a holder in due course from Rexrode.

D. *Reacquirers.* A person who reacquires an instrument is entitled to the same status as that person held previously. For example, a holder in due course negotiates an instrument and subsequently reacquires it from someone other than a holder in due course. That person may still maintain the position of a holder in due course. However, a holder not in due course may not better his or her position by reacquiring the instrument from a holder in due course. For example, in VI-C above, Siege could never acquire the rights of a holder in due course by reacquiring the note.

PERSONAL AND REAL DEFENSES

VII. There are two types of defenses available to parties primarily liable (maker on a note and acceptor on a draft) and secondarily liable (drawers and indorsers) on an instrument: personal and real. *Personal defenses* merely render obligations voidable; they are not available against a holder in due course. However, *real defenses* create void obligations and are allowed against all holders. (See Figure 5-8.)

A. *Note:* The Federal Trade Commission (FTC) has adopted a rule abolishing the holder-in-due-course doctrine *as it relates to installment sales contracts used to finance retail purchases involving consumer goods.* This rule in effect gives the installment buyer the right to assert *any* defenses and claims arising from a seller's misconduct against any credit company or bank which subsequently purchases the credit contract from the seller.

1. The rule is designed to protect consumers' rights against *sellers* when consumers

FIGURE 5-8 DEFENSES AVAILABLE TO PARTIES PRIMARILY OR SECONDARILY LIABLE ON A NEGOTIABLE INSTRUMENT

REAL (void obligation) (Available against holder in due course)	PERSONAL (voidable obligations) (Not available against a holder in due course)

Incapacity
    Minority (in states where voidable)
    Mental (in states where void)
    Intoxication (in states where void)
    Duress (in states where void)
Fraud in the execution
 	
    Exceptions:
      Impostor
Forgery   Fictitious payee
      Negligence
Unauthorized signature
Illegality
Material alteration
Discharge in bankruptcy
	Lack of consideration
	Breach of contract
	Fraud in the inducement
	Duress
	Undue influence
	Discharge of parties
	Payment before maturity
	Conditional delivery
	Delivery of incomplete instrument
	Nondelivery (complete or incomplete)
	Dishonored check

purchase consumer goods on credit and become obligated to make payments to a financial institution.

2. Sellers are required to insert a specific notice in any installment sales contract used to finance retail purchases which expressly preserves the buyer's defenses against any credit company or bank which subsequently purchases the contract.

3. The rule also applies in the following circumstances:

   a. To credit sales transactions in which the seller and a financial institution have a prearranged agreement for direct loans to the buyer for purposes of paying the purchase price.

   b. Where the seller engages in loan referrals to the buyer.

4. The rule does *not* apply to:

   a. Checks issued for payment for goods or services purchased by a consumer;

   b. Transactions by persons other than consumers (a consumer is a person who buys goods or services for personal, family, or household use);

   c. Purchases of real estate, investment securities, or utility services; and

   d. Purchases for a price in excess of $25,000.

B. *Personal defenses* are defenses which usually arise between the original parties to the instrument, i.e., the maker-payee or the drawer-payee.

   1. *Lack of consideration.* That which will be sufficient consideration in a simple contract will also be sufficient consideration between parties to a negotiable instrument. For example, A executed and issued a note to his son as a gift. The note was merely a promise to pay unsupported by consideration and unenforceable by the son. However B, a holder in due course who received the note from the son, would take the note free from A's defense of lack of consideration.

   2. *Breach of contract.* A holder in due course may collect on an instrument even though the payee did not perform the payee's part of the contract for which the negotiable instrument was executed and issued. For example, D executed and delivered a draft to E in exchange for E's promise to build a garage. The garage was not constructed. E negotiated the draft to a holder in due course, who takes free of D's defense of breach of contract.

3. *Fraud in the inducement.* Where a maker or drawer executes and issues a negotiable instrument induced by a payee's fraud, the maker or drawer cannot use the defense of fraud against a holder in due course.

4. *Duress or undue influence.* This occurs when a payee threatens a maker or drawer and thereby acquires an instrument payable to the payee's order or when a payee utilizes a confidential or fiduciary relationship with a maker or drawer and wrongfully induces a maker or drawer to execute and issue an instrument to the payee's order.

5. *Discharge of parties.* A holder in due course takes free of the defense of any prior discharge of one or more parties. For example, Z was an indorser on a note payable in the amount of $1,000. W, the owner (holder) of the note, accepted $150 from Z and gave her a discharge of any secondary liability. Z's indorsement was not scratched out, nor was any notation of Z's discharge made on the note. W negotiated the note to M, a holder in due course. Z remains secondarily liable to M.

6. *Payment before maturity.* A maker or drawer of an instrument who pays it before maturity and still allows the instrument to circulate cannot assert payment as a defense against a holder in due course. For example, T was a maker on a note issued to S, the payee. Prior to the note's due date, T paid the face value of the note to S but did not take possession of the note. S negotiated the note to V, a holder in due course. T must pay the face value of the note to V.

7. *Nondelivery of an instrument, whether complete or incomplete.* The defense of nondelivery of an instrument is not available against a holder in due course; e.g., an instrument payable to bearer is stolen and subsequently negotiated to a holder in due course.

8. *Delivery of an incomplete instrument.* The defense of unauthorized completion of a blank instrument is not available against a holder in due course. For example, a maker gives a blank instrument to be completed by inserting a specified amount, and subsequently the payee fills in an unauthorized or incorrect amount.

9. *Conditional delivery of a completed instrument.* This occurs when a person executes a negotiable instrument and conditions its payment upon the happening of a specified event. For example, M executes a note payable to P on an oral condition that no payment will be made until M sells her home.

C. *Real defenses* [3-305(2)]. These defenses are available against all holders, even against a holder in due course. They arise out of circumstances which create void obligations under the statutes or common law of the state wherein the transaction occurred (see Figure 5-8). *Note:* If a maker's, drawer's, acceptor's, or indorser's negligence caused (substantially contributed to) the real defense to arise, that person is precluded from asserting a real defense. For example, Nora completed a negotiable promissory note payable to bearer in every detail except that she omitted to state the amount in the spaces provided. She left the note on the top of her office desk. An employee stole the note and negotiated it to a holder in due course. As another example, Elmer lost his checkbook but failed to report the loss to his drawee. The checks were found by Opal, who forged Elmer's name and issued the check to Retail. Retail negotiated the check to a depository bank for collection. As a third example, an acceptor of a draft paid it upon presentment without noticing that the amount of the check was raised from $100,000 to $1,000,000 subsequent to the time of acceptance. As a fourth example, a holder indorsed a negotiable promissory note in blank and negligently allowed it to be stolen, and it was subsequently negotiated by the thief to a holder in due course. (See XXI-B-3-d below for more examples of a drawer's negligence.)

1. *Legal incapacity.* State laws govern whether incapacity will be a personal or real defense.
   a. *Minority* is a real defense when it is allowed as a defense to a simple contract under state law.
   b. *Mental incapacity* is a real defense where a state law provides that all contracts made by a mentally incompetent person are null and void. If, however, state law provides that contracts to which a mentally incapacitated person is a party are merely voidable, mental incapacity is a personal defense.
   c. *Intoxication.* State laws will determine whether this is a real or personal defense.
   d. *Duress.* State laws will determine whether this is a real or personal defense.
2. *Void obligations.* If an obligation originates in such a way that it is void from its inception under state laws, it is a real defense.
   a. *Fraud in the execution.* This defense arises out of a situation when an individual, because of misrepresentation, has been induced to sign an instrument without knowledge of, or opportunity to gain knowledge of, the character or terms of the instrument. For example, F signs a receipt, not realizing that his signature is being transposed onto a negotiable instrument hidden beneath the receipt, or an illiterate person is told she is signing a receipt when in reality she is signing a negotiable instrument.
   b. *Forgery and unauthorized signature.* A person who does not execute a negotiable instrument cannot be held liable to any holder presenting an instrument containing that person's forged or unauthorized signature (3-404). See the discussion in XXI-B-3-d below for important exceptions to this rule.
   c. *Illegality.* As a general rule, where a negotiable instrument is issued in connection with an illegal transaction, the instrument will be void and the party primarily liable will have illegality available as a real defense. However, not all illegal transactions are void under state statutes. Therefore, a negotiable instrument issued in connection with a transaction which was merely voidable under a state statute would give rise to a personal rather than a real defense.
3. *Material alteration.* When an alteration changes the original obligation of a party to a negotiable instrument, it is considered a material alteration and creates a real defense only to the extent of the alteration (3-407). For instance, the amount payable on a note is changed from $100 to $1,000. A holder in due course has a valid claim for only $100.
4. *Discharge in bankruptcy.*

PRESENTMENT FOR ACCEPTANCE AND PAYMENT

VIII. In general, proper presentment is necessary to hold secondary (drawers and indorsers) parties liable upon the instrument [3-501(1)]. Any demand upon a party to pay or accept an instrument is a presentment. A holder must first present an instrument for payment or acceptance and then give notice of dishonor to parties who are secondarily liable in order to preserve their liability on the instrument [3-501(1)(2)].

A. *Place of presentment.* When an instrument is payable or to be accepted at a bank within the United States, the instrument must be presented for payment or acceptance at that bank. Presentment may be made at the residence or place of business of the person who is going to pay or accept the instrument where no place for payment or acceptance is specified in the instrument [3-504(c)].

B. *Presentment for payment or acceptance* may be made personally, by mail, or through a clearinghouse [3-504(a)(b)].

1. An instrument must be presented for payment or acceptance to the drawee or primary party or some person who is authorized to make or refuse to make payment or acceptance.
   a. A person to whom presentment is made has a right to:
      (1) Request exhibition of the instrument;
      (2) Identification of the person presenting the instrument;
      (3) The production of the instrument at a proper place;
      (4) A signed receipt on the instrument for any type of payment or the surrender of the instrument upon full payment.
   b. If the person presenting the instrument does not comply with any of these, the presentment is not proper.
2. A person making presentment is entitled to have the time for presentment extended in order to comply with requests made by the person to whom he or she is making presentment.

C. Instruments must be presented for payment or acceptance at the proper time (3-503).
   1. Instruments payable on a stated date must be presented for acceptance on or before that date and must be presented for payment on that specific date.
   2. Instruments payable after sight must be presented for payment or acceptance within a reasonable time after date or issue, whichever is later.
      a. A reasonable time is determined by the nature of the instrument and the circumstances surrounding its issue.
      b. A reasonable time for presentment with respect to the secondary liability of a drawer of an uncertified check is thirty days after date or issue, whichever is later.
      c. In the situation of an indorser, a reasonable time elapses seven days after the indorsement.

IX. *Presentment for acceptance.* Upon acceptance of a draft, a drawee assumes primary liability to any holder thereof. See VIII above.
   A. *Acceptance* is the drawee's signed engagement written on the instrument to honor the draft as presented [3-410(1)].
      1. Acceptance usually takes place by the drawee writing the word "accepted" on the face of the note and then signing and dating it.
      2. However, the drawee's signature alone written on the face of the instrument may constitute an acceptance, if so intended.
   B. *Certification* is an acceptance by a drawee bank of a check whereby the bank unconditionally promises to pay the check from specifically appropriated funds when it is subsequently presented for payment. Once a check is certified upon request of a *holder*, the drawer and all prior indorsers are discharged [3-411(1)].
   C. Most drafts need not be presented for acceptance. However, the following types of drafts must be presented for acceptance:
      1. Drafts that explicitly state that they must be presented for acceptance.
      2. Drafts payable at a place other than the residence or place of business of the drawee.
      3. Drafts payable after sight or where acceptance is necessary in order to determine the maturity of the instrument; e.g., a draft payable twelve days after sight means it is payable twelve days after it is presented to the drawee.

X. *Presentment for payment* at the proper place and time and in the proper manner is necessary to charge any indorser with liability. See VIII above.

XI. *Notice of dishonor* (3-508). An instrument is dishonored when it is presented for payment or acceptance, and payment or acceptance is refused or cannot be made within the allowed time. There are two purposes for giving notice of dishonor: first to inform parties that are secondarily liable that the maker or acceptor has failed to meet his or her obligation, and second to advise secondary parties that they will be required to make payment on the instrument.

    A. Notice of dishonor will usually be given by the holder. However, any person who may be compelled to pay the instrument may give notice to any other person who may be liable.

    B. Notice of dishonor may be given by returning the unpaid instrument bearing a stamp, ticket, or some type of memorandum stating that the instrument was not paid or accepted. However, any type of notice that provides knowledge of the dishonor and informs any secondary parties that they may be liable is sufficient, whether it be oral or in writing.

    C. Notice of dishonor must be given [3-508(2)]:

        1. By a bank before midnight of its next banking day following the banking day on which the instrument is dishonored.

        2. By any other person before midnight of the third business day after receipt of the notice of dishonor.

    D. Failure to give notice or an unexcused delay in giving notice within the required time period causes all indorsers to be discharged.

XII. *Protest* (3-509). A protest is a written notice that an instrument has been dishonored. Protest is necessary only on drafts drawn or payable outside the United States, i.e., foreign instruments.

XIII. *Excused or delayed presentment, notice of dishonor, and protest.* The UCC provides for two circumstances whereby presentment, notice, and protest are excused [3-511(1)]:

    A. Where the holder does not have notice that an instrument is due. For example, an instrument has an acceleration clause which has become operative because of a default; however, the holder had no way of knowing that it was overdue.

    B. Where the delay in presentment is due to circumstances beyond the control of the holder. For example, a storm incapacitates all means of communication for a period of time past the due date of the instrument.

XIV. *Waiver of presentment, notice, and protest.* The requirements of presentment, notice, and protest may be waived by the drawer or any indorser [3-511(5)(6)].

    A. By a drawer in writing on the face of the instrument.

    B. By an indorser either in writing on the back of the instrument or by indorsing "payment guaranteed" or "collection guaranteed."

LIABILITY OF PARTIES TO AN INSTRUMENT

XV. *Liability of parties.* There are three potential liabilities that persons may be subject to in dealing with negotiable instruments. These liabilities are primary and secondary liability for the face amount of the instrument and liability for damages as a result of breach of implied warranties made upon transfer of the instrument. (See Figure 5-9.) No person can be primarily or secondarily liable for the face amount of an instrument unless that person's signature appears thereon. All persons whose signatures appear on the instrument possess some type of primary or secondary contractual obligation to pay its face amount. They also may be additionally liable for breach of implied warranties that arise upon transfer or negotiation of the instrument and accrue to transferees for value. A person whose signature does *not* appear on the instrument may be liable only for breach of implied warranties made upon transfer or negotiation of the instrument for value. For example, Alwes purchased a negotiable promissory note payable to

FIGURE 5-9   LIABILITY OF PARTIES TO COMMERCIAL PAPER

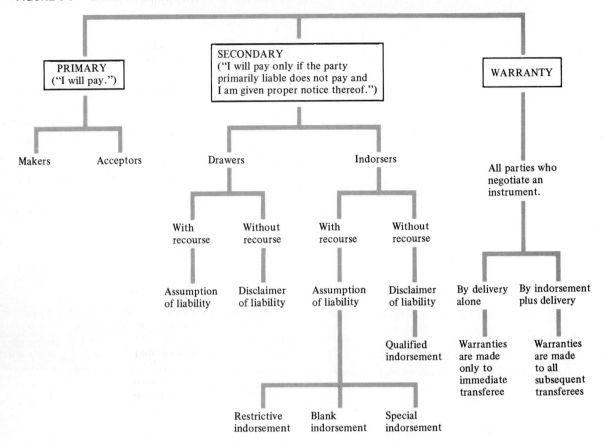

bearer. Alwes sold the note to Stacy for value without indorsing it. Alwes is not primarily or secondarily liable, but he may be liable for breach of implied warranties. See XVI below.

A. *Primary parties.* A maker of a note and an acceptor of a draft possess *primary liability.* A drawee has no liability whatsoever *on the instrument* prior to its acceptance. Only upon acceptance does a drawee become an acceptor and acquire primary liability for the face amount of the draft. Primary parties unconditionally promise to pay the face amount of the instrument upon its presentment for payment [3-413(1)].

B. *Secondary parties* have secondary liability. A drawer after acceptance of a draft and all unqualified indorsers are secondarily liable for the face amount of the instrument. *Secondary liability* means that certain conditions must be fulfilled before the duty to pay the face amount arises. These conditions precedent are presentment for payment to a party primarily liable, receipt of notice of dishonor, and in some instances protest.

   1. The drawer engages that he or she will pay the face amount of the draft to the holder or any indorser if the acceptor dishonors the draft. The drawer may disclaim this liability by drawing "without recourse," i.e., a qualified engagement [3-413(2)].

2. The indorser engages that he or she will pay the instrument according to its tenor if it is dishonored upon presentment *and* the indorser is given the necessary notice of dishonor (3-414).

   a. This liability runs to any holder and any subsequent indorser.

   b. An indorser may disclaim secondary liability by indorsing "without recourse."

   c. Indorsers are assumed to be liable to one another in the order in which they indorsed the instrument.

C. *Accommodation parties.* An accommodation party (cosignor) is one who signs a negotiable instrument in any capacity for the purpose of lending his or her name and credit to another party to the instrument [3-415(1)].

   1. The obligation of the accommodation party is dependent on the capacity in which he or she signed. The accommodation party may sign as maker, drawer, acceptor, or indorser.

   2. An accommodation party is not liable to the party accommodated; if the accommodation party pays the instrument, a right of recourse exists against that party [3-415(5)].

D. *Unauthorized signatures, representatives, and imposters.*

   1. An unauthorized agent who signs an instrument in the principal's name is in the same category as a forger. Both a forger and an unauthorized agent are personally liable on the instruments upon which their signatures appear [3-404(1)].

   2. If an authorized representative signs an instrument but does not indicate that he or she is an agent or who the principal is, the agent is personally liable.

   3. If an authorized agent signs and states he or she is an agent but does not disclose the name of the principal, then between the immediate parties, the principal is liable. However, the principal is not liable to any subsequent holders.

   4. If an authorized agent signs the principal's name and his or her own and does not disclose that he or she is signing in a representative capacity, the principal is liable and the agent is also personally liable.

   5. There are three different situations relating to "imposters."

      a. *Imposter rule:* An imposter contacts a person, represents to be someone else, and persuades the person to issue an instrument in the name of the person who the imposter represents himself or herself to be. The imposter indorses the instrument in the payee's name and places it into circulation. The drawer is liable on the instrument.

      b. *Fictitious payee rule:* An employee who has authority to execute and issue checks issues a check to a named payee who is fictitious. The employee indorses and cashes the check. The drawer is liable on the instrument.

      c. *Faithless employee rule:* An employee provides the employer with the name of a person to whom the employer is indebted. The employer issues a check payable to its creditor; the employee is given possession of it, indorses it with the payee's name, and negotiates the instrument. The drawer is liable.

WARRANTIES ON TRANSFER

XVI. *Warranties in general.* Certain implied warranties attach to the assignment or negotiation of commercial paper and the presentment of these types of instruments for payment or acceptance. Warranties enable a party who has been held liable on an instrument to recover the loss against a prior transferor.

A. *Warranties on transfer.* Any person who negotiates an instrument and receives value for it makes certain implied warranties [3-417(2)]. Where the transfer is made by *indorsement and delivery*, the warranties apply to the immediate transferee and also to any subsequent holders who take the instrument in good faith. Where the transfer is made by *delivery only*, the warranties accrue only to the benefit of the transferor's immediate transferee. The warranties implied by a transferor either by indorsement and delivery or by delivery alone are as follows:

1. The transferor has good title to the instrument;
2. All signatures are genuine or authorized;
3. The instrument has not been materially altered. For example, Smythe executed and delivered a check for $250 payable to the order of P. P properly indorsed the check and delivered it to Hallam. Hallam changed the amount of the check to $2,500 and properly negotiated it to H, a holder in due course. P and Smythe are liable to H only for $250, the original tenor of the check. In addition, H can recover actual damages ($2,250) from Hallam for breach of warranty.
4. No defense is available against the transferor (*Exception:* A qualified indorser warrants only that he or she has *no knowledge of* any defense); and
5. The transferor has no knowledge of any insolvency proceedings instituted with respect to the maker, acceptor, or drawer of an unaccepted instrument.

B. *Warranties on presentment.* A person presenting an instrument for payment or acceptance makes the following warranties to the payor or acceptor [3-417(1)(a)(b)(c)].

1. That person has good title to the instrument. For example, Maker executes and delivers a negotiable note payable to the order of Payee. The note was stolen by Thief before Payee could indorse it. Thief forged Payee's indorsement and sold the note to Innocent. Innocent presented the note to Maker and received payment. Payee remained owner of the note and is entitled to be paid the face amount from Maker. Maker, in turn, can collect from Innocent for the latter's breach of the implied warranty (upon presentment) that he had good title to the note.
2. The instrument has not been altered.
3. That person has no knowledge that the signature of the maker or drawer is unauthorized.
4. *Exception:* The warranties upon presentment stated in the first two parts in B above are not made by a holder in due course who receives payment in good faith to:
   a. A maker or drawer with respect to their own signatures;
   b. An acceptor of a draft with respect to the drawer's signature; and
   c. An acceptor of a draft who had accepted *before* it was acquired by the holder in due course. This rule applies whether the alteration occurred before or after the acceptance.

DISCHARGE (RELEASE OF LIABILITY OF PARTIES)

XVII. *Discharge.* The following are the *only* situations in which a discharge is effective [3-601(1)]. *No discharge is effective against a holder in due course unless the holder has notice of the discharge upon taking the instrument* (3-602).

A. *Payment or satisfaction.* Payment to a holder discharges the liability of the paying party to the extent of such payment or satisfaction.

1. Payment will not result in discharge when the paying party pays in bad faith, as when the paying party knows the holder has acquired the instrument by theft or through a previous holder who had acquired it by theft.
2. Payment will not discharge a payor who pays in a manner inconsistent with a restrictive indorsement.

B. *Tender of payment.* Tender is a readiness and willingness to pay the instrument when it is due at the place specified. Any party making tender in full payment to a holder at or after payment is due is discharged *to the extent of all subsequent liability for interest, costs, and attorney fees.* That person is not relieved of liability for the face amount of the instrument or any interest accrued up to that time.

   1. The holder's refusal of a tender completely discharges any party who has a right of recourse against the party making tender. For example, Maker tenders payment to Holder, who refuses the tender. Indorsers are wholly discharged of their secondary liability.

C. *Cancellation and renunciation.* Neither a cancellation nor a renunciation need be supported by consideration to be effective.

   1. *Cancellation.* A holder who intends to do so may discharge any party to the instrument by mutilating or destroying the instrument, or by any indication of intent to cancel on the face of the instrument or indorsement. For instance, the holder may cross out a party's signature, write the word "cancel" on the instrument, or strike out the signature of the parties the holder wishes to discharge.

   2. *Renunciation.* A holder may renounce his or her rights by a writing "signed and delivered," or by surrendering the instrument, to the party the holder wishes to discharge. The renunciation must be in writing and must be absolute and unconditional.

D. *Impairment of recourse or collateral.* An indorser normally has a right of recourse against primary parties, prior indorsers, or the drawer, in the case of a draft. If any of the rights of the indorser are affected by the action or inaction of the holder, the indorser is discharged from liability on the instrument.

   1. An indorser is discharged to the extent that the holder, without consent and without an express reservation of rights against the indorser:

      a. Releases or agrees not to sue any person against whom the indorser, as known to the holder, has a right of recourse. For example, M is the maker of a note in the amount of $500 payable to P. The note has been indorsed by P, Q, and R. H, the holder, received $40 from P and released P of her secondary liability. Q and R are discharged from their secondary liability.

      b. Agrees to suspend the right to enforce the instrument against the party;

      c. Discharges a prior indorser. For example, M is a maker of a note payable to P. The note has been indorsed by P, X, Y, and Z. H, the holder, scratched out X's name as a personal favor to X. P remains secondarily liable. Y and Z are discharged from secondary liability.

      d. Unjustifiably impairs any collateral given by or on behalf of the indorser or any person against whom the indorser has a right of recourse. For example, M, a maker of a note payable to P, gave collateral to P as security for the promise to pay. The note was subsequently indorsed by A, B, C, D, and E. In each negotiation A, B, C, D, and E received possession of the collateral. H, a holder and last possessor of the collateral, wrongfully caused the collateral to substantially deteriorate. A, B, C, D, and E are discharged of their secondary liability.

E. *Reacquisition.* Intervening parties are discharged when a prior holder reacquires the instrument. For example, M is a maker of a note payable to P. The note is indorsed by P, A, B, C, D, and E in that order. Thereafter, B repurchases the note. P, A, and B remain secondarily liable. D and E are discharged of their secondary liability.

F. *Fraudulent and material alteration.* Any alteration of an instrument which is both fraudulent and material will cause a discharge of any party if the obligation of that party is changed thereby.

G. *Certification of a check.* When a holder obtains a certification of a check from a drawee bank, the drawer and all prior indorsers are discharged.

H. *Acceptance varying a draft.* When a holder assents to an acceptance by a drawee which varies the terms of the draft, the drawer and all indorsers are discharged.

I. *Unexcused delay in presentment, notice of dishonor, or protest (3-502).*

    1. *Indorser.* Any indorser is discharged if presentment or notice of dishonor is delayed or not given without a proper excuse.

    2. *Drawer.* A drawer who has funds in his or her drawee bank is not automatically discharged by a holder's unexcused failure to make proper presentment or to give proper notice of dishonor. However, the drawer will be discharged upon proving that he or she suffered a financial loss as a result of the holder's action or inaction.

J. *An act which would discharge a simple contract.* Any party is discharged from liability to another party by any act or agreement with such party which would discharge a simple contract or the payment of money, e.g., release, rescission, novation, or an accord and satisfaction [3-601(2)].

BANK DEPOSITS AND COLLECTIONS

XVIII. A check is freely transferable and a transferee thereof can become a holder in due course. Therefore, the rules previously discussed that apply to all commercial paper govern the rights and duties of parties to a check. In addition, article 4 of the UCC provides special rules governing the rights and duties between a customer (depositor), the customer's bank, and other banks in the check collection chain. The following terminology is important to the study of bank deposits and collections.

A. *Account* is any account with a bank and includes a checking, time, interest, or savings account [4-104(1)(a)].

B. *Banking day* is that part of any day in which a bank is open to the public for purposes of carrying out its banking functions [4-104(1)(c)].

C. *Clearinghouse* is any association of banks or other payors regularly clearing items [4-104(1)(d)].

D. *Item* is any instrument for the payment of money even though it is not negotiable. It does not include money [4-104(1)(g)], e.g., checks, notes, drafts, matured bonds, or bond coupons.

E. *Settle* is to pay in cash, by clearinghouse settlement, in a charge or credit or as otherwise instructed. Settlement may be provisional or final [4-104(1)(j)].

F. *Customer* is any person having an account with a bank or for whom a bank has agreed to collect items. It includes a bank carrying an account with another bank [4-104(1)(e)].

G. *Depository bank* is the first bank to which an item is transferred for collection notwithstanding that it is also the payor bank [4-105(a)].

H. *Payor bank* is a bank where an item is payable as drawn or accepted [4-105(b)].

I. *Intermediary bank* is any bank, except the depository or payor bank, to which an item is transferred in the course of collection [4-105(c)].

J. *Collecting bank* is any bank handling an item for collection, except the payor bank [4-105(d)].

K. *Presenting bank* is any bank presenting an item, except a payor bank [4-105(e)].

RIGHTS AND DUTIES OF THE PAYOR BANK

XIX. The payor bank (i.e., drawee) owes an absolute duty to its depositor (i.e., drawer) to honor (i.e., pay) checks *only* as ordered by its drawer.

A. *Bank's duty to pay checks.* A payor bank is under a duty to its depositor to pay checks so long as there are sufficient funds in the depositor's account. The bank is liable to a depositor for any actual damages caused by its wrongful dishonor of a check (4-402).

1. A check presented to a drawee bank must be paid prior to the close of business on the day of presentment.
2. A bank is not obligated to pay an uncertified check presented more than six months after its date.
3. A bank may rightfully charge the account of a legally incompetent or deceased depositor prior to the time it acquires actual notice of such incompetence or death (4-405).
   a. Even with knowledge of death, the bank is allowed ten days following the date of death to pay or certify checks drawn by the deceased.

B. *Orders to stop payment of checks.* Proper orders from a depositor to stop payment on checks must be followed by a payor-depository bank (4-403).
1. A stop-payment order is an oral or written notice from a depositor to a depository-payor bank not to pay an instrument when it is presented for payment.
   a. Only the depositor, not a payee or indorser, is given the right to stop payment on an uncertified check.
   b. A bank cannot rightfully follow a stop-payment order on a certified check. Upon certification, the bank becomes primarily liable to any holder of the instrument.
   c. In order for a stop-payment order to be valid, it must be received by the bank at a time and in a manner as to afford the bank reasonable opportunity to comply.
   d. Stop-payment orders have a limited duration [4-403(2)].
      (1) An oral order is effective for fourteen days.
      (2) A written order is effective for six months unless renewed in writing within that period.
2. A bank which pays a check in violation of a proper stop-payment order is liable to its depositor. However, its liability extends only to the amount of actual loss resulting from the bank's failure to obey the order [4-403(3)].

C. A bank is under no duty to certify a check. If it does certify a check, upon the request of either the drawer or the holder, the bank has a duty to pay the amount of the instrument to its holder upon presentment [3-411(1)(2)].
1. Where a holder obtains the certification, the drawer and all prior indorsers on the check are discharged.
2. Where a drawer obtains the certification, the drawer retains secondary liability. However, prior indorsers are discharged.

DEPOSIT AND COLLECTION OF CHECKS

XX. Deposit and collection of checks (see Figures 5-10 and 5-11).
   A. *Deposit of checks.*
   1. In order to hold an indorser or drawer liable on an uncertified check, it must be deposited by the holder within a reasonable time (3-502).
      a. To hold the indorser's secondary liability, a reasonable time is presumed to be seven days after the indorsement [3-503(2)(b)].
      b. To hold a drawer of a check liable, a reasonable time is presumed to be thirty days after date or issue, whichever is later [3-503(2)(a)].
      c. Where a bank is presented with a check more than six months after its date, the bank is under no duty to honor the check unless it is certified (4-404).

FIGURE 5-10 COLLECTION OF CHECKS

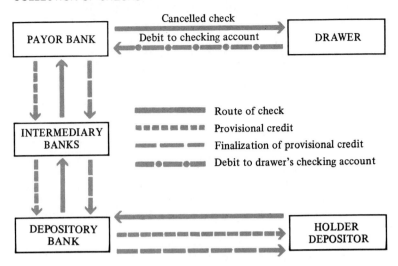

2. Presentment for deposit must be at a reasonable hour during a banking day [3-503(4)].

    a. A bank may fix a cutoff hour of 2 P.M. or later for deposits.

    b. Any deposit made after the bank's cutoff hour may be treated as received at the beginning of the next banking day.

3. A depository bank is entitled to receive the indorsement of a depositor. Where the indorsement is missing, the bank may supply the indorsement itself.

B. *Collection of checks.*

    1. A depositor is usually given a *provisional credit* upon depositing a check in a bank [4-201(1)].

        a. The credit remains provisional until the check deposited has cleared and is honored by the drawee bank.

        b. Because the credit is provisional, the depository bank may charge-back the amount of the check if it fails to clear the collecting process and is not honored by the drawee bank.

            (1) This is true even though the depositor has already drawn checks against the provisional credit.

            (2) The depository bank has a security interest in the deposited check, any accompanying documents, or the proceeds thereof until it receives final payment through the collection process [4-208(1)].

    2. All *collecting banks* are considered to be agents or subagents of the original depositor [4-201(1)].

        a. The original depositor continues to be the owner of the check until it is paid by the drawee bank.

        b. The original depositor bears the risk of loss in the event of nonpayment of the check or insolvency of one of the collecting banks prior to final settlement.

    3. The initial collecting bank is under a duty to the depositor to exercise ordinary care during the collecting process. Such care must be used (4-202):

        a. In presentment of the check for payment;

        b. In sending notice of dishonor;

        c. In settling for the check when final settlement is received by the bank.

FIGURE 5-11   DISHONOR OF CHECKS: REVERSAL OF THE COLLECTION PROCESS

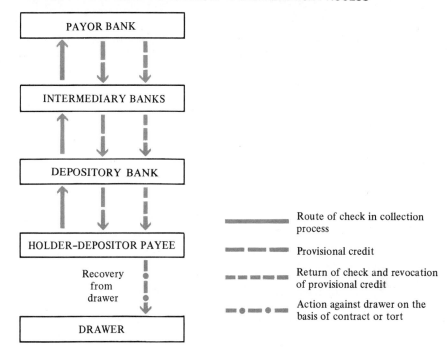

4. Any collecting bank is not liable for the negligence, default, mistake, or insolvency of another bank in the collection process.

PAYMENT OF CHECKS AND FINAL SETTLEMENT

XXI. Payment of checks and final settlement conclude the bank deposit and collection process.

    A. *Payment of checks* (see Figures 5-10 and 5-11).

        1. Any credit that is given by a bank upon receipt of a check is provisional and does not become final until final payment has been made by the payor bank [4-201(1)].

            a. The code adopts the "first-in, first-out" rule, and therefore, the credits first given are held to be the first withdrawn [4-208(2)].

            b. A check is "finally paid" by a payor bank when the bank has done any of the following [4-213(1)]:

                (1) Paid the check in cash;

                (2) Irrevocably settled for the check with a presenting bank;

                (3) Completed the process of posting the check to the presenting bank's account; or

                (4) Made a provisional settlement for a check but subsequently failed to revoke the settlement in proper time and manner.

    B. *Final settlement.*

        1. Final payment of a check by the payor bank automatically changes all provisional credits or settlements of other banks in the collection chain into final payments [4-213(3)].

a. Upon final payment, the agency status between the depositor and the collecting banks is ended.

b. Where there are no provisional credits or settlements between banks in the collection chain, each bank makes payment to the other by means of *bank drafts*.

2. Depositors do not have the right to withdraw provisional credits or settlements. However, current banking practice permits such withdrawals. If the check is dishonored after such withdrawal, the depository bank and each collecting bank has a right to *charge-back* the amount of provisional credit or settlement given [4-212(4)].

   a. A right of charge-back can be exercised only against provisional credits or settlements.

   b. The right to charge-back is terminated when final payment for the check is made.

   c. Each bank must return the check and send notice of charge-back prior to a midnight deadline or within a reasonable time after it learns of the facts.

   d. A failure to charge-back or to claim a refund does not affect other rights of the bank against the customer or any other party.

3. There are certain circumstances in which proceeds can be recovered even after final settlement (4-207).

   a. Each customer or collecting bank who obtains payment or acceptance of an item makes the following *warranties in favor of the payor bank* [4-207(1)]:

   (1) That the customer or collecting bank has good title to the item or is authorized to obtain payment or acceptance on behalf of the party who has a good title;

   (2) That the customer or collecting bank has no knowledge that the signature of the drawer is unauthorized. (*Exception:* This warranty is not made by any customer or collecting bank that is a holder in due course);

   (3) That the item has not been materially altered. (*Exception:* This warranty is not made by any customer or collecting bank that is a holder in due course.)

   b. Each customer or collecting bank who transfers any item and receives settlement makes the following *warranties in favor of its transferee and to any subsequent collecting bank* [4-207(2)]:

   (1) That the customer has good title or is authorized to obtain payment or acceptance on behalf of the party who has good title;

   (2) That all signatures are genuine or authorized;

   (3) That the item has not been materially altered;

   (4) That no defense of any party is good against the customer; and

   (5) That the customer has no knowledge of insolvency proceedings against the drawer or the acceptor.

   c. In addition, each customer and collecting bank that transfers an item and receives settlement engages to take up the item upon dishonor and necessary notice of dishonor [4-207(2)].

   d. A drawee (i.e., payor bank) has an absolute duty to pay a check *only* according to the order of the drawer (customer). On the other hand, the customer has a duty to exercise reasonable care in writing and issuing a check and in examining his or her bank statement and items to discover the unauthorized signature, alterations, or any other irregularities on the check [4-406(1)]. (See Figure 5-12.)

FIGURE 5-12   LIABILITY OF A DRAWEE BANK TO ITS DRAWER

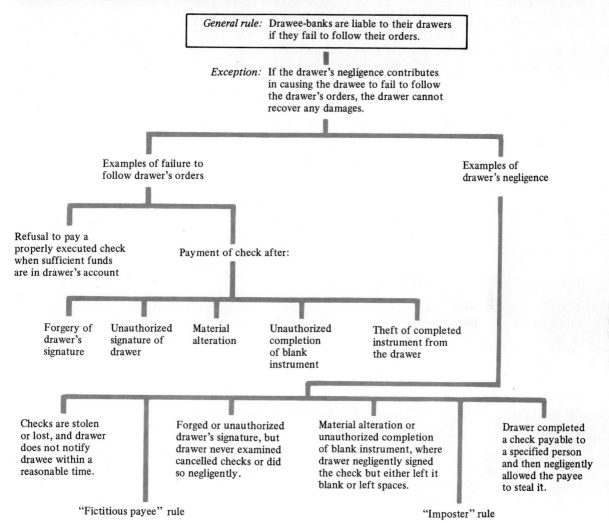

(1) Upon discovery of any such irregularity, the customer must notify the bank promptly.

(2) Failure to examine and notify the bank as required will prevent the customer from asserting a defense of unauthorized signature or any alteration on the item.

(3) Where the customer fails to examine and notify the bank of irregularities but the bank itself failed to exercise ordinary care to discover the irregularities, the customer is not precluded from asserting his or her defenses of unauthorized signature and material alteration on the item.

SELF-QUIZ

To check your understanding of the key words and concepts and the accuracy of your answers to the questions, refer to the text material as referenced by page number.

KEY WORDS AND CONCEPTS

Commercial paper   **148**
Drawer   **148**
Drawee   **148**
Time draft   **148**
Sight draft   **148**
Bank draft   **148**
Trade acceptance   **148**
Check   **148**
Cashier's check   **148**
Certified check   **148**
Maker   **148**
Simple promissory note   **148**
Collateral note   **148**
Installment note   **148**
Mortgage note   **148**
Judgment note   **149**
Dishonor   **162**
Primary liability   **163**
Secondary liability   **163**
Accommodation party   **165**
Imposter rule   **165**
Warranties   **165**
Discharge   **166**
Account   **168**
Banking day   **168**
Clearinghouse   **168**
Certificate of deposit   **149**
Negotiable instrument   **149**
Money   **150**
Order paper   **151**
Bearer paper   **152**
Negotiation   **153**
Special indorsement   **154**
Blank indorsement   **154**
Restrictive indorsement   **154**
Qualified indorsement   **155**
Holder   **156**
Holder in due course   **156**
Personal defense   **158**
Real defense   **158**
Presentment   **161**
Acceptance   **162**
Item   **168**
Settle   **168**

Customer   **168**
Depository bank   **168**
Payor bank   **168**
Intermediary bank   **168**
Collecting bank   **168**
Presenting bank   **168**
Final settlement   **171**
Charge-back   **172**

QUESTIONS

1. Describe the various types of commercial paper. Identify the parties to each instrument. **(148)**
2. List and explain the requirements for negotiability. **(149)**
3. Contrast the rights of a holder in due course of an instrument with those of an assignee. **(156)**
4. What are the rights of a holder in due course? When can a holder in due course be held liable on an instrument? **(158)**
5. What rules are applied to resolve ambiguities on the face of an instrument? **(152)**
6. How is an instrument negotiated? Identify, explain, and give several examples of the different types of indorsements. **(153)**
7. How does one acquire the status of a holder in due course? **(156)**
8. List all of the personal and real defenses available to a party primarily liable. When can they be used and against whom? **(158)**
9. What is presentment? What is its effect and why is it necessary? **(161)**
10. How does presentment for payment differ from presentment for acceptance? **(162)**
11. What are the rights of a holder when an instrument has been dishonored? **(164)**
12. What are the duties of a holder when an instrument has been dishonored? **(162)**
13. Who is primarily liable on an instrument issued payable to an impersonator? **(165)**
14. Describe warranties on transfer and warranties on presentment. To and from whom are these warranties made? **(165)**
15. What is the legal effect of certification of a check by a holder in respect to the liability of the drawee-acceptor, prior indorsers, and the drawer? By a drawer? **(162, 169)**
16. When is an indorser discharged on an instrument? When is a maker or acceptor discharged? **(166)**

17. What are the rights of a bank if it wrongfully pays a check? **(172)**
18. What are the rights and duties of a collecting bank? **(170)**
19. Describe the collection procedure for a check.
20. What is the legal relationship between a depositor and the collecting bank? **(170)**
21. What are the rights and duties of a payor bank? **(168)**

SELECTED QUESTIONS AND UNOFFICIAL ANSWERS

OBJECTIVE QUESTIONS

Select the best answer for each of the following items. Mark only one answer for each item. Answer all items.

NOVEMBER 1980

1. Who among the following can personally qualify as a holder in due course?
   a. A payee.
   b. A reacquirer who was not initially a holder in due course.
   c. A holder to whom the instrument was negotiated as a gift.
   d. A holder who had notice of a defect but who took from a prior holder in due course.

2. The Mechanics Bank refused to pay a check drawn upon it by Clyde, one of its depositors. Which of the reasons listed below is *not* a proper defense for the bank to assert when it refused to pay?
   a. The bank believed the check to be an overdraft as a result of its misdirecting a deposit made by Clyde.
   b. The required indorsement of an intermediary transferee was missing.
   c. Clyde had orally stopped payment on the check.
   d. The party attempting to cash the check did not have proper identification.

3. Your client, Globe, Inc., has in its possession an undated instrument which is payable 30 days after date. It is believed that the instrument was issued on or about August 10, 1980, by Dixie Manufacturing, Inc., to Harding Enterprises in payment of goods purchased. On August 13, 1980, it was negotiated to Desert Products, Inc., and thereafter to Globe on the 15th. Globe took for value, in good faith and without notice of any defense. It has been learned that the goods shipped by Harding to Dixie are defective. Which of the following is correct?
   a. Since the time of payment is indefinite, the instrument is non-negotiable and Globe can *not* qualify as a holder in due course.
   b. By issuing an undated instrument payable 30 days after date, Dixie was reserving the right to avoid liability on it until it filled in or authorized the filling in of the date.
   c. Since the defense involves a rightful rejection of the goods delivered, it is valid against Globe.
   d. Globe can validly fill in the date and will qualify as a holder in due course.

4. A CPA's client has an instrument which contains certain ambiguities or deficiencies. In construing the instrument, which of the following is *incorrect*?
   a. Where there is doubt whether the instrument is a draft or a note, the holder may treat it as either.
   b. Handwritten terms control typewritten and printed terms, and typewritten terms control printed terms.
   c. An instrument which is payable only upon the happening of an event that is uncertain as to the time of its occurrence is payable at a definite time if the event has occurred.
   d. The fact that the instrument is antedated will not affect the instrument's negotiability.

5. Smith buys a TV set from the ABC Appliance Store and pays for the set with a check. Later in the day Smith finds a better model for the same price at another store. Smith immediately calls ABC trying to cancel the sale. ABC tells Smith that they are holding him to the sale and have negotiated the check to their wholesaler, Glenn Company, as a partial payment on inventory purchases. Smith telephones his bank, the Union Trust Bank, and orders the bank to stop payment on the check. Which of the following statements is correct?
   a. If Glenn can prove it is a holder in due course, the drawee bank, Union Trust, must honor Smith's check.
   b. Union Trust is *not* bound or liable for Smith's stop payment order unless the order is placed in writing.
   c. If Union Trust mistakenly pays Smith's check

two days after receiving the stop order, the bank will *not* be liable.

d. Glenn can *not* hold Smith liable on the check.

6. Marshall Franks purchased $1,050 worth of inventory for his business from Micro Enterprises. Micro insisted on the signature of Franks' former partner, Hobart, before credit would be extended. Hobart reluctantly signed. Franks delivered the following instrument to Micro:

January 15, 1980

We, the undersigned, do hereby promise to pay to the order of Micro Enterprises, Inc., One Thousand and Fifty Dollars ($1,050.00) on the 15th of April, 1980.

Marshall Franks
Marshall Franks

Norman Hobart
Norman Hobart

Memo:
N. Hobart signed as an
accommodation for Franks

Franks defaulted on the due date. Which of the following is correct?

a. The instrument is non-negotiable.

b. Hobart is liable on the instrument but only for $525.

c. Since it was known to Micro that Hobart signed as an accommodation party, Micro must first proceed against Franks.

d. Hobart is liable on the instrument for the full amount and is obligated to satisfy it immediately upon default.

7. Rapid Delivery, Inc., has in its possession the following instrument which it purchased for value.

March 1, 1980

Thirty days from date, I, Harold Kales, do hereby promise to pay Ronald Green four hundred dollars and no cents ($400.00). This note is given for value received.

Harold Kales
Harold Kales

Which of the following is correct?

a. The instrument is negotiable.

b. The instrument is non-negotiable, and therefore Rapid has obtained no rights on the instrument.

c. Rapid is an assignee of the instrument and has the same rights as the assignor had on it.

d. The instrument is non-transferable on its face.

8. Harrison obtained from Bristow his $11,500 check drawn on the Union National Bank in payment for bogus uranium stock. He immediately negotiated it by a blank indorsement to Dunlop in return for $1,000 in cash and her check for $10,400. Dunlop qualified as a holder in due course. She deposited the check in her checking account in the Oceanside Bank. Upon discovering that the stock was bogus, Bristow notified Union National to stop payment on his check, which it did. The check was returned to Oceanside Bank, which in turn debited Dunlop's account and returned the check to her. Which of the following statements is correct?

a. Dunlop can collect from Union National Bank since Bristow's stop payment order was invalid in that the defense was only a personal defense.

b. Oceanside's debiting of Dunlop's account was improper since she qualified as a holder in due course.

c. Dunlop can recover $11,500 from Bristow despite the stop order, since she qualified as a holder in due course.

d. Dunlop will be entitled to collect only $1,000.

9. An otherwise valid negotiable bearer note is signed with the forged signature of Darby. Archer, who believed he knew Darby's signature, bought the note in good faith from Harding, the forger. Archer transferred the note without indorsement to Barker, in partial payment of a debt. Barker then sold the note to Chase for 80% of its face amount and delivered it without indorsement. When Chase presented the note for payment at maturity, Darby refused to honor it, pleading forgery. Chase gave proper notice of dishonor to Barker and to Archer. Which of the following statements best describes the situation from Chase's standpoint?

a. Chase can *not* qualify as a holder in due course for the reason that he did *not* pay face value for the note.

b. Chase can hold Barker liable on the ground that Barker warranted to Chase that neither Darby nor Archer had any defense valid against Barker.

c. Chase can hold Archer liable on the ground that

Archer warranted to Chase that Darby's signature was genuine.

d. Chase can *not* hold Harding, the forger, liable on the note because his signature does not appear on it and thus, he made no warranties to Chase.

46. Anderson agreed to purchase Parker's real property. Anderson's purchase was dependent upon his being able to sell certain real property that he owned. Anderson gave Parker an instrument for the purchase price. Assuming the instrument is otherwise negotiable, which one of the statements below, written on the face of the instrument, will render it non-negotiable?
a. A statement that Parker's cashing or indorsing the instrument acknowledges full satisfaction of Anderson's obligation.
b. A statement that payment of the instrument is contingent upon Anderson's sale of his real property.
c. A statement that the instrument is secured by a first mortgage on Parker's property and that upon default in payment the entire amount of the instrument is due.
d. A statement that the instrument is subject to the usual implied and constructive conditions applicable to such transactions.

MAY 1980

15. Mask stole one of Bloom's checks. The check was already signed by Bloom and made payable to Duval. The check was drawn on United Trust Company. Mask forged Duval's signature on the back of the check and cashed the check at the Corner Check Cashing Company which in turn deposited it with its bank, Town National Bank of Toka. Town National proceeded to collect on the check from United. None of the parties mentioned was negligent. Who will bear the loss assuming the amount *cannot* be recovered from Mask?
a. Bloom.
b. Duval.
c. United Trust Company.
d. Corner Check Cashing Company.

19. Gomer developed a fraudulent system whereby he could obtain checks payable to the order of certain repairmen who serviced various large corporations. Gomer observed the delivery trucks of repairmen who did business with the corporations, and then he submitted bills on the bogus letterhead of the repairmen to the selected large corporations. The return envelope for payment indicated a local post office box. When the checks arrived, Gomer would forge the payees' signatures and cash the checks. The parties cashing the checks are holders in due course. Who will bear the loss assuming the amount *cannot* be recovered from Gomer?
a. The defrauded corporations.
b. The drawee banks.
c. Intermediate parties who indorsed the instruments for collection.
d. The ultimate recipients of the proceeds of the checks even though they are holders in due course.

21. An instrument is order paper when it is
a. Payable to the order of cash on its face.
b. Indorsed to John Smith by Marvin Frank, the payee.
c. Payable to the order of Marvin Frank and indorsed in blank.
d. Payable to a specified person or bearer.

22. Barber has in his possession a negotiable instrument which he purchased in good faith and for value. The drawer of the instrument stopped payment on it and has asserted that Barber does *not* qualify as a holder in due course since the instrument is overdue. In determining whether the instrument is overdue, which of the following is *incorrect*?
a. A reasonable time for a check drawn and payable in the United States is presumed to be 30 days after issue.
b. A reasonable time for a check drawn and payable in the United States is presumed to be 20 days after the last negotiation.
c. All demand instruments, other than checks, are *not* overdue until a reasonable time after their issue has elapsed.
d. The instrument will be deemed to be overdue if a demand for payment had been made and Barber knew this.

23. A formal protest of dishonor must be made in order to hold the drawer or indorsers liable for all of the following *foreign* instruments *except*
a. Drafts.
b. Promissory notes.
c. Trade acceptances.
d. Checks.

24. Dodson drew a check to the order of Swanson for services which were partially rendered. The check was left blank because the exact amount was *not* known at the time of issue. The understanding between Dodson and Swanson was that Swanson would complete the job, fill in the check for the exact amount due which was estimated as $650, but which would in no event exceed $700. Swanson failed to complete the work as agreed, but filled in the amount of the check for $1,000. He then negotiated it to Irwin in satisfaction of a $500 debt, with the balance paid to Swanson in cash. Swanson has disappeared, Dodson stopped payment and Irwin is seeking to collect the $1,000 from Dodson. What will Irwin be able to collect?

a. Nothing.
b. $500.
c. $700.
d. $1,000.

25. A holder in due course will take an instrument free from which of the following defenses?
a. Claims of ownership on the part of other persons.
b. Infancy of the maker or drawer.
c. Discharge in insolvency proceedings.
d. The forged signature of the maker or drawer.

30. Robb stole one of Markum's blank checks, made it payable to himself, and forged Markum's signature to it. The check was drawn on the Unity Trust Company. Robb cashed the check at the Friendly Check Cashing Company which in turn deposited it with its bank, the Farmer's National. Farmer's National proceeded to collect on the check from Unity Trust. The theft and forgery were quickly discovered by Markum who promptly notified Unity. None of the parties mentioned was negligent. Who will bear the loss, assuming the amount *cannot* be recovered from Robb?

a. Markum.
b. Unity Trust Company.
c. Friendly Check Cashing Company.
d. Farmer's National.

MAY 1979

25. Martindale Retail Fish Stores, Inc., purchased a large quantity of fish from the Seashore Fish Wholesalers. The exact amount was *not* ascertainable at the moment, and Martindale, rather than waiting for the exact amount, gave Seashore a check which was blank as to the amount. Seashore promised *not* to fill in any amount until it had talked to Martindale's purchasing agent and had the amount approved. Seashore disregarded this agreement and filled in an amount that was $300 in excess of the correct price. The instrument was promptly negotiated to Clambake & Company, one of Seashore's persistent creditors, in payment of an account due. Martindale promptly stopped payment. For what amount will Martindale be liable to Clambake? Why?

a. Nothing because Martindale can assert the real defense of material alteration.
b. Nothing because Clambake did not give value and the stop order is effective against it.
c. Only the correct amount because the wrongful filling in of the check for the $300 excess amount was illegal.
d. The full amount because the check is in the hands of a holder in due course.

26. Filbert Corporation has in its possession an instrument which Groves, the maker, assured Filbert was negotiable. The instrument contains several clauses which are *not* typically contained in such an instrument, and Filbert is *not* familiar with their legal effect. Which of the following will adversely affect the negotiability of the instrument?

a. A promise to maintain collateral and to provide additional collateral if the value of existing collateral decreases.
b. A term authorizing the confession of judgment on the instrument if *not* paid when due.
c. A statement to the effect that the instrument arises out of the November 1, 1978, sale of goods by Filbert to Groves.
d. A statement that it is payable only out of the proceeds from the resale of the goods sold by Filbert to Groves on November 1, 1978.

Answers to Objective Questions

November 1980			May 1980	
1. a	**6.** d		**15.** d	**23.** b
2. a	**7.** c		**19.** a	**24.** d
3. d	**8.** c		**21.** b	**25.** a
4. c	**9.** b		**22.** b	**30.** b
5. c	**46.** b			

May 1979	
25. d	**26.** d

Explanation of Answers to Objective Questions

NOVEMBER 1980

1. (a) The correct answer is (a) since the payee is the only holder who can meet the requirements of a holder in due course. A holder in due course must be a holder who gives executed value for the instrument (cannot be a gift). The holder in due course may have no knowledge of the fact that the instrument (principal only) is overdue nor knowledge of any defense on the instrument when he or she receives it. A holder in due course must also take the instrument in good faith. Answer (b) is incorrect since a holder who does not qualify as a holder in due course cannot better his rights by transferring the instrument through a HIDC. Answer (c) is incorrect because the holder failed to give value. The holder in answer (d) cannot qualify as HIDC since he has knowledge of a defense, but the holder does receive the rights of a HIDC since he acquired the instrument through a HIDC.

2. (a) Answer (a) is not a proper defense for the bank to assert when it refused to pay. The bank is at fault by misdirecting the funds and has a duty to pay the check. Answers (b), (c), and (d) are all proper defenses for the bank. The oral stop payment order in answer (c) would effectively keep the bank from paying the check for a 14 day period.

3. (d) An undated note is considered dated as of the day of issue. Thus Globe, the holder, has the authority to fill in the date with the day of issuance. After dating the instrument, Globe meets all the requirements of a HIDC. The fact that Globe received an undated instrument will not destroy its HIDC status. The time of payment is considered definite as soon as the appropriate date is entered. Answer (c) describes a personal defense (failure of consideration) which would not be good against a HIDC.

4. (c) Answer (c) is the statement that is incorrect. In order to qualify as a draft, an instrument must be payable on demand or at a definite time. In the event the instrument rests on an uncertainty with respect to time (i.e., payable on the death of a certain person) it is nonnegotiable. To qualify as a negotiable instrument, one must be able to determine a definite time for payment from the face of the instrument. Answers (a), (b) and (d) all state proper rules of construction.

5. (c) The correct answer is (c) since the bank is only liable to the drawer if failure to obey stop payment order caused the drawer a loss. Since Smith has no grounds for rescinding the sale, the Union Trust bank has no liability. Answer (a) is incorrect since a payee has no right to compel payment of a check by drawee bank. There is no privity of contract between the payee and drawee bank. Answer (b) is incorrect because the stop payment order can be oral or written. An oral order is effective for 14 days and a written order is effective for 6 months. A stop payment order does not destroy the drawer's liability on the instrument unless he has a valid defense; therefore, answer (d) is false.

6. (d) An accommodating party (Hobart) is someone who lends his name to the instrument as security. Such a party is liable in the position he signs the instrument. In this case, Hobart signed as a co-maker and is therefore, primarily liable for the face value of the instrument. Micro can go against either Franks or Hobart on the due date. Hobart will be able to seek redress against Franks, the accommodated party. Therefore, answer (d) is correct. The instrument meets all the requirements of negotiability, thus answer (a) is incorrect.

7. (c) Before an instrument qualifies as a negotiable instrument it must be payable to order or to bearer. This instrument does not contain these words of negotiability; thus the law of assignments applies to the transfer of this nonnegotiable instrument. The assignee has the same rights as the assignor concerning this instrument. Thus answer (c) is correct.

8. (c) The only defenses good against a holder in due course are real defenses. In this case the only defense Bristow can assert is fraud in the inducement, which is a personal defense, not good against a holder in due course. As a result, answer (c) is correct and Dunlop can recover the full $11,500 from Bristow. Bristow's only recourse will be against Harrison. Answer (a) is incorrect since the stop payment order requires the bank to refuse payment of the instrument. Oceanside's actions were proper under the circumstances making answer (b) incorrect. Answer (d) is also incorrect since Dunlop would be HIDC to the face value of the instrument since his check constitutes giving executed value for a negotiable instrument.

9. (b) Barker, having received value for the instrument, has warranty liability to Chase, the immediate holder. Barker grants five warranties, one of which is that no defense is good on the instrument. Answer (b) is correct since this warranty was breached. If a holder performs the full agreed upon consideration or value promised for the instrument, he is a holder in due course to the face value of the instrument. This makes answer (a) incorrect. Answer (c) is incorrect because Archer's failure to endorse the instrument only extends his warranty liability (including the warranty that states all signatures are genuine) to the immediate holder, Barker. Answer (d) is incorrect since Harding is liable for the forgery he placed on the instrument.

46. (b) Answer (b) will render the instrument nonnegotiable since such a statement would cause the instrument to be conditional by making payment dependent on an uncertain event. Answer (d) would not be placing any conditions on the instrument that would not already be present by operation of law. If the instrument states that it is "subject to" another agreement then this would condition the promise or order and the instrument would be nonnegotiable. Normally a negotiable instrument can contain no other promise except the promise to pay money. However, the negotiable character of the instrument will not be destroyed by a second promise that concerns security for the instrument such as answer (c).

MAY 1980

15. (d) Corner Check Cashing Company must bear the loss because as a holder obtaining payment, it warrants that it has good title to the instrument. However, it does not have good title because the forgery prevented good title from passing. Therefore answers (a) and (c) are incorrect because of Corner Check Cashing Company's warranty of good title. Answer (b) is incorrect because Duval has a real defense in that his indorsement was forged. Corner Check Cashing Company's only recourse is to recover from Mask.

19. (a) Normally forgeries of the payee's signature would be sufficient to relieve the defrauded corporations of any liability on these instruments. However, a drawer who voluntarily transfers payment to an imposter (Gomer) must bear the loss if a holder in due course subsequently tries to collect. There-

fore, answer (a) is correct. Forgery is usually a real defense that would be good against all subsequent holders in due course but the imposter exception would allow the banks, intermediate parties and the recipients to avoid the loss. The rationale for such a result is the fact that the defrauded corporations were in the best position to keep the defense (forgery) from occurring.

21. (b) Answer (b) is correct because this is a special indorsement. An instrument is order paper if payable to the order of a named party on the face or has as its last indorsement a special indorsement. Answer (a) is incorrect because an instrument payable to the order of cash or bearer creates bearer paper. In determining the type of paper, the indorsements on the back are considered first. Therefore, answer (c) is incorrect since a blank indorsement creates bearer paper. Answer (d) is incorrect because a special indorsement is payable to a named person and signed by the indorser.

22. (b) Under the law of commercial paper to qualify as a holder in due course, the holder must have no knowledge that the instrument is overdue. A check is considered overdue if outstanding more than 30 days after issue. All other demand instruments are overdue after a reasonable time has elapsed, or if the holder is aware demand has been made for payment. Therefore, answer (b) is incorrect because an instrument payable on its face to a specified person or bearer creates bearer paper (instead of order paper), because a special indorsement is payable to a named person and signed by the indorser.

23. (b) A formal protest of dishonor is only necessary on drafts drawn or payable outside the United States. Since checks and trade acceptances are forms of a draft, formal protest of dishonor would be required. This is not true of a promissory note.

24. (d) Irwin qualifies as a holder in due course and therefore can defeat any personal defense. The unauthorized completion of an incomplete instrument is a personal defense. Dodson's negligence precludes his claiming a real defense. Irwin can collect the full $1,000 from Dodson. Dodson's only recourse would be to sue Swanson.

25. (a) A holder in due course takes an instrument free of all personal defenses, but not real defenses.

Infancy, forgery of a necessary signature and discharge in bankruptcy are real defenses and are available against a holder in due course. Answer (a) is correct because the only personal defense present in the possible answers is claims of ownership on the part of other persons.

30. (b) If the drawee bank (Unity Trust Company) pays a check on which the drawer's signature (Markum) was forged, the bank is bound by the acceptance and the drawee can only recover the money paid from the forger (Robb). Normally a person who presents an instrument for payment makes three warranties. These warranties are: warranty of title; warranty of no knowledge that the signature of the drawer is unauthorized; warranty of no material alterations. However, a holder in due course or someone with the rights of a holder in due course does not warrant to the drawee bank that the drawer's signature is genuine because the drawer bank is in a better position to determine the genuineness of the drawer's signature. Therefore, the drawee bank should bear the loss.

MAY 1979

25. (d) Even though an unauthorized completion of the check is a real defense, a holder in due course may enforce the check as completed. Thus Martindale will be liable to Clambake for the full amount of the check. Therefore, answers (a) and (c) are incorrect. Answer (b) is incorrect because Clambake did give value since it accepted the check in payment of an account due, and the payment of an antecedent debt is considered to be value for purposes of negotiable instruments.

26. (d) A clause in an instrument stating that it is payable only out of the proceeds from the resale of certain goods would adversely affect the negotiability of the instrument, i.e., the instrument is not unconditional if payment is limited to a particular source. An instrument must be unconditional to be negotiable.

ESSAY QUESTIONS AND ANSWERS

MAY 1981 (Estimated time: 15 to 20 minutes)

2. Part a. Oliver gave Morton his 90-day negotiable promissory note for $10,000 as a partial payment for the purchase of Morton's business.

Morton had submitted materially false unaudited financial statements to Oliver in the course of establishing the purchase price of the business. Morton also made various false statements about the business' value. For example, he materially misstated the size of the backlog of orders. Morton promptly negotiated the note to Harrison who purchased it in good faith for $9,500, giving Morton $5,000 in cash, a check for $3,500 payable to him which he indorsed in blank and an oral promise to pay the balance within 5 days. Before making the final payment to Morton, Harrison learned of the fraudulent circumstances under which the negotiable promissory note for $10,000 had been obtained. Morton has disappeared and the balance due him was never paid. Oliver refuses to pay the note.

Required Answer the following, setting forth reasons for any conclusions stated.

In the subsequent suit brought by Harrison against Oliver, who will prevail?

Answer Harrison will prevail, but only to the extent of "value," here $8,500, given for the negotiable promissory note. The primary issue in the case is the "value" requirement for holding in due course. The facts reveal that Harrison purchased the instrument in good faith, that it was not overdue, and, at the time the negotiation took place, Harrison had no knowledge of the fraudulent circumstances under which the instrument was originally obtained from Oliver. The facts indicate that the note was negotiable and that the negotiation requirement was satisfied.

The Uniform Commercial Code section dealing with "taking for value" provides that a holder, here Harrison, takes for value to the extent that the agreed consideration has been performed. Certainly, the payment of the $5,000 in cash constitutes value. The code further provides that when a holder gives a negotiable instrument for the instrument received, he has given value. Although this provision is primarily concerned with the giving of one's own negotiable instrument, it is obvious that the negotiation of another's negotiable instrument as payment is value. However, the promise to pay an agreed consideration is not value even though it constitutes consideration.

2. Part b. McCarthy, a holder in due course, presented a check to the First National Bank, the drawee bank named on the face of the instrument.

The signature of the drawer, Williams, was forged by Nash who took the check from the bottom of Williams' check book along with a cancelled check in the course of burglarizing Williams' apartment. The bank examined the signature of the drawer carefully, but the signature was such an artful forgery of the drawer's signature that only a handwriting expert could have detected a difference. The bank therefore paid the check. The check was promptly returned to Williams, but he did not discover the forgery until thirteen months after the check was returned to him.

Required Answer the following, setting forth reasons for any conclusions stated.

1. Williams seeks to compel the bank to credit his account for the loss. Will he prevail?
2. The facts are the same as above, but you are to assume that the bank discovered the forgery before returning the check to Williams and credited his account. Can the bank in turn collect from McCarthy the $1,000 paid to McCarthy?
3. Would your answers to 1 and 2 above be modified if the forged signature was that of the payee or an indorser rather than the signature of the drawer?

Answer

1. No. Williams will not prevail. The Uniform Commercial Code imposes upon the depositor the responsibility for reasonable care and promptness in discovering and reporting his unauthorized signature. In any case, the depositor must discover and report his unauthorized signature within one year from the time the items (checks) are made available to him. The latter rule applies irrespective of lack of care on the part of either the bank or depositor. This absolute rule is based in part upon the rationale that, after certain periods of time have elapsed in respect to commercial transactions, finality is the most important factor to be considered. Thus, after this amount of time has elapsed, existing expectations and relations are not to be altered.

2. No. The bank cannot collect from McCarthy. The Uniform Commercial Code places the burden upon the bank to know at its peril the signature of its drawer. Therefore, when the bank has paid on the forged signature of a depositor, it cannot recover the loss by seeking collection from a party who has received payment in good faith.

3. The first answer (b.1.) would be changed in that the law allows the depositor a three-year period in which to discover the forged signature of the payee or an indorser. Thus, if both the bank and depositor are not negligent (as it would appear from the excellence of the forgery), the loss rests with the bank. However, if it can be shown that the depositor was negligent (for example, he disregarded a notice from the proper party that he had not received payment), the bank will prevail if it was in no way negligent.

The restated circumstances also change the second answer (b.2.) A bank is not deemed to know the signatures of indorsers; therefore, the bank may recover its loss from McCarthy, the party collecting on the item. Section 3-417 of the Uniform Commercial Code provides that a party receiving payment on the instrument warrants to the payor that he has good title to the instrument.

MAY 1978 (Estimated time: 25 to 30 minutes)

2. Part a. Your CPA firm was engaged to audit the Meglo Corporation. During the audit you examined the following instrument:

April 2, 1977

Charles Noreen
21 West 21st Street
St. Louis, Missouri

I, Charles Noreen, do hereby promise to pay to Roger Smith, Two Thousand Dollars ($2,000) one year from date, with 8% interest upon due presentment.

FOR: Payment for used IBM typewriters.

Charles Noreen

Meglo purchased the instrument from Smith on April 10, 1977, for $1,700. Meglo received the instrument with Smith's signature and the words "Pay to the order of Meglo Corporation" on the back. Upon maturity, Meglo presented the instrument to Noreen, who refused to pay. Noreen alleged that the typewriters were defective and did not satisfy certain warranties given in connection with the purchase of the used IBM typewriters which were guaranteed for one year. Noreen had promptly notified Smith of this fact and had told him he would not pay the full amount due.

Required Answer the following, setting forth reasons for any conclusions stated.

1. Is the instrument in question negotiable commercial paper?
2. Assuming that the instrument is negotiable, does Meglo qualify as a holder in due course entitled to collect the full $2,000?
3. Assuming that the instrument is negotiable, is Noreen's defense valid against a holder in due course?
4. Assuming that the instrument is nonnegotiable, what is the legal effect of the transfer by Smith to Meglo?

Answer

1. No. Although it meets all of the other requisites of negotiability pursuant to the Uniform Commercial Code, it lacks the specific terminology of negotiability. That is, it is neither payable to Smith's "order" nor payable to "bearer." Consequently, it is a nonnegotiable promissory note. This defect is not cured by Smith's indorsement despite the fact he used the words "pay to the order of." The indication of the nature of the transaction is legally insignificant.

2. Yes. The note is not overdue, and Meglo took it for value and without notice or knowledge of any defect in it. The only possible assertion that could be made by Noreen to defeat Meglo's status as a holder in due course is that the size of the discount was so large as to indicate a lack of good faith. In the absence of any further information, a $300 discount on a one-year note such as this is not of such amount as to suggest a lack of good faith. Under these circumstances Meglo would collect the full $2,000.

3. No. It is a mere personal defense and as such would not prevail against a subsequent holder in due course.

4. Since the instrument is not negotiable it cannot be "negotiated" to another person so as to enable him to qualify as a holder in due course. However, the transferor does assign all his rights to collect on the promise. Therefore, even if the typewriters were defective, Meglo would be entitled to sue on the promise and collect the amount due, decreased by damages for breach of warranty.

2. Part b. Marvin Farber cashed a check for Harold Kern which was made to the order of Charles Walker by Marglow Investments & Se-

curities. The check had the following indorsements on the back:

1. *Charles Walker*
2. without recourse
   Doris Williamson
3. Pay to the order of Harold Kern
   Jack Dixon
4. Pay to the order of Marvin Farber

Kern neglected to sign his indorsement when he gave the check to Farber, and Farber did not notice this until the following day. Before Farber could locate Kern and obtain his signature, Farber learned that Walker had fraudulently obtained the check from Marglow (the drawer). Farber finally located Kern and obtained his signature. Farber promptly indorsed the check in blank and cashed it at National Bank. National Bank presented the check for payment through normal banking channels, but it was dishonored by Marglow's bank pursuant to a valid stop order. National Bank contacted Farber and informed him of the situation. Farber repaid the amount and the check was returned to him with National Bank's blank indorsement on the back.

Required Answer the following, setting forth reasons for any conclusions stated.

1. Identify the type of indorsement and indicate the liability for each indorsement numbered 1, 2, and 3 above.
2. Will Farber prevail in a legal action seeking payment of the check by Marglow?

Answer

1. Walker (indorsement 1) is a blank indorser. A blank indorsement specifies no particular indorsee and may consist of a mere signature. Williamson (indorsement 2) is a "without recourse" or qualified indorser. As such, she does not guarantee payment. Furthermore, the warranty that no defense of any party is good against the indorser, which is given by other indorsers, is limited by a without-recourse indorsement to a warranty that *the indorser has no knowledge of such defense*.

Dixon (indorsement 3) is a special indorser. A special indorsement specifies the person to whom or to whose order it makes the instrument payable.

Any instrument specially indorsed becomes payable to the order of the special indorsee and may be further negotiated only by that indorsement.

Indorsers in general have contract liability and also give certain warranties upon transfer. The Uniform Commercial Code provides that, unless otherwise agreed, indorsers are liable to one another in the order in which they indorse. This is presumed to be the order in which their signatures appear on the instrument. Both blank and special indorsers state that upon dishonor and notice, they will pay the instrument according to its tenor at the time of their indorsement to the holder or any subsequent indorser. The obligation is, in effect, a contractual undertaking to act as a guarantor. Walker and Dixon are subject to this liability; Williamson is not.

2. Yes. Although Farber cannot personally qualify as a holder in due course because he had notice of the defense (fraud) asserted by Marglow prior to the completion of the negotiation, he can assert the standing of his transferor (Kern). Thus Farber will prevail.

Farber could not assert a subsequent indorser-transferor's standing as a holder in due course (his bank's) in that the Uniform Commercial Code provides that a prior holder who had notice of a defense or claim against him cannot improve his position by taking it from a later holder in due course.

CHAPTER

6

Secured Transactions

The following is a generalized listing of subjects to be tested through the May 1983 Uniform CPA Examination.

Article 9 (Secured Transactions) of the Uniform Commercial Code (as amended in 1972), which pertains to security in personal property, is covered under this topic. The Article applies to personal property used as security for a debt and to outright sales of accounts receivable and chattel paper. Creation, attachment, and perfection of a security interest, and the various priorities and rights of creditors and third parties are included.[1]

The AICPA Board of Examiners has adopted a new content specification outline for the business law section of the Uniform CPA Examination, *to be effective with the November 1983 examination*. The outline lists the following topics to be tested under the title "Secured Transactions."

    D. Secured Transactions
        1. Attachment of Security Agreements
        2. Perfection of Security Interests
        3. Priorities
        4. Rights of Debtors, Creditors, and Third Parties[2]

I. Whenever goods are sold and delivered, services are rendered, or money is lent in exchange for a promise to pay in the future, a credit transaction takes place.
    A. If some form of collateral is given as security for payment of a debt or other obligation, the credit is a *secured credit*.
    B. Where the credit is given on the debtor's unsupported promise to pay, the credit is an *unsecured credit*.

---

[1] AICPA, *Information for CPA Candidates*, Copyright © 1975, 1979, by the American Institute of Certified Public Accountants, Inc.
[2] AICPA, *Business Law—Content Specification Outline*, approved by the AICPA Board of Examiners on August 31, 1981.

PRE-UCC SECURED CREDIT DEVICES

II. The following secured credit devices are identified below by their pre-UCC legal names. Under the UCC, each is now known as a "secured transaction."

    A. *Pledge* is a bailment of personal property as security for some debt or obligation. For example, Farmer transferred his tractor to Bank as security for a loan.

    B. *Bill of sale with a disfeasance clause* is a sale wherein one person transfers title to goods to another on the condition that if the goods are not paid for, title reverts to the seller.

    C. *Chattel mortgage* is a transfer of some legal or equitable right in personal property or creation of a lien thereon as security for payment of money or performance of some act. The debtor is the owner of the personal property mortgaged subject to the creditor's rights or lien.

    D. *Conditional sale* is a sale in which the seller reserves title to the goods, although possession is delivered to the buyer, until the purchase price is paid.

UCC SECURITY INTERESTS

III. Generally article 9 of the UCC codifies and expands the precode chattel security law to provide a simplified and unified structure of secured financing transactions [9-102(2)].

    A. Its purpose is to replace different precode security devices with a single device known as a security interest and to establish a uniform set of laws and nomenclature for all secured transactions. (See Figure 6-1.)

    B. Article 9 of the code applies to any transaction, regardless of its form, in which the parties intended to create a security interest in personal property or fixtures [9-102(1)(a)].

    C. Refer to Figure 6-2 for an overview of the fundamentals associated with a secured transaction.

DEFINITIONS

IV. Definitions under the UCC.

    A. *Security interest* is an interest in personal property or fixtures which secures a debt or other obligation [1-201(37)].

    B. *Debtor* is any person who has subjected personal property as security for a debt or other obligation [9-105(1)(d)].

    C. *Secured party* is any person in whose favor there is security interest [9-105(1)(m)].

    D. *Collateral* is any personal property which is subject to the security interest [9-105(c)].

    E. *Security agreement* is an agreement which invests a creditor with a security interest in the personal property or fixtures of a debtor [9-105(1)(l)].

FIGURE 6-1 A SECURED TRANSACTION

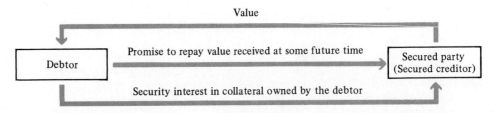

FIGURE 6-2 FUNDAMENTALS OF SECURED TRANSACTIONS

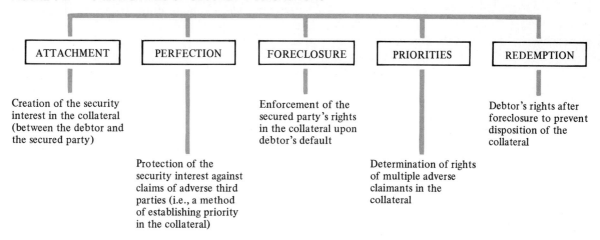

F. *Buyer in the ordinary course of business* is a person who, in good faith and without knowledge of adverse ownership rights or a security interest in a third party, buys goods in the ordinary course of business from a person in the business of selling goods of that kind [1-201(9)].

G. *Purchase-money security transaction* is a sale in which a seller retains an interest in the goods sold to a buyer to secure all or part of the purchase price or in which a creditor advances funds or incurs obligations to enable a debtor to acquire rights in or to use the collateral if such value is in fact so used (9-107).

H. *After-acquired property* is personal property acquired by a debtor after a security interest has attached which itself becomes subject to the previously created security interest [9-104(1)].

I. *Floating lien* is a security interest in constantly changing collateral, e.g., inventory, accounts receivable, or contract rights.

J. *Attachment* is the creation of an enforceable security interest between the debtor and the secured party [9-203(1)(2)].

K. *Proceeds* includes whatever is received upon the sale, exchange, collection, or other disposition of collateral or proceeds. Insurance payable by reason of loss or damage to the collateral is proceeds, except to the extent that it is payable to a person other than a party to the security agreement. Money, checks, and deposit accounts are "cash proceeds." All other proceeds are "noncash proceeds" [9-306(1)].

CLASSIFICATION OF COLLATERAL

V. Collateral under the UCC is classified as follows:

    A. *Tangibles* include all property or "goods" which are movable at the time the security interest attaches, including fixtures to real estate, minerals before extraction, and timber to be removed under a contract for sale [9-105(1)(h)].

        1. *"Goods"* are further classified into consumer goods, farm products, inventory, and equipment. The same "good" may fall into different classifications at different times, depending on the principal use to which the property is subjected at the time or the nature of the good.

a. *Consumer goods* are goods used or purchased primarily for personal, family, or household use, e.g., appliances, household furniture, recreational vehicles, and automobiles used for personal reasons [9-109(1)].

b. *Farm products* are crops, livestock, or supplies used or produced in farming operations, or products of crops or livestock (ginned cotton, wool-clip, maple syrup, milk and eggs, or unborn young of animals) so long as they are still in possession of the debtor engaged in farming [9-109(3)].

c. *Inventory.* Goods are inventory if (1) they are held by a person for sale or lease or to be furnished under contracts of service; (2) they are raw materials or work in process; or (3) they are materials used or consumed in a business, i.e., retailer's goods, wholesaler's goods, and manufacturer's materials used or consumed in business [9-109(4)], e.g., packages, cartons, or fuel.

d. *Equipment* is goods used or purchased for use primarily in business (including farming or a profession), e.g., a lawyer's office furniture, machinery in a factory, or a furniture delivery truck [9-109(2)].

B. *Intangibles.* This classification includes:

1. *Instruments*, commercial paper, and investment securities such as notes, drafts, checks, bonds, and stocks [9-105(1)(i)];

2. *Documents of title*, such as bills of lading and warehouse receipts [2-105(f)];

3. *Accounts* are rights to payment carried on open accounts for goods sold or leased or services rendered which are *not evidenced by* instruments or chattel paper whether or not they have been earned by performance. The UCC no longer distinguishes between accounts receivable and contract rights (9-306).

4. *General intangibles*, such as franchises, patents, literary royalty rights, and copyrights (9-106);

5. *Chattel paper* is any writing or writings which evidences both a debt and security interest in, or lease of, specific goods, e.g., the retail installment contract itself [9-105(b)];

6. *Money* is a medium of exchange authorized or adopted by a domestic or foreign government as a part of its currency [1-201(24)].

C. *Fixtures.* Goods are fixtures "when they become so related to particular real estate that an interest in them arises under real estate law" [9-313(1)]. That is, they are legally considered part of the real estate, e.g., kitchen cabinets and built-in microwave oven, a central air-conditioning unit, an overhead crane in a warehouse.

ATTACHMENT OF SECURITY INTERESTS

VI. Obtaining an enforceable security interest under the UCC (between the debtor and the secured party) (9-203). (See Figure 6-3.)

A. *Attachment* (creation). A security interest cannot attach (i.e., come into being as enforceable between the debtor and the secured party) until all three of the following conditions exist.

1. A *written agreement* that it attach which contains a reasonable identification (description) of the collateral securing the debt (9-110). When the security interest covers crops growing or to be grown or timber to be cut, the land must also be described [9-203(1)(a)]. If the secured interest is to attach to after-acquired property, the intent to do so must be indicated clearly in the agreement.

a. When the collateral is in the possession of a secured party, the agreement need not be in writing, e.g., a pledge.

b. When the debtor is allowed to retain possession of the collateral, the security agreement must always be in writing.

c. The security agreement need be signed only by the debtor.

• **FIGURE 6-3**   CREATION OF AN ENFORCEABLE SECURITY INTEREST
(BETWEEN DEBTOR AND SECURED PARTY)

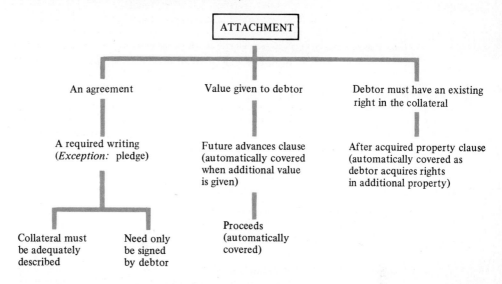

2. *Value given to the debtor* by the secured party (value may encompass virtually any other type of consideration sufficient to support a contract) [1-201(44)], i.e., any currently bargained for legal detriment.

3. *A right in the collateral belonging to the debtor.* For example, a debtor has no rights in an account until it comes into existence, in fish until they are caught, in crops until they are planted, in livestock until they are conceived, in timber until it is cut, in a contract until the contract has been made, and in minerals until they are extracted [9-204(2)].

B. *Future advances, after-acquired property, and proceeds.*

1. The UCC allows a security agreement to include a provision covering future advances [9-204(3)]. For example, in a security agreement, a creditor gave to the debtor a line of credit in the amount of $50,000. The creditor initially advanced credit to the debtor in the amount of $10,000. The agreement provided that the balance of the credit was to be extended to the debtor in four equal annual installments.

   a. The financing statement may be drafted to include past, present, and future indebtedness.

   b. However, the security interest does not attach until value is *actually* given.

2. The UCC allows creation of a security interest in after-acquired property (property that the debtor does not currently own) by a properly worded security agreement and a filed financing statement [9-204(1)]. For example, a security interest is given in all of the office equipment the debtor now owns as well as all property in which the debtor may "hereafter acquire" ownership (i.e., a floating lien).

   a. Security interest does not attach until the debtor acquires an interest in the collateral.

   b. Such a security interest may be defeated if the debtor acquires some or all of the new property subject to a purchase-money security agreement which is filed by the secured creditor within ten days after the debtor receives possession. (See Figure 6-4.)

FIGURE 6-4   PURCHASE-MONEY SECURITY AGREEMENT: TEN-DAY SECRET LIEN

EXAMPLE 1

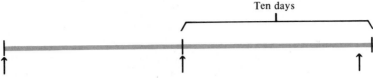

Nonpurchase money security agreement containing an after-acquired property clause. A financing statement is filed at this time. The collateral is equipment.

The same debtor buys additional property under a *purchase money* security agreement. The debtor *takes possession* of the collateral.

Purchase money secured creditor files interest within 10 days. Having done so, creditor takes priority over previously filed (perfected) non-purchase money security agreement which contained an after-acquired property clause.

EXAMPLE 2

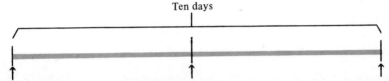

Purchase money security agreement attached. However, creditor did not perfect (file) interest at this time. The buyer (debtor) did *receive possession* at this time.

Debtor now subjects the same personal property to a second secured transaction (a nonpurchase money secured transaction). This security interest is perfected at this time by filing or otherwise.

Purchase money secured creditor files security interest at this time. Having done so within 10 days, creditor takes priority over previously filed (perfected) nonpurchase money security interest in the same property.

    c. *Note:* The UCC has in effect abolished the "floating lien" on *consumer goods.* It prohibits the attachment of a security interest under an after-acquired property clause pertaining to consumer goods other than accessions unless the debtor acquired the consumer goods within ten days after the secured party gave value to the debtor. For example, D borrowed $4,000 from C and included her personal automobile as collateral in the security agreement. The agreement also contained an after-acquired property clause. Eighteen days after the loan, D purchased a television set. D subsequently defaulted on her debt to C. C claimed that the television set was subject to the security interest. The television set did not become additional security under the after-acquired property clause.

    3. *Proceeds.* The UCC allows a security interest to be created in proceeds of collateral described in the security agreement (9-306). Review the definition of "proceeds" at IV-K above.

        a. Unless proceeds are expressly excluded, a security interest automatically continues in any identifiable proceeds of collateral in favor of the secured party [9-203(3)]. For example, Retail gave a security interest in her inventory to Lender. Retail sold an automobile from her inventory to Buyer. Buyer gave cash, a check, a trade-in automobile, and a promissory note in payment. The cash, check, trade-in, and note are proceeds and are subject to Lender's security interest. As another example, casualty insurance payments received by a debtor as a result of damage or destruction of insured collateral are "proceeds."

        b. The security interest continues in the collateral notwithstanding its sale, exchange, or other disposition unless the disposition was authorized by the secured party in the security agreement or otherwise [9-306(2)]. *Exception:* A buyer in the ordinary course of business takes free of a security interest created by the seller even though it may be perfected and even though the buyer knew of its existence [9-307(1)]. See VIII-C-2 below.

PERFECTION OF SECURITY INTERESTS

VII. *Preserving a security interest under the UCC* (between the secured party and third persons). Third parties include subsequent secured creditors, trustee for a bankrupt debtor, purchaser of the collateral from the debtor, and subsequent lien creditors. Upon perfection, the security interest held by the secured party will take precedence over subsequent third-party claims to the collateral. Perfection cannot occur prior to attachment of the security interest [9-303(1)]. For example, Idot executed and delivered to Mono a promissory note for the amount of a loan together with a signed security agreement designating Idot's garden tractor as collateral. Mono immediately filed a financing statement. Because Idot did not need the money immediately, she agreed to and did receive the loan ten days later. The security interest was not perfected at the time of filing. Attachment and perfection occurred ten days after filing. Had an intervening security interest been properly perfected, it would have taken priority over Mono's security interest in the garden tractor. Perfection can be accomplished in three ways: filing of a financing statement, change in possession of the collateral, or attachment alone. (See Figure 6-5.)

  A. *Perfection by filing* (public notice) (9-302).

   1. Filing of a *financing statement* (9-402). Most security interests can be perfected only by the filing of a financing statement that meets the following minimum requirements. (See Figure 6-6.)

   a. It must be signed by the debtor;

   b. It must state the names of the secured party and the debtor;

   c. It must state the mailing address of the secured party and the debtor;

FIGURE 6-5   PERFECTING A SECURITY INTEREST

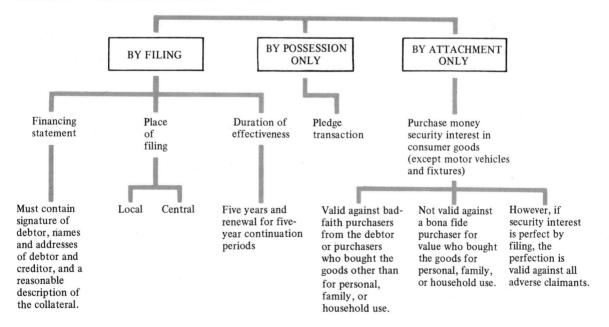

FIGURE 6-6   FORMAL REQUISITES OF A FINANCING STATEMENT

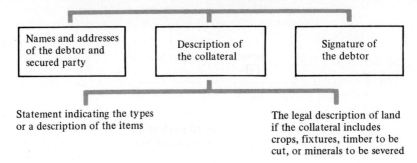

d. It must reasonably describe the collateral. Details need not be given. For example, the following descriptions would be sufficient: "dining room set," "farm tractors," "inventory," and "all the goods owned by me."

(1) A security interest in after-acquired property of the debtor may be perfected by clearly indicating an intent to do so in the financing statement.

(2) If the financing statement covers timber, minerals, or crops or includes goods that are to become fixtures, the financing statement must also describe the real estate involved.

(3) The security interest in proceeds is a continuously perfected security interest *if* the security interest in the original collateral was perfected, *but* it ceases to be a perfected security interest and becomes unperfected ten days after receipt of the proceeds by the debtor *unless*:

(*a*) A filed financing statement covers the original collateral *and* the proceeds are the type of collateral in which a security interest can be perfected by filing in the same place where the financing statement has been filed; or

(*b*) A financing statement has been filed covering the original collateral, *and* the proceeds are identifiable cash proceeds; or

(*c*) The security interest in the proceeds is perfected by an appropriate filing or otherwise *before* the expiration of the ten-day period. A security interest can be perfected (with the exception of the ten-day automatic perfection and that provided in 1-a, b above) only by the same method as that required for perfection of a security interest in the original collateral.

e. Any amendments to the financing statement must be signed by both the debtor and the secured creditor.

2. *Place of filing* (9-401) (see Table 6-1). The proper place to file in order to perfect a security interest is as follows:

a. When the collateral is equipment used in farming operations; farm products; accounts, contract rights, or general intangibles arising from or relating to the sale of farm products by a farmer; or consumer goods, the place of filing it is as follows (local filing):

(1) In the office of the Recorder of Deeds in the county of the debtor's residence; or

(2) If the debtor is not a resident of this state, then in the office of the Recorder of Deeds in the county where the goods are kept.

b. When the collateral is crops, the place of filing is in the office of the Recorder of Deeds in the county where the land on which the crops are growing or are to be grown is located (local filing).

   c. When the collateral is goods which are fixtures or are to become fixtures at the time the security interest attaches, the place of filing is in the office where a mortgage on the real estate concerned would be filed or recorded [9-401(1)(a)] (local filing).

   d. In all other cases, the place of filing is in the office of the secretary of state (central filing).

3. *Exceptions to filing for perfection.*

   a. No filing is necessary to perfect a security interest when the security interest is a purchase-money security interest in consumer goods other than motor vehicles or fixtures [9-302(1)(d)]. However, this type of perfection (by attachment alone) is not effective against a purchaser of the consumer goods from the debtor who purchases the goods for personal, household, or family use without knowledge of the existing security interest. (See Figure 6-5.)

   b. A security interest in collateral in possession of the secured creditor is perfected so long as possession continues.

   c. Security interests in motor vehicles including accessories need not be filed to be perfected where state law requires the security interest to be noted on the certificate of title.

   d. An assignment of an *"insignificant"* part of the outstanding accounts of the assignor as security need not be filed to be perfected against third-party claimants.

   e. An assignment for the benefit of all of the transferor's creditors need not be filed in order to be perfected against third-party claimants.

   f. A security interest in proceeds has automatic perfection for ten days after the debtor's receipt of the proceeds. Review VII-A-1d(3) above.

   g. The security interests in instruments and documents have automatic perfection for twenty-one days after they attach but only to the extent that they were given for new value. Thereafter, filing is necessary for continued perfection against third-party claimants.

4. *Length of time filing is effective.* Unless otherwise stated in the financing statement, each filing is effective for five years [9-403(2)].

5. *Continuation statement.* The duration of the effectiveness of a filed security interest can be extended by a filing of a continuation statement. Each extension provides an additional five years' protection to the security party [9-403(3)].

6. *Termination statement.* Filing of a termination statement removes a perfected security interest from the record (9-404).

B. *Perfection by possession.* A security interest in collateral which is in the possession of a secured party is perfected against all third parties. This is the typical pledge or field warehousing situation [9-302(1)(a), 9-305]. (See Table 6-1.)

C. *Perfection by attachment only.* In the following transactions a security interest is perfected even though there has not been a filing or a change in possession of the collateral. However, the perfection is effective only against certain third parties [9-302(1)(d)]. (See Figure 6-7 and Table 6-1.)

1. A *purchase-money security interest in consumer goods* other than motor vehicles or fixtures. *Note:* Perfection in this situation is effective against everyone except a bona fide purchaser for value who buys the goods for personal, family, or household use [9-307(2)]. An example is a neighbor who purchases the goods for personal use at a garage or rummage sale. However, the security interest can be perfected against everyone if the secured party files a financing statement.

TABLE 6-1 PERFECTION OF SECURITY INTERESTS

Type of collateral	Perfection by possession, i.e., pledge or field warehousing	Perfection by central filing	Perfection by local filing	Perfection by attachment	Retroactive automatic perfection
1. Goods under purchase-money security interest (except motor vehicles inventory and fixtures)	X		X	Applies to consumer goods only; effective only against purchasers from the debtors who buy for nonpersonal, household, or family purposes	Automatic perfection for ten days after debtor's receipt of goods; creditor has a grace period of ten days within which to perfect permanently by possession or filing; applies to all goods
2. Goods under non-purchase-money security interest (except motor vehicles and fixtures)	X		X		
3. Fixtures			X (fixture filing)		
4. Motor vehicles (including vehicle accessories)					
a. Where state law requires security interest to be noted on the certificate of title		Compliance with the certificate of title statute is required			
b. Where state law requires title registration but does not require notation of security interest on the certificate of title	X	X — If the vehicle is taken by the debtor to another state, the perfection continues for a period of 4 months			
5. Chattel paper (installment sales contracts containing a negotiable promissory note)	X	X			
6. Documents of title (payable in goods) issued for new value, e.g., bills of lading and warehouse receipts					
a. Negotiable	X				
b. Nonnegotiable	X	X			Nonnegotiable documents — Automatic perfection for twenty-one days after attachment without filing or possession; creditor has a grace period of twenty-one days after attachment to permanently perfect by possession or filing

Collateral			
7. Instruments (payable in money) issued for new value, e.g., drafts and notes including investment securities but excluding instruments that are a part of chattel paper			
a. Negotiable instruments	X		
b. Nonnegotiable instruments	X		Same as above
8. Money	X		
9. Letters of credit	X		
10. Accounts (nonfarm) transfer of a "significant" amount of the assignor's outstanding accounts		X	X Only when an "insignificant" amount of the outstanding accounts is assigned
11. Accounts (farm)		X	
12. Minerals		X	
13. Timber		X Only if timber is to be cut	
14. Proceeds from collateral (including inventory)	X	Filing of a security interest in the original collateral constitutes an automatic filing as to proceeds; the automatic perfection of proceeds becomes unperfected ten days after receipt of the proceeds by the debtor unless: 1. A filed financing statement covers the original collateral and the proceeds are of the type that can be perfected by the same type of filing; or 2. A filed financing statement covers the original collateral and the proceeds are identifiable cash proceeds; or 3. A security interest in the proceeds is perfected by an appropriate filing before the expiration of the ten-day grace period.	Automatic and temporary perfection exists for ten days after a debtor's receipt of proceeds
15. Consignment of goods for sale	X		

FIGURE 6-7 TYPES OF SECURITY INTERESTS PERFECTED BY ATTACHMENT ALONE

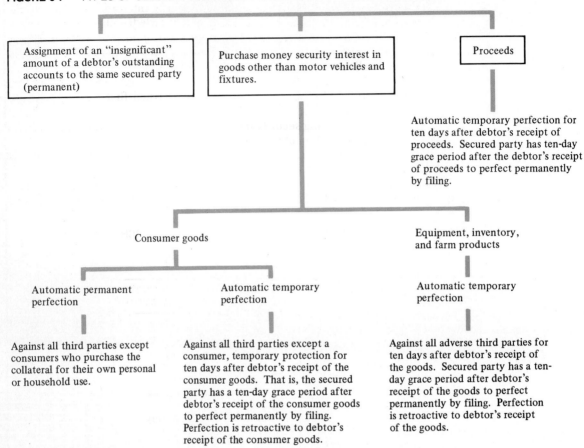

PRIORITIES BETWEEN CONFLICTING SECURITY INTERESTS AND SUBSEQUENT PURCHASERS

    VIII. *Priorities.* The UCC provides rules for determining priorities between conflicting security interests in the same collateral and determining the rights of a subsequent purchaser of secured collateral. [For our purposes, only the general rules governing priorities and a few important exceptions are considered. (See Figure 6-8.)]

    A. *Purchase-money security interest priority* [9-312(4)].

        1. A purchase-money security interest in collateral other than inventory, motor vehicles, and fixtures takes priority over intervening conflicting interests in the same collateral or its proceeds if it is perfected when the debtor receives possession of the collateral or within ten days thereafter. (See Figure 6-7 and Table 6-1.)

            a. If the necessary filing occurs prior to or within ten days after the debtor receives possession, perfection of the security interest relates back to the date of possession.

            b. The purchase money security interest is a *"secret lien"* for a period of ten days after the debtor takes possession of the collateral, unless the secured party files before the end of the ten-day period.

c. The purchase-money secured party who filed within the ten-day period has priority over any intervening conflicting security interests even though the latter had been filed first and he or she had knowledge of their existence.

B. If the security interest is *a non-purchase-money security interest* or if a purchase-money security interest is not filed within ten days after the debtor received possession of the collateral, the following general rules apply [9-312(5)].

  1. If all conflicting security interests are perfected by filing, the first interest filed receives priority, regardless of which interest attached first and regardless of whether it attached before or after filing.

  2. If none of the conflicting security interests are perfected by filing, the priority is in the order of perfection of the interest (i.e., take possession or file).

  3. If none of the security interests are perfected, the priority is in the order of attachment.

C. The *general rules governing priorities* between a secured creditor and subsequent purchasers of the collateral or other conflicting interests are as follows:

FIGURE 6-8   PRIORITIES BETWEEN CONFLICTING INTERESTS AND SUBSEQUENT PURCHASERS

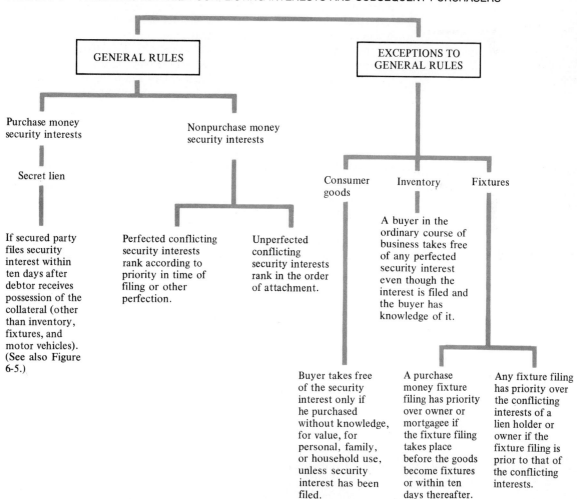

1. Where *consumer goods* are sold, the buyer takes priority over a security interest, even though perfected, *if* the buyer buys without knowledge of the security interest, pays value, and uses it for personal, family, or household purposes, *unless* prior to the purchase the secured party has filed a financing statement covering such goods [9-307(2)].

2. A *buyer in the ordinary course of business* takes free from any security interest created by the seller in inventory goods, even though the security interest is perfected and even though the buyer knows of its existence [9-307(1)].

3. A *buyer of farm products in ordinary course of business* takes free of an unperfected security interest if the buyer pays value and receives delivery without knowledge of the security interest and before it is perfected.

4. *Fixtures* (9-313).

   a. As a general rule, a *"fixture filing"* is necessary to protect a secured party against both existing and future interests in the real estate, even where the security interest attaches to goods before they become fixtures.

      (1) A *non-purchase-money security interest* in a fixture is protected only if the fixture filing is made prior to the filing or recording of a conflicting real estate interest.

      (2) A *purchase-money security interest* in a fixture is protected as follows:

         (a) Against prior real estate interests (except construction mortgages), the purchase-money security interest has priority if the fixture filing takes place within ten days after the goods become fixtures.

         (b) Against subsequent holders of real estate interests, the interest has priority if the fixture filing takes place prior to the filing or recording of the real estate interest.

   b. The UCC defines *fixture filing* as "the filing in the office where a mortgage on real estate would be filed or recorded of a financing statement covering goods which are or are to become fixtures" [9-313(1)(b)]. A fixture filing must provide the following information:

      (1) Show that it covers a fixture;

      (2) Recite that it is to be filed for record in the real estate records;

      (3) Contain a description of the real estate; and

      (4) Show the name of the owner of record if the debtor does not have an interest of record in the real estate.

   c. On default, the secured party having priority in the fixture may remove it from the real estate on the condition that the secured party reimburse any lien holder or owner of the real estate for any physical injury caused during the removal. The secured party, however, has no duty to reimburse the parties for depreciation of market value of the real estate caused by the removal.

5. *Priority of future advances* against intervening parties. An intervening party may be a lien creditor, a conflicting secured party, or a purchaser of the collateral who acquires adverse interests between the time the original security interest (that provides for future advances) is perfected and the time when future advances are made.

   a. An *intervening lien creditor* takes subject to subsequent advances under a perfected security interest if they are made:

      (1) Before he or she became a lien creditor, or

      (2) Without knowledge of the lien, or

      (3) Within forty-five days after he or she became a lien creditor, or

      (4) *"Pursuant to a commitment"* (i.e., the security agreement obligated the secured creditor to make future advances) entered into without knowledge of the lien.

b. *Intervening buyers* (other than buyers of inventory in the ordinary course of business) take subject to subsequent advances under a perfected security interest if they are made:

    (1) within forty-five days after the purchase, or

    (2) the secured creditor making the advance had knowledge of the sale of the collateral by the debtor, whichever occurs first, *unless*

    (3) the advances are made "pursuant to a commitment" entered into without knowledge of the purchase.

c. *Intervening conflicting security interests* take subject to subsequent advances under a security interest perfected by filing or possession according to the general rules stated in B above.

    (1) The future advance has the same priority as the first advance under a perfected security interest.

    (2) If a commitment is made before or while the security interest is perfected by filing or possession, the priority of the advances is the same as that of the perfected security interest.

6. A *holder in due course* of a negotiable instrument takes it free from *any* security interest. See Chapter 5.

7. A *holder to whom a negotiable document of title has been duly negotiated* (i.e., the "person entitled under the document") takes the document free from *any* security interest. See Chapter 4.

8. A *bona fide purchaser for value* of an investment security takes free from *any* security interest. See Chapter 4.

9. A *trustee in bankruptcy,* as a lien creditor of a bankrupt debtor, has priority under the following circumstances:

    a. The security interest was perfected after the date of filing of the petition in bankruptcy;

    b. The perfected security interest constitutes the giving of a preference to the secured creditor over other creditors of the bankrupt;

    c. The security interest was created with the intent to defraud other creditors of the debtor.

    d. See Chapter 8 for a detailed discussion of the rights of a trustee in bankruptcy over collateral owned by a debtor.

DEFAULT, REPOSSESSION, AND DISPOSITION OF COLLATERAL

  IX. Default by the debtor and foreclosure by the secured party (9-503, 9-504). (See Figure 6-9.)

    A. *Right to possession.* On default, the secured party is entitled to possession of the collateral (9-503). (See Figure 6-10.)

      1. The secured party may *repossess* the collateral from the debtor so long as it is done without a breach of peace.

      2. If the collateral is bulky and difficult to remove, the secured party may have it rendered useless and sell it on the debtor's premises.

      3. The secured party may require the debtor to assemble the collateral and make it available at a place designated by the secured party which is reasonably convenient to both parties.

      4. If the collateral is goods in process, the secured creditor may complete the goods, if such completion is commercially reasonable, and thereafter exercise the right to dispose of the collateral.

      5. If the collateral is accounts receivable, general intangibles, chattel paper, or instruments, the secured creditor "forecloses" on the collateral by notifying each

FIGURE 6-9 CREDITOR'S RIGHTS AND DUTIES UPON DEBTOR'S DEFAULT

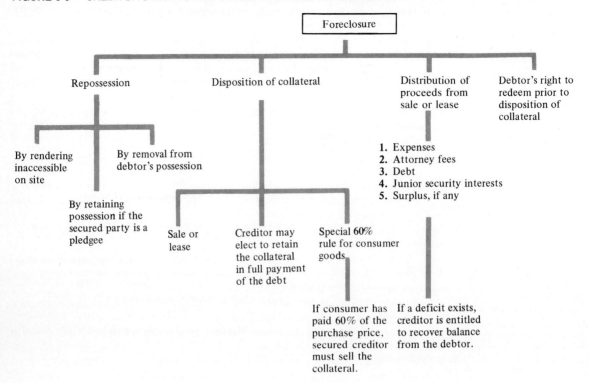

obligor of the debtor's default and instructing the obligor to make future payments to the secured creditor rather than to the debtor.

6. If the collateral is a fixture, the secured creditor having priority is allowed to remove (sever) it from the real estate. The secured creditor is liable to the owner of the real estate for any physical damage caused by the removal.

B. *Disposition of the collateral.* Once a secured creditor is in possession, it must act in a commercially reasonable manner in exercising its right to sell, lease, propose retention where allowed, or in any other disposition. The secured party may dispose of the collateral in the following ways [9-504(1)]. (See Figure 6-11.)

1. By *private or public sale;*
2. By *lease;* or
3. *In any manner* calculated to produce the greatest commercial benefit to all parties concerned. However, the method of disposal must be *commercially reasonable.*
4. *Notice of sale* must be given to the debtor and to others who have a perfected security interest in the collateral or who have an interest known to the secured party. *Exception:* perishable goods.
5. *Consumer goods (special rule)* (9-505).
   a. Secured party must sell *(compulsory sale)* if 60 percent or more of the purchase price or debt has been paid by the debtor unless after default the debtor waives the right to a sale of the collateral in a signed writing.
   b. If less than 60 percent has been paid *or* if the security interest is in collateral other than consumer goods, the secured party in possession may propose (in writing) to retain the collateral in satisfaction of the debt. If no written objec-

FIGURE 6-10   METHODS OF REPOSSESSION OF COLLATERAL BY SECURED PARTY

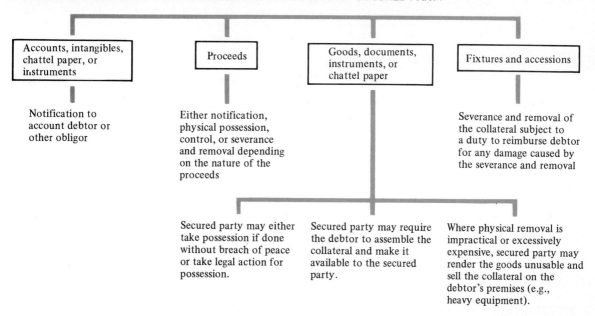

tion is made to the proposal within twenty-one days, the creditor's election becomes final.

    6. If the creditor properly retains the collateral, the debtor is discharged.

C. *Distribution of proceeds.* The order of distribution of proceeds is as follows [9-504(1)]:

    1. Expenses of retaking, holding, and preparing for sale;

    2. Reasonable attorney fees and legal expenses;

    3. Satisfaction of the indebtedness;

    4. Junior security interests if written notice of demand is given before distribution;

    5. Surplus, if any, to the debtor.

D. *Rights of debtor and duties of secured party* (see Figure 6-9).

    1. *Debtor* or any secondarily secured party has an absolute right to redeem the collateral at any time before the secured party disposes of the collateral or enters

FIGURE 6-11   RIGHTS OF SECURED PARTY TO DISPOSE OF COLLATERAL

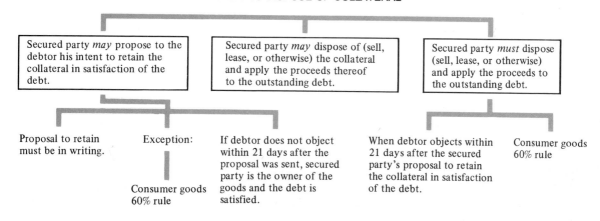

into a contract for its "disposition" (sale, lease, or retention of collateral) (9-506). For the debtor or secondarily secured party to redeem, that party must tender payment of all amounts due the secured party, including expenses incurred in retaking, holding, and preparing the collateral for disposition. To the extent provided in the security agreement, the redeeming party is liable for reasonable attorney's fees and legal expenses.

2. *Secured party's liability for damages.* The secured party is liable to the debtor for damages or may suffer the loss of the right to recover any deficiency on the debt if the secured party fails to comply with the UCC (9-507). For example, Conner financed a new car with Trust Company. After Conner missed four payments, Trust Company repossessed the car and notified him that unless he paid the balance owed, the car would be sold. Eighteen months later the car was sold at a private sale. The court held that Trust Company's delay and method of sale violated its duty to act with commercial reasonableness and barred recovery of any deficiency from the debtor. As another example, the secured creditor repossessed secured equipment upon default of the creditor. It did not dispose of it, propose to retain it, or indicate that it would deduct its value from the amount demanded from the debtor. The court refused to award the creditor the balance due on the debt.

SELF-QUIZ

To check your understanding of the key words and concepts and the accuracy of your answers to the questions, refer to the text material as referenced by page number.

KEY WORDS AND CONCEPTS

QUESTIONS

1. Define and distinguish between the following security agreements. Although the UCC does not refer to them by name, the UCC governs the security interests they create.
   a. Pledge **(186)**
   b. Bill of sale with a defeasance clause **(186)**
   c. Chattel mortgage **(186)**
   d. Conditional sales contract **(186)**
   e. Purchase-money transaction **(187)**

2. What three conditions must exist for a security interest to attach to specific collateral? **(188)**

3. What is meant by perfecting a security interest? **(191)**

4. What are the requirements of a valid financing statement? **(191)**

5. When is a security interest perfected? **(191)**

6. Must a secured transaction agreement always be in writing? **(188)** If not, under what circumstances can it be oral? **(188)**

7. What are the four types of goods classified by the UCC on the basis of the nature of the collateral or its use for the purposes of filing requirements? **(187)**

8. As a general rule, filing is necessary to perfect all security interests. However, there are exceptions. Name them. **(191)**

9. What are two important instances when a third party (a person other than the secured party or debtor) can take free of a security interest even though the security interest has been perfected? **(197)**

10. Once a security interest is perfected by filing, how long does this protection exist? Once the protection terminates, can it be extended, i.e., "continued"? If so, how and for how long? **(193)**

11. What is meant by a termination statement? How is it used in relation to a secured transaction? **(193)**

12. What are the rights of a secured creditor upon default by the debtor? **(199)**

13. What is the debtor's right of redemption? **(201)** How and when must the debtor exercise this right? **(201)**

14. Under what circumstances may the secured creditor retain the collateral in satisfaction of the secured creditor's security interest after the debtor's default? **(200)**

15. Why is it important for a secured creditor to perfect his or her security interest? **(191)**

16. What is the nature of a security interest as it exists under the UCC? How does it differ from the interests created under laws prior to the UCC? **(186)**

SELECTED QUESTIONS AND UNOFFICIAL ANSWERS

OBJECTIVE QUESTIONS

Select the best answer for each of the following items. Mark only one answer for each item. Answer all items.

NOVEMBER 1980

31. In the course of an examination of the financial statements of Control Finance Company for the year ended September 30, 1980, the auditors learned that the company has just taken possession of certain heavy industrial equipment from Arrow Manufacturing Company, a debtor in default. Arrow had previously borrowed $60,000 from Control secured by a security interest in the heavy industrial equipment. The amount of the loan outstanding is $30,000. Which of the following is correct regarding the rights of Control and Arrow?

a. Control is *not* permitted to sell the repossessed equipment at private sale.

b. Arrow has *no* right to redeem the collateral at any time once possession has been taken.

c. Control is *not* entitled to retain the collateral it has repossessed in satisfaction of the debt even though it has given written notice to the debtor and he consents.

d. Arrow is *not* entitled to a compulsory disposition of the collateral.

32. The Jolly Finance Company provides the financing for Triple J Appliance Company's inventory. As a part of its sales promotion and public relations campaign, Jolly Finance placed posters in Triple J's stores indicating that Triple J is another satisfied customer of Jolly and that the goods purchased at Triple J are available through the financing by Jolly. Jolly also files a financing statement which covers the financed inventory. Victor Restaurants purchased four hi-fi sets for use in its restaurants and had read one of the Jolly posters. Triple J has defaulted on its loan and Jolly Finance is seeking to repossess the hi-fi sets. Which of the following is correct?

a. Jolly has a perfected security interest in the hi-fi sets which is good against Victor.

b. Victor's knowledge of the financing arrangement between Jolly and Triple J does *not* affect its rights to the hi-fi sets.

c. Jolly's filing was unnecessary to perfect its security interest in Triple J's inventory since it was perfected upon attachment.

d. The hi-fi sets are consumer goods in Victor's hands.

33. The Gordon Manufacturing Company manufactures various types of lathes. It sold on credit 25 general-use lathes to Hardware City, a large retail outlet. Hardware City sold one of the lathes to Johnson for use in his home repair business, reserving a security interest for the unpaid balance. However, Hardware City did *not* file a financing statement. Johnson's creditors are asserting rights against the lathe. Which of the following statements is correct?

a. The lathe is a consumer good in Johnson's hands.

b. No filing was necessary to perfect a security interest in the lathe against Johnson's creditors.

c. Gordon Manufacturing could assert rights against the lathe sold to Johnson in the event Hardware City defaults in its payments.

d. The lathe was inventory in both Gordon and Hardware's hands and is equipment in Johnson's, and both Gordon and Hardware City must file to perfect their interests.

34. The Town Bank makes collateralized loans to its customers at 1% above prime on securities owned by the customer, subject to existing margin requirements. In doing so, which of the following is correct?

a. Notification of the issuer is necessary in order to perfect a security interest.

b. Filing is a permissible method of perfecting a security interest in the securities if the circumstances dictate.

c. Any dividend or interest distributions during the term of the loan belong to the bank.

d. A perfected security interest in the securities can only be obtained by possession.

35. Bass, an automobile dealer, had an inventory of 40 cars and 10 trucks. He financed the purchase of this inventory with County Bank under an agreement dated July 7 that gave the bank a security interest in all vehicles on Bass' premises, all future acquired vehicles, and the proceeds thereof. On July 11, County Bank properly filed a financing statement that identified the collateral in the same way that it was identified in the agreement. On Oc-

tober 1, Bass sold a passenger car to Dodd for family use and a truck to Diamond Company for its hardware business. Which of the following is correct?

a. The security agreement may *not* provide for a security interest in future acquired vehicles even if the parties agree.

b. The passenger car sold by Bass to Dodd continues to be subject to the security interest of the County Bank.

c. The bank's security interest is perfected as of July 7 despite the fact it was *not* filed until July 11.

d. The security interest of the County Bank does *not* include the proceeds from the sale of the truck to Diamond Company.

36. Retailer Corp. was in need of financing. To secure a loan, it made an oral assignment of its accounts receivable to J. Roe, a local investor, under which Roe loaned Retailer on a continuing basis, 90% of the face value of the assigned accounts receivable. Retailer collected from the account debtors and remitted to Roe at intervals. Before the debt was paid, Retailer filed a petition in bankruptcy. Which of the following is correct?

a. As between the account debtors and Roe, the assignment is *not* an enforceable security interest.

b. Roe is a secured creditor to the extent of the unpaid debt.

c. Other unpaid creditors of Retailers Corp. who knew of the assignment are bound by its terms.

d. An assignment of accounts, to be valid, requires the debtors owing the accounts to be notified.

37. The Secured Transactions Article of the Code recognizes various methods of perfecting a security interest in collateral. Which of the following is *not* recognized by the Code?

a. Filing.

b. Possession.

c. Consent.

d. Attachment.

38. Which of the following is included within the scope of the Secured Transactions Article of the Code?

a. The outright sale of accounts receivable.

b. A landlord's lien.

c. The assignment of a claim for wages.

d. The sale of chattel paper as a part of the sale of a business out of which it arose.

22. Williamson purchased from Dilworth Hardware a new lathe for his home workshop for cash. Two weeks later, Williamson was called by the Easy Loan Company. Easy explained to Williamson that it had been financing Dilworth's purchases from the manufacturers and that to protect its interest it had obtained a perfected security interest in Dilworth's entire inventory of hardware and power tools, including the lathe which Williamson bought. Easy further explained that Dilworth had defaulted on a payment due to Easy, and Easy intended to assert its security interest in the lathe and repossess it unless Williamson was willing to make payment of $200 for a release of Easy's security interest. If Williamson refuses to make the payment, which of the following statements is correct?
a. Williamson will *not* take free of Easy's security interest if he was aware of said interest at the time he purchased the lathe.
b. Even if Williamson had both actual notice and constructive notice via recordation of Easy's interest, he will prevail if Easy seeks to repossess the lathe.
c. Easy's security interest in the lathe in question is invalid against all parties unless its filing specifically described and designated the particular lathe Williamson purchased.
d. Williamson must pay the $200 or the lathe can be validly repossessed and sold to satisfy the amount Dilworth owes Easy and any excess paid to Williamson.

23. Two Uniform Commercial Code concepts relating to secured transactions are "attachment" and "perfection." Which of the following is correct in connection with the similarities and differences between these two concepts?
a. They are mutually exclusive and wholly independent of each other.
b. Satisfaction of one automatically satisfies the other.
c. Attachment relates primarily to the rights against the debtor and perfection relates primarily to the rights against third parties.
d. It is *not* possible to have a simultaneous attachment and perfection.

24. Which of the following requirements is *not* necessary in order to have a security interest attach?
a. There must be a proper filing.
b. The debtor must have rights in the collateral.

c. Value must be given by the creditor.
d. Either the creditor must take possession or the debtor must sign a security agreement which describes the collateral.

25. In respect to obtaining a purchase money security interest, which of the following requirements must be met?
a. The property sold may only be consumer goods.
b. Only a seller may obtain a purchase money security interest.
c. Such a security interest must be filed in all cases to be perfected.
d. Credit advanced to the buyer must be used to obtain the property which serves as the collateral.

26. Vista Motor Sales, a corporation engaged in selling motor vehicles at retail, borrowed money from Sunshine Finance Company and gave Sunshine a properly executed security agreement in its present and future inventory and in the proceeds therefrom to secure the loan. Sunshine's security interest was duly perfected under the laws of the state where Vista does business and maintains its entire inventory. Thereafter, Vista sold a new pickup truck from its inventory to Archer and received Archer's certified check in payment of the full price. Under the circumstances, which of the following is correct?
a. Sunshine must file an amendment to the financing statement every time Vista receives a substantial number of additional vehicles from the manufacturer if Sunshine is to obtain a valid security interest in subsequently delivered inventory.
b. Sunshine's security interest in the certified check Vista received is perfected against Vista's other creditors.
c. Unless Sunshine specifically included proceeds in the financing statement it filed, it has *no* rights to them.
d. The term "proceeds" does *not* include used cars received by Vista since they will be resold.

14. Wilcox Laboratories, Ltd., manufactures medical equipment for sale to medical institutions and retailers. Wilcox also sells directly to consumers in its wholly-owned retail outlets. Wilcox has created a subsidiary, Wilcox Finance Corporation, for the purpose of financing the purchase of its products by the various customers. In which of the following situations does Wilcox Finance *not* have to file a financing statement to perfect its security interest against competing creditors in the equipment sold by Wilcox?

a. Sales made to medical institutions.

b. Sales made to consumers who purchase for their own personal use.

c. Sales made to retailers who in turn sell to buyers in the ordinary course of business.

d. Sales made to any buyer when the equipment becomes a fixture.

15. Kelmore Appliances, Inc., sells various brand name appliances at discount prices. Kelmore maintains a large inventory which it obtains from various manufacturers on credit. These manufacturer-creditors have all filed and taken secured interests in the appliances and proceeds therefrom which they have sold to Kelmore on credit. Kelmore in turn sells to hundreds of ultimate consumers; some pay cash but most buy on credit. Kelmore takes a security interest but does *not* file a financing statement for credit sales. Which of the following is correct?

a. The appliances in Kelmore's hands are consumer goods.

b. Since Kelmore takes a purchase money security interest in the consumer goods sold, its security interest is perfected upon attachment.

c. The appliance manufacturers can enforce their secured interests against the appliances in the hands of the purchasers who paid cash for them.

d. A subsequent sale by one of Kelmore's customers to a bona fide purchaser will be subject to Kelmore's secured interest.

18. Migrane Financial does a wide variety of lending. It provides funds to manufacturers, middlemen, retailers, consumers, and home owners. In all instances it intends to create a security interest in the loan transactions it enters into. To which of the following will Article 9 (Secured Transactions) of the Uniform Commercial Code *not* apply?

a. A second mortgage on the borrower's home.

b. An equipment lease.

c. The sale of accounts.

d. Field warehousing.

20. Bigelow manufactures mopeds and sells them through franchised dealers who are authorized to resell them to the ultimate consumer or return them. Bigelow delivers the mopeds on consignment to these retailers. The consignment agreement clearly states that the agreement is intended to create a security interest for Bigelow in the mopeds delivered on consignment. Bigelow wishes to protect itself against the other creditors of and purchasers from the retailers who might assert rights against the mopeds. Under the circumstances, Bigelow

a. Must file a financing statement and give notice to certain creditors in order to perfect his security interest.

b. Will have rights against purchasers in the ordinary course of business who were aware of the fact that Bigelow had filed.

c. Need take *no* further action to protect himself, since the consignment is a sale or return and title is reserved in Bigelow.

d. Will have a perfected security interest in the mopeds upon attachment.

21. Johnson loaned money to Visual, Inc., a struggling growth company, and sought to obtain a security interest in negotiable stock certificates which are traded on a local exchange. To perfect his interest against Visual's other creditors, Johnson

a. Need do nothing further in that his security interest was perfected upon attachment.

b. May file or take possession of the stock certificates.

c. Must take possession of the stock certificates.

d. Must file and give the other creditors notice of his contemplated security interest.

MAY 1978

49. Gladstone Warehousing, Inc., is an independent bonded warehouse company. It issued a warehouse receipt for 10,000 bales of cotton belonging to Travis. The word "NEGOTIABLE" was conspicuously printed on the warehouse receipt it issued to Travis. The warehouse receipt also contained a statement in large, clear print that the cotton would only be surrendered upon return of the receipt and payment of all storage fees. Travis was a prominent plantation owner engaged in the cotton-growing business. Travis pledged the warehouse receipt with Southern National Bank in exchange for a $50,000 personal loan. A financing statement was *not* filed. Under the circumstances, which of the following is correct?

a. Travis' business creditors *cannot* obtain the warehouse receipt from Southern National unless they repay Travis' outstanding loan.

b. The bank does *not* have a perfected security interest in the cotton since it did *not* file a financing statement.

c. Travis' personal creditors have first claim, superior to all other parties, to the cotton in question because the loan was a personal loan and constituted a fraud upon the personal creditors.

d. The fact that the word "NEGOTIABLE" and the statement regarding the return of the receipt were conspicuously printed upon the receipt is *not* binding upon anyone except Travis.

50. Vega Manufacturing, Inc., manufactures and sells hi-fi systems and components to the trade and at retail. Repossession is frequently made from customers who are in default. Which of the following statements is correct concerning the rights of the defaulting debtors who have had property repossessed by Vega?

a. Vega has the right to retain all the goods repossessed as long as it gives notice and cancels the debt.

b. It is unimportant whether the goods repossessed are defined as consumer goods, inventory, or something else in respect to the debtor's rights upon repossession.

c. If the defaulting debtor voluntarily signs a statement renouncing his rights in the collateral, the creditor must nevertheless resell them for the debtor's benefit.

d. If a debtor has paid sixty percent or more of the purchase price of consumer goods in satisfaction of a purchase money security interest, the debtor has the right to have the creditor dispose of the goods.

Answers to Objective Questions

November 1980		November 1979	
31. d	35. c	22. b	25. d
32. b	36. a	23. c	26. b
33. d	37. c	24. a	
34. d	38. a		

May 1979		May 1978	
14. b	20. a	49. a	50. d
15. b	21. c		
18. a			

Explanation of Answers to Objective Questions

NOVEMBER 1980

31. (d) Upon default the secured party normally has the right to retain (or sell) the collateral to satisfy the obligation. However, the secured party cannot retain the collateral if it is consumer goods and the debtor has paid 60% or more of the obligation. In such a case the debtor is entitled to a compulsory disposition of the goods. Control's security interest is in equipment not consumer goods, and Arrow has been paid only 50% of the obligation. Thus Arrow is not entitled to a compulsory disposition. Answer (d) is correct. Control can sell the possessed equipment at either a public or private sale. Either type of sale must be handled in a commercially reasonable manner. Thus answer (a) is incorrect. Arrow can redeem the collateral at any time up to when it is sold by paying the full obligation plus the expenses of the secured party. Control could retain the collateral if written notice of such was sent to the debtor and this debtor did not object within 21 days. This makes answers (b) and (c) incorrect.

32. (b) A purchaser takes free of a perfected security interest in inventory if the purchaser buys from a dealer of goods in the ordinary course of business, even though the purchaser has knowledge of the security interest. In this question the hi-fi sets are inventory and Victor would qualify as a purchaser in the ordinary course of business. Thus answer (b) is correct and answer (a) is incorrect. Automatic perfection by attachment only occurs when a purchase-money security interest is taken in consumer goods. Jolly is taking a security interest in inventory, thus there would be no automatic perfection by attachment. This makes answers (c) and (d) incorrect.

33. (d) The correct answer is (d) because the lathe is inventory, goods held for sale, in the hands of Gordon and Hardware. In Johnson's possession the lathe would be equipment, items used primarily in a business. Consumer goods are those items bought for use primarily for personal, family or household purposes, making answer (a) incorrect. Filing the financing statement was necessary for perfection because the lathe was inventory and automatic perfection by attachment only applies to a security interest in consumer goods. This makes answer (b) incorrect. Answer (c) is incorrect because a purchaser in the ordinary course of business (Johnson) will defeat a prior perfected security interest in inventory.

34. (d) A perfected security interest in securities can only be obtained by possession. An exception to this rule is when the creditor temporarily returns the security to the debtor (for sale, exchange, etc.). In such situations the creditor's security interest remains perfected for 21 days. However, a bona fide purchaser of the security will defeat the creditor's security interest. Thus answer (d) is correct. To perfect a security interest in securities there is no need to notify the issuer. Dividends and interest earned during the secured transaction are the property of the debtor.

35. (c) Answer (c) is correct because the security interest is perfected as of July 7, not July 11. Answer (a) is incorrect because after acquired property clause is very typical of a security agreement that creates a security interest in inventory. This provision creates a floating lien. Answer (b) is incorrect because a purchase in the ordinary course of business (Dodd) defeats a prior perfected security interest in inventory. Proceeds include what is received upon sale of the collateral. County Bank does have a perfected security interest in the proceeds from the sale of a truck because the security agreement states proceeds are covered. The general rule states that security interest in proceeds is automatically perfected for a 10-day period if the security interest in the original collateral was perfected. However, if the security agreement states that the security interest is to cover proceeds, the perfected security interest will continue beyond the 10-day period without any additional filing. Thus answer (d) is incorrect.

36. (a) A nonpossessary security interest in accounts can only be created by a written security agreement. Retailer Corp. and Roe engaged in an oral assignment of the accounts which would be unenforceable. Answer (a) is correct. A nonpossessary security interest in accounts can only be perfected by filing a financing statement.

37. (c) The correct answer is (c) since consent is not a recognized method of perfecting a security interest. Filing, possession and attachment are all methods of perfecting a security interest in collateral [answers (a), (b), and (d)].

38. (a) The only item listed that is within the scope of article 9 (secured transactions) is the outright sale of accounts receivable.

NOVEMBER 1979

22. (b) Williamson is a buyer in the ordinary course of business and will defeat the rights of a secured creditor such as Easy Loan Company even if Williamson had both actual notice and/or constructive notice of Easy's security interest. Answer (a) is incorrect because Williamson will take free of Easy's security interest as stated above even if he was aware of the interest at the time he purchased the lathe. Answer (c) is incorrect because Easy's security interest would be valid against appropriate parties if the security agreement contains a description which identifies the collateral. Answer (d) is incorrect as explained above, because Williamson purchased in good faith, paid value and dealt with a person who regularly deals in goods involved.

23. (c) The similarity and difference between the concepts of attachment and perfection are that attachments relate primarily to the rights of the secured party against the debtor and the collateral, whereas perfection relates primarily to the secured party's rights in the collateral against third parties. Attachment and perfection are not mutually exclusive and wholly independent of each other as in answer (a) since both are required to establish an effective secured transaction. Answer (b) is incorrect because satisfaction of one of these concepts does not automatically satisfy the other. To that extent, they are independent and the requirements of each must be satisfied. Answer (d) is incorrect because it is possible in limited circumstances to have a simultaneous attachment and perfection. This occurs in purchased money security interests in consumer goods.

24. (a) In order to have a security interest attached, it is not necessary that there be a proper filing. However, answers (b), (c), and (d) set out the 3 requirements which must be satisfied before a security agreement can attach in the collateral: the debtor must have rights in the collateral; value must be given by the creditor; and the creditor must take either possession of the collateral or the debtor must sign a security agreement which describes the collateral.

25. (d) In order to obtain a purchase money security interest, credit must be advanced to the buyer which is in fact used to obtain the property which serves as the collateral. For example, the seller or a third party can lend the purchase price to the buyer. Answer (a) is incorrect because the concept of a purchase money security interest is not limited to consumer goods. Answer (b) as stated above is not correct because either a seller or other lender may obtain a purchase money security interest under appropriate circumstances. Answer (c) is incorrect because a purchase money security interest need not be filed in consumer goods transactions in order to be perfected.

26. (b) Under the facts given, Sunshine's security interest in the certified check that Vista received is perfected against Vista's other creditors. Answer (c) is incorrect because the security interest attaches to proceeds automatically without special mention in the financing statement. Answer (d) is incorrect because the term "proceeds" is broad enough to include anything received in exchange for the collateral including used motor vehicles, i.e., "trade ins." Answer (a) is incorrect because Sunshine covered itself in the executed security agreement by stating that the security agreement covered both present and future inventory. Therefore, an amendment is unnecessary every time Vista receives a substantial number of vehicles from the manufacturer.

MAY 1979

14. (b) A purchase money security interest is automatically perfected without the necessity of filing a financing statement if the purchaser is a consumer who purchases for his own personal use. Answers (a), (c), and (d) are incorrect because in each of these cases a secured creditor must file a financing statement to perfect its security interest against competing creditors.

15. (b) When a creditor takes a purchase money security interest in consumer goods, the security interest is perfected upon attachment. Hence no filing is required by Kelmore. Answer (a) is incorrect because the appliances in Kelmore's possession before the sale would be classified as inventory and not as consumer goods. Answer (c) is incorrect because consumers who buy from dealers in the ordinary course of business take free and clear

of pre-existing security interests even if they have knowledge of the security interests. Answer (d) is incorrect because a subsequent sale by one of Kelmore's customers to another bona fide consumer would not be subject to Kelmore's security interest. However, a subsequent purchaser would be subject to Kelmore's security interest if Kelmore had filed a financing statement at the time of the original consumer sale, rather than relying on perfection by attachment only.

18. (a) The requirement is the transaction type not covered by Article 9 of the Uniform Commercial Code. This article regulates any transaction that is intended to create a security interest in personal property. However, Article 9 expressly excludes mortgages on real property. These transactions continue to be regulated by the mortgage statutes of the various states. Equipment leases, the sale of accounts, and field warehousing, as in answers (b), (c), and (d), are transactions covered by Article 9.

20. (a) Bigelow, the manufacturer-seller, in delivering inventory to retailers, must file a financing statement and give separate notice to certain creditors (inventory financiers with after-acquired clauses) in order to perfect his security interest. Answer (b) is incorrect because purchasers who buy from dealers in the ordinary course of business take free of a security interest even if they are aware of the security interest. Answer (c) is incorrect because the consignment intended to create a security interest in personal property, and therefore the filing requirements of Article 9 must be complied with even though the transaction was in the form of a consignment. Answer (d) is incorrect because automatic perfection of a security interest upon attachment applies only for a purchase money security interest in consumer goods.

21. (c) Stock certificates are classified by Article 9 of the UCC as instruments. Instruments may only be perfected by possession. Filing is not a permitted means of perfection nor is perfection by attachment alone. Therefore answers (a), (b), and (d) are incorrect.

MAY 1978

49. (a) Southern National Bank, by taking possession of the negotiable warehouse receipt, has perfected a security interest. The bank will not give up the negotiable document until the loan is repaid or it will lose perfection of its security interest. Answer (b) is incorrect because a financing statement need not be filed because possession of a negotiable document perfects a security interest in the goods represented by the document. Answer (c) is incorrect because taking a personal loan is not a fraud upon existing personal creditors and would not give the personal creditors any rights in the security. Answer (d) is incorrect because the word "negotiable" conspicuously printed on the warehouse receipt along with the statement is binding on all parties involved in the transaction.

50. (d) A secured creditor must sell consumer goods, i.e., cannot repossess and keep, if the debtor has paid 60% or more for them, unless the debtor waives this right in a signed writing. Answer (a) is incorrect because the creditor may propose to retain repossessed goods, but the creditor must sell them if the debtor objects. Answer (b) is incorrect because the distinction between consumer goods and other goods is important. Other goods may be retained unless the debtor objects, while consumer goods 60% paid for must be sold unless the debtor waives his right to a sale. Answer (c) is also incorrect because a defaulting debtor may voluntarily renounce his rights in the collateral and the creditor need not resell them for the debtor's benefit.

ESSAY QUESTIONS AND ANSWERS

May 1981 (Estimated time: 15 to 20 minutes)

3. Part a. Walpole Electric Products, Inc., manufactures a wide variety of electrical appliances. Walpole uses the consignment as an integral part of its marketing plan. The consignments are "true" consignments rather than consignments intended as security interests. Unsold goods may be returned to the owner-consignor. Walpole contracted with Petty Distributors, Inc., an electrical appliance wholesaler, to market its products under this consignment arrangement. Subsequently, Petty became insolvent and made a general assignment for the benefit of creditors. Klinger, the assignee, took possession of all of Petty's inventory, including all the Walpole electrical products. Walpole has demanded return of its appliances asserting that the relationship created by the consignment between itself and Petty was one of agency and that Petty

never owned the appliances. Furthermore, Walpole argues that under the consignment arrangement there is no obligation owing by Petty at any time, thus there is nothing to secure under the secured transactions provisions of the Uniform Commercial Code. Klinger has denied the validity of these assertions claiming that the consignment is subject to the Code's filing provisions unless the Code has otherwise been satisfied. Walpole sues to repossess the goods.

Required Answer the following, setting forth reasons for any conclusions stated.
1. What are the requirements, if any, to perfect a true consignment such as discussed above?
2. Will Walpole prevail?

Answer

1. In order to prevail against the creditors of a party to whom goods have been consigned, the consignor may do one of three things according to the Uniform Commercial Code (section 2-326):
a. Comply with applicable state law providing for a consignor's interest to be evidenced by a posted sign. Most states do not have such statutes.
b. Establish that the person conducting the business is generally known by his creditors to be substantially engaged in selling the goods of others. This is either not the case or is difficult to prove.
c. Comply with the filing provisions of Article 9: Secured Transactions. From a practical standpoint, this last course of action appears to be the most logical, if not the only, choice.
Article 9 (section 9-114) requires that a consignor comply with the general filing requirements of the code (section 9-302) and also give notice in writing to the creditors of the consignee who have a perfected security interest covering the same type of goods. The written notice must be given before the date of filing by the consignor and received within five years before the consignee takes possession of the goods. The notice must state that the consignor expects to deliver goods on consignment to the consignee and must contain a description of the goods.

2. No. Walpole will not prevail. Whether a consignment is a "true" consignment (an agency relationship) or is intended as a security interest, the Uniform Commercial Code requires that notice be given to creditors of the consignee.

A consignment is governed by sections from two articles of the code: Article 2: Sales and Article 9:

Secured Transactions. Section 2-326 treats a consignment as a "sale or return" because "the goods are delivered primarily for resale." Section 2-326(3) provides the following:

> Where goods are delivered to a person for sale and such person maintains a place of business at which he deals in goods of the kind involved, under a name other than the name of the person making delivery, then with respect to claims of creditors of the person conducting the business the goods are deemed to be on sale or return. The provisions of this subsection are applicable even though an agreement purports to reserve title to the person making delivery until payment or resale or uses such words as "on consignment" or "on memorandum."

It is obvious from the facts, that Walpole's marketing arrangement is covered by the above language. The code further provides that the creditors of the consignee will be able to assert claims against goods sold on a sale or return basis unless some form of notice is given.

3. Part b. Lebow Woolens, Inc., sold several thousand bolts of Australian wool on credit to Fashion Plate Exclusives, Inc., a clothing manufacturer, obtaining a duly executed security agreement and a financing statement. Fashion Plate became delinquent in meeting its payments. Lebow subsequently discovered that a miscaptioned financing statement for a $12,500 sale had been filed under the name of Fashion Styles Limited, another customer. Lebow took the following actions. First, on August 11, 1980, it repossessed the bolts of wool which were not already altered by Fashion Plate. This amounted to some 65% of the invoice in question. Next on August 20, 1980, it filed a corrected financing statement covering the sale in question. Dunbar, another creditor of Fashion Plate's, levied against Fashion Plate's inventory, work in process, and raw materials on August 13th and obtained a judgment of $14,000 against Fashion Plate, an amount in excess of the value of the Lebow bolts of wool. The judgment was obtained and entered on August 18, 1980. Dunbar asserts its rights as a lien judgment creditor.

Required Answer the following, setting forth reasons for any conclusions stated.
In a lawsuit to determine the rights of the parties, how should the competing claims of Lebow and Dunbar be decided?

Answer Lebow will prevail to the extent of the 65 percent of the bolts of wool that it repossessed on August 11, 1980. Since Lebow obtained possession of 65 percent of the shipment prior to attachment or judgment by Dunbar, Lebow's security interest with respect to those goods had been perfected as of August 11. The original erroneous filing is invalid against the creditors of Fashion Plate. Lebow's security interest was not perfected by filing initially, and, therefore, Lebow will not prevail over the rights of Dunbar, a subsequent lien creditor of Fashion Plate. The facts of the case indicate that the security interest was not perfected by filing until August 20, 1980. However, prior to that time Dunbar levied against the goods on August 13 and obtained a judgment against Fashion Plate on August 18, 1980. Both dates are prior to the August 20 filing by Lebow; thus, the lien creditor would have priority over Lebow's claim based exclusively on perfection by filing. Perfection can also be accomplished by possession, but if perfection by either method precedes the time that the lien creditor obtains rights against the property, it prevails.

MAY 1980 (Estimated time: 17 to 20 minutes)

4. Part a. After much study and deliberation, the marketing division of Majestic Enterprise, Inc., has recommended to the board of directors that the corporation market its products almost exclusively via consignment arrangements instead of other alternative merchandising-security arrangements. The board moved favorably upon this proposal.

Required Answer the following, setting forth reasons for any conclusions stated.
What are the key legal characteristics of a consignment?

Answer A consignment is a selling arrangement between the owner, called the *consignor*, and the party who is to sell the goods, called the *consignee*. The consignee is appointed the agent to sell the owner's merchandise. The following are the key characteristics.
1. Title to the goods remains at all times with the consignor.
2. The consignee is at no time obligated to buy or pay for the goods.
3. The consignee receives a commission for the goods sold.
4. The proceeds belong to the consignor.

4. Part b. Norwood Furniture, Inc., found that its credit rating was such that it was unable to obtain a line of unsecured credit. National Bank indicated that it would be willing to supply funds based upon a "pledge" of Norwood's furniture inventory which was located in two warehouses. The bank would receive notes and bearer negotiable warehouse receipts covering the merchandise securing the loans. An independent warehouseman was to have complete control over the areas in the warehouse set aside as field warehousing facilities. The Hastings Field Warehousing Corporation was selected to serve as the independent warehouseman. It was to retain keys to the posted area in which the inventory was contained. Negotiable bearer warehouse receipts were issued to Norwood when it delivered the merchandise to Hastings. The receipts were then delivered by Norwood to National to secure the loans which were made at 80% of the market value of the furniture indicated on the receipts. Upon occasion, Norwood would take temporary possession of the furniture for the purpose of packaging it, surrendering the warehouse receipt for this limited purpose. As orders were filled out of the field warehouse inventory, the requisite receipt would be relinquished by National, the merchandise obtained by Norwood, and other items substituted with a new receipt issued.

Required Answer the following, setting forth reasons for any conclusions stated.
1. Based upon the facts given, is the field warehousing arrangement valid?
2. When does a security interest in the negotiable warehouse receipts attach?
3. What, if anything, is necessary to perfect a security interest in goods covered by negotiable warehouse receipts?
4. What are the dangers, if any, that National faces by relinquishing the warehouse receipts to Norwood?

Answer

1. Yes. Independent dominion and control by the field warehouseman is the essential test that must be met in order to create a valid security inter-

est in the field warehoused goods. If the debtor (Norwood) were allowed to retain dominion and control of the goods placed in the field warehouse on its premises, the validity of the field warehousing arrangement would be questionable. But where the warehouseman is an independent warehousing company and where the formalities are adhered to (that is, posting, and the keys are in the warehouseman's exclusive control), the arrangement will withstand an attack upon its validity.

2. The Uniform Commercial Code provides that a security interest attaches when
a. The collateral is in possession of the secured party pursuant to agreement or the debtor has signed a security agreement that contains a description of the collateral.
b. Value has been given.
c. The debtor has rights to the collateral.
Typically the security interests in such situations arise upon delivery of the warehouse receipts to the creditor.

3. Nothing. A security interest in goods covered by negotiable documents may be perfected by taking possession of the documents. When possession is obtained, no filing is necessary.

4. The danger inherent in relinquishing the negotiable document of title to Norwood is that he may "duly negotiate" it to a holder. The code provides that "such holders take priority over an earlier security interest even though perfected. Filing . . . does not constitute notice of the security interest to such holders. . . ."

Negotiation of a negotiable bearer document of title is by delivery alone. The instrument is "duly negotiated" when negotiated "to a holder who purchases it in good faith without notice of any defense against or claim to it on the part of any person and for value, unless it is established that the negotiation is not in the regular course of business or financing or involved receiving the document in settlement or payment of a money obligation."

PART
FOUR

Debtor-Creditor Relationships and Consumer Protection (10%)*

Chapter 7
Suretyship

Chapter 8
Bankruptcy

Chapter 9
Federal Consumer Protection
Legislation and Bulk Sales

---

* This percentage allocation represents the relative weight to be given to this *area* of business law on the Uniform CPA Examinations beginning in November 1983. It also indicates the approximate percentage of the total achievable test score to be assigned to this *area* of business law for each Uniform CPA Examination beginning in November 1983.

CHAPTER

7

Suretyship

The following is a generalized listing of subjects to be tested through the May 1983 Uniform CPA Examination.

Included in this topic are the identification and characteristics of the surety relationship, the various rights of the parties to the relationship, the surety's defenses, and the cosurety relationship.[1]

The AICPA Board of Examiners has adopted a new content specification outline for the business law section of the Uniform CPA Examination, *to be effective with the November 1983 examination*. The outline lists the following topics to be tested under the title "Suretyship."

   B. Suretyship
      1. Liabilities of Sureties and Cosureties
      2. Release of Sureties
      3. Subrogation and Contribution[2]

I. The rights, duties, and liabilities of a surety are substantially the same as those of the guarantor. This chapter will distinguish the two only in several important areas. Where no distinction is indicated, the rights, duties, and liabilities of the surety and guarantor should be considered as identical. Unless otherwise indicated, the words *surety* or *suretyship* will include within their meaning *guarantor* and *guaranty*, respectively.

---

[1] AICPA, *Information for CPA Candidates*, Copyright © 1975, 1979, by the American Institute of Certified Public Accountants, Inc.
[2] AICPA, *Business Law–Content Specification Outline*, approved by the AICPA Board of Examiners on August 31, 1981.

DEFINITIONS

II. An understanding of the meaning of the following terms is important to the study of the subject of suretyship:

A. *Absolute or unconditional guaranty* is an unconditional undertaking by a guarantor that the principal debtor will pay the debt or perform his or her obligation, i.e., a promise of payment or performance on a contract upon default of the principal debtor without any conditions precedent attached to the promise.

B. *Collateral guaranty* is a contract in which the guarantor undertakes *to pay damages* resulting from the failure of the principal debtor to perform his or her duties under an existing contract. To distinguish from a suretyship, a surety undertakes to do the very thing that the principal debtor has promised to do upon the principal debtor's default.

C. *Conditional guaranty* is one which depends upon some extraneous event beyond the mere default of the principal debtor, such as notice to the guarantor of the principal debtor's default and/or reasonable diligence in exhausting collection remedies against the principal debtor.

D. *Continuing guaranty* is one relating to a future liability of the principal debtor under successive transactions, which either continues the liability or from time to time renews it after it has been satisfied.

E. *Special guaranty* is one which is available only to the particular person to whom it is offered or addressed. It is distinguished from a general guaranty, which operates in favor of any person who may accept it.

F. *Limited guaranty* is one where the guarantor undertakes a liability of a principal debtor limited to a specified transaction or for a specified period of time.

G. *Indemnity contract* is a two-party contract involving a binding promise made to a potential debtor (not to the creditor as in a guaranty) to reimburse that debtor for a debt or other obligation not currently existing but that may occur in the future, e.g., a fire insurance policy.

H. *Suretyship* is a contract in which one person (*surety*) is obligated to perform the exact promise that a second person *(principal debtor)* is obligated to perform for a third person *(creditor)*. In its broadest definition, it includes any obligation to pay, answer for, or satisfy the debt, default in performance, or wrong of another person, association, or entity. For example, construction bonds, fidelity bonds, purchasers of real estate who assume and agree to pay an existing mortgage, unqualified indorsers, and accommodation indorsers on commercial paper (i.e., drafts and promissory notes). The surety's promise is always made to the creditor. If the "surety's" promise is made to the debtor, it is a promise to indemnify not a promise to answer for the debt or default of another as is required for a suretyship relationship. (See Figure 7-1.)

I. *Guarantee for collection.* In this type of guaranty, the creditor must give the guarantor notice of the principal debtor's default and legally attempt to collect from the principal debtor as a condition precedent to recovery from the guarantor.

J. *Cosureties* are sureties *for the same principal debtor for the same debt* or other obligation.

K. *Subsurety* is a surety for a surety on the same debt or other obligation.

L. *Surety bond* is a contractual obligation by a *compensated surety* (i.e., one who is in the business of being a surety for pay) to pay an agreed-upon sum of money upon the failure of the bonded person to perform a specified duty owed to a third person. For example, a fidelity bond issued to a bank to reimburse it for embezzlements by its employees or a construction bond issued to an employer of a general building contractor to guarantee the performance of such contractor. Other types of surety

FIGURE 7-1   SURETYSHIP AND GUARANTY RELATIONSHIP

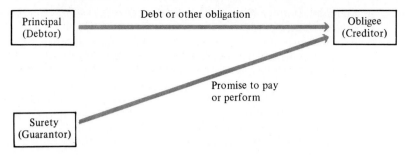

bonds are issued to guarantee performance of officers of the court, such as executors, guardians, or conservators.

SURETYSHIP: A CONTRACTUAL RELATIONSHIP

III. The suretyship relationship is based on contract. For a legally binding suretyship to exist, all the requisite elements of a contract must be present; i.e., offer and acceptance, reality of consent, legally sufficient consideration, legality of subject matter and objectives, legal capacity of parties, and a legally sufficient writing signed by the surety (see Chapter 2).

  A. *Statute of Frauds.* Under the Statute of Frauds, suretyship contracts (including a guaranty) must be evidenced by a writing in order to be enforceable. The writing must be signed by the surety and contain a statement of the surety's promise.

   1. The *"leading object"* or *"primary purpose"* rule is an exception to the requirement of a writing signed by a surety. A surety's oral promise is binding whenever it is made to benefit the surety rather than the principal debtor.

   2. Some examples of the application of the "primary purpose" rule follow:

   a. Hurich was a shareholder and creditor in TMH, Inc., a closed corporation. TMH, Inc., ran short of cash and was threatened with insolvency. Hurich orally induced his girl friend, Irene, to lend TMH, Inc., money on the false promise that he would repay the loan to her if the corporation was not able to. The court enforced Hurich's oral promise as being one that was made for the personal benefit of the promisor (surety).

   b. Tom is a commercial tenant of Alan at an extremely valuable property located in downtown Utica. The property is subject to a $750,000 mortgage with Bank. Alan became hardpressed for money and became erratic in making mortgage payments to Bank. Bank threatened to foreclose. Upon hearing this, Tom orally assured Bank that they need not worry because the mortgage payments would be paid, either by Alan or by himself. Tom's oral promise falls within the primary purpose rule and is enforceable.

   c. Del credere agent. A *del credere agent* is one who sells goods on credit to purchasers in behalf of his or her principal and for an additional commission, guarantees the solvency and performance of each purchaser. Since a del credere agent is a surety, this oral guarantee is enforceable under the primary purpose rule.

  B. *Suretyship and indemnity contracts compared.*

   1. Suretyship contracts, with the exception mentioned above, must be in writing to be enforceable. An oral indemnity contract is enforceable.

   2. A surety's promise is made to a creditor. The promise is to answer for an existing obligation or one that is to come into existence simultaneously with the surety's binding obligation. For example, Albert said, "Go ahead, Julius, sell that car to Andrea; if she doesn't pay for it within three years, I will." Julius sold the automobile to Andrea. The underlying debt and the suretyship undertaking occurred simultaneously. As another example, Nelson owed Lamar $6,000 under a contract to purchase an automobile. Nelson became unemployed. Hearing of Nelson's unemployment, Lamar asked Nelson's father, Ralph, to become a surety on the obligation. He did so in exchange for a reduction of the debt to $5,000. Ralph's promise was to answer for a preexisting debt. If the promises by Albert and Ralph were reduced to writing, signed by Albert and Ralph, respectively, each would be legally bound as a surety. On the other hand, the promise in an indemnity contract is made *to a potential debtor* to reimburse the latter for a loss or for the payment of a debt that may occur *in the future*. For example, a casualty insurance policy or an indemnity bond.

RIGHTS OF THE SURETY

IV. Surety's rights against the principal debtor (see Figure 7-2).

A. *Indemnity* (reimbursement). If a surety is compelled to pay or perform upon the default of the principal debtor, the surety is entitled to reimbursement from the principal debtor. Exceptions to this rule are as follows:

1. A discharge in bankruptcy of the principal debtor will release the duty to indemnify the surety.

2. A surety's payment of the debt or performance of the obligation after having received notice of principal debtor's defense against the creditor will cause the surety to lose the right of indemnity.

3. A *"gift surety"* (i.e., one who does not receive any actual value for his or her promise) is not entitled to indemnity. Contrast the definition of "gift surety" with that of a "compensated surety" appearing at VIII-C-2 below. *Note:* A person may be a gift surety even though the promise by the surety is supported by legally sufficient consideration. For example, Dora promised Eileen that if Eileen would loan Agnus $5,000 Dora would "make good" on the loan if Agnus did not repay it. Dora neither bargained for nor received any value from Agnus or Eileen. Dora is a "gift surety." Her promise is legally binding because she received a presently bargained for legal detriment from Eileen in exchange for her promise to act as a surety; i.e., Eileen loaned money to Agnus even though she was under no previous obligation to do so.

4. A surety can never recover from the principal debtor more than the amount that the surety paid the creditor.

B. *Subrogation.* A surety who pays a creditor "steps into the shoes of a creditor"; that is, the surety acquires the identical claim or right that the creditor possessed against the principal debtor. For example, D borrows money from C and as a security for the loan pledges 300 shares of stock to C. S agrees to act as surety to D in the transaction. If D defaults and S is required to pay the debt of D, S is entitled to hold the 300 shares of stock as security in seeking to enforce the rights of indemnity against D.

FIGURE 7-2   SURETY'S RIGHTS AGAINST THE PRINCIPAL DEBTOR

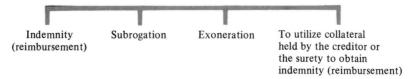

| Indemnity (reimbursement) | Subrogation | Exoneration | To utilize collateral held by the creditor or the surety to obtain indemnity (reimbursement) |

1. The surety is subrogated only to the extent of his or her payment. For example, Vince was a surety on a $10,000 debt to the extent of $8,000. George, the creditor, held collateral as security that amounted to $6,000. Vince was forced to pay George $8,000 upon the principal debtor's default. Vince, by virtue of his rights of subrogation and indemnity, is a secured creditor to the amount of $6,000 (i.e., the collateral held by the secured creditor, George) and an unsecured creditor of the principal debtor in the amount of $2,000.

C. *Exoneration.* When the debt or obligation for which the surety has given his or her promise has become due, the surety may take legal action to enforce the debt or obligation against the principal debtor and cosureties if the creditor has failed to do so. For example, Samuel is a surety on a debt owed by Saul to Daniel. Daniel (creditor) holds ample *collateral* as security for the payment of the debt. Saul is in default on the debt. Daniel refuses to apply the collateral to the debt and seeks payment from Samuel (surety). Samuel is without liquidity. He would suffer irreparable harm if required to raise money by sale or mortgage of his property, or by taking it out of his business. Samuel is entitled to decree in equity against Saul (principal debtor), exonerating Samuel (surety) from his duty to pay.

1. If cosureties were present, the decree could also be entered against the cosureties to exonerate Samuel except as to his own share of the obligation. The decree of exoneration is enforced by a levy against the property of the principal debtor and the cosureties, respectively. The property levied upon could be in the possession of the principal debtor or in the hands of the creditor or cosurety as security for the debt at the time of levy of execution.

2. The surety's lawsuit for exoneration does not hinder the creditor's right to proceed to judgment and execution against the surety. The creditor's right to recover against the surety arises immediately upon the default of the principal debtor. The creditor *need not* resort to collateral in its possession prior to recovery from the surety.

D. *Utilization of collateral.* The surety has the right to *resort to collateral* held either by himself or by the creditor in the exercise of the right of indemnity from the principal debtor.

V. Surety's rights against a cosurety (see Figure 7-3).

A. *In general.* To be cosureties, all sureties must be sureties for the same principal debtor and for the same debt of obligation. Cosureties may assume equal or unequal portions of the debt or other obligation. For example, Surety A agreed to be surety to the extent of $20,000, surety B to the extent of $10,000, and surety C to the extent of $30,000 on a total debt of $30,000.

FIGURE 7-3   RIGHTS AMONG COSURETIES

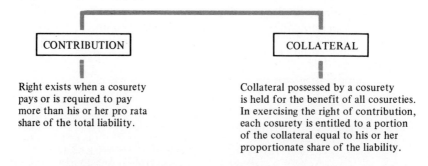

CONTRIBUTION	COLLATERAL
Right exists when a cosurety pays or is required to pay more than his or her pro rata share of the total liability.	Collateral possessed by a cosurety is held for the benefit of all cosureties. In exercising the right of contribution, each cosurety is entitled to a portion of the collateral equal to his or her proportionate share of the liability.

B. *Contribution.* A surety is entitled to *pro rata* (i.e., in a proportion that each surety's risk bears to the total amount of risk assumed by all cosureties) contribution from cosureties upon payment of a debt or performance of an obligation for which others are also sureties.

1. A surety need not exercise his or her right of indemnity against the principal debtor prior to eligibility for contribution from cosureties.
2. In settlement of liability (i.e., contribution) each cosurety is entitled to share pro rata in any collateral held by the creditor or cosurety as security for the performance of the principal debtor's obligation. Each cosurety is entitled to share the collateral in a proportion that his or her dollar amount of risk bears to the total dollar amount of risk assumed by all sureties.
3. The following formula can be used to calculate the dollar amount of pro rata contribution due from cosureties or the pro rata share of the collateral held by a cosurety when one cosurety is obligated to pay the entire debt or to perform the obligation.

$$\frac{\text{Dollar amount of risk assumed by a cosurety}}{\text{Total dollar amount of risk assumed by all cosureties}} \times \begin{array}{c}\text{dollar amount}\\\text{of debt paid by}\\\text{a cosurety}\end{array} = \begin{array}{c}\text{dollar amount of}\\\text{pro rata contribution}\\\text{due from a cosurety}\end{array}$$

Using the amounts stated in V-A above, and assuming that cosurety C paid the entire debt, the calculations are as follows:

Risk assumed:	Surety A:	$20,000	
	Surety B:	$10,000	
	Surety C:	$30,000	
		$60,000	Total risk assumed

$$\text{Cosurety A:} \quad \frac{\$20,000}{\$60,000} \times \frac{\$30,000}{1} = \$10,000$$

$$\text{Cosurety B:} \quad \frac{\$10,000}{\$60,000} \times \frac{\$30,000}{1} = \$ 5,000$$

$$\text{Cosurety C:} \quad \frac{\$30,000}{\$60,000} \times \frac{\$30,000}{1} = \$15,000$$

Surety C, having paid the entire debt of $30,000, is entitled to $5,000 from cosurety B and $10,000 from cosurety C.

C. *Pro rata share of collateral held by a cosurety.* A cosurety who is obligated to pay a creditor upon the default of the principal debtor is entitled to share pro rata in collateral held by any cosurety. To compute the cosurety's pro rata share of the collateral held by any cosurety substitute the value of the collateral (or the value of the proceeds from the sale of the collateral) for the dollar amount of debt paid by a cosurety in the formula stated above. *Note:* In the problem above, if a cosurety was in possession of collateral valued at $18,000, each cosurety would be entitled to share in the collateral as follows:

Cosurety A: $\frac{1}{3}$ or $ 6,000

Cosurety B: $\frac{1}{6}$ or $ 3,000

Cosurety C: $\frac{1}{2}$ or $ 9,000
$18,000   Total value of collateral

D. *Reduction of liability upon discharge or release by the creditor.* The discharge or release of one cosurety results in a reduction of the liability of the remaining cosurety or cosureties to the extent of the released cosurety's pro rata share of the total debt (i.e., the amount that the remaining sureties would have been able to recover from the cosurety had he not been discharged or released under their right of contribution). For example, A, B, and C are cosureties on a debt in the amount of $15,000. The creditor released B. A and C are only obligated to the creditor in the amount of $10,000 should either have to pay upon default of the principal debtor.

VI. Surety's rights against subsurety.

    A. *In general.* A surety owes a duty to a subsurety to pay the agreed amount of debt or perform the agreed-upon obligation upon the default of the principal debtor.

    B. *Contribution.* No right of contribution exists between the surety and the subsurety.

    C. *Subsurety's right of indemnity.* If the surety does not pay the amount owed to the creditor upon the default of the principal debtor and the subsurety is compelled to pay, the subsurety has the right of indemnity against the surety.

    D. *Collateral in possession of surety.* In pursuing his or her right of indemnity against the surety, the subsurety is entitled to use any collateral held by the surety as security for the principal debtor's performance of the obligation.

VII. Surety's rights against the creditor (see Figure 7-4).

    A. *Subrogation.* The surety has the right to be subrogated to the rights of the creditor upon the surety's payment in full to the principal debtor.

        1. The right exists even though the principal debtor did not know that the creditor had obtained a surety for the obligation.

        2. Some rights of the creditor to which the surety may be subrogated are:

            a. A mortgage on real estate owned by the principal debtor;

            b. A security interest in the collateral under article 9 of the Uniform Commercial Code;

            c. The right to collect attorney fees upon the principal debtor's promissory note;

            d. The right to confess judgment against the principal debtor on a promissory note; or

            e. A priority in bankruptcy.

        3. The creditor has the duty to take all legal measures to effect the surety's right of subrogation. For example, assign all rights against principal debtor; supply all requisite indorsements of promissory notes, stocks or bonds; and release all rights to collateral held as security.

    B. *Notice of default.* As a general rule, a creditor is under no duty to give notice of the principal debtor's default to the surety. The conditional guaranty and the guarantee for collection are exceptions.

        1. A *conditional guaranty* may provide that the creditor's demand for payment from the principal debtor, notice of default to the surety, and an attempt to collect from the principal debtor are conditions precedent to the surety's (guarantor's) liability.

FIGURE 7-4   SURETY'S RIGHTS AGAINST CREDITOR

| Set-off | Subrogation: To acquire the legal status of the creditor as against the debtor (e.g., secured creditor or pledgee of collateral) | To utilize collateral held by the creditor to obtain indemnity (reimbursement) from the debtor | Under a conditional guaranty or guarantee for collection, to force the creditor to take legal steps to recover from the debtor prior to proceeding against the creditor after default |

2. A *guarantee for collection* obligates the creditor, upon default of the principal debtor, to exercise "due diligence" to obtain payment from the principal debtor prior to proceeding against the surety (guarantor). "Due diligence" means to sue the principal debtor, obtain a judgment, and have a levy of execution on the judgment be returned unsatisfied (i.e., the principal debtor or his or her property could not be located or if located, were of insufficient value to satisfy the judgment).

C. *Collateral in possession of the creditor.*

    1. The creditor owes a duty to the surety to retain, safeguard, and refrain from *legally impairing collateral* in his or her possession (see also VIII-C below).

    2. Upon payment of the debt by the surety to the creditor, the surety has the right to proceed against the collateral held by the creditor in order to exercise the right of indemnity (reimbursement) against the principal debtor. The surety has a right to the collateral even though he or she did not bargain for the right and did not previously know that collateral was being held by the creditor.

D. *Refusal of payment.* A surety has the right to refuse payment to the creditor for the following reasons:

    1. *Breach of contractual condition precedent to payment.* To be entitled to payment the creditor must have complied with all conditions precedent agreed upon in a conditional guaranty or a guarantee for collection. These conditions precedent were discussed in VII-B-1, **2** above.

    2. *Defenses.* A surety may refuse payment if it has available to it any ordinary contractual defense or any special suretyship defense against the creditor (see VIII below).

SURETY'S DEFENSES AGAINST THE CREDITOR

VIII. The surety may assert three types of defenses against the creditor; his own *ordinary contractual defenses,* contractual defenses possessed by the principal debtor, and special suretyship defenses (see Figure 7-5).

A. *Surety's own contractual defenses.* Some of the surety's contractual defenses are as follows:

    1. Absence of legally sufficient consideration for the suretyship promise;

    2. Breach of contract by the creditor;

    3. Lack of legal capacity to contract on the part of the surety;

    4. Illegality of the suretyship transaction or its purpose;

    5. Mutual mistake of fact by the surety and the creditor;

    6. Duress or undue influence exerted upon the surety by the creditor;

    7. Statute of Limitations has expired on the creditor's cause of action against the surety for default of the principal debtor;

    8. Right to set-off (deduct) any debt owed by the creditor to the surety against the amount of debt guaranteed by the surety;

    9. Statute of Frauds was not complied with because the suretyship was not evidenced by a legally sufficient writing signed by the surety.

B. *Contractual defenses available to the principal debtor.* The surety has the right to assert most contractual defenses available to the principal debtor which arose out of the basic transaction by which the debt or obligation came into existence. In other words, if the principal debtor is not liable to the creditor, the surety is not liable. *Exceptions:* The following defenses available to the principal debtor are not available to the surety:

    1. Insolvency or discharge in bankruptcy of the principal debtor; and

    2. Lack of legal capacity of the principal debtor.

FIGURE 7-5 SURETY'S DEFENSES AGAINST CREDITOR

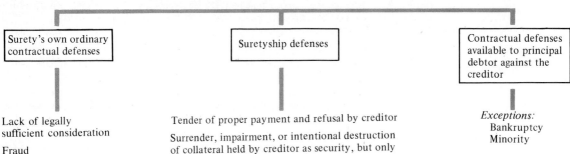

Surety's own ordinary contractual defenses	Suretyship defenses	Contractual defenses available to principal debtor against the creditor

Lack of legally sufficient consideration

Fraud

Duress

Undue influence

Mutual mistake

Lack of legal capacity

Illegality (at the time of the contract or subsequently)

Statute of Frauds

Set-off

Statute of Limitations

Tender of proper payment and refusal by creditor

Surrender, impairment, or intentional destruction of collateral held by creditor as security, but only to the extent surrendered, impaired, or destroyed

Discharge of the debtor

1. Payment in full to creditor
2. Complete performance of the obligation by the debtor
3. Release of the debtor by the creditor, but only to the extent released
4. Novation (i.e., substitution of debtors)

Discharge or release of a cosurety by the creditor, but only to the extent of the discharged or released cosurety's pro rata share of the entire debt

A binding material alteration (increase in risk to the surety) of the obligation without the consent of the surety

Exception: Compensated surety

Exceptions:
Bankruptcy
Minority

C. *Suretyship defenses.* In addition to ordinary contractual defenses, the surety may assert the following special suretyship defenses (see Figure 7-5).
1. *Discharge of the principal debtor.* Any event that legally discharges the debt or obligation of the principal debtor also has the effect of discharging the debt or obligation of the surety to the same extent. For example:
   a. A legally binding release given by the creditor to the principal debtor;
   b. Payment in full to the creditor by the principal debtor;
   c. Complete performance of the obligation by the principal debtor;
   d. A *novation* entered into by the principal debtor, the creditor, and a substitute debtor whereby the latter becomes the principal debtor and the existing principal debtor is released from debt or other obligation.
2. *Increase in the surety's risk* as a result of events subsequent to the surety's undertaking will *discharge the surety.* A change in the surety's risk occurs whenever there is any alteration of the original terms and conditions of the contract that created the debt or other obligation owed by the principal debtor. A gratuitous surety is completely discharged if the creditor does anything that varies the surety's risk. However, a "compensated," commercial surety is discharged only if the creditor's action caused a "binding material" increase in the risk. Even so, the compensated, commercial surety is discharged only to the extent of the increased risk. Some examples of how this defense may arise are as follows:

a. **Surety bond.** A bonded employer neglects to give notice to the surety that the employer increased the money-handling responsibilities of several covered employees from $10,000 to $100,000. *Result:* Surety is discharged.

b. Creditor and debtor increase the interest rate to be paid by the debtor under the original obligation. *Result:* Surety is discharged.

c. Surety agreement is to indemnify performance of a partnership consisting of three partners. Subsequently, one partner withdraws. *Result:* Surety is discharged.

d. Creditor gives the debtor a *legally binding extension of time* within which to pay the debt. *Result:* Surety is discharged unless:

    (1) Surety is amply protected by collateral. For example, the amount of the debt is $50,000 and the surety holds $75,000 worth of bonds as security.

    (2) Surety is a compensated (paid) surety. A *compensated surety* is one that *is in the business* of being a surety for pay. For example, a bonding or insurance company.

    (3) Surety is a continuous guarantor. For example, Acme Surety Company agrees with 1st Bank to be surety on any loans made by 1st Bank to Trix Company during the 1982 year for a total amount of $100,000. Trix Company received loans from 1st Bank in March, May, and July, all to be repaid within six months after the date of each loan. On the due date of the March loan Trix Company received a one-month extension of time and in exchange gave 1st Bank common stock to hold as security for repayment of all loans. The surety is not discharged.

3. A *tender of proper payment* by the principal debtor or the surety to the creditor, coupled with the creditor's refusal thereof, discharges the surety. *It does not discharge the debtor.* It merely terminates the accrual of interest on the debt.

4. *Surrender, release, or impairment of collateral* (i.e., property held as additional security) by the creditor will discharge the surety, *but only to the extent* of the value of the collateral surrendered, released, or impaired. The following are examples of surrender, release, or impairment of collateral by a creditor:

a. Janis loaned money to Sharp. Sharp gave 2,000 shares of common stock to Janis to hold as security. Nolan agreed to be surety on the debt. Several weeks later Janis sold 1,000 of the shares to Lucky, a bona fide purchaser for value. Nolan is discharged to the extent of the value of the 1,000 shares at the time they were sold.

b. A creditor, holding bonds as security for a debt, surrendered the bonds to the principal debtor without permission from the surety. The surrender of the bonds released the surety to the extent of their value at the time of the surrender.

c. The creditor, upon the default of the principal debtor, sold the collateral without giving prior notice of the sale to the surety. A creditor does have the right to sell collateral and use the proceeds to satisfy the debt. However, prior to doing so, he or she must notify the surety.

d. A creditor failed to file a Uniform Commercial Code financing statement covering the collateral and consequently lost its priority over the collateral to third persons.

5. A *creditor's concealment of material information* (i.e., information pertaining to the risk assumed by the surety) from the surety prior to the latter's undertaking of the risk gives rise to a defense of fraud. For example, a creditor knew that the principal debtor had lied to a prospective surety about his or her financial condition. The creditor failed to warn the surety. The creditor is guilty of fraud and the surety's undertaking is voidable.

6. *Failure of creditor to give conditional guarantor notice of default* by the principal debtor as required under a conditional guaranty (see VII-B-1 above).

7. *Failure of creditor to use "due diligence"* to obtain payment from the principal debtor as required by a guarantee for collection (see VII-B-2 above).

8. *Special note: Decrease in the surety's risk.* No modification of the original obligation by the principal debtor and the creditor will release the surety if the modification is beneficial to the surety, i.e., it decreases the surety's risk. For example, The principal debtor gave collateral to the creditor or the principal debtor and creditor reduced the rate of interest payable on the debt.

RIGHTS OF THE CREDITOR

IX. Creditor's rights against principal debtor.

    A. *Payment.* Unless the principal debtor has a defense, the creditor has the right to receive the exact payment or performance specified in the contract with the principal debtor.

    B. *Collateral in possession of the creditor.*

        1. *Right to possession.* As security for full payment of the debt or complete performance of the obligation, the creditor has exclusive right to possession of the collateral and any income thereon.

        2. *Return of collateral prior to default.* The creditor has a duty to return the collateral and any income thereon to the principal debtor only upon receipt of full payment of the debt or complete performance of the obligation.

        3. *Option to resort to collateral upon default.* Upon default the creditor has the following alternatives:

            a. Decline to resort to the collateral and proceed against the principal debtor, the surety, or both; or

            b. Resort to the collateral immediately. If the creditor does resort to the collateral for payment:

                (1) Any excess collateral or its proceeds must be returned to the principal debtor; or

                (2) If the collateral or its proceeds are not sufficient to satisfy the debt, the creditor can recover the deficiency from either the principal debtor, a surety, or any cosurety.

    C. *Collateral in possession of the surety.* Upon default of the principal debtor the creditor has the following options:

        1. *Decline to resort to collateral* and proceed against the principal debtor, surety, or both.

        2. *Resort immediately to the collateral* held by the surety. The creditor has this right even though the creditor is also in possession of collateral. If the creditor does resort to collateral held by a surety:

            a. Any excess collateral or its proceeds must be returned to the principal debtor; or

            b. If the collateral or its proceeds are not sufficient to satisfy the debt, the creditor can recover the deficiency from either the principal debtor or the surety.

X. Creditor's rights against the surety (including cosureties) (see Figure 7-6).

    A. *Payment.* Upon default of the principal debtor, the creditor is entitled to immediate payment from the surety even though the creditor or surety or both are in possession of ample collateral as security for the debt or performance. *Exceptions:* Conditional guaranty and guarantee for collection (see VII-D-1, 2 above).

    B. *Collateral in possession of the surety or cosurety.*

FIGURE 7-6   CREDITOR'S RIGHTS AGAINST SURETY

To immediate payment upon debtor's default without notice or previous demand for payment from the debtor *Exceptions:* Conditional guaranty or guarantee for collection	Subrogation to the rights of a surety in possession of collateral	To utilize collateral held by the surety to obtain payment from the debtor	To demand and receive payment without first resorting to collateral possessed by either the creditor or the surety

1. *Prior to default.* The surety owes to the creditor a duty to retain, safeguard, and to refrain from legally impairing the collateral or any income thereon.
   a. The surety must not release the collateral to the principal debtor before the creditor is fully paid or receives complete performance.
   b. The creditor's negligent or willful damage or destruction of the collateral is a violation of his or her duty.
   c. A creditor who intentionally causes any lien or security interest to attach to collateral has legally impaired the collateral. For example, a surety held bearer bonds as collateral. The surety pledged the bonds as security for a personal loan from a bank. At the time the bank made the loan it had no knowledge that the bonds were not owned by the surety and that they were being held as collateral under a suretyship. The bank has priority in the bonds over the creditor.
2. *Upon default.* Upon default, the creditor has two alternative remedies. He may:
   a. *Decline to resort to any collateral* (i.e., in his or her possession or in the possession of the surety) and proceed immediately against the surety and cosurety or the debtor for payment; or
   b. *Resort to the collateral held by the surety.* If the creditor does resort to the collateral for payment:
      (1) Any excess collateral or its proceeds must be returned to the principal debtor, or
      (2) If the collateral or its proceeds are not sufficient to satisfy the debt, the creditor can recover the deficiency from either the surety, any cosurety, or the principal debtor.

RIGHTS OF THE PRINCIPAL DEBTOR

XI. Principal debtor's rights against the creditor (see Figure 7-7).
   A. *Payment.* The creditor has a duty to accept proper tender of payment either from the principal debtor or from the surety. Refusal of proper tender of payment does not discharge the principal debtor. It *does* prevent the further accrual of interest on the debt. *Note:* Such refusal *does* discharge the surety.
   B. *Collateral in possession of the creditor.*
      1. Prior to default, the creditor has a duty to retain, safeguard, and refrain from legally impairing the collateral or income therefrom in his or her possession.
         a. A creditor is liable to the principal debtor for willful or negligent damage, loss, or destruction of collateral entrusted to the creditor by the principal debtor.
         b. If proper payment is tendered or made prior to default, the creditor must return the collateral and any income thereon to the principal debtor.

FIGURE 7-7   CREATOR'S DUTIES TO PRINCIPAL DEBTOR

Exercise "due diligence" to collect from a conditional guarantor or a guarantor under a guarantee for collection	To retain and safeguard collateral in creditor's possession	To return excess proceeds after utilization of collateral to obtain payment
To accept payment upon proper tender by debtor or surety	To return collateral upon payment of the debt prior to default	

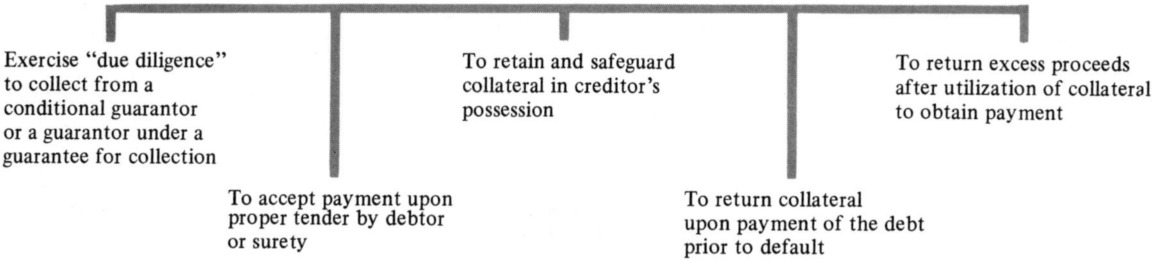

      c. After default the creditor has the option to either resort to the collateral or to proceed immediately against the principal debtor or the surety.

        (1) If the creditor does resort to the collateral for payment:

           (*a*) The creditor must return any excess collateral or its proceeds to the principal debtor; and

           (*b*) If the collateral or its proceeds are not sufficient to satisfy the debt, the creditor may proceed against the principal debtor or the surety for the deficiency.

           (*c*) The reasons why a creditor may not choose to resort to collateral are that the collateral may not currently have a ready market, it may have lost a substantial amount of its value, or a resort to the collateral may involve too much time.

    C. *Notice of default.* A principal debtor is not entitled to notice that the debt or obligation is due or past due. The creditor may immediately proceed against the principal debtor personally or resort to any collateral upon default by the principal debtor.

  XII. Principal debtor's rights against the surety (see Figure 7-8).

    A. *Rights prior to payment by the surety.*

      1. *Contractual or other defenses.* A principal debtor has the right to assert any contractual or other defenses he or she may have against either the creditor or the surety or both to eliminate the liability to pay or perform the obligation. These rights are usually asserted in two ways: one in a lawsuit by the principal debtor against the creditor to rescind the contract with the creditor and thereby eliminate the underlying debt or other obligation; and the other as a defense to a lawsuit filed for exoneration filed by the surety. Some examples of defenses are, fraud, lack of legal capacity to contract, lack of legally sufficient consideration, duress, undue influence, illegality of the transaction or its purpose, prior release

FIGURE 7-8   SURETY'S DUTIES TO PRINCIPAL DEBTOR

To retain and safeguard collateral in surety's possession prior to default	To return collateral upon payment of the debt prior to default	To pay the debt upon default	To return to the debtor any excess proceeds after utilization of collateral to obtain indemnity (reimbursement)
	To return to the debtor all income from collateral not required to be used to obtain indemnity (reimbursement)		

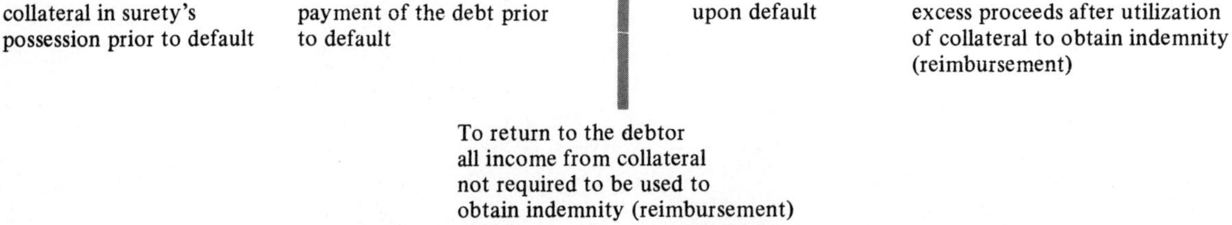

of the debt, and mutual mistake of fact. A discharge in bankruptcy is also a defense to the principal debtor. *Note:* These defenses (with the exception of lack of legal capacity of the principal debtor to contract and the insolvency or discharge in bankruptcy of the principal debtor) are also available to the surety along with his or her own contractual and surety defenses to be asserted against the creditor should the latter demand payment from the surety (see VIII above).

   2. *Damages or injunction.* The principal debtor can sue for an injunction against a surety to prevent damage, destruction, or legal impairment of collateral entrusted to the surety by the principal debtor. If such damage, destruction, or legal impairment has already occurred, the principal debtor can either recover damages or assert any one of the above-mentioned wrongful acts as a defense or set-off against any claims by the surety.

   3. *Return of collateral in possession of the surety.* The principal debtor is entitled to return of collateral in possession of the surety in the following circumstances:
      a. The principal debtor paid the creditor in full prior to default;
      b. The principal debtor has a valid defense against the creditor; and
      c. After default of the principal debtor and full payment by the surety to the creditor, the surety was indemnified by the principal debtor.

B. *Rights after payment by the surety.*

   1. *Contractual and suretyship defenses.* As a general rule, after the surety has paid the creditor, the surety is entitled to be indemnified by the principal debtor and to be subrogated to the creditor's rights in any collateral in the latter's possession (see IV-A, B above). The principal debtor has a right to assert the following defenses to a surety's claim for indemnity:
      a. Discharge in bankruptcy;
      b. Partial payment (a surety is never entitled to indemnification of and subrogation to more than the amount paid to the creditor);
      c. The surety paid or performed after having received notice of one or more of the principal debtor's defenses against the creditor;
      d. The surety was a "gift surety." Only "compensated sureties" are entitled to indemnity and subrogation; or
      e. The time period provided for in a Statute of Limitations had expired on the surety's cause of action for indemnity.

   2. *Return of collateral.* The principal debtor is entitled to excess proceeds and income from his or her collateral after the surety had resorted to the collateral and obtained full indemnification.

SELF-QUIZ

To check your understanding of the key words and concepts and the accuracy of your answers to the questions, refer to the text material as referenced by page number.

KEY WORDS AND CONCEPTS

QUESTIONS

1. What is the single most important factor used to identify a suretyship? **(215)**
2. What is a contract of indemnity? **(215)**
3. Why is it important to distinguish between a suretyship and a contract of indemnity? **(216)**
4. What two types of promises to answer for the debt or default of another receive distinctly different treatment under the law of suretyship? **(215)** How is the treatment different? **(220)**
5. Must all suretyship contracts be in writing in order to be enforceable? **(216)**
6. Explain the "leading object" or "primary purpose" rule exception to the Statute of Frauds. **(216)**
7. Compare the rights of "gift surety" with those of a "compensated surety." **(217, 223)**
8. Explain the concept of subrogation. **(217)**
9. Which parties to a suretyship transaction are entitled to subrogation? **(217)** When? **(220)**
10. Why is it important to a party to have the right of subrogation? **(220)**
11. Exoneration is an equitable remedy available to a surety only under unusual circumstances. What are those circumstances? **(218)**
12. A surety is entitled to contribution from cosureties. Explain the formula used to determine the share of the debt that the surety must bear. **(218)**
13. What is the effect of the discharge or release of a cosurety by the creditor? **(219)**
14. Under what circumstances must a surety be given notice of the principal debtor's default? **(220)**
15. List some of the rights possessed by a creditor to which a surety may be subrogated. **(220)**
16. What are the duties of a creditor in possession of collateral? **(224)** Of a surety in possession of collateral? **(224)**
17. What are the options available to a surety or creditor in possession of collateral upon the default of the principal debtor? **(224)**
18. List three types of defenses available to a surety against the creditor. **(221)**
19. Which two defenses are available to the principal debtor but are not available to the surety? **(221)**
20. List the suretyship defenses. **(222)**
21. How may the risk assumed by a surety be increased so as to give rise to a surety defense? **(222)**
22. Explain what is meant by the "impairment of collateral." **(223)**
23. What option does a creditor who is in possession of collateral have upon the default of the principal debtor? **(224)**
24. List the duties of a creditor or surety in possession of collateral. Prior to default by the principal debtor? **(224)** After default? **(225)**

SELECTED QUESTIONS AND UNOFFICIAL ANSWERS

OBJECTIVE QUESTIONS

Select the best answer for each of the following items. Mark only one answer for each item. Answer all items.

MAY 1981

35. Doral is the surety on a loan made by Nelson to Gordon. Which statement describes Doral's legal relationship or status among the respective parties?

a. As between Gordon and Doral, Doral has the ultimate liability.

b. Upon default by Gordon and payment by Doral, Doral is entitled to subrogation to the rights of Nelson or to obtain reimbursement from Gordon.

c. Doral is a fiduciary insofar as Nelson is concerned.

d. Doral is *not* liable immediately upon default by Gordon, unless the agreement so provides.

36. Don loaned $10,000 to Jon, and Robert agreed to act as surety. Robert's agreement to act as surety was induced by (1) fraudulent misrepresentations made by Don concerning Jon's financial status and (2) a bogus unaudited financial statement of which Don had no knowledge, and which was independently submitted by Jon to Robert. Which of the following is correct?

a. Don's fraudulent misrepresentations will *not* provide Robert with a valid defense unless they were contained in a signed writing.

b. Robert will be liable on his surety undertaking despite the facts since the defenses are personal defenses.

c. Robert's reliance upon Jon's financial statements makes Robert's surety undertaking voidable.

d. Don's fraudulent misrepresentations provide Robert with a defense which will prevent Don from enforcing the surety undertaking.

37. Welch is a surety on Stanton's contract to build an office building for Brent. Stanton intentionally abandoned the project after it was 85% completed because of personal animosity which developed toward Brent. Which of the following is a correct statement concerning the rights or responsibilities of the various parties?

a. Any modification of the contract, however slight and even if beneficial to Welch, will release Welch.

b. Welch would be ordered to specifically perform the completion of the building if Brent sought this remedy.

c. Neither Stanton's failure to give Welch prior notice of its intention to abandon the project *nor* its actual abandonment of the project will release Welch.

d. Welch can*not* engage a contractor to finish the job and obtain from Brent the balance due on the contract.

38. Reginald, who is insolvent, defaulted on a loan upon which Jayne was the surety. Edward, the creditor, demanded payment from Jayne of the amount owed by Reginald. The loan was also secured by a mortgage which Edward has the right to foreclose. Which of the following is Jayne's best legal course of action?

a. Seek specific performance by Reginald.

b. Refuse to pay until Reginald has been petitioned into bankruptcy and the matter has been decided by the trustee in bankruptcy.

c. Pay Edward and resort to the subrogation rights to the collateral.

d. Refuse to pay because Edward must first resort to the collateral.

39. Overall, Inc., owns 100% in the stock of Controlled Corporation, each being a separate entity. Overall telephoned the Factory Supply Company and ordered $400 of miscellaneous merchandise. Overall told Factory to ship the supplies to Controlled and Overall would pay for them. Factory did so and now seeks recovery of the price or damages. Which of the following is correct?

a. Overall is a surety.

b. The Statute of Frauds will *not* bar Factory from recovering from Overall.

c. Controlled is the principal debtor.

d. Overall and Controlled are jointly and severally liable on the contract.

MAY 1980

36. Dilworth provided collateral to Maxim to secure Dilworth's performance of an obligation owed to Maxim. Maxim also obtained the Protection Surety Company as a surety for Dilworth's performance. Dilworth has defaulted and Protection has discharged the obligation in full. Which of the following is the correct legal basis for Protection's assertion of rights to the collateral?

a. Promissory estoppel.

b. Exoneration.

c. Indemnification.

d. Subrogation.

39. Nolan Surety Company has agreed to serve as a guarantor of collection (a form of conditional guaranty) of the accounts receivable of the Dunbar Sales Corporation. The duration of the guarantee is one year and the maximum liability assumed is

$3,000. Nolan charged the appropriate fee for acting in this capacity. Which of the following statements *best* describes the difference between a guarantor of collection and the typical surety relationship?

a. A guaranty need *not* be in writing provided the duration is less than a year.

b. The guarantor is *not* immediately liable upon default; the creditor must first proceed against the debtor.

c. A guaranty is only available from a surety who is a compensated surety.

d. A guaranty is only used in connection with the sale of goods which have been guaranteed by the seller.

41. Simpson and Thomas made separate contracts of suretyship with Allan to guarantee repayment of a $12,000 loan Allan made to Parker. Simpson's guarantee was for $12,000 and Thomas' for $8,000. In the event Simpson pays the full amount ($12,000), what may he recover from Thomas?

a. Nothing since their contracts were separate.

b. $4,800.

c. $6,000.

d. $8,000.

42. Moncrief is a surety on a $100,000 obligation owed by Vicars to Sampson. The debt is also secured by a $50,000 mortgage to Sampson on Vicars' factory. Vicars is in bankruptcy. Moncrief has satisfied the debt. Which of the following is a correct statement?

a. Moncrief is a secured creditor to the extent of the $50,000 mortgage and a general creditor for the balance.

b. Moncrief would not be entitled to a priority in bankruptcy, even though Sampson could validly claim it.

c. Moncrief is only entitled to the standing of a general creditor in bankruptcy.

d. Moncrief is entitled to nothing in bankruptcy since this was a risk he assumed.

44. Cornwith agreed to serve as a surety on a loan by Super Credit Corporation to Fairfax, one of Cornwith's major customers. The relationship between Fairfax and Super deteriorated to a point of hatred as a result of several late payments on the loan. On the due date of the final payment, Fairfax appeared 15 minutes before closing and tendered payment of the entire amount owing to Super. The office manager of Super told Fairfax that he was too late and would have to pay the next day with additional interest and penalties. Fairfax again tendered the payment, which was again refused. It is now several months later and Super is seeking to collect from either Cornwith or Fairfax or both. What are Super's rights under the circumstances?

a. It cannot collect anything from either party.

b. The tender of performance released Cornwith from his obligation.

c. The tender of performance was too late and rightfully refused.

d. Cornwith is released only to the extent that the refusal to accept the tender harmed him.

MAY 1979

1. Martinson borrowed $50,000 from Wisdom Finance Company. The loan was evidenced by a nonnegotiable promissory note secured by a first mortgage on Martinson's ranch. One of the terms of the note required acceleration of repayment in the event that Wisdom "deemed itself insecure." When the value of the property declined, Wisdom notified Martinson that pursuant to the terms of the note, it "deemed itself insecure" and demanded that either additional collateral or an acceptable surety be provided. Martinson arranged for Clark, a personal friend, to act as surety on the loan. Clark signed the note as an indorser and Wisdom agreed in writing *not* to accelerate repayment of the loan during the life of the debt. Martinson has defaulted. Which of the following is a correct statement?

a. Clark's promise is *not* supported by consideration, hence is unenforceable.

b. Clark is a guarantor of collection and his obligation is conditioned upon Wisdom's first proceeding against Martinson.

c. Release of the mortgage by Wisdom would release Clark to the extent of the value of the property.

d. Wisdom must first foreclose the mortgage before it can proceed against Clark.

5. Dunlop loaned Barkum $20,000 which was secured by a security agreement covering Barkum's machinery and equipment. A financing statement was properly filed covering the machinery and equipment. In addition, Delson was a surety on the Barkum loan. Barkum is now insolvent and a petition in bankruptcy has been filed against him. Delson paid the amount owed ($17,000) to Dunlop. The property was sold for $12,000. Which of the following is correct?

a. Delson has the right of a secured creditor to the $12,000 via subrogation to Dunlop's rights and the standing of general creditor for the balance.

b. To the extent Delson is *not* fully satisfied for the $17,000 he paid Dunlop, his claim against Barkum will *not* be discharged in bankruptcy.

c. Delson's *best* strategy would have been to proceed against Barkum in his own right for reimbursement.

d. Delson should have asserted his right of exoneration.

6. Quinn was the sole owner of Sunnydale Farms, Inc. The business was in dire need of additional working capital in order to survive. Click Company was willing to loan Sunnydale $12,000, but only if Click obtained a security interest in Sunnydale's machinery and equipment and a promise from Quinn to guarantee repayment of the loan. Click obtained both. Sunnydale was subsequently adjudged bankrupt. Click filed a reclamation claim for the machinery and equipment which was denied by the trustee in bankruptcy. The property was sold at public auction for $10,500. Click negotiated a settlement with the trustee whereby it received the $10,500 proceeds on the sale in full settlement of its claim against the bankrupt. Which of the following is a correct statement?

a. Where a surety is the sole owner of the stock of the corporation whose debt he guarantees, he is a compensated surety.

b. Click first had to exhaust his remedies against the property before he could sue Quinn.

c. Quinn must pay Click the $1,500 difference, plus interest.

d. The settlement released Quinn from his surety obligation.

7. Crawford and Blackwell separately agreed to act as sureties on a loan of $25,000 by Lux to Factor. Each promised to pay the full $25,000 upon default of Factor. Lux subsequently released Blackwell from his surety undertaking. Which of the following is a correct statement?

a. The release has *no* effect upon Crawford's right to contribution if he is obligated to pay.

b. The release of Blackwell had *no* effect upon Crawford's liability.

c. The release of Blackwell also totally released Crawford.

d. The release of Blackwell also released Crawford to the extent of $12,500.

Answers to Objective Questions

May 1981		May 1980	
35. b	38. c	36. d	42. a
36. d	39. b	39. b	44. b
37. c		41. b	

May 1979	
1. c	6. d
5. a	7. d

Explanation of Answers to Objective Questions

MAY 1981

35. **(b)** A surety, who satisfies the obligation of the debtor, will be subrogated to the rights of the creditor. The right of subrogation means that upon satisfaction of the creditor, the surety has the same rights as the creditor had against the debtor. This includes the rights in any collateral the creditor might be holding to insure performance by the principal debtor. The surety also has the right of reimbursement which means once the surety satisfies the obligation, the principal debtor must repay the surety. Answer (a) is incorrect because the principal debtor, not the surety, always has ultimate liability. Answer (c) is incorrect since there is no fiduciary relationship between surety and creditor. Answer (d) is incorrect because normally a surety is immediately liable upon default by the debtor. Only in a guaranty of collection does the creditor have to exhaust his remedies against debtor before being able to proceed against the surety.

36. **(d)** If the creditor obtains the surety's promise by fraud, the surety has a valid defense against the creditor. The fact that the creditor's fraud was not contained in a signed writing (answer a) will not invalidate the surety's defense. Answer (b) is incorrect because the fact that fraud in the inducement is a personal defense has relevance only under the law of negotiable instruments, not the law of suretyship. Fraud by the principal debtor on the surety will not permit the surety to avoid liability to the creditor (answer c).

37. (c) Unless the contract is a conditional guaranty, it is unnecessary for creditors to give notice of the debtor's default to the surety. With or without notice, upon default the surety is liable for the performance guaranteed under the agreement. Answer (a) is incorrect because any modifications of the contract that have the possibility of increasing the surety's risk would release the surety. Brent could sue the surety for compensatory damages, not specific performance; therefore, answer (b) is incorrect. Answer (d) is incorrect since if Welch, the surety, did satisfy the obligation by engaging a contractor to finish the job, Welch could collect the balance due on the agreement.

38. (c) Upon payment by the surety, the surety will be subrogated (stand in the shoes of the creditor) to the rights of the creditor. Edward, the creditor, had a right to foreclose the mortgage; therefore, when Jayne pays the obligation, she also has the right to foreclose on the mortgage. Answer (a) is incorrect because money damages would be a sufficient remedy, consequently specific performance would not be available. Answer (b) is incorrect since bankruptcy of the principal debtor is not a defense that the surety can use against the creditor. Answer (d) is incorrect since the creditor has no obligation to resort to the collateral before proceeding against the surety for satisfaction. However, if the creditor does not use the collateral, he must hold the collateral for the benefit of the surety.

39. (b) Overall's promise is not a promise to pay the debt of another. Consequently, it need not be in writing to be enforceable because it does not fall within the suretyship section of the Statute of Frauds. Answers (a), (c), and (d) are incorrect because the agreement is a third party beneficiary contract, not a suretyship agreement. Controlled never incurred an obligation concerning the goods delivered to them. Overall is the debtor who entered a contract with Factory for the benefit of Controlled.

36. (d) Once a surety satisfies the obligation the surety is subrogated to the rights of the creditor. The surety is said to stand in the shoes of the creditor once the surety pays the debt. Promissory estoppel relates to consideration requirements of a contract. Exoneration is the surety's right to force the principal debtor to pay the debt on the due date

if the surety is able to prove the debtor has sufficient funds. Indemnification is a right of an insured against an insurer.

39. (b) Guaranty of collection is a special form of suretyship agreement. The guarantor of collection is only liable if the creditor has attempted to collect from the principal debtor and was unable to do so. The normal surety is liable when the loan or obligation is due irrespective of whether the creditor has attempted to collect from the debtor. A guaranty is a promise to pay the debt of another, thus the statute of frauds would normally require that it be in writing. A guaranty can arise from a non-compensated, as well as a compensated, surety. A guaranty can be used in connection with all types of contracts.

41. (b) Simpson and Thomas would be co-sureties since they are guaranteeing the same obligation. If one co-surety satisfies the full obligation he then has the right of contribution, meaning that the other surety must contribute his proportionate share. Since Simpson guaranteed the full $12,000 and Thomas only guaranteed $8,000, their proportionate shares would be in a 3-to-2 ratio. Thus Thomas must pay Simpson $4,800.

42. (a) Once Moncrief, the surety, satisfies the debt, he is subrogated to the rights of Sampson, the creditor. Thus he becomes a secured creditor to the extent of the mortgage ($50,000) and a general creditor for the balance. Moncrief would have the same rights in the bankruptcy proceeding as Sampson could have exercised.

44. (b) The tender of performance by the principal debtor completely releases the surety from his obligation. However, such tender does not release the principal debtor if the contractual duty consists of the obligation to pay money. If the contractual duty consisted of anything but the obligation to pay money, then the tender of such performance would have also released Fairfax.

1. (c) Clark became a surety by indorsing the existing promissory note. Since Clark is a surety, release of the collateral by the creditor (Wisdom) would release the surety (Clark) to the extent of the value of the collateral released. Answer (a) is incorrect because Clark's promise to act as surety by indorsing the promissory note was supported by consideration: the creditor agreed not to accelerate repayment of the loan during the life of the debt. Answer (b) is incorrect because Clark is a surety, and his obligation is not conditioned upon Wisdom's first proceeding against Martinson. Clark is liable if Martinson does not pay the note when it is presented to him at maturity. Answer (d) is incorrect because Wisdom need not foreclose the mortgage before it can proceed against Clark. Clark is responsible immediately upon default, presentment, or notice of dishonor.

5. (a) When a surety properly pays a debtor's obligation, the surety is subrogated to the creditor's interest in property held as security for performance of the obligation. Accordingly the surety may enforce any lien, pledge, or mortgage which secured the debt. To the extent that the sale of the property fails to pay off the surety, the surety would become a general creditor in the bankruptcy action for the balance. Answer (b) is incorrect because an unpaid surety's claim will be discharged in bankruptcy just as a normal creditor's claim. Answer (c) is incorrect because once the debtor is adjudicated a bankrupt, the only option open to the surety would be to file as a creditor in the bankruptcy action. Answer (d) is incorrect because once the debtor has been adjudicated bankrupt the trustee controls the debtor's property and the remedy of exoneration will not be permitted. Exoneration is the right of a surety to require the debtor to pay the creditor if the debtor has the assets to do so.

6. (d) Release of a debtor by the creditor releases the surety also. Thus the settlement negotiated between the trustee in bankruptcy and creditor released Quinn, the surety, from any further obligation. Thus answer (c) is incorrect because Quinn need not pay Click the creditor the $1,500 deficiency. Answer (b) is incorrect because Quinn agreed to be an ordinary surety, for which there is no requirement that the creditor exhaust his remedies against the property. Answer (a) is incorrect because a surety is not compensated merely because he is the sole stockholder of a corporation whose debt he guarantees.

7. (d) Unless there is a reservation of rights by the creditor against the co-sureties, release of one co-surety reduces the other co-surety's obligation by the same amount. Hence the release of Blackwell also released the co-surety, Crawford, to the extent of one-half the debt, or $12,500. Answers (a), (b), and (c) are incorrect because the actions of Lux did not totally release Crawford, but they did have an effect upon Crawford's liability and right to contribution.

ESSAY QUESTIONS AND ANSWERS

NOVEMBER 1980 (Estimated time: 15 to 20 minutes)

3. Part a. Hardaway Lending, Inc., had a 4 year $800,000 callable loan to Superior Metals, Inc., outstanding. The loan was callable at the end of each year upon Hardaway's giving 60 days written notice. Two and one-half years remained of the four years. Hardaway reviewed the loan and decided that Superior Metals was no longer a prime lending risk and it therefore decided to call the loan. The required written notice was sent to and received by Superior 60 days prior to the expiration of the second year. Merriweather, Superior's chief executive officer and principal shareholder, requested Hardaway to continue the loan at least for another year. Hardaway agreed, provided that an acceptable commercial surety would guarantee $400,000 of the loan and Merriweather would personally guarantee repayment in full. These conditions were satisfied and the loan was permitted to continue.

The following year the loan was called and Superior defaulted. Hardaway released the commercial surety but retained its rights against Merriweather and demanded that Merriweather pay the full amount of the loan. Merriweather refused, asserting the following.

- There was no consideration for his promise. The loan was already outstanding and he personally received nothing.
- Hardaway must first proceed against Superior before it can collect from Merriweather.
- Hardaway had released the commercial surety, thereby releasing Merriweather.

Required Answer the following, setting forth reasons for any conclusions stated.

Discuss the validity of each of Merriweather's assertions.

Answer The first two defenses asserted by Merriweather are invalid. The third defense is partially valid.

Consideration on Hardaway's part consisted of

forging the right to call the Superior Metals loan. The fact that the loan was already outstanding is irrelevant. By permitting the loan to remain outstanding for an additional year instead of calling it, Hardaway relinquished a legal right, which is adequate consideration for Merriweather's surety promise. Consideration need not pass to the surety; in fact, it usually primarily benefits the principal debtor.

There is no requirement that the creditor first proceed against the debtor before it can proceed against the surety, unless the surety undertaking expressly provides such a condition. Basic to the usual surety undertaking is the right of the creditor to proceed immediately against the surety. Essentially, that is the reason for the surety.

Hardaway's release of the commercial surety from its $400,000 surety undertaking partially released Merriweather. The release had the legal effect of impairing Merriweather's right of contribution against its cosurety (the commercial surety). Thus, Merriweather is released to the extent of ⅓ [$400,000 (commercial surety's guarantee)/ $1,200,000 (the aggregate of the cosureties' guarantees)] of the principal amount ($800,000), or $266,667.

CHAPTER

8

Bankruptcy

The following is a generalized listing of subjects to be tested through the May 1983 Uniform CPA Examination.

The Federal Bankruptcy Act is the basis for questions dealing with bankruptcy. This topic includes methods of dealing with financial failure in lieu of bankruptcy, voluntary and involuntary petitions in bankruptcy, administration of the bankrupt's estate, preferences, priorities, exemptions, duties of a bankrupt, and the effect of a discharge on the bankrupt's debts.[1]

The AICPA Board of Examiners has adopted a new content specification outline for the business law section of the Uniform CPA Examination, *to be effective with the November 1983 examination*. The outline lists the following topics to be tested under the title "Bankruptcy."

A. Bankruptcy
1. Voluntary and Involuntary Bankruptcy
2. Effects of Bankruptcy on Debtor and Creditors
3. Reorganizations[2]

PURPOSE

I. *Purpose* of the Bankruptcy Reform Act of 1978 (hereinafter referred to as the "act") is to modernize bankruptcy law and improve its administration to accomplish the following objectives:

---

[1] AICPA, *Information for CPA Candidates*, Copyright © 1975, 1979 by the American Institute of Certified Public Accountants, Inc.
[2] AICPA, *Business Law—Content Specification Outline*, approved by the AICPA Board of Examiners on August 31, 1981.

A. To distribute a debtor's assets equitably among any creditors (liquidation) to give the debtor a "new" start; and

B. To provide an honest debtor in a desperate monetary situation a chance to be financially rehabilitated (reorganization, or adjustment of debts of an individual with regular income); and

C. To establish a new bankruptcy court system to become effective April 1, 1984. Each federal judicial district will contain a special bankruptcy court with exclusive jurisdiction in bankruptcy under the act and exclusive authority over all of the debtor's property, wherever located in the United States.

DEFINITIONS

II. The following definitions are important to the study of the provisions of the act.

  A. *Insolvency*

    1. With reference to a *debtor* (person or entity), *other than a partnership*, insolvency is the financial condition in which the debtor's debts exceed the fair value of all the debtor's assets, excluding property

      a. Exempted, and

      b. Fraudulently transferred by the debtor.

    2. A *partnership is insolvent* when the total value of partnership debts is greater than the total fair value of:

      a. All of the partnership's property (exclusive of property transferred, concealed, or removed with intent to hinder, delay, or defraud creditors); plus

      b. The sum of the value of each general partner's separate property (partners' personal assets) in excess of property exempted by the act or state law.

  B. An *order of relief* is the equivalent of an adjudication of bankruptcy under prior bankruptcy law. It is a court order finding that a debtor is bankrupt within the provisions of the act.

  C. *Bankruptcy* is a procedure whereby a debtor is subjected to one of the following:

    1. *Liquidation.* The debtor's nonexempt assets are sold or otherwise disposed of and the proceeds are distributed for the benefit of creditors (see V below).

    2. *Reorganization.* The debtor is allowed to avoid liquidation by the establishment of a plan to rearrange legal interests of creditors and/or shareholders, to sell or distribute any or all property of the debtor, to merge or consolidate, to satisfy or modify any existing liens, to extend maturity dates or change interest rates on debt securities, or to issue new securities (see VI below).

    3. *Adjustment of debts.* An individual debtor is allowed to avoid liquidation under a plan whereby the debtor's debts are adjusted and subsequently repaid periodically out of future income (see VII below).

  D. A *custodian* includes:

    1. A receiver or trustee of any of the debtor's property appointed other than under the provisions of the act;

    2. An assignee under a general assignment for the benefit of the debtor's creditors; or

    3. A trustee, receiver, or agent appointed by law or authorized by contract to take charge of a debtor's property for the purpose of enforcing a lien against it or for the purpose of administering it for the benefit of the debtor's creditors.

  E. *Court of bankruptcy* is a federal court in which a petition in bankruptcy is filed. Each federal judicial district contains a bankruptcy court as an adjunct to the district court for that district.

  F. *Discharge in bankruptcy* is a court-ordered release of an individual debtor from the duty to pay his or her debts upon liquidation or rehabilitation.

G. *Trustee* is a person elected by the creditors or appointed by the court of bankruptcy to act as the representative of the debtor and in so doing to collect, administer, and liquidate the debtor's nonexempt estate.

H. *Farmer* is a person who obtained 80 percent of his or her gross income from farming during the taxable year immediately preceding the taxable year in which a petition in bankruptcy was filed against him or her.

I. *Insiders:*
  1. If the debtor is an individual, insiders include:
   a. A relative (an individual related by marriage or blood within the third degree) of a debtor or of a general partner of the debtor;
   b. The partnership in which the debtor is a general partner;
   c. A general partner of the debtor; or
   d. A corporation of which the debtor is a director, an officer, or a person in control.
  2. If the debtor is a corporation, insiders include:
   a. An officer or director or person in control of the debtor;
   b. A partnership in which the debtor is a general partner;
   c. A general partner of the debtor; or
   d. A relative (an individual related by marriage or blood within the third degree) of a general partner, officer, director, or person in control of the debtor.
  3. If the debtor is a partnership, insiders include:
   a. A general partner in the debtor;
   b. Any relative (an individual related by marriage or blood within the third degree) of any general partner or person in control of the debtor;
   c. Any other partnership in which the debtor is a general partner;
   d. A general partner of the debtor; or
   e. A person in control of the debtor.
  4. An affiliate, or insider of an affiliate as if such affiliate were the debtor; and
  5. A managing agent of the debtor.

J. *Relative* means an individual related by marriage or blood within the third degree as determined by the common law.

K. *Equity security holder* means an owner of an *equity security* of the debtor, such as a share of stock in a corporation, an interest of a limited partner in a limited partnership; or a warrant or right to purchase, sell, or subscribe to a share of stock in a corporation or limited partnership.

L. *Plan.* A plan in bankruptcy is a method of reorganization or the adjustment of the debts of a debtor *without* liquidation.

M. *Party in interest* includes the debtor, creditor, equity security holder, trustee, creditor's committee, and equity security holders' committee.

N. *Individual with regular income* is an individual, other than a stock broker or a commodity broker, whose income is sufficiently stable and regular to enable him or her to make payments under an adjustment of debts plan.

O. *Debtor in possession* is an individual or entity who, at the discretion of the court, is allowed to remain in possession and control of his or her assets and business *during reorganization* proceedings.

P. A *claim* is a right to receive payment from the debtor.

Q. *"Property of the estate"* includes any property owned by the debtor at the filing of a bankruptcy petition including any increment thereto *and* all property acquired by the debtor in alimony, by inheritance, and life insurance proceeds within 180 days after the filing of a petition in bankruptcy. Earnings by an individual debtor after the filing of a bankruptcy petition are *not* included in the estate.

III. The following are methods of dealing with financial failure in lieu of bankruptcy i.e., creditors' rights other than in bankruptcy).

    A. *Foreclosure* on property subject to a debt or other obligation.

        1. Real estate mortgages (see Chapter 10).

        2. Secured transactions involving personal property (see Chapter 6).

    B. *Attachment* or *garnishment* is the process of obtaining legal rights in a debtor's property so that it may be sold and its proceeds applied to the debt after a judgment is secured by a creditor.

        1. Attachment is used to obtain legal rights in the property of a debtor that is in the debtor's possession.

        2. Garnishment is used to obtain legal rights in the property of a debtor that is in the possession of a third person.

        3. The creditor is required to post a bond to protect the debtor should the debtor fail to obtain a judgment.

    C. *Execution.*

        1. After a judgment is secured by a creditor, that creditor may have the court issue a *writ of execution.*

        2. The writ of execution orders a sheriff to take possession and sell any of the debtor's nonexempt property, and use the proceeds to pay the judgment debt.

    D. A *creditors' composition* is a contract between the debtor and one or more of his or her creditors in which the latter agree to accept an immediate payment of part of the debt owed to each of them in exchange for a discharge of their claims against the debtor.

        1. The payments may be voidable under the provisions of the act as a fraudulent or preferential transfer.

        2. As a general rule, the composition is not binding on nonparticipating creditors.

    E. *Assignment for benefit of creditors.* An assignment for the benefit of creditors is a contract between the debtor and one or more of the debtor's creditors in which the debtor agrees to transfer his or her assets to an "assignee" or "trustee" (usually a creditor) for the purpose of liquidation and a pro rata distribution of the debtor's assets among the creditors, in exchange for the promise of each creditor to discharge the debtor.

        1. The assignee (usually a creditor) receives legal title to the property.

        2. The assignee is a "custodian" under the act. Therefore, the assignment will justify the entry of an order of relief in an involuntary proceeding in bankruptcy filed by the debtor's creditors.

        3. Nonparticipating creditors are *not* bound to the terms of the assignment.

        4. The assignment may be voidable under the provisions of the act as a fraudulent or preferential transfer.

    F. *Receivership.* A court may appoint a *receiver* to care for and preserve a debtor's property pending the outcome of a lawsuit filed by creditors to collect unpaid debts. The purpose of the appointment is to prevent a debtor from "wasting" assets before they can be used to satisfy debts owing to creditors.

        1. A creditor, who has charged the interest of a partner with a judgment debt, may apply to a court for the appointment of a receiver for the partner's interest.

        2. A judgment creditor of an insolvent corporation (in the equity sense, i.e., not able to meet obligations as they become due) may file a lawsuit in equity for appointment of a receiver for the purposes of liquidating the assets of the corporation for the benefit of creditors.

FIGURE 8-1 TYPES OF BANKRUPTCY RELIEF

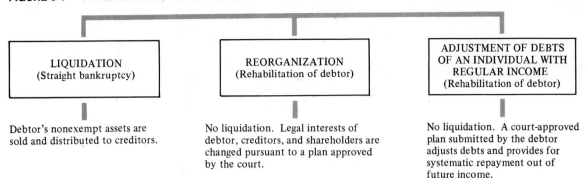

3. A receiver is a "custodian" under the act. Therefore, the appointment will also justify the entry of an order of relief against the debtor in an involuntary proceeding in bankruptcy filed by the debtor's creditors.

G. *Rescission of voidable fraudulent conveyances.* All conveyances and transfers of property by the debtor to third parties in fraud of creditors can be legally set aside (i.e., voided) and made subject to the claims of creditors.

1. *Common law fraud.* Conveyances or transfers by the debtor that are made *with the specific intent* to hinder, delay, or defraud creditors are fraudulent.

2. *Uniform Fraudulent Conveyances Act.* Most states have enacted the Uniform Fradulent Conveyance Act or a similar statute. These laws *create a presumption of fraud* whenever a debtor conveys or transfers property in exchange for inadequate consideration while insolvent or when the conveyance or transfer renders him or her insolvent. If the debtor fails to prove the absence of fraud, fraud is implied in law, and the conveyance or transfer is voidable.

LIQUIDATION (STRAIGHT BANKRUPTCY), REORGANIZATION, AND ADJUSTMENT OF DEBTS

IV. The act provides three major types of relief for debtors and creditors, one through liquidation of a *debtor's estate* (Chapter 7 case), the second through reorganization of the debtor's legal obligations without liquidation (Chapter 11 case) and the third, adjustment of debts of an individual with regular income (Chapter 13 case). (See Figure 8-1.) Bankruptcy cases under Chapters 7 and 11 can be initiated by either a voluntary or involuntary *petition in bankruptcy.* A case under Chapter 13 can be instituted only by a voluntary petition of the individual debtor.

LIQUIDATION (STRAIGHT BANKRUPTCY)

V. The following procedures are involved in liquidation of a bankrupt's estate under Chapter 7 of the act.

A. *Voluntary petition.* Debtors may initiate a bankruptcy proceeding against themselves by filing a petition in bankruptcy with the bankruptcy court. (See Figure 8-2.)

1. The debtors can be any individual, partnership, association, or corporation other than:

a. Governmental units (i.e., municipalities);

FIGURE 8-2   FILING OF PETITIONS IN BANKRUPTCY CASES

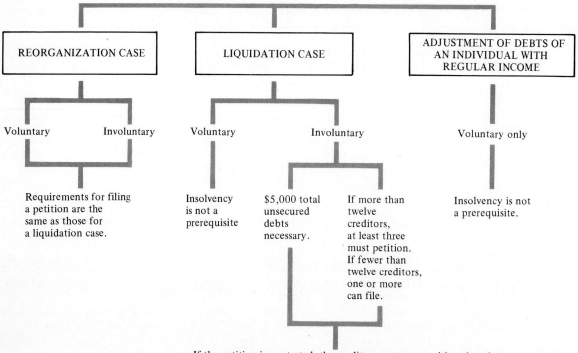

REORGANIZATION CASE	LIQUIDATION CASE	ADJUSTMENT OF DEBTS OF AN INDIVIDUAL WITH REGULAR INCOME

Voluntary   Involuntary

Voluntary   Involuntary

Voluntary only

Requirements for filing a petition are the same as those for a liquidation case.

Insolvency is not a prerequisite

$5,000 total unsecured debts necessary.

If more than twelve creditors, at least three must petition. If fewer than twelve creditors, one or more can file.

Insolvency is not a prerequisite.

If the petition is contested, the creditors must prove either that the debtor is unable to meet his or her obligations as they become due or that a custodian (a liquidator) of the debtor's assets or business was appointed for the benefit of creditors.

    b. Railroads;

    c. Insurance companies;

    d. Banks;

    e. Savings and loan associations; or

    f. Credit unions.

  2. A single petition may be filed by husband and wife to establish a *joint case* in bankruptcy.

    a. The petition must be filed with the mutual consent of the spouses.

    b. After the institution of the joint case, the court will determine whether or not and to what extent the debtors' estates are to be consolidated.

  3. The *debtor need not be insolvent* to file a petition.

  4. The *filing* of a voluntary petition for liquidation also *constitutes an automatic order of relief* (adjudication of bankruptcy) by the court.

  5. For a partnership to file a voluntary petition, all partners must consent.

B. *Involuntary petition.*

  1. An involuntary petition is one instituted by one or more creditors against a nonconsenting debtor who owes *unsecured* debts totaling $5,000 or more to one or more creditors (see Figure 8-2). In addition:

    a. If there are twelve (12) or more creditors, at least *three* (3) creditors must join in the petition; or

b. If there are fewer than twelve (12) creditors, *one* or more creditors may file the petition.

2. The act abolishes the concept of "acts of bankruptcy." Consequently, the creditor need not allege in the petition and prove that the debtor committed an act of bankruptcy.

3. An involuntary petition in bankruptcy is permitted against any debtor who is an individual, partnership, association, or corporation, *except:*

    a. Municipalities;

    b. Railroads;

    c. Banks;

    d. Farmers and ranchers;

    e. Charitable organizations and foundations; and

    f. Churches and schools.

4. A partnership petition by less than all of the general partners must be treated as an involuntary petition.

C. *Automatic stay of all judicial proceedings against a debtor.* Upon the filing of a voluntary or involuntary petition, all judicial proceedings and other debt collection efforts against the debtor are suspended.

1. The stay prevents any creditor from obtaining an advantage over other creditors.

2. It protects the debtor from harassment, collection efforts, and foreclosure actions by creditors.

3. No lien (judicial or otherwise) can be created or enforced against the debtor's estate after the automatic stay.

D. *The petition for liquidation,* whether voluntary or involuntary, is *not* binding upon the debtor. The debtor has an absolute right to convert a liquidation case into one of the rehabilitation cases (i.e., a Chapter 13, "Reorganization" or a Chapter 11, "Adjustment of Debts of an Individual with Regular Income"). Once the debtor exercises this right it is lost forever. *Note:* A debtor may always convert a rehabilitation case into a liquidation case.

E. *Order of relief (adjudication of bankruptcy).* (See Figure 8-3.)

1. The filing of a voluntary petition constitutes an automatic order of relief.

2. In an involuntary case, the bankruptcy court will decree an order of relief only in the following circumstances:

    a. The debtor did not contradict (deny) (contest) the involuntary petition and demand a trial; or

    b. If the debtor does contradict (deny) (contest) the involuntary petition, after a trial the court will issue an order of relief against the debtor, only if the bankruptcy court finds that:

        (1) The debtor is generally not paying his or her debts as they become due (i.e., a variation of the old insolvency in the equity sense test); *or*

        (2) A *custodian* (liquidator) of the debtor's property was "appointed" or took possession during the 120-day period preceding the filing of the involuntary petition (i.e., a receiver, a trustee, or an assignee under a general assignment by the debtor, was "appointed" or took possession of the debtor's property for the benefit of all of the debtor's creditors).

F. *Appointment or election of a trustee in a liquidation case is mandatory* (see Figure 8-4).

1. Promptly after the order of relief, the court *must appoint* a disinterested person as *interim trustee* in the case. The interim trustee serves until the creditors elect a permanent trustee.

2. If the creditors do not elect a *permanent trustee* at the first meeting of creditors,

FIGURE 8-3 ORDER OF RELIEF (ADJUDICATION OF BANKRUPTCY)

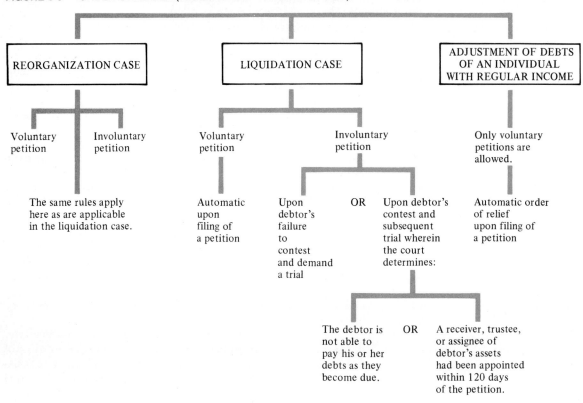

the interim trustee, appointed by the court, serves as permanent trustee in the case.

3. Upon the death, removal, resignation, or inability of a trustee to serve, the creditors may elect a *successor trustee*. If the creditors fail to elect a successor trustee, the court may appoint a trustee in the case.

4. Upon appointment of a trustee, the debtor's possession and control of his or her estate is terminated and is assumed by the trustee.

G. *Meeting of creditors.*

1. The court *must* call the first meeting of creditors within a reasonable time after the order of relief.

2. The court *is not* allowed to preside at or attend the creditors' meeting.

3. The debtor must attend the creditors' meeting and submit to examination under oath.

4. In a *liquidation case*, the creditors may elect a person to serve as permanent trustee in the case. If a permanent trustee is not elected by the creditors, then the court-appointed interim trustee becomes the permanent trustee in the case. If a trustee dies, resigns, or is removed for cause, the creditors may elect a successor trustee to fill the vacancy.

   a. *To be eligible to vote* a creditor must possess an allowable, undisputed, fixed, liquidated, and unsecured claim. A *creditor is not eligible to vote if* he or she has an interest materially adverse (e.g., a holder of substantial equity securities in the debtor) to the interests of *unsecured creditors*, or is an insider, or is a *secured creditor*.

b. No election for trustee can be held unless requested by at least 20 percent in amount of allowable claims.

c. To be elected trustee, a person must receive the affirmative vote of a majority of votes cast of creditors holding at least 20 percent in amount of the claims actually voted.

5. Creditors who are eligible to vote for a trustee *may* elect a *creditors' committee* composed of three to eleven unsecured creditors who possess allowable claims. The function of the creditors' committee is to:

a. Consult with the trustee;

b. Make recommendations to the trustee in respect to performance of the trustee's duties; and

c. Submit to court any question affecting the administration of the bankrupt's estate.

H. *Claims of creditors*

1. Filing proofs of claim:

a. A provable claim may be filed by a creditor, the debtor, or by the trustee.

b. Claims must be filed within six months after the first creditors' meeting.

2. Only provable and allowable claims are permitted to be filed with the trustee. A provable claim is not always allowable.

a. To be a *provable claim* it must be in writing, signed by the creditor, debtor or trustee, and filed within six months of the first creditors' meeting.

b. A provable claim is automatically an *allowable claim* unless "a party in interest" objects to it. Upon proper objection, the court will disallow the following claims:

(1) Any claim subject to any defense available to the trustee under common law, state statute, or the act.

(2) A claim that is unenforceable against the debtor because of a contractual defense such as fraud, duress, usury, lack of consideration, undue influence, illegality, Statute of Frauds, minority, or Statute of Limitations.

FIGURE 8-4   APPOINTMENT OF TRUSTEE

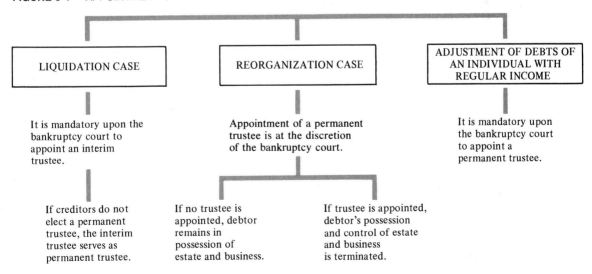

(3) A claim for interest that had not accrued (earned) prior to the date of the petition in bankruptcy (unmatured interest).

(4) A claim to the extent that the creditor can offset against the claim the amount of debt owing to the debtor from the creditor.

(5) A property tax claim to the extent that the tax due exceeds the value of the property.

(6) A claim by an insider or the attorney of the debtor to the extent that it exceeds the reasonable value of the insider's or attorney's services.

(7) A claim by a landlord of the debtor for damages caused by the debtor's termination of a lease to the extent that the claim exceeds:

    (a) The rent established by the lease for the greater of one year or 15 percent of the remaining term of the lease not to exceed three years, *plus*,

    (b) Any unpaid rent due under the lease on the earlier of the date of the filing of the bankruptcy petition, or the date on which the lessor repossessed or the debtor surrendered the leased property.

(8) A claim for damages by the employer of the debtor for breach of the employment contract to the extent that it exceeds:

    (a) The salary or wages established by the employment contract for one year following the earlier of the date of the filing of the petition; and

    (b) The termination of the performance of the employment contract.

REORGANIZATION

VI. *Reorganization in bankruptcy* is an alternative to liquidation. Procedures involved in *reorganization* of a bankrupt's estate are provided in Chapter 11 of the act.

  A. *Purpose.* The purpose of the reorganization provisions of the act is to provide a means by which an individual or a business can preserve its value through a rearrangement of the interests of the debtor, creditors, or equity security holders *without* subjecting the bankrupt's estate to liquidation. Chapter 11 is primarily designed to aid the large corporate debtor.

  B. *Petition for reorganization.* Either a voluntary (by the debtor) or involuntary (by the debtor's creditors) petition for reorganization can be filed (see Figure 8-2). (Under the previous Bankruptcy Act, a debtor's creditors could not file a petition for reorganization, but were limited to filing a petition for liquidation.)

    1. The prerequisites for filing a petition for reorganization are essentially the same as those required for petitions for liquidation cases under Chapter 7. For a review of these requirements see V-A, B above and Figure 8-2.

    2. The filing of a petition in reorganization (as in a liquidation case) causes an automatic stay of judicial or other creditor proceedings against the debtor (see V-C above).

  C. *Persons or organizations eligible to be debtors.* Those who were eligible to be debtors in a liquidation case are also eligible to be debtors in a reorganization case under Chapter 11. In addition a *railroad* can subject itself or be subjected to reorganization proceedings. Those not eligible to be debtors are:

    1. A governmental unit;

    2. An insurance company, bank, savings and loan association, or credit union; or

    3. A stockbroker or commodity broker.

    Note: A railroad is allowed to be a debtor under reorganization but not under liquidation procedures in bankruptcy.

D. *Order of relief* (see Figure 8-3). The same rules for a court decree of an order of relief apply here as apply to petitions for liquidation in bankruptcy covered in V-A, B above.

E. *Appointment of trustee or examiner is discretionary* with the bankruptcy court. However, the court will usually appoint a trustee for "cause" (i.e., the fraud, incompetence, dishonesty, or mismanagement on the debtor's part). (See Figure 8-4.)

   1. At any time prior to a confirmation of a plan of reorganization, the court, at its discretion, may appoint a permanent trustee if such appointment is in the interests of creditors, equity security holders, and any other interests in the estate. *If no trustee is appointed, the debtor automatically remains in possession and control of its estate (i.e., its assets and business).*

      a. A *debtor in possession* has most of the rights and duties of a trustee.

      b. Like a trustee, the debtor in possession is a separate entity apart from the debtor and may sue or be sued in such independent, separate legal capacity.

   2. If a trustee is not appointed, any party in interest prior to the confirmation of a reorganization plan, may request the court to appoint an *examiner*.

      a. The court will appoint an examiner if:

         (1) The appointment is in the interests of creditors, any security holders, and other interests in the estate; or

         (2) The debtor's fixed, liquidated, unsecured debts, other than debts for goods, services, or taxes, or owing to an insider, exceed $5,000,000.

      b. The court may order the examiner to conduct an appropriate investigation of the debtor, including allegations of fraud, dishonesty, incompetence, misconduct, mismanagement or irregularity in the management of the debtor's affairs.

   3. Upon the removal, resignation, death, or inability of a trustee or examiner to serve, the court may appoint a successor trustee or examiner.

   4. Upon the appointment of a trustee or examiner, the debtor's possession and control of his or her estate is terminated.

F. *Creditors and equity security holders' meetings.*

   1. Mandatory appointment of a creditor committee. As soon as practical after the order of relief, the *court must appoint at least one committee of creditors who possess unsecured claims.*

   2. On the request of a party in interest, the court may appoint a committee of equity security holders or additional committees of creditors if necessary to assure adequate representation of creditors or of *equity security holders.*

   3. Powers and duties of committees. Any committee appointed by the court has the following powers and duties:

      a. To hire one or more attorneys, accountants, or other agents to perform services for the committee;

      b. To consult with the trustee or debtor in possession of the debtor's estate;

      c. To investigate the acts, conduct, assets, liabilities, and financial condition of the debtor, or the operation of the debtor's business, and any other relevant matter;

      d. To participate in the formulation of a reorganization plan and collect and file acceptances of the plan with the court;

      e. To request the appointment of a trustee or examiner if none has been previously appointed; and

      f. To perform any other services as are in the interest of parties represented in the bankruptcy proceeding.

G. *Claims of creditors and equity security holders' interests.*
  1. Creditors and equity security holders need not file proof of claim or interest in a reorganization case. *Note:* Such proof *is* required in a liquidation case.
  2. Any claim or interest included on the debtor's schedules is deemed to be a filed proof of claim or interest in a reorganization case. *Note:* The debtor is required to file a *list of creditors*, a *schedule of assets and liabilities*, and a *statement of his financial affairs* (i.e., a debtor's schedule). If the debtor does not do so, the trustee must provide the list, schedule, and statement.

H. *Filing, contents, acceptance, and confirmation of a plan of reorganization.*
  1. *Filing the plan of reorganization:*
     a. The debtor may file a plan with a petition commencing a voluntary case or at any time during a voluntary or involuntary case.
     b. The debtor in possession (i.e., no trustee has been appointed) has the *exclusive right* to file a plan during the first 120 days of a reorganization case (i.e., 120 days after the date of the order of relief).
     c. Thereafter, any party in interest (debtor, trustee, a creditor, creditors' committee, equity security holders' committee, or an equity security holder) may file a plan if:
        (1) A trustee has been appointed;
        (2) The debtor in possession did not file a plan within 120 days after the date of the order of relief, or
        (3) A plan filed by the debtor was not accepted.
  2. *Required contents of the plan of reorganization.* A plan must include the following:
     a. Designation of separate classes of claims and interests;
     b. Identification of any class of claims or interests that are to be impaired (i.e., alteration of any legal, equitable, and contractual rights) by the plan;
     c. Identification of any class of claims or interests not impaired by the plan;
     d. Specification of the treatment (i.e., nature of the impairment) of any class of claims or interest impaired under the plan;
     e. Provide the same treatment for each claim or interest of a particular class;
     f. Provide adequate means for execution of the plan, such as;
        (1) Retention by the debtor of all or any part of the property in the bankrupt's estate,
        (2) Transfer of all or any part of the property in the bankrupt's estate to one or more entities (i.e., an individual, partnership, corporation, estate, trust, or governmental unit),
        (3) Merger, or consolidation of the bankrupt with another individual, partnership, or corporation,
        (4) Sale of all or any part of the property of the estate or distribution of all or any part of the property of the estate to a party in interest,
        (5) Satisfaction or modification of any lien,
        (6) Cancellation or modification of any debt instrument,
        (7) Extension of maturity dates, changes in interest rates, or other terms of outstanding securities (ie., stocks, bonds, warrants, etc.),
        (8) Issuance of new securities of the bankrupt or of any entity referred to in (2) and (3) above.
     g. The *plan must prohibit* the issuance of *nonvoting equity* (ownership) securities (i.e., limited partnership interests, stocks, etc.). The plan must also provide for an appropriate distribution of voting power among the various classes of equity securities.
  3. *Acceptance of the plan of reorganization.*

a. The holder of an allowable claim or interest may accept or reject the plan.
   b. The holders' acceptance or rejection is valid only if in compliance with the law governing the adequacy of disclosure of information to the holders.
   c. No acceptance of a plan is required from holders of claims or interests that are not impaired by the plan.
   d. A class of claims has accepted a plan if it is accepted by creditors holding at least two-thirds in amount and more than one-half in number of allowed claims of the class.
   e. A class of equity interests has accepted a plan if it is accepted by holders of such interests that hold at least two-thirds in amount of the allowed interests of such class.

4. *Confirmation of the plan of reorganization.*
   a. If all the requirements of the act are satisfied, the court is required to confirm a plan.
   b. Only one plan may be confirmed by the court.
   c. Effect of confirmation. Once a plan is confirmed it is binding on the debtor, creditors, and equity security holders whether or not their claim or interest is impaired and whether or not they have accepted the plan. It is also binding on any other person or organization affected by the plan.
   d. The court may revoke an order of confirmation if it was procured by fraud.

I. *Conversion to liquidation proceedings or dismissal of a reorganization case.*

1. The debtor has the absolute right to convert a reorganization case to a liquidation case, *unless:*
   a. A trustee has been appointed to take title, possession, and control of the debtor's estate (the debtor is *not* a "debtor in possession");
   b. The case is an involuntary reorganization case; or on the request of someone other than the debtor.
   c. The case was converted to a reorganization case.

2. The court may convert a reorganization case to a liquidation case or dismiss a reorganization case for cause, whichever is in the best interests of creditors and the estate. Causes for conversion or dismissal include:
   a. Continuing loss or diminution of the estate without a reasonable likelihood of rehabilitation;
   b. Inability to bring about a plan;
   c. Unreasonable and prejudicial delay by the debtor;
   d. Failure to propose a plan according to the provisions of the act;
   e. Denial of confirmation of every proposed plan;
   f. Inability to bring about substantial performance of a confirmed plan;
   g. Material default by a debtor of a confirmed plan; and
   h. Termination of a plan by reason of performance of its terms.

3. The court may convert a reorganization case to an "Adjustment of Debts of an Individual with Regular Income" case under Chapter 13 if:
   a. The debtor requests a conversion, and
   b. The debtor has not been discharged of any claims by virtue of the confirmation of a plan under the reorganization case.

ADJUSTMENT OF DEBTS: INDIVIDUAL WITH REGULAR INCOME

VII. Adjustment of debts of an individual with regular income under Chapter 13 of the act is another alternative to liquidation.
   A. *Purpose.* The purpose of the provisions of this chapter is to allow an individual with regular income, including debtors engaged in business (self-employed persons)

wage earners, and persons receiving investment income, or pension, welfare, or social security benefits to adjust their debts and make repayment of their debts out of future income. Both secured and unsecured debts may be adjusted. This procedure provides to the debtor the following benefits:

1. It protects the individual debtor's assets from liquidation;
2. It prevents harassment of the debtor by creditors;
3. It tends to enhance the credit rating of the individual debtor; and
4. The debtor is allowed to retain all property (i.e., the debtor need not surrender any property as would be a requirement in a liquidation case).

B. *Individuals eligible to be a debtor under Chapter 13.*
   1. Debtor must be an individual, not an organization; and the debtor's unsecured debts must total less than $100,000, with secured debts totaling less than $350,000.
   2. Chapter 13 proceedings *are* available to self-employed persons who are engaged in business.
   3. An individual's income is "regular" if it is sufficiently periodic and stable so that the agreed-upon payments under a Chapter 13 plan can be made.

C. *Commencement of a case under Chapter 13.* A case *may only be commenced by the filing of a voluntary petition* by an eligible individual debtor. A debtor cannot be forced into an adjustment of debts case (see Figure 8-2).

D. *Order of relief.* The filing of the voluntary petition constitutes an automatic order of relief and all judicial proceedings and collection efforts against the debtor are automatically stayed (suspended). (See Figure 8-3.)

E. *Appointment of a trustee.*
   1. The court *must* appoint a trustee in all Chapter 13 cases.
   2. The trustee's duties are essentially identical to the duties of a trustee in a liquidation case.
   3. If the individual debtor is engaged in business, the trustee has the additional investigative powers of a trustee under a reorganization case (see Figure 8-4).

F. *Debtor engaged in business.* Unless the court orders otherwise, a debtor engaged in business may operate that business subject to limitations and conditions provided by the court, the trustee, or in the act.

G. *Claims of creditors.* Whether a creditor's claim is provable and allowable is governed by essentially the same rules determining provable and allowable claims under a liquidation case (see V-H-1, 2 above).

H. *Filing, contents, and confirmation of a plan of adjustment of debts.*
   1. *Filing:*
      a. The debtor has the exclusive right (as well as duty) to propose (file) a plan of rehabilitation (i.e., an individual debt-repayment plan).
      b. *No other party is allowed to file a plan.* The creditors cannot force a plan upon the debtor.
   2. *Contents of a plan:*
      a. The plan must provide for:
         (1) Submission of sufficient future earnings or other future income of the debtor to the control of the trustee as is necessary to carry out the plan;
         (2) Full payment of all claims entitled to priority under the act (see X below);
         (3) The same treatment for each claim with a particular class, if the plan classifies claims; and
         (4) Payments of claims over a period of not longer than three years. The court may approve a longer period, but never more than five years.

b. The plan may modify the rights of holders of secured as well as unsecured claims.

3. *Confirmation of a plan:*

    a. The court may confirm a plan if:

        (1) It satisfies the provisions of the act;

        (2) It is proposed in good faith;

        (3) It is in the best interests of creditors;

        (4) The plan is feasible;

        (5) It is accepted by the holder of each allowed secured claim; and

        (6) The requisite fees and charges have been paid.

    b. After confirmation of a plan, the court may order any entity from which the debtor receives income to pay all or part of such income to the trustee.

    c. The effect of a confirmation of a plan is to bind the debtor and each creditor to the terms of the plan whether or not:

        (1) The claim of the particular creditor is provided for in the plan, and

        (2) The particular creditor has accepted, rejected, or objected to the plan.

    d. Confirmation of a plan vests title to all property of the estate in the debtor, free and clear of any claim of any creditor provided for in the plan. In addition, creditors must stop all collection efforts and suspend interest and late charges on most debts.

    e. Creditors are barred from attempting to collect from a bankrupt's codebtor (e.g., one who has cosigned a note with the bankrupt debtor) as long as a repayment plan is in effect. This rule *applies only* to collection of consumer debt (i.e., debts incurred primarily for a personal, family, or household purpose).

4. If the debtor does not file a plan or if the court does not approve the debtor's plan, the creditors are free to force the debtor into involuntary (liquidation) bankruptcy.

5. *Discharge of the debtor:*

    a. The court must enter a discharge as soon as practicable after the debtor completes payments under the plan.

    b. A discharge relieves the debtor from all unsecured debts that were disallowed or provided under the plan except nondischargeable debts as provided in the act (see XIV below).

RIGHTS OF A TRUSTEE, EXAMINER, AND DEBTOR IN POSSESSION

VIII. *Rights of a trustee, examiner, or debtor in possession in bankruptcy:* Unless noted otherwise, the rights of the trustee, examiner, and the debtor in possession are essentially the same. The trustee has the right to:

A. Sue or be sued in such capacity;

B. Possess title (at the time of appointment, a trustee is vested with title) to all of the debtor's nonexempt property;

C. In a liquidation case, the trustee's primary right (and duty) is to collect the bankrupt's assets and reduce them to cash; in a reorganization case, the trustee must collect assets, but the assets will not be reduced to cash;

D. Hire one or more attorney, accountant, appraiser, auctioneer, or other professional person to aid the trustee in carrying out his or her duties;

E. Operate the business of the debtor if authorized by the court (the debtor is not in possession);

F. Investigate in a reorganization case where the court has allowed the debtor to operate the business (this right is not available to a debtor in possession);

G. Possession and control of all property of the estate including all books, records, documents, and papers pertaining to the property of the estate;

H. *Rescind (avoid) voidable preferences, obligations, and transfers.* The trustee has the right and duty to avoid any transfer made by a debtor or any obligation (including liens and security interests) incurred by him or her, if such transfers or obligations are voidable under the common law, state or federal statutes, or the act. The trustee has a right and duty to avoid the following transactions:

1. A fraudulent transfer under the *Uniform Fraudulent Conveyance Act* adopted by a state in which the transaction occurred (see III-G-2 above).

2. A trustee can avoid *statutory liens* on the property of the debtor if:
   a. The lien becomes effective:
   (1) After a bankruptcy case is filed, or
   (2) During an insolvency proceeding against a debtor (other than a bankruptcy case), or
   (3) When a custodian is appointed or takes possession of the debtor's property, or
   (4) During the insolvency of the debtor; or
   b. The lien would *not* have been perfected or enforceable against a bona fide purchaser on the date of the filing of the petition, whether or not such a purchaser exists.
   c. Examples of statutory liens are:
   (1) For rent;
   (2) Mechanics liens,
   (3) Federal tax liens on negotiable instruments and investment securities.

3. Under the *Common Law or statute*, in any situation where the debtor could have avoided (i.e., rescinded) a contract and recovered his or her property. For example, fraud, duress, mutual mistake, or lack of legal capacity to contract.

4. A *voidable preferential transfer* (i.e., conveyance, payment of money, or lien) is one that is made or given by a debtor to the creditor, that if it were allowed, would enable the creditor to receive a greater percentage of the claim than the creditor would have received in distribution of the debtor's assets in a liquidation case or if the transfer had not been made. A voidable preferential transfer will be held to exist under the following circumstances. (See Figure 8-5.)
   a. The transfer is made "to or for the benefit of a creditor":
   (1) In payment of a *previously owed (antecedent) debt;*
   (2) Made *while the debtor was insolvent;* i.e., a debtor's liabilities exceed his or her assets, exclusive of the value of fraudulent transfers and property exempted under the act. (*Note:* The trustee need not provide evidence that the debtor was insolvent at the time of the transfer. *A debtor is presumed to be insolvent during the ninety days preceding a petition in bankruptcy.* The creditor has the burden of proving otherwise.); and
   (3) Made *within ninety days prior to the filing of the petition* (start of a bankruptcy case); *or*
   b. The transfer is made to or for the benefit of an *insider* (see II-I above):
   (1) *Up to one (1) year* before the date of filing of the petition, and
   (2) The *creditor-insider knew or had reasonable grounds to believe that the debtor was insolvent* at the time of the transfer. *Note:* The trustee must prove that the debtor was insolvent at the time of the transfer to the creditor-insider and that the latter knew or had reasonable grounds to believe that the debtor was insolvent at that time.

FIGURE 8-5 VOIDABLE PREFERENCES (TRANSFERS AND LIENS)

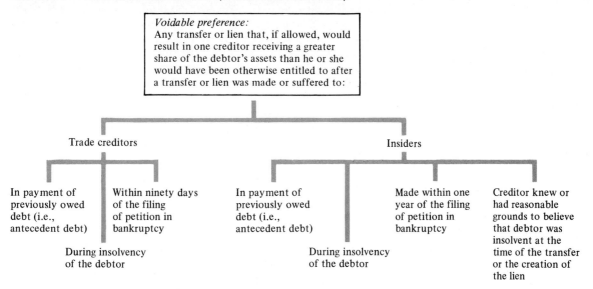

c. Examples of voidable preferences are:

(1) Cargo, a retailer, owned and sold television sets. He found it extremely difficult to meet all of his obligations as they came due and went out of business on January 1, 1981. On that date, he owed creditors $50,000 and owned assets valued at $30,000. On March 15, 1981, Color TV, Inc., a creditor, accepted some $1,800 worth of television sets remaining in Cargo's inventory and, in exchange, gave Cargo a full discharge of an $1,800 debt. On May 20, 1981, Cargo filed a voluntary petition in bankruptcy. The transfer of the television sets is a voidable transfer.

(2) Assume that in the example stated above, Cargo retained ownership of the television sets and instead signed a security agreement granting Color TV, Inc., a security interest in the television sets. The security interest is also a voidable preference.

(3) X, Y, and Z were partners. X, a playboy, was constantly being pursued by his personal creditors. Y and Z were aware of this. On May 1, 1981, X, Y, and Z reorganized their partnership. Under the new partnership agreement, X was required to contribute capital in the amount of $150,000. He did so by executing and delivering a deed to the partnership that conveyed to it fee simple absolute ownership in an office building. On April 10, 1982, X's creditors filed an involuntary petition in bankruptcy against X. The trustee can avoid the conveyance as a voidable preference.

(4) Saro, a creditor sued Ruiz, her debtor upon the latter's default on a debt. The lawsuit was filed on July 3, 1980, and Saro received a judgment in her favor against Ruiz on August 12, 1980. At the time, Ruiz owned assets of $750,000 and possessed liabilities of $920,000. Saro recorded her judgment on August 30, 1980, and it became a lien against Ruiz's farm on that date. On October 16, 1980, Ruiz filed a voluntary petition in bankruptcy. The involuntary judgment lien is a voidable preference.

(5) Zayre, Inc., leased a restaurant from Dodge for forty years. Ten years later Zayre, Inc., became insolvent. It was ten months behind on rental payments to Dodge. Dodge terminated the lease according to the terms of the lease agreement and repossessed the restaurant. One month later Zayre, Inc., was subjected to an involuntary petition in bankruptcy and adjudicated a bankrupt. The trustee filed a lawsuit to void the termination of the lease on the grounds that it was a voidable transfer. The court agreed with the trustee, voided the termination, and included the market value of Zayre, Inc.'s unexpired interest in the lease (i.e., thirty years) as an asset in the bankrupt debtor's estate.

d. *Time of transfer or obligation (perfection).* For purposes of determining whether a transfer or obligation is a voidable preference, *the transfer or obligation is deemed to have been made at the time it is perfected, not necessarily when it is actually made.* Perfection (and consequently "transfer" or "obligation") takes place at the moment when a debtor's other unsecured creditors could not subsequently acquire a superior legal interest (right) in the same property.

(1) *Real estate.* Perfection of title to real estate or a lien on real estate occurs at the time the debtor could no longer transfer clear title to that real estate to a bona fide purchaser for value; i.e., at the time the deed or lien is recorded or the grantee or lienholder takes possession of the real estate. See Chapter 10.

(2) *Personal property.* Perfection of personal property or a security interest in personal property occurs at the moment that the debtor's unsecured creditors are legally precluded from reaching that property or interest by attachment, garnishment, or execution; i.e., when the transferee-creditor takes possession of the debtor's property, or in the case of nonpossessory security interests, when the transfer is properly perfected by filing (see Chapter 6).

(3) For example, a solvent debtor, 200 days prior to a petition in bankruptcy, transferred an apartment house to a noninsider unsecured creditor in payment of an antecedent debt. The creditor inadvertently failed to record her deed until thirty days prior to the petition in bankruptcy. At the time the deed was recorded, the debtor was insolvent. The transfer is deemed to take place within the ninety day period, and since all other elements are present, the transfer is a voidable preference.

(4) As another example, D obtained a loan from C and at the same time gave C a security interest in D's present and future accounts receivables. Under article 9 of the UCC, filing of a financing statement is necessary to perfect a security interest in accounts receivable against judgment lien creditors. C did not file a financing statement until 120 days later, at which time D was insolvent. Eighty days after C filed the financing statement D's other creditors filed an involuntary petition in bankruptcy against D. The security interest given by D to C is deemed to have been given for an antecedent debt, while D was insolvent and within ninety days of bankruptcy. Consequently, the transfer is a voidable preference.

e. *Exceptions:* The following transactions are *not* voidable even though they contain all the elements of a "voidable" preference listed in VIII-H-4 above.

(1) The transfer is a *contemporaneous exchange for new value* given to the debtor. For example, a debtor, within the ninety-day period, buys goods and pays immediately by issuing a check to the creditor;

(2) It was made in payment of a debt incurred *in the ordinary course of business* or *financial affairs* of the debtor and the transferee *within forty-five days* after the debt was incurred; e.g., an insolvent debtor purchases business inventory for cash, pays his or her utility bills, and satisfies accounts payable; or

(3) A purchase money security interest given to a creditor and filed within ten days after the security interest attached (see Chapter 6).

5. *Fraudulent transfers and obligations under the provisions of the Bankruptcy Act* (see Figure 8-6).

   a. The trustee may avoid any transfer of property of the debtor or any obligation incurred by the debtor, that was *made or incurred within one year of the date of filing of the petition,* under any one of the following circumstances:

   (1) *Actual fraud.* The debtor made such transfer or incurred such obligation with *actual intent to hinder, delay, or defraud* any past or future creditor of the debtor (debtor's insolvency is not required), *or*

   (2) *Bankruptcy fraud.* The debtor *received less than a reasonably equivalent value* in exchange for such transfer or obligation (i.e., constructive fraud); and

   (a) Was *insolvent* at the time of the transaction *or became insolvent* as a result of it; or

   (b) Was *engaged in business possessing an unreasonably small amount of capital*; or

   (c) *Intended to incur debts* that would be *beyond his or her ability to pay.*

FIGURE 8-6   FRAUDULENT TRANSFERS OR DEBTS

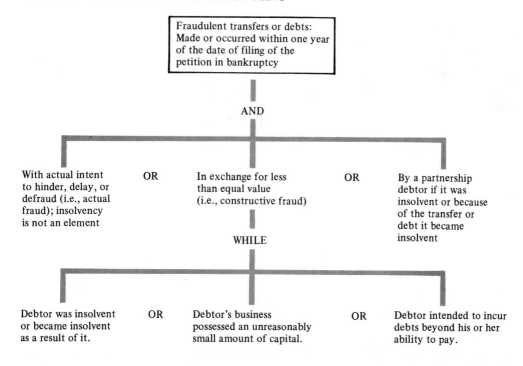

b. A *trustee of a partnership debtor may avoid any transfer* of property or debtor's obligation incurred *within one year* of the date of the filing of the petition *if* the *debtor was or thereby became insolvent* (debtor's intent to hinder, delay or defraud is not required).

6. *Statute of Limitations:* To avoid a preference or a fraudulent transfer of obligation under the provisions of the act, the trustee must take appropriate legal action prior to the earlier of:

   a. *Two years* after the appointment of a trustee, and
   b. The time the bankruptcy case is closed or dismissed.

I. Sell, use, and lease property in the bankrupt's estate.

J. Reject executory (i.e., totally unperformed) contracts of the bankrupt, and

K. Obtain credit if the trustee is authorized to operate the business of the debtor.

DUTIES OF A TRUSTEE, EXAMINER, OR DEBTOR IN POSSESSION

IX. Duties and powers of a trustee, examiner, or debtor in possession in bankruptcy are as follows:

A. *To collect, administer, and reduce to money the "property of the estate"* in the best interest of all parties in interest (see II-Q above); (the duty to reduce to money is present only in a liquidation case under Chapter 7 of the act);

B. *To make an accounting* of all property received;

C. *To investigate the financial affairs of the debtor* (this duty does not apply to the debtor in possession);

D. *To examine proofs of claims* and to object to the allowance of improper claims;

E. *To oppose the discharge of the debtor, if advisable;*

F. *To furnish such information* about the estate and its administration *as is requested by a party in interest;*

G. *To avoid all voidable preferences* and fraudulent transfers and obligations made or incurred by the debtor (see VII-H-4,5 above).

H. *To file periodic reports,* including a statement of receipts and disbursements if the operation of the debtor's business is authorized by the court;

I. *Of utmost loyalty* (the trustee, examiner, and debtor in possession owe a fiduciary duty to all interested parties); and

J. *To advise and counsel a debtor in an "adjustment of debts of an individual with regular income" case* as well as to adjust the rehabilitation plan, with the court's permission, to any changed needs of the debtor.

PRIORITIES

X. The following expenses and claims have priority in the following order.

A. *Secured debts of creditors. Note:* Secured (lien) creditors are also unsecured creditors to the extent that their liens on the collateral are not sufficient to pay their claims.

B. *Administrative expenses,* and any fees and charges assessed against the estate; e.g., expenses of preserving the estate, taxes incurred by the estate, and wages or fees for services of an accountant or attorney or other person.

C. In an involuntary case, *unsecured debts arising in the ordinary course of the debtor's business or financial affairs after a bankruptcy case has commenced but prior to the earlier of the appointment of the trustee or the order of relief* (i.e., while debtor is in possession of the business with permission of the bankruptcy court). This priority does not apply in voluntary bankruptcy cases.

D. Claims for *wages, salaries, or commissions earned* (including sick leave, severance, and vacation pay) by an individual *within ninety days* of the date of the filing of the petition to the extent of $2,000 for each such employee.

E. Claims for *contributions to employee benefit plans* (fringe benefits) arising from services rendered within 120 days before the earliest of the date of the filing of the petition or the cessation of the debtor's business to the extent of the number of employees covered by the plan multiplied by $2,000 less the total amount of wages, salaries, or commissions paid to an employee under D above.

F. Unsecured claims of individuals (consumers) to the extent of $900 for *deposits of money with the debtor to apply to the purchase* or *lease of property*, or *purchase of services* for the personal, family, or household use of such individual *that were not delivered or provided*; e.g., lay-away deposits on a retail purchase; payment for a one-year membership in a health club; or rent; or damage deposits held by a landlord.

G. *Taxes (federal, state and local)* that have accrued prior to the date of filing of the petition.

H. Claims of *unsecured nonpriority creditors*.

I. Any remaining *balance* of money is paid *to the debtor*.

EXEMPTIONS

XI. The act exempts specified items of property from the *individual* bankrupt's estate. If a joint case is filed by a married couple, each spouse is entitled to the exemptions. (See Figure 8-7.)

A. An *individual* debtor may *exempt property* by filing a list of exempt property with the court. He or she may choose to exempt one of the following:

1. Property exempt from creditors under the law of the state in which he or she has established residence; or
2. Property exempted under the act.
3. A state may pass legislation confining the debtor to selecting only the state exemptions.

B. Under the act, the following items of property are exempt:

1. *Homestead.* Real or personal property the debtors or their dependents use as a *residence*, not to exceed $7,500 in value.
2. *Motor vehicle.* Debtor's interest in one *motor vehicle* not to exceed $1,200 in value.
3. *Household items.* Debtor's interest, not to exceed $200 in value, in each item of household furnishings or goods, wearing apparel, appliances, books, animals,

FIGURE 8-7   EXEMPTIONS FROM BANKRUPTCY: DEBTOR'S CHOICE

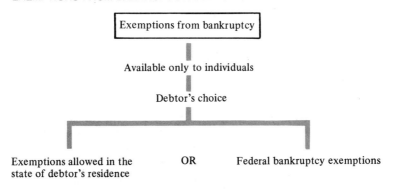

crops, or musical instruments used primarily by the debtor or the debtor's dependent for personal, family, or household purposes. There is no item or aggregate monetary limitation for this exemption.

4. *Personal jewelry.* Debtor's total interest, not to exceed $500 in value, in jewelry used primarily for personal, family, or household purposes.

5. *Professional trade items.* Debtor's total interest, not to exceed $750 in value, in tools, implements, or professional books used in the trade of the debtor or the debtor's dependent.

6. Any *unmatured life insurance contract* owned by the debtor, other than a credit life insurance contract.

7. Any professionally *prescribed health aids* for the debtor or the debtor's dependent; e.g., wheelchairs, crutches, respirators, braces, etc.

8. The debtor's right to receive:
   a. Social security, unemployment compensation, or local public assistance benefits;
   b. Veterans' benefits;
   c. Accident and sickness, disability, or unemployment benefits; or
   d. Alimony, support, or separate maintenance to extent necessary to support the debtor and the debtor's dependents;

9. The debtor's right to receive:
   a. An award under a crime victim's reparation law;
   b. A payment on account of the wrongful death of a person of whom the debtor was a dependent to the extent reasonably necessary to support the debtor and the debtor's dependents;
   c. Life insurance proceeds from a policy on the life of a person of whom the debtor was a dependent to extent reasonably necessary to support the debtor and the debtor's dependents;
   d. A payment (not to exceed $7,500) on account of personal injury to the debtor or to a person of whom the debtor is a dependent; or
   e. A payment for loss of future earnings of the debtor or a person of whom the debtor is or was a dependent to the extent reasonably necessary to support the debtor or the debtor's dependents.

10. *Avoidance of liens or security interests on exempt property:* A debtor may avoid a lien on security interest on his or her property *to the extent that such lien or security interest impairs an exemption,* if such lien is:
    a. A judicial lien; or
    b. A nonpossessory, *non-*purchase-money security interest in exempted property, such as:
       (1) Household furnishings and goods, wearing apparel, appliances, books, animals, crops, musical instruments, or jewelry held primarily for personal, family, or household use of the debtor or the debtor's dependent;
       (2) Tools, implements, or professional books used in the trade of the debtor or the debtor's dependent; and
       (3) Professionally prescribed health aids for the debtor or the debtor's dependent.

11. *Redemption of consumer secured debt:* An *individual debtor may redeem exempted tangible personal property* (intended primarily for personal, family, or household use) *from a lien* securing a (non-purchase money) dischargeable *consumer debt* by payment to the secured creditor of the fair market value of the goods or the amount of the secured debt if the secured debt is less; e.g., X owned a dining room set. He borrowed $2,000 and allowed the dining room set

to become collateral for the loan. X is now in bankruptcy. The market value of the dining room set is $1,200 and the outstanding secured debt is $1,850. X may redeem the dining room set by surrendering it or paying to the secured creditor $1,200. The remaining amount of the debt ($650) is unsecured and would be discharged in bankruptcy.

DUTIES OF A BANKRUPT

XII. The debtor is under a duty to:
  - **A.** File a list of creditors, a schedule of assets and liabilities, and a statement of the debtor's financial affairs;
  - **B.** Cooperate with the trustee as necessary to enable the trustee to perform the trustee's duties;
  - **C.** Surrender to the trustee all property of the estate and any recorded information, including books, documents, records, and papers, relating to the property of the estate;
  - **D.** Appear for examination at meetings of creditors;
  - **E.** Attend the hearing to grant or refuse the debtor's discharge; and
  - **F.** Comply with all lawful orders of the court.

DISCHARGE IN BANKRUPTCY

XIII. A discharge is a release of a debtor from any obligations to creditors. *Only an individual can be granted a discharge under the act.*
  - **A.** The following are *grounds upon which the court may deny a debtor a discharge in bankruptcy.*
    1. The debtor is not an individual;
    2. The debtor, with the intent to hinder, delay, or defraud, has or has permitted the transfer, removal, destruction, mutilation, or concealment of either:
       - **a.** The debtor's property *within* one year before the date of the filing of the petition; or
       - **b.** The property of the estate, *after* the date of the filing of the petition;
    3. The debtor has without justification, concealed, destroyed, mutilated, falsified, or failed to keep and preserve any books, documents, records, and papers from which the debtor's financial condition might be ascertained;
    4. The debtor has committed a bankruptcy crime. A *bankruptcy crime* includes "knowingly and fraudulently" making a false oath or account, presentation of a false claim, giving or receiving money in exchange for acting or refusing to act, and withholding relevant books and records from an officer of the estate;
    5. The failure of the debtor to explain satisfactorily any loss of assets or deficiency of assets to meet the debtor's liabilities;
    6. The refusal of a debtor to:
       - **a.** Obey any lawful order of the court; or
       - **b.** Testify after having been granted immunity.
    7. The debtor's commission of an act stated in grounds 2 through 6 above during the year before the date of the filing of the petition or during the case, *in connection with another bankruptcy case concerning an insider;*
    8. The debtor has been granted a discharge in a case commenced within six years prior to the present bankruptcy case. The six-year rule does not apply if the debtor has repaid 70 percent of the debts under a Chapter 13 repayment plan.
    9. The approval of the court of a waiver of discharge executed by the debtor.

B. *Revocation of discharge.* The court may revoke a discharge on any one of the following grounds:
   1. The debtor obtained a discharge through fraud;
   2. The debtor acquired a right to property that was the property of the estate and fraudulently concealed the acquisition from the trustee; or
   3. The debtor refused to obey a lawful order or to testify after having been granted immunity.

CLAIMS NOT DISCHARGED IN BANKRUPTCY

XIV. Only claims against individuals can be discharged. A discharge *does not* relieve an individual debtor from liability for any of the following debts or claims:
   A. *Taxes (federal, state, or local)* whether or not a claim for such tax was filed or allowed; and for taxes with respect to which the debtor made a fraudulent return.
   B. *Money, property, services,* or an extension of time, renewal, or refinance of credit *obtained by innocent or fraudulent misrepresentation* or by use of a fraudulent written statement respecting the debtor's or an insider's financial condition and upon which the creditor reasonably (justifiably) relied.
   C. *Claims known to the debtor, not scheduled in time for proof and allowance,* unless the creditor had notice or actual knowledge of the case in time to file the claim.
   D. *Debts created by embezzlement, misappropriation, or by fraud while acting in a fiduciary capacity.*
   E. *Debts arising from willful and malicious torts,* such as:
      1. Injury or damage to the person or property of others; or
      2. Conversion of the property of others.
   F. For *alimony, maintenance, or support* of the debtor's spouse, former spouse, or child of the debtor.
   G. For *student, educational loans* made by a governmental unit or a nonprofit institution of higher education:
      1. If such loans have been due and owing for five (5) years; and
      2. A nondischarge will not impose an undue hardship on the debtor and the debtor's dependents.
   Note: Such loans include direct student, educational loans, as well as insured and guaranteed loans.

DEBTOR'S PROMISE TO PAY A DEBT DISCHARGED IN BANKRUPTCY

XV. An agreement by the debtor and creditor to reaffirm a debt dischargeable in bankruptcy is enforceable only if:
   A. The agreement was entered into *before* the discharge was granted; and
   B. The bankruptcy court advised the debtor at a hearing of the consequences of reaffirmation and that the debtor is not required by law to reaffirm a discharged debt; and
   C. The debtor does not rescind such agreement within "30 days after the agreement becomes enforceable" (i.e., within thirty days after the hearing); and
   D. In the case of a consumer debt of an individual debtor not secured by real property, the bankruptcy court has approved the agreement as not imposing an undue hardship on the debtor or the debtor's dependents and is in the debtor's best interest.

SUMMARY OF BANKRUPTCY EVENTS

XVI. The following is a summary of the events in bankruptcy in the order that they will most likely occur.

    A. Filing of a voluntary or involuntary petition.

    B. An automatic stay of legal proceedings against the debtor by creditors upon filing of a petition in bankruptcy.

    C. Order of relief (adjudication of bankruptcy).

    D. Appointment of trustee; or debtor is allowed to remain in possession; or the appointment of an examiner.

    E. First meeting of creditors and/or equity security holders.

    F. Filing of proof of claims.

    G. Filing of plans of reorganization or adjustment of debts of an individual with regular income.

    H. Avoidance of voidable transfers and preferences by the trustee.

    I. Acceptance or rejection of a plan by creditors and by equity security holders, if in an appropriate bankruptcy case.

    J. Confirmation or rejection of a plan by the bankruptcy court.

    K. Conversion of cases if ordered or allowed by the court.

    L. Exemption of certain property owned by the debtor.

    M. Possible redemption of consumer secured debt by the debtor.

    N. Distribution of the debtor's nonexempt assets to pay expenses and claims according to priorities.

    O. Discharge or denial of discharge of the debtor.

    P. Possible revocation of discharge of the debtor.

CRIMINAL OFFENSES

XVII. The United States Code defines various "bankruptcy crimes" for which bankrupts, officers of the court, *and* any other person may be prosecuted, found guilty, fined, and/or imprisoned.

    A. A "bankruptcy crime" can be committed before, during or after bankruptcy proceedings.

    B. A trustee, other officer of the court, or *any other person* commits a *bankruptcy crime* under the following circumstances:

        1. Fraudulent appropriation for personal use any property from the bankrupt estate;

        2. Embezzlement;

        3. Unlawful transfer of any property from the bankrupt estate;

        4. Secretion or destruction of any documents belonging to the bankrupt estate;

        5. Fraudulent concealment from the trustee or other court officer, any property belonging to the bankrupt estate;

        6. Make a false oath during a bankruptcy proceeding;

        7. Present a false claim or proof under oath against the estate of a debtor;

        8. Receive any material amount of property from the debtor after a petition is filed with the intent to violate the provisions of act;

        9. Receive or attempt to obtain any money or property in exchange for an act or the forbearance from acting in any proceeding under the act; or

       10. Conceal, destroy, mutilate, or falsify any document affecting or relating to the property or affairs of the debtor.

SELF-QUIZ

To check your understanding of the key words and concepts and the accuracy of your answers to the questions, refer to the text material as referenced by page number.

KEY WORDS AND CONCEPTS

QUESTIONS

1. What are the available methods of dealing with financial failure in lieu of bankruptcy? Explain some of the distinguishing features of each. **(238)**
2. What are the steps in the administration of a bankrupt's estate during a bankruptcy case? **(258)**
3. Who may file a voluntary petition in bankruptcy and/or an involuntary petition under Chapters 7, 11, and 13 of the act? **(239)**
4. What requirements are necessary in order to file a voluntary petition? An involuntary petition? **(240)**
5. Identify and explain the purposes of the three most important types of bankruptcy cases. **(239)**
6. What is the significance of an order of relief? **(236)**
7. What are the rights and duties of a trustee in bankruptcy? Of an examiner? A debtor in possession? **(249, 254)**
8. List and explain the preferences and transfers that are voidable by the trustee in bankruptcy. In regard to point of time, what preferences given to insiders may be avoided by the trustee in bankruptcy? **(250)**
9. What is the importance of the first creditors' meeting? Identify the parties who may legally attend a creditors' meeting. **(242)**
10. What are the requirements for a proof of claim by a creditor? Are all provable claims allowable? **(243)**
11. Who may submit a plan of reorganization? Must any plan be accepted or confirmed? **(246)**
12. List the types of claims in order of their priority under the act. **(254)**
13. Identify the property owned by the bankrupt that is exempt from creditors. **(255)**
14. What are the duties of a bankrupt? **(257)**
15. What is a bankruptcy crime? What effect does it have on the bankrupt? **(259)**
16. What debts are discharged in bankruptcy? **(258)**

17. Who is the only "person" that is dischargeable in bankruptcy? **(257)**

18. What is the legal significance of a debtor's "reaffirmation agreement"? **(258)**

19. Under what circumstances can a reorganization case be converted to a liquidation case? **(247)**

20. Identify the parties that are bound by a bankruptcy court confirmation of a reorganization plan. **(247)**

21. Explain an "adjustment of debts of an individual with regular income" bankruptcy case. Can this type of case be commenced by a corporation, partnership, or association? **(247)** Can it be commenced by the filing of an involuntary petition? **(248)**

22. Under which bankruptcy case(s) is it mandatory for the court to appoint a trustee? **(243)**

23. Explain the dual legal capacity possessed by a "debtor in possession." **(245)**

24. Define an "automatic stay in judicial proceedings against the debtor." When does it occur? **(241, 245, 248)**

25. Who may submit a plan for "adjustment of debts of an individual with regular income"? What are the consequences if the plan is rejected? **(248)**

26. What must be established in order for the court to issue an order of relief in an involuntary liquidation or reorganization case? **(242)**

27. Can a wife and husband file a "joint case" in a bankruptcy case? **(240)**

28. Define a "provable claim" in bankruptcy. **(243)**

29. List the required contents of a plan of reorganization. **(246)**

SELECTED QUESTIONS AND UNOFFICIAL ANSWERS[1]

OBJECTIVE QUESTIONS

Select the best answer for each of the following items. Mark only one answer for each item. Answer all items.

MAY 1981

40. A client has joined other creditors of the Martin Construction Company in a composition agreement seeking to avoid the necessity of a bankruptcy proceeding against Martin. Which statement describes the composition agreement?

a. It provides a temporary delay, *not* to exceed six months, insofar as the debtor's obligation to repay the debts included in the composition.

b. It does *not* discharge any of the debts included until performance by the debtor has taken place.

c. It provides for the appointment of a receiver to take over and operate the debtor's business.

d. It must be approved by all creditors.

41. In a bankruptcy proceeding, the trustee

a. Must be an attorney admitted to practice in the federal district in which the bankrupt is located.

b. Will receive a fee based upon the time and fair value of the services rendered, regardless of the size of the estate.

c. May *not* have had any dealings with the bankrupt within the past year.

d. Is the representative of the bankrupt's estate and as such has the capacity to sue and be sued on its behalf.

42. Haplow engaged Turnbow as his attorney when threatened by several creditors with a bankruptcy proceeding. Haplow's assets consisted of $85,000 and his debts were $125,000. A petition was subsequently filed and was uncontested. Several of the creditors are concerned that the suspected large legal fees charged by Turnbow will diminish the size of the distributable estate. What are the rules or limitations which apply to such fees?

a. None, since it is within the attorney-client privileged relationship.

b. The fee is presumptively valid as long as arrived at in an arm's-length negotiation.

c. Turnbow must file with the court a statement of compensation paid or agreed to for review as to its reasonableness.

d. The trustee must approve the fee.

43. If a secured party's claim exceeds the value of the collateral of a bankrupt, he will be paid the total amount realized from the sale of the security and will

a. Not have any claim for the balance.

b. Become a general creditor for the balance.

c. Retain a secured creditor status for the balance.

---

[1] AICPA, *Uniform CPA Examination–Questions and Unofficial Answers* have been modified wherever appropriate to conform them to the Bankruptcy Reform Act of 1978 that became effective on October 1, 1979.

d. Be paid the balance only after all general creditors are paid.

44. In order to establish a preference under the federal bankruptcy act, which of the following is the trustee required to show where the preferred party is *not* an insider?

a. That the preferred party had reasonable cause to believe that the debtor was insolvent.

b. That the debtor committed an act of bankruptcy.

c. That the transfer was for an antecedent debt.

d. That the transfer was made within 60 days of the filing of the petition.

MAY 1980

3. The federal bankruptcy act contains several important terms. One such term is "insider." The term is used in connection with preferences and preferential transfers. Which among the following is *not* an "insider"?

a. A secured creditor having a security interest in at least 25% or more of the debtor's property.

b. A partnership in which the debtor is a general partner.

c. A corporation of which the debtor is a director.

d. A close blood relative of the debtor.

10. Bunker Industries, Inc., ceased doing business and is in bankruptcy. Among the claimants are employees seeking unpaid wages. The following statements describe the possible status of such claims in a bankruptcy proceeding or legal limitations placed upon them. Which one is an *incorrect* statement?

a. They are entitled to a priority.

b. If a priority is afforded such claims, it *cannot* exceed $2,000 per wage earner.

c. Such claims *cannot* include vacation, severance, or sick-leave pay.

d. The amounts of excess wages *not* entitled to a priority are mere unsecured claims.

31. Merchant is in serious financial difficulty and is unable to meet current unsecured obligations of $25,000 to some 15 creditors who are demanding immediate payment. Merchant owes Flintheart $5,000 and Flintheart has decided to file an involuntary petition against Merchant. Which of the following is necessary in order for Flintheart to validly file?

a. Flintheart must be joined by at least two other creditors.

b. Merchant must have committed an act of bankruptcy within 120 days of the filing.

c. Flintheart must allege and subsequently establish that Merchant's liabilities exceed Merchant's assets upon fair valuation.

d. Flintheart must be a secured creditor.

35. Hapless is a bankrupt. In connection with a debt owed to the Suburban Finance Company, he used a false financial statement to induce it to loan him $500. Hapless is seeking a discharge in bankruptcy. Which of the following is a correct statement?

a. Hapless will be denied a discharge of any of his debts.

b. Even if it can be proved that Suburban did *not* rely upon the financial statement, Hapless will be denied a discharge either in whole or part.

c. Hapless will be denied a discharge of the Suburban debt.

d. Hapless will be totally discharged despite the false financial statement.

MAY 1979

16. Barkam is starting a new business, Barkam Enterprises, which will be a sole proprietorship selling retail novelties. Barkam recently received a discharge in bankruptcy, but certain proved claims were unpaid because of lack of funds. Which of the following would be a claim against Barkam?

a. The unpaid amounts owed to secured creditors who received less than the full amount after resorting to their security interest and receiving their bankruptcy dividend.

b. The unpaid amounts owed to trade suppliers for goods purchased and sold by Barkam in the ordinary course of his prior business.

c. A personal loan by his father made in an attempt to stave off bankruptcy.

d. The unpaid amount of taxes due to the United States which became due and owing within three years preceding bankruptcy.

19. Marigold, Inc., was in extreme financial difficulty. Hargrove, one of its persistent creditors, insisted upon payment of the entire amount due on the shipments of goods to Marigold over the past four months or it would sue Marigold and obtain a judgment against it. In order to dissuade Hargrove from taking such action, Marigold persuaded Hargrove to accept its note which was secured by a second mortgage on Marigold's warehouse. Hargrove filed the mortgage on November 1, 1979, the same day that the note and mortgage were executed. On February 1, 1980, Marigold concluded that things were hopeless and filed a voluntary petition in bankruptcy. The trustee in bankruptcy is attacking the validity of the mortgage as voidable. Which of the following is correct?

a. The mortgage is *not* voidable since it was filed the same day it was obtained.

b. The fact that Marigold was delinquent on its payment to Hargrove establishes that Hargrove knew that Marigold was insolvent in the bankruptcy sense.

c. The antecedent indebtedness requirement necessary to establish a voidable preference has *not* been satisfied under the facts given.

d. Whether Marigold was insolvent in the bankruptcy sense is irrelevant insofar as deciding whether or not the mortgage is voidable.

23. Hance, doing business as Hance Fashions, is hopelessly insolvent. As a means of staving off his aggressive creditors and avoiding bankruptcy, Hance has decided to make a general assignment for the benefit of his creditors. Consequently, he transferred all his nonexempt property to a trustee for equitable distribution to his creditors. What are the legal consequences of Hance's actions?

a. A debtor may *not* make an assignment for the benefit of creditors if he has been adjudicated a bankrupt and discharged within the preceding six years.

b. All his creditors must participate in the assignment and distribution of property if a majority in number and amount participate.

c. Upon distribution of all his assigned property to the participating creditors, he is discharged from all liability.

d. He has committed an act that would be grounds for a court to enter an order of relief after being petitioned into bankruptcy by his creditors.

24. Markson is a general creditor of Black. Black filed a voluntary petition in bankruptcy. Markson is irate and wishes to have the bankruptcy court either deny Black a general discharge or at least *not* have his debt discharged. The discharge will be granted and it will include Markson's debt even if

a. It is unscheduled.

b. Markson extended the credit based upon a fraudulent financial statement.

c. Markson was a secured creditor who was *not* fully satisfied from the proceeds obtained upon disposition of the collateral.

d. Black had received a previous discharge in bankruptcy within six years.

50. Jane Sabine was doing business as Sabine Fashions, a sole proprietorship. Sabine suffered financial reverses and began to use social security and income taxes withheld from her employees to finance the business. Sabine finally filed a voluntary petition in bankruptcy. Which of the following would *not* apply to her as a result of her actions?

a. She would remain liable for the taxes due.

b. She is personally liable for fines and imprisonment.

c. She could justify her actions by showing that the use of the tax money was vital to continuation of the business.

d. She may be assessed penalties up to the amount of taxes due.

Answers to Objective Questions

May 1981		May 1980	
40. b	**43.** b	**3.** a	**31.** a
41. d	**44.** c	**10.** c	**35.** c
42. c			

May 1979	
16. d	**24.** c
19. d	**50.** c
23. a	

Explanation of Answers to Objective Questions[1]

MAY 1981

40. (b) A composition with creditors is an agreement made between a debtor and creditors whereby the creditors agree with one another and the debtor to accept less than the full amount due. The composition does not discharge any of the debts until performance by the debtor has taken place. However, the agreement is valid from the time made.

---

[1] Explanations of answers to objective questions 19 and 23 of May 1979 have been modified by the author wherever appropriate in order to reflect the provisions of the new Bankruptcy Reform Act that became effective on October 1, 1979.

Answer (a) is incorrect because a valid composition discharges the unpaid portion of the debts and does not merely provide a temporary delay. Answer (c) is incorrect because a composition does not provide for an appointment of receiver which is called a receivership. Answer (d) is incorrect because it need not be approved by all creditors, only those who wish to participate.

41. (d) A trustee is the representative of the estate and has the capacity to sue and be sued. Answer (a) is false since a trustee is either elected by creditors or appointed by a judge to liquidate the estate. There is no requirement that the trustee be an attorney. Answer (b) is also incorrect since a trustee is compensated using a specified percentage of the estate, not by reference to value or amount of services rendered. Answer (c) is incorrect since it is permissible for the trustee to have dealings with the debtor within the prior year.

42. (c) According to the Rules of Bankruptcy Procedure, it is necessary to file a proof of claims against the debtor's estate. The filing must be timely (within a six-month period) or the claim will be barred. A claim that is filed on time is given prima facie validity and is approved unless there is an objection by one of the creditors. Answer (a) is incorrect since all claims are subject to filing and review. Answer (b) is also false because a fee may result from an arm's-length negotiation and still be disallowed by Bankruptcy Procedure. Claims for services by an attorney of the debtor, to the extent a fee exceeds a reasonable value for services rendered, are disallowed. The court must approve the reasonableness of the claim even if the transaction is an arm's-length negotiation. Answer (d) is false because it is the courts, not the trustee, which approve the fees.

43. (b) A secured creditor has a security interest in the personal property of the debtor which is acting as collateral for the debt. In a bankruptcy proceeding, there is an order of priorities concerning distribution of the debtor's estate. Secured creditors are given first priority in the sense that property subject to a valid security interest is not part of the estate for distribution purposes but belongs to the secured creditor to the extent of his security interest. The secured party can either take the property or its cash equivalent. If the value of the property is insufficient to satisfy the claim, the secured creditor becomes a general creditor for the balance. After all secured creditors and priority claims are fully satisfied, all general creditors then share in the remaining assets of the debtor's estate. Answers (a), (b), and (d) are incorrect because the secured party does have a claim for the balance, but only as an unsecured general creditor.

44. (c) In order to establish a preference under the Bankruptcy Reform Act, the trustee is required to show that the transfer was made in payment of an antecedent debt (a debt incurred prior to the transfer as contrasted with a present transfer for value). As a result of such a transfer the preferred party receives more than he would in the bankruptcy proceedings. Answer (a) is untrue since, under the new Bankruptcy Reform Act of 1978 in order for the trustee to establish a preference, it is no longer a requirement to prove that the preferred party have reasonable cause to believe that the debtor is insolvent. Answer (b) is incorrect since, under the Act of 1978, acts of bankruptcy no longer exist. Answer (d) is incorrect since the transfer must be made within 90 days, not 60 days, of the filing of the bankruptcy petition.

MAY 1980

3. (a) Answer (a) is correct because a secured creditor is not an "insider" for the purposes of a preferential transfer. However, a partner is an insider with regard to the partnership, a director is an insider concerning the corporation, and a close relative is an insider to the debtor.

10 (c) Under the Bankruptcy Reform Act of 1978, a priority is given to claims of wage earners up to an amount of $2,000 per claimant, provided wages were earned within 90 days of the filing of the petition. This priority does include claims from vacation, severance and sick leave pay; therefore, answer (c) is the correct answer. If the individual wage earner's claim exceeds $2,000 it falls to the last priority under unsecured claims (general creditors).

31. (a) If the debtor has 12 or more creditors, 3 or more creditors who are owed at least $5,000 (together) above any security interest can file. Answer (b) is incorrect because the 1978 Bankruptcy Reform Act no longer includes "acts of bankruptcy." Answer (c) describes insolvency in the "bankruptcy" sense which is not required for involuntary bankruptcy. There is no need for Flintheart to be a secured creditor in order to sign an involuntary petition.

35. (c) If the debtor supplies false information to obtain credit, the debt incurred will not be discharged in a bankruptcy proceedings. Answer (a) is incorrect because only the debt involving the false information will not be discharged. All other dischargeable debts will be terminated at the end of the bankruptcy proceedings. Answer (b) is incorrect because the creditor must rely on the false information before the resulting debt becomes nondischargeable. Answer (d) is incorrect because Hapless will be denied a discharge of the Suburban debt.

16. (d) Any unpaid amount of taxes due to the United States or to any state or subdivision thereof from within three years preceding bankruptcy is not discharged by the bankruptcy proceeding. The unpaid balances owed to secured creditors, as in answer (a), or unpaid amounts owed to trade suppliers for goods purchased, as in answer (b), or a personal loan from the bankrupt's father made in an attempt to stave off bankruptcy, as in answer (c), are all items which would be discharged in bankruptcy. Once these claims are discharged, the bankrupt would no longer have to pay them.

19. (d) Marigold, Inc., made a voidable preference by giving Hargrove a second mortgage since it gave Hargrove a preferential position over other creditors on a prior debt. Whether Hargrove knew that Marigold was insolvent in the bankruptcy sense or equity sense is irrelevant in deciding whether the mortgage constitutes a voidable preference. Answer (a) is incorrect since the mortgage is a voidable preference. Answer (b) is incorrect because Marigold's delinquency on its payments to Hargrove does not establish that Hargrove knew or should have known that Marigold was insolvent (liabilities exceed FMV of assets). Answer (c) is incorrect because the problem clearly indicates that the mortgage was given to Hargrove in consideration of an antecedent or pre-existing debt.

23. (d) By making a general assignment for the benefit of creditors, Hance may be petitioned into bankruptcy by his creditors. A general assignment for the benefit of creditors is grounds for the court to issue an order of relief against a debtor. The assignor's insolvency in this situation is immaterial. Answer (a) is incorrect because a discharge in bankruptcy within the preceding six years only bars a present discharge of any unpaid debts. The question makes no mention of a previous discharge in bankruptcy. Answer (b) is incorrect because all creditors need not participate in the assignment and distribution of property. Those creditors who choose not to participate may pursue other remedies such as petitioning the debtor into bankruptcy. Answer (c) is incorrect because the distribution of assigned property to the participating creditors does not necessarily discharge the debtor from all further liability.

24. (c) The requirement is the situation in which Markson's debt will be discharged. When a debtor files a voluntary petition in bankruptcy, a discharge will be granted and will include any amounts owed to secured creditors who were not fully paid from the proceeds of the collateral. A previous discharge within six years, as in answer (d), will bar a current discharge in bankruptcy. Also a debt will not be discharged in bankruptcy if the debt was created upon a fraudulent financial statement, as in answer (b), or has not been scheduled, as in answer (a). An unscheduled debt is one that has not been listed by the debtor and the creditor did not have notice of the bankruptcy proceeding.

50. (c) The requirement is the statement that would not apply to Jane Sabine's actions. An employer who withholds social security and income taxes from employees may not justify using such funds to finance her business even if such action were vital to continuation of the business. Such action is a criminal act and would subject the perpetrator to absolute liability. Even should she be adjudicated a bankrupt, she would, as in answer (a), remain personally liable for taxes due. As in answer (b), she would be personally liable for fines and imprisonment. Also in answer (d), she may be assessed penalties up to the amount of the taxes due (100%).

ESSAY QUESTIONS AND ANSWERS

MAY 1977 (Estimated time: 18 to 20 minutes)

7. Part a. The MIB Corporation has been petitioned into bankruptcy. The petition was filed May 1, 1980. Among its creditors are the following:

A. *Viscount Machine Manufacturing, Inc.* Viscount, a wholly owned subsidiary, sold MIB two tractor trailers on November 1, 1979, and filed and recorded its financing statement on March 15, 1980, after it learned that MIB was in severe financial difficulty. The outstanding balance due Viscount is $9,000 which is the current fair market value of the two tractor trailers. Viscount is attempting to repossess the tractor trailers in order to recover its outstanding balance.

B. *Second National County Bank* Second National holds a first mortgage on the real estate where MIB has its principal plant, office, and warehouse. The mortgage is for $280,750 representing the unpaid balance due on the original $350,000 mortgage. The property was sold for $290,000, its fair market value as established by bids received by the trustee. The mortgage was taken out two years ago and duly filed and recorded at that time.

C. *Marvel Supply Company* Marvel, a major supplier of parts, delivered $10,000 worth of parts to MIB on April 17, 1980. Upon delivery Marvel received 50% cash and insisted on the balance by the end of the month. When the balance was not paid, Marvel obtained from MIB a duly executed financing statement which Marvel filed on May 2, 1980.

D. *Sixty-five wage earners* This class of employee is mainly composed of the machine operators and others employed in MIB's plant and warehouse. They were not paid for the final month. All were paid at the minimum wage level and each has a claim for $400 which equals $26,000 in total.

E. *Federal, state, and local taxing authorities* MIB owes $6,800 in back taxes.

F. *Administration costs* These total $12,000.

G. *Various general creditors* Excluding items A through F stated above, general creditors have provable claims of $1,614,900. The bankrupt's total estate consists of $850,000 of assets in addition to the real estate described in B.

Required Answer the following, setting forth reasons for any conclusions stated.

1. Discuss the legal implications and the resulting rights of each of the persons or entities described above in A through G as a result of the facts given and the application of bankruptcy law to them.

2. What is the bankruptcy dividend (percentage on the dollar) that each general creditor will receive? Show calculations in good form.

Answer

1. A. *Viscount Machine Manufacturing, Inc.* Viscount has a preference which is voidable under the bankruptcy laws. Viscount is an "insider." The trustee can attack the security interest asserted by Viscount because it was not perfected until March 15, 1980, which is between 90 days and one (1) year prior to the filing of the petition against MIB, and in addition, the creditor had reasonable cause to believe that the debtor was insolvent in the bankruptcy sense. Therefore, its secured position with respect to the tractor trailers will be denied, and it is placed in the general creditor category with respect to its $9,000 claim.

B. *Second National County Bank* Second National is a bona fide secured creditor and as such will be paid in full ($280,750) from the proceeds of the sale of the real estate. The balance of the proceeds ($9,250) will be added to the funds which potentially are available to the general creditors.

C. *Marvel Supply Company* Marvel Supply is a general creditor in the amount of $5,000. Filings made after the date of bankruptcy are invalid. The $5,000 cash payment does not present a problem in that it merely represents a contemporaneous exchange of one type of the debtor's assets for another at fair market value.

D. *Sixty-five wage earners* The wage earners are entitled to a priority of $400 each, payable after the administration costs but before taxes. Each employee is entitled to a priority not to exceed $2,000 for wages earned within the ninety days preceding the filing of the bankruptcy petition.

E. *Federal, state, and local taxing authorities* The unpaid taxes in question are also a priority item. They rank after the administration costs and the wage earners' claims. It should be noted that wage earners' claims which are entitled to priority and taxes which became due within three years preceding bankruptcy are not discharged in a bankruptcy proceeding.

F. *Administration costs* As indicated above, administration costs (court, attorneys', trustees', and accountants' fees, etc.) are entitled to the first priority available against the unsecured assets of the debtor.

G. *Various general creditors*   The general creditors are entitled to a pro rata distribution of MIB's assets after all secured creditors and priority items are paid.

2. *Computation of Bankruptcy Dividend*

Assets Available to General Creditors

Before adjustments (G)		$ 850,000
Increased by excess proceeds		
from sale of real estate (B)		9,250
Subtotal		859,250
Less priorities:		
Administrative costs (F)	$12,000	
Sixty-five wage earners (D)	26,000	
Federal, state, and local taxing		
authorities (E)	6,800	44,800
Total assets available to general creditors		$ 814,450

Liabilities of General Creditors

As stated (G)		$1,614,900
Increased by:		
Viscount's claim (A)	$ 9,000	
Marvel's claim (C)	5,000	14,000
Total		$1,628,900

Assets available ($814,450) ÷ liabilities applicable ($1,628,900) = 50% on the dollar; that is, 50 cents per dollar will be paid to general creditors.

CHAPTER
9

Federal Consumer Protection Legislation and Bulk Sales

The following is a generalized listing of subjects to be tested through the May 1983 Uniform CPA Examination.

... problems arising as a result of a bulk purchase, covered by Article 6 (Bulk Sales) of the Uniform Commercial Code, are included, on the AICPA Uniform Examination.[1]

The AICPA Board of Examiners has adopted a new content specification outline for the business law section of the Uniform CPA Examination, *to be effective with the November 1983 examination.* The outline lists the following topics to be tested under the titles "Federal Consumer Protection Legislation" and "Bulk Transfers."

C. Bulk Transfers
  1. Publication, Notification, and Other Requirements
  2. Rights of Pre-Sale Creditors
  3. Rights of Post-Sale Creditors
  4. Effects of Security Interests
D. Federal Consumer Protection Legislation
  1. Consumer Credit Protection Act
  2. Magnuson-Moss Federal Warranty Act
  3. Regulation of Deceptive Practices Pursuant to Section 5, Federal Trade Commission Act[2]

FEDERAL CONSUMER PROTECTION LEGISLATION

To protect consumers, the Congress of the United States enacted the Federal Trade Commission Act and numerous other important regulatory statutes (see Figure 9-1). To

---

[1] AICPA, *Information for CPA Candidates.* Copyright © 1975, 1979, by the American Institute of Certified Public Accountants, Inc.
[2] AICPA, *Business Law–Content Specification Outline,* approved by the AICPA Board of Examiners on August 31, 1981.

FIGURE 9-1   CONSUMER PROTECTION LEGISLATION

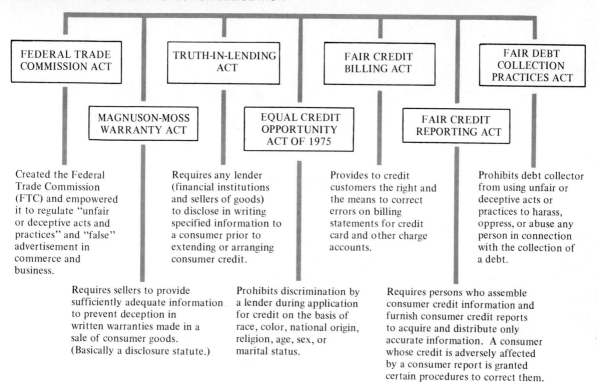

ensure compliance with the provisions of these laws, Congress created the Federal Trade Commission (FTC).

FEDERAL TRADE COMMISSION ACT (As Amended) AND THE FEDERAL TRADE COMMISSION (FTC)

I. The Federal Trade Commission Act, as amended, established the FTC and granted it authority to control "unfair methods of competition" and "deceptive acts and practices" in or affecting interstate commerce. The FTC's role in controlling "unfair methods of competition" is discussed in Chapter 17. Its role in regulating unfair or deceptive acts and trade practices under section 5 of the Federal Trade Commission Act is covered in this chapter.

    A. *Nature of the FTC.* The FTC is a federal administrative agency that possesses broad investigative, rulemaking, and regulatory power (see Chapter 16).

    B. *FTC Enforcement Authority.* The FTC's enforcement authority is civil in nature; it does not have criminal enforcement authority.

    C. *Jurisdiction.* The FTC has sole enforcement authority of the provisions of the Federal Trade Commission Act as amended and *concurrent* enforcement authority with the U.S. Attorney General and other enforcement agencies with regard to the following federal consumer protection laws:[1]

---

[1] The laws listed in 1–6 and 13 are *not* subject to examination on the Uniform CPA Examination, and consequently will not be discussed in this book. The laws listed in 7–12 are subject to examination by the AICPA on the Uniform CPA Examinations beginning in November of 1983. They are discussed in the sections that follow.

1. Fur Products Labeling Act;
2. Wool Products Labeling Act;
3. Food Drug and Cosmetic Act;
4. Flammable Fabrics Act;
5. Lanham Trade-Mark Act;
6. Fair Packaging and Labeling Act;
7. Magnuson-Moss Warranty—Federal Trade Commission Improvement Act;
8. Consumer Credit Protection Act (i.e., Truth in Lending Act);
9. Equal Credit Opportunity Act;
10. Fair Credit Reporting Act;
11. Fair Credit Billing Act;
12. Fair Debt Collection Practices Act; and
13. Electronic Funds Transfer Act

D. *Unfair or deceptive acts or practices under section 5 of the Federal Trade Commission Act.* The FTC has authority to regulate unfair or deceptive acts or practices involving advertising, warranties, and credit. A prohibited act or practice is one that is false, deceptive, misleading, or unfair. The deception may be expressed or implied from the act or practice. Actual deception of a consumer need not be proved by the FTC; it need only establish that the act or practice is unfair or that it has the potential to deceive a consumer. Some examples of prohibited acts or practices are as follows:

1. *Invalid, unreasonable, or unsubstantiated claims.* A firm must have a reasonable basis for making a claim that its product will perform as advertised. Claims of product performance must be substantiated prior to their advertisement. The following claims have been held to be in violation: That certain maternity garments eliminate the discomforts of pregnancy or promote safe and easy childbirth; that a bust cream will beneficially affect the structure and firmness of the breasts; that a certain oil additive reduces oil consumption; that the use of a certain mouthwash prevents colds and sore throats; or that certain liver pills are a cure or remedy for liver disorders.

2. *Bait advertising* (i.e., "bait and switch"). Bait advertising occurs whenever a product is offered for sale for a specified price and the advertiser, at the time of the advertisement, does not intend or want to sell the specified product, but in reality intends and wants to sell a different product at a higher price. The following conduct and activities are evidence that an advertiser-seller has engaged in a "bait and switch" deceptive practice:
   a. Refuse to show or sell the advertised product;
   b. Fail to stock and have available an adequate quantity of the advertised product;
   c. Use compensation plans that encourage salespersons to sell products other than those advertised;
   d. Refuse to agree to deliver the advertised product within a reasonable time after the sale;
   e. Discredit (i.e., disparage) any attribute of the advertised product or any service that is provided with it, either before or after the sale; or
   f. Fail to make delivery of the advertised product within a reasonable amount of time after the sale or intentionally deliver defective goods.

3. *Fraudulent, false, or misleading advertisements or representations about the performance, character, composition, quality, or source of the goods being sold.*
   a. Both the advertiser and its advertising agency can be liable. An advertising agency is liable when it either develops a fraudulent, false, or misleading

advertisement for the advertiser or knowingly uses such an advertisement provided by the advertiser. The advertiser is liable for all such advertisements that it approves.

  b. Some examples of fraudulent, false, or misleading advertisements are as follows:
    (1) Rabbit fur is represented to be seal;
    (2) Veneer as solid wood;
    (3) Secondhand goods as new;
    (4) Cigars made from tobacco grown in the United States were represented as "Havana" cigars;
    (5) Use of an *undisclosed* mock-up or prop instead of the actual product, article, or substance represented in a test, experiment or demonstration as visual proof of a claim made for a product. For example: An advertisement on TV represented plexiglass sprinkled with sand to be sandpaper, showed the advertiser's shaving cream being applied to its surface, and a razor easily "shaving" the "sandpaper." As another example: A soup advertiser failed to advise TV viewers that it added marbles to its depicted bowl of soup to give the appearance that its soup contained a large quantity of vegetables and meat.

4. *Price deception.* This type of deception occurs whenever an advertisement is designed to lead prospective purchasers to believe that they will be charged a lower price when in reality they will not. For example:
  a. An advertisement advises prospective consumers that they are to receive "free" goods when in reality they are not free; e.g., "buy one and get one free," but the price of one exceeds the regular price of the product; or
  b. The price of a product is referred to as the "regular price" when in reality the advertiser had not recently sold the product at that price during the regular course of its business; or
  c. The product is advertised as "free," but in reality the prospective purchaser is required to buy another product in order to obtain the "free" one.

5. *Endorsements.* An endorsement is the expression of an actual opinion, belief, or experience as to the merits of a product or service. An endorsement is held to be deceptive if:
  a. The endorser does not use the product;
  b. The endorser is represented as an expert when in reality he or she is not, e.g., "scientist," "doctor," "dentist," or "auto racer."
  c. The endorser is an expert but did not examine the products so as to support the expressed opinions or conclusions; or
  d. The endorser compared competing products or services but did not examine and evaluate such products or services.

6. *Disparagement.* False disparagement (discredit) of a competitor or a competitor's product is an unfair or deceptive trade practice. Comparison advertising is not deceptive if the superiority claims made within it are based upon results of reliable tests that accurately establish significant comparative superiority over competitive brands. For example: "The Pepsi Challenge," in which persons were asked to sample taste unidentified Coca Cola and Pepsi and then reveal which sample they preferred.

7. *Product name imitation.* It is a deceptive practice for a firm to adopt the same name or one that is similar to the well-known (i.e., has consumer acceptance) name of a competitor's product.

8. *Written warranties.* See II below.

9. *Credit.* See III below.

10. *Collection of debts.* See VI below.

E. *Door-to-door sales of consumer goods: FTC cooling-off rule.* An FTC rule makes it an "unfair or deceptive act or practice" for a door-to-door seller to fail to give a consumer written notice of the right to cancel a home solicitation sale of $25 or more within three business days after the date of the contract.

    1. The three-business-day period does not begin to run until the consumer is given notice of the right to cancel.

    2. Upon a cancellation, the consumer is not liable for any finance charges, the creditor is obligated to return any downpayment, and any security interest is void.

    3. If the seller does not pick up the product in the consumer's possession within twenty days after notice of cancellation, the seller's rights to the product are lost.

    4. The FTC rule applies only to home solicitation sales. It does not apply to purchases by mail or phone, or purchases of real estate, insurance, or investment securities.

F. *Authority of the FTC* (see Figure 9-2). To ensure compliance with the provisions of federal consumer protection legislation, the FTC has the authority to:

    1. *Investigate alleged violations.* The FTC can investigate alleged violations either upon its own initiative or upon complaint by a consumer.

    2. *Promulgate trade regulation rules.* The FTC can create rules and regulations that carry the force of law to enforce the intent and purposes of consumer protection legislation. These rules and regulations may define and identify acts or practices that are unfair or deceptive;

    3. *Initiate administrative quasi-judicial proceedings.* The FTC can issue a formal complaint against an alleged violator and have its case tried before an FTC administrative law judge;

    4. *Issue cease and desist orders* against a violator of its rules;

    5. *Impose fines* upon violators of cease and desist orders or FTC trade regulation rules;

    6. *Rescind or reform* (i.e., change) consumer contracts;

FIGURE 9-2   SANCTIONS AND REMEDIES UNDER THE FEDERAL TRADE COMMISSION ACT

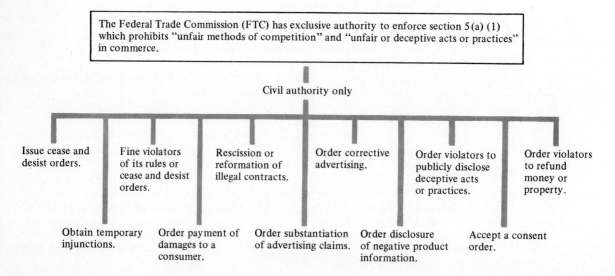

7. *Order refunds of money or property* to consumers;

8. *Obtain temporary injunctions* to stop unfair or deceptive acts or practices;

9. *Order payment of damages* to consumers;

10. *Order corrective advertising* to remedy the effect of previous deceptive advertising and to curtail future deceptions. For example, the manufacturer of Listerine mouthwash was ordered to state in its advertisements of the product that Listerine will not prevent colds or sore throats. As another example, an oil manufacturer, after action by the FTC, agreed to advertise that the results of its product tests, as previously advertised, cannot be relied upon to support claims that STP oil additive reduces oil consumption;

11. *Order substantiation (i.e., documentation) of advertising claims.* For example, Sears, Roebuck & Co. was ordered by the FTC to substantiate its advertised claim that its "do-it-yourself dishwasher" required "no scraping and no pre-rinsing";

12. *Order an advertiser to disclose positive or negative product information.* For example, a land developer was required to disclose to potential buyers the risks of purchasing undeveloped land. As another example, cigarette ads were required to contain the Surgeon General's warning of the potential hazard of smoking cigarettes;

13. *Order a violator to publicly disclose* ("confess") its unfair or deceptive acts or practices (as an example, a land developer found in violation was ordered to expend a large amount of money to advertise that it had been found guilty of deceptive practices and that persons who previously purchased underdeveloped land from the violator had the right to rescind their contracts); and

14. *Accept a consent order.* A *consent order* is an agreement between the FTC and an alleged violator wherein the FTC waives its right to prosecute the alleged violator and the alleged violator, without an admission of guilt, agrees to accept the complaint, findings, and orders made by the FTC. Once accepted by the FTC, the consent order has the binding effect of a formal, adjudicatory decree of an administrative agency. For example, the FTC accepted a consent order prohibiting a drug company from making disease-prevention claims for its household disinfectants.

MAGNUSON-MOSS WARRANTY: FEDERAL TRADE COMMISSION IMPROVEMENT ACT

II. The Magnuson-Moss Warranty Act was enacted for the purpose of minimizing deception in *written warranties* made in conjunction with the sale of consumer goods and to require sellers to provide to consumers adequate information to evaluate written warranties.

  A. In general:
  1. The stated purposes of the act are to:
     a. Improve the adequacy of information available to consumers in connection with written warranties;
     b. Prevent deception; and
     c. Improve competition in the marketing of consumer products.
  2. The act applies only to *consumer products* and to *merchants.*
  3. *Service contracts* as substitutes for written warranties are also regulated by the act.
  4. The act *does not* require merchants to make any warranties, oral or written. *However,* if a written warranty is made, it must comply with the provisions of the act. *Oral warranties are not covered by the act.*

5. The act creates a dual classification of warranties, i.e. "full" warranties and "limited" warranties.
6. The act provides for a method of resolving disputes with consumers through informal procedures.
7. The act creates a federal court action for consumers, including *a class action.*
8. The act empowers the Federal Trade Commission and the Department of Justice to take action against deceptive warranties pending trial.
9. The act supersedes state laws relating to warranties in the area of disclaimer of implied warranties.

B. Scope of coverage—Definitions.

1. *Supplier* (i.e., merchant) is any person engaged in the business of making a consumer product directly or indirectly available to consumers, e.g., a manufacturer or seller.
2. *Warrantor* is "any supplier or other person who gives or offers to give a written warranty or who is or may be obligated under an implied warranty."
3. *Consumer* is a buyer of any consumer product, his or her transferee, or any other person who is entitled by state law or the terms of the warranty to enforce the obligations of the warranty.
4. *Consumer product* is "any tangible personal property which is distributed in commerce and which is normally used for personal, family, or household purposes."
5. *Written warranty* includes:
   a. Any written affirmation of fact or written promise made in connection with the sale of a consumer product that relates to the *nature, quality, or performance* of material or workmanship over a specified period of time; or
   b. Any written undertaking in connection with the sale by a supplier *to refund, replace, or take other remedial action* with respect to the product in the event that the product fails to meet the specifications set forth in the undertaking.
6. *Deceptive warranty* is one that is false or misleading or that would mislead a reasonable person exercising due care.

C. *Disclosures required in the written warranty.* The act empowers the FTC to adopt rules prescribing the information that must be stated in a written warranty pertaining to a consumer product sold at a price in excess of $5. The FTC, by rule, requires disclosure, but only for products costing over $15.

1. The act allows the FTC rules to require the inclusion of the following items in written warranties. The FTC *has* issued a rule requiring the "full and conspicuous" disclosure of these items of information "in simple and readily understood language" in written warranties.
   "(1) The clear identification of the names and addresses of the warrantors.
   (2) The identity of the party or parties to whom the warranty is extended.
   (3) The products or parts covered.
   (4) A statement of what the warrantor will do in the event of a defect, malfunction, or failure to conform with such written warranty—at whose expense—and for what period of time.
   (5) A statement of what the consumer must do and expenses he must bear.
   (6) Exceptions and exclusions from the terms of the warranty.
   (7) The step-by-step procedure which the consumer should take in order to obtain performance of any obligation under the warranty, including the identification of any persons or class of persons authorized to perform the obligations set forth in the warranty.

(8) Information respecting the availability of any *informal dispute settlement procedure* offered by the warrantor and a recital, where the warranty so provides, that the purchaser may be required to resort to such procedure before pursuing any legal remedies in the courts.

(9) A brief, general description of the legal remedies available to the consumer.

(10) The time at which the warrantor will perform any obligations under the warranty.

(11) The period of time within which, after notice of a defect, malfunction, or failure to conform with the warranty, the warrantor will perform any obligations under the warranty.

(12) The characteristics or properties of the products, or parts thereof that are not covered by the warranty.

(13) The elements of the warranty in words, or phrases which would not mislead a reasonable, average consumer as to the nature or scope of the warranty" (Sec. 102a).

2. *FTC rulemaking power.* The FTC is directed to prescribe rules requiring that the terms of any written warranty be made available to a consumer prior to a sale of a consumer product. The FTC has issued a rule on *presale availability of written warranties.* Sellers may use any one of the following four alternatives to make warranties available to prospective buyers prior to sale.

a. Display the warranty text in close conjunction to the product;

b. Maintain a binder containing the warranties;

c. Display a package disclosing the warranty text; or

d. Display a sign containing the warranty text. (Catalog and mail order sellers may either print the full text of the warranty in the catalog or solicitation or disclose that the warranty text is available free on request.)

D. *Designation of written warranties.* Any warrantor warranting a consumer product costing the consumer more than $15 must *conspicuously* designate the written warranty as either a "full (statement of duration) warranty" or a "limited warranty."

1. A *"full warranty"* is one that meets the following *federal minimum standards* required by the act:

"(1) such warrantor must, as a minimum, remedy (i.e., fix or repair) such consumer product within a reasonable time and without charge, in the case of a defect, malfunction, or failure to conform with such written warranty;

(2) notwithstanding section 108(b), such warrantor may not impose any limitation on the duration of any implied warranty on the product;

(3) such warrantor may not exclude or limit consequential damages for breach of any written or implied warranty on such product, unless such exclusion or limitation conspicuously appears on the face of the warranty; and

(4) if the product (or a component part thereof) contains a defect or malfunction after a reasonable number of attempts by the warrantor to remedy defects or malfunctions in such product, such warrantor must permit the consumer to elect either a refund for, or replacement without charge of, such product or part (as the case may be). The Commission may by rule specify for purposes of this paragraph, what constitutes a reasonable number of attempts to remedy particular kinds of defects or malfunctions under different circumstances. If the warrantor replaces a component part of a consumer product, such replacement shall include installing the part in the product without charge."

2. If a written warranty does not meet the federal minimum standards, the warranty must be conspicuously designated as a *"limited" warranty.*

3. The warrantor cannot impose any duty upon the consumer as a condition precedent to the warrantor's remedies for a defective consumer product.

4. A full warranty extends to any consumer with respect to a consumer product; i.e., privity of contract is not required for a consumer to claim the benefits of a full warranty.

E. *Service contracts.* A supplier or warrantor may enter into a service contract with the consumer in addition or in lieu of a written warranty if its terms and conditions are clearly and conspicuously disclosed in simple and readily understood language.

F. *Designation of representatives.*

   1. A warrantor may designate a representative to perform his duties under the written or implied warranty.

   2. A designation does not relieve the warrantor of its duties.

G. *Limitation on disclaimer of implied warranties.*

   1. No supplier can disclaim or modify any implied warranty to a consumer if:

      a. The supplier had made a written warranty to the contrary; or

      b. At the time of the sale, or ninety days thereafter, the supplier enters into a service contract with the consumer.

   2. Implied warranties may be limited in duration to the duration of a written warranty so long as the time limit is reasonable and conscionable. This rule *applies only to* limited warranties.

      a. The limitation must be set forth in clear and unmistakable language and be prominently displayed on the face of the warranty.

      b. A limitation of the duration of an implied warranty prevents the written warranty from meeting the federal minimum requirements for a "full warranty."

   3. Any disclaimer, modification, or limitation in violation of the provisions of the act is void for purposes of state law and this act.

H. *Remedies of the consumer.*

   1. *Informal settlement procedure:*

      a. The FTC is authorized to prescribe rules setting forth the minimum requirements for any such procedure. The FTC has issued a rule that sets forth the specific duties of a warrantor who elects to provide for an *informal dispute settlement procedure* in the terms of a warranty.

      b. One or more warrantors *may* establish an informal dispute settlement procedure if:

         (1) The procedure is established by a warrantor;

         (2) Such procedure meets the requirements of the FTC rules; and

         (3) The warrantor incorporates in the written warranty a requirement that the consumer resort to such procedure prior to taking any legal action to enforce a remedy under the act.

   2. *Consumer lawsuits.* A consumer individually or in a class action may resort to a civil lawsuit in a state or federal court for damages or any other available remedy under the act, provided that the consumer has resorted to any existent informal settlement procedures.

   3. *Damages and costs.* A consumer who *successfully* prosecutes a lawsuit is entitled to damages or other legal and equitable relief (i.e., rescission and restitution). In addition, the consumer may recover court costs and expenses, including attorney fees.

I. *Injunction.* The FTC and the U.S. Attorney General are authorized to file lawsuits to obtain injunctions for the following reasons:

   1. To restrain any warrantor from making deceptive warranties;

   2. To restrain any person from failing to comply with any requirement imposed by the act.

J. The act does not invalidate or supersede the Federal Trade Commission act. A violation of any of the act's warranty provisions is a "deceptive act or practice" in violation of the Federal Trade Commission Act.

K. *State law superseded.* State law is superseded by the act in the following respects.

   1. If a written, full, or limited warranty is given by the seller or if a service contract is entered into with the buyer, implied warranties cannot be disclaimed or modified. *Exception:* The *duration* of the implied warranty may be limited to the duration of a limited written warranty of reasonable duration if such limitation is conscionable and is set forth in clear and unmistakable language and prominently displayed on the face of the warranty.

   2. Any state requirement relating to labeling or disclosure with respect to written warranties or performance thereunder is not valid if:

   a. The written warranty is also within the scope of the act (or rules thereunder); and

   b. It is not identical to the requirements of the act (or any rules thereunder).

CONSUMER CREDIT PROTECTION ACT (TRUTH IN LENDING ACT)
(As Amended by the Truth in Lending Simplification and Reform Act of 1980)

   III. The *Truth in Lending Act,* Regulation Z, and the Truth in Lending Simplification and Reform Act were established to minimize deceptive credit practices by lending institutions by requiring a written disclosure to the borrower or potential borrower of the true cost of credit.

   A. *Power to make rules.* The Truth in Lending Act empowered the Board of Governors of the Federal Reserve System to promulgate rules to fulfill its purposes.

   B. *Regulation Z.* Regulation Z was promulgated by the Board of Governors (i.e., the *Federal Reserve Board*) to implement the act. The objective of the act and Regulation Z is to require lenders to disclose enough information about credit charges to enable consumers to compare one lender's credit charges with those of others, thereby having the opportunity to make an informed choice.

   C. *Creditors covered.* Anyone who offers, extends, or arranges consumer credit on a regular basis (i.e., is in the business of doing so) *in connection with a loan of money or the sale of real or personal property or services* is subject to regulation under the Truth in Lending Act. Some examples are banks, savings and loan associations, consumer finance companies, credit unions, and retailers or other sellers that sell on installment contract. Another example would be any retailer or other seller that regularly arranges credit for its customers with a consumer finance company, bank, or other financial institution.

   1. *Consumer credit* is credit granted to a *natural person* for personal, family or household purposes.

   2. *Exemptions from coverage.* Truth in Lending does not apply to:

   a. Extension of credit for business or government purposes;

   b. A transaction involving credit of more than $25,000. Two major exceptions to the $25,000 maximum are all consumer credit transactions involving real property (e.g., real estate mortgages) and all secured transactions involving personal property used or expected to be used as the principal residence of a consumer (e.g., a mobile home).

   c. Corporations, associations, partnerships, trusts, and estates;

   d. Transactions in investment securities by a broker-dealer registered with the Securities Exchange Commission (SEC); e.g., the purchase of stocks, bonds, and other investment securities on margin account; and

   e. All loans or credit extensions primarily for agricultural purposes; e.g., production, harvest, exhibition, marketing, transportation, processing, or manufacturing of agricultural products by a farmer (who is a natural person) including farmland, a farm residence, and personal property and services used primarily in farming.

D. Truth in Lending categorizes all consumer credit transactions as being either closed end or open end.

1. *Closed end credit* occurs whenever a debtor and creditor, at the time of the credit transaction, agree on an extension of credit for a specified period of time, the total amounts and number of payments to be made, and the due date of each payment; e.g., real estate mortgages, consumer loans from finance companies, and retail installment sales contracts.

2. *Open end credit* is an arrangement between a creditor and a potential debtor under which a series of consumer credit transactions are consummated and the debtor has the option either to pay off the debt in specified minimum installments or to pay any outstanding balance in full; e.g., retail revolving credit accounts and credit transactions involving credit cards.

E. *Disclosure requirements.* A covered lender must comply with Truth in Lending disclosure requirements either when a finance charge is or may be imposed *or* when the credit agreement provides that the debt is payable in *more* than four installments (i.e., the *Four Installment Rule promulgated by the Federal Reserve Board*).

1. If a transaction involves one or more debtors, the lender need only make disclosure to the primary debtor.

2. If a transaction involves two or more lenders, only one must make the required disclosure.

3. A creditor who *properly* uses model disclosure forms and clauses published by the Federal Reserve Board is deemed to be in compliance with the disclosure requirements of Truth in Lending.

4. *Closed end credit disclosure.* A covered lender (creditor) must provide to the debtor (consumer) a written *disclosure statement* (or a Federal Reserve Board model disclosure form, if available) "before the credit is extended" (i.e., before a debtor-creditor relationship is created) that includes at a minimum the following information:

a. *Total dollar amount of finance charges*, i.e., the direct and indirect cost of credit. Examples of costs that must be included in the finance charge are interest, application for loan fees, time/price differential (i.e., the cash/credit differential), service charge, finder's fee, carrying charge, points (i.e., prepaid interest on real estate mortgage loans), credit reports and investigation fees, credit life or disability insurance premiums *if* such insurance is required as a condition of the extension of credit and property (i.e., casualty) or liability insurance if it is required as a condition of the extension of credit *and* the creditor requires the consumer to buy it from or through the creditor. The creditor need not itemize the types and amounts of the finance charges;

b. *Annual percentage rate* (APR), i.e., the cost of credit expressed as an annual rate;

c. *Amount financed*, i.e., the total dollar amount of credit extended. Although the creditor is not required to provide an itemization of the amount financed, the creditor must advise the debtor of his or her right to receive a written itemization upon request;

d. *Total dollar amount of all installments to be made;*

e. *Number and due dates of installment payments;*

f. *Total sale price* (required only for credit sales, not for loans). The sale price must include the amount of any downpayment;

g. *Late charge,* i.e., the amount and under what circumstances payable;

h. *Any security interest taken in goods purchased;*

i. *Prepayment refund,* if any;

j. *Prepayment penalty, if any;*

k. *Reference to credit contract documents* must be made for additional information pertaining to default, acceleration clause, rebates, nonpayment of debt, and penalties; and

l. *Assumption* (required only for residential mortgage transactions). The creditor must disclose whether or not a subsequent purchaser or assignee is allowed to assume the debtor's mortgage debt.

5. *Open end credit disclosure.* The creditor must provide two types of disclosure, an initial statement and periodic statements.

    a. *Initial statement.* Under Regulation Z, the creditor must provide an initial statement to the debtor "before the first transaction is made on any open end credit account" that discloses the following information:

        (1) Finance charge:

            (*a*) *How* the finance charge will be calculated.

            (*b*) *When* the finance charge will be imposed.

            (*c*) The *balance* on which a finance charge will be calculated.

            (*d*) The *types of charges* that will be included in the finance charge, e.g., interest and service charges.

        (2) Annual percentage rate (APR);

        (3) Other charges;

        (4) Security interests taken to secure the credit;

        (5) Minimum periodic payment required; and

        (6) Notice of the debtor's rights under the Fair Credit Billing Act. Such notice is required once each year. It can be included here or in a periodic statement.

    b. *Periodic statements.* A periodic statement must be sent to the debtor at the end of each "billing cycle" in which there is either a finance charge *or* a closing debit or credit account balance of more than one dollar. A periodic statement must contain the following disclosures:

        (1) Amounts and dates of extension of credit and a description of any goods purchased in each open end transaction made during the billing period. *Exception:* Creditors who carry less than 15,000 accounts *if* they gave the debtor a brief description of the goods at the time of the sale and the creditor treats any inquiry from a debtor about his or her statement as an allegation of a billing error under the Fair Credit Billing Act (see IV below).

        (2) Amount of any finance charge;

        (3) Annual percentage rate (APR);

        (4) Periodic percentage rates, e.g., 0.86 percent monthly;

        (5) Balance at start of billing period, i.e., "old balance";

        (6) Balance at the end of the billing period, i.e., "new balance";

        (7) Amounts and identification of credits to the account;

        (8) Address for debtor to send billing inquiries;

        (9) Date, if any, within which payments can be made to apply to "new balance" so as to avoid additional finance charges.

F. The act *does not* prescribe the amount of interest or other finance charges to be charged to consumers. It merely requires their disclosure.

G. *Residential mortgage transactions–Disclosures and right of rescission* (i.e., cooling-off period). A three-business-day *"cooling-off period and the right to re-*

scind is provided to consumers *who use their residence as collateral* (including a mobile home or a trailer used as a principal residence) for a mortgage loan. The cooling-off period and right to rescind *do not apply* to a first mortgage given to purchase a residence, i.e., a purchase-money mortgage.

   1. The lender must make the disclosures required by the Truth in Lending Act (see III-E-4 above).
   2. The lender must give the consumer notice of the consumer's right to cancel during the cooling-off period.
   3. The consumer has the right to cancel the transaction for a period of three business days following either the date of the transaction or the date of receipt of written notice from the lender of the right to cancel.
   4. If the transaction is properly canceled, the lender must return any deposits within twenty days after cancellation, the consumer is not liable for any charges, and the mortgage lien is void.

H. *Deceptive advertising.* The Truth in Lending Act placed advertising of credit terms under the jurisdiction of the Federal Trade Commission (FTC).
   1. Bait advertising is illegal. Potential lenders are in violation if they advertise credit terms that they do not normally offer on a regular basis to their customers.
   2. If an advertisement contains any mention of credit, it must disclose, at a minimum, the downpayment, if any, the repayment terms, and the annual percentage rate (APR).

I. *Credit card liability.* The Truth in Lending Act provides the following limitations on the liability of credit card holders for the unauthorized use of credit cards issued in their names:
   1. A card holder incurs no liability if the issuer is notified of loss or theft of the credit card prior to the time the unauthorized use occurred;
   2. Prior to notification of the issuer of the loss or theft of a credit card, the card holder's liability for unauthorized use is limited to an amount up to $50, but only if:
      a. The card was accepted by the card holder, i.e., signed or used by the card holder;
      b. The issuer notified the card holder of the potential liability; and
      c. The issuer provided the card holder a stamped, self-addressed notification form and envelope to be mailed to the issuer upon loss or theft of the credit card; and
   3. If the conditions in 2 above are not met, credit card holders have no liability for the unauthorized use of a credit card issued in their names.

J. *Limitation on garnishment of wages.* The Truth in Lending Act restricts garnishment of a debtor's wages.
   1. Garnishment of any debtor's wages by any and all of the debtor's creditors is limited to the lesser of 25 percent of the disposable earnings (i.e., salary less deductions) of debtor or the amount by which the debtor's weekly disposable earnings exceed thirty times the federal minimum hourly wage.
   2. An employer is prohibited from discharging an employee for one or more garnishment of the latter's wages for any one debt by the same creditor. However, if the employee's wages are subjected to garnishment by two or more creditors (i.e., for more than one debt), the employer may discharge the employee.
   3. This provision is enforced by the Secretary of Labor.

K. *Civil and criminal liability.* Violators of the disclosure requirements of the Truth in Lending Act are subject to the following civil and criminal liabilities.
   1. Civil remedy of rescission of the credit transaction plus court costs and attorney fees.

2. Civil liability to the consumer for actual damages, if any, plus a penalty of twice the amount of finance charges in the transaction, but not less than $100 or more than $1,000, plus any court costs and attorney fees.
3. Criminal liability for *willful* violations of a fine up to $5,000 or imprisonment up to one year, or both.

EQUAL CREDIT OPPORTUNITY ACT

IV. *Discrimination prohibited.* The Equal Credit Opportunity Act makes it unlawful for a creditor to discriminate against a consumer during an application for credit, in the extension or denial of credit, or in the termination of an existing line of credit on the basis of race, color, national origin, religion, age, sex, marital status, or receipt of public aid.

A. It is a violation for a lender to even ask an applicant for information regarding the applicant's race, color, national origin, religion, age, sex, marital status, or receipt of public aid. *Exception:* A lender may inquire into and take into consideration information about an applicant's spouse under the following circumstances:
1. The spouse is to be jointly liable on the account;
2. The applicant is relying upon alimony, separate maintenance, or child support payments to support the credit application;
3. The applicant intends to allow the spouse to use the credit account;
4. The applicant indicated that he or she plans to rely on the spouse's income for repayment of the debt; or
5. The applicant lives in a community property state.

B. *Notice of acceptance or reasons for rejection.* Applicants for credit must be notified of acceptance or rejection within thirty days of the date of credit application. A *detailed* explanation of the reasons for rejection must be provided to a consumer who is denied credit or whose credit is terminated. For example, "Your current monthly wages are too low"; "Your numerous defaults in the past on debts owing to other creditors is the reason for our denial of credit"; or "The amount of your current debts is too high."

C. *Sanctions and remedies.* A creditor, in violation of the act, is subject to the following sanctions and remedies:
1. *Actual damages.* A consumer can recover actual damages suffered as a result of a violation;
2. *Punitive damages.* The court can award punitive damages up to $10,000 to any injured individual and in a class action award consumers as a class up to $500,000 or 1 percent of a violator's net worth, whichever is lesser (i.e., a creditor's maximum liability for any one violation);
3. Court costs; and
4. Attorney fees.

D. *Class actions.* Class action lawsuits are permitted by the act; i.e., one person sues not only as an individual but also in behalf of all other members of a class of persons who were "injured" as a result of the violation of the act.

FAIR CREDIT REPORTING ACT (An Amendment to the Truth in Lending Act)

V. The purpose of the *Fair Credit Reporting Act* is to require consumer reporting agencies to acquire and disseminate *accurate* information in a consumer report to those who provide credit, insurance, or employment to consumers.

A. *Exemptions.* The act does *not* apply to business or commercial credit transactions (i.e., nonconsumer credit).

B. *Definitions.*

    1. A *consumer reporting agency* is any person, corporation, agency, or governmental unit that regularly assembles or evaluates consumer information for the purpose of furnishing consumer reports to third parties.

    2. A *consumer report* is any communication (including credit guides and blacklists) by a "consumer reporting agency" pertaining to consumer's creditworthiness, standing, capacity, or reputation intended to be used to determine a consumer's eligibility for:

        a. Credit or insurance for personal, family, or household purposes, or

        b. Employment purposes, i.e., hiring or discharge of an employee.

    3. *Investigative consumer report* is a report or portion of a report that contains information about a consumer's character, general reputation, personal characteristics, or mode of living obtained through personal interviews of persons *other than the consumer*. It is much more personal in nature than a consumer report.

C. *Duties of consumer reporting agency.*

    1. *Ordinary care, i.e., lack of negligence.* A consumer reporting agency has a duty to establish and follow "reasonable procedures to assure maximum possible accuracy" of information concerning the consumer who is the subject of its reports.

        a. This duty relates not only to its investigative, but also to collection of information and reporting activities (i.e., preparation and updating reports, revealing the contents of files, and correcting errors).

        b. *Creditor defense.* If an agency has established reasonable procedures and exercised ordinary care, it is not liable to a consumer for unintentional violations due to a bona fide error. Under the act, clerical, calculation, computer malfunction, and programming and printing errors are considered to be bona fide errors.

    2. *Notice of investigative consumer reports.* An investigative consumer report cannot be prepared unless:

        a. The consumer is given written notice that such report is being prepared within three days of the time the report is requested, and

        b. The consumer is informed that he or she has the right to know the nature and scope of the personal investigation to be made.

    3. *User access to consumer reports.* A consumer reporting agency can furnish consumer reports to users only under the following circumstances.

        a. Pursuant to court order;

        b. Upon written request of the consumer who is the subject of the report; and

        c. To a person that the agency has reason to believe intends to use the report on behalf of the consumer in connection with the following:

            (1) A credit transaction (i.e., consumer not commercial);

            (2) Employment purposes (i.e., hiring or discharge);

            (3) Insurance (i.e., personal not business); or

            (4) Application for a government license or other benefit.

    4. *Consumer access to information.* Upon the reasonable request of a properly identified consumer, a consumer reporting agency must disclose the following information:

        a. The nature and substance of the information on file (except medical information). *Note:* The agency need not show the consumer the actual contents of its file;

        b. The source of the information (except the sources of material compiled in an investigative consumer report);

        c. The identity of the recipients of any consumer report that was furnished either for employment purposes within the last two years or for credit, insurance, or any other purposes within the last six months prior to the date of the request to reveal information.

5. *Disputed information.* If any information in the consumer report is disputed by the consumer, the consumer reporting agency must reinvestigate within a reasonable time unless it has reasonable grounds to believe that the dispute by the consumer (debtor) is frivolous or irrelevant. After the reinvestigation, it must either:

   a. Delete any inaccurate or unverifiable information from the consumer report and, if the consumer so requests, notify the recipients of a report mentioned in VI-C-4 above; or

   b. If the dispute is not resolved, the consumer's position must be made a part of the report, and if the consumer so requests, it must be provided to the recipients of a report mentioned in VI-C-4 above.

6. *"Stale" information.* Certain "stale" information cannot be included in any consumer report, such as:

   a. Bankruptcies over ten years old, and

   b. Any other adverse information older than seven years.

E. *Sanctions and remedies.* The act provides the following sanctions and remedies for a violation of its provisions:

1. *Damages.* A consumer can recover from a violator as follows:

   a. Willful violation: actual damages, punitive damages, and court costs and attorney fees;

   b. Innocent or negligent violation: actual damages, court costs and attorney fees;

   c. *Class actions.* Class actions for punitive damages are permitted under the act; i.e., one person injured as a result of a violation of the act can sue for and recover damages as an individual as well as in behalf of other members of the same class who were injured as a result of the same violation; and/or

2. *Criminal liability.* A criminal fine and/or imprisonment may be imposed on:

   a. Any person who obtains information on a consumer report from a consumer reporting agency under false pretenses; or

   b. Any officer or employee of a consumer reporting agency who knowingly or willfully provides such information to an unauthorized person.

F. *Enforcement.* The act is enforced by the Federal Trade Commission (FTC) and other federal agencies.

FAIR CREDIT BILLING ACT (An Amendment to the Truth in Lending Act)

VI. The purpose of the *Fair Credit Billing Act* is to protect consumers against unfair and inaccurate credit billing practices in regard to open-end credit. The act requires a creditor to respond to inquiries by its consumer credit customer that allege a billing error in any statement of any open-end credit account.

A. Definitions.

1. *Consumer.* A consumer is a "natural person" who applies for or obtains credit for "personal, family, or household purposes." Consequently, a trust or an association, partnership, corporation, or other company is not entitled to protection under the act.

2. *Open end credit* occurs whenever a consumer is extended credit in a number of separate credit transactions over an unlimited period of time and is given the right to either pay off the debt in installments at a specified rate of interest or pay any outstanding balance in full. For example, credit extended through credit cards, retail revolving credit contracts, a credit union, bank, or other financial institution's open-end loan account.

3. *Billing error.* A "billing error" includes:
      a. An actual error in the amount of a charge;
      b. A charge for goods or services that the consumer did not actually receive or that the consumer refused to accept delivery on the grounds that the goods or services did not conform to the contract;
      c. Any charge that the consumer alleges he or she did not incur;
      d. A charge for which the consumer requested clarification and for which clarification is needed; and
      e. A credit or payment that was not posted to the customer's account.
B. *Billing error correction procedures.* The act requires that creditors establish and maintain billing error correction procedures whereby their debtors can allege billing errors and have such allegations resolved within a specified period of time.
   1. The creditor must give written notice and explanation to the debtor of the latter's rights and duties under the Fair Credit Billing Act at least once each year. Such notice may be included in the creditor's initial disclosure statement or in any subsequent periodic statement.
   2. A copy of the billing error correction procedures must be made available to the debtor upon request.
   3. The procedures must inform the debtor-consumer of the following:
      a. The debtor-consumer must give the creditor *written notice* of any alleged billing error;
      b. The duties of the creditor upon receipt of a complaint; and
      c. The rights of the debtor-consumer against the creditor if a complaint is ignored or an error is not corrected.
C. *Duty of the debtor-consumer.* The debtor must notify the creditor of an alleged billing error within sixty days of the billing date. The notification must be *in writing and contain an explanation* of the reasons for the allegation of billing error.
D. *Duties of the creditor.*
   1. Upon receipt of proper written notice of an alleged billing error from the debtor, the creditor must either correct the error in the credit account or conduct an investigation.
      a. The creditor must acknowledge receipt of such notice within thirty days of its receipt, unless the creditor corrects the debtor's statement within that time.
      b. Within two billing cycles but no later than ninety days, the creditor must either correct the alleged error or explain why the creditor believes the statement is correct.
      c. During the investigation of the alleged billing error, the creditor is prohibited from threatening or issuing an adverse credit report on the debtor.
      d. Prior to any response by the creditor, the creditor, an attorney, or a collection agency is prohibited from sending collection letters or taking collection action in respect to the billing error in dispute.
   2. The creditor must credit the debtor's account promptly after receipt of any payment on account.
   3. The creditor must refund any overpayment upon the request of the debtor. If no request for refund is made, the creditor may credit the debtor's account in the amount of the overpayment.
E. *Remedies of the debtor-consumer.*
   1. *Forfeiture of the right to collect.* The creditor forfeits its right to collect the lesser of the amount of the billing error in dispute or $50 in the following circumstances:
      a. It did not establish billing error correction procedures;
      b. It failed to follow its billing error correction procedures; or

c. It was negligent in carrying out its billing error correction procedures.

2. *Damages.* A debtor can recover any actual damages suffered as a result of a creditor's violation of any provision of the act. For example, actual damages suffered to a consumer's credit rating or standing as a result of a creditor's erroneous report or statement to a consumer credit reporting agency.

FAIR DEBT COLLECTION PRACTICES ACT (An Amendment to the Truth in Lending Act)

VII. The purpose of the *Fair Debt Collection Practices Act* is to protect consumers from harassment, abuse, and unfair or fraudulent acts or practices in the attempt to collect or collection of consumer debts by debt collectors.

A. Definitions.

1. *Consumer debt* is an obligation incurred primarily for personal, family, or household purposes.

2. *Debt collector* is any person or agency whose primary business is to attempt to collect or collect debts *owed to others.* The act does not apply to a lender or a credit seller who attempts to collect its own debt by itself or by its attorney.

3. *Prohibited practices.* It is a violation of the act for a debt collector in connection with collection of a debt to:

a. Use or threaten physical violence or use profanity;

b. Threaten arrest or imprisonment;

c. Use unfair, unconscionable, or illegal means of collection;

d. Publish a "deadbeat" list, i.e., a list of consumers who allegedly refuse to pay debts;

e. Harass, oppress, or abuse *any person.* For example, falsely state on a telephone that a member of the debtor's family had an accident so as to induce the debtor to accept a collect call;

f. Use false, deceptive, or misleading means or representations;

g. Take or threaten to take the property of the debtor;

h. Simulate a governmental agency or legal process;

i. Design, compile, and furnish deceptive collection forms;

j. Take a check postdated by more than five days from the debtor and thereafter deposit such check without written notice of intent to do so not less than three days prior to the deposit;

k. Solicit a postdated check for the purpose of threatening criminal prosecution;

l. Depositing or threatening to deposit a postdated check prior to its date;

m. Make *any* contact with the debtor under the following circumstances:

(1) At an unusual time or place "which is known or should be known to be inconvenient." A convenient time is assumed to be between 8 A.M. and 9 P.M.;

(2) When the debt collector learns that the debtor is represented by an attorney and the debt collector knows or can obtain the attorney's name;

(3) At the debtor's place of employment if the debt collector knows or has reason to know that such communication is not permitted;

(4) After the debtor has advised the debt collector in writing that the debtor refuses to pay the debt and that the debt collector is to stop any future communication;

n. Communicate *in regard to the debt* with third parties other than the debtor's attorney, spouse, a consumer reporting agency, or the creditor. A debt collector can contact a third person only for the purpose of locating the debtor. In making such contact, the debt collector may not reveal that he or she is a "debt collector" unless expressly requested to do so by the third person. Even then, the debt collector cannot discuss the debt. If the debtor is a minor, the debt collector is allowed to communicate with the debtor's parents.

    o. Communicate with the debtor by postcard or by use of an envelope that indicates that it was sent by a debt collector.

4. *Debt collector's initial communication with the debtor.*

    a. Within five days after its first communication with the consumer (debtor), the debt collector must advise the consumer in writing of the following information:

        (1) The amount of the debt;

        (2) The name of the creditor;

        (3) Notice that unless the consumer disputes the debt in writing within thirty days, the debt collector can assume that the debt is valid without any further verification; and

        (4) A statement that if the consumer notifies the debt collector in writing within thirty days that the debt or any portion thereof is disputed, the collector must stop all collection efforts *until* verification of the debt is obtained. After verification is obtained, the debt collector can resume debt collection against the consumer-debtor.

    b. A consumer-debtor can stop the debt collector from making any further contact *after the initial communication* by doing any one of the following: Advise the debt collector that he or she refuses to pay the debt; *or* Notify the debt collector that the debtor is represented by an attorney. *Any* contact subsequent to the time of the consumer's notification is a violation of the act. After such notification, the debt collector's only remedy is to file a lawsuit against the consumer on the debt.

5. *Sanctions and remedies.* Violators of the act are subject to civil liability for damages and Federal Trade Commission (FTC) imposed sanctions.

    a. *The Federal Trade Commission* (FTC) has authority to regulate "unfair or deceptive acts or practices" in connection with the collection of consumer debt. Violations of the act are unfair or deceptive acts or practices (see I-F above).

    b. *Civil liability for damages.* A debtor may recover the following damages and expenses from a violator:

        (1) Actual damages suffered by the debtor;

        (2) Punitive damages up to $1,000;

        (3) Court costs; and

        (4) Attorney fees.

BULK TRANSFERS (Article 6 of the UCC)

Article 6 of the Uniform Commercial Code (UCC) was enacted to protect creditors from unscrupulous or fraudulent merchants who sell out their stock in trade (i.e., inventory) to anyone for any price, keep the proceeds from such sale, and disappear without paying their creditors. This protection is provided by the requirement that the merchant-seller's creditors be given advance notice of the impending sale. The advance notice affords creditors the opportunity to take legal measures to protect their interest prior to the bulk sale. (See Figure 9-3.)

    VIII. *General rule.* If the required advance notice is not given, the bulk transfer is not effective against any creditor of the transferor. "Any creditor" means only those creditors having claims against the transferor that arose *prior to* the bulk transfer [6-109].

FIGURE 9-3   "BULK SALES" ACT

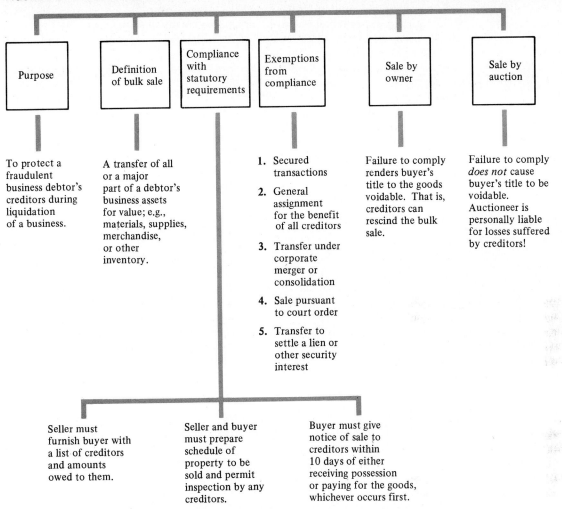

Purpose	Definition of bulk sale	Compliance with statutory requirements	Exemptions from compliance	Sale by owner	Sale by auction
To protect a fraudulent business debtor's creditors during liquidation of a business.	A transfer of all or a major part of a debtor's business assets for value; e.g., materials, supplies, merchandise, or other inventory.		1. Secured transactions 2. General assignment for the benefit of all creditors 3. Transfer under corporate merger or consolidation 4. Sale pursuant to court order 5. Transfer to settle a lien or other security interest	Failure to comply renders buyer's title to the goods voidable. That is, creditors can rescind the bulk sale.	Failure to comply *does not* cause buyer's title to be voidable. Auctioneer is personally liable for losses suffered by creditors!

Seller must furnish buyer with a list of creditors and amounts owed to them.	Seller and buyer must prepare schedule of property to be sold and permit inspection by any creditors.	Buyer must give notice of sale to creditors within 10 days of either receiving possession or paying for the goods, whichever occurs first.

Note: If sale is by auction (not by seller), the auctioneer has the ultimate responsibility to ensure compliance with the "Bulk Sales" Act.

   A. Definitions.
      1. *Bulk transfer* [6-102]. A *bulk transfer* is any transfer not in the ordinary course of business of a major part of (i.e., value not quantity) or all the materials, supplies, merchandise, or other inventory of a transferor's business by an enterprise subject to article 6 of the UCC [6-102(1)]. A transfer of a substantial part of equipment is a bulk transfer only if it is made in connection with a bulk transfer of inventory, but not otherwise [6-102(2)]. The creation of a security interest is not a bulk transfer [6-103].
      2. *Enterprise.* An *enterprise*, under article 6 of the UCC, is one whose principal business is the sale of merchandise from stock, including one which manufactures what is sold [6-102(3)].
   B. *Exemptions.* Transfers exempted from article 6 are as follows:

1. Transfers as security for a debt or other obligation (secured transactions);
2. A general assignment for the benefit of all creditors;
3. Transfers in settlement of a lien or other security interest;
4. Sales by executors, administrators, receivers, trustees in bankruptcy, or any public official under court order;
5. Sales made pursuant to court order of dissolution or reorganization of a corporation;
6. A transfer to a new business enterprise organized to take over and continue the business if public notice of the takeover is given and the new enterprise assumes the debts of the transferor and the latter does not receive a legal interest in the new enterprise superior to creditors' claims; and
7. A transfer to a person who maintains a known place of business in the state, who becomes bound to pay the debts of the transferor in full and gives public notice of that fact, and who is solvent after becoming so bound [6-103].

C. *Sale by owner (nonauction).* A *bulk transfer (sale) by the owner* (transferor) of the goods is *ineffective* against the owner's (transferor's) creditors *unless* all of the following requirements are met [6-104]. Compare with "sale by auction" discussed below.

1. List of creditors, schedule of property, and notice to creditors.
   a. *List of creditors.* The transferor must furnish to the transferee a complete and accurate list of all the transferor's creditors that includes their names and addresses and the amounts owed to each [6-104(1)(a), (2)]. The list must be signed by the transferor and sworn to or affirmed.
      (1) A bulk transfer is not rendered ineffective by errors or omissions in the list of creditors unless the transferee had knowledge of such errors and omissions.
   b. *Schedule of property.* The transferor and the transferee must prepare a schedule of the property transferred that is sufficient to identify it [6-104(1)(b)].
   c. *Preservation of list of creditors and schedule of property.* The transferee must preserve the list and schedule for six months after the bulk transfer and permit inspection of them by any of the transferor's creditors. The transferee may fulfill its duty by filing them with the proper public official (i.e., with the county clerk in the county where the property is located at the time of transfer or in some states, with the secretary of state) [6-104(1)(c)].
   d. *Notice to creditors.* The *transferee* must give notice of the transfer to all persons named on the list of creditors and to all persons who are known to the transferee to hold or assert claims against the transferor [6-105].
      (1) The notice must be given at least ten days before the transferee takes possession of the goods or pays for them, whichever occurs first [6-105].
      (2) It must be delivered personally or sent by registered mail to all creditors on the list [6-107(3)].
      (3) The notice must state [6-107].
         (a) That a bulk transfer is about to be made;
         (b) The names and business addresses of the transferor and transferee;
         (c) Whether or not all debts of the transferor are to be paid in full from the proceeds of the transfer, and if so, the address to which creditors should send their bills. If the debts are not to be paid in full, the notice must state:
            i. The location and description of the property to be transferred and an estimated amount of the transferor's total debt;

        ii. The address where the list of creditors and schedule of property may be inspected;

        iii. Whether the proceeds of the transfer are to be used to pay existing debts, and if so, the amount of the debts and to whom owing; and

        iv. Whether the transfer is for new consideration and if so, the amount of such consideration and the time and place of payment.

2. *Rights and remedies of creditors prior to a bulk transfer.* Upon receipt of notice that a bulk transfer is to take place, creditors may utilize whatever remedies are available to them under state or federal law. Some examples of remedies available to creditors are:

a. Attachment;

b. Levy of execution on the goods;

c. File an involuntary petition in bankruptcy against the transferor;

d. Injunction; or

e. File a lawsuit requesting a court to appoint a receiver.

3. *Rights and remedies of creditors after the bulk transfer.* Only those creditors of the transferor who held claims based on transactions or events occurring *before* the bulk transfer are protected.

a. *Effect of compliance.* Upon *compliance* with the requirements of article 6 of the UCC, the transferee acquires valid title to the goods free from all creditors of the transferor.

    (1) A transferee who received a list of creditors from the transferor, who properly notified each creditor on the list, did not know that the name of a creditor was omitted, and had no knowledge of the existence of such creditor's claim, is held to have complied with the requirements of the statute and takes title to the goods free from the claim of the omitted creditor.

    (2) A transferee who was in collusion with the transferor to defraud creditors takes voidable title. The creditors can have the transfer set aside even though the requirements of article 6 of the UCC were complied with.

b. *Effect of noncompliance.* Noncompliance *causes the transfer to be ineffective only against those creditors of the transferor who did not receive the required notice* (i.e., pretransfer creditors, not posttransfer creditors; see 3, above).

    (1) *Remedies of creditors.* The pretransfer creditors who did not receive the required notice may disregard the transfer and take the following legal action:

        (*a*) Levy execution on the goods in the possession of the purchasers;

        (*b*) Sue for an attachment;

        (*c*) Sue for an appointment of a receiver to take title to the goods in possession of the purchasers;

        (*d*) File an involuntary petition in bankruptcy against the transferor. The trustee in bankruptcy would then take steps to set aside the ineffective transfer.

    (2) *Statute of limitations.* No lawsuit may be filed to set aside an ineffective transfer nor a levy of execution made against the goods more than six months after the date on which the transferee took possession of the goods. *Exception:* If the transfer was concealed from creditors, the period is six months after the discovery of the transfer [6-111].

    (3) *Purchasers from the transferee* [6-110].

        (*a*) A purchaser of the goods from the transferee who does not pay value *or* who takes with notice of the noncompliance, takes title subject to such noncompliance.

(b) A *bona fide purchaser* (i.e., one who pays value in good faith without notice of noncompliance) takes title free from all claims of the bulk transferor's creditors.

D. *Bulk sale by auction.* The provisions of article 6 applying to bulk transfers by owners equally apply to *bulk sales by auction,* with the exception of those indicated below [6-108].

1. *Compliance.* The special requirements for a proper auction sale in bulk include:

a. The seller must furnish *the auctioneer* a sworn list of creditors and assist in the preparation of a schedule of the property to be sold [6-108(2), 6-104)].

b. The *auctioneer must* receive and retain this list and allow inspection by creditors, for six months, or properly file a list of creditors and schedule of property [6-108(3)(a)].

c. The *auctioneer must* give notice at least ten days before the auction to those creditors on the list and any others known to him or her [6-108(3)(b)].

2. *Effect of noncompliance.* The failure to comply with these duties by the auctioneer does not affect the validity of the sale or title of the purchasers of the goods (contrast with defective bulk sale by owner) [6-108(4)].

3. *Auctioneer's personal liability.* If the auctioneer knows that the auction is a bulk sale, yet fails to comply with the requirements of article 6 of the UCC, the auctioneer is personally liable to creditors of the transferor as a class to the extent of the net proceeds of the auction [6-108(4)].

E. *Security interests under article 9 of the UCC.*

1. *Buyer not in the regular course of business.* A person, who purchases all or a major part of an enterprise's inventory or all or a major part of equipment if it is sold in conjunction with a bulk sale, is a transferee in bulk and consequently is not a buyer in the regular course of business (see VIII-A-1 above).

2. *Priorities.* Secured creditor versus transferee in bulk.

a. *Unperfected security interests* (i.e., not filed). A transferee in bulk takes priority over the rights of any unperfected security interests in the goods to the extent that the transferee *gives value* and receives delivery of the goods *without knowledge* of the security interest and *before it is perfected* [9-301(1)(c)], i.e., filed.

b. *Perfected (i.e., filed) security interests.* If a secured creditor files a *purchase-money security interest before or within ten days* after the *collateral comes into the possession of the debtor* (i.e., the bulk transferor), the secured party takes priority over the rights of a transferee in bulk that arise between the time the security interest attaches and the time of filing [9-301(2)]. For example, on April 1, 1981, Manufacturer sold farm machinery to Dealer. Dealer is in the business of selling farm machinery to farmers. On the date of the sale, Manufacturer and Dealer entered into a security agreement whereby Manufacturer obtained a security interest in the machinery to secure payment of the purchase price of $1,000,000. Retailer received delivery of the machines on May 1, 1981. During the month of April 1981, Dealer fell upon hard times financially and decided to sell all of its inventory to Jacklin. On May 6, 1981, Jacklin, in good faith without notice of Manufacturer's security interest, purchased the machinery for $700,000. Manufacturer filed its financing statement on May 9, 1981. Manufacturer's security interest takes priority over the rights of Jacklin, a transferee in bulk.

SELF-QUIZ

To check your understanding of the key words and concepts and the accuracy of your answers to the questions, refer to the text material as referenced by page number.

KEY WORDS AND CONCEPTS

QUESTIONS

1. Name the three broad powers possessed by the FTC as a federal administrative agency. **(269)**
2. List and explain at least six unfair or deceptive acts or practices that violate consumer protection legislation or FTC rules. **(270)**
3. List the previolation and postviolation remedies available to the FTC against alleged or proved violators. **(272)**
4. Review the provisions of the Magnuson-Moss Warranty—Federal Trade Commission Improvement Act. **(273)**
5. What rulings has the FTC issued under the authority of the Magnuson-Moss Warranty—Federal Trade Commission Improvement Act? **(274)**
6. Explain the provisions of Regulation Z under the Truth in Lending Act. **(277)**
7. Identify the persons and transactions that are exempt from the provisions of the Truth in Lending Act. **(277)**
8. What information must be disclosed to a consumer in a "disclosure statement"? **(278)**
9. What limitation has been placed on a creditor's right to garnishee the wages of a consumer? **(280)**
10. Name two types of consumer contracts in which a consumer has three business days to cancel all obligations thereunder. **(272, 279)**

11. Under what circumstances can a lender or creditor make inquiries relating to the marital status or spouse of an applicant for credit or a debtor? **(281)**

12. What is the purpose of the Fair Credit Reporting Act? **(281)**

13. What information is a consumer entitled to from a consumer reporting agency when his or her credit rating has been adversely affected or application for credit, insurance, or employment has been rejected? **(282)**

14. What remedies are available to a consumer who disputes the accuracy of a consumer report? **(283)**

15. Can anyone other than a consumer reporting agency be criminally liable under the Fair Credit Reporting Act? If your answer is yes, identify the persons and explain the circumstances under which they may be held liable. **(283)**

16. What is the duty of a consumer reporting agency upon receipt of a request for an investigative consumer report from a prospective user? **(282)**

17. What are the duties of a creditor upon receiving written notice of an alleged billing error from a debtor? **(284)**

18. List at least ten practices prohibited under provisions of the Fair Debt Collection Practices Act. **(285)**

19. How can debtors force debt collectors to stop future contacts with them? **(285)**

20. What are the legal requirements for a valid bulk transfer under the UCC? By owner (nonauction)? **(288)** By an auctioneer? **(290)**

21 What are the rights of creditors after a defective bulk transfer by an owner (nonauction)? **(289)** By an auctioneer? **(290)**

22. How can a transferee in a defective bulk transfer free the goods from the claims of the transferor's creditors? **(290)**

23. Discuss the rights of secured creditors after the goods subject to security interests are transferred in a bulk transfer. **(290)**

SELECTED QUESTIONS AND UNOFFICIAL ANSWERS

Select the best answer for each of the following items. Mark only one answer for each item. Answer all items.

AUTHOR'S OBJECTIVE QUESTIONS

1. Grey purchased an automobile from Door Auto Sales on a retail installment contract. Grey signed a promissory note that contained an acceleration clause that provided that the entire debt would become due upon default of any one installment. Door Auto Sales did not disclose the existence of the clause in its installment contract. Grey sued Door Auto Sales for violation of the Truth in Lending Act. Which of the following statements is correct?

a. The acceleration clause is a "default penalty" and must be disclosed by the lender in the installment contract.

b. An acceleration clause is required to be disclosed but only in a separate writing called a disclosure statement.

c. An acceleration clause need not be disclosed unless it provides for a default or delinquency charge for late payment.

d. A required disclosure under the Truth in Lending Act cannot be made in a promissory note signed by the debtor.

2. Ajax, Inc., obtained in its name a credit card issued by Allied Express Company. Ajax, Inc., allowed its officers to use its credit card for personal reasons. Each officer was obligated to assume liability with the corporation for all credit charges. Ajax, Inc., sent numerous complaints to Allied Express of billing errors. Allied Express did not acknowledge Ajax's complaints and cancelled the credit card without explanation. Ajax sued Allied Express for violation of the Fair Credit Billing Act. Which of the following statements is incorrect?

a. Ajax, Inc., is a consumer and is entitled to the protection afforded by the Fair Credit Billing Act.

b. The Fair Credit Billing Act does apply to open-end consumer credit as established by the issuance of a credit card.

c. The Fair Credit Billing Act requires a creditor (i.e., credit card issuer) to acknowledge receipt of proper complaints of billing errors, investigate, and correct the account or explain why a credit account won't be corrected.

d. A "proper" complaint of billing error is one made in writing.

3. Which of the following is *not* covered by the pro-

visions of the Magnuson-Moss Warranty—Federal Trade Improvement Act?

a. Consumer products.
b. Written warranties.
c. Oral warranties.
d. Enforcement authority of the FTC.

4. On May 1, 1981, at his home, Arco, an attorney, was induced to enter into a contract for the purchase of $1,100 worth of stereo music recording tapes. The salesperson had been in the neighborhood calling on another customer when he remembered that Arco, a friend, had at one time expressed an interest in buying music recording tapes. Arco gave the salesperson $350 as a downpayment. On May 2, 1981, Arco decided that he did not need any more tapes. Which of the statements below is incorrect?

a. Arco cannot cancel the contract in the absence of fraud, duress, or undue influence.
b. The salesperson committed an "unfair or deceptive act or practice."
c. Arco cannot cancel the contract after May 3, 1981.
d. If Arco notifies the seller on May 2, 1981, that he cancelled the purchase and the seller refuses to refund the downpayment, Arco can ask the FTC to order the seller to make the refund.

5. Which of the following is *not* a remedy available to the FTC against violators of federal consumer protection laws?

a. Issue a cease and desist order.
b. Order corrective advertising.
c. Impose criminal sanctions under a violator.
d. Impose a civil fine.

6. A door-to-door salesperson for Esso Publications negotiated a magazine subscription contract with Cox at the latter's home. Cox made a downpayment of $4.25. The salesperson advised Cox that the balance owed was $125.75 and that he could pay it in five installments. The contract itself did not disclose the total purchase price, the balance due, or indicate any interest or other finance charges. Cox defaulted without making another payment. Esso attempted to collect by demanding payment in several collection letters. Cox sued Esso and alleged a violation of the Truth in Lending Act. Which of the following statements is incorrect?

a. Esso is liable to Cox for a penalty of twice the amount of finance charges, but never less than $100 or more than $1,000.

b. Esso may also be assessed court costs and attorney fees.
c. Esso did not violate the Truth in Lending Act because Cox was not obligated to pay any interest.
d. A creditor must provide a debtor-consumer a written disclosure statement that reveals, among other required facts, the total cash price of the goods, the amount of finance charges, the annual percentage rate of charges, and the number and due dates of installment payments, if any.

7. Which one of the following loans would be subject to the provisions of the Truth in Lending Act?

a. A personal loan from a father to a daughter to apply to the purchase of an automobile.
b. A loan to an individual for business purposes.
c. A loan to an association, trust, estate, partnership, or corporation.
d. A loan of $24,000 to an individual to be applied to the purchase price of a home.

8. Lena obtained an auto loan from Bank where she and her husband had a joint checking account. Lena signed a promissory note for the amount of the loan. The note contained an acceleration clause that allowed Bank to declare the entire amount of the note due if Bank deemed itself insecure or upon default of any monthly payment. The note also authorized Bank to apply any funds owned by Lena and held by Bank to satisfy the debt. Bank learned that Lena's husband had declared bankruptcy. It thereupon accelerated the debt and used the funds from the joint checking account as an offset against the debt due on the note. Lena sued the Bank for violating the Equal Credit Opportunity Act by accelerating the note on the basis of her husband's bankruptcy rather than her own creditworthiness. Which of the following statements is correct?

a. Bank will lose because a creditor may never use the income, debts, or past credit history of one spouse to deny or terminate credit to the other.
b. Bank will win because the Equal Credit Opportunity Act only applies to discrimination on the basis of marital status during application for credit.
c. Bank will lose because an acceleration clause is against public policy and void under article 9 of the Uniform Commercial Code.
d. Bank will win because a creditor who extends credit to a spouse in justifiable reliance upon a

joint savings or checking account held in the name of both spouses is entitled to take into consideration the creditworthiness of both spouses.

9. TRX, a consumer reporting agency, had issued many consumer reports on Bonnie for many years. During those years, Bonnie had complained personally and in writing that the reports contained stale and inaccurate information about her. In December 1981, Bonnie applied for a home mortgage loan. The bank ordered a consumer credit report on Bonnie from TRX. Bonnie learned that the report contained erroneous information provided by her creditors. As a result of Bonnie's efforts, her creditors advised TRX that the information they had furnished earlier was erroneous. TRX sent the uncorrected report to Bonnie's bank without any attempt to correct the report or verify the accuracy of its contents. Bonnie sued TRX for violation of the federal Fair Credit Reporting Act. Which of the following statements is correct?

a. If a willful violation is established, Bonnie cannot be awarded punitive damages.

b. TRX is liable to Bonnie for any actual damages she suffered and may be assessed court costs and attorney fees.

c. TRX can successfully assert the following defense: "Our only duty under the act is to report what we are told."

d. TRX is liable because the act prohibits disclosure of personal information about a consumer.

10. In certain circumstances, a consumer reporting agency must disclose to a consumer that the consumer is the subject of a requested consumer report, that it intends to conduct an investigation, and that the consumer has the right to know the nature and scope of the investigation. The use of one of the sources below would require disclosure. Which one is it?

a. Prior and current employers for purposes of obtaining information about a consumer's past and present salaries or wages.

b. Court and other official records for purposes of determining whether a consumer was declared bankrupt and to ascertain the existence of judgments and liens.

c. A consumer's ex-wife, neighbor, or ex-employer for the purposes of determining the consumer's alcohol or drug use.

d. Creditors for purposes of obtaining the consumer's past credit history.

11. Which one of the following has primary *civil* enforcement authority of the provisions of the Magnuson-Moss Warranty Act—Federal Trade Commission Act, Consumer Credit Protection Act (Truth in Lending Act), Equal Credit Opportunity Act, Fair Credit Billing Act, Fair Credit Reporting Act, and the Fair Debt Collection Practice Act?

a. Federal Trade Commission (FTC).

b. U.S. Attorney General.

c. Board of Governors of the Federal Reserve System, i.e., the Federal Reserve Board.

d. A state attorney general.

12. When Roberts graduated from college, he still owed money on a student loan. Unable to collect the debt, the university turned over the account to Bureau Collections, Inc., for collection. An employee of Bureau telephoned Roberts on several occasions demanding payment. Roberts wrote to Bureau and advised that he would not pay the debt and he did not wish to be bothered. Bureau did not respond to Roberts' letter by mail or phone for six months. At that time, a new employee telephoned Roberts and demanded payment. Roberts sued Bureau for violation of the federal Fair Debt Collection Practices Act. Which of the following statements is incorrect?

a. The alleged debt is not a consumer debt and consequently the Fair Debt Collection Practices Act is not applicable.

b. Bureau violated the act because it failed to send to Roberts within five days of its initial communication written notice of the amount of debt, the name of the debtor, and that if Roberts disputed the debt in writing within thirty days, it would have to stop collection until it verified the debt.

c. Bureau violated the act because it contacted Roberts after he had advised it in writing that he would not pay the debt and did not wish to be contacted in the future.

d. The act applies to Bureau only if it were engaged in the business of collecting debts of others.

13. Which of the following is *not* a prohibited act or practice under the provisions of the Fair Debt Collection Practices Act?

a. Threatening debtors to blacklist them with a local Merchants' Retail Credit Association.

b. Collection telephone calls and telegrams made and sent to debtors and their relatives at midnight.

c. Send a postcard to a debtor at the debtor's home or place of employment that bears the following statement: "Dear Customer: We made you a loan because we thought that you were honest."

d. A personal contact by the debt collector with the debtor at the debtor's residence at 6 P.M. on a Friday evening.

14. Tom, a merchant, decided to go out of business. He hired Ross, an auctioneer, to dispose of all of his inventory and equipment. Ross and Tom prepared a list of Tom's unsecured creditors and a schedule of the inventory and equipment to be auctioned. Through an oversight, Ross failed to advise Tom's creditors of the time, place, and date of the auction sale. After the sale, Ross immediately contacted Tom's creditors, apologized for his failure to give notice, and advised them that he had turned over all the proceeds from the sale to Tom. The proceeds amounted to only 40 percent of Tom's total debt. Tom's creditors sued Ross and the purchasers at the auction sale. Which of the following statements is correct?

a. The auctioneer, Ross, complied with the provisions of article 6 of the UCC.

b. The auction sale of the equipment is not a bulk transfer.

c. Ross is personally liable to Tom's creditors as a class in the amount of the net proceeds of the auction.

d. The auction sale by Ross is ineffective to pass title to the goods to the purchasers at the auction sale.

15. Under the provisions of the Consumer Credit Protection (Truth in Lending Act), a disclosure statement need *not* contain one of the following. Which one is it?

a. Annual percentage rate (APR) that indicates the annual cost of the loan stated as a percentage.

b. Finance charges, i.e., the dollar amount of the cost of the loan.

c. Surety or sureties on the loan.

d. Downpayment, cash price, number, and due dates of installments, total amount financed, and an explanation of any delinquency or default charges.

Answers to Author's Objective Questions

1. c	**4.** a	**7.** d	**10.** c	**13.** d
2. a	**5.** c	**8.** d	**11.** a	**14.** c
3. c	**6.** c	**9.** b	**12.** a	**15.** c

Explanation of Answers to Author's Objective Questions

1. (c) The Truth in Lending Act requires disclosure of finance charges, the annual percentage rate (APR) of finance charges, and any prepayment, default, or delinquency penalties. An acceleration clause, in itself, merely accelerates the due date of the total debt under an installment note. It does not establish finance charges or provide for penalties. Answer (a) is incorrect because an acceleration clause is not a "default penalty." Answers (b) and (d) are incorrect because the required "disclosure statement" may be printed on the installment (loan) contract, a security agreement, the face of a promissory note, or on a separate writing.

2. (a) Ajax, Inc., is not a consumer. A "consumer" is a natural person who obtains credit for personal, family, or household purposes. Ajax, Inc., is a legal entity and consequently is not afforded the protection of the Fair Credit Billing Act. Answer (b) is correct because the Fair Credit Billing Act does apply to open-end credit accounts created by issuance of credit cards. Answers (c) and (d) are correct because the Fair Credit Billing Act requires that upon receipt of a *written* complaint of a billing error, the creditor must acknowledge the complaint to the consumer unless the error is corrected within thirty days; if not, to investigate and thereafter either correct the account or inform the consumer within ninety days of the receipt of notice as to why the error will not be corrected.

3. (c) The Magnuson-Moss Warranty Act does not apply to oral warranties. Oral warranties are governed by the common law and the Uniform Commercial Code. Answer (a) is incorrect because the act specifically applies to consumer products, i.e., those products purchased for personal, family, and household use. Answer (b) is incorrect. The act does not require merchants to make any warranties. However, if the merchant does make a written warranty, the merchant must conspicuously designate it as either a "full warranty" or a "limited warranty" and meet the minimum disclosure requirements of the act. Answer (d) is incorrect because the act gives the FTC authority to promulgate any rules necessary to enforce its provisions. The FTC also has enforcement authority over any merchant whose written warranties are false, misleading, or deceptive.

4. (a) An FTC rule permits a consumer to cancel a home solicitation sale in excess of $25 within three days after the date of the sale. Arco is a consumer, as he purchased the tapes for his personal use. The right to cancel does not depend on proof of fraud, duress, or undue influence. Answer (b) is correct because the above-mentioned FTC rule makes it an "unfair or deceptive act or practice" for a door-to-door seller to fail to give a consumer written notice of the right to cancel a purchase. Answer (c) is correct because the consumer cannot cancel the contract after expiration of three days after the date of the sale. Answer (d) is correct because the FTC has authority to order a violator of its rule to refund money to a consumer.

5. (c) The FTC has civil enforcement authority only. It cannot impose criminal sanctions upon a violator. Answers (a), (b), and (d) are incorrect because they are civil remedies that are available for use by the FTC.

6. (c) Merchants who regularly extend credit are subject to the *written* disclosure requirements of the Truth in Lending Act whenever they offer or extend consumer credit for which a finance charge is or may be imposed or which pursuant to any agreement the credit is or may be payable in more than four installments. The credit extended by Esso came within the provisions of the act, as the balance owed by Cox was to be paid in five installments. The act does not prescribe the amount or type of finance charges which can be made by a creditor. It imposes the duty upon those who extend credit on a regular basis to consumers to fully inform the latter in writing of the total amount of finance charges, the annual percentage rate, the total amount financed, the total cash price of the goods or services, and the number and due dates of installment payments, if any. Answers (a) and (b) are correct because a violator of the act is subject to stated penalties and may be assessed court costs and attorney fees. Answer (d) is correct for the reasons stated above.

7. (d) The Truth in Lending Act applies to consumer credit. Consumer credit is credit of an amount less than $25,000 extended to a natural person for personal, family, or household use. The $24,000 loan to an individual to be applied to the purchase price of a home is consumer credit. In fact, the act applies to all consumer credit real estate

transactions, regardless of the amount of credit extended. Answer (a) is incorrect because the act applies only to those persons or entities that extend credit to consumers on a regular basis, i.e., are in the business of extending consumer credit. Answer (b) is incorrect because the act applies only to consumer credit. This loan was made for a business purpose. Answer (c) is incorrect because a consumer is a natural person. Associations, trusts, estates, partnerships, and corporations are not natural persons and consequently are not "consumers" under the provisions of the act.

8. (d) All inquiries of or information about the financial condition or credit history of a spouse are not discriminatory practices under the Equal Credit Opportunity Act. Such inquiries and information are allowed whenever the applicant or the circumstances indicate that the creditworthiness of a spouse is being used by an applicant to secure or maintain credit. In this problem, Bank justifiably relied on the joint checking account in making the loan. Since each joint tenant has the absolute right to make withdrawals, Lena's husband could have depleted the funds in the joint account. Answer (a) is incorrect for reasons stated above. Answer (b) is incorrect because the act not only applies during the application of credit but also to denial of credit or termination of existing credit. Answer (c) is incorrect because an acceleration clause is valid if its purpose is to aid the creditor to collect the debt evidence by a note. For example, acceleration upon default by the debtor on an installment payment or if the creditor, in good faith, deems itself insecure.

9. (b) A credit reporting agency has a duty to follow reasonable procedures to assure accuracy of its reports. TRX is negligent for sending the erroneous report after receiving notice of error. Under the circumstances, the agency had a duty to investigate and check the information for its accuracy. Answer (a) is incorrect because a court can award punitive damages to a consumer against a willful violator of the act. Answer (c) is incorrect because a credit reporting agency's duty to a consumer goes beyond merely transcribing whatever information is furnished by a consumer's creditors or others. It must use ordinary care to assure the accuracy of the information obtained and if the consumer challenges the accuracy of the information, it must conduct a reasonable investigation. Answer (d) is incorrect because the act does permit disclosure of personal information about a consumer pursuant to court order, upon request of the consumer, or to persons that the agency has reason to believe intend to use the information on behalf of the consumer in connection with credit, employment, or insurance.

10. (c) Prior written notice of the nature and scope of an intended future investigative consumer report must be given to a consumer not later than three days after a request for such a report is made by a potential user. An investigative consumer report contains information about the consumer's character, reputation, personal characteristics, habits, education, mode of living, and other personal information. The intent to contact an ex-wife, neighbor or ex-employer for the purposes stated would require prior disclosure. Answers (a), (b), and (d) are incorrect because this information may be obtained and reported in a consumer report without prior notice to the consumer.

11. (a) Compliance with these laws is enforced by the Federal Trade Commission (FTC) since their violations are considered to be unfair or deceptive acts or practices in commerce. Answer (b) is incorrect because the U.S. Attorney General's primary concern is the prosecution of criminal violations. Answer (c) is incorrect because the Federal Reserve Board has primary responsibility to prescribe regulations under the Truth in Lending Act and to interpret provisions of the Equal Credit Opportunity Act. Answer (d) is incorrect because state attorney generals are not charged with the enforcement of federal consumer protection laws.

12. (a) A debt incurred by a student to pay for college expenses is a consumer debt. It is an obligation incurred primarily for a personal purpose. Answer (b) is correct because the act requires such notice to be sent and Bureau failed to do so. Answer (c) is correct because the act provides that it is a violation for a debt collector to make any contact with a consumer debtor after the collector receives written notification from the debtor that he or she refuses to pay the debt and does not wish to be contacted any further. Answer (d) is correct because the act regulates only the collection activities of persons or entities that engage in debt collection on a regular basis.

13. (d) A debt collector is allowed to communicate with the debtor at a convenient time and place. The debtor's home is considered a convenient place. Unless special circumstances exist, 8 A.M. to 9 P.M. is considered a convenient time. Answer (a) is incorrect because it is a violation for a debt collector to use unfair or unconscionable means to collect a debt or to communicate with third parties other than the debtor's attorney, the creditor, or a consumer reporting agency. Answer (b) is incorrect because the act makes it unlawful for a debt collector to harass, oppress, or abuse *any* person in connection with the collection of a debt. Answer (c) is incorrect for two reasons: (1) it is a violation for a debt collector to communicate with a debtor by postcard, and (2) a debt collector is prohibited by the act to use deceptive or misleading representations in connection with the collection of a debt.

14. (c) Failure of an auctioneer to perform his or her duties under article 6 of the Uniform Commercial Code causes the auctioneer to be personally liable to the creditors of the bulk transferor for sums owing to them up to but not exceeding the net proceeds from the auction. Article 6 of the UCC requires that the auctioneer give notice of the auction to all persons named on the list of creditors at least ten days before it occurs. Ross failed to give the required notice and consequently is personally liable to Tom's creditor to the extent of the proceeds from the auction, i.e., 40 percent of the total debts. Answer (a) is incorrect for the reason stated above. Answer (b) is incorrect because a transfer of a substantial part of equipment is a bulk transfer if it is made in connection with a bulk transfer of inventory. The facts state that all of Tom's inventory and equipment were transferred. Answer (d) is incorrect because the auctioneer's failure to perform any duties under article 6 of the UCC does not affect the validity of the sale or the title of the purchasers.

15. (c) The Truth in Lending Act does not require disclosure of the identity of the surety on a consumer loan. The purpose of this act is to require sufficient disclosure about credit charges to enable consumers to make an informed choice of credit offered by lenders. Answers (a), (b), and (d) are incorrect because the act requires that this type of credit information be disclosed in a written disclosure statement given to a prospective borrower prior to the extension of credit.

ESSAY QUESTIONS AND ANSWERS

NOVEMBER 1974 (Estimated time: 12 to 18 minutes)

4. Part b. During your examination of the financial statements of Wyatt Associates, Inc., for the fiscal year ended June 30, 1974, you discovered the following facts relating to a transaction with Flinko Corporation. The transaction occurred during April 1974.

Flinko, one of Wyatt's major competitors, was insolvent in the equity sense, i.e., it could not meet the claims of its current creditors. Wyatt offered to purchase all of Flinko's assets, including furniture, fixtures, equipment, materials, supplies, inventory, and any and all other assets owned by Flinko. Wyatt's offering price equaled 105 percent of the total of all outstanding claims of Flinko's creditors. Flinko agreed to satisfy all creditors' claims out of the proceeds of sale and to hold Wyatt harmless from any claims of creditors. Meglo, Flinko's president and sole stockholder, accepted the offer. However, Meglo notified no one of the sale, absconded with the entire proceeds, and has not been heard from since.

Required Discuss the legal and the financial-reporting implications of the above transaction to Wyatt. Ignore antitrust considerations.

Answer Wyatt will have to pay the claims of the creditors of Flinko or hold all of the assets it purchased from Flinko for the benefit of its creditors.

The transaction in question is a bulk transfer (often referred to as a *bulk sale*) and is ineffective against any creditor of the seller (transferor) unless the buyer (transferee) requires the seller (transferor) to furnish a list of the seller's existing creditors. Furthermore, the buyer (transferee) is required to give notice to any known creditors of the seller (transferor) ten days prior to taking possession of the goods or when it pays for them, whichever happens first.

Obviously, Wyatt has not fulfilled these requirements. Wyatt neither requested much less obtained, a list nor did it give notice to Flinko's creditors. Therefore, it must suffer the consequences. Wyatt's only recourse is to attempt to recover against the missing Meglo.

As recovery from Meglo is highly improbable, Wyatt has incurred a loss in the amount of the claims of Flinko's creditors, which must be recorded in the fiscal year ended June 30, 1974, creating a related liability of the same amount. The June 30, 1974, balance sheet should include any unpaid claims at that date. The loss should be reported in the income statement, probably as an extraordinary item.

PART
FIVE

Property, Estates and Trusts, and Insurance (10%)*

---

* This percentage allocation represents the relative weight to be given to this *area* of business law on the Uniform CPA Examinations beginning in November 1983. It also indicates the approximate percentage of the total achievable test score to be assigned to this *area* of business law for each Uniform CPA Examination beginning in November 1983.

CHAPTER

10

Property

The following is a generalized listing of subjects to be tested through the May 1983 Uniform CPA Examination.

This topic is concerned primarily with real property law, although the distinction between real and personal property is also included. Among the subjects covered are the various estates in land, conveyances of real property, the landlord-tenant relationship, and real property mortgages.[1]

The AICPA Board of Examiners has adopted a new content specification outline for the business law section of the Uniform CPA Examination, *to be effective with the November 1983 examination*. The outline lists the following topics to be tested under the title "Real and Personal Property."

A. Real and Personal Property
   1. Distinctions Between Realty and Personality
   2. Easements and Other Nonpossessory Interests
   3. Types of Ownership
   4. Landlord-Tenant
   5. Deeds, Recording, Title Defects, and Title Insurance
B. Mortgages
   1. Characteristics
   2. Recording Requirements
   3. Priorities
   4. Foreclosure[2]

---

[1] AICPA, *Information for CPA Candidates*, Copyright © 1975, 1979, by the American Institute of Certified Public Accountants, Inc.
[2] AICPA, *Business Law—Content Specification Outline*, approved by the AICPA Board of Examiners on August 31, 1981.

THE NATURE OF PROPERTY

    I. Definition. *Property*, as a legal concept, is a right or group of rights a person possesses in something that is protected by law.

    II. Types of property. The word "property" is used in common law and statutes to mean both real and personal property.

        A. *Real property* consists of land and things of a permanent nature contained there or affixed to it, including the surface of the earth and the area above and beneath the surface, e.g., soil, air, growing trees, minerals, buildings, and lakes.

        B. *Personal property* (personalty) is all property not established as real property. Personal property may be classified as tangible (corporeal) or intangible (incorporeal).

            1. *Tangible personal property* (chose in possession) is movable property subject to its owner's right of immediate possession and control, e.g., automobiles, furniture, and goods.

            2. *Intangible personal property* (chose in action) is that kind of property which in its physical form is of little value but which, when enforced by legal action, realizes its full representative value, e.g., stock certificate, promissory note, draft, bill of lading, account receivable, warehouse receipt, patent, and copyright.

FIXTURES AND TRADE FIXTURES

    III. Personal property annexed to real property is either a fixture or a trade fixture.

        A. *Fixtures* are articles of personal property which have been attached in some manner to land or a building so as to become permanent parts of it. Once personal property becomes a fixture, it is the property of the owner of the land to which it is attached or used.

            1. As a general rule, the *intent* of the parties will determine when personal property has become a fixture. The parties may, by agreement, expressly provide as to the ownership of personal property attached to land. For example, a landlord and tenant agree that the building the tenant is to erect is to remain the tenant's personal property and be removed prior to the expiration of the tenant's lease.

            2. If there is no agreement as to intentions of the parties, the following guidelines are used to determine their intent.

                a. *Physical relation of the personal property to the land.* As a general rule, if the personal property has been so annexed that it cannot be moved without materially damaging the land, building, or the personal property itself, it is a fixture, e.g., plumbing, heating, wiring, or bricks.

                b. *Purpose of adaptation of the fixture.* As a general rule, if the personal property annexed is necessary or natural to the use of the land or a building, it is considered a fixture, e.g., movable steps leading to front door, storm screens, trees, shrubs, and central air conditioning or heating.

                c. *Interest in the land of the person affixing the personal property to the land.* If an owner of the land annexes personal property, it is considered a fixture. Where the annexor is someone other than the owner, such as a tenant, the intent must be determined from the physical relationship of the personal property to the land and its purpose or adaption.

        B. *Trade fixtures* are items of personal property installed and attached to leased premises by a tenant and used by the tenant in the tenant's trade or business. (See Figure 10-1.)

            1. The tenant is entitled to remove trade fixtures at any time prior to the expiration of the lease unless the fixture has become an integral part of the land or building

FIGURE 10-1   ELEMENTS OF A TRADE FIXTURE

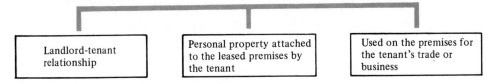

and its removal would cause material damage to the land, the building, or the fixture itself.

   2. The tenant must reimburse the landlord for any damage caused by the tenant's removal of a trade fixture.

C. Rights of claimants to fixtures (see Chapter 6).

THE CONCEPT OF OWNERSHIP

  IV. *Ownership* is defined as the right to control, possess, enjoy, and dispose of property in a manner not contrary to law. (See Figure 10-2.)

    A. Ownership of land includes rights in land of others, e.g., right to lateral support of soil, right to light and air, and the right to be free from nuisances on adjoining properties.

    B. Ownership of property includes the right to be free from the wrongful trespasses of other persons or their property.

    C. Ownership is not absolute or unrestricted. It is limited by the rights of other persons and by powers of government. (See Figure 10-2.)

      1. By rights of other persons. An owner of property may not exercise his or her rights so as to wrongfully injure the person or property of another.

      2. By powers of government. Every owner's rights are subject to the following powers of government:

        a. *Eminent domain* (the inherent power to take title to private property for public purpose by paying a just compensation, without the consent of the owner);

        b. *Police power* (the inherent power to regulate the use of private property for the public health, safety, morals, or welfare);

        c. *Taxation* (the inherent power to tax for purposes of regulation or revenue);

        d. *Escheat* (the inherent power to take title to property owned by a person who died without heirs).

    D. Property may be owned by one person or simultaneously with two or more persons.

      1. *Tenancy in severalty* is ownership of property by one person alone.

      2. *Concurrent* (multiple) *ownership* occurs when two or more persons acquire undivided ownership rights in the same parcel of property (real or personal).

FIGURE 10-2   RIGHTS TO LAND AND RESTRICTIONS ON PROPERTY OWNERSHIP

a. Their ownership rights may be identical and equal; e.g., joint tenancy, or A and B own a life estate.

b. Their ownership rights may be identical but not equal; e.g., tenancy in common whereby one tenant owns a one-third interest and the other owns a two-thirds interest, or A has a life estate and B owns the remainder.

CONCURRENT (JOINT) OWNERSHIP

V. Types of concurrent (multiple) ownership (coownership) (cotenancy), in property (see Figure 10-3).

A. *Joint tenancy.* A joint tenancy exists whenever two or more persons own an entire estate and also an equal undivided part thereof.

1. Joint tenancy ownership consists of the unities of time, title, interest, and possession and carries with it the right of survivorship.

FIGURE 10-3   TYPES OF CONCURRENT (JOINT) OWNERSHIP

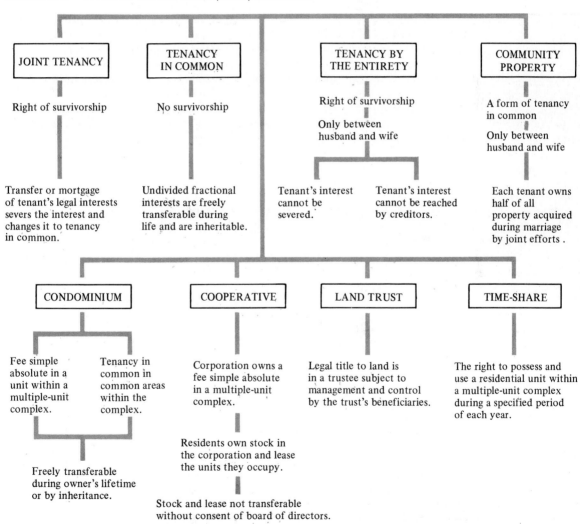

a. At common law, a joint tenancy cannot be created unless the unities of time, title, interest, and possession are obtained by the coowners simultaneously.

  (1) An owner in severalty could avoid the common law rule by a conveyance to an intermediary party ("a straw man") who in turn reconveyed the estate to the original owner and others as joint tenants.

  (2) Many states have nullified the common law rule by a statute providing that the unities need not be acquired simultaneously.

b. Joint tenancy has the characteristic of *survivorship*.

  (1) Upon the death of a joint tenant, the tenant's interest passes to surviving joint tenants. The last surviving tenant becomes an owner in severalty.

  (2) Joint tenancy is not an inheritable estate.

2. A joint tenancy can be created only by express grant, purchase, or devise.

  a. The law will not imply a joint tenancy.

  b. The deed, will, or other instrument must clearly show that the intention was to create a joint tenancy, e.g., "to A and B, as joint tenants, with right of survivorship."

  c. Where the intention to create a joint tenancy is not clearly indicated, the court will declare that a tenancy in common resulted, e.g., "to A and B," or "to A and B jointly."

3. A joint tenant may *sever* an undivided interest in the following ways:

  a. By a conveyance of an interest during the tenant's lifetime.

  (1) After such conveyance, the interest becomes an interest in tenancy in common.

  (2) Where two or more joint tenants remain after severance, they own the remaining undivided interest in joint tenancy as between themselves. The severed interest is owned in tenancy in common.

  b. By obtaining a *partition*. A partition has the effect of dividing the property and causing each person's interest to be owned in severalty.

4. A tenant who is in possession of jointly owned property owes a duty to the cotenants not to commit *waste*. Waste occurs whenever a cotenant acts or fails to act in relationship to the land and thereby impairs its value, e.g., failing to pay taxes, causing a substantial change in the use of the land, or destroying improvements on the land.

B. *Tenancy in common.* A tenancy in common exists whenever two or more persons own an undivided fractional interest in the same estate other than as joint tenants or tenants by entirety.

  1. It may be created by grant or devise or be implied by law.

  2. Tenants in common need not own equal interests.

  3. Their interests are freely transferable during each tenant's lifetime and are inheritable by will or intestate succession.

  4. There is no right of survivorship in tenancy in common ownership.

  5. As in joint tenancy, each cotenant may obtain a partition of the property.

  6. A tenant who is in possession of property owned in common owes a duty to the cotenants not to commit *waste*. Waste occurs whenever a cotenant acts or fails to act in relationship to the land and thereby impairs its value, e.g., failing to pay taxes, causing a substantial change in the use of the land, or destroying improvements on the land.

C. *Tenancy by the entirety.* A tenancy by the entirety is essentially a special joint tenancy that can exist only between husband and wife.

  1. It is created by conveyance to husband and wife "as joint tenants" or "jointly."

  2. Neither tenant can sever his or her interest without the consent of the other.

3. The interest of either tenant cannot be reached by that tenant's individual creditors.

D. *Community property*. The definition of "community property" varies among states where this type of coownership is allowed.

    1. As a general rule, states with community property laws recognize two types of property ownership between husband and wife.

        a. Separate property.

            (1) It is property owned by a spouse prior to marriage or subsequently acquired by one spouse alone during marriage by inheritance or by a gift.

            (2) Separate property is solely and absolutely owned by a spouse.

        b. Community property.

            (1) Community property is property acquired by one spouse during marriage by joint effort with the other.

            (2) Each spouse owns one-half of all community property.

E. *Condominium ownership*.

    1. Each owner owns solely and absolutely (a fee simple) the unit he or she exclusively occupies.

    2. Each owner also has a tenancy in common interest in all other parts of the condominium land and buildings shared and used in common with other owners.

F. *Cooperative ownership*.

    1. The real estate is owned by a corporation.

    2. The corporation in turn is owned by the shareholders of the corporation, who are also lessees of the units within the cooperative.

G. *Land trust*. A land trust is a statutory trust. It cannot be created under the common law. It is a type of trust where, by deed, a trustee receives complete record (legal) title to real estate restricted by a concurrent agreement whereby the beneficiary or beneficiaries retain full management and control (power of direction) over the real estate. This type of trust must not be confused with the Massachusetts (business) Trust, which is created by agreement under the common law and in which the trustee acquires not only legal title to the trust property but also absolute control of its management.

H. *Time-share ownership* is a unique method of obtaining the benefits of condominium ownership and at the same time sharing the use of residential units with other owners of the same condominium.

    1. This type of ownership is especially desirable in a recreational setting in which the purchaser desires a vacation home for only that part of a year during which the purchaser plans to occupy the home. For example, high-rise buildings at an oceanside resort are delared into a condominium.

    2. The individual units are sold to multiple buyers, granting each buyer the right to use the units during a specified part of each year.

ESTATES IN LAND

VI. An *estate* is a right in land that is either presently possessory or may become possessory in the future (future interest). An estate may be owned in severalty by one person or concurrently with others. Different estates may be owned simultaneously by two or more different persons in the same parcel of land.

A. *Possessory estates*. These estates are classified on the basis of their duration. There are *freehold* estates (those existing for an indefinite length of time) and *nonfreehold* estates (those existing for a determinable length of time).

1. *Freehold estates.*

    a. *Fee simple absolute.* The owner possesses all of the rights a person may have in a parcel of land. (See Figure 10-4.)

        (1) It is freely transferable during the lifetime of its owner.

        (2) It is an inheritable estate either by will or by intestate succession.

        (3) It has no time limit on its existence.

    b. *Life estate.* A *life estate* is one whose duration is measured by the life or lives of one or more persons (who may or may not be its owners). If its duration is measured by the life of a person other than the owner (life tenant), it is called a life estate pur autre vie.

        (1) It is not inheritable and terminates upon the death of the person or persons by whose life it is measured.

        (2) It is freely transferable by sale or gift during the lifetime of its owner (life tenant).

        (3) The life tenant (owner of the life estate) has the exclusive right to possess, use, and derive income from the land during the duration of the estate.

        (4) The life tenant owes the following duties:

            (*a*) To pay taxes levied on the land;

            (*b*) To make ordinary repairs; and

            (*c*) Not to commit waste.

                i. A life tenant commits waste when the life tenant acts or fails to act in respect to the land he or she possesses so as to impair its value, e.g., failing to make ordinary repairs, changing the use of the land from agriculture to mining, excessively cutting timber, or destroying buildings.

                ii. The life tenant is liable for damages caused by waste to the owner

FIGURE 10-4   FEE SIMPLE ABSOLUTE

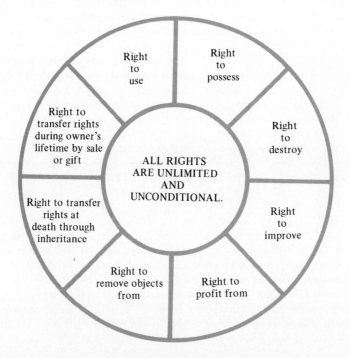

of the future interest in the same land, i.e., the reversioner or remainderman.

    iii. The owner of a future interest in the same land may obtain an injunction against the life tenant restraining the life tenant from committing waste.

    (5) Life estates are created either by a conveyance from an owner of the estate (a conventional life estate) or by operation of law (a legal life estate).

        (a) *Conventional life estates* are usually created through the use of deeds, wills, and trusts, e.g., "to C for life."

        (b) *Legal life estates* are created by state law regardless of the intent of any party, e.g., dower and homestead.

  c. *Fee simple determinable* (qualified fee) (base fee). A fee simple determinable is a fee simple subject to a condition, e.g., "to C so long as the land is used for agricultural purposes only."

    (1) When the condition occurs, ownership of the estate automatically reverts (reversion) to the person (reversioner) who created the estate or to his or her heirs.

    (2) The interest retained by a grantor of a fee simple determinable is a *possibility of reverter*.

  d. *Fee simple on a condition subsequent.* A fee simple on a condition subsequent is a fee simple that may be ended voluntarily by its grantor or the grantor's heirs upon the happening of a contingency, e.g., "to A on the condition that the land never be used for industrial purposes."

    (1) The estate does not terminate automatically upon the happening of the contingency.

    (2) The person (reversioner) who owns the reversion at the time the contingency occurs must exercise the *right of entry* to end the estate and cause its reversion.

2. *Nonfreehold estates* (leasehold estates). See XII below.

B. *Nonpossessory estates* (future interests). A future interest is a presently existing estate in land. However, it does not entitle its owner to use and possession of the land until the termination of a preceding estate or the occurrence of a condition or both. The future interest may be a reversion or a remainder. (See Figure 10-5.)

1. *Reversion.* A reversion is the estate remaining with a person after that person has conveyed some but not all of the rights in land to another person for a limited duration.

  a. The following estates are accompanied by a reversion:

    (1) A life estate where the estate is to return to the grantor upon the death of the person by whose life the estate is measured, e.g., "to A for life."

    (2) A life estate with a contingent remainder, e.g., "to A for life, then to C if C is age twenty-one and living in Illinois." If the contingency has not occurred at the death of the life tenant, the estate will automatically revert to its grantor or the grantor's heirs.

    (3) A fee simple determinable (qualified fee) (base fee). The future interest created is the reversionary interest called the *possibility of reverter*.

    (4) A fee simple on a condition subsequent. The future interest created is the reversionary interest, called the *right of entry*.

  b. Reversions are inheritable and freely transferable during the lifetime of the owner of the reversionary estate.

2. *Remainder.* A remainder is a presently existing estate in land in which the actual use and possession of the land is postponed. Remainders are classified as being either vested or contingent.

FIGURE 10-5 ESTATES IN LAND

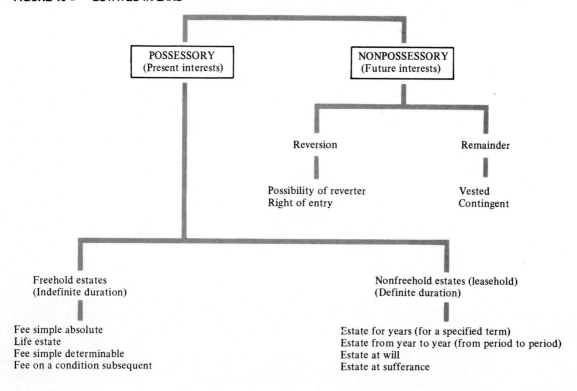

a. A *vested remainder* is an estate in land whereby the right to use and possess depends only upon the termination of a preceding estate, e.g., "to C for life with remainder to B and his heirs."

(1) It is an inheritable estate.

(2) It is freely transferable during its owner's lifetime.

b. A *contingent remainder* is an estate in land whereby the right to use and possess depends not only upon the termination of a preceding estate but also upon the happening of a contingency, e.g., "to C for life with remainder to B if he survives C."

EASEMENTS, PROFITS, AND LICENSES

VII. Other rights in real property.

    A. *Easements.* An easement is a limited right to use the land owned by another person for a specific purpose and in a specific manner.

        1. Dominant and servient estates.

            a. The *dominant estate* is the land for whose benefit an easement was created.

            b. The *servient estate* is the land which is subjected to the burden of the easement.

        2. Easements may be appurtenant or in gross. (See Figure 10-6.)

            a. *Easement appurtenant* is created for use in connection with another parcel of land. It cannot be created without two parcels of land.

                (1) Easements appurtenant *"run with the land"*; that is, the benefit to the

dominant estate and the burden to the servient estate continue regardless of any change in ownership of either estate.

    (2) The easement is irrevocable.

    (3) The following are examples of easements appurtenant:

        (*a*) A right-of-way over another person's adjoining parcel of land;

        (*b*) A common driveway on a boundary line between two lots, each lot owned by a different person.

b. An *easement in gross* is created for the use of a specific person or entity. It is not intended for use in connection with another parcel of land.

    (1) Easements in gross may be personal or commercial in nature.

        (*a*) A *personal easement in gross* is not transferable and terminates upon its owner's death.

        (*b*) A *commercial easement in gross* is freely transferable during the life of its owner.

    (2) The following are examples of easements in gross:

        (*a*) If Y sells a parcel of land to X, reserving to himself the right to use a lake on the land for swimming purposes, Y owns a personal easement in gross;

        (*b*) Utility easements (commercial easement in gross);

        (*c*) Railroad right-of-ways (commercial easement in gross).

3. Creation of easements.

    a. An easement is an interest in land, and therefore any contract, grant, or reservation creating an easement must be in a writing as required by the Statute of Frauds.

    b. Easements are created in the following ways:

        (1) By agreement. Easements may be created by contract.

        (2) By grant or reservation in a deed.

        (3) By implication. This easement is created by operation of law regardless of the intent of the parties. The following are the requisite elements of an easement by implication:

        (*a*) One person owns two tracts of land;

FIGURE 10-6 TYPES AND CHARACTERISTICS OF EASEMENTS

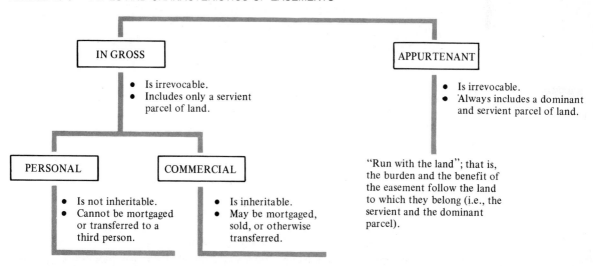

(b) That person subjects the use of one tract for the benefit of the other tract;

(c) The use is apparent;

(d) The use is continuous;

(e) The use is necessary; and

(f) At some time thereafter, the owner sells one of the tracts of land to another person.

(g) Some examples of easements by implication are:

    i. Jones owns lots A and B. Sewage from his house on lot B drains through an underground pipe running across lot A. There is a visible catch basin on the surface of lot A. If Peters buys lot A, she will own it subject to an implied easement for sewage drainage across her lot.

    ii. Amos owns two adjacent parcels of land. Both parcels are improved with homes. Amos resides in the home on lot A and leases lot B with its improvements to Y. A driveway runs down the boundary line of the adjacent lots and is used for ingress and egress purposes for both lots. Amos subsequently conveyed Lot B to James. A party driveway easement was created by implication.

(4) By sale by reference to subdivision plat.

(5) By prescription. An easement by prescription arises when an unauthorized person uses another's property adversely, openly, notoriously, and continuously for a period of time established by statute, usually five to twenty years.

(6) By necessity. An easement by necessity arises when a person receives a conveyance of a parcel of land under such circumstances that he or she does not have access to the land except through adjoining land owned by strangers or the grantor. That person is entitled to a reasonable right of way over the land of the grantor.

4. Termination of easements. Easements are terminated in the following ways:

a. By expiration of the duration of the easement;

b. By fulfillment of the purpose for which it was created. For example, a right of way easement is granted for purposes of construction of a nuclear power plant. The easement will end at the time the plant is completed.

c. By a written release;

d. By a merger of the dominant and servient estates. For example, the dominant and servient estates become owned by the same person.

e. By intentional abandonment of the easement. For example, a manufacturing corporation owned a railroad right-of-way as a means to transport ore to its processing plant. The corporation removed the rails and ties and tore down its processing plant. The easement was extinguished.

f. By destruction of the servient estate;

g. By prescription (the owner of the servient estate prevents the use of the easement for the prescribed statutory period of time).

B. *Profit a prendre.* A profit is an interest in land which carries with it the right to remove soil or the produce of soil, e.g., the right to remove gravel, natural gas, oil, coal, timber, or minerals.

1. It may be created by agreement, grant, or reservation or by prescription.

2. It may be classified as a profit appurtenant or one in gross.

3. Profits are terminated in the same ways as are easements.

C. *License.* A license is a revocable authorization to use land that is in the possession

of someone other than the licensee, e.g., permission to hunt on the land owned by another.
1. It can be created orally or in writing.
2. It is personal in nature and consequently is not transferable or inheritable.
3. It is not an estate in land.

PUBLIC RESTRICTIONS ON OWNERSHIP

VIII. Public restrictions on ownership of real property are as follows:
  A. *Eminent domain.* The right of eminent domain is the inherent power of government to *take title* to private property for public use in exchange for just compensation without the owner's consent.
  B. *Police power.*
    1. Police power is the inherent power of government to *regulate the use* of land for the public health, safety, morals, and general welfare of the community.
    2. The power to regulate use of land is exercised in the following ways:
      a. Subdivision regulations;
      b. Zoning laws;
      c. Building codes.
  C. *Taxation.*
    1. A real estate tax is a lien upon the land which renders title to the land unmarketable until the lien is discharged.
    2. A real estate tax may be levied against land in the following ways:
      a. As an annual tax for general revenue purposes; or
      b. As a special assessment to provide revenue to fund public improvements adjacent to the land taxed, e.g., roads and alleys.

PRIVATE RESTRICTIONS ON OWNERSHIP

IX. Private restrictions on ownership of real property are as follows:
  A. *Nuisance.*
    1. An owner of real estate may not use the property so as to wrongfully interfere with the reasonable use and enjoyment of land owned by another.
    2. The remedies of damages and injunction are available to an injured party.
  B. *Waste.*
    1. Where one or more persons have concurrent rights in the same parcel of land, the person rightfully in possession has a duty to the coowners to refrain from doing any act which impairs the value of the land. For example, coowner in possession has a duty to pay taxes, make necessary repairs, etc.
    2. Examples of persons owing a duty not to commit waste are:
      a. A mortgagor in possession to the mortgagee;
      b. A life tenant in possession to a reversioner;
      c. A life tenant in possession to a remainderman;
      d. A joint tenant in possession to cotenants;
      e. A leasehold tenant to the landlord;
      f. A tenant in common in possession to the cotenants.
    3. The remedies of damages and injunction are available to the injured party against the person who committed the waste.
  C. *Conditions.* A condition is a restriction on use of land provided for in a deed accompanied by a possibility of reverter or a right of entry. See VI-A-1, c, d above.
  D. *Restrictive covenants.*

1. Restrictive covenants are limitations on use of land imposed by private persons on the land of others by provisions in a contract or deed, e.g., building set-back lines, style of architecture of building to be constructed, maximum height of structures, limitation to residential use only, or prohibition on the sale of intoxicating liquor.
2. A grantor may impose restrictive covenants by including them in a deed, whether the land conveyed is a single lot or multiple lots in a subdivision.
3. Restrictive covenants "run with the land" and therefore are binding on all subsequent owners of the land.
4. The present owner of the land intended to be benefited by the restriction is entitled to enforce the covenant. If it is clear that the restriction was intended to benefit an entire tract of land such as a subdivision, an owner of any parcel in the tract has the right to enforce the covenant.
5. Restrictive covenants are enforced by an injunction to restrain a violation. If the injunction is disobeyed, it is enforced by contempt of court proceedings that could result in a fine or imprisonment or both.
6. A court will not grant an injunction under the following circumstances:
   a. A substantial or complete change has been allowed to occur in the characteristics of the neighborhood in violation of the covenant;
   b. A property owner who asks for an injunction has violated the restriction;
   c. The time limit (statutory, by deed, or by contract) on the restriction has expired.

E. *Liens* (see Figure 10-7).
1. *Mortgages.* See XIII below.
2. Security interests in fixtures. See Chapter 6.
3. *Judgment lien.* A judgment rendered by a court against a debtor creates a lien that attaches to all of the real estate owned by the debtor within the state.
4. *Mechanic's lien.* A mechanic's lien is acquired by persons who furnish labor or materials for the construction or improvement of the land and buildings.
   a. The lien may be enforced against any legal or equitable interest in the property subject to the lien.
   b. The following persons can acquire a mechanic's lien:
      (1) General contractors;
      (2) Subcontractors;
      (3) Materialmen, such as lumberyards;
      (4) Laborers, such as electricians, plumbers, bricklayers, carpenters, etc.
   c. The lien must be filed (recorded) in the county where the improved property is located within a period of time specified by statute.
   d. Once properly filed (recorded), the lien dates back to the time that labor or materials were furnished.
   e. Filing (recordation) of the lien is necessary to perfect it against the owner of

FIGURE 10-7   LEGAL STRUCTURE OF A LIEN

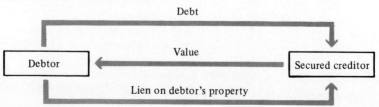

the property, any future judgment lien creditor of the owner, or a subsequent purchaser of the property.

    f. The lien is enforced by foreclosure and sale of property subject to the lien.

    g. The lien is discharged by payment or by a release of lien granted by the lienholder.

    h. Since the mechanic's lien is an encumbrance on title, a release of lien must be filed (recorded) to clear title of record and make it marketable.

ACQUISITION OF TITLE TO REAL PROPERTY

X. Title to real property can be acquired in the following ways:

  A. *Eminent domain.*

    1. Federal and state governments have the power to acquire title to land without the consent of its owner under the following conditions:

      a. Due process of law must be followed.

      b. The property must be taken for public use. *Exception:* Where property is taken for urban renewal purposes (a public purpose), it need not be subsequently subjected to public use.

      c. Just compensation for the property taken must be paid to the owner and any other person having an interest, such as a lessee or remainderman.

    2. The power of eminent domain may be delegated to railroads, utilities, and local governmental units.

    3. *Condemnation* is the legal proceeding by which title to property is taken by eminent domain. Usually, this proceeding is begun only if a voluntary transfer of title cannot be obtained.

  B. *Adverse possession.*

    1. A private person who has no interest in a parcel of land may acquire title to it by adversely possessing it for a statutory period of time, usually from five to twenty years.

    2. For possession to result in ownership, it must be hostile to the present owner's title, actual, exclusive, notorious, and continuous during the statutory period of time.

    3. Continuous adverse possession by different persons may be accumulated to satisfy the required statutory period. Such cumulation is called *tacking.*

    4. An adverse possessor must file a lawsuit called a *bill to quiet title* in order to establish ownership of record.

  C. Purchase at a *foreclosure sale*. A foreclosure sale is an involuntary sale of a debtor's title to land pursuant to an agreement between a debtor and creditor or by decree of a court, e.g., upon default of a mortgage, foreclosure of a tax lien, foreclosure of a mechanic's lien, or foreclosure of a judgment lien.

  D. Purchase at a *partition sale*. A partition sale is a court-ordered sale for purposes of severing undivided interests in land such as joint tenancies and tenancies in common.

  E. *Accretion.* Accretion is the process by which one owner of land acquires title to land of another through the gradual imperceptible deposits of sand or soil as a result of natural causes, such as water or wind.

  F. *Escheat.* The legal process by which a state or county can acquire title to land owned by a person who dies without a valid will and without leaving any heirs is called escheat.

  G. *Inheritance* (testate and intestate succession) (see Chapter 11).

  H. *Community property.* Title to one-half of all community property is automatically vested in each spouse when it is acquired during marriage, regardless of whose name legal title is taken in. Property acquired by a spouse before marriage or by gift or inheritance during marriage is not considered community property.

I. Contracts for the sale of real property and conveyance of title by deed.

1. *Contracts for the sale of real property.* The types of contracts, their formation, validity, enforcement, remedies for breach, transfer of rights, and discharge of contractual obligations are discussed in Chapter 2.

   a. In general. A contract for the sale of real property *does not convey legal title* to the property. Legal title is conveyed to the buyer by deed.

      (1) Upon completion of the contract, the buyer acquires *equitable title*. Equitable title entitles the buyer to the following rights:

         (*a*) To file (record) the contract of record; and

         (*b*) To insure the property against loss by fire or other peril.

   b. The buyer and seller are coowners of the real property until absolute (legal) title is conveyed to the buyer by delivery and acceptance of a deed from the seller.

2. *Common provisions found in contracts for the sale of real property.*

   a. *Parties.* Every sales contract for real property must identify the seller or buyer to be enforceable.

   b. *Quality of title* to be conveyed. Unless otherwise provided in the contract, the seller is obligated to convey a fee simple absolute.

   c. *Legal description.* The contract must contain a description of the property sufficient to provide a reasonably certain identification. A formal legal description may be provided as follows:

      (1) By reference to the Rectangular Survey System;

      (2) By reference to recorded plat; or

      (3) By reference to metes and bounds.

   d. *Price.* The purchase price and the method and time of its payment must be stated without ambiguity. If not so stated, the contract is incomplete and unenforceable.

   e. *Form of deed* to be delivered.

      (1) If the contract is silent as to the type of deed to be delivered to the buyer, most states allow the seller to give a deed *without* covenants (warranties).

      (2) The usual deeds provided for in contracts are (these deeds are subsequently defined and explained in this chapter):

         (*a*) General warranty;

         (*b*) Special warranty;

         (*c*) Grant, bargain, and sale;

         (*d*) Quitclaim.

   f. *Title exceptions.*

      (1) Unless the contract provides otherwise, the seller must convey *"marketable" title*, and the buyer is obligated to accept nothing less.

         (*a*) A title is nonmarketable unless it is free from all liens, encumbrances, and restrictions and any reasonable question as to its validity.

         (*b*) If the seller cannot deliver a marketable title at the time called for by the contract, the buyer may consider the contract breached.

      (2) The seller may protect himself or herself by providing in the contract that the seller is to convey title subject to specified encumbrances and restrictions commonly referred to as *title exceptions*. For example:

         (*a*) Existing leases not expiring prior to delivery of deed;

(b) Special tax assessments;

(c) General real property taxes;

(d) Existing restrictive covenants;

(e) Outstanding mortgages;

(f) Easements of record;

(g) Encroachments.

g. *Forfeiture of earnest money.*

(1) Contracts customarily provide for a down payment or earnest money deposit to be paid by the buyer to the seller.

(2) A forfeiture clause allows a seller, upon the buyer's default, to void the contract and retain the buyer's money as liquidated damages.

(3) Forfeiture clauses are valid so long as the amount agreed upon is not so large as to constitute a penalty.

h. *Apportionment or proration of charges.* Contracts usually provide for adjusting or prorating one or more of the following items as of the date of delivery of possession or deed to the buyer:

(1) General real estate taxes or special assessments;

(2) Prepaid rents;

(3) Prepaid insurance premiums;

(4) Utility charges;

(5) Interest on outstanding mortgages to be assumed or taken subject to by the buyer;

(6) Prepaid fuel or supplies on hand.

i. *Evidence of title.*

(1) Unless otherwise agreed in the contract, a seller is not obligated to furnish the buyer evidence that the title is good and marketable. The buyer would have to investigate the title for his or her own protection and at the buyer's own expense.

(2) A contract can provide that the seller furnish any one of the following forms of *evidence of title*:

(a) *Abstract of title.* An abstract of title is a written history of recorded (filed) instruments and legal proceedings which have affected title to the property, commencing with government ownership and brought up to current date.

(b) *Title insurance policy.* A title insurance policy provides for indemnification of the buyer and/or the mortgagee against loss incurred by reasons of defects in title.

(c) *Torrens certificate.*

i. The Torrens system of registration of titles has been adopted by only a few cities and counties in the United States.

ii. The Torrens certificate is evidence of title which has been initially registered in an owner by court proceedings.

iii. No future conveyance of the property or encumbrance is valid unless entered on the original registered title certificate.

iv. Attorney's certificate of title. When an attorney's certificate of title is required, no formal abstract of title is prepared. The attorney conducts a search of the public records. Based on what is revealed by the examination, the attorney will issue the written opinion (certificate of title) of the current status of the title.

j. *Risk of loss.*

(1) Unless provided otherwise in the contract or by statute, most state courts have held that the risk of loss or damage to the premises is on the buyer

as soon as the buyer has become bound to the contract of sale. For example, Holmes entered into a contract for the sale of his house and lot with Watson. A week before Watson was to receive title from Holmes, the house was totally destroyed by fire. Watson is obligated to pay the full purchase price.

   (2) The buyer may be fully protected by including a clause in the contract which allows the buyer to void the contract if the premises are totally or substantially destroyed by fire or other casualty prior to taking of possession or delivery of deed.

   (3) *Uniform Vendor and Purchasers Act.* Many states have adopted the Uniform Vendor and Purchaser Risk Act, which provides that the seller retains the risk of loss until the buyer receives a deed from the seller or the buyer is given possession of the premises, which ever occurs first.

k. *Escrow provision.* The contract may provide that the sales transaction be completed by the use of an escrow arrangement.

   (1) An *escrow arrangement* is a contract between the seller, the buyer, and an escrow agent. (See Figure 10-8.)

   (2) The escrow agent is an agent of both the seller and the buyer.

   (3) The seller and buyer obligate themselves to deliver to the escrow agent all documents and monies necessary to complete the transaction.

   (4) The escrow agent is obligated to complete the transaction pursuant to the terms of the sales contract between the seller and buyer.

   (5) An escrow arrangement protects the buyer against the death or other incapacity of the seller and assures the seller that the purchase price is available to complete the transaction. For example, if, before the death or incompetency of the seller or buyer, a properly executed deed is deposited in escrow (under a valid contract of sale and escrow agreement) and is later delivered by the escrow agent in compliance with the escrow conditions, its delivery (transfer of title) "relates back" to the date that the deed was deposited under the "doctrine of relation back."

l. *Possession.* Unless agreed upon otherwise, the right of possession passes to the buyer at the time the buyer receives the deed from the seller.

m. *Time of essence.*

   (1) Where the contract does not provide that time is of the essence, the buyer or the seller has a reasonable time after the closing date to comply with the terms of the contract.

FIGURE 10-8   ESCROW ARRANGEMENT

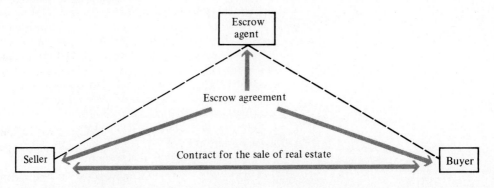

(2) If the contract provides that time is of the essence, failure of the seller or buyer to perform on the agreed-upon date places that party immediately in default.

3. *Requirements for a valid conveyance by deed:*
  a. A deed must be in writing.
  b. The deed must be signed by the grantor or a duly authorized agent (*attorney in fact* appointed by grant of *a power of attorney*).
  c. Seal, attestation, and acknowledgment. In most states, a seal, attestation, or acknowledgment is not required.
    (1) A deed is under *seal* when it contains a statement that it is sealed or contains words such as "Seal" or "Witness my hand and seal."
    (2) An *attestation* is the act of witnessing a grantor's signature at the grantor's request and signing the deed as a witness.
    (3) An *acknowledgment* is a formal declaration by the grantor before an authorized official (notary public, judge, or military officer) that the deed was executed freely and voluntarily by the grantor.
  d. Description. The Statute of Frauds requires that the deed describe the property so that it is clearly identifiable and distinguishable from other parcels of real property.
  e. Consideration. As a general rule, consideration is not required to support a valid deed.
  f. Parties to a deed.
    (1) A deed is void unless it names an existing grantor and grantee and identifies them with reasonable certainty.
    (2) A grantor must have legal capacity in order to convey title by deed.
      (*a*) A deed executed by an adjudicated incompetent is void, e.g., a ward of a guardian.
      (*b*) A deed executed by a nonadjudicated incompetent is voidable, e.g., a minor.
  g. *Granting clause.* A granting clause identifies the estate being conveyed and includes words of conveyance.
    (1) If there is no clear indication of the estate being conveyed, the law presumes that the grantor intended to convey a fee simple absolute.
    (2) Every deed must contain words of conveyance. Examples are:
      (*a*) "Convey and warrant";
      (*b*) "Grant, bargain, and sell";
      (*c*) "Convey and quitclaim";
      (*d*) "Quitclaim all interest";
      (*e*) "Remise, release, and quitclaim."
    (3) Words of conveyance indicate the grantor's intention to make a present transfer of title. They also identify the grantor's warranties, if any, to the grantee. (See 4-c below.)
  h. *Delivery of the deed* by the grantor.
    (1) In order for title to transfer, the deed must be "delivered" to the named grantee or the grantee's agent during the lifetime of the grantor.
    (2) *Delivery* is the intent of the grantor that the deed shall presently transfer title to the grantee.
    (3) Delivery can be accomplished in two ways.
      (*a*) *Actual delivery.* Actual delivery is the unconditional physical delivery of a deed by the grantor to the grantee or the grantee's agent with the intent to transfer title.
      (*b*) *Constructive delivery.* Constructive delivery occurs (even though

there is no actual delivery prior to the death or incapacity of the grantor) if the grantor, during the grantor's lifetime, indicates by words or conduct that the executed deed should operate immediately to convey title to the grantee. Examples are delivery in escrow and a grantor who, prior to death, executes and mails a deed to the grantee.

  i. Acceptance of the deed by the grantee.

    a. As a general rule, a grantee must accept the deed from the grantor for title to pass.

    b. Acceptance may be express or may be implied from the conduct of the grantee.

4. Optional provisions commonly found in deeds.

    a. Exceptions and reservations. The deed may provide exceptions and/or reservations in the grant made in the deed, e.g., an exception of a certain acreage, or reservation of mineral rights.

    b. Habendum.

      (1) The *habendum* establishes the quantity of the estate conveyed to the grantee.

      (2) Any limitation, encumbrance, or restriction is stated in the habendum. For example:

        (*a*) A limitation by reservation of a life estate or by a declaration of trust;

        (*b*) Agreement by the grantee to take *"subject to"* or *"assume and agree to pay"* a mortgage;

        (*c*) A list of restrictive covenants controlling the future use of the property being conveyed.

    c. *Covenants (warranties) of title.*

      (1) Covenants (warranties) of title may be expressly stated in a deed or implied from the words of conveyance used by the grantor.

      (2) The following covenants may be express or implied in a deed:

        (*a*) Covenant of seizen (a promise by the grantor that the grantor possesses title and has a right to convey it);

        (*b*) Covenant of quiet enjoyment (a promise by the grantor that the grantor or any other person having a better title will not disturb the grantee's possession);

        (*c*) Covenant against encumbrances (a promise by the grantor that there are no existing encumbrances on the title to the property);

        (*d*) Covenant of further assurance (a promise by the grantor that the grantor will execute or obtain all necessary additional documents to perfect title in the grantee;

        (*e*) Covenant of warranty forever (a promise by a grantor that the grantor will forever warrant title to the property).

      (3) In many states, the five covenants of title are implied by law when the grantor uses such phrases of conveyance as "convey and warrant" or "warrant generally."

      (4) Phrases of conveyance such as "grant, bargain, and sell," "convey and quitclaim," or "quitclaim all interest" do not imply covenants as a matter of law.

      (5) Covenants do not guarantee that *any* title will transfer to the grantee by the deed. If the grantee receives no title or title is defective, the grantee's only recourse is to sue the grantor for damages based on breach of covenant.

      (6) The first three covenants bind the grantor only to the immediate grantee,

while the remaining two covenants bind the grantor to not only the immediate grantee but also any subsequent grantee.

    5. Types of deeds.

        a. *Quitclaim deed.*

            (1) A quitclaim deed usually contains phrases of conveyance such as "remise, release, and quitclaim," "convey or quitclaim," or "quitclaim all interest."

            (2) It contains no convenants (warranties), express or implied.

            (3) It transfers whatever interest the grantor possesses at the time of the delivery of the deed to the grantee. It does not warrant that the grantor has any interest or that the interest the grantor does possess is of a particular quality.

        b. *General warranty deed.*

            (1) A general warranty deed usually contains phrases of conveyance such as "convey and warrant" or "warrant generally."

            (2) It contains all five covenants (warranties) of title, i.e., seizen, quiet enjoyment, encumbrance, further assurance, and warranty forever.

            (3) General warranty covenants apply to all defects, those coming into existence while the grantor possesses title as well as those which occurred prior thereto.

        c. *Special warranty deed.*

            (1) A special warranty deed usually contains phrases of conveyance such as "warrant specially." In some states the word "grant" alone is sufficient.

            (2) It contains the same covenants (warranties) as the general warranty deed.

            (3) It differs from the general warranty deed in that the grantor covenants only against defects of title which arose during the time the grantor possessed title.

        d. *Specialty deeds.*

            (1) These deeds usually take the form of either a special warranty deed or a quitclaim deed.

            (2) They derive their names either from the fiduciary status of the grantor or from the special purpose they fulfill.

            (3) Examples of specialty deeds are deed of trust, deed in trust, trustee's deed, executor's deed, deed of gift, administrator's deed, guardian's deed, deed in partition, deed of release, and deed in foreclosure.

ACQUISITION OF TITLE TO PERSONAL PROPERTY

    XI. Title to personal property is acquired in the following ways.

        A. *Purchase and sale* (see Chapter 3).

        B. *Abandoned, lost, or mislaid property.*

            1. Abandoned property.

                a. Property is abandoned when its owner relinquishes possession of it with the intent to part forever with title.

                b. Title to abandoned property is acquired by any person who takes possession of it with the intent to own it.

            2. *Lost property.*

                a. Property is lost when its possessor accidentally parts with possession of it and does not know of its location.

                b. The finder of lost property acquires the right of possession of it as against everyone except the true owner or its prior possessor.

3. *Mislaid property.*

    a. Property is mislaid when its possessor voluntarily places it somewhere and forgets its location.

    b. The owner of the premises where the property is found is entitled to possession of it as against everyone except the true owner or the person who mislaid the property.

C. *Inheritance* (see Chapter 11).

D. *Occupation.*

    1. A person may acquire title to unowned property by taking possession of it with the intent to obtain title.

    2. Abandoned property and wildlife are examples of unowned property.

E. *Gift.* A gift is a voluntary transfer of title to property from one person (donor) to another (donee), without any consideration received in exchange.

    1. The elements of a gift are:

        a. The transferor must *intend to presently transfer title* to a specific item of property.

        b. The donor must *irrevocably "deliver"* the property to the transferee (donee) or to the transferee's agent with the intent of investing ownership.

        (1) Delivery may be actual or constructive.

            (*a*) *Actual delivery* is accomplished by the physical transfer of the subject of the gift from the donor to the donee.

            (*b*) *Constructive delivery* is the transfer from the donor to the donee of a symbol which indicates an intent to deliver, e.g., a key to an automobile, a passbook to a savings account, or a key to a safe-deposit box.

        (2) A valid delivery may be made by the donor to a third person with irrevocable instructions to deliver to the donee, e.g., to an escrowee or agent of the donee.

        c. The donee must accept delivery for the gift to become effective.

    2. Types of gifts.

        a. *Inter vivos.* An *inter vivos gift* is an unconditional *lifetime irrevocable* transfer of title to property from one person to another without any consideration in exchange.

        b. *Causa mortis.* A *causa mortis gift* is a *revocable* transfer of title to property from one person to another *given in contemplation of death as a result of sickness or peril.* A *causa mortis* gift is revoked in the following ways:

        (1) The donor indicates an intent to revoke prior to death.

        (2) The donor recovers from sickness or the peril ceases to exist. The revocation is automatic under these circumstances.

        (3) The donee dies prior to the donor.

F. *Accession.* Accession is the annexation or adding of new value to an item of personal property owned by another through labor and materials.

    1. When the labor and materials are annexed pursuant to agreement, the owner of the property improved receives title to the accessions, e.g., a tune-up (labor and materials) to an automobile engine under a contract between its owner and a garage mechanic.

    2. Labor and materials may be added to another's property without the owner's consent.

        a. Innocent wrongful improver.

        (1) If the improvements are severable, the innocent improver retains title to them.

        (2) If the improvements are not severable, the owner of the property retains title to the property in its improved condition *unless*:

(a) The identity of the original property is changed as a result of the improvement; or

(b) The value of the labor and materials added is in excess of the value of the property in its original state.

(c) In either case, the party losing title to property is entitled to recover the value of the property lost.

b. Wilful and wrongful improver.

(1) As a general rule, the original owner is entitled to the property in its improved state and the wilful improver is not entitled to recover the value of labor and services.

(2) A wilful improver may acquire title as against the original owner only under the following circumstances:

(a) The identity of the original property is hopelessly lost; or

(b) The value of the improved property is almost entirely due to the labor of the improver, and this value is far in excess of the original item.

(c) The original owner is entitled to recover the value of the property taken.

G. *Confusion.* Confusion is the intermingling of goods owned by two or more persons in such a manner that the property of each cannot be identified and separated.

1. Confusion arises frequently with respect to fungible goods, e.g., grain, oil, pipe, cattle, poultry, coal, and gravel.

2. Confusion may be caused by nature or by the innocent or wilful act of one or more of the owners.

a. Confusion caused by nature or by the innocent act of a party.

(1) If the amount of goods owned by each party is known, the parties are owners of the mass as tenants in common in proportion to their respective amounts.

(2) If the amount of goods owned by each party is not known, the parties are equal owners of the mass as tenants in common.

b. Confusion caused by the wilful act of a party.

(1) If the amount of goods owned by each party is known and the mass still contains an amount of goods equal to the total amount confused, the parties are owners of the mass as tenants in common in proportion to their respective amounts.

(2) If the amount of goods owned by each party is known but the mass does not contain an amount of goods equal to the total amount confused, the wilful confusor must bear the loss caused by the deficiency.

(3) If the amount of goods owned by each party is not known, the wilful confusor loses title to his or her share and the remaining parties are equal owners of the mass as tenants in common.

LANDLORD-TENANT RELATIONSHIP

XII. Landlord and tenant.

A. Nature and creation of this relationship.

1. Nature.

a. A *lease* is both a contract and a conveyance whereby the owner (landlord-lessor) of real property is bound to give exclusive possession and control of all or part of the property to another person (tenant-lessee) for a temporary period of time.

(1) The tenancy created is a possessory estate in land.

(2) The lease, as a contract, is personal property.

      b. The most outstanding chracteristic of a lease is that it continues for a definite term and always carries with it the duty of the tenant to pay rent to the landlord.

      c. If the amount of rent is not stated, the tenant is obligated to pay a reasonable amount, i.e., the rental market value of similar property.

   2. Creation. The formation and validity of the lease is governed by the law of contracts as discussed in Chapter 2.

B. Types of tenancy.

   1. *Tenancy for years* (tenancy for a definite term).

      a. This tenancy terminates automatically at the end of the specified term.

      b. Notice is not required to be given by the landlord or tenant in order to terminate the tenancy.

      c. Death of either the landlord or the tenant does not terminate the tenancy.

   2. *Tenancy from year to year* (tenancy from period to period), e.g., month to month, year to year, or six months to six months.

      a. This tenancy is usually created in the following ways:

         (1) By an agreement to pay rent periodically without a fixed duration of the lease;

         (2) By an existing tenant holding over after the termination of a tenancy for a definite term.

      b. It may be terminated by either the landlord or the tenant upon giving the required statutory notice.

         (1) Most states require thirty days to terminate a month-to-month tenancy, sixty days to terminate a year-to-year tenancy, and seven days to terminate a week-to-week tenancy.

   3. *Tenancy at will.*

      a. It may be terminated by either the landlord or the tenant upon giving the required statutory notice, usually thirty days.

      b. Death of either the landlord or the tenant terminates this tenancy.

   4. *Tenancy at sufferance.*

      a. A tenant at sufferance is a trespasser.

      b. This type of tenancy arises from the following circumstances:

         (1) A tenant holds over after the expiration of a lease; or

         (2) A mortgagor in default refuses to vacate the premises after a mortgagee's foreclosure.

      c. The landlord can evict the tenant as a trespasser by instituting legal proceedings.

      d. If the landlord allows the tenant at sufferance to remain in possession and accepts payment of rent, a new lease is impliedly created (a tenancy for a definite period or a tenancy from period to period).

C. Covenants implied in a lease. A landlord impliedly makes the following covenants to the tenant by virtue of the lease.

   1. Covenant that the landlord possesses *the right of possession* that the landlord purports to transfer to the tenant.

      a. The covenant is not a promise to deliver possession.

      b. The covenant is breached only when someone other than the landlord has the superior right of possession.

      c. It is not breached if the tenant is unable to obtain possession because of the occupation of the premises by a trespasser, e.g., a previous tenant wrongfully holding over.

   2. Covenant that the landlord will not disturb the *quiet enjoyment* of the premises after the tenant is in possession.

a. The covenant is violated if the tenant is dispossessed by someone owning superior title.

   b. The covenant is violated if the landlord's actions materially interfere with the tenant's use and enjoyment of the premises, e.g., failing to make agreed-upon repairs or stopping heat or water from entering the leased premises.

    (1) To terminate the lease for breach of this covenant, the tenant must abandon the premises.

    (2) Upon rightful abandonment a *constructive eviction* occurs, and the tenant's obligations under the lease terminate.

D. Rights and duties of the landlord.

  1. The landlord retains a reversionary interest in the leased property and is entitled to possession upon the termination of the lease.

  2. The landlord is entitled to *rent* when it is due. If rent is not paid when due, the landlord has the following remedies:

    a. The landlord may sue for rent and allow the lease to continue.

    b. The landlord may choose to end the lease and sue for eviction and damages.

    c. Some states grant a statutory lien (distress for rent) to the landlord for unpaid rent on personal property owned by the tenant.

  3. The landlord may recover for damages to the premises caused by the tenant's intentional or negligent acts.

  4. The landlord has a duty to warn the tenant of latent (hidden) defects in the premises leased. The landlord need not warn the tenant of patent (obvious) defects.

  5. The landlord has a duty to repair those premises which remain under his or her control.

  6. The landlord has no duty to make improvements or to repair leased premises unless such duty has been assumed in the lease. In some states, a statutory duty is imposed on a landlord to improve and repair *apartments* so as to maintain them in a habitable condition.

  7. The landlord has the duty to pay real estate taxes unless otherwise agreed in the lease.

E. Rights and duties of the tenant.

  1. The tenant has the right to exclusive possession during the duration of the lease unless otherwise agreed in the lease. The lease may give the landlord the right to enter upon the premises for the following reasons:

    a. To make improvements or to repair the premises;

    b. To inspect the premises; or

    c. To show the premises to prospective new tenants.

  2. The tenant has the right to terminate the lease if the landlord has caused actual (physical) or constructive (landlord breached the covenant of quiet enjoyment) eviction.

  3. As a general rule, the tenant has a duty to make ordinary repairs.

  4. The tenant has a duty not to use the leased premises in such a manner as to intentionally or negligently injure the person or property of the landlord or any other person found on the leased premises.

  5. A tenant is entitled to remove trade fixtures prior to the expiration of the lease.

  6. The tenant has the duty to pay *rent*.

    a. If the amount of rent is not agreed upon, the tenant is obligated to pay a reasonable rent.

    b. Rent is payable at the end of the term of the lease unless expressly or impliedly agreed otherwise.

    c. Unless the promises of the landlord and tenant are made dependent of each other in the lease, the failure of the landlord to perform does not terminate the tenant's duty to pay rent; e.g., landlord's failure to keep the promise to repair does not relieve the tenant of the duty to pay rent.

F. Assignment of a lease or sublease.

    1. *Assignment.* An assignment is the transfer by a tenant to a third person of *all* of the tenant's remaining rights in an existing lease.

        a. The tenant remains liable to the landlord under the terms of the lease.

        b. As a general rule, the assignee is liable to both the landlord and the tenant-assignor for the covenants in the lease that run with the land. These covenants are:

            (1) To pay rent;

            (2) To insure the premises;

            (3) To repair the premises; and

            (4) To pay taxes.

        c. Unless there is a specific provision in a lease voiding an attempted assignment, leases are freely assignable.

    2. *Sublease.* A sublease is the transfer by a tenant to a third person of less than all of the tenant's remaining rights in an existing lease, e.g., a sublease of one room of three currently being leased, a sublease for a term less than the unexpired term of an existing lease, or a sublease of the entire unexpired term of an existing lease subject to a right of reentry upon a condition.

        a. The sublessee is liable to the sublessor (tenant) according to the terms of the sublease.

        b. The sublessee is not liable for nonperformance of the covenants in the original lease.

        c. The sublessee is legally the tenant of the sublessor. The sublessee is not the tenant of the original landlord.

        d. Without a provision in a lease voiding an attempted sublease, leases can be freely sublet.

G. Transfer of the landlord's interest.

    1. A landlord may freely transfer or mortgage the leased premises.

    2. The grantee or mortgagee will acquire the interest subject to any existing leases.

    3. For a grantee to receive the future benefits of any existing leases, the grantee must receive an assignment of them.

H. Wrongful *abandonment* of the premises by the tenant. If the tenant wrongfully vacates the leased premises before the lease expires, the landlord is entitled to the following alternative remedies.

    1. The landlord may accept the tenant's abandonment (surrender), treat the lease as ended, and relet the premises in the landlord's behalf.

    2. The landlord may refuse to terminate the lease and sue the tenant for rent as it becomes due.

    3. The landlord may refuse to terminate the lease and relet the premises as an agent in behalf of the tenant.

        a. The landlord must give notice of the action to the tenant.

        b. The landlord is entitled to recover from the wrongdoing tenant the deficiency between the rent and the rent paid by the new tenant. If the rent from the new tenant is in excess of that due from the original tenant, the landlord must hold the excess for the original tenant.

        c. If the landlord fails to give notice of intention to relet for the tenant's account, a *surrender* by operation of law will occur, terminating the original lease.

I. Termination of a tenancy. Leases terminate as follows:

    1. By *expiration of the duration* of the lease;

2. By an *exercise of the right to terminate* provided for in the terms of the lease, e.g., for failure to repair or pay rent;

3. By *actual eviction*, when the landlord physically dispossesses the tenant of part or all of the premises;

4. By *constructive eviction*, in which the landlord causes a breach of the implied covenant of quiet enjoyment and the tenant abandons the premises;

5. By *surrender*, when:
  a. The tenant wrongfully abandons the premises; and
  b. The landlord, by words or conduct, indicates an acceptance of the tenant's abandonment.

6. By *destruction* of the leased premises.
  a. Where a lease includes land and its improvements (buildings, etc.), damage or destruction of the improvements *does not* cause the lease to terminate.
  b. A lease of one apartment in an apartment building is terminated upon the substantial damage or total destruction of the leased apartment.

7. The property subject to the lease is taken by *condemnation* under the power of the eminent domain.

MORTGAGES

XIII. Real estate mortgages (see Figure 10-9 for the legal structure of a mortgage).

A. *Definitions*.

  1. *Mortgage* is, in most states, a conveyance of an interest in land by one person (mortgagor-debtor) to another person (mortgagee-creditor) as a security for payment of a debt or some other obligation.
    a. The mortgagor retains title to the land.
    b. The mortgagee acquires a *nonpossessory lien* upon the land.

  2. *Purchase-money mortgage* is one created to obtain the purchase price of the land upon which the mortgage lien is to attach. A non-purchase-money mortgage is given upon land already owned by the mortgagor.

  3. *Deed of trust* (trust deed) is a form of mortgage in that the debtor (trustor) conveys the land to a disinterested person (trustee) in trust for the benefit of a creditor (beneficiary) as security for the payment of a debt or some other obligation. (See Figure 10-10.)
    a. As a general rule, a deed of trust creates the same rights and duties as a mortgage.
    b. The trustee holds legal "title" with power only to sell the land if the debtor defaults, i.e., power of sale.

FIGURE 10-9   LEGAL STRUCTURE OF A MORTGAGE

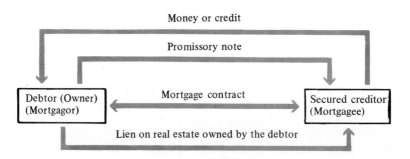

FIGURE 10-10 LEGAL STRUCTURE OF A DEED OF TRUST SECURITY (LIEN) DEVICE

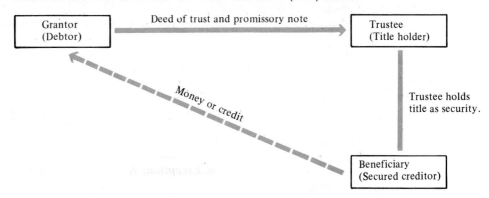

    c. It is commonly used where the amount borrowed is large and has been obtained from a large number of creditors.

B. *Form of mortgage.*

  1. A mortgage is a conveyance of an interest in land and consequently must be executed with the same formalities as a deed and delivered to the mortgagee. See X above.

  2. Common provisions found in a mortgage are as follows:

    a. Identification of the parties (mortgagor and mortgagee);

    b. Description of the land subject to the *mortgage lien*;

    c. Amount of debt secured, future advances, rate of interest, and terms of repayment;

    d. Assignment to the mortgagee of the right to rents and profits from the land, to be exercised only upon default;

    e. A release and waiver of homestead rights;

    f. Covenants (promises) by the mortgagor:

      (1) To pay all indebtedness secured by the mortgage;

      (2) To execute and deliver a promissory note made payable to the mortgagee;

      (3) To maintain possession, to repair, and to not commit waste;

      (4) To permit inspection of the property by the mortgagee;

      (5) To keep the property free from all liens;

      (6) To pay all general taxes and special assessments when due;

      (7) To keep the property insured;

      (8) To allow the mortgagee to declare the entire debt due upon any default (acceleration clause);

      (9) To allow the mortgagee to petition a court immediately for a decree of foreclosure upon any default;

     (10) To allow the mortgagee to petition a court for appointment of a receiver to collect rents and profits during foreclosure proceedings;

     (11) To allow the mortgagee to take possession and collect rents and profits after foreclosure sale and the entry of a deficiency judgment against the mortgagor.

    g. A *defeasance clause* which provides that the conveyance in the mortgage is null and void upon the performance of the mortgagor.

C. *Liabilities created by the mortgage.*

  1. A personal obligation evidenced by a promissory note;

  2. A lien (security interest) on property evidenced by the mortgage contract.

D. *Recording (filing) the mortgage.*

    1. A mortgage need not be recorded to be valid between the mortgagor and mortgagee.

    2. A mortgage must be recorded to protect the mortgagee's lien against subsequent interests which may be acquired in the property.

        a. It must be recorded in the recording office of the county where the mortgaged property is located.

        b. Recordation gives *constructive notice* (public) of the mortgagee's lien to all third persons.

        c. A recorded mortgage takes priority over any subsequent interests which may be acquired in the mortgaged property.

E. *Property subject to be mortgaged.*

    1. As a general rule, any interest in real property, *presently owned*, may be the subject of a mortgage. *Exception:* A mortgage may contain an *after-acquired property clause.*

        a. Such a clause causes the existing mortgage lien to attach to property subsequently acquired by the mortgagor.

        b. The lien does not attach to after-acquired property until title is acquired by the mortgagor.

    2. Improvements. All improvements on the mortgaged property at the time of the mortgage or added in the future are subject to the mortgage lien.

    3. Fixtures.

        a. Fixtures not subject to an existing security interest become subject to the lien of the mortgage.

        b. Priority between a security interest in a fixture and a mortgage lien is established by the rules found in article 9 of the UCC. (Secured transactions involving fixtures were discussed in Chapter 6.)

    4. Crops.

        a. Crops growing on mortgaged land are subject to the mortgage lien.

        b. If the crops are severed prior to default on the mortgage indebtedness, the mortgagor has absolute title in them.

    5. The following are examples of interests in real property that can be mortgaged:

        a. A fee simple;

        b. A life estate;

        c. A reversion;

        d. A vested remainder;

        e. An option to buy real property;

        f. A right to receive rent;

        g. A tenant's leasehold interest.

F. *Rights and duties of the mortgagor.*

    1. Unless otherwise agreed, the mortgagor has the following rights:

        a. To possession of the property until *default*, foreclosure, and sale;

        b. To repair and improve the property;

        c. To obtain and keep rents and profits from the property; and

        d. To insure the premises.

    2. A mortgagor may lease, sell, give away, or transfer title (equity) by will or descent, subject only to the lien of the mortgage. The value of the *mortgagor's equity* is equal to the difference between the market value of the property and the amount of the outstanding mortgage debt at any given point of time.

    3. The title (equity) is subject to execution by the mortgagor's judgment creditors.

    4. Dower exists in the title (equity).

    5. Mortgagor's equity of redemption and right of redemption.

    a. *Equity of redemption*. After default and before foreclosure sale, the mortgagor may redeem the property by payment of all principal and interest due on the mortgage note.

    b. *Right of redemption*. After foreclosure sale, most states allow a mortgagor a period of time, usually one year, to reinstate the debt and mortgage by paying to the purchaser at foreclosure sale the amount of the purchase price plus the statutory rate of interest.

  6. The mortgagor has the following duties:

    a. To pay the agreed-upon indebtedness when due;

    b. To pay general taxes and special assessments;

    c. To refrain from committing waste (impairment of the security), i.e., failure to pay taxes, destruction of improvements, or failure to discharge a prior lien;

    d. To perform all covenants in the mortgage.

G. *Rights and duties of the mortgagee.*

  1. The mortgagee is entitled to a lien on the property.

  2. The mortgagee is entitled to payment of principal and interest when due.

  3. The mortgagee may insure the mortgaged property although there is no duty to do so under common law.

  4. The mortgagee may transfer the debt and mortgage to a third person.

  5. The mortgagee has the remedies of damages or injunction against the mortgagor for waste.

  6. The mortgagee may foreclose the mortgage upon default by the mortgagor.

  7. If the proceeds of a foreclosure sale are not sufficient to pay the mortgage indebtedness, the mortgagee is entitled to recover any deficiency from the mortgagor.

  8. The mortgagee has the following duties:

    a. Not to interfere with the mortgagor's possession, use, and enjoyment of the property;

    b. To turn over any proceeds from foreclosure sale which are in excess of the indebtedness;

    c. To perform all covenants in the mortgage.

H. *Transfer of mortgagor's interest (equity)*. The mortgagor may sell the mortgaged property at any time without the mortgagee's consent unless otherwise provided in the mortgage agreement.

  1. Transfer subject to the mortgage. If a buyer takes title to property *subject to* an existing mortgage, the buyer does not become personally liable for the mortgage debt.

    a. The property remains subject to the mortgage lien.

    b. The mortgagor remains personally liable on the mortgage debt.

  2. Transfer with an assumption of the mortgage. If a buyer takes title to property and *assumes and agrees to pay* the mortgage debt (third-party beneficiary contract). (See Figure 10-11.)

    a. The property remains subject to the mortgage lien;

    b. The mortgagor remains personally liable on the mortgage debt as a surety;

    c. Upon default and foreclosure sale, the mortgagee may recover any deficiency from either the mortgagor or the buyer.

  3. Transfer by *novation*. The transfer by novation occurs when the mortgagee agrees to release the mortgagor from personal obligation and to accept the buyer as a substitute mortgagor. The mortgage lien continues on the property.

I. *Transfer of the mortgagee's interest.*

  1. The mortgage and the note it secures are freely assignable.

FIGURE 10-11 TRANSFER OF TITLE TO MORTGAGED REAL ESTATE

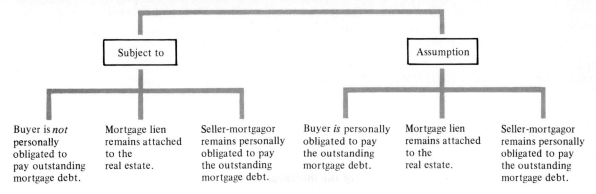

2. An assignment of the mortgage note carries with it the mortgage lien even though the mortgage itself is not assigned.
3. A partial assignment of the debt carries with it a pro rata portion of the mortgage lien.
4. An assignment of a mortgage is a transfer of an interest in land and therefore can be recorded.
   a. Recordation of the assignment is not constructive notice to the mortgagor.
      (1) A mortgagor must be given actual notice of the assignment by the mortgagee.
      (2) If the mortgagor does not receive actual notice and makes payment to the original mortgagee, the mortgagor is discharged of personal obligation.
   b. *Recordation* is necessary to protect an assignee's interest against subsequent assignees of the same debt.
J. *Multiple mortgages on the same parcel of property.*
   1. A *recorded* mortgage takes priority over all prior unrecorded mortgages and all subsequent mortgages, whether recorded or not.
   2. All subordinate mortgage liens are erased if, on foreclosure sale, the proceeds are sufficient only to discharge the superior mortgage.

RECORDATION: PRIORITIES BETWEEN CONFLICTING LEGAL INTERESTS

XIV. All states have statutes allowing recordation of instruments that affect title to real property. (See Figure 10-12.)
   A. *Place of recordation.* As a general rule, a public office in the county where the real property is located is the designated place for recordation.
   B. *Types of instruments which can be recorded* are:
      1. Deeds;
      2. Contracts for sale of real property;
      3. Installment land contracts;
      4. Leases;
      5. Mortgages;
      6. Powers of attorney to sell real property;
      7. Releases of mortgages;
      8. Assignments of mortgages;
      9. Profits *a prendre*;
      10. Easements.

Chapter 10: Property 329

FIGURE 10-12 RECORDATION OF REAL PROPERTY INSTRUMENTS OR DOCUMENTS

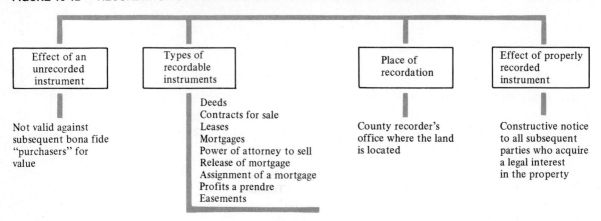

C. *Purpose of recordation.* The following are the two purposes of recordation:
1. To provide a means of protecting existing estates or other interests in real property; and
2. To protect interests of *bona fide subsequent purchasers* against secret, unrecorded interests.

D. *Effect of a recorded instrument.* A properly recorded instrument gives *constructive notice* of the interest it represents to any person who subsequently acquires another interest in the property.

E. *Effect of an unrecorded instrument:*
1. It is valid between the parties to it.
2. An unrecorded instrument is not valid against a subsequent bona fide purchaser.
   a. A bona fide purchaser is a party who has *paid value* for an estate or other interest in land *without actual or constructive notice* of an already existing estate or interest in the same parcel of land.
      (1) A purchaser has actual notice when the purchaser knows of a prior unrecorded estate or other interest.
      (2) A purchaser has constructive notice of all recorded estates or interests in land.

SELF-QUIZ

To check your understanding of the key words and concepts and the accuracy of your answers to the questions, refer to the text material as referenced by page number.

KEY WORDS AND CONCEPTS

QUESTIONS

1. What are the private and public restrictions on ownership of property? **(311)**
2. What is the most important distinction between a joint tenancy and a tenancy in common? **(303)**
3. How does a freehold estate differ from a nonfreehold estate? **(305)**
4. Explain the difference between a conventional and a legal life estate. **(307)**
5. What are the rights and duties of a life tenant? **(306)**
6. List four inheritable estates in land. **(306)**
7. List and explain the ways easements may be created and terminated. **(309)**
8. Who has the right to enforce restrictive covenants? **(312)**
9. List nine ways title can be acquired to real property. **(313)**

10. List and explain the provisions commonly found in a contract for the sale of real property. **(314)**

11. List and explain the important features of a deed. **(317)**

12. List and explain five covenants implied in a warranty deed. **(318)**

13. Can a quitclaim deed convey title? **(319)**

14. In what ways may title to personal property be acquired? Explain. **(319)**

15. What are the rights and duties of a landlord and tenant toward each other? **(323)**

16. What effect does an assignment and sublease have upon the liabilities created by the original lease? **(324)**

17. List and explain the ways a lease may be terminated. **(324)**

18. What two liabilities are created by a mortgage? **(325)**

19. What interests in property can be made subject to a mortgage? List some examples. **(327)**

20. List and explain the rights and duties of a mortgagor and mortgagee to each other. **(328)**

21. Explain the liabilities of the mortgagor and a purchaser of mortgaged property after completion of each of the following transactions:
    a. A buyer takes title "subject to" the mortgage. **(329)**
    b. A buyer takes title and "assumes and agrees to pay" the mortgage. **(329)**
    c. A buyer takes title under a novation. **(328)**

22. Must an instrument evidencing an interest in real property be recorded in order to be valid? **(330)**

23. What is the purpose of recordation? **(329)**

24. What is the effect of an unrecorded instrument? **(330)**

SELECTED QUESTIONS AND UNOFFICIAL ANSWERS

OBJECTIVE QUESTIONS

Select the best answer for each of the following items. Mark only one answer for each item. Answer all items.

MAY 1981

52. Glover Manufacturing, Inc., purchased a four-acre tract of commercially zoned land. A survey of the tract was made prior to the closing, and it revealed an unpaved road which passed across the northeast corner of the land. The title search revealed a mortgage held by Peoples National Bank, which was satisfied at the closing by the seller out of the funds received from Glover. The title search did not indicate the existence of any other adverse interest which would constitute a defect in title. There was no recordation made in connection with the unpaved road. Which of the following statements is correct regarding Glover's title and rights to the land against the claims of adverse parties?

a. The unpaved road poses *no* potential problem if Glover promptly fences off the property and puts up "no trespassing" signs.

b. Glover does *not* have to be concerned with the unpaved road since whatever rights the users might claim were negated by failing to record.

c. The mere use of the unpaved road as contrasted with the occupancy of the land can *not* create any interest adverse to Glover.

d. The unpaved road revealed by the survey may prove to be a valid easement created by prescription.

53. Golden sold his moving and warehouse business including all the personal and real property used therein, to Clark Van Lines, Inc. The real property was encumbered by a duly-recorded $300,000 first mortgage upon which Golden was personally liable. Clark acquired the property subject to the mortgage but did not assume the mortgage. Two years later, when the outstanding mortgage was $260,000, Clark decided to abandon the business location because it had become unprofitable and the value of the real property was less than the outstanding mortgage. Clark moved to another location and refused to pay the installments due on the mortgage. What is the legal status of the parties in regard to the mortgage?

a. Clark took the real property free of the mortgage.

b. Clark breached its contract with Golden when it abandoned the location and defaulted on the mortgage.

c. Golden must satisfy the mortgage debt in the event that foreclosure yields an amount less than the unpaid balance.

d. If Golden pays off the mortgage, he will be able to successfully sue Clark because Golden is subrogated to the mortgagee's rights against Clark.

54. Tremont Enterprises, Inc., needed some additional working capital to develop a new product line. It decided to obtain intermediate term financing by giving a second mortgage on its plant and warehouse. Which of the following is true with respect to the mortgages?
a. If Tremont defaults on both mortgages and a bankruptcy proceeding is initiated, the second mortgagee has the status of general creditor.
b. If the second mortgagee proceeds to foreclose on its mortgage, the first mortgagee must be satisfied completely before the second mortgagee is entitled to repayment.
c. Default on payment to the second mortgagee will constitute default on the first mortgage.
d. Tremont can *not* prepay the second mortgage prior to its maturity without the consent of the first mortgagee.

47. Gilgo has entered into a contract for the purchase of land from the Wicklow Land Company. A title search reveals certain defects in the title to the land to be conveyed by Wicklow. Wicklow has demanded that Gilgo accept the deed and pay the balance of the purchase price. Furthermore Wicklow has informed Gilgo that unless Gilgo proceeds with the closing, Wicklow will hold Gilgo liable for breach of contract. Wicklow has pointed out to Gilgo that the contract says nothing about defects and that he must take the property "as is." Which of the following is correct?
a. Gilgo can rely on the implied warranty of merchantability.
b. Wicklow is right in that if there is *no* express warranty against title defects, none exists.
c. Gilgo will prevail because he is entitled to a perfect title from Wicklow.
d. Gilgo will win if the title is *not* marketable.

48. Marks is a commercial tenant of Tudor Buildings, Inc. The term of the lease is five years and two years have elapsed. The lease prohibits subletting, but does *not* contain any provision relating to assignment. Marks approached Tudor and asked whether Tudor could release him from the balance

of the term of the lease for $500. Tudor refused unless Marks would agree to pay $2,000. Marks located Flint who was interested in renting in Tudor's building and transferred the entire balance of the lease to Flint in consideration of his promise to pay Tudor the monthly rental and otherwise perform Marks' obligations under the lease. Tudor objects. Which of the following statements is correct?
a. A prohibition of the right to sublet contained in the lease completely prohibits an assignment.
b. The assignment need *not* be in writing.
c. The assignment does *not* extinguish Marks' obligation to pay the rent if Flint defaults.
d. The assignment is invalid without Tudor's consent.

11. Carr owns 100 acres of undeveloped land on the outskirts of New Town. He bought the land several years ago to build an industrial park in the event New Town grew and prospered. The land was formerly used for grazing and truck gardening. A subsequent inspection revealed that several adjacent landowners recently had been using a shortcut across his land in order to reach a newly constructed highway. Which of the following is a correct statement?
a. There is a danger that the adjacent landowners will obtain title by adverse possession.
b. Since Carr has properly recorded his deed, the facts do *not* pose a problem for him.
c. There is a danger that an easement may be created.
d. Since the adjacent landowners are trespassers, Carr has nothing to fear.

20. Monrad is contemplating making a contract for the purchase of certain real property. Which of the following is *incorrect* insofar as such a contract is concerned?
a. It must meet the requirements of the statute of frauds.
b. If the agreement is legally consummated, Monrad could obtain specific performance.
c. The contract is nonassignable as a matter of law.
d. An implied covenant of marketability applies to the contract.

26. Dombres is considering purchasing Blackacre. The title search revealed that the property was willed by Adams jointly to his children, Donald and Martha. The language contained in the will is unclear as to whether a joint tenancy or a tenancy in common was intended. Donald is dead and Martha has agreed to convey her entire interest by quitclaim deed to Dombres. The purchase price is equal to the full fair market price of the property. Dombres is *not* interested in anything less than the entire title to the tract. Under the circumstances, which of the following is correct?

a. There is a statutory preference which favors the finding of a joint tenancy.
b. Whether the will created a joint tenancy or a tenancy in common is irrelevant since Martha is the only survivor.
c. Dombres will *not* obtain title to the entire tract of land by Martha's conveyance.
d. There is *no* way or means whereby Dombres may obtain a clear title under the circumstances.

NOVEMBER 1979

10. Marcross and two business associates own real property as tenants in common that they have invested in as a speculation. The speculation proved to be highly successful, and the land is now worth substantially more than their investment. Which of the following is a correct legal incident of ownership of the property?

a. Upon the death of any of the other tenants, the deceased's interest passes to the survivor(s) unless there is a will.
b. Each of the co-tenants owns an undivided interest in the whole.
c. A co-tenant can *not* sell his interest in the property without the consent of the other tenants.
d. Upon the death of a co-tenant, his estate is entitled to the amount of the original investment, but *not* the appreciation.

39. Lantz sold his moving and warehouse business, including all the personal and real property used therein, to Mallen Van Lines, Inc. The real property was encumbered by a duly-recorded $300,000 first mortgage upon which Lantz was personally liable. Mallen acquired the property subject to the mortgage but did *not* assume the mortgage. Two years later, when the outstanding mortgage was $260,000, Mallen decided to abandon the business location because it had become unprofitable and the value of the real property was less than the outstanding mortgage. Mallen moved to another location and refused to pay the installments due on the mortgage. What is the legal status of the parties in regard to the mortgage?

a. Mallen breached its contract with Lantz when it abandoned the location and defaulted on the mortgage.
b. Mallen took the real property free of the mortgage.
c. If Lantz pays off the mortgage, he will be able to successfully sue Mallen because Lantz is subrogated to the mortgagee's rights against Mallen.
d. Lantz must satisfy the mortgage debt in the event that foreclosure yields an amount less than the unpaid balance.

Answers to Objective Questions

May 1981		November 1980	
52. d	**54.** b	**47.** d	**48.** c
53. c			

May 1980		November 1979	
11. c	**26.** c	**10.** b	**39.** d
20. c			

Explanation of Answers to Objective Questions

MAY 1981

52. (d) An easement can be created by prescription when a person uses someone else's land in a wrongful, open and notorious manner continuously for the period of time prescribed by statute (normally 20 years). Answer (a) is incorrect because, if the property was not fenced until after the statutory period had expired, the easement would have already been created by prescription. Answer (b) is incorrect because an easement gained by prescription is valid without recording such interest. Answer (c) is incorrect because adverse use creates an easement, while adverse occupancy (adverse possession) results in ownership of the property.

53. (c) Golden, the original debtor, must satisfy the mortgage debt in the event that the foreclosure yields an amount less than the unpaid balance. Golden was originally liable on the mortgage, and no novation or release was granted by the mortgagor when Golden sold the warehouse to Clark. Answer (a) is incorrect because Clark did not take the property free of the mortgage. The property was subject to the mortgage at all times, but Clark was not personally liable as he did not *assume* the mortgage.

Answer (b) is incorrect because Clark bought the property only *subject* to the mortgage and therefore, did not breach his agreement with Golden when he abandoned the location and stopped making the mortgage payments. Answer (d) is incorrect because Golden will not be able to sue Clark because Clark did not contract to be liable on the mortgage debt. Thus, there is no one for Golden to be subrogated to.

54. (b) Upon foreclosure, the first mortgagee has priority and must be paid in full before any payment is made to a subsequent mortgagee (second or third mortgagees). Answer (a) is incorrect because a second mortgagee remains a secured creditor in the bankruptcy proceedings although his interest is inferior to a first mortgagee. The doctrine of marshalling of assets may help a second mortgagee since it allows him to compel a first mortgagee to foreclose on other property available to the first mortgagee as security before foreclosing on property which a second mortgagee has a claim on. Answer (c) is incorrect because default of the second mortgage does not constitute a default of the first mortgage. Answer (d) is incorrect since second mortgages are sometimes obtained for a short period of time and can be paid off before maturity without consent of first mortgagee.

NOVEMBER 1980

47. (d) In a contract for the sale of real property, unless expressly disclaimed there is an implied promise that the seller will provide a marketable title. A marketable title is one reasonably free from doubt. It does not contain: encumbrances; encroachments; restrictions, except for zoning laws. However, to be marketable, a title does not have to be perfect. Third parties may have rights to temporary use and possession of the property. Thus answer (d) is correct and answers (b) and (c) are incorrect. Answer (a) is incorrect because the implied warranty of merchantability is granted in a sale of goods by a merchant not in the sale of real property.

48. (c) A tenant may engage in an assignment or a sublease unless expressly prohibited by the lease. An assignment of the lease is the transfer by the lessee of his entire interest without reserving any right of re-entry. The assignor remains liable on the lease despite the assignment. Answer (c) is correct. Answer (a) is incorrect because a clause in the lease

prohibiting a sublease does not prohibit an assignment. Since there were 3 years left on the lease when assigned it was not capable of being performed within one year and consequently the agreement to transfer such an interest must be in writing [answer (b)]. There is no need for the landlord to consent to the assignment unless the lease expressly prohibited assignment.

MAY 1980

11. (c) One method of creating an easement is by prescription. This occurs when a person uses someone else's land in a wrongful, continuous, open and notorious manner for the prescribed statutory period of time. The adjacent landowner appears to be engaging in this type of use. The landowners are merely using the property, not possessing it, thus adverse possession is not present. Prescription can occur even though the owner has recorded the deed. Anyone obtaining an easement would initially be a trespasser since the use must be wrongful.

20. (c) Real property contracts are assignable; thus, the statement in answer (c) is incorrect making answer (c) the correct answer. The Statute of Frauds demands the sale of an interest in real property to be in writing, thus answer (a) is correct. Answer (b) is correct because specific performance is an available remedy for breach of real property contract. The seller impliedly covenants that the title being transferred is marketable (reasonably free from doubt).

26. (c) When the deed is unclear as to whether a joint tenancy or tenancy in common was intended, there is a statutory presumption in favor of tenancy in common. Thus, Donald and Martha were tenants in common and when Donald died his interest passed to his heirs. Thus, if Dombres wanted to obtain the entire title, he would have to purchase the interest of Donald's heirs, as well as Martha's interest.

NOVEMBER 1979

10. (b) The correct legal incident of ownership of property as tenants in common is that each of the co-tenants owns an undivided interest in the whole. Answer (a) is incorrect because upon the death of any of the other tenants in common, the deceased tenant's interest will pass to his heirs and not to the surviving co-tenants. Answer (c) is incorrect because a co-tenant in common can sell his interest in the property without the consent of the other co-tenants. Answer (d) is incorrect because upon the death of a co-tenant, his estate owns the same interest as the decedent.

39. (d) Lantz, the original debtor, must satisfy the mortgage debt in the event that the foreclosure yields an amount less than the unpaid balance. Lantz was originally liable on the mortgage, and no novation or release was granted by the mortgagee when Lantz sold the warehouse to Mallen. Answer (a) is incorrect because Mallen bought the property only subject to the mortgage and therefore, did not breach his agreement with Lantz when Mallen abandoned the location and stopped making the mortgage payments. Answer (b) is incorrect because Mallen did not take the property free of the mortgage. The property was subject to the mortgage at all times, but Mallen was not personally liable as he did not assume the mortgage. Answer (c) is incorrect because Lantz will not be able to sue Mallen because Mallen did not contract to be liable on the mortgage debt. Thus, there is no one for Lantz to be subrogated to.

ESSAY QUESTIONS AND ANSWERS

MAY 1979 (Estimated time: 15 to 20 minutes)

5. Part a. Hammar Hardware Company, Inc., purchased all the assets and assumed all the liabilities of JoMar Hardware for $60,000. Among the assets and liabilities included in the sale was a lease of the building in which the business was located. The lessor-owner was Marathon Realty, Inc., and the remaining unexpired term of the lease was nine years. The lease did not contain a provision dealing with the assignment of the leasehold. Incidental to the purchase, Hammar expressly promised JoMar that it would pay the rental due Marathon over the life of the lease and would hold JoMar harmless from any future liability thereon.

When Marathon learned of the proposed transaction, it strenuously objected to the assignment of the lease and to the occupancy by Hammar. Later, after this dispute was resolved and prior to expiration of the lease, Hammar abandoned the building and ceased doing business in that area. Marathon has demanded payment by JoMar of the rent as it matures over the balance of the term of the lease.

Required Answer the following, setting forth reasons for any conclusions stated.

1. Was the consent of Marathon necessary in order to assign the lease?
2. Is JoMar liable on the lease?
3. If Marathon were to proceed against Hammar, would Hammar be liable under the lease?

Answer

1. No. In the absence of a restriction on the right to assign specifically stated in the lease, a lessee may assign his leasehold interest to another. Only in unusual circumstances, where the lease involves special elements of personal trust and confidence as contrasted with mere payment for occupancy, will the courts limit the right to assign.

2. Yes. Although JoMar may effectively assign the lease, which in effect is an assignment of the right to occupy the leasehold premises and a delegation of its duty to pay Marathon, it cannot shed its liability to Marathon for the rental payments. In the absence of a release, JoMar remains liable. The transaction described in the fact situation is in the nature of a surety relationship.

3. Yes. Marathon is a third-party creditor beneficiary of Hammar's promise to JoMar. As such, Marathon can assert rights on the promise even though it was not a party to the contract. Marathon is not barred by lack of privity or the fact that it gave no consideration to Hammar for the promise.

5. Part b. The Merchants and Mechanics County Bank expanded its services and facilities as a result of the economic growth of the community it serves. In this connection, it provided safe deposit facilities for the first time. A large vault was constructed as a part of the renovation and expansion of the bank building. Merchants purchased a bank vault door from Foolproof Vault Doors, Inc., for $65,000 and installed it at the vault entrance. The state in which Merchants was located had a real property tax but did not have a personal property tax. When the tax assessor appraised the bank building after completion of the renovation and expansion, he included the bank vault door as a part of the real property. Merchants has filed an objection claiming the vault door was initially personal property and remains so after installation in the bank.

There are no specific statutes or regulations determinative of the issue. Therefore, the question will be decided according to common law principles of property law.

Required Answer the following, setting forth reasons for any conclusions stated.

1. What is the likely outcome as to the classification of the bank vault door?
2. The above situation involves a dispute between a tax authority and the owner of property. In what other circumstances might a dispute arise with respect to the classification of property as either real or personal property?

Answer

1. Based upon the facts of the problem and the legal criteria discussed below, the vault door will probably be classified as real property. The criteria applicable are these:

- Annexation—the mode and degree to which the chattel is physically attached to the real property.
- Adaptation—the extent to which the chattel is used in promoting the purpose for which the real property is used.
- Intention—whether the chattel was intended as a permanent improvement of the real property.

Applying these criteria to the facts demonstrates that the degree of annexation of a vault door is by necessity very high. Furthermore, the adaptation of the personal property (the vault door) to the use of the real property by the bank also argues for a finding in favor of real property classification. Finally, the last criterion, the intent of the bank to make a permanent improvement of the real property, appears to have been satisfied. Taking these criteria together, it would appear that the bank door has become real property.

2. In addition to tax collectors, disputes involving the categorization of property as real or personal have arisen in respect of—

- Real property mortgagees versus creditors of the same debtor who have a security interest in personal property (chattel mortgagees).
- Landlord versus tenant upon expiration of the lease and the question of what property may be removed.
- Takers under a will versus the executor in cases where different takers will receive the property, based upon its classification.
- The seller versus the purchaser of real property, where a dispute arises concerning the removal of certain property by the seller.
- The mortgagor versus mortgagee, when the question arises regarding what property is included under the scope of the mortgage.

CHAPTER

11

Administration of Estates and Trusts

The following is a generalized listing of subjects to be tested through the May 1983 Uniform CPA Examination.

This topic includes the administration of a decedent's estate and administration of a trust. The Uniform Principal and Income Act is the prevailing statute applicable in the area of allocation of trust principal and income.[1]

The AICPA Board of Examiners has adopted a new content specification outline for the business law section of the Uniform CPA Examination, *to be effective with the November 1983 examination*. The outline lists the following topic to be tested under the title "Administration of Estates and Trusts."

C. Administration of Estates and Trusts.[2]

INTESTATE SUCCESSION

  I. Inheritance by *intestate succession*.
    A. Where no valid will has been executed, or if a valid will does not provide for distribution of an entire estate, the decedent is said to have died totally or partially *intestate*. The applicable state statute prescribes the persons who will inherit the decedent's property as well as the proportionate amount of property each is to receive.

---

[1] AICPA, *Information for CPA Candidates*, Copyright © 1975, 1979, by the American Institute of Certified Public Accountants, Inc.
[2] AICPA, *Business Law—Content Specification Outline*, approved by the AICPA Board of Examiners on August 31, 1981.

1. Rules of descent and distribution are statutory. Their purpose is to assure an orderly transfer of title to real and personal property and to carry out what probably would be the wishes of the decedent.
2. *Descent* is the vesting of title to real estate by operation of law in heirs immediately upon the death of their ancestor. *Note:* Title to personal property of a decedent is vested in the personal representative (executor or administrator) for distribution under the provisions of the applicable state statute.
3. *Distribution* is the apportionment and division of a decedent's intestate property, under authority of a court, by the personal representative (executor or administrator).
4. All states have a statute of descent and distribution.

B. The following rules for descent and distribution of intestate property are representative of those found in many state statutes:
1. If a spouse and one or more descendants are living, spouse takes one-third of all property, children share equally in two-thirds, and any descendants of deceased children share *per stirpes* (i.e., equally in the share that their deceased parent would have taken if living).
2. If no spouse is living but one or more descendants are living, children share equally in all property, and descendants of deceased children share *per stirpes*.
3. If a spouse is living but there are no surviving descendants, the surviving spouse takes all of the deceased spouse's property.
4. If there is no spouse and no descendants surviving but a brother, sister, parent, or descendant of a deceased brother or sister is living, then parents, brothers, and sisters share equally in all property (allowing a sole surviving parent a double share). Descendants of a deceased brother or sister share *per stirpes*.
5. The typical intestate succession statute continues distribution through maternal and paternal grandparents and their descendants, maternal and paternal great-grandparents and their descendants, and collateral heirs.
6. Finally, if no spouse survives or no known relative of the decedent is living, the real estate escheats to the county in which it is located and the personal property escheats to the county of which the decedent was a resident.

WILLS AND CODICILS: TESTATE SUCCESSION

II. Inheritance, testamentary distribution, wills, and codicils (see Figure 11-1).
A. Definitions.
1. *Will* is a legal declaration of the wishes of a natural person called the *testator*, providing for distribution of the testator's property after death.
2. *Devise* is a gift of real estate through a will.
a. *General devise* is a gift of real estate by a testator without a specific description of it; e.g., "I devise all my land."

FIGURE 11-1   INHERITANCE BY WILL OR INTESTATE SUCCESSION

    b. *Specific devise* is a gift of specifically identified real estate; e.g., "I devise my Sunset Lake estate."

  3. *Legacy* is a gift of personal property through a will.

    a. *General (legacy) bequest* is a gift of personal property payable out of the general assets of the testator, e.g., a gift of $100.

    b. *Specific (legacy) bequest* is a gift of specifically identified item of personal property, e.g., a grandfather clock.

  4. *Testate* is the circumstance of a person who died leaving a will.

B. In general. Individual states have enacted statutes providing for the kinds of property or interests that may be disposed of by will and prescribing the formalities that must be observed in the execution of a will. Any estate that the owner may transfer during the owner's lifetime may be disposed of by will. A will may be revoked during the life of the testator and becomes legally effective and operative only upon the death of the testator.

C. *Testamentary capacity* must be present to execute a valid will.

  1. The most common minimum age required for executing a valid will is eighteen.

  2. A will made by persons who do not have mental capacity or who are under a legal disability is voidable. A lack of mental capacity or legal disability may be caused by the following:

    a. Insanity;

    b. Undue influence;

    c. Duress;

    d. Mistake;

    e. Fraud; or

    f. Execution of a will with an intent other than testamentary.

D. Types of wills.

  1. *Holographic will* is a will written entirely in the handwriting of the testator.

  2. *Nuncupative will* is an oral will and can be made only when the testator is in a last illness. These wills are permitted in only a few states.

  3. *Soldiers' and sailors' wills* may be oral or written and need not be made in accordance with formalities required for other types of wills. These wills are required to be signed by the testator. They need not be attested to by witnesses.

  4. *Conditional will* is one which takes effect only on the happening of a specified condition. For example, the son of a decedent must be married before he may receive his devise.

  5. *Joint will* is one which contains the same provisions for two or more persons. Each testator makes testamentary disposition in favor of the other. Both must make and sign the will jointly. Most states provide that the execution of a joint will results in a binding contract, and subsequently the will *is irrevocable*.

  6. *Formal (statutory) will* is a written instrument, executed with the formalities required by law, whereby a person makes a disposition of his or her property to take effect after death.

E. Requirements of a formal (statutory) will—*execution* (see Figure 11-2).

  1. It must be signed by the testator; and

  2. It must be signed by the testator in the presence of at least two disinterested witnesses who attest to the will, each of whom must sign his or her name as a witness in the presence of each other as well as in the presence of the testator. The witnesses must be disinterested; that is, they must not stand to gain or lose financially as a result of the validity or nonvalidity of the will in question.

  3. The testator must declare the will to be the last will and testament at the time of affixing his or her signature. The testator need not reveal the contents of the will to the attesting witnesses.

FIGURE 11-2   FORMATION AND REVOCATION OF WILLS AND CODICILS

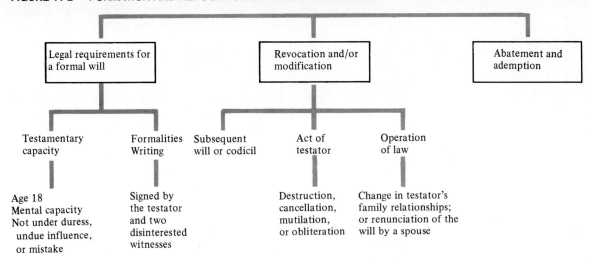

4. The *attestation* by witnesses includes a recitation that the will was signed, that it was declared by the testator as the last will and testament, and that the witnesses, at the request of the testator, in the testator's presence and in the presence of each other, signed their names as attesting witnesses.

F. Revocation and/or modification of wills by means of codicil or subsequent will.

   1. A *codicil* is a supplement or an addition to an existing will.

   2. All requirements for a valid will are necessary for a valid codicil.

   3. Where a codicil or subsequent will does not expressly revoke a prior will, the following rules apply:

      a. A subsequent will or codicil revokes a prior will insofar as it is inconsistent with the prior will;

      b. The prior will is revoked impliedly if the testator disposes of the entire estate in the codicil or subsequent will.

G. Revocation and/or modification of wills other than by codicil or subsequent will may be accomplished as follows:

   1. By physical action by the testator.

      a. A will may be revoked by the deliberate and intentional destruction, cancellation, or mutilation of the will itself, e.g., tearing, cutting, obliterating, or burning with intent to revoke.

      b. In some states, a partial revocation may be accomplished by erasures or obliteration of a part of the will if the testator intended not to revoke the entire will or codicil.

   2. By operation of law.

      a. A will may be revoked by implication from certain changes in the family relations of the testator, e.g., marriage, the birth of a child, or the adoption of a child.

      b. As a general rule, a subsequent divorce will impliedly revoke any existing testamentary provision for a spouse. This is especially true when the divorce is coupled with a property settlement.

      c. A surviving spouse in some states has a statutory *right to renounce a will* and to receive a statutory intestate share of the estate. The will is revoked only as to those provisions which are favorable to the renouncing spouse.

(1) This right is absolute, and court approval is not required.

(2) In order to exercise this right, the surviving spouse must execute and file a written renunciation within a statutorily prescribed time.

H. Abatement and ademption.

1. *Abatement* is a process of reducing devises and bequests during the administration of an estate when the total available assets in the estate are insufficient to satisfy the provisions of a will.

2. *Ademption* occurs when a specific bequest or devise becomes impossible to perform because of circumstances or events occurring after the execution of a will.

3. Suppose Green's assets are worth $50,000 when he bequeaths and devises $10,000 to his good friend Bone, $10,000 to his good friend Jones, his farm to his son Alfred, and the residue of the estate to his daughter Sue. Suppose further that at the time of Brown's death only $15,000 remains, with the farm having been sold to pay unforeseen debts. Both Jones and Bone would receive $7,500. Their gifts are said to have *abated*. Alfred would receive nothing since the special devise has been sold. The daughter, Sue, would also receive nothing since the $30,000 that Brown had intended her to inherit was not available. The gifts to Alfred and Sue are said to have *adeemed*.

I. Wills can incorporate extrinsic documents or other writings by reference. The following requirements must be met in order for a document or other writing to be incorporated in a will by reference:

1. The extrinsic documents must actually be in existence;

2. The will must also state that the document is in existence at the time of the execution of the will;

3. The testator must manifest intent to incorporate the document; and

4. The testator must describe the incorporated document sufficiently to identify it. For example, "I hereby adopt and reaffirm the bequests and devises made by me in my letter to my son, John, dated May 1, 1980."

ADMINISTRATION OF DECEDENTS' ESTATES (PROBATE)

III. In general. Whether a person dies intestate or leaves a will, it is necessary that an efficient and impartial method exist to protect the interests of creditors, to carry out testamentary provisions, and to identify those persons entitled to property under the applicable wills and the statutes of descent and distribution.

A. *Administrator* (man) or *administratix* (woman) is a person appointed by a court to administer the estate of a testate or intestate deceased person, i.e., the legal representative of a deceased person's estate. This person is hereinafter referred to as the administrator.

B. *Executor* (man) or *executrix* (woman) is a person appointed by a testator or the court to carry out the directions and requests in the will and to dispose of the property according to the will after death. This person is hereinafter referred to as the executor.

C. Duties of the administrator or executor include:

1. A fiduciary duty to the estate, i.e., a duty of absolute and unconditional loyalty;

2. To post a bond to ensure faithful performance of his or her duties unless the requirement of a bond is excused by the will; and

3. To collect all assets, pay all debts and expenses, and transfer title to the decedent's property according to the decedent's will and, if there was no will, according to the law.

IV. The steps in administration of a decedent's estate are as follows:

A. A petition to appoint either an executor or administrator is filed.

B. The executor or administrator is appointed by the court.

C. Where the decedent died testate, all copies of the will must be proved before the court by the witnesses.

    1. The witnesses must testify as to the validity of all signatures on the will and to the mental condition of the testator at the time of the execution of the will.

    2. If witnesses are dead or cannot be located, proof of their handwriting is necessary. Upon proof of the will, a formal decree will be entered, admitting the will to probate.

D. Proof of heirship is required whether the decedent died testate or intestate. *Proof of heirship* is the identification of and notice to those persons who may be entitled under the law to a decedent's property.

E. The personal representative (executor or administrator) must collect and preserve all of the decedent's assets and then file an inventory of the total of the estate with the court.

F. The personal representative has a duty to invest proceeds prudently and otherwise manage the estate.

G. The personal representative is under a duty to publish a notice that all claims and debts against the decedent's estate must be filed and proved within a certain period of time.

H. Thereafter, the personal representative must pay filed and proved claims in the following order of priorities:

    1. Federal and state death and income taxes;

    2. Widow's award (a cash allowance entitled to the widow pending final settlement);

    3. Funeral expenses;

    4. Secured creditors;

    5. General creditors;

    6. Final distribution to appropriate devises or legatees or heirs.

I. The personal representative must file a final report with the court and petition that the representative be finally discharged from his or her duties and that the estate be closed.

J. The final step in administration is an order by the court discharging the personal representative from his or her duties and closing the decedent's estate.

TRUSTS

V. Definition. A *trust* occurs whenever legal title to property is held by one person (trustee) for the use and benefit of another person (beneficiary). (See Figure 11-3.)

VI. Essential elements for the creation of a trust.

    A. A trust must have at least two parties, i.e., *a trustee and existing, identifiable beneficiary or beneficiaries*.

    B. The settlor must expressly or impliedly manifest an *intention* to create a trust.

    C. The settlor must have an *existing right in the trust corpus* at the time of its creation.

    D. The *trust corpus* must be identified with reasonable certainty.

    E. The *purpose* of the trust must be specified. It must be a lawful purpose. If not, it is void.

VII. Formalities of a trust.

    A. A trust may be created either orally or in writing. However, an express trust of real property must be in writing under the Statute of Frauds.

    B. A contract is not necessary for a valid declaration of trust; i.e., neither an agreement or consideration is required. For example, S deposited 2,000 shares of common

FIGURE 11-3 LEGAL STRUCTURE OF A TRUST

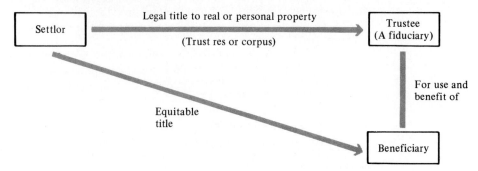

stock in a bank and declared a trust as a gift of the income from the stock to Z for ten years.

VIII. Parties to a trust.

    A. *Settlor* is the person who declares (creates) the trust.

        1. The settlor may also be a trustee or beneficiary but not both.

        2. The settlor may revoke the trust only if the trust instrument so provides.

        3. The settlor must have the legal capacity to make a contract.

    B. *Trustee* is the person who receives and holds title to property in trust.

        1. The trustee may be any person or entity possessing legal capacity to hold title to property.

        2. A person or entity cannot be forced to serve as a trustee.

        3. If a trustee accepts the trust, the trustee is invested with legal title to the trust property.

        4. If the trustee does not accept or does not have the capacity to serve as a trustee, a court will appoint a trustee. A court will never allow a trust to fail for lack of a trustee.

        5. The three primary *duties of the trustee* are as follows:

            a. The trustee must carry out the purpose of the trust as provided for in the trust agreement.

            b. The trustee must act with *prudence and care* (prudent investor rule) in the administration of the trust so as to conserve trust capital and realize income consistent with the security of the capital.

                (1) Some states restrict investments to those made only from a prescribed list.

                (2) Other states are more permissive; however, the trustee carries the burden of showing that a prudent choice was made if the investment was not on the prescribed list.

                (3) Trust instrument provision may allow the trustee wide discretion as to types of investments. The discretion allowed may include investments not within a statutory list. This wide discretion does not relieve a trustee from the general duty of prudence and care.

            c. The trustee owes a *fiduciary duty* to the beneficiary.

        6. The *powers of a trustee* are determined by:

            a. The law of the state in which the trust is established; and

            b. The provisions in the instrument which created the trust.

        7. The *liabilities of trustee* are as follows:

            a. The trustee is personally liable on contracts made on behalf of the trust (unless the contract provides otherwise). However, the trustee may be reimbursed from trust property.

    b. The trustee is personally liable for torts committed by the trustee or by agents of the trustee. However, as in the case of contracts, the trustee may be reimbursed from trust property.

  8. *Termination of a trustee's duties.*

    a. The trustee may resign at any time if serving without compensation or without a written agreement as to duration.

    b. If the trustee is a compensated trustee or has signed an agreement to serve as trustee for a specified duration, the trustee may be relieved of his or her duties only under the following circumstances:

      (1) By order of court;

      (2) By consent of all the beneficiaries; or

      (3) By discharge or release in accordance with the terms of trust instrument.

C. *Beneficiary* is the equitable owner of the trust and the person entitled to its benefits, unless otherwise provided in the trust declaration.

  1. The beneficiary may be any person, entity, or thing (e.g., cats, houses, charities, etc.), including the settlor.

  2. Unless specifically restricted by the trust instrument, a beneficiary's interest may be:

    a. Attached by creditors;

    b. Sold by the beneficiary to a third person; or

    c. Passed to heirs, if the beneficiary held more than a life estate in the trust.

D. Other legal parties.

  1. *Income beneficiary* is a person or persons entitled to receive the current income produced by the trust property, e.g., current interest on bonds owned by the trust.

  2. *Remainderman* is a person or persons who have the right to receive the title to trust property upon accomplishment of the trust purpose or termination of the trust. If the duration of the trust was twenty-five years with the yearly income going to B and the remainder going to C, C would not receive any income or yearly interest. However, C would own the entire trust property after the expiration of twenty-five years.

  3. The income beneficiary and the remainderman may be one and the same person or persons.

  4. *Reversioner* is the person entitled to receive title to the trust property after the trust ends when no remainderman is named. For example, in a trust declared by S "to T in trust with income payable to B for her life," the settlor is the reversioner.

E. As a general rule, a trust is a legal entity for tax purposes and is taxable as such.

IX. Types of trusts (see Figure 11-4).

A. *Express trust* is created by the intentional act of the settlor. This type may be either *inter vivos* or *testamentary* (created by a will).

  1. An *inter vivos trust* comes into existence during the lifetime of the settlor.

  2. A *testamentary trust* is one which comes into existence upon the death of the settlor. It must comply with the formalities for a will.

  3. *Charitable trust* may be either *inter vivos* or testamentary.

    a. A charitable trust differs from a private trust as follows:

      (1) The purpose of the trust is to fulfill some general or specific social purpose.

      (2) The time duration is unlimited.

      (3) The beneficiaries need not be definite and identifiable persons. For example, a trust to provide medical payments for the poor in LaSalle, Illinois.

FIGURE 11-4   CLASSIFICATION OF TRUSTS

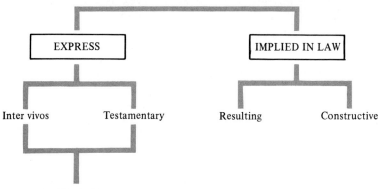

1. Charitable
2. Spendthrift
3. Totten

    b. The *cy pres doctrine* is applicable only to charitable trusts. The doctrine is applied whenever a settlor manifests a general charitable intent to benefit a specified charity but that charity does not or never did exist. Rather than cause the trust to fail for lack of a beneficiary, the court will itself designate a beneficiary which is most closely in keeping with the settlor's general charitable intent. For example, a trust fund set up to aid in the abolition of slavery. Before the trust came into existence, slavery was abolished. To prevent the trust from failing for lack of a beneficiary, the court declared the trust to remain in effect for the benefit of the black race.

    4. *Spendthrift trust* may be either *inter vivos* or testamentary. It is created by a trust agreement which prohibits any transfer of a beneficiary's rights by assignment or otherwise and prevents creditors of the beneficiary from attaching (obtaining) the trust principal or its income until it is actually paid to the beneficiary.

    5. *Totten trust* (savings bank trust) is a deposit of money in a bank "in trust" for another person.

        a. A mere deposit is not sufficient to support irrevocability of the totten trust.

        b. The following factors are considered by courts to ascertain the existence of an irrevocable totten trust (no individual factor is conclusive as to the existence of the trust):

           (1) An express statement by the depositor of the intent to create the trust;

           (2) Notice by the depositor to the beneficiary of the deposit in trust;

           (3) Delivery of a savings bankbook to the beneficiary;

           (4) Failure of depositor to withdraw the balance before death; and

           (5) A close relationship of depositor to beneficiary.

    6. *Massachusetts (business) Trust* (see Chapter 15, XXIV). This type of trust is a form of a business organization rather than a "pure" trust as explained in this chapter.

    7. *Real estate investment trust (REIT)* (see Chapter 15, XXV).

B. *Implied trust* is one created by operation of law.

    1. *Resulting trust* is a trust which arises out of a presumed intention of a settlor to create a trust when the intent to do otherwise is not adequately expressed. A resulting trust may be implied in law under the following circumstances:

        a. Failure of an express trust for any reason;

TABLE 11-1   ALLOCATION TO TRUST PRINCIPAL (CORPUS) AND INCOME
The Uniform Principal and Income Act (See page 348)

Description of event	Allocated to principal	Allocated to income
Receipts		
1. Consideration received for sale or exchange of trust principal (corpus)	X	
2. Receipt of repayment of loan from trust principal (corpus)	X	
3. Replacement or change in the form of principal (corpus)	X	
4. Proceeds from insurance on property forming part of the principal (corpus)	X	
5. Stock dividend	X	
6. Distributions upon liquidation of a corporation	X	
7. Rent receipts from lease of trust real or personal property		X
8. Interest received on money loaned including prepayment penalties		X
9. Stock split	X	
10. Stock warrants (a writing, evidencing the right to purchase shares or other securities, issued to the trust as owner of shares of stock)	X	
11. Proceeds from the sale of stock owned by the trust	X	
12. Cash dividends paid on trust stock		X
13. A right to purchase stock or bonds of a corporation *other than* that of the distributing corporation		X
14. Liquidating dividends, i.e., cash dividends paid out of stated capital or paid in surplus	X	
15. Script or property dividends		X
Expenditures		
1. Improvements, i.e., expenditures for repairs, or maintenance, the effect of which is to materially or substantially increase the value of trust property (traditional rules of capitalization)	X	
2. Expenditures for the purpose of merely preserving the normal operating efficiency or utility of depreciable trust assets		X
3. Ordinary expenses incurred in the administration, management, or preservation of trust property, e.g., payments for property insurance, payment of assessed recurring taxes on trust property, interest expense, and utilities		X
4. A reasonable allowance for depreciation of trust property		X
5. Court costs, attorney fees, or other fees if expenses relate primarily to protection or preservation of income beneficiary's interests		X
6. Costs, expenses, and fees expended by a trustee to protect the income of the trust		X
7. Costs, expenses, and fees expended by a trustee to defend the trust or the title to any trust corpus	X	
8. Expenses for preparation of trust corpus for sale or lease	X	
9. Real estate taxes on trust corpus		X
10. Casualty insurance premiums on trust corpus		X
11. Loss on sale of rental property owned by the trust	X	
12. Capital gains distribution from mutual fund shares owned by the trust		X
13. Amortization payment to liquidate a mortgage on trust corpus	X	

b. An express trust is fully performed without exhausting the trust property;

c. Where one party (A) pays the purchase price of property but title is taken in the name of another party (B) without the intention of making a gift. The presumption here is that the parties intended B to hold the property for the benefit of A, and B will be treated as a trustee upon a resulting trust.

2. *Constructive trust* is a remedial device in the form of a trust created by operation of law to prevent unjust enrichment.

    a. It arises regardless of the intentions of the parties.

    b. A constructive trust will be declared to exist whenever one person acquires money or property from another under the following circumstances:

        (1) By breach of that person's fiduciary duty. For example, a corporate executive who makes an undisclosed profit in a deal with the corporation will be treated as a trustee for the corporation to the extent of the profit;

        (2) By wrongful killing of another in order to acquire a benefit. For example, the beneficiary of a life insurance policy murders the named insured;

        (3) By fraud, mistake, duress, or undue influence.

ALLOCATIONS TO TRUST INCOME OR PRINCIPAL (CORPUS)

X. The trustee has a duty to properly allocate trust increments and expenses to either *trust principal (corpus)* or *trust income*. The Uniform Principal and Income Act which has been adopted by most states provides the rules that must be followed by a trustee in making allocations to either principal (corpus) or income. (See Table 11-1.)

XI. Termination of the trust.

    A. Methods.

        1. End of the term specified in the trust declaration.

        2. Achievement of the trust purpose.

        3. Merger. The legal and equitable estate become vested in the same person. For example, the life tenant of the trust sells his or her interest to the owner of the vested remainder.

        4. Failure of trust purpose.

            a. A private or charitable trust terminates if its performance becomes illegal or impossible.

            b. A charitable trust will not terminate because of impossibility of performance if the *cy pres* doctrine is applicable. See IX-A-3-b above.

    B. Duties of the trustee upon termination of the trust.

        1. The trustee must transfer title to trust property to those persons entitled to it under the trust declaration within a reasonable time after the trust terminates.

        2. The trustee's legal interest in the trust property and his or her fiduciary duty terminate when the trustee has made a proper distribution of the trust property, together with any accumulated income.

SELF-QUIZ

To check your understanding of the key words and concepts and the accuracy of your answers to the questions, refer to the text material as referenced by page number.

KEY WORDS AND CONCEPTS

QUESTIONS

1. Do federal or state statutes govern testamentary and intestate succession? **(338)**
2. What is the importance of intestate succession to a decedent's heirs? **(338)**
3. Explain the difference between holographic, nuncupative, soldiers' and sailors', conditional, and joint wills. **(340)**
4. What are the requirements of a formal will? **(340)**
5. In what manner may a will be revoked? **(341)**
6. Describe the duties of an executor and an administrator. **(342)**
7. List the steps in the administration of a decedent's estate. **(342)**
8. What property is included in the administration of a decedent's estate? **(343)**
9. Name the parties to a trust and explain their respective rights, duties, and legal or equitable interests. **(344)**
10. What is trust property? **(343)**
11. What are the legal requirements for a valid trust? **(343)**
12. List and explain the duties of a trustee. **(344)**
13. Distinguish between the following types of trusts:
    a. Express and implied **(346)**
    b. *Inter vivos* and testamentary **(345)**
    c. Charitable and private **(345)**
    d. Spendthrift and totten **(346)**
    e. Resulting and constructive **(346)**
14. Identify the distinction between trust income and trust corpus, and explain how each may be increased or diminished. **(347)**
15. List the methods by which a trust may be terminated. **(347)**
16. Review Table 11-1. **(347)**

SELECTED QUESTIONS AND UNOFFICIAL ANSWERS

OBJECTIVE QUESTIONS

Select the best answer for each of the following items. Mark only one answer for each item. Answer all items.

MAY 1981

49. With respect to trusts, which of the following states an *invalid* legal conclusion?
a. The trustee must obtain the consent of the majority of the beneficiaries if a major change in the investment portfolio of the trust is to be made.
b. For federal income tax purposes, a trust is entitled to an exemption similar to that of an individual although *not* equal in amount.
c. Both the life beneficiaries of a trust and the ultimate takers have rights against the trustee, and the trustee is accountable to them.
d. A trust is a separate taxable entity for federal income tax purposes.

50. The last will and testament of Jean Bond left various specific property and sums of money to relatives and friends. She left the residue of her estate equally to her favorite niece and nephew. Which of the various properties described below will become a part of Bond's estate and be distributed in accordance with her last will and testament?
a. A joint savings account which listed her sister, who is still living, as the joint tenant.
b. The entire family homestead which she had owned in joint tenancy with her older brother

who predeceased her and which was still recorded as jointly owned.
c. Several substantial gifts that she made in contemplation of death to various charities.
d. A life insurance policy which designated a former partner as the beneficiary.

51. Shepard created an inter vivos trust for the benefit of his children with the remainder to his grandchildren upon the death of his last surviving child. The trust consists of both real and personal property. One of the assets is an apartment building. In administering the trust and allocating the receipts and disbursements, which of the following would be *improper*?
a. The allocation of forfeited rental security deposits to income.
b. The allocation to principal of the annual service fee of the rental collection agency.
c. The allocation to income of the interest on the mortgage on the apartment building.
d. The allocation to income of the payment of the insurance premiums on the apartment building.

NOVEMBER 1980

45. The Marquis Trust has been properly created and it qualifies as a real estate investment trust (REIT) for federal income tax purposes. As such, it will
a. Be taxed as any other trust for income tax purposes.
b. Have been created under the Federal Trust Indenture Act.
c. Provide limited liability for the parties investing in the trust.
d. Be exempt from the Securities Act of 1933.

49. James Gordon decided to create an inter vivos trust for the benefit of his grandchildren. Gordon wished to bypass his own children and to provide an independent income for his grandchildren. He did not, however, wish to completely part with the assets he would transfer to the trust. Therefore, he transferred the assets to the York Trust Company in trust for the benefit of his grandchildren irrevocably for a period of 21 years. In relation to the Gordon trust and the rights and duties of the parties in respect to it
a. Such a trust is quite useful in skipping generations and tying up the ownership of property, since its duration can be potentially infinite.

b. The trust is *not* recognized as a legal entity for tax purposes, thus Gordon must include the trust income with his own.
c. York has legal title to the trust property, the grandchildren have equitable title, and Gordon has a reversionary interest.
d. If the trust deed is silent on the point, York must *not* sell or otherwise dispose of the trust assets without Gordon's advice and consent.

50. Paul Good's will left all of his commercial real property to his wife Dorothy for life and the remainder to his two daughters, Joan and Doris, as tenants in common. All beneficiaries are alive and over 21 years of age. Regarding the rights of the parties, which of the following is a correct statement?
a. Dorothy may *not* elect to take against the will and receive a statutory share instead.
b. The daughters *must* survive Dorothy in order to receive any interest in the property.
c. Either of the daughters may sell her interest in the property without the consent of their mother or the other daughter.
d. If only one daughter is alive upon the death of Dorothy, she is entitled to the entire property.

51. Larson is considering the creation of either a lifetime (inter vivos) or testamentary (by his will) trust. In deciding what to do, which of the following statements is correct?
a. If the trust is an inter vivos trust, the trustee must file papers in the appropriate state office roughly similar to those required to be filed by a corporation to qualify.
b. An inter vivos trust must meet the same legal requirements as one created by a will.
c. Property transferred to a testamentary trust upon the grantor's (creator's) death is *not* included in the decedent's gross estate for federal tax purposes.
d. Larson can retain the power to revoke an inter vivos trust.

52. An executor named in a decedent's will
a. Must consent to serve, have read the will, and be present at the execution of the will.
b. Need *not* serve if he does *not* wish to do so.
c. Must serve without compensation unless the will provides otherwise.
d. Can *not* be the principal beneficiary of the will.

28. The Astor Bank and Trust Company is the trustee of the Wayne Trust. A significant portion of the trust principal has been invested in AAA rated public utility bonds. Some of the bonds have been purchased at face value, some at a discount, and others at a premium. Which of the following is a proper allocation of the various items to income?

a. The income beneficiary is entitled to the entire interest without dilution for the premium paid but is *not* entitled to the proceeds attributable to the discount upon collection.

b. The income beneficiary is entitled to the entire interest without dilution and to the proceeds attributable to the discount.

c. The income beneficiary is only entitled to the interest less the amount of the premium amortized over the life of the bond.

d. The income beneficiary is entitled to the full interest and to an allocable share of the gain resulting from the discount.

40. Waldorf's last will and testament named Franklin as the executor of the will. In respect to Franklin's serving as executor, which of the following is correct?

a. He serves without compensation unless the will provides otherwise.

b. He is at liberty to purchase the estate's property the same as any other person dealing at arm's length.

c. Waldorf must have obtained Franklin's consent in writing to serve as executor.

d. Upon appointment by the court, he serves as the legal representative of the estate.

Answers to Objective Questions

May 1981			
49. a	**51.** b		
50. b			

November 1980		
45. c	**51.** d	
49. c	**52.** b	
50. c		

May 1980	
28. a	**40.** d

Explanation of Answers to Objective Questions

May 1981

49. (a) A trust is a fiduciary relationship wherein one person (trustee) holds legal title to property for the benefit of another (beneficiary). A trustee has the power to do what is necessary to fulfill the terms of the trust. A trustee cannot speculate, must diversify and can make major changes in an investment portfolio without the consent of beneficiaries. Answer (b) is not incorrect because a simple trust is entitled to a $300 per year exemption for federal tax purposes which is similar to an individual's exemption. Answer (c) is not incorrect because a trustee is a fiduciary to the beneficiaries and can take no personal advantage from his position. All beneficiaries can sue for mismanagement, conversion or waste by the trustee. A trustee must also keep trust assets separate from his personal assets and be accountable for both trust assets and his actions. Answer (d) is not an incorrect statement since a trust is a separate taxable entity for federal income tax purposes although it may not be subject to any tax.

50. (b) A joint tenancy is a form of concurrent property ownership in which the joint tenants have a right of survivorship in the property concurrently held. Thus, if a joint tenant dies, that tenant's interest in the property is divided equally among the surviving joint tenants. The deceased tenant's interest in the property will not pass to his heirs. Since Jean had full ownership of the property upon her brother's death and on her death, such property is properly included in her estate. Answer (a) is incorrect because, upon Jean's death, her sister will receive full ownership of the savings account regardless of any provision to the contrary in a will. Answer (c) is incorrect since gifts made in contemplation of death are irrevocable once made. Answer (d) is incorrect since a life insurance policy will pass to the named beneficiary without regard to the will of the deceased.

51. (b) An inter vivos trust comes into existence while the settlor (grantor) is living. The allocation of trust items to principal and income is governed by the Uniform Principal and Income Act (adopted by most states). Allocations made to trust principal include: original trust property, proceeds and gains from sale of trust property, insurance received on destruction of property, new property purchased with principal or proceeds from the principal, stock dividends and splits and a reserve for depreciation. Disbursements from trust principal are for reduction of indebtedness, litigation over trust property, permanent improvements and costs related to purchase/sale of trust property. Income includes profits from trust principal, e.g., rent, interest, cash dividends and royalties. Expenses from income include interest, insurance premiums, taxes, repairs, and depreciation. The annual service fee should be allocated to income because it is an expense associated with administration and management of trust property. It should not be allocated to principal. Answers (a), (c), and (d) are all proper allocations to income.

NOVEMBER 1980

45. (c) The certificateholders (owners) of a real estate investment trust have limited liability. Their liability is limited to their investment in the trust similar to the limited liability of a shareholder in a corporation and a limited partner. Thus answer (c) is correct. Answer (d) is incorrect because the sale of an interest in a real estate investment trust is the sale of a security under the Securities Act of 1933. Consequently, the seller of these interests would have to comply with the registration requirements of this act. A real estate investment trust does not fall within the provisions of the Federal Trust Indenture Act. This makes answer (b) incorrect. The normal trust, as distinguished from a real estate investment trust, is a taxable entity for income tax purposes, while a real estate investment trust is not a taxable entity. Ordinary income passes through to the investors and each investor pays income tax on his/her share.

49. (c) A trust is a fiduciary relationship in which one person, the trustee, has legal title to the property and another person, the beneficiary, has equitable title. Upon termination of the trust, the property is disposed of according to the stated desires of the settlor (creator of the trust). Thus answer (c) is correct. Answer (a) is incorrect because a trust is considered a taxable entity for income tax purposes. If a trust deed is silent, the trustee has the authority to sell trust property if necessary to carry out the trust purpose. This makes answer (d) incorrect. Answer (a) is incorrect because the rule against perpetuities states that the duration of a trust cannot be infinite and can never exceed "a life in being plus 21 years." The rationale behind this rule is to prevent the tying up of title to property for an unreasonable length of time.

50. (c) The will created a life estate in Dorothy, the wife, and a vested remainder in fee simple that the daughters owned as tenants in common. This means that the daughters' ownership rights to the property came into existence when Paul, the decedent, died, even though their right of possession does not occur until Dorothy dies and her life estate terminates. One daughter could sell her interest without the consent of either of the other two parties. Answer (c) is correct. Answer (a) is incorrect because a spouse under the concept of statutory share has the right to denounce the will and elect to take stated share (normally 1/3) of the dead spouse's estate. Answer (d) is incorrect because the daughters received the remainder as tenants in common, not as joint tenants. Tenancy in common does not have the right of survivorship, thus if one of the daughters predeceased Dorothy, the interest of the dead daughter would pass by the deceased daughter's estate.

51. (d) A settlor may revoke a trust if the trust instrument reserves this right. Thus answer (d) is correct. Creation of an inter vivos (living) trust only need be in writing when the trust involves real property or where performance is not capable of being completed in one year from the date of creation. Inter vivos trusts involving personal property can be oral. Testamentary trusts must meet the same legal requirements for a valid will (i.e., in writing, signed, witnessed, etc.). Thus answers (a) and (b) are incorrect. Answer (c) is incorrect because property in a testamentary trust is considered to have been transferred at the decedent's death and is therefore part of the decedent's gross estate for federal estate tax purposes.

52. (b) An executor is the personal representative of the decedent that is named in a will. If the decedent died intestate then the court would appoint an administrator as the personal representative. The person named as executor can decline to serve in which case the court will then appoint a substitute. If the will does not provide compensation for the services of an executor the court will order that the person serving in this capacity receive a reasonable fee for services rendered. The executor can be the principal beneficiary of the will, but need not have read the will nor be present at the signing of the will.

28. (a) Normally the income beneficiary is entitled to all interest earned by the items making up the corpus of the trust and the principal beneficiary is charged with any loss or gain relevant to the value of the corpus of the trust. Thus, answer (a) is correct.

40. (d) An executor is the legal representative of an estate when the decedent died testate (with a valid will). The executor has the right to be compensated unless the will denies such right. He is in a fiduciary relationship with the estate and thus is not like any other person dealing at arm's length. There is no need to obtain the consent in writing of the individual designated as executor. Naturally, the designated person can decline serving in such a capacity.

ESSAY QUESTIONS AND ANSWERS

MAY 1976 (Estimated time: 7 to 10 minutes)

7. Part b. You have been assigned by a CPA firm to work with the trustees of a large trust in the preparation of the first annual accounting to the court. The income beneficiaries and the remaindermen are in dispute as to the proper allocation of the following items on which the trust indenture is silent:

1. Costs incurred in expanding the garage facilities of an apartment house owned by the trust and held for rental income.
2. Real estate taxes on the apartment house.
3. Cost of casualty insurance premiums on the apartment house.
4. A two-for-one-stock split of common stock held by the trust for investment.
5. Insurance proceeds received as the result of a partial destruction of an office building which the trust owned and held for rental income.
6. Costs incurred by the trust in the sale of a tract of land.
7. Costs incurred to defend title to real property held by the trust.

Required

1. Explain briefly the nature of a trust, the underlying concepts in the allocation between principal and income, and the importance of such allocations.
2. Indicate the allocations between principal and income to be made for each of the above items.

Answer

1. A trust generally involves a transfer of income-producing property (principal) by will, deed, or indenture to a trustee who takes legal title to the property subject to a fiduciary obligation to manage and conserve the property for the benefit of others who are described as beneficiaries. A trust generally provides that the trustee shall invest the trust principal and pay the income therefrom to the income beneficiary and at the termination of the trust transfer the trust principal to the remainderman. The property that composes the principal of the trust may change from time to time as the trustee sells and reinvests the proceeds.

The will or trust agreement can provide the rules for allocation of items between principal and income. In the absence of specific trust provisions, the law of the jurisdiction in which the trust is located will govern. For this purpose, most jurisdictions have adopted the Uniform Principal and Income Act or some variation thereof. Income produced by the investment and management of the trust principal is kept separate for distribution to the income beneficiary. However, ordinary operating expenses incurred by the trust in generating earnings are charged against income. Similarly, expenses incurred in acquiring or protecting the trustee's title to principal are charged against principal. Thus, the allocation between principal and income of a trust is of great importance because it affects the respective benefits derived from the trust by the income beneficiary and the remainderman.

2. (1) Principal, (2) income, (3) income, (4) principal, (5) principal, (6) principal, (7) principal.

CHAPTER

12

Insurance

The following is a generalized listing of subjects to be tested through the May 1983 Uniform CPA Examination.

Under this topic primary emphasis is placed upon life and property insurance in relation to the successful management of a business. The topic embraces matters such as insurable interests in individuals and property, assignability of insurance policies, coinsurance, and other standard policy provisions.[1]

Note: Life insurance will no longer be a subject to be tested on the Uniform CPA Examination beginning with the November 1983 examination.[2]

The AICPA Board of Examiners has adopted a new content specification outline for the business law section of the Uniform CPA Examination, *to be effective with the November 1983 examination.* The outline lists the following topics to be tested under the title "Fire and Casualty Insurance."

    D. Fire and Casualty Insurance
      1. Coinsurance
      2. Multiple Insurance Coverage
      3. Insurable Interest[3]

---

[1] AICPA, *Information for CPA Candidates, Copyright* © 1975, 1979 by the American Institute of Certified Public Accountants, Inc.

[2] AICPA, *Business Law—Content Specification Outline,* approved by the AICPA Board of Examiners on August 31, 1981.

[3] AICPA, *Business Law—Content Specification Outline,* approved by the AICPA Board of Examiners on August 31, 1981.

NATURE AND PURPOSE

I. Insurance is a device used to distribute and equalize individual losses.
   A. *Nature.*
      1. *Insurance* is a contract to transfer risk of financial loss.
      2. An insurance contract is not a wagering agreement. A wagering agreement creates a risk which did not previously exist. An insurance contract transfers an existing risk.
      3. An insurer, in exchange for consideration called a *premium*, obligates itself to pay an insured or the insured's beneficiary a specified amount for financial loss caused by specific peril or perils. (See Figure 12-1.)
   B. *Purpose.*
      1. The primary purpose of insurance is to provide protection from the occurrence of a contingent event over which an insured has little or no control.
      2. A secondary purpose is to provide a means of accumulating savings, e.g., an endowment life insurance contract.

DEFINITIONS

II. The following definitions are important to the study of insurance:
   A. *Application* is a request for insurance made by a party applying for an insurance policy.
   B. *Policy* is a written contract of insurance.
   C. *Loss* is a financial injury resulting from the occurrence of the contingency insured against by a policy of insurance.
   D. *Peril* is a risk, hazard, or contingency insured against by a policy of insurance.
   E. *Beneficiary* is the person to whom the proceeds (face value or accumulated cash values) of an insurance policy are payable.
   F. *Insurer* is the insurance company with whom a contract of insurance is made.
   G. *Insured* is any person who acquires insurance on property in which that person has an insurable interest or a person upon whose life an insurance policy is effected.
   H. *Owner* of an insurance policy is a person who possesses the right to exercise the various rights provided for in the insurance policy. The owner usually is also the insured; however, this need not be the case.
   I. *Insurable interest* is present whenever a person has a legal or equitable interest in the property or life insured such that that person will suffer a financial loss by its destruction or a financial benefit from its preservation. An insurable interest is necessary to have a valid insurance contract.
   J. *Binder* is an agreement for insurance. It may provide for insurance coverage effective immediately upon its execution or subsequently upon the occurrence of a condition precedent.
   K. *Nonforfeiture option* is the right of an owner of a life insurance policy to receive its accumulated cash value if the policy terminates for nonpayment of premiums.

FIGURE 12-1   LEGAL STRUCTURE OF AN INSURANCE CONTRACT

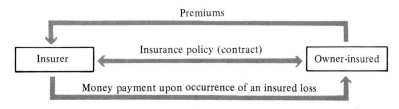

L. *Settlement option* is the right of an owner of an insurance policy or its beneficiary to specify the manner of distribution of proceeds (face value or accumulated cash values) of the policy.

M. *Lapse* is the termination of insurance coverage for failure of the insured to pay premiums when due.

N. *Valued policy* is one in which an agreed evaluation is placed on property at the time the policy is issued. The insurer obligates itself to pay the insured the agreed-upon value of the policy upon total destruction of the insured property, e.g., a fire insurance policy. The agreed-upon value must be paid regardless of the value of the insured property at the time of the total loss.

O. *Open (nonvalued) policy* is one in which the insurer is obligated to pay the insured the amount of actual loss subject to a maximum amount stated in the policy, e.g., a fire insurance policy.

P. *Blanket (floating) policy* is an open policy which covers a class of constantly changing property at a specified location, e.g., inventory or fungible goods.

FORMATION OF INSURANCE CONTRACTS

III. As a general rule, the insurance policy must meet the same legal requirements as any other contract in order to be valid. (See Figure 12-2.)

    A. *Offer and acceptance.*

        1. *Life and health insurance contracts.* Where no binder is issued, the following common law rules apply:

            a. An application accompanied by the first premium is an offer. Acceptance occurs when the insurer delivers the policy to the applicant.

            b. An application submitted without the first premium is merely an invitation to the insurer to submit an offer.

                (1) The tender of a policy to the applicant is the offer.

                (2) Acceptance occurs when the applicant pays the first premium to the company.

            c. Binders. When a premium is paid with the application *and a binder is issued*, a contract results; however, the effective date of insurance coverage is dependent upon the provisions of the binder.

        2. *Casualty (property) insurance contracts.* The existence of an offer and acceptance is not dependent upon the payment of a premium or a delivery of the policy. The protection becomes effective the moment the applicant and the insurance agent (broker) agree as to the coverage and identify the insurer.

FIGURE 12-2   ELEMENTS OF A VALID INSURANCE CONTRACT

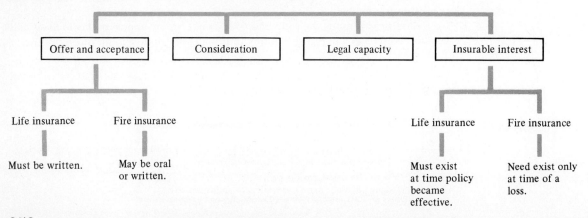

  a. The application of the insured is usually the offer.

  b. The application may be made in writing or by an oral request for coverage.

  c. Acceptance occurs at the time that the agent (broker) or the insurer indicates an acceptance of the application.

  d. A binder, when used in respect to casualty (property) insurance, provides immediate and temporary protection until the insurer completes an investigation of the risk and decides whether to issue a policy.

B. *Consideration* is necessary for a binding insurance contract.

C. *Legal capacity.* For an insurance policy to be legally binding, the parties to it must be legally competent to enter into a contract.

D. *Form.*

 1. Most states require life insurance contracts to be in writing.

 2. Casualty (property) insurance contracts may be oral or in writing.

E. *Insurable interest.* An insurable interest in the life or property insured is required in both life and casualty (property) insurance.

 1. Where no insurable interest exists, the policy is void. The insurer may deny the validity of the policy. The insurer is obligated to refund all unearned premiums to the insured.

 2. In respect to life insurance, the insurable interest in the life of the insured must exist *at the time the policy is issued.* It need not exist thereafter.

 3. In the case of casualty (property) insurance, the insured must have an insurable interest in the property only *at the time of loss.*

 4. The following persons or entities have insurable interests in life:

  a. Spouses in the lives of each other;

  b. Parents in the lives of their children;

  c. Children in the lives of their parents;

  d. Any dependent person in the life of the person providing support;

  e. An employer in the life of a key employee;

  f. Partners in the lives of each other;

  g. Shareholders of a close corporation in the lives of each other;

  h. A creditor in the life of his or her debtor to the extent of the debt;

  i. Every person in his or her own life.

 5. The following persons or entities have an insurable interest in property:

  a. Owners of property, including tenants in common, joint tenants, life tenants, and remaindermen;

  b. Lessee in property leased;

  c. Bailee in property bailed;

  d. Pledgee in property pledged;

  e. Mortgagee in property mortgaged;

  f. Buyer and seller in a contract for sale of property (real estate or personal property);

  g. Trustee in trust corpus;

  h. Shareholder of a close corporation in the property owned by the corporation.

F. A casualty (property) insurance contract *is* a contract of indemnity. A life insurance contract *is not* a contract of indemnity.

LIFE INSURANCE

 IV. Life insurance policies are classified as term, ordinary, limited-payment, and endowment insurance.

  A. Classification of life insurance policies (see Table 12-1).

   1. *Term* insurance.

TABLE 12-1 LIFE INSURANCE POLICY FEATURES COMPARED
Life Insurance and Life Insurance Contracts

Policy features	Ordinary (whole) life	Limited-pay life	Endowment	Term
Length of coverage	Permanent	Permanent	Temporary	Temporary
Death benefit (face value)	Yes	Yes	Yes	Yes
Cash values	Yes	Yes	Yes	No
Loan values	Yes	Yes	Yes	No
Length of time premiums payable	Until death or age 100	Until death or to a stated age	Until death or for a maximum stated period of time (endowment period)	Until death or until expiration of a stated term
When face value payable	At death or age 100	At death or age 100	At death during endowment period, or at the end of the endowment period	At death during term only

    a. The insurer is obligated to pay the face value of the policy only if the insured's death occurs within the specified term.
    b. Term insurance has no cash or loan value. It is the only type of life insurance that does not have a savings feature.
    c. Term policies are generally guaranteed renewable and convertible.
        (1) *Guaranteed renewable* means the insured has the right to renew the policy after each term without proof of insurability, up to a specified age.
        (2) *Guaranteed convertible* means the insured has the right to convert the term coverage to some other type of policy at his or her election.
    d. The insured is required to pay premiums for the specified term in order to maintain coverage.
  2. *Ordinary (straight) (whole)* life insurance.
    a. The insurer is obligated to pay the face value of the policy either upon the death of the insured or upon attainment of age 100, whichever occurs first.
    b. Ordinary life policies have cash and loan values which increase with the age of the policy. These values represent the savings feature of the policy.
    c. The insured is required to pay premiums until he or she dies or attains age 100, at which time the policy is paid in full.
  3. *Limited-payment* life insurance. The difference between this type and ordinary life is that the insured is required to pay premiums for only a specified number of years. At the end of that time, the policy is paid in full. If the insured's death occurs prior to that time, the insurer is obligated to pay the face value of the policy.
  4. *Endowment* insurance.
    a. The insurer is obligated to pay the face value of the policy upon the death of the insured or after the expiration of a specified period of time (endowment period).
    b. Endowment policies have cash and loan values which increase during the endowment period.
    c. The insured is required to pay premiums during the endowment period.

B. Common provisions included in life insurance policies.

1. *Grace period clause.* This clause allows the insured a specified period (usually thirty or thirty-one days) after the premium due date to pay a delinquent premium to prevent a lapse of the policy.

2. *Entire contract clause.* This clause provides that the policy and the application constitute the entire contract.

3. *Suicide clause.* This clause provides that the insurer is not liable on the policy in the event of suicide by the insured (while sane or insane) within a stated period of time after the policy is issued (usually two years).

4. *Misstatement-of-age clause.* If the insured had misstated his or her age, this clause allows the insurer to adjust the benefits so that the amount payable is only the amount the premium paid would have purchased at the correct age.

5. *Incontestability clause.* This clause prevents the insurer from contesting the policy on the basis of an applicant's fraud, misrepresentation, or concealment after the policy has been in force for a period of time (usually two years) during the lifetime of the insured. The clause does not prevent an insurer from contesting a policy on the following grounds:
   a. No insurable interest existed at the date the policy was issued.
   b. Someone other than the insured (an impostor) took the physical examination required by the insurer.
   c. The policy was taken out with intent to subsequently murder the insured.
   d. The insured misrepresented his or her age. Under the misstatement-of-age clause, proceeds payable can be adjusted to reflect the benefits actually purchased by the premiums paid, based on the insured's correct age.

6. *Reinstatement clause.* This clause allows the insured to reinstate a terminated policy upon meeting the following conditions:
   a. Reinstatement must be requested within (three) five years after date of premium default (if it has not been surrendered for its cash value).
   b. The insured must provide proof of insurability.
   c. The insured must pay all overdue premiums with interest at a rate specified in the policy.
   d. The insured must pay all outstanding loans on the policy with interest.

7. *Dividend options.* An applicant for a participating life insurance policy (one that pays dividends) is allowed to choose one of the following ways of receiving payment of dividends:
   a. Paid in cash to the owner of the policy;
   b. Applied to payment of premiums;
   c. Remain on deposit with the insurer at interest;
   d. Used to purchase paid-up additional insurance coverage;
   e. Added to cash value for purpose of paying up the policy in fewer years or causing the face value to mature earlier.

8. *Nonforfeiture options.* An owner of a life insurance policy may elect to surrender the policy to the insurer and receive any accrued cash value in the form of cash or paid-up permanent insurance coverage.

9. *Policy loan provision.* This provision gives the owner of an insurance policy the right to borrow its cash value without terminating the insurance coverage.

10. *Automatic premium loan provision.* This provision gives the insurer the right to automatically pay premiums from policy cash values and thereby prevent a lapse of the policy.

11. *Settlement options.* An owner of a life insurance policy or the beneficiary may elect any one of the following settlement options:
    a. Allow proceeds to remain on deposit with the insurer at interest;

b. Receive proceeds in equal installments over a fixed period of time (fixed-period option);

c. Receive the proceeds in fixed amount installments until all proceeds have been paid (fixed-amount option);

d. Receive equal installments payable during the life of the beneficiary (life annuity);

e. Receive the proceeds in a lump sum.

C. *Beneficiary designation.*

  1. A beneficiary may be designated as *revocable* or *irrevocable*.

    a. *Revocable.* The owner of the policy may change the beneficiary at any time prior to the insured's death without the consent of the beneficiary.

    b. *Irrevocable.* An irrevocable beneficiary is a coowner of the insurance policy. No rights under the policy can be exercised without the irrevocable beneficiary's consent.

  2. A beneficiary is not required to have an insurable interest.

  3. The following can be named beneficiaries by the owner of a life insurance policy:

    a. The owner;

    b. The insured;

    c. The insured's estate;

    d. A person other than the owner or insured;

    e. A trustee of a trust;

    f. An executor or administrator of the owner or insured.

D. *Rights of creditors in life insurance benefits and values.*

  1. Creditors of an insured who is not the owner of the policy have no rights to life insurance benefits or values either before or after the policy matures (by death or endowment).

  2. Rights of an owner's creditors.

    a. Prior to maturity (by death or endowment).

      (1) Owner is not a bankrupt.

        (*a*) If the policy is payable to the owner, the owner's estate, or the owner's legal representative, the cash values are subject to the owner's creditors.

        (*b*) If the policy is payable to other beneficiaries (revocably or irrevocably), the cash value cannot be reached by an owner's creditors.

      (2) Owner is a bankrupt.

        (*a*) If the policy is payable to the owner, the owner's estate, or the owner's legal representative, the cash value passes to the trustee in bankruptcy for the benefit of the owner's creditors.

        (*b*) If the policy is payable to other beneficiaries, the owner's creditors may or may not reach the cash value, depending upon the type of beneficiary designation and state exemption statutes.

          i. Irrevocable beneficiary designation. The cash value is not subject to the owner's creditors.

          ii. Revocable beneficiary designation. The cash value is subject to the owner's creditors unless it is exempt by state statute, for example a state statute exempting insurance values where the beneficiary is a spouse, parent, child, or other dependent of an insured.

    b. At maturity (death or endowment).

      (1) If the policy is payable to the owner, the owner's estate, or the owner's legal representative, the proceeds are subject to the owner's creditors.

   (2) If the policy is payable to other beneficiaries (revocably or irrevocably), the proceeds are not subject to the owner's creditors.
  3. Rights of a beneficiary's creditors (other than an owner, the owner's estate, or the owner's representative).
   a. Prior to maturity (death or endowment). Regardless of whether the designation is revocable or irrevocable, the cash value is not subject to the beneficiary's creditors.
   b. At maturity (death or endowment). As a general rule, proceeds payable to a beneficiary can be reached by the beneficiary's creditors. *Exception:* Where the beneficiary designation contains a spendthrift clause, the proceeds cannot be reached by the beneficiary's creditors until they have been paid to the beneficiary.
E. *Assignment of a life insurance contract (policy).*
 1. If the owner of the policy reserved the right to change the beneficiary (revocable designation), the contract is freely assignable.
 2. If the right to change beneficiaries was not reserved (irrevocable designation), the policy cannot be assigned without the consent of the beneficiary.
F. *Subrogation.* The right of subrogation is not available to an insurer on a life policy against a third person who caused the death of an insured.
G. *Business uses of life insurance.*
 1. *Key man insurance.*
  a. Employer is the applicant, owner, and beneficiary of the policy and the premium payor.
  b. Employee is named the insured.
  c. Ordinary or limited payment life insurance is usually used.
 2. *To provide employee fringe benefits.*
  a. Deferred-compensation employee benefits funded by life insurance cash values.
   (1) Employer is the applicant, owner, and beneficiary of the policy and the premium payor.
   (2) Employee is the insured.
   (3) The policy is chosen so that the accumulated cash value at the date of the employee's retirement is equal to an amount necessary to provide the employee a previously agreed upon pension (annuity).
   (4) Ordinary or limited-payment life insurance is usually used.
  b. Split-dollar insurance.
   (1) Employer is the applicant and owner of the policy.
   (2) Employee is named the insured.
   (3) Employee, employee's estate, or employee's dependents are named beneficiaries.
   (4) Ordinary life insurance is usually used.
   (5) Employee is given the option to purchase the policy from the employer for its cash value upon termination of employment.
   (6) Employer and employee share payment of premiums according to the following formula:
    (*a*) The employer pays the amount of each yearly premium which equals the annual increase in cash value. The employee pays the balance of the annual premium.
    (*b*) When the increase in cash value is equal to or greater than the annual premium, the employer is obligated to pay the full annual premium. The employee is no longer obligated to pay anything.

(7) Upon the death of the employee (insured), the employer is entitled to be paid an amount equal to the cash value of the policy at the time of death. The named beneficiary is paid the excess up to the face value of the policy.

3. *Credit life insurance* (see Figure 12-3).
    a. Creditor is the applicant, owner, beneficiary, and premium payor.
    b. Debtor is the insured.
    c. The amount of insurance carried is roughly equal to the outstanding debt.
    d. Term insurance is the type of insurance used.

4. *Mortgage protection life insurance* (see Figure 12-4).
    a. Mortgagor (owner of property subject to a mortgage lien) is the applicant, insured, owner, and premium payor.
    b. Mortgagor, mortgagor's estate, or mortgagor's dependents are named beneficiaries.
    c. The amount of insurance carried is roughly equal to the outstanding debt.
    d. Term insurance is the type of insurance used.

5. *Business continuation (buy and sell) agreements funded by life insurance death proceeds.* These agreements are commonly used by individual proprietors, partners, or shareholders of close corporations.
    a. Individual proprietor business continuation plan.
        (1) The individual proprietor enters into a contract with a son or daughter or a key employee in which the latter agrees to purchase and the proprietor agrees to sell the business at a stated value upon the death of the proprietor.
        (2) The contract requires the purchaser (son, daughter, or key employee) to purchase a life insurance policy on the life of the proprietor in an amount equal to the purchase price of the business.
        (3) The purchaser of the business is the applicant, owner, beneficiary, and premium payor.
        (4) Ordinary life insurance is the type of insurance purchased.
        (5) Heirs of the deceased proprietor are bound by the terms of the business continuation contract.
    b. *Entity and cross-purchase-type business continuation agreements* for partnerships and close corporations.

FIGURE 12-3   CREDIT LIFE INSURANCE

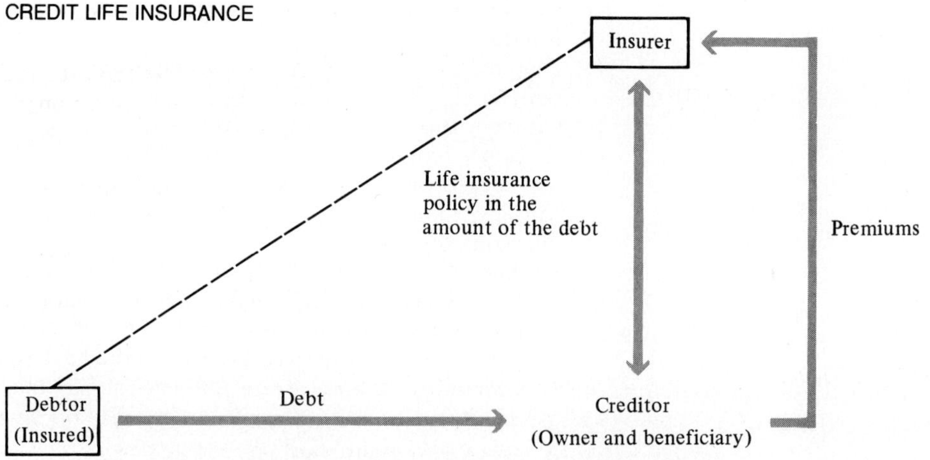

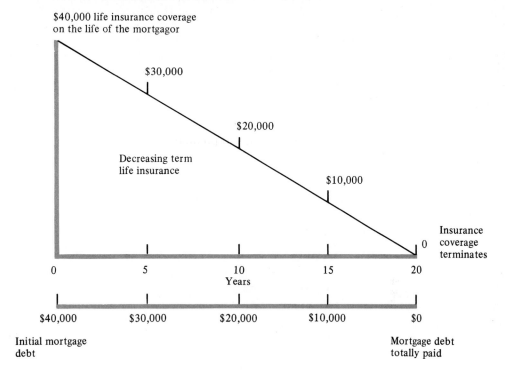

FIGURE 12-4   MORTGAGE PROTECTION LIFE INSURANCE:
20 YEARS, $40,000 DECREASING TERM LIFE INSURANCE

$40,000 life insurance coverage
on the life of the mortgagor

$30,000

$20,000

Decreasing term
life insurance

$10,000

Insurance
0   coverage
terminates

0   5   10   15   20

Years

$40,000 $30,000 $20,000 $10,000 $0

Initial mortgage
debt

Mortgage debt
totally paid

(1) In both the entity and cross-purchase plans, the owners (partners or shareholders) enter into a contract in which each agrees to purchase a proportionate ownership interest of each other upon his or her death and at a stated value.

(2) In the entity plan, the contract requires the entity (partnership or corporation) to purchase a life insurance policy on each of the lives of the owners (partners or shareholders) in an amount equal to the value of his or her ownership interest in the firm.

(3) In the entity plan, the entity is the applicant, owner, beneficiary, and premium payor.

(4) In the cross-purchase plan, the contract requires each owner (partner or shareholder) to purchase a life insurance policy on the lives of every other owner in an amount sufficient to pay for the proportionate ownership interest to be acquired.

(5) In the cross-purchase plan, each owner (partner or shareholder) is the applicant, owner, beneficiary, and premium payor.

(6) In both plans, ordinary life insurance is the type used.

(7) In both plans, the heirs of a deceased owner (partner or shareholder) are legally bound by the terms of the business continuation contract.

FIRE AND CASUALTY INSURANCE: FIRE INSURANCE

V. The Standard Fire Insurance Policy is used throughout the United States to provide indemnity for losses caused by fire and lightning to insured premises.

A. Fire policies are classified as follows:

   1. Valued policy. See II-N above.

   2. Open (nonvalued) policy. See II-O above.

   3. Blanket (floating) policy. See II-P above.

B. *Basic coverage.* The Standard Fire Insurance Policy provides coverage for loss to insured property by fire or lightning.

   1. A fire insurance policy covers loss caused by a hostile fire. It does not cover loss caused by a friendly fire.

      a. A *hostile fire* is one that burns where it is not intended to be confined.

      b. A *friendly fire* is one that burns in the place where it is intended to burn, e.g., a fireplace, a furnace, or a trash-burning container.

   2. The Standard Fire Insurance Policy generally covers direct damage to the structure and its contents by fire; indirect damage caused by smoke, heat, water, and chemicals used to extinguish the fire; damage caused by the efforts of firefighters in extinguishing the fire; and damage to property that is being removed to protect it from the fire.

C. *Optional additional coverage.* Additional coverage is available by amendment to the Standard Fire Insurance Policy. These amendments (attachments) are called "*forms*," "*endorsements*," or "*riders*." The amendments may be used to provide any or all of the following additional coverages:

   1. Damage caused by weight of ice, snow, and sleet;

   2. Appurtenant structures;

   3. Fair rental value of a dwelling during its restoration;

   4. "*Extended coverage*" (i.e., insurance against the perils of windstorm, hail, explosion, riot, riot attending a strike, civil commotion, aircraft, vehicles, and smoke);

   5. Vandalism and malicious mischief;

   6. Theft;

   7. Debris removal;

   8. Earthquake and volcanic eruption;

   9. Breakage of glass;

   10. Freezing the pipes;

   11. Collapse of buildings; or

   12. Falling objects.

D. *Recovery of loss.* Amount of recovery for loss is governed by the terms of the insurance contract.

   1. Partial destruction of the insured property. The amount recoverable is the actual loss sustained, but not in excess of the maximum amount provided in the policy.

   2. Total destruction of the insured property.

      a. Under a valued policy, the insured is entitled to recover the stated amount of the policy. The amount bears no relationship to the fair market value of the insured property at the time of loss.

      b. Under an open (nonvalued) policy, the insured is entitled to recover the amount of actual loss (fair market value at the time of loss) incurred, limited by the maximum amount of the coverage of the policy.

E. Common provisions included in fire insurance contracts.

   1. *Coinsurance clause.*

      a. This clause requires the insured to insure property at a stated percentage of its current value in order to recover the face amount of the policy.

      b. When the insured does not carry insurance equal to the agreed-upon percentage of current value of the property, recovery under the policy is based on the following formula:

$$\frac{\text{Dollar amount of insurance carried}}{\text{Dollar amount of insurance required to be carried}} \times \text{loss} = \text{dollar amount of recovery}$$

c. For example, an insured carried a fire insurance policy in the amount of $60,000 which contained an 80 percent coinsurance clause. A fire occurred, causing $60,000 damage to the insured property. At the time of the loss, the market value of the insured property was in the amount of $100,000. Computation of the amount of recovery is as follows:

$$\frac{\$60,000}{\$100,000 \times .80} \times \$60,000 = \$45,000$$

d. An insured can never recover more than the face amount of the policy. For example, Jones owned a building which was covered by a fire insurance policy in the amount of $60,000. The policy contained a 90 percent coinsurance clause. The building was totally destroyed by fire. The building was valued at $100,000. The insured can recover only $60,000, the face amount of the policy, even though the amount of the recovery using the formula would be $66,666.66.

$$\frac{\$60,000}{\$100,000 \times .90} \times \$100,000 = \$66,666.66$$

2. *Pro rata clause.* This clause provides that if the insured has multiple fire policies covering the same risk, any loss must be apportioned among the insurers. Each insurer is liable only for that portion of the loss which its coverage bears to the total coverage. Recovery under each of the multiple fire policies is computed as follows:

$$\frac{\text{Dollar amount of coverage under policy 1}}{\text{Total dollar amount of coverage under all policies}} \times \text{loss} = \frac{\text{dollar amount of recovery}}{\text{under policy 1}}$$

$$\frac{\text{Dollar amount of coverage under policy 2}}{\text{Total dollar amount of coverage under all policies}} \times \text{loss} = \frac{\text{dollar amount of recovery}}{\text{under policy 2}}$$

Recovery under policy 1 + recovery under policy 2 = loss suffered by the insured

For example, Smith has a total of $80,000 of coverage on a building, of which company X provides 20,000 coverage and company Y provides $60,000 coverage. Under a pro rata clause, company X is obligated to pay one-fourth and company Y is obligated to pay the remaining three-fourths of a loss.

3. *Beneficiary* designation. The beneficiary is the person or persons entitled to the proceeds in the event of loss.

  a. The insured is usually the named beneficiary; however, this need not be the case.

  b. Mortgagors and mortgagees.

  (1) If a mortgagee (creditor) requires the mortgagor (debtor) to carry fire insurance on the mortgaged property for the benefit of the mortgagee, the latter is protected to the extent of his or her interest.

  (2) If there is no provision in the mortgage requiring the mortgagor to insure for the mortgagee's benefit, the mortgagee has no rights in the proceeds of a fire policy taken out by the mortgagor.

  (3) "Loss payable" clause in a fire policy requires payment to the mortgagee as the mortgagee's "interest may appear," and the balance of the proceeds are payable to the mortgagor.

4. *Cancellation.* Either the insured or the insurer may cancel the policy upon giving notice.
5. *Notice and proof of loss.* Most policies require the insured to give *immediate* (construed by the courts to mean a reasonable time after the loss) notice of loss, together with proof of loss (inventory) within a specified period of time.
6. *Assignment* of the insurance contract or its proceeds.
   a. Prior to a loss, a fire insurance policy is not assignable without the consent of the insurer.
   b. After a loss, the insured's right to receive proceeds is freely assignable without the insurer's permission.
7. *Subrogation.* An insurer, after paying the insured for a loss caused by the intentional act or negligence of a third person, is subrogated to the rights of the insured against the third person.
8. *Conditions and exclusions.* The Standard Fire Insurance Policy contains several provisions that limit or deny coverage under certain circumstances.
   a. *Concealment of fraud provision.* This provision voids the policy if, before or after a loss, the insured wilfully concealed or misrepresented a fact or circumstance material to the risk assumed, e.g., false proof of loss or fraudulent statement as to the structure insured.
   b. *Excluded perils.* Damages caused by enemy attack by armed forces, invasion, order of governmental authority, neglect of the insured at or after a loss, and loss by theft.
   c. *Bullion, money, documents, and evidences of debt.* Accounts, bills, currency, deeds, evidences of debt, money, securities, bullion, and manuscripts are excluded from coverage.

LIFE AND FIRE INSURANCE COMPARED

VI. Table 12-2 illustrates some important distinctions between life insurance and fire insurance.

TABLE 12-2 LIFE INSURANCE AND FIRE INSURANCE DISTINGUISHED

	Life insurance	Fire insurance
Amount of proceeds payable	All policies are valued	Both valued and open (nonvalued) policies are issued
Formation of the insurance contract	Must be in writing	May be oral or written
Insurable interest	Must exist only at the time the policy is issued	Need exist only at the time of the loss
Contract of indemnity	No	Yes
Right of subrogation	No	Yes
Assignment of contract or proceeds	Freely assignable prior to and after a loss	Prior to loss, not assignable without consent of the insurer. After a loss, freely assignable

VII. Accident and health insurance, automobile, property and liability insurance, and workers' compensation insurance are also considered "casualty" insurance by some authorities in the insurance industry.

A. *Formation of casualty insurance contracts:* As a general rule, contract law governs the legal existence and validity of a casualty insurance contract. See Chapter 2. In addition, some aspects of casualty insurance are given special legal treatment. For example, the legal concepts of indemnity, subrogation, and insurable interest apply to casualty insurance contracts. See also III above.

B. *Accident and health insurance policies.* These types of policies provide protection against the loss of wages or against hospital, surgical, and medical expenses incurred as a result of sickness or accidental bodily injury. Included within these policies are the following types of coverages.

   1. *Disability income coverage* provides payments, based on a specified percentage of an incapacitated insured's weekly or monthly income, to the insured during periods of disability to compensate for loss of income caused by illness or accidental (i.e., not self-inflicted) bodily injury.

   a. To be considered *"disabled"*, many policies provide that the insured must be unable to perform the duties of his or her own occupation. Other policies provide that the insured must be unable to perform the duties of *any* occupation in order to be considered disabled.

   b. Some disability policies also include a lump-sum death and dismemberment benefit that is payable upon the death of the insured, loss of sight, or loss of limbs caused by accident.

   2. *Medical expense coverage* provides for the reimbursement for expenses that result from sickness and accidental (i.e., not self-inflicted) bodily injury. This type of coverage is classified as follows:

   a. *Hospital expense coverage* provides reimbursement for room and board charges and miscellaneous hospital expenses up to specified maximum amounts incurred by an insured while confined in a hospital.

   b. *Surgical expense coverage* provides reimbursement for surgical expenses, based on a surgical schedule that lists the amounts payable for specified surgical procedures.

   c. *Regular medical expense coverage* provides reimbursement for expenses incurred as a result of home, office, or hospital physician visits (i.e., nonsurgical).

   d. *Major medical expense coverage* provides protection for catastrophic losses as a result of illness or accident. It provides reimbursement for a large variety of hospital, surgical, physician, and other medical expenses. It is distinguished from a regular medical expense policy in the following ways.

   (1) It has high policy maximum limits, e.g., $25,000, $50,000, or even $100,000.

   (2) It contains fewer exclusions from coverage.

   (3) It provides deductibles in amounts as high as $1,000.

   (4) It contains a *"coinsurance"* clause whereby the insured is obligated to share a portion of each dollar of expense with the insurer. For example, under an 80 percent "coinsurance" clause, the insurer is obligated to pay 80 percent of each dollar in excess of the policy deductible. The insured is responsible for the balance.

C. *Automobile insurance policies.*

    1. These policies provide protection against the following four types of losses.

        a. Loss that results from the insured's legal liability (fault) for damages to third persons arising out of the ownership or use of an insured automobile, e.g., bodily injury and property damage coverage.

        b. Medical expenses incurred by an insured, members of the insured's household, or the insured's passengers as a result of an accident involving an automobile, e.g., medical payments coverage.

        c. Loss that results from damage to or theft of the insured automobile, e.g., collision and comprehensive coverage.

        d. Loss that results from bodily injury to the insured, resident relatives, and any other person occupying an insured automobile and caused by a driver of an uninsured automobile, a "hit and run" driver, or a driver whose insurance company became insolvent within one year from the date of the accident.

    2. The four basic types of coverages under an automobile insurance policy are liability, medical payments, physical damage, and uninsured motorist.

        a. *Liability coverage* obligates the insurer to pay any damages the insured is legally obligated to pay to third persons for bodily injury or property damage arising out of the ownership, maintenance, or use of the insured automobile. It provides two maximum limits of liability.

            (1) *"Per person" limitation* prescribes the maximum dollar amount the insurer will pay for bodily injury to any one person.

            (2) *"Per occurrence" limitation* establishes the maximum dollar amount the insurer will pay to all persons for injuries to their person and property in any one accident.

            (3) These dollar amount limitations are commonly expressed as follows: $50,000/$100,000/$25,000. The first number represents the per person bodily injury limit, the second represents the per occurrence bodily injury limit, and the third represents the per occurrence property damage limit.

        b. *Medical payments coverage* obligates the insurer to pay (regardless of any fault on the part of the insured) the medical expenses of the following classes of persons, subject to a maximum dollar limitation per person.

            (1) Insured and members of the insured's household who are injured while occupying or through being struck by any automobile.

            (2) Passengers who are injured while occupying the insured automobile.

        c. *Physical damage* coverage obligates the insurer to pay (regardless of any fault on the part of the insured) to the insured the actual amount of loss the insured has suffered as a result of damage to or theft of the insured automobile. This provision provides two basic types of coverage: collision and comprehensive.

            (1) *Collision.* This coverage obligates the insurer to pay for loss in excess of any deductible caused by collision to the insured automobile. A *deductible* is a specified amount of the first dollar amount of any loss that must be paid by the insured; $100, $200, or even $300 deductibles are common.

                (*a*) Collision coverage is issued with or without a deductible.

                (*b*) The insured can recover even if the insured's negligence caused the loss.

                (*c*) Collision includes upset or an impact of the insured automobile with any other object.

            (2) *Comprehensive* is an all-risk type of property insurance coverage that obligates the insurer to reimburse the insured for loss to the insured automobile caused other than by collision.

(*a*) The coverage includes breakage of glass and loss caused by missiles, falling objects, fire, theft (of the insured automobile), explosion, earthquake, windstorm, hail, water, flood, malicious mischief or vandalism, riot or civil commotion, and collision with a bird or animal.

(*b*) This coverage may also be issued with or without a deductible.

(*c*) The insured can recover even though the insured's negligence contributed to the loss.

(*d*) Personal effects found within the insured automobile are not usually covered under the comprehensive coverage.

d. *Uninsured motorist coverage* obligates the insurer to pay to an insured person the amount of damages for bodily injury that an insured person could legally collect (on the basis of fault) from an uninsured motorist, a "hit and run" driver, or a driver whose automobile insurance company became insolvent within one year from the year of the accident.

(1) The following persons are usually designated "insured persons" under this coverage:

(*a*) The insured named as such in the policy and his or her family who are also members of the insured's household. These persons are covered even though they are not injured while occupying an automobile.

(*b*) Any person injured while occupying an insured automobile with the permission of the named insured.

(2) Recovery is usually limited to damages as a result of bodily injury.

(3) The coverage contains "per person" and "per occurrence" maximum limits of recovery. The usual minimum limits are the minimum limits of liability insurance required to be carried by motorists under a state's financial responsibility law.

(4) Where the injured insured person and that person's insurance company cannot agree as to the existence of liability on the part of the *"uninsured motorist"* or on the amount of damages, the parties have two courses of action available to them.

(*a*) The insured may file a lawsuit against the "uninsured motorist" wherein the latter's fault and the amount of damages are determined by a court; or

(*b*) The insured or the insurer can submit the insured's claim to arbitration before the American Arbitration Association. *Arbitration* is the submission of a dispute between persons to a disinterested person (arbitrator) for hearing and decision.

(5) Uninsured motorist coverage should not be confused with *underinsured motorist coverage*, which is available by endorsement to a basic automobile policy.

(*a*) The underinsured motorist is a driver of an automobile whose automobile liability insurance coverage is not sufficient to pay the amount of damages suffered by a person who was injured as a result of underinsured motorist's fault.

(*b*) Underinsured motorist coverage obligates the insurer to pay to its injured insured, subject to the dollar amount limitations of its policy, the amount of damages that remain unpaid because of the inadequate liability insurance coverage of the underinsured motorist.

D. *Workers' compensation.* See Chapter 18.

SELF-QUIZ

To check your understanding of the key words and concepts and the accuracy of your answers to the questions, refer to the text material as referenced by page number.

KEY WORDS AND CONCEPTS

Application   **355**
Insurance policy   **355**
Loss   **355**
Peril   **355**
Beneficiary   **355**
Insurer   **355**
Insured   **355**
Owner   **355**
Insurable interest   **355, 357**
Binder   **355**
Nonforfeiture value   **359**
Settlement option   **359**
Lapse   **356**
Valued policy   **356**
Casualty insurance   **363**
Exclusion   **366**
Disabled   **367**
Disability income coverage   **367**
Liability coverage   **368**
Collision   **368**
Uninsured motorist coverage   **369**
Underinsured motorist coverage   **369**
Arbitration   **369**
Open (nonvalued) policy   **356**
Blanket (floating) policy   **356**
Grace period clause   **359**
Entire contract clause   **359**
Suicide clause   **359**
Misstatement-of-age clause   **359**
Incontestability clause   **359**
Reinstatement clause   **359**
Automatic premium loan   **359**
Revocable beneficiary   **360**
Irrevocable beneficiary   **360**
Coinsurance clause   **364**
Pro rata clause   **365**
Endorsement   **364**
Rider   **364**
Extended coverage   **364**
Medical expense coverage   **367**
Major medical expense coverage   **367**
Comprehensive coverage   **368**
Deductible   **368**

"Per person" limitation   **368**
"Per occurrence" limitation   **368**

QUESTIONS

1. What are the essential elements of a binding life insurance contract? **(356)** A fire insurance contract? **(356)**
2. Explain the effect of lack of an insurable interest in respect to the validity of an insurance policy. **(357)**
3. In respect to a life and to a fire insurance policy, when must the insurable interest exist? Who must possess the insurable interest? **(357)**
4. List those persons or entities who have an insurable interest in the life of each other. **(357)**
5. List those persons or entities who have an insurable interest in property. **(357)**
6. Are life and fire insurance policies contracts of indemnity? Explain **(366)**
7. List and explain the four basic classifications of life insurance policies. **(357)**
8. Discuss the rights that creditors of an owner, insured, or beneficiary may have in the proceeds of a life insurance policy. **(360)**
9. Are life and fire insurance policies assignable? If so, when and under what circumstances? **(366)**
10. Is the right of subrogation available to life and fire insurers? **(366)**
11. List and explain six business uses of life insurance. **(361)**
12. A fire insurance policy provides coverage against which type of fire? **(364)**
13. Can an insured under a fire insurance policy recover an amount of his or her actual loss in excess of the face amount of the policy? **(364)**
14. State the formula used to compute the amount of actual loss payable under a coinsurance clause of a fire insurance policy. **(365)**
15. List the six important distinctions between life and fire insurance. **(366)**
16. What benefits are payable under the medical expense coverage of an accident and health insurance policy? **(367)**
17. Distinguish between a major medical expense and a regular medical expense insurance policy. **(367)**
18. Explain the four basic coverages under an automobile insurance policy. **(368)**

19. What two courses of action does an injured insured have under uninsured motorist coverage when an agreement cannot be reached with the insurer as to its liability for damages caused by an uninsured motorist? **(369)**

SELECTED QUESTIONS AND UNOFFICIAL ANSWERS

OBJECTIVE QUESTIONS

Select the best answer for each of the following items. Mark only one answer for each item. Answer all items.

MAY 1981

48. Burt owns an office building which is leased to Hansen Corporation under the terms of a long-term lease. Both Burt and Hansen have procured fire insurance covering the building. Which of the following is correct?

a. Both Burt and Hansen have separate insurable interests.

b. Burt's insurable interest is limited to the book value of the property.

c. Hansen has an insurable interest in the building, but only to the extent of the value of any additions or modifications it has made.

d. Since Burt has legal title to the building, he is the only party who can insure the building.

NOVEMBER 1980

53. Bernard Manufacturing, Inc., owns a three-story building which it recently purchased. The purchase price was $200,000 of which $160,000 was financed by the proceeds of a mortgage loan from the Cattleman Savings and Loan Association. Bernard immediately procured a standard fire insurance policy on the premises for $200,000 from the Magnificent Insurance Company. Cattleman also took out fire insurance of $160,000 on the property from the Reliable Insurance Company of America. The property was subsequently totally destroyed as a result of a fire which started in an adjacent loft and spread to Bernard's building. Insofar as the rights and duties of Bernard, Cattleman, and the insurers are concerned, which of the following is a correct statement?

a. Cattleman Savings and Loan lacks the requisite insurable interest to collect on its policy.

b. Bernard Manufacturing can only collect $40,000.

c. Reliable Insurance Company is subrogated to Cattleman's rights against Bernard upon payment of Cattleman's insurance claim.

d. The maximum amount that Bernard Manufacturing can collect from Magnificent is $40,000, the value of its insurable interest.

55. Morse is seeking to collect on a property insurance policy covering certain described property which was destroyed. The insurer has denied recovery based upon Morse's alleged lack of an insurable interest in the property. In which of the situations described below will the insurance company prevail?

a. The property has been willed to Morse's father for life and, upon his father's death, to Morse as the remainderman.

b. The insured property does *not* belong to Morse, but instead to a corporation which he controls.

c. Morse is *not* the owner of the insured property but a mere long-term lessee.

d. The insured property belongs to a general trade debtor of Morse and the debt is unsecured.

MAY 1980

47. Rollo Trading Corporation insured its 15 automobiles for both liability and collision. Poindexter, one of its salesmen, was in an automobile accident while driving a company car on a sales trip. The facts clearly reveal that the accident was solely the fault of Connors, the driver of the other car. Poindexter was seriously injured, and the automobile was declared a total loss. The value of the auto was $2,850. Which of the following is an *incorrect* statement regarding the rights and liabilities of Rollo, its insurer, Poindexter, and Connors?

a. Rollo's insurer has *no* liability whatsoever since the accident was the result of Connors' negligence.

b. Rollo's insurer is liable for $2,850, less any deductible, on the collision policy, but will be subrogated to Rollo's rights.

c. Rollo's insurer must defend Rollo against any claims by Poindexter or Connors.

d Poindexter has an independent action against Connors for the injuries caused by Connors' negligence.

48. Hazard & Company was the owner of a building valued at $100,000. Since Hazard did not believe that a fire would result in a total loss, it procured two standard fire insurance policies on the property. One was for $24,000 with the Asbestos Fire Insurance Company and the other was for $16,000 with the Safety Fire Insurance Company. Both policies contained standard pro rata and 80% coinsurance clauses. Six months later, at which time the building was still valued at $100,000, a fire occurred which resulted in a loss of $40,000. What is the total amount Hazard can recover on both policies and the respective amount to be paid by Asbestos?

a. $0 and $0.
b. $20,000 and $10,000.
c. $20,000 and $12,000.
d. $40,000 and $20,000.

12. Charleston, Inc., had its warehouse destroyed by fire. Charleston's property was insured against fire loss by the Conglomerate Insurance Company. An investigation by Conglomerate revealed that the fire had been caused by a disgruntled employee whom Charleston had suspended for one month due to insubordination. Charleston seeks to hold its insurer liable for the $200,000 loss of its warehouse. Which of the following is correct insofar as the dispute between Charleston and the Conglomerate Insurance Company?

a. Since the loss was due to the deliberate destruction by one of Charleston's employees, recovery will be denied.
b. Conglomerate must pay Charleston, but it will be subrogated to Conglomerate's rights against the wrongdoing employee.
c. The fact that the employee has been suspended for one month precludes recovery against Conglomerate.
d. Arson is excluded from the coverage of most fire insurance policies, and therefore Conglomerate is *not* liable.

38. Glick was the owner of a factory valued at $100,000. He procured a fire insurance policy on the building for $40,000 from Safety Insurance Company, Inc. The policy contained an 80% coinsurance clause. The property was totally destroyed by fire. How much will Glick recover from the insurance company?

a. $20,000.
b. $32,000.
c. $40,000.
d. Glick will recover nothing because he did *not* meet the coinsurance requirements.

45. The usual fire insurance policy does *not*

a. Have to meet the insurable interest test if this requirement is waived by the parties.
b. Provide for subrogation of the insurer to the insured's rights upon payment of the amount of the loss covered by the policy.
c. Cover losses caused by the negligence of the insured's agent.
d. Permit assignment of the policy prior to loss without the consent of the insurer.

2. Wilson obtained a fire insurance policy on his dairy farm from the Columbus Insurance Company. The policy was for $80,000 which was the value of the property. The policy was the standard fire insurance policy sold throughout the United States. A fire occurred late one night and caused a $10,000 loss. Which of the following will prevent Wilson from recovering the full amount of his loss from Columbus Insurance?

a. The coinsurance clause.
b. Wilson had a similar policy with another insurance company for $40,000.
c. The fact that 50% of the loss was caused by smoke and water damage.
d. The fact that his negligence was the primary cause of the fire.

7. Stein bought an office building valued at $200,000. The fire insurance policy contained a 100% coinsurance clause. Stein insured the building for $120,000. Subsequently, a fire caused damage of $40,000 to the building. Which of the following is the correct amount Stein will recover?

a. $40,000.
b. $24,000.
c. $13,333.
d. Nothing because the building was *not* insured for 100% of its value.

Answers to Objective Questions

Explanation of Answers to Objective Questions

MAY 1981

48. (a) A person has an insurable interest in property if he will benefit by its continued existence or suffer from its destruction and has a legal or equitable interest in the property (e.g., a mortgagee, mortgagor, tenant in rented property, or partner in partnership property). Both Burt (owner of legal title) and Hansen (tenant in leased property) have an insurable interest, therefore, answer (a) is true. Answer (b) is incorrect because Burt has an insurable interest to the extent of any economic loss he might suffer. Such a loss would normally be measured by market value of the property, not book value. Answer (c) is also false because the tenant has an insurable interest for the amount of economic loss he will suffer in the event the property is destroyed. This amount may be greater or less than the value of the additions or modifications. The tenants would measure their economic loss in reference to items such as the expense of finding a new office building or new business space.

NOVEMBER 1980

53. (c) Answer (c) is correct because under a fire insurance policy an insurer who pays a claim is subrogated (succeeds to the rights of the insured) to any rights that the insured had against a third party. Answer (a) is incorrect since Cattleman, as mortgagee, has an insurable interest to the extent of the outstanding debt ($160,000). If the policy is a valued policy then Bernard will collect $200,000. If it is an open policy then Bernard will collect the market value of the building at the time of destruction up to a maximum of $200,000. Thus answer (b) and (d) are incorrect.

55. (d) Concerning a property insurance policy, the insured must have an insurable interest in the property both at the time the policy is issued and when the loss occurs. To have an insurable interest in property, a person must have both a legal interest and a possibility of monetary loss. An unsecured creditor does not have an insurable interest in the property of the debtor. However, a vested remainderman would have an insurable interest, as would a shareholder in the property of the corporation, and as would a lessee in the property that is the subject of the leasehold.

MAY 1980

47. (a) Rollo Trading Corporation's insurer does have liability even though the accident was the result of Connors' negligence. Rollo had collision coverage under the insurance policy, therefore the insurer is liable for any damages to Rollo's car caused by collision, irrespective of whose negligence caused the damage. Most policies contain $50- or $100-deductible clauses concerning collision coverage. One of the insurer's obligations under an auto insurance policy is to defend the insured against any lawsuits arising from operation of the vehicle covered by the policy. Poindexter has a right to sue Connors for injuries caused by Connors' negligence.

48. (c) When there is a partial loss for property covered under a policy with a co-insurance clause. the following formula is applied to determine the recovery:

$$\frac{\text{Face value of policy}}{\text{Fair value of property} \times \text{co-insurance \%}} \times \text{Loss}$$
$$= \text{Recovery}$$

$$\frac{\$16,000}{\$100,000 \times 80\%} \times \$400,000 = \$20,000$$

$$\frac{\$24,000}{\$100,000 \times 80\%} \times \$40,000 = \$12,000$$

Thus answer (c) is the correct answer.

NOVEMBER 1979

12. (b) Under the facts, Conglomerate must pay Charleston, the insured, but Conglomerate upon payment will be subrogated to the Charleston rights against the employee who committed arson. Answer (a) is incorrect since the typical fire policy does not exclude recovery by the insured if a fire is caused by deliberate or negligent destruction by the insured's employees. Answer (c) is incorrect because the fact that the employee has been suspended for 1 month is of no legal consequence. Answer (d) is incorrect because arson by anyone other than the insured is generally an included risk under standard fire insurance policies.

38. (c) Glick, the owner of the factory, should recover $40,000. Fire loss recovery is limited to 1) the amount of the loss, 2) the face value of the policy, and 3) the coinsurance limitation. Coinsurance clauses make the insured a coinsurer if the insured does not carry adequate insurance coverage, e.g., 80% of asset fair market value. Here Glick carried $40,000 insurance but the insurance contract required $80,000 (80% of $100,000 in value). Thus, Glick became a coinsurer for 50% ($40,000/$80,000) of the loss. The resulting coinsurance limitation is $50,000 (50% of $100,000) but Glick's recovery is further limited to $40,000—the face value of the policy.

45. (d) The usual fire insurance policy does not permit assignment of the fire policy prior to loss without the consent of the insuror. However, any insurance payments payable by a policy may be assigned. Answer (a) is incorrect because a valid fire insurance policy claim would have to meet the insurable interest test. Any attempt to waive this requirement would be in violation of public policy. It would be highly unusual for a fire insurance company to waive the insurable interest test. Answer (b) is incorrect because the typical fire insurance policy does provide for subrogation of the insurance company to the insured's right upon payment by the insurance company. Answer (c) is incorrect because the usual fire insurance policy does cover losses when the loss is incurred as a result of the negligence of the insured's agent or employees.

MAY 1979

2. (b) When a property owner has insured his property with more than one insurance company, each insurance company is required to pay a pro rata share of the loss. If Wilson had both an $80,000 policy and a $40,000 policy on the same property, the $80,000 policy must pay two-thirds and the

$40,000 policy one-third of any loss (limited to $80,000 and $40,000 respectively). Answer (a) is incorrect because a coinsurance clause applies only when the property owner has underinsured his property; Wilson insured his property for its value. Answer (c) is incorrect since damage from smoke and water in addition to fire damage is recoverable under the standard fire policy sold in the United States. Answer (d) is incorrect since negligence is not a bar to recovery under a standard fire insurance policy.

NOVEMBER 1978

7. (b) A co-insurance clause requires the insured to maintain insurance equal to a specified percentage of the value of his property. If a loss occurs, the insurer will only pay a proportionate share of the loss if the insured has not carried insurance equal to the specified percentage of value of the insured asset. The formula is: recovery = actual loss × amount of insurance ÷ co-insurance percentage × the value of insured property. The recovery, however, is also limited to the lesser of the amount of the policy and the amount of the loss. In this case: ($40,000 × $120,000) ÷ (100% × $200,000) = $24,000.

ESSAY QUESTIONS AND ANSWERS

NOVEMBER 1974 (Estimated time: 5 to 10 minutes)

7. Part c. Marvel Enterprises, Inc., contracted to buy Jonstone's factory and warehouse. The contract provided that if title did not pass to Marvel prior to October 1, 1974, Marvel would have the right to possession on that date pending conveyance of title upon delivery of the deed. The contract also provided that the purchase price was to be adjusted depending upon the actual acreage conveyed as determined by an independent survey. This provision was subject to a further stipulation: the maximum purchase price would not exceed $450,000 nor be less than $425,000 as long as the survey did not reveal major variances nor render title unmarketable.

All the requisite paperwork was not in order by October 1, 1974, and Marvel exercised its option to take possession on that date. Concurrently, Marvel obtained a fire insurance policy on the factory and warehouse effective October 1, 1974. The closing was finally scheduled for October 17, 1974. The survey confirmed the acreage described in the contract of sale, and Marvel tendered the balance of the purchase price on October 17, 1974. During the interim period, however, the factory and warehouse were totally destroyed by fire and Marvel seeks to recover on its fire insurance policy. The insurance company denies liability.

Required Discuss Marvel's rights to recover from the insurance company.

Answer Marvel will recover against the insurance company for the value of the insured property destroyed, i.e., the factory and warehouse.

The insurance company is undoubtedly asserting a lack of insurable interest on Marvel's part in that legal title had not been transferred to it at the time of the fire. However, where a purchaser, pursuant to a contract of sale of real property, takes possession of the premises prior to the closing, the risk of loss is his. Thus, the insurable interest requirement has been satisfied and Marvel may recover. It may also be argued that a valid insurable interest is created by the contract alone.

NOVEMBER 1972 (Estimated time: 10 to 15 minutes)

6. Part a. You have been assigned to review the insurance coverage as of June 30, 1972, of Foley & Co., a partnership. As part of your work you inspect the correspondence file with Foley's insurance agent. The file reveals that Foley has filed a number of claims with Adams Insurance which remain unpaid. You extracted the following facts from the correspondence file regarding each unpaid claim.

Foley dispatched an order on November 11, 1971, to Western Computer Co. accompanied by its check in full payment for 1,000 computer components to be shipped by boat, FAS Vessel at Western's home port. The parts were labeled, packed, crated, and picked up for delivery to the pier. On the way to the pier, the truck caught fire and the goods were completely destroyed. Foley sent a claim to Adams for recovery under its blanket insurance policy which covers "all goods in Foley's possession, owned by it, or to which it had any legally recognizable insurable interest."

Adams denies liability on the policy, claiming:
a. The risk of loss had not passed to Foley.
b. Foley did not have any legally recognized insurable interest.

Required Is Adams correct in either of its contentions? Explain.

Answer Yes as to risk of loss. No as to insurable interest. Since the contract was FAS Vessel at Western's home port, the risk of loss remains with Western until the goods arrive and are unloaded at that point. However, the Uniform Commercial Code provides for "an insurable interest in the purchaser of goods upon identification of existing goods to the contract." Thus, under the facts presented, identification to the contract having been clearly made, Foley can recover from Adams for any insured loss. If Adams pays Foley, Adams will be subrogated to any rights Foley would have against Western.

6. Part c. During January 1972, Cragsmoore, one of Foley's employees, negligently dropped a lighted cigar on some packing material which caught fire and totally destroyed the warehouse and the goods stored therein. The warehouse and contents were covered by a $2 million fire insurance policy which contains a 90 percent coinsurance clause. The loss was subsequently appraised at $2.5 million.

Foley seeks to recover for the loss. Adams denies any and all liability; or, in the alternative, claims that it is not obligated to pay the full $2 million.

Required What can Foley recover? Explain.

Answer $2 million. One of the risks assumed by an insurer is the negligence of the insured, including its employees. Thus, despite Cragsmoore's negligence, Foley can recover for the destruction of its warehouse and the goods stored therein. In addition, the coinsurance clause does not apply to a total destruction of the insured property. Hence, Foley will recover the face amount of the policy. If Adams pays Foley, Adams will be subrogated to any rights Foley would have against Cragsmoore.

PART

SIX

Business Organizations (15%)*

Chapter 13
Agency

Chapter 14
Partnerships

Chapter 15
Corporations and Other Forms of
Business Organizations

---

* This percentage allocation represents the relative weight to be given to this *area* of business law on the Uniform CPA Examinations beginning in November 1983. It also indicates the approximate percentage of the total achievable test score to be assigned to *this* area of business law for each Uniform CPA Examination beginning in November 1983.

CHAPTER

13

Agency

The following is a generalized description of the subject matter to be tested through the May 1983 Uniform CPA Examination.

> . . . the area of agency with the main focus upon the subject of imposition of liability in contract and tort by the agent upon his principal. This area of law may be tested in situations relating to proprietorships, partnerships, or corporations.[1]

The AICPA Board of Examiners has adopted a new content specification outline for the business law section of the Uniform CPA Examination, *to be effective with the November 1983 examination*. The outline lists the following topics to be tested under the title "Agency."

A. Agency
1. Formation and Termination
2. Liabilities of Principal for Tort and Contract
3. Disclosed and Undisclosed Principals
4. Agency Authority and Liability[2]

NATURE OF AGENCY

I. *Consensual in nature.* An agency relationship is created by the mutual assent of two parties. The mutual assent need not meet the requisites of a contract, and consequently one person may agree to act as an agent as a gift of his or her services to another. It is a relationship wherein two persons have agreed that one of them is to act on behalf of the other to effect contractual, personal, or commercial transactions with a third party or parties.

---

[1] AICPA, *Information for CPA Candidates*, Copyright © 1975, 1979, by the American Institute of Certified Public Accountants, Inc.

[2] AICPA, *Business Law—Content Specification Outline*, approved by the AICPA Board of Examiners on August 31, 1981.

SCOPE OF AGENCY

II. In its broadest definition, the term "agency" includes all relationships in which one person is acting in any manner or activity with the permission and in behalf of another. This definition includes the agency relationships of principal to agent, employer to employee (master to servant), and employer to independent contractor.

    A. In its narrowest definition, the term *"agency"* includes only the relationship of principal to agent. In the principal-agent relationship, the agent is given authority from the principal to enter into contracts with third parties on behalf of the principal. (See Figure 13-1.)

        1. *Principal.* The principal is the person who has authorized another to contract on his or her behalf. The word "person" includes an individual, association, partnership, and corporation.

        2. *Agent.* An agent is the person who has agreed to contract on behalf of a principal pursuant to the authority granted by a principal. An individual, association, partnership, or corporation may also serve as an agent.

    B. The principal may or may not control or have the right to control the physical conduct of the agent in the performance of the agent's services on behalf of the principal. See III below.

TYPES OF AGENCY RELATIONSHIPS

III. Agency relationships may be classified as follows: principal to agent, employer to employee (master to servant), and employer to independent contractor. These classifications are based on: (1) The nature of the services performed by the employee (servant) or agent; and (2) the amount of control that the employer or principal exercises or retains over the physical conduct of the employee (servant) or agent in the performance of the employee or agent's services. (See Figure 13-2.)

    A. *Principal-agent.* The following requirements must be met to create a principal-agent relationship (see Figure 13-1):

        1. The agent must receive *authority to enter contracts* with third persons *in behalf of the principal;*

        2. The agent must owe a fiduciary duty to the principal; and

        3. The agent must be subject to a minimum amount of control or right to control by the principal with the performance of the matters entrusted the agent.

FIGURE 13-1   PRINCIPAL, AGENT, AND THIRD-PARTY RELATIONSHIP

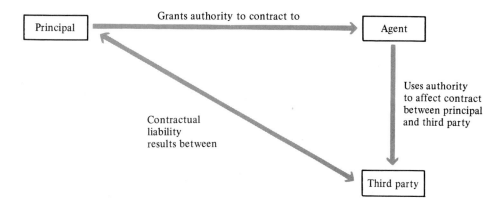

FIGURE 13-2 TESTS TO DETERMINE LEGAL NATURE OF EMPLOYMENT RELATIONSHIPS

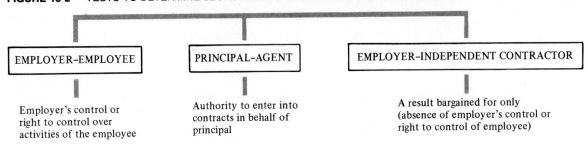

B. *Employer-employee (master-servant).* This relationship is determined from both the degree of control that the employer exercises or retains over the physical conduct of the *employee* and the nature of services performed by the employee.

1. An employee's conduct in the performance of services is subject to a *high degree of actual control, or* the employer retains *the right to exert a high degree of control.* Examples of evidence of control are:

   a. Services are required to be performed on the employer's premises;

   b. Hourly wages are paid;

   c. The employer has the right to establish or has established the time that the employee must begin or end services;

   d. The employee must use the employer's tools;

   e. Lunch periods and times for coffee breaks are established by the employer;

   f. The employer controls or reserves the right to control the methods by which the employee is to produce specified results on behalf of the employer (master).

2. As a general rule, a "pure" employee performs duties of a ministerial (non-decision-making) nature and has no authority to enter into contracts on behalf of the employer, e.g., a factory employee or a truck driver.

3. An employee may or may not also be an agent. An employee who has been given authority by the employer to enter into contracts on its behalf is also an agent, e.g., a retail clerk.

4. A person is an employee even though not compensated for his or her activities so long as that person is subject to a high degree of actual control or the right to control by the employer.

C. *Employer-independent contractor.* Distinction between the employer relationship and the *independent contractor* relationship is based on the degree of control retained over the conduct of the person performing the service.

1. The independent contractor is obligated *to produce a result only* and is free to pursue his or her own methods in the performance of the work *without control over his or her activities* by the employer. For example, Juno hired Elmo to paint her house for $500. No restrictions on time for performance, use of equipment, or materials were imposed. Elmo is an independent contractor.

2. The independent contractor may also be an agent. In the example given above, Juno gave Elmo authority to buy paint and other materials and to charge them to Juno's account. Elmo is an independent contractor *and* an agent.

D. It is important to distinguish between a "pure" employee, an agent, and a "pure" independent contractor for the following reasons:

1. Employers and principals are liable to third parties in *respondeat superior* for torts committed by their employees and agents in the scope of their employment or agency. See XIII below;

2. An employer of a "pure" independent contractor is not ordinarily liable to third persons in respondeat superior for the torts committed by the independent contractor; and

3. A "pure" employee or "pure" independent contractor cannot bind its employer to contracts negotiated with third parties in the employer's behalf.

CREATION OF THE AGENCY RELATIONSHIP

IV. As a general rule, no formalities are required to create an agency relationship (i.e., principal-agent, employer-employee, or employer-independent contractor). Consideration is not essential. The agency relationship may be created in the following ways. (See Figure 13-3.)

A. *By contract or agreement* between the parties. The contract or agreement may be expressed or implied.

    1. An *express contract or agreement* (oral or written). As between the parties, the general principles of contract law determine the enforceability of the contract or agreement. Unless a contract exists, the agency relationship is not binding upon the parties to it. A contract which creates an agency relationship is not required to be in writing unless it falls within the Statute of Frauds. For example, the Statute of Frauds requires contracts which by their terms cannot be possibly performed within a year to be in writing.

    2. An *implied contract or agreement* (implied from words or conduct). For example; Retailer advertised a special sale to be held at her store. Business was so good that Retailer's two employees were having difficulty handling all the customers. Jack, a customer, stepped behind a counter and assisted Retailer's employees. Retailer saw Jack but did not object. The conduct of Retailer and Jack created an agency relationship. If Jack was allowed to sell goods, he would be an employee and an agent. If Jack did not sell goods, he would be considered an employee.

B. *Agency by operation of law* (authority implied in law). An agency relationship by operation of law is implied regardless of the express or implied intentions of the parties. The following are circumstances which give rise to an agency relationship by operation of law.

FIGURE 13-3   CREATION OF AGENCY

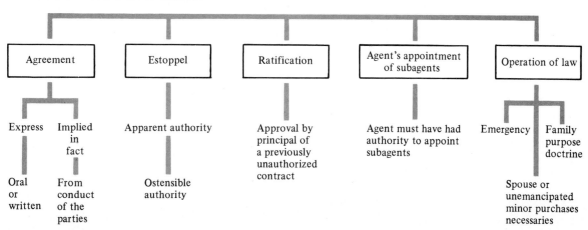

1. A nonresident motorist statute which appoints the secretary of state an agent of the nonresident motorist for the purpose of serving legal process.
2. A spouse is an agent of the other for the purchase of necessaries when the latter does not supply them.
3. An unemancipated infant (minor) is an agent of the parent for the purchase of necessaries when the latter does not supply them.
4. Emergency. Any action taken by an agent or employee in an emergency which is reasonably necessary to protect an employer's interest gives rise to an agency.
   a. For example, a truck driver hires X to guard his employer's truck and its contents after a mechanical breakdown renders the truck inoperative; or
   b. A trainman hires a doctor to treat passengers after a train accident.
5. *Family purpose doctrine.* An agency relationship for tort liability purposes arises whenever an automobile registered in a parent's name is used, with the parent's consent, for a family purpose by various members of the family. Not all states follow this doctrine.

C. *Agency by estoppel* (ostensible agent, apparent authority). An agency relationship by estoppel arises whenever one person (principal) by his or her conduct clothes another (agent) with apparent authority which causes a third person to justifiably believe that such person is an agent.
1. The term *"apparent authority"* is properly used only *when there is merely the appearance of authority but in fact authority does not exist.*
2. *The appearance of authority of the agent must be due to the words or conduct of the principal.*
3. For examples, see VIII-C-1 below.

D. By *ratification.* Ratification is an approval of a prior unauthorized act of an actual agent or of the act of a purported agent (a stranger) which relates to the commission of the act with the same effect as if the act were originally authorized. For example, Doris was hired to manage Jane's grocery store. Doris, without actual authority from Jane, borrowed $4,000 from Bank in order to meet the monthly payroll. When Doris informed Jane of her action, Jane replied, "That's OK with me, but watch your liquidity next month." A ratification occurred. As another example, assume that Doris did not personally inform Jane of the loan but that Jane first learned of the loan when she received notice from Bank that it was due and payable. Jane paid off the loan. Jane ratified the previously unauthorized loan.
1. It may be in the form of express language, or it may be implied from the conduct of the principal.
2. To have a valid ratification, the following conditions have to be satisfied:
   a. The agent or purported agent must have purported to act on behalf of the principal;
   b. The principal must have been capable of authorizing the act both at the time of the act and when the principal ratified, e.g., legal capacity;
   c. The principal must ratify the entire act;
   d. The principal must ratify before the third party withdraws;
   e. The acts ratified must be legal; and
   f. The principal must have had full knowledge of all *material facts* pertaining to the unauthorized act.
3. The ratification need not be communicated to anyone in order to be effective. As a practical matter, however, communication may be necessary in order to provide proof.
4. Ratification releases the agent from liability to both the principal and third persons for exceeding the agent's authority, i.e., contractual liability *but not* tortious liability.

E. By agent's appointment of subagents.

    1. Definition. A *subagent* is a person employed by an agent with the express or implied consent of the principal to assist the agent in transacting the business of the principal.

    2. General rule. An agent does not have the authority to appoint a subagent.

        a. The principal may grant the agent express authority to appoint a subagent.

        b. *Implied authority* to appoint a subagent may be inferred from the following circumstances:

            (1) The nature of the principal's business (implied in fact);

            (2) Custom and usages of trade (implied in fact);

            (3) Prior dealings between the principal, agent, and subagent (implied in fact); or

            (4) Emergency (implied in law). See IV-B-4 above.

        c. Some examples that illustrate implied authority to appoint a subagent follow:

            (1) Link was employed as a land buyer for Train. Train wanted enough land to construct an industrial complex in Georgia. It was customary for professional land buyers during acquisition of industrial sites to obtain the services of real estate brokers. Link hired ABC brokerage to find sellers and secure options to purchase land. ABC is a subagent (i.e., an independent contractor).

            (2) Ace gave Dan authority to sell goods. Ace furnished Dan an automobile for his use in selling. Dan, on many occasions, allowed Pete to use Ace's automobile to assist Dan in selling Ace's goods. Ace knew this and happily accepted offers and contracts to sell goods procured by Pete. Pete is a subagent (i.e., an agent-independent contractor).

            (3) Avco, a truck driver employed by Fargo, suffered a heart attack while driving Fargo's truck on a remote stretch of highway in Wyoming. A passing motorist stopped to assist him. Luke, a passenger in the automobile, volunteered to drive the truck to the nearest town, 100 miles away, while Avco was rushed to the hospital. Avco, who was unable to drive, accepted Luke's offer. Luke is a subagent (i.e., an employee).

    3. If an appointment of a subagent is authorized, the subagent is the agent of the principal.

    4. If the appointment of a subagent is not authorized, the subagent is the agent of the original agent.

LEGAL CAPACITY OF PRINCIPAL

V. Capacity to be a principal. Any "person," if legally competent to enter into contracts, may act through an agent. The extent of the principal's capacity will determine the legal status of the agreement appointing the agent and any contracts entered into by the principal's agent with third persons, i.e., whether it is valid, voidable, or void. For example, a principal is a minor (i.e., under eighteen years of age), or the principal is a court-adjudicated incompetent (i.e., a guardian or conservator has been appointed).

LEGAL CAPACITY OF AGENT

VI. Since the act of the agent is by law the act of the principal, it is immaterial whether the agent has full legal capacity to make a contract. The agent is merely a "conduit" through whom authority to contract is transmitted from the agent's principal to a third person. (See Figure 13-4.)

FIGURE 13-4   AGENT AS A CONDUIT

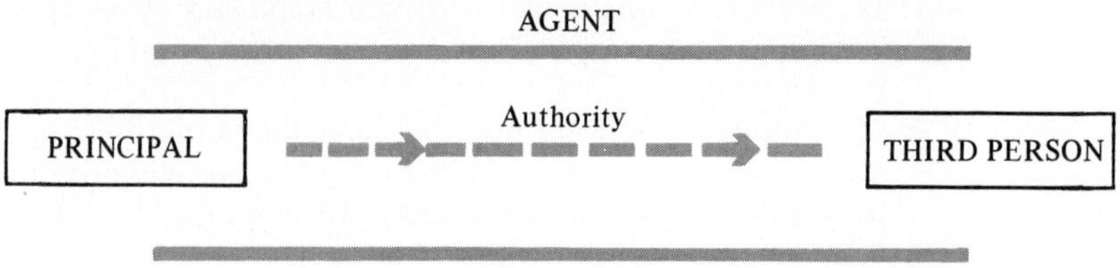

AGENT

PRINCIPAL $\longrightarrow$ Authority $\longrightarrow$ THIRD PERSON

Note: Legally, the act of the agent is the act of the principal.

A. Between principal and agent, the contract of agency may be voidable or void; but between the principal and the third person who dealt with the agent, an authorized contract is valid. For example, P, an adult, hired A, a minor, as her agent to sell an automobile. A sold the automobile in behalf of P to Z, an adult. The agency contract between P and A is voidable by A, the minor. P and Z are bound to the contract for the sale of the automobile.

B. *Some* mental capacity is necessary for an agent. Therefore, infants of tender years, lunatics, and imbeciles under certain factual situations may be legally held incompetent to act even as agents, e.g., persons for whom legal guardians or conservators have been appointed by a court (i.e., adjudicated incompetents).

C. As a general rule, associations and entities also have legal capacity to act as agents.
   1. A partnership can be an agent.
   2. As a general rule, a corporation has legal capacity to be an agent unless its articles of incorporation prohibit such activity.
   3. An unincorporated association, through its members as individuals, can also act as an agent.

CLASSIFICATION OF AGENTS

VII. All agents may be classified according to the authority that they derive from the principal and the nature of the activities that they perform in the principal's behalf.

A. All agents are either actual or ostensible.
   1. *Actual agent* is a person given express or implied authority to act in behalf of another.
   2. *Ostensible agent* (apparent authority) (agent by estoppel) is a person who *is not* an actual agent but who is held out by the principal to a third person as having authority to act in behalf of the principal. See VIII-C below.

B. Types of agents.
   1. *General agent* is one employed to transact all the business of the principal or all of the principal's business of a particular kind in a particular place, e.g., a person hired to manage your restaurant.
   2. *Special agent* is one employed to act for the principal only in a specific transaction or only for a particular purpose or class of work. A special agent is not given entire control over a class of work. A special agent is not given entire control over a particular business but is given only authority to do certain acts, e.g., attorney at law, auctioneer, real estate broker, or factor.
   3. *Universal agent* is an agent employed to transact any and all of the contracts of the principal, e.g., "blanket power of attorney."
   4. *Del credere agent* is an agent who sells goods on credit and guarantees the solvency of the purchaser and the latter's performance of the contract. A del

credere agent is liable to the principal if the purchaser defaults. For example, P hired A to sell P's goods on credit. As a part of the agreement, P obligated herself to pay to A an additional commission in exchange for A's obligation to guarantee each buyer's solvency and his or her performance of the purchase contract. See also III-A-2-c in Chapter 7.

SCOPE OF AGENT'S AUTHORITY

VIII. A fundamental rule of law of agency is that the principal is only liable in contract for the authorized contracts of an agent. An agent may receive authority to act in the following ways (see Figures 13-3 and 13-5):

A. *Express authority* is authority which is expressly conferred upon the agent by the principal. Express authority may be:

   1. Written; or
   2. Oral.

   P orally or in writing requests her agent, A, to sell P's auto for $1,500; A's authority to sell the auto is express.

B. *Implied in fact* authority is the authority to perform those acts which are usually and customarily performed in conducting the transactions or activities expressly authorized by a principal. An agent is impliedly authorized to transact or perform those acts which are reasonably necessary to carry out the agent's express authority.

   1. The authority is to perform those acts which are not specifically stated in the agent's express authority.
   2. It is based on implied consent of the principal.
   3. The test of the scope of the agent's implied authority is the *justified belief of the agent* as to the extent of the agent's authority. Some factors to consider in establishing the extent of an agent's implied authority are:

   a. Nature of the agency;
   b. Whether the agent is a special or general agent;
   c. Custom or usages of trade;
   d. Prior dealings between principal and agent; and
   e. Such other facts and circumstances which indicate the implied consent of the principal.

   4. Examples of factual situations giving rise to implied authority:

FIGURE 13-5   TYPES OF AUTHORITY

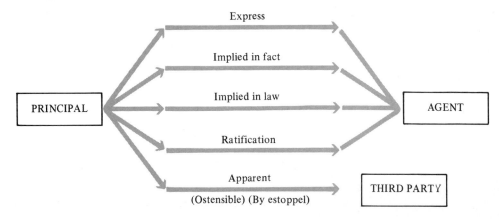

a. P authorized A to manage his apartment house at a commission of 5 percent of rentals collected, and nothing more is said to A. The authority implied (not exclusive) is to:

(1) Hire a janitor;

(2) Purchase fuel for heating;

(3) Arrange for painting and repairs as needed;

(4) Occasionally redecorate an apartment; and

(5) Enter into lease agreements.

b. P instructs her agent, A, to drive P's new auto from Chicago to Los Angeles and says nothing further. The authority implied (not exclusive) is to:

(1) Buy oil and gasoline in the principal's name to enable the agent to drive from Chicago to Los Angeles;

(2) Make ordinary automobile repairs at the principal's expense.

c. Dee was hired to sell a pickup truck for Mack. Dee gave Mack possession of the truck. Mack has the implied authority to collect the purchase price for the truck. An agent rightfully in possession of goods that he or she has the express authority to sell also has implied authority to collect the purchase price.

C. *Apparent* authority (ostensible authority) (by estoppel). An agent's apparent authority is determined by analyzing the relation *between the principal and third person*.

1. *Test.* Apparent authority is that authority which the *principal by his or her conduct has led a third party*, acting as a reasonable and prudent person, justifiably to believe is conferred on the "agent" by the principal. For example:

a. P writes a letter to A authorizing her to sell P's auto and sends a copy of the letter to C, a prospective purchaser. *Result:* A has express authority to sell the auto and apparent authority as to C.

b. P on the following day writes a letter to A revoking the authority to sell the auto but does not send a copy of the second letter to C, who is not otherwise informed of the revocation. *Result:* A has no actual authority to sell the auto. However, as to C, A continues to have apparent authority.

c. A, in the presence of P, tells C that she is P's agent to buy lumber, and P does not deny A's statement. C, in reliance upon the statement, ships lumber to P on A's order. A also orders lumber from D. *Result:* P is bound to C, although in fact A had no actual authority. P would not be liable to D. As to D, neither actual authority nor apparent authority existed.

2. *Secret limitations on an agent's express authority.* When the principal has created apparent authority, the secret limitations imposed upon the agent's express authority are not binding on third persons. For example, A hired B as a manager of a supermarket. A reserved the exclusive right to purchase inventory for the store. A week later, a supplier who did not know of the restriction on B's express authority accepted B's offer to purchase $100,000 worth of canned goods. The supplier did know that B was the manager of the supermarket. A is bound to the contract with the supplier. See also XVIII below.

D. *Implied in law authority.* Review IV-B above.

E. *Ratification* (i.e., retroactive grant of authority). Review IV-D above.

DISCLOSED AND UNDISCLOSED PRINCIPALS

IX. Principals may be disclosed, partially disclosed, or undisclosed. (See Figure 13-6.)

A. *Disclosed principal.* A principal is disclosed when both the existence of the agency and the identity of the principal are known to the third party.

1. The principal is bound by all contracts negotiated by the agent *in the name of the principal*, provided that the agent has acted within the scope of his or her

FIGURE 13-6 LIABILITY OF PRINCIPAL FOR ACTS OF AGENT

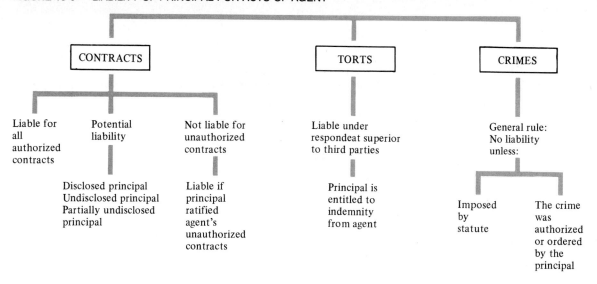

authority, express, implied, or apparent, or that the principal has ratified the unauthorized acts of the agent.

2. The agent *is not usually bound to the terms* of any contract the agent is authorized *or* even unauthorized to negotiate in behalf of the principal.

3. However, an agent can make a contract in his or her own name. In such a case, the agent becomes one of the contracting parties and is personally liable on the contract. For example, an agent:

   a. Joins the principal as joint obligor on a contract, note, or draft;

   b. Guarantees the performance of the contract by the principal, in which event the agent is liable as a surety;

   c. Acts for an undisclosed or partially undisclosed principal. See IX-B below;

   d. Signs a promissory note or a draft without indicating representative capacity (i.e., agency). The following signatures are illustrative: "For Levy Corporation, /s/ Edmund Durz"; /s/ "Edmund Durz, for Levy Corporation"; or /s/ "Edmund Durz."

      (1) Examples of positions of representative capacity are: president, agent, director, trustee, executor, vice president, secretary, comptroller, treasurer, and purchasing agent.

      (2) To eliminate personal liability on the note or draft the agent must clearly indicate that he or she is signing only in a representative capacity, for example, "Levy Corporation, by /s/ Edmund Durz, President."

B. *Partially disclosed principal or undisclosed principal.*

   1. Definitions.

      a. A principal is *partially disclosed* when the existence of the agency is known to the third person but the identity of the principal is not known to the third person. For example, ABC, a food broker, contracted to purchase olives from Ajax. The olives were purchased for TWX. At the time of the contract, Ajax did not know of TWX but did know that ABC was a food broker. TWX is a partially disclosed principal.

      b. An agent acts for an *undisclosed principal* when the agent appears to be acting only in his or her own behalf and the third person with whom the agent is dealing has no knowledge that the agent is acting as agent. For example, Railroad was hired by Beth Steel Co. to obtain options to purchase land in its behalf from farmers in XYZ county. It instructed Railroad to negotiate the options in Railroad's name. Railroad followed instructions and obtained options to purchase totalling $2 million. Beth Steel Co. is an *undisclosed principal.*

2. The principal is a party to the contract and is fully liable to the third person, provided that the agent has acted within the scope of authority, express or implied, or that the principal has ratified the unauthorized acts of agent.

3. The agent is also liable on the contract with the third person. For the agent to avoid personal liability on the contract, the contract with the third person must clearly indicate that the agent is not to be bound.

4. Upon discovery of the identity of the principal, the third person has an *irrevocable election* to hold either the principal *or* the agent to the contract.
   a. What constitutes an election is a question of fact.
   b. Most courts hold that the third person has not made an irrevocable election until:
      (1) The third person learns of the existence of the principal and learns the principal's identity; and
      (2) The third person asserts a claim against the principal *or* agent by filing a lawsuit *and* receiving a judgment against one or the other. For example, X was authorized by Y to purchase an apartment house from T in behalf of Y. T and Y disliked each other immensely. X negotiated and purchased the apartment house from T. For spite, Y refused to go through with the deal. After T sued Y and received a judgment, she discovered that Y was insolvent. T is barred from suing and recovering from X.

INCOMPETENT AND NONEXISTENT PRINCIPALS: AGENT'S LIABILITY

X. An agent may be liable either for damages or to the terms of a contract when the agent acts for an incompetent principal, a principal lacking full capacity, or a nonexistent principal. (See Figure 13-7.)

A. *Liability on the contract.*

1. Agents are personally bound to the terms of a contract that they enter into with a third party in behalf of a nonexistent principal. For example:
   a. A promoter is personally bound to contracts entered into on behalf of a corporation that is being newly organized but is not yet legally in existence (i.e., its application for incorporation has not yet been approved by the state). See III-B-2 in Chapter 15.
   b. A principal dies before the agent and the third party enter into a contract. Death of a principal automatically terminates an agent's authority to contract.
   c. An agent is liable as a party to the terms of a contract with a third person when the agent *knows* that the principal is legally incompetent. That is, a principal has been declared legally incompetent by a court on the basis of insanity, habitual intoxication, or for any other reason.

B. *Liability for damages.* Agents, when acting in behalf of their principals, make implied in law warranties that they possess actual or implied in fact authority to contract and that their principals have contractual capacity at the time that the agents enter into the contracts on behalf of the principals. If either of these warranties is breached, the agent is liable for any damages suffered by the third party as a result.

FIGURE 13-7 AGENT'S LIABILITY TO THIRD PARTIES

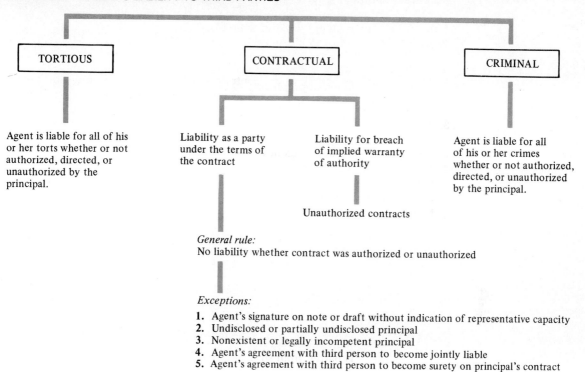

Agent is liable for all of his or her torts whether or not authorized, directed, or unauthorized by the principal.

Liability as a party under the terms of the contract

Liability for breach of implied warranty of authority

Unauthorized contracts

Agent is liable for all of his or her crimes whether or not authorized, directed, or unauthorized by the principal.

General rule:
No liability whether contract was authorized or unauthorized

Exceptions:
1. Agent's signature on note or draft without indication of representative capacity
2. Undisclosed or partially undisclosed principal
3. Nonexistent or legally incompetent principal
4. Agent's agreement with third person to become jointly liable
5. Agent's agreement with third person to become surety on principal's contract

1. The following are exceptions to the agent's liability for breach of warranty:
   a. The agent and the third person agreed that the agent does not warrant authority;
   b. The third person had actual or implied knowledge that the agent was without authority or that the agent was acting for an incompetent principal.
   c. A principal who had capacity at the time of the contract or who subsequently acquired it ratified (approved or assented to) the previously unauthorized contract by the agent. The ratification relates back to the time of the original contract.
2. Liability is imposed on the agent even though the agent acted honestly and in good faith in the mistaken belief that he or she had authority or that the principal was legally competent.

AGENT'S CONTRACTUAL LIABILITY TO THIRD PERSONS: AUTHORIZED AND UNAUTHORIZED CONTRACTS

XI. Agent's liability to third person on authorized or unauthorized contracts (see Figure 13-7).
   A. *General rule.* The agent *is not bound to the terms* of an authorized or an unauthorized contract that the agent negotiated on behalf of the principal with a third party.
   B. *Exceptions.* The following are five important exceptions to this rule.
      1. An agent signed a promissory note, check, or other draft but did not clearly indicate that it was signed in a representative capacity, e.g., "Jerry Jiminez." To

prevent liability on the terms of a contract, note, check, or other draft, the agent should sign as follows: "Coprox Corporation, by Jerry Jiminez, agent" or "Bendrax Company, by Ralph Eakins, Treasurer."

2. Agents who contract in behalf of a partially disclosed and undisclosed principal. See IX above.

3. Agents who contract in behalf of a nonexistent principal or those who knowingly act for an incompetent principal. See X above.

4. Agents who expressly agree to be jointly liable on the contract with the principal.

5. Agents who agree to act as sureties to guarantee the principal's performance (liability).

AGENT'S TORT AND CRIMINAL LIABILITY

XII. Agents are liable for their own torts and crimes. (See Figure 13-8.)

A. *Torts.* An agent is always liable for his or her own tort. This is true whether or not the tort was committed while the agent was acting with or without authority from the principal or that the principal may have directed the agent to commit the tort. Examples of torts are fraud (i.e., deceit), duress, conversion, negligence, false imprisonment, libel, slander, interference with the contractual rights of another person, and commercial bribery.

1. The fact that the principal is also liable for the agent's tort under the concept of respondeat superior does not relieve the agent of tort liability. See XIII-A below.

2. A principal who has been held liable for the agent's tort is entitled to *indemnity* (i.e., reimbursement) from the agent in the amount of damages paid to third persons.

B. *Crimes.* An agent is always liable for crimes. This is true even though the principal authorized or ordered the agent to commit the crime. The agent is liable even though the principal is also liable for the agent's crime.

PRINCIPAL'S TORT AND CRIMINAL LIABILITY

XIII. *The following rules apply only to the employer (master)-employee (servant) relationship,* i.e., the "agency" relationship wherein the principal controls or possesses the right to control the "agent's" physical activities during the performance of the "agent's" duties. (See Figures 13-6 and 13-8 and review II and III above.)

A. *Tort liability.* A principal is liable to third persons for tortious acts committed by an agent under the following circumstances:

1. The principal expressly authorizes the agent to commit a tort. For example, P authorizes A to fraudulently misrepresent his product to C. C trusts A and purchases the product. P is liable to C for damages.

2. Doctrine of *respondeat superior.* A principal is liable for any tort committed by the agent, even though not expressly authorized by the principal, if the tort is committed by the agent while acting within the scope of the agent's employment.

a. An agent is acting within the scope of employment if:

(1) The agent is performing acts of the kind he or she was authorized to perform;

(2) The agent's acts are not unreasonably outside the time or area where such performance was to occur; or

(3) The purpose of the acts performed was to serve the principal.

FIGURE 13-8   RESPONDEAT SUPERIOR CONCEPT OF LIABILITY

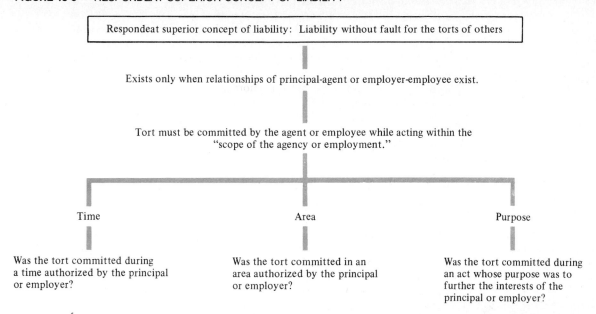

Respondeat superior concept of liability: Liability without fault for the torts of others

Exists only when relationships of principal-agent or employer-employee exist.

Tort must be committed by the agent or employee while acting within the "scope of the agency or employment."

Time

Area

Purpose

Was the tort committed during a time authorized by the principal or employer?

Was the tort committed in an area authorized by the principal or employer?

Was the tort committed during an act whose purpose was to further the interests of the principal or employer?

    b. It is no defense to the principal that the principal selected the agent with greatest care, that the agent was properly trained, or that the principal gave the agent specific instructions *not* to do the tortious act or make the tortious representation.

    3. For example, an agent assaulted a customer while attempting to collect on one of the principal's accounts, or a sales agent, on the way to call on a potential buyer, negligently drove his automobile into a bus and severely injured its passengers.

B. *Criminal liability.* A principal is not ordinarily liable for the criminal acts of agents unless (see Figure 13-7):

    1. The principal directed or authorized the crime. For example, an agent, in her anxiety to acquire a very large manufacturer's account, asked from her principal and received permission to criminally bribe (commercial bribery) an officer and a director of the manufacturer; or

    2. A statute prescribes liability, e.g., antitrust laws, sale of liquor to minors, and antipollution laws.

AGENT'S DUTIES TO THE PRINCIPAL

    XIV. The following are duties of the agent to the principal:

        A. *To exercise care and skill,* i.e., not to be negligent in the performance of services;

        B. *To personally perform all services* on behalf of the principal unless otherwise authorized. For example, the agent received actual or implied in fact authority to hire subagents;

        C. *To disclose any information* to the principal that does or could materially affect the subject matter of the agency. Full disclosure is required even though the agent may acquire the information outside the scope of the agent's employment;

        D. *To keep and render accounts.* The agent must keep a record of and account for all money or property received from the principal or the third party;

E. *To act only as authorized* by the principal;

F. *To obey reasonable instructions* from the principal;

G. *Not to act for a third person* in a transaction authorized by the principal. If the agent does so without the principal's consent, the transaction is voidable by the principal. If done without the consent or knowledge of the principal and the third person, the transaction is voidable by both the principal and the third person. In either case, the agent will not be entitled to any pay for services, as the agent's actions constituted a breach of the agent's duty of loyalty to both persons. One person cannot legally "serve two masters" in the same transaction;

H. *Fiduciary duties.* The agent owes the following fiduciary duties to the principal:

    1. Utmost loyalty and good faith;

    2. Not to take personal advantage of economic opportunities rightfully belonging to the principal;

    3. To make full and honest disclosure to the principal;

    4. Not to personally use or disclose confidential information obtained in the course of the agency, for example, customer lists, trade secrets, marketing techniques, or future marketing plans.

    5. Not to make any secret profit or compensation out of the subject matter of the agency. All secret profits and compensation belong to the principal, and the agent is under a duty to account.

    6. Examples of breach of fiduciary duties are as follows:

        a. Zack was employed by Ezra to obtain uranium leases. Zack worked for three weeks. During that time he learned of a valuable uranium deposit in Redacre. Zack quit his job with Ezra and immediately acquired a uranium lease on Redacre in his own name.

        b. Tillis employed Dale to sell textbooks on credit only. Dale secured orders for textbooks in the amount of $10,000, collected down payments in the amount of $1,000, and absconded.

        c. P employed Z to sell P's excavating machinery. Z was authorized to repair and maintain the machinery during the time it was in her possession. Z leased the machinery to contractors and pocketed the rent.

        d. Brad employed Sara as a full-time salesperson. Sara used part of her time to sell competing products made by Brad's competitor.

        e. Tab was employed as a purchasing agent for Fallon. Tab learned of an opportunity to make a purchase from a new supplier. Tab, thinking that Fallon was satisfied with her existing suppliers, neglected to inform her of the opportunity of dealing with a new supplier.

PRINCIPAL'S DUTIES TO THE AGENT

XV. The following are the duties of the principal to the agent:

    A. *To compensate the agent* (if the contract states no definite amount, the principal is obligated to pay the fair value of the agent's services);

    B. *To reimburse the agent for expenditures* of personal funds in the course of doing business for the principal;

    C. *To perform the contract* with the agent;

    D. *To refrain from unreasonably interfering* in the agent's work;

    E. *To inform the agent of existing risks* unknown to the agent;

    F. *To render an accurate account* to the agent of money or other things due the agent;

    G. *Not to harm the agent's reputation.*

XVI. Termination of the agent's authority between the principal and agent may be by:

A. *Mutual agreement of the parties:*

　　1. By the terms of the original contract or agreement which created the agency. For example, the contract recites that the agent "has thirty days to sell my 1980 Ford pickup truck"; or

　　2. At any time subsequent thereto by mutual assent to terminate.

B. *Fulfillment of the purpose of the agency:*

　　1. If the purpose is fulfilled by the agent, termination occurs at the time that the last act necessary to accomplish the purpose of the agency is completed. For example, A was hired by P to negotiate options to purchase 1,000 acres of land. Six months later A acquired an option that brought the total acreage under option to 1,000.

　　2. If the purpose is fulfilled by someone other than the agent, the agency terminates when agent receives notice thereof.

C. *Revocation by the principal:*

　　1. The principal has the power (not necessarily the right) to renounce the agency and withdraw at will.

　　2. If the principal revokes the agency in breach of contract, the principal is liable to the agent for damages.

　　3. Even though the revocation may be a breach of contract with the agent, it is an effective termination of the agency between the principal and the agent.

D. *Renunciation by the agent:*

　　1. The agent has the *power* (as does the principal) to renounce the agency and terminate it at will. The agent (as well as the principal) is liable for damages if such renunciation constitutes a breach of the agency contract. For example, A was hired by P to act as an industrial sales agent for a period of five years. After two years, A secured a better position and refused to work for P. The agency is terminated. A is liable to P for damages for breach of contract.

　　2. The law makes a distinction between the power and right to terminate an agency.

E. *Bankruptcy of the principal.* Knowledge by the agent of the principal's bankruptcy is necessary to terminate the agent's authority to act in behalf of the principal.

F. *Bankruptcy of the agent.*

G. *Death of the principal.* As a general rule, death of the principal automatically results in termination of the agency.

H. *Death of the agent.*

I. *Insanity of the principal.*

J. *Insanity of the agent* (depends on degree of insanity or whether agent is adjudicated a lunatic).

K. *Change in business conditions.* Any change such that the agent as a reasonable person should realize that if the principal knew of it, the latter would revoke the agent's authority to act upon the agreement is sufficient to terminate the agency For example, Adams had actual authority to sell Vern's goods at $2,500 per unit. Adams learned that the current market value for the same goods was $3,200 per unit. Adams's authority to sell at $2,500 per unit is terminated.

L. *Loss or destruction of the specific subject matter upon which the existence of the agency depends.* For example, P gives A his boat to sell. The boat is totally destroyed by a tornado.

M. *Loss of qualification of principal or agent.* This usually occurs whenever the agent's authority depends on the principal maintaining a license to do business, and the license is revoked.

N. *Disloyalty of agent.* Disloyalty occurs whenever an agent acquires or asserts any interest adverse to that of the principal, i.e., a breach of fiduciary duty.

O. *Subsequent illegality of the subject matter involved in the agency.* For example, an agent is employed to sell a particular pesticide, and subsequently a statute is passed declaring its sale to be illegal.

P. *Note:* An agency may have been legally terminated (i.e., authority to contract on behalf of another with third persons) between the ex-principal and ex-agent, but the possibility of the principal becoming bound thereafter for the ex-agent's contract still exists. See VIII-C above and XVIII below.

IRREVOCABLE AGENCY

XVII. Irrevocable agency (an *agency coupled with an interest*) arises when an agent acquires from the principal an interest which is either a security interest or a property interest in the subject matter of the agency in addition to the agent's employment and salary.

A. The authority of the agent is irrevocable by the principal.

B. Neither death, insanity, nor bankruptcy of the principal will cause an agency coupled with an interest to terminate. Examples of irrevocable agencies:

   1. A bailment in which the bailee is given the right to sell bailed goods if storage charges are not paid by bailor.

   2. A makes a loan to P. A receives a mortgage from P giving her the right to sell the mortgaged property in case of a default by P.

   3. A, an agent of P, has the authority to collect accounts on behalf of P. In addition, P gave to A the right to apply monies collected to the payment of A's salary and commissions.

D. An irrevocable agency terminates automatically upon the fulfillment of its purpose or upon the subsequent illegality of its subject matter or performance.

E. All other types of agencies are revocable by the principal. For example, the principal can terminate the agent's actual authority to contract in behalf of the principal merely by expressing the intent to do so to the agent or to the third party.

REQUIREMENT OF NOTICE TO THIRD PARTIES OF TERMINATION OF AGENCY

XVIII. Notice to third parties from the principal is required upon termination of the agency between the principal and the agent. Failure of the principal to give third parties notice of the termination of the agency may result in creation of apparent (ostensible) (authority by estoppel) authority. The rule applies even though the termination was by the agent rather than the principal. It is immaterial whether the termination was wrongful or rightful. For example, Paul was the sole proprietor of a farm equipment retail store. Edmunds was Paul's key employee and manager. Edmunds had authority to sell and collect on accounts. Paul sold his store and business to Edmunds and retired. Paul did not give notice to third parties of the change in ownership. Edmunds continued to sell in behalf of Paul and collected $150,000 from customers. He then absconded with the money. Paul is liable on the contracts executed by Edmunds. The customer need not pay a second time for the goods.

A. *Actual notice.* Actual notice is required to be given to all persons who had prior dealings with the agent or principal. Actual notice is effective when received.

B. *Constructive notice.* Public notice is required to persons who have not had prior dealings with the agent or principal but who knew of the existence of the agency, e.g., publication in a newspaper. Constructive notice is effective at the time it is properly published even though never read.

SELF-QUIZ

To check your understanding of the key words and concepts and the accuracy of your answers to the questions, refer to the text material as referenced by page number.

KEY WORDS AND CONCEPTS

QUESTIONS

1. Describe how an agency may be created. **(381)**
2. Differentiate between a principal-agent relationship, a master-servant relationship, and an independent contractor on the basis of liability assumed by the principal. **(380)**
3. Who has legal capacity to be a principal? An agent? **(383)**
4. What are the various types of authority an agent may possess? **(385)**
5. A principal may be disclosed, partially disclosed, or undisclosed. Discuss the liabilities of the principal and agent to the third person under each of these situations. **(386)**
6. When is a principal liable for an agent's torts? **(390)**
7. What are the legal implications when an agent acts without authority? **(385, 389)**
8. When is an agent liable for the agent's own torts? **(390)**
9. What are the agent's duties to the principal? **(391)**
10. What are the principal's duties to the agent? **(392)**
11. How can an agency be terminated between the principal and agent? Between the principal and the third person? **(393)**
12. Under what circumstances is an agent bound to the terms of a contract entered into with third parties in behalf of the principal? When is an agent liable for breach of warranty of authority? **(389)**

SELECTED QUESTIONS AND UNOFFICIAL ANSWERS

OBJECTIVE QUESTIONS

Select the best answer for each of the following items. Mark only one answer for each item. Answer all items.

MAY 1981

29. Barton, a wealthy art collector, orally engaged Deiter to obtain a rare and beautiful painting from Cumbers, a third party. Cumbers did not know that Barton had engaged Deiter to obtain the painting for Barton because as Barton told Deiter "that would cause the price to skyrocket." Regarding the liability of the parties if a contract is made or purported to be made, which of the following is correct?

a. Since the appointment of Deiter was oral, *no* agency exists, and any contract made by Deiter on Barton's behalf is invalid.

b. Because Barton specifically told Deiter *not* to

reveal for whom he (Deiter) was buying the painting, Deiter can *not* be personally liable on the contract made on Barton's behalf.

c. If Deiter makes a contract with Cumbers which Deiter breaches, Cumbers may, after learning of the agreement between Barton and Deiter, elect to recover from either Barton or Deiter.

d. If Deiter makes a contract to purchase the painting, without revealing he is Barton's agent, Cumbers has entered into a contract which is voidable at his election.

30. Moderne Fabrics, Inc., hired Franklin as an assistant vice president of sales at $2,000 a month. The employment had no fixed duration. In light of their relationship to each other, which of the following is correct?

a. Franklin has a legal duty to reveal any interest adverse to that of Moderne in matters concerning his employment.

b. If Franklin voluntarily terminates his employment with Moderne after working for it for several years, he can *not* work for a competitor for a reasonable period after termination.

c. Moderne can dismiss Franklin only for cause.

d. The employment contract between the parties must be in writing.

31. Sly was a general agent of the Cute Cosmetics Company with authority to sell, make collections, and adjust disputes. Sly was caught padding his monthly expense account by substantial amounts and was dismissed. Cute hired another general agent, Ready, to replace Sly. Ready was slowly but steadily calling upon Sly's accounts to make sales and was informing them that Sly's services had been terminated. Cute also published a notice in the appropriate trade journals and the local newspaper announcing the replacement of Sly with Ready. Sly, after he was let go, called on all the customers who had outstanding accounts payable and quickly made whatever collections he could in cash and absconded. Which of the following statements is correct regarding Cute's legal right against the customers?

a. Cute can regain possession of the goods since title did *not* pass because Sly's actions constituted a fraud.

b. Cute can obtain payment from the customers despite Sly's wrongful acts since it had published a notice of Sly's dismissal.

c. Cute will have to absorb the loss since Sly had

continuing implied authority to make collections.

d. Cute will have to absorb the loss unless Cute can prove the customers had actual notice of Sly's dismissal.

32. Marcross is an agent for Fashion Frocks, Ltd. As such, Marcross made a contract for and on behalf of Fashion Frocks with Sowinski Fabrics which was not authorized and upon which Fashion has disclaimed liability. Sowinski has sued Fashion on the contract asserting that Marcross had the apparent authority to make it. In considering the factors which will determine the scope of Marcross' apparent authority, which of the following would *not* be important?

a. The custom and usages of the business.

b. Previous acquiescence by the principal in similar contracts made by Marcross.

c. The express limitations placed upon Marcross' authority which were *not* known by Sowinski.

d. The status of Marcross' position in Fashion Frocks.

33. Duval Manufacturing Industries, Inc., orally engaged Harris as one of its district sales managers for an 18-month period commencing April 1, 1980. Harris commenced work on that date and performed his duties in a highly competent manner for several months. On October 1, 1980, the company gave Harris a notice of termination as of November 1, 1980, citing a downturn in the market for its products. Harris sues seeking either specific performance or damages for breach of contract. Duval pleads the Statute of Frauds and/or a justified dismissal due to the economic situation. What is the probable outcome of the lawsuit?

a. Harris will prevail because he has partially performed under the terms of the contract.

b. Harris will lose because his termination was caused by economic factors beyond Duval's control.

c. Harris will lose because such a contract must be in writing and signed by a proper agent of Duval.

d. Harris will prevail because the Statute of Frauds does *not* apply to contracts such as his.

34. Jason Manufacturing Company wished to acquire a site for a warehouse. Knowing that if it negotiated directly for the purchase of the property the price would be substantially increased, it employed Kent, an agent, to secure lots without disclosing that he was acting for Jason. Kent's authority was evidenced by a writing signed by the proper officers of Jason. Kent entered into a contract in his own name to purchase Peter's lot, giving Peter a negotiable note for $1,000 signed by Kent as first payment. Jason wrote Kent acknowledging the purchase. Jason also disclosed its identity as Kent's principal to Peter. In respect to the rights and liabilities of the parties, which of the following is a correct statement?

a. Peter is *not* bound on the contract since Kent's failure to disclose he was Jason's agent was fraudulent.

b. Jason, Kent and Peter are potentially liable on the contract.

c. Unless Peter formally ratifies the substitution of Jason for Kent, he is *not* liable.

d. Kent has *no* liability since he was acting for and on behalf of an existing principal.

NOVEMBER 1980

26. A power of attorney is a useful method of creation of an agency relationship. The power of attorney

a. Must be signed by both the principal and the agent.

b. Exclusively determines the purpose and powers of the agent.

c. Is the written authorization of the agent to act on the principal's behalf.

d. Is used primarily in the creation of the attorney-client relationship.

27. Agents sometimes have liability to third parties for their actions taken for and on behalf of the principal. An agent will *not* be personally liable in which of the following circumstances?

a. If he makes a contract which he had no authority to make but which the principal ratifies.

b. If he commits a tort while engaged in the principal's business.

c. If he acts for a principal which he knows is nonexistent and the third party is unaware of this.

d. If he acts for an undisclosed principal as long as the principal is subsequently disclosed.

28. Mayberry engaged Williams as her agent. It was mutually agreed that Williams would *not* disclose that he was acting as Mayberry's agent. Instead he was to deal with prospective customers as if he were

a principal acting on his own behalf. This he did and made several contracts for Mayberry. Assuming Mayberry, Williams or the customer seeks to avoid liability on one of the contracts involved, which of the following statements is correct?

a. Williams has *no* liability once he discloses that Mayberry was the real principal.

b. Mayberry must ratify the Williams contracts in order to be held liable.

c. The third party may choose to hold either Williams or Mayberry liable.

d. The third party can avoid liability because he believed he was dealing with Williams as a principal.

29. Park Manufacturing hired Stone as a traveling salesman to sell goods manufactured by Park. Stone also sold a line of products manufactured by a friend. He did *not* disclose this to Park. The relationship was unsatisfactory and Park finally fired Stone after learning of Stone's sales of the other manufacturer's goods. Stone, enraged at Park for firing him, continued to make contracts on Park's behalf with both new and old customers that were almost uniformly disadvantageous to Park. Park, upon learning of this, gave written notice of Stone's discharge to all parties with whom Stone had dealt. Which of the following statements is *incorrect*?

a. Park can bring an action against Stone to have him account for any secret profits.

b. Prior to notification, Stone retained some continued authority to bind Park despite termination of the agency relationship.

c. New customers who contracted with Stone for the first time could enforce the contracts against Park if they knew that Stone had been Park's salesman but were unaware that Stone was fired.

d. If Park had promptly published a notification of termination of Stone's employment in the local newspapers and in the trade publications, he would *not* be liable for any of Stone's contracts.

30. Michaels appointed Fairfax as his agent. The appointment was in writing and clearly indicated the scope of Fairfax's authority and also that Fairfax was *not* to disclose that he was acting as an agent for Michaels. Under the circumstances

a. Fairfax is an agent coupled with an interest.

b. Michaels must ratify any contracts made by Fairfax on behalf of Michaels.

c. Fairfax's appointment had to be in writing to be enforceable.

d. Fairfax has the implied and apparent authority of an agent.

31. Magnus Real Estate Developers, Inc., wanted to acquire certain tracts of land in Marshall Township in order to build a shopping center complex. To accomplish this goal, Magnus engaged Dexter, a sophisticated real estate dealer, to represent them in the purchase of the necessary land without revealing the existence of the agency. Dexter began to slowly but steadily acquire the requisite land. However, Dexter made the mistake of purchasing one tract outside the description of the land needed. Which of the following is correct under these circumstances?

a. The use of an agent by Magnus, an undisclosed principal, is manifestly illegal.

b. Either Magnus or Dexter may be held liable on the contracts for the land, including the land that was *not* within the scope of the proposed shopping center.

c. An undisclosed principal such as Magnus can have *no* liability under the contract since the third party believed he was dealing with Dexter as a principal.

d. An agent for an undisclosed principal assumes *no* liability as long as he registers his relationship to the principal with the clerk of the proper county having jurisdiction.

33. Wanamaker, Inc., engaged Anderson as its agent to purchase original oil paintings for resale by Wanamaker. Anderson's express authority was specifically limited to a maximum purchase price of $25,000 for any collection provided it contained a minimum of five oil paintings. Anderson purchased a seven-picture collection on Wanamaker's behalf for $30,000. Based upon these facts, which of the following is a correct legal conclusion?

a. The express limitation on Anderson's authority negates any apparent authority.

b. Wanamaker can *not* ratify the contract since Anderson's actions were clearly in violation of his contract.

c. If Wanamaker rightfully disaffirms the unauthorized contract, Anderson is personally liable to the seller.

d. Neither Wanamaker *nor* Anderson is liable on the contract since the seller was obligated to ascertain Anderson's authority.

50. Ozgood is a principal and Flood is his agent. Ozgood is totally dissatisfied with the agency relationship and wishes to terminate it. In which of the following situations does Ozgood *not* have the power to terminate the relationship?

a. Ozgood and Flood have agreed that their agency is irrevocable.

b. Flood has been appointed as Ozgood's agent pursuant to a power of attorney.

c. Flood is an agent coupled with an interest.

d. The agency agreement is in writing and provides for a specific duration which has *not* elapsed.

40. Dolby was employed as an agent for the Ace Used Car Company to purchase newer model used cars. His authority was limited by a $3,000 maximum price for any car. A wholesaler showed him a 1938 classic car which was selling for $5,000. The wholesaler knew that Ace only dealt in newer model used cars and that Dolby had never paid more than $3,000 for any car. Dolby bought the car for Ace, convinced that it was worth at least $7,000. When he reported this to Williams, Ace's owner, Williams was furious but he nevertheless authorized processing of the automobile for resale. Williams also began pricing the car with antique car dealers who indicated that the current value of the car was $4,800. Williams called the wholesaler, told him that Dolby had exceeded his authority, that he was returning the car, and that he was demanding repayment of the purchase price. What is the wholesaler's *best* defense in the event of a lawsuit?

a. Dolby had apparent authority to purchase the car.

b. Dolby's purchase was effectively ratified by Ace.

c. Dolby had express authority to purchase the car.

d. Dolby had implied authority to purchase the car.

45. What fiduciary duty, if any, exists in an agency relationship?

a. The agent owes a fiduciary duty to third parties he deals with for and on behalf of his principal.

b. The principal owes a fiduciary duty to his agent.

c. The agent owes a fiduciary duty to his principal.

d. There is *no* fiduciary duty in an agency relationship.

1. Wilcox works as a welder for Miracle Muffler, Inc. He was specially trained by Miracle in the procedures and safety precautions applicable to installing replacement mufflers on automobiles. One rule of which he was aware involved a prohibition against installing a muffler on any auto which had heavily congealed oil or grease or which had any leaks. Wilcox disregarded this rule, and as a result an auto caught fire causing extensive property damage and injury to Wilcox. Which of the following statements is correct?

a. Miracle is *not* liable because its rule prohibited Wilcox from installing the muffler in question.
b. Miracle is *not* liable to Wilcox under the workmen's compensation laws.
c. Miracle is liable irrespective of its efforts to prevent such an occurrence and the fact that it exercised reasonable care.
d. Wilcox does *not* have any personal liability for the loss because he was acting for and on behalf of his employer.

2. Halliday engaged Fox as her agent. It was mutually agreed that Fox would *not* disclose that he was acting as Halliday's agent. Instead he was to deal with prospective customers as if he were a principal acting on his own behalf. This he did and made several contracts for Halliday. Assuming Halliday, Fox, or the customer seeks to avoid liability on one of the contracts involved, which of the following statements is correct?

a. The third party may choose to hold either Fox or Halliday liable.
b. The third party can avoid liability because he believed he was dealing with Fox as a principal.
c. Halliday must ratify the Fox contracts in order to be held liable.
d. Fox has *no* liability once he discloses that Halliday was the real principal.

3. Smith has been engaged as a general sales agent for the Victory Medical Supply Company. Victory, as Smith's principal, owes Smith several duties which are implied as a matter of law. Which of the following duties is owed by Victory to Smith?

a. *Not* to compete.
b. To reimburse Smith for all expenditures as long as they are remotely related to Smith's employment and *not* specifically prohibited.
c. *Not* to dismiss Smith without cause for one year from the making of the contract if the duration of the contract is indefinite.
d. To indemnify Smith for liability for acts done in good faith upon Victory's orders.

4. Winter is a sales agent for Magnum Enterprises. Winter has assumed an obligation to indemnify Magnum if any of Winter's customers fail to pay. Under these circumstances, which of the following is correct?

a. Winter's engagement must be in writing regardless of its duration.
b. Upon default, Magnum must first proceed against the delinquent purchaser-debtor.
c. The above facts describe a *del credere* agency relationship and Winter will be liable in the event his customers fail to pay Magnum.
d. There is *no* fiduciary relationship on either Winter's or Magnum's part.

Answers to Objective Questions

May 1981		November 1980	
29. c	32. c	26. c	29. d
30. a	33. c	27. a	30. d
31. d	34. b	28. c	

November 1979		May 1979	
31. b	50. c	40. b	45. c
33. c			

May 1978	
1. c	3. d
2. a	4. c

Explanation of Answers to Objective Questions

MAY 1981

29. **(c)** Upon learning the identity of the undisclosed principal, the third party may sue the agent and the principal but may only elect to recover from one of them. Answer (a) is incorrect because an agency relationship could result from an express (oral or written) or implied agreement as well as by estoppel. Answer (b) is incorrect because an agent for an undisclosed or partially disclosed principal is fully liable for performance on contracts the agent makes. This is true even though the contracts are within the agent's scope of authority. Answer (d) is incorrect since the fact that an agency relationship is undisclosed will not allow the third party to avoid liability under a contract made by an agent acting within the scope of his authority.

30. **(a)** An agency relationship is a fiduciary relationship which means that the agent owes great trust and loyalty to the principal while acting as an

agent. An agent with interests adverse to his principal must disclose these facts to the principal. Answer (b) is incorrect since the employment contract did not contain a restrictive covenant prohibiting competition. The agent may work for a competitor but has a duty not to disclose confidential information if detrimental to his old principal. Answer (c) is incorrect because a principal can normally dismiss the agent without cause even though the principal may be liable for breach. Answer (d) is incorrect since the contract is capable of being performed in one year; the oral contract is enforceable.

31. (d) Termination of an agency relationship can occur by operation of law (e.g., death or insanity of either party, bankruptcy of the principal) or by acts of the parties (e.g., terms of the agreement, mutual recission, unilateral acts of either party). When termination occurs by acts of the parties, the principal must give actual notice to all parties who had previously dealt with the agent. All parties that knew of the relationship but had never dealt with Sly need only receive constructive notice through publication in an appropriate trade journal or newspaper. Answer (b) is incorrect since Cute did not give actual notice to the prior customers. Consequently, Sly retained apparent authority, not implied, to make collections and sell goods. Therefore, answers (a) and (b) are incorrect.

32. (c) A third person's reasonable interpretation of a principal's representations measures apparent authority. Express limitations on Marcross' authority, which were not known by Sowinski, are called secret limitations. These limitations do not alter an agent's apparent authority since the third party can assume there are no limits on the agent's normal authority unless informed to the contrary. Answer (a) is incorrect since an agent's normal authority is measured in relation to the custom and usages of the business. Answer (b) is incorrect since previous acquisitions will influence a third party's interpretation of an agent's authority. Answer (d) is incorrect because apparent authority may be inferred from the position or status of the agent.

33. (c) The Statute of Frauds provides that contracts not performable within one year must be in writing to be enforceable. Since the Duval-Harris contract cannot be performed within one year (18 month duration), it is required to be in writing to be enforceable. Answer (a) is incorrect since Harris'

past performance would allow him to recover any amount owed him from services rendered before termination. However, it will not enable him to enforce the executory portion (unperformed part) of the oral contract. Answer (b) is incorrect since the economic factors cited by Duval would not be proper grounds for avoidance of the contract. Economic factors do not qualify as an objective impossibility which would excuse Duval's duty to perform. Answer (d) is incorrect since the Statute of Frauds does apply.

34. (b) All three parties are potentially liable on the contract. A principal, whether disclosed, undisclosed or partially disclosed, will be liable for the contracts of his agent if these agreements are within the scope of the agent's express, implied or apparent authority. Answers (a) and (c) are incorrect because an undisclosed agency relationship is not fraudulent or illegal and will effectively bind the third party to the agreement without that party's subsequent ratification. Answer (d) is incorrect because an agent, acting on behalf of an undisclosed or partially disclosed principal, is personally liable for performance of the contract even though the agreement was within the agent's scope of authority.

NOVEMBER 1980

26. (c) A power of attorney is a written document authorizing another to act as one's agent. The written authorization must only be signed by the principal. Besides the express authority granted in the power of attorney, the agent can also have implied and apparent powers by which to bind the principal. Thus, answer (c) is correct.

27. (a) The correct answer is (a) since an agent, after the principal ratifies an unauthorized act, is acting within his authority and is free of any liability on the contract. An agent is personally liable for all torts he commits; therefore, answer (b) is incorrect. An agent is liable if he acts for a principal which he knows is non-existent and knows the third party is unaware of this. Thus, answer (c) is incorrect. If an agent contracts for an undisclosed principal the agent remains liable to the third party even though he is acting within the scope of his authority. The agent, however, has recourse against the principal. The third party can sue either the principal or agent. As a result, answer (d) is incorrect.

28. (c) In an undisclosed principal relationship, the third party has the option of holding the principal or agent liable, making answer (c) correct. Answer (a) is incorrect since in an undisclosed principal relationship the agent is always liable even though acting within the scope of his authority. Answer (b) is incorrect because Williams had been expressly authorized to make these contracts. Consequently, there would be no need for Mayberry to ratify these agreements. They are binding due to Williams' express authority. Answer (d) is incorrect because an undisclosed principal relationship is legal. The only time an undisclosed principal could not enforce an agreement against the third party would be when the contract specifically excluded an undisclosed principal as a party to the agreement.

29. (d) When termination of an agency relationship occurs by means other than operation of law (such as unilateral action upon the part of the principal) the principal is obligated to give two types of notice. First, constructive notice by publication to all third parties who have had no prior dealings with the agent. This is effective to terminate the agent's authority to bind the principal even if the third party does not read the publication. Secondly, the principal must give actual notice to all parties that had prior dealings with the agent. If the principal does not give proper notice upon termination the agent has apparent authority to bind the principal. This makes answer (d) correct since it contains the incorrect statement. An agency is a fiduciary relationship in which the agent owes good faith and loyalty to the principal. The agent is precluded from dealing for his own interests (secret profits). Violation of the agent's fiduciary duty allows the principal to sue for the secret profits. This makes answer (a) incorrect because it contains a true statement.

30. (d) The correct answer is (d). This is a legal contract establishing Fairfax as an agent with express, implied and apparent authority. Answer (a) is incorrect because an agent coupled with an interest is a relationship where the agent has a property or security interest in the relationship (beyond sharing in the commissions) and as a result the principal cannot terminate the relationship. The principal needs to ratify only those contracts outside the agent's scope of authority (express or implied). This explains why answer (b) is false. Answer (c) is incorrect since the creation of a principal agency rela-

tionship through contract needs to be in writing only if it is not capable of being performed in one year.

NOVEMBER 1979

31. (b) Either Magnus (the undisclosed principal) or Dexter (the agent) may be held liable on the contract for all land entered into by Dexter on Magnus's behalf including the parcel not wanted by Magnus. Dexter executed the contract within the scope of the agency relationship and thus Dexter's actions are binding on Magnus. Also, Dexter is liable on each of the contracts because he failed to disclose that he was acting as agent for Magnus Corporation. Answer (a) is incorrect because the practice of using an agent to represent an undisclosed principal has been accepted by the courts as being legal and ethical. Answer (c) is incorrect because an undisclosed principal has full liability under a contract made by his agent even though the third party is not aware of the existence of the principal at the time of the contract. Answer (d) is incorrect because there is no provision for an agent of an undisclosed principal registering his relationship with any public official. In order to avoid liability, the agent must fully disclose his principal before the contract is made.

33. (c) If the principal, Wanamaker, rightfully disaffirms the unauthorized contract by Anderson, the agent, Anderson is personally liable to the seller on the theory of the implied warranty of authority. Anderson warranted to the seller that he had authority to bind Wanamaker to the sale contract. Answer (a) is incorrect because an express limitation on an agent's authority does not negate any apparent authority. Apparent authority is based on prior action and on what is customary in the general business community. Answer (b) is incorrect because Wanamaker, the principal, could ratify the contract made by Anderson since Anderson was purporting to act for Wanamaker. Answer (d) is incorrect because the agent is always liable on a contract that he makes on behalf of his principal on the theory that he warrants to the third party that he has authority. The seller should have ascertained Anderson's authority in order to assure that he had an enforceable contract against Wanamaker.

50. (c) Normally, a principal has the power to terminate an agency relationship even though it would constitute a breach to do so. However, where the agency is an agency coupled with an interest, i.e., where the agent owns part of the subject matter, the principal does not have the power to terminate the relationship. Answer (a) is incorrect because a principal can elect to terminate and be liable for breach of contract even though he has agreed that the agency is irrecoverable. Answer (b) is incorrect because an appointment of an agent pursuant to a power of attorney does not deprive the principal of the power to terminate the relationship. Answer (d) is incorrect because an agency agreement, even if in writing, and even if it provides for a specific duration, can be terminated by the principal in violation of the agreement. However, this action does subject the principal to a suit for damages.

MAY 1979

40. (b) After discovering that the agent had disobeyed instructions and exceeded his authority, Ace nevertheless proceeded to process the car for resale. This constitutes an effective ratification since it is approval after the fact. Answer (a) is incorrect because the wholesaler knew from previous dealings that Ace Used Car Company only dealt in newer model used cars and Dolby had never paid more than $3,000 for any car; thus apparent authority is missing. Answer (c) is incorrect because Dolby had express instructions not to pay more than $3,000 and to purchase only newer model vehicles. Answer (d) is incorrect because implied authority is that authority which is deemed necessary to carry out an agent's express authority. Since he did not have express authority, he did not have implied authority either.

45. (c) In an agency relationship the agent owes a fiduciary duty to his principal. Therefore answer (d) is incorrect since it states there is no fiduciary duty in an agency relationship. Answer (a) is incorrect since an agent owes no fiduciary duty to third parties with whom he deals on behalf of his principal. Answer (b) is incorrect because generally speaking the principal owes no fiduciary duty, since the principal is not required to subordinate his own interest for the benefit of his agent. The duty the principal owes to the agent is to compensate him in accordance with the contract, and to reimburse and indemnify the agent for money expended or expenses incurred by the agent for the benefit of the principal.

MAY 1978

1. (c) The principal or employer is liable for injurious acts caused by its agents or employees who are acting within the course and scope of their employment. The fact that the principal had a rule designed to prevent such an injurious act is not a legal defense. Thus answer (a) is incorrect. Answer (b) is incorrect because the employer is liable to the employee under the workmen's compensation laws for a job-related injury even if the employee disobeyed instructions or was negligent. Answer (d) is incorrect because even though the employer is liable, the negligent employee is not excused from personal liability for negligent acts. If Miracle is held liable, e.g., for property damage by the lessor, Miracle will be subrogated to the third party's rights against Wilcox.

2. (a) Halliday is an undisclosed principal. A third party who contracts with the agent of the undisclosed principal may choose to hold either the agent or principal liable. Answer (b) is incorrect because third-party unawareness of the principal does not release the principal from any contract. Answer (c) is incorrect because an undisclosed principal is liable for contracts made by the agent and ratification by the principal is not necessary. Answer (d) is incorrect because an agent who acts for an undisclosed principal remains liable even after the principal is disclosed.

3. (d) A principal (employer) owes a duty to its agent (employee) to indemnify the agent for acts carried out in good faith upon the principal's (employer's) behalf. Answer (a) is incorrect because a principal owes no duty not to compete with its agent. It is the agent who has a duty not to compete with its principal. Answer (b) is incorrect because a principal has the duty to reimburse an agent only for expenditures directly related to employment. Answer (c) is incorrect because agency agreements of an indefinite duration are generally implied to continue from pay period to pay period and may be terminated by notice of either party.

4. (c) An agent who sells on credit and guarantees the accounts to his principal is known as a del credere agent. Answer (a) is incorrect because a del credere agent's guarantee is not a suretyship agreement and is not required to be in writing.

Answer (b) is incorrect because Winter promised to indemnify Magnum if the customers failed to pay; the agreement did not require Magnum to try to collect from the customers. Answer (d) is incorrect because as an agent, Winter is a fiduciary and owes the duty of loyalty, good faith, obedience, duty to account, not to commingle, etc.

ESSAY QUESTIONS AND ANSWERS

MAY 1980 (Estimated time: 10 to 13 minutes)

5. Part a. Vogel, an assistant buyer for the Granite City Department Store, purchased metal art objects from Duval Reproductions. Vogel was totally without express or apparent authority to do so, but believed that his purchase was a brilliant move likely to get him a promotion. The head buyer of Granite was livid when he learned of Vogel's activities. However, after examining the merchandise and listening to Vogel's pitch, he reluctantly placed the merchandise in the storeroom and put a couple of pieces on display for a few days to see whether it was a "hot item" and a "sure thing" as Vogel claimed. The item was neither "hot" nor "sure" and when it didn't move at all, the head buyer ordered the display merchandise repacked and the entire order returned to Duval with a letter that stated the merchandise had been ordered by an assistant buyer who had absolutely no authority to make the purchase. Duval countered with a lawsuit for breach of contract.

Required Answer the following, setting forth reasons for any conclusions stated.
   Will Duval prevail?

Answer Yes. Despite the stated lack of express or apparent initial authority of Vogel, Granite City Department Store's agent, there would appear to be a ratification by the principal.
   It is clear from the facts stated that Granite would not have been liable on the Vogel contract if the head buyer had immediately notified Duval and returned the goods. Instead the head buyer retained the goods and placed some on display in an attempt to sell them. Had they proved to be a "hot" item, undoubtedly the art objects would have been gratefully kept by Granite. Granite wants to reject the goods if they don't sell but wants to have the benefits if they do sell. Such conduct is inconsistent with a repudiation based upon the agent's lack of express

or apparent authority. The retention of the goods for the time indicated, the attempted sale of the goods, and a failure to notify Duval in a timely way, when taken together, constitute a ratification of the unauthorized contract.

5. Part b. Foremost Realty, Inc., is a real estate broker that also buys and sells real property for its own account. Hobson purchased a ranch from Foremost. The terms were 10% down with the balance payable over a 25 year period. After several years of profitable operation of the ranch, Hobson had two successive bad years. As a result, he defaulted on the mortgage. Foremost did not want to foreclose, but instead offered to allow Hobson to remain on the ranch and suspend the payment schedule until Foremost could sell the property at a reasonable price. However, Foremost insisted that it be appointed as the irrevocable and exclusive agent for the sale of the property. Although Hobson agreed, he subsequently became dissatisfied with Foremost's efforts to sell the ranch and gave Foremost notice in writing terminating the agency. Foremost has indicated to Hobson that he does not have the legal power to do so.

Required Answer the following, setting forth reasons for any conclusions stated.
   Can Hobson terminate the agency?

Answer No. The facts reveal an agency coupled with an interest and therefore an irrevocable agency. Most agency-principal relationships are terminable by either party. However, one clearly recognized exception to this generally prevailing rule is that the agency may not be terminated when the agent has an interest in property that is the subject of the agency. This agency, coupled with an interest rule, applies here since the creditor (Foremost Realty, Inc.) has the requisite interest in the property because it is the mortgagee-creditor of the defaulting mortgagor-debtor. Thus, the appointment by Hobson of Foremost as the irrevocable agent for the sale of the mortgaged property cannot be terminated unilaterally by Hobson.

NOVEMBER 1977 (Estimated time: 20 to 25 minutes)

5. Duval was the agent for Sunshine Pools, Inc. He sold pools, related equipment, and accessories for Sunshine. Holmes, president of Tilden Sporting

Equipment, Inc., approached Duval and offered him an excellent deal on a commission basis if he would secretly sell their brand of diving boards and platforms instead of the Sunshine products. Duval agreed. The arrangement which was worked out between them was to have Duval continue to act as a general sales agent for Sunshine and concurrently act as the agent for an "undisclosed" principal in respect to Tilden diving boards. He could then sell both lines to new pool customers and go back to prior customers to solicit sales of the Tilden boards. Duval was not to mention his relationship with Tilden to the prospective customers, and of course, no mention of these facts would be made to Sunshine. Duval was told to use his discretion insofar as effectively misleading the prospective customers about whose diving board they were purchasing.

Things went smoothly for the first several months until Tilden began to manufacture and ship defective diving boards. Subsequently, Tilden became insolvent, and Holmes absconded with advance payments made by purchasers including those who had purchased from Duval.

Required Answer the following, setting forth reasons for any conclusions stated.

a. What are the rights of the various customers against Duval?

b. What are the rights of the various customers against Tilden and/or Holmes?

c. What rights does Sunshine have against Duval?

d. What rights does Sunshine have against Tilden and/or Holmes?

Answer

a. Duval has potential liability based upon two separate legal theories: the undisclosed principal doctrine and the theory of fraud. Duval led the customers to believe that the diving boards were Sun-shine products. Thus, at a minimum, he would not be disclosing his true principal, or he may have been intentionally misstating the facts so as to make it appear that the purchaser was obtaining all Sunshine products. The rule is clear that an agent is personally liable on the contracts when acting for an undisclosed principal. Thus, the customers can sue Duval and recover on this basis. Alternatively, fraud may be asserted, and if proved, liability will attach in that the agent is responsible for his torts even though committed in an agency capacity.

b. Tilden, an undisclosed principal, is liable for the contracts made for and on its behalf even though its identity was not initially disclosed. Furthermore, Tilden would be liable for the tort of conversion committed by Holmes who absconded with advance payments made by purchasers. Tilden also would be liable for breach of warranty with respect to defective goods delivered to the various customers. Finally, Holmes would be personally liable for the conversion of the customers' advance payments.

c. Duval has breached his fiduciary duty by selling a competing item without his principal's knowledge and consent. Therefore, he can be dismissed, and he can be required to account for any profits he has realized as a result of his breach of contract and trust.

d. Sunshine could proceed against Tilden based upon Tilden's intentional interference with a contractual relationship. This well-recognized tort occurs, as it did here, when a party intends to induce the breach of a contract or interfere with the performance of a contract (here the Sunshine-Duval contract) with the knowledge of the existence of that contract and the belief that such breach or interference will follow. In addition, Sunshine would have an action against Holmes personally as a result of his tortious conduct even though Holmes acted in his capacity as president of Tilden.

CHAPTER

14

Partnerships

The following is a generalized description of subjects to be tested through the May 1983 Uniform CPA Examination.

Another major area is partnership law, which encompasses the characteristics of the partnership and limited partnership; the rights, duties, and liabilities of the partnership and the partners among themselves and to third parties; and the rights of the various parties upon dissolution. These topics are based upon the Uniform Partnership Act and the Limited Partnership Act.[1]

The AICPA Board of Examiners has adopted a new content specification outline for the business law section of the Uniform CPA Examination, *to be effective with the November 1983 examination*. The outline lists the following topics to be tested under the title "Partnerships."

B. Partnerships
1. Formation and Existence of Partnerships
2. Liabilities and Authority of Partners
3. Transfer of Partnership Interest
4. Dissolution and Winding Up[2]

NATURE AND DEFINITION OF A GENERAL PARTNERSHIP

I. A *partnership* is an association of two or more persons to carry on a business for profit as coowners (see Figure 14-1). Each partner in a *general partnership* is both an agent and a principal in respect to other partners and consequently owes a fiduciary duty to

---

[1] AICPA, *Information for CPA Candidates*, Copyright © 1975, 1979, by the American Institute of Certified Public Accountants, Inc.
[2] AICPA, *Business Law—Content Specification Outline*, approved by the AICPA Board of Examiners on August 31, 1981.

FIGURE 14-1 ELEMENTS OF A GENERAL PARTNERSHIP

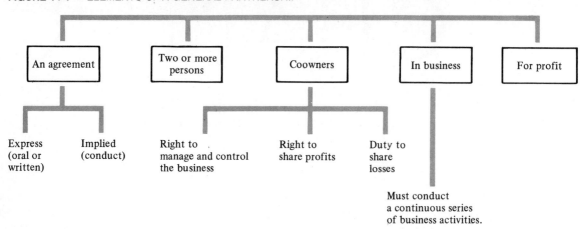

every other partner. *Note:* Because partners are in a principal-agent relationship to each other, the law of agency as discussed in Chapter 13 is fully applicable to their relationship in respect to each other and with third parties. In addition to the law of agency, the Uniform Partnership Act provides special rules which define the rights and duties of partners.

A. *Agreement.* No partnership can exist without an express or implied agreement by two or more persons to conduct themselves as partners. If their relationship includes all the elements of a partnership, a partnership results even though they actually believed that they were acting otherwise. For example, X, Y, and Z were partners under a written partnership agreement. X died. Y and Z continued operating the business without executing another partnership agreement. Subsequently, a dispute arose between Y and Z as to whether Z was entitled to compensation for his services as provided for in the written partnership agreement between X, Y, and Z. Although X's death caused an automatic dissolution of the partnership, Y and Z's continuing to do "business as usual" created a new partnership by implication between Y and Z pursuant to the terms of the previous partnership agreement.

B. *Business.* As a general rule, an association to conduct only one transaction is not considered the conduct of business and consequently is not a partnership. X, Y, and Z agree to combine their abilities and resources to sell a farm which they recently inherited from their grandfather. Generally, "business" includes multiple activities intended to carry on a trade or profession. Associations created to conduct one transaction are usually held to be joint ventures by the courts.

C. *Coowners.* Coownership involves the right to share in the profits of the business, the duty to share in its losses, the right to make management decisions, and the right to possess and use partnership property for partnership purposes. The right to share in profits, the right to take part in management, and the duty to share in losses are the strongest indicia of coownership. Partnership coownership should not be confused with joint ownership of property, i.e., joint tenancy, tenancy in common, community property, condominium, or tenancy by the entireties. Partnership property is owned by the partnership as a business entity even though its title may legally be taken in the name of an individual partner. See VIII-B below.

D. *Profits.* The sharing of gross profits does not of itself establish a partnership. Section 7(4) of the Uniform Partnership Act provides that the receipt by a person of a share of profits of a business is prima facie (i.e., in the first instance) evidence that

that person is a partner. This section also provides that no such inference shall be drawn if such profits are received in payment:

1. Of a debt, by installments or otherwise;
2. As wages of an employee;
3. As rent to a landlord even though the payment may vary with the profits of the business;
4. As interest on a loan;
5. As an annuity to a widow or executor of a deceased partner; or
6. As consideration for the sale of the goodwill of a business or other property by installment or otherwise.

FORMATION OF THE PARTNERSHIP AGREEMENT

II. An *agreement* is essential to the formation of every partnership.
  A. It may be *express or implied* from the conduct and activities of the parties.
  B. It may be *oral or in writing. Exception:* A contract to form a partnership that is to continue for a period longer than one year must be in writing under the provisions of the Statute of Frauds.

CHARACTERISTICS OF A GENERAL PARTNERSHIP

III. The following are distinctive characteristics of a partnership.
  A. It is an express or implied contract.
  B. Each partner is an agent and principal to other partners for partnership purposes. (See Figure 14-2.)
  C. Each partner owes a fiduciary duty to each other partner. (See Figure 14-2.)
  D. Although a partnership is *not a legal entity*, it is recognized as an entity in the following circumstances:
    1. For bookkeeping purposes;
    2. In the *marshaling of assets*;
    3. Title to property;
    4. Right to sue and be sued where statutes permit; and
    5. Adjudication as bankrupt where statutes permit.
  E. The partnership itself pays no income taxes on its profits.
  F. Each partner is entitled to a share of the partnership profits and must contribute to partnership losses.
  G. Each partner has the right to possess and use partnership property for partnership purposes.
  H. Each partner has an equal right to manage and control the business.

GENERAL PARTNERSHIPS DISTINGUISHED FROM CORPORATIONS

IV. A general partnership is distinguished from a corporation as follows (see Table 14-1):
  A. A partnership can be created by an agreement of the partners. A corporation can come into existence only through statutory authorization.

FIGURE 14-2   RELATIONSHIP OF PARTNERS TO EACH OTHER

Fiduciary duty

TABLE 14-1 CHARACTERISTICS OF CORPORATIONS AND GENERAL PARTNERSHIPS

	Corporations	General partnerships
Formation	Only under statutory authorization	By agreement of the parties
Duration	Perpetual, for a specific purpose, or for a specified term	Agreed term, life of any partner, or a specified purpose
Entity	Separate legal entity	Not a separate legal entity
Liability	Owners (shareholders) do not have individual liability; corporation incurs liability as a legal entity	General partners are individually liable for all obligations
Agency	A shareholder is neither a principal nor an agent of the corporation	Each partner is both a principal and an agent of the copartners
Transfer of interest	In absence of express restrictions, ownership interest (stock) may be freely transferred to outsiders	New partnership agreement is required to admit or to change partners; a partner may transfer the rights to receive profits and his or her share upon liquidation
Capital	Capital may be obtained by sale of stock or bonds	New capital secured only by loans, increase in membership, or new capital contributions by existing partners
Doing business	The business activities of a corporation must be authorized by a specified percentage of directors at a duly constituted formal meeting	Unanimity of partners, formal or informal, is usually required for matters affecting material aspects of partnership business; otherwise, majority decision prevails
Fiduciary duty	Shareholders do not owe a fiduciary duty to the corporation	Each partner owes a fiduciary duty to the copartners
Management	Shareholders do not participate in management; the corporation is managed by the board of directors	All general partners have a right to be involved in management responsibilities and decisions

B. A partnership is not a separate legal entity apart from the individual partners. A corporation is a legal entity.

C. Partnership existence may be limited to an agreed-upon term. A corporation's life can be perpetual.

D. A change of partners requires a new partnership agreement, while the shareholders of a corporation may change without any alteration in the legal status of a corporation.

E. Each partner is entitled to an equal right to manage and control the business and other activities of the partnership. The business of a corporation is managed by a board of directors elected by the shareholders.

F. Each general partner is individually liable for all obligations of the partnership. Shareholders of a corporation are not individually liable for corporate obligations.

G. Partners are entitled to a share of the profits of the partnership. Shareholders do not have an absolute right to compel the corporation to distribute profits in the form of dividends.

LEGAL CAPACITY TO BECOME A PARTNER

V. Any "person" who is legally competent to enter into contracts may become a member of a legally binding partnership. The Uniform Partnership Act defines "person" as an individual, a partnership, a corporation, or an association.

A. *Individuals.* Contract law determines an individual's legal capacity to contract. A partner's agreement to become a partner may be voidable on the basis of minority, intoxication, mental infirmity, fraud, duress, undue influence, etc.

    1. *Minors.* Minors (i.e., persons under age eighteen) do not have full contractual capacity to contract, yet they can become partners.

        a. Their agreement to become a partner is voidable only by themselves. Therefore, if they do not rescind their partnership obligation, they are legally entitled to all the rights granted them under the partnership agreement.

            (1) Prior to attaining the age of majority (age eighteen), a partner has the right to rescind (disaffirm) the partnership agreement and avoid any liability to copartners and to some extent some or all personal liability to partnership creditors.

            (2) Upon disaffirmance (rescission), a minor is entitled to the return of capital contributions and his or her share of profits *only* to the extent that such action will not impair the rights of partnership creditors who became creditors prior to the disaffirmance. For example, X, a minor, became a partner of Y and Z and contributed $50,000 in capital. Y and Z did not make capital contributions. The partnership is solvent. It has assets of $80,000 and liabilities of $60,000. X rescinded the partnership agreement, caused dissolution, and demanded the return of her $50,000 capital contribution. X is entitled to the return of $20,000.

B. *Corporations.* Unless prohibited by statute or its articles of incorporation, a corporation has legal capacity to be a partner.

C. *Partnerships.* Under the Uniform Partnership Act, a partnership can be a member of another partnership. It is an entity for this purpose.

D. *Associations.* Associations, acting through their individual members, have legal capacity to become members of partnerships.

TYPES OF PARTNERSHIPS

VI. Partnerships are classified as follows:

A. A *general partnership* is one in which all partners have unlimited liability for partnership debts.

B. A *limited partnership* is one in which one or more partners are general partners, and one or more of the other partners' liabilities are limited to the extent of their investments. See XIII below.

C. A partnership may be further classified as trading or nontrading.

    1. A *trading partnership* is one that is engaged in buying, selling, or leasing goods, real estate, or other property in the regular course of its business for profit.

    2. A *nontrading partnership* is one engaged in providing services in the regular course of its business for profit, for example, attorneys, accountants, and doctors.

D. *Partnership by estoppel.* It is not an actual partnership in that it does not arise from the expressed or implied in fact agreement of the "partners." Although each person is not actually a partner of the others, they all possess the liability of partners to third persons. It is a partnership imposed by law rather than one entered into voluntarily by the parties involved. A partnership by estoppel is held to exist whenever the following circumstances are present:

1. Persons not actually partners to one another by reason of words or conduct hold themselves out to third persons as being partners; and
2. The third persons have *changed their position in reliance* upon the assumed partnership existence. For example, A, B, and C decided to form a computer services corporation. None of them knew that a corporation could be formed only by compliance with the formal requirements of a state incorporation law. A, B, and C drew up a written agreement between themselves called "Articles of Incorporation" and proceeded to sell computer services. They consulted one another whenever a business decision was required. They shared losses as well as profits. They subsequently became insolvent and were sued by their creditors, who had no idea that A, B, and C believed that they were doing business as a corporation. A, B, and C are personally liable to the creditors as partners. They will be estopped from claiming otherwise.

TYPES OF PARTNERS

VII. Partners are classified as follows:
  A. *Real partner* is an actual partner as coowner of a business for profit. A real partner may be active or inactive and may or may not be known to the general public.
  B. *Ostensible partner* has consented to be held out as a partner whether he or she is a real partner or not. Usually created by estoppel.
  C. *General partner* is a partner whose liability for partnership indebtedness is unlimited.
  D. *Silent partner* is a real partner who has no voice and takes no part in partnership business.
  E. *Secret partner* is a real partner whose membership in the partnership is not disclosed to the public.
  F. *Dormant partner* is a real partner who is both a silent and a secret partner.
  G. *Limited partner* is a member of a limited partnership who is liable for firm indebtedness only to the extent of his or her capital contribution (investment). Limited partnerships are discussed in XIII below.

PARTNERSHIP PROPERTY, TENANCY IN PARTNERSHIP, AND PARTNERS' "INTEREST IN THE PARTNERSHIP"

VIII. The Uniform Partnership Act provides special rules that apply to partnership property and partners' legal interests in the partnership.
  A. *Transfer of title to partnership property.* Title to real property may be acquired and transferred by the partnership in the partnership name as well as in the names of individual partners.
    1. Partnership property whose *title is held in the name of the partnership*. Title to partnership property so held cannot be transferred (sale or gift) without proper authority from partners. This is so even though a transferee may be a bona fide purchaser for value without actual knowledge of a partner's lack of authority to transfer title.
    2. Partnership property whose *title is held in the name of one or more partners*. Title to partnership property held in the name of one or more partners cannot be transferred without proper authority to do so from partners. *Exception:* A bona fide purchaser for value from a partner in whose name title to the real estate is held receives absolute and valid title even though the partner lacked authority to transfer title. A bona fide purchaser for value is one who takes title in exchange

for value and does so without knowledge, actual or constructive, of the partner's lack of authority.

B. *Partnership property.* Property in possession of a partnership and used in the course of its business may or may not be partnership property. Partnership property is all real estate or personal property owned by the partnership, even though its title is held in the names of one or more partners. Title is said to be held in the name of a person when a writing such as a deed or bill of sale names that person as owner. Such "paper title" is not conclusive evidence of ownership. Whether property is owned by a partnership (i.e., partnership property) or the partners is important for the following reasons: (1) Partnership property is subject to the rights of partnership creditors; (2) Partnership creditors have priority over the personal creditors of partners in regard to partnership property; (3) A partner's personal creditors have priority over partnership creditors in property personally owned by partners (i.e., nonpartnership property); and (4) Neither partnership nor partners' personal creditors have any rights to property possessed by the partnership but owned by a third person. The following facts considered in their entirety are used to determine whether a specific item of property is partnership property:

1. It is carried on the books as partnership property.
2. It was purchased with partnership funds.
3. Title to it was taken in the partnership name.
4. The partnership pays taxes levied upon it.
5. Income from the property is treated as partnership funds.
6. The partners declare the property to be partnership property.

None of these facts alone is conclusive evidence of ownership.

C. *Partner's rights in partnership.* A partner's rights in a partnership are as follows:

1. *Rights in specific partnership property*, i.e., the right to possess and use partnership property for partnership purposes.
2. An *"interest in the partnership,"* i.e., the right to a share of profits, surplus, and goodwill; the return of any capital contribution; and the right to receive repayment of any loan the partner made to the partnership.
3. *Right to participate in management.* See X-A-1 below.

D. *Tenancy in partnership.* All partnership property is owned by partners by tenancy in partnership. It is a special type of joint ownership that has similar characteristics to a joint tenancy. The characteristics are:

1. Each partner has the right to possess it only for partnership purposes;
2. A right of survivorship exists in surviving partners; i.e., a partner or partners living at the death of a partner continue ownership in tenancy in partnership. This is another way of saying that a partner's ownership of partnership property is not inheritable by will or intestate succession.
3. Title to partnership property cannot be transferred by a partner without authority to do so from other partners. *Exception:* Partnership property held in the name of a partner that is transferred to a bona fide purchaser for value. See VIII-A above.
4. Partnership property is legally immune from attachment or execution by personal (i.e., nonpartnership) creditors of a partner. A partner's personal creditors can only proceed against a partner's "interest" in the partnership. See E below.
5. No rights of dower in partnership real estate accrue to a deceased partner's widow.

E. *Partner's "interest in the partnership."* As stated previously, a partner's "interest in the partnership" is the partner's share of profits, surplus, goodwill, right to repayment of loans, and right to the return of capital contributions. (See Figure 14-3.)

FIGURE 14-3 A GENERAL PARTNER'S "INTEREST IN THE PARTNERSHIP"

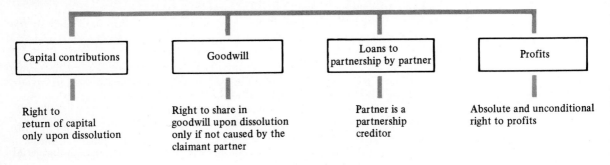

1. A partner's interest is personal property.
2. A partner can assign the interest to a third party. The assignee does not become a partner. The partner-assignor remains a partner.
3. The assignment of a partner's interest does not cause a dissolution of the partnership.

PARTNERSHIP CAPITAL

IX. *Partnership capital* is the sum total of the money and property contributed by the partners and dedicated to permanent use in the business.

    A. Except upon dissolution, no partner may withdraw any part of a capital contribution without the consent of all partners.

    B. A partner, by terms of the agreement, may contribute no capital but only skill and services or use of a certain property rather than the property itself, e.g., use of a building but not title.

    C. A careful distinction must be made between *partnership capital and a loan by a partner* for the following reasons:

        1. A partner is entitled to repayment of a loan without any new agreement with the copartners, but a withdrawal of capital by a partner requires a new partnership agreement.

        2. A debt owing to a partner has priority rights over the rights of partners to return of capital upon liquidation of the partnership.

        3. Loans to a partnership from its partners automatically draw interest without an agreement to that effect. However, capital contributions can draw interest only if that is previously agreed upon by the partners.

RIGHTS AND DUTIES OF PARTNERS

X. The rights and duties of partners among themselves are governed by the provisions of the partnership agreement. If the partnership agreement is silent as to the rights and duties, the following rules are applied by the courts.

    A. Rights of partners as owners of the partnership (see Figure 14-4).

        1. *Management.* Unless expressly denied the right to manage, each partner has the right to take part in management activities and decisions in a partnership.

            a. A decision of the majority prevails on all matters involving the method or manner in which the ordinary functions of the business are or will be conducted, e.g., establishing prices, discounts, levels of inventory, and production schedules. As another example, to execute a deed to a vacant lot held in the partnership's name, which was acquired as the site of a future office for the partnership, is a plan obviously beyond the present capabilities of the majority.

    b. Unanimous action by the partners is required if the action taken or to be taken is in any way contrary to the original agreement of the partners or if the action would alter the original agreement. For example:

      (1) To add a completely new product line of business;

      (2) To change the previously agreed upon formula for sharing losses;

      (3) To move the home office of the partnership from the east to the west coast of the United States;

      (4) To add B as a partner, with B being willing to contribute a substantial amount of new capital;

      (5) To confess judgment in certain actions and thereby avoid incurring the cost of defense;

      (6) To agree to submit other disputed claims to arbitration which a partner believes will prove less costly than civil litigation;

      (7) To dispose of all the partnership personal property, with a partner having received what is believed to be a good offer from a newly founded firm;

      (8) To assign all the assets to a bank in trust for the benefit of creditors, hoping to work out satisfactory arrangements without the problems of formal bankruptcy; or

      (9) To alter the respective interests of the parties in the profits by decreasing one partner's share to 40 percent and increasing the other partners' shares accordingly.

2. *Inspection of the books.* Each partner has an absolute right to inspect and receive copies of any partnership books and records in the possession of any other partner.

3. *Sharing of profits and losses.* Each partner is entitled to a share of partnership profits and is liable for partnership losses.

    a. The formula for sharing profits is established by the express or implied agreement of the partners.

    b. If there is no agreement as to sharing of profits, partners share equally without regard to the extent of a partner's capital contribution or the extent of the partner's services rendered.

    c. Losses are shared in the same proportion as profits.

FIGURE 14-4   RIGHTS OF A GENERAL PARTNER

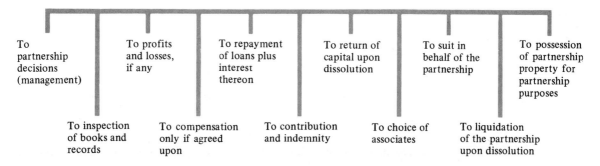

4. *Compensation.* Unless otherwise agreed, partners are not entitled to compensation for services rendered to the partnership. Their recourse is only to the profits of the partnership.
5. *Repayment of loans.* A partner who makes a loan ("advance") beyond the amount of capital which that partner has agreed to contribute is entitled to a return of the amount loaned.
   a. Unless otherwise agreed, a partner is automatically entitled to receive interest on the amount loaned.
   b. Loans have priority over capital contributions upon liquidation of the partnership.
6. *Contribution and indemnity.* A partner who pays more than his or her share of partnership expenses, debts, or other obligations has a right to contribution from the copartners unless:
   a. The partner acts in bad faith;
   b. The partner negligently causes the necessity for payment; or
   c. The partner has previously agreed to bear the expense, debt, or other obligation alone.
7. *Return of capital contributions.* Unless otherwise agreed, each partner is entitled to the return of his or her capital contribution.
   a. Until it is paid to the partner, it remains a liability of the partnership.
   b. Unless otherwise agreed, a partner *is not* entitled to receive interest on a capital contribution.
8. *Right to choose associates.* No partner may be forced to accept another person as a partner. For example, Poltz, a partner, sold (assigned) his partnership interest to Windom. Windom demanded the rights of partner. Windom is not a partner.
9. *Right to sue other partners.*
   a. *Actions at law* are generally not allowed in disputes involving partnership affairs.
   b. *Actions in equity.* A partner is entitled to the equitable remedy of an accounting under the following circumstances:
      (1) Where the partner is wrongfully excluded from the partnership business or possession of its property by other partners;
      (2) Where this right exists under the terms of any agreement;
      (3) Where a partner is accountable as a fiduciary; and
      (4) Where other circumstances render an accounting just and reasonable as determined by a court.
10. *Rights of partners in specific partnership real or personal property.* See also VIII-D above.
    a. Each partner has an equal right to possess and use partnership property for partnership purposes.
    b. A partner cannot assign the right in specific partnership property.
    c. A partner's interest in specific partnership property is not subject to attachment or execution by individual creditors.
    d. Upon the death of a partner, that partner's rights in partnership property pass to the surviving partner or partners (tenancy in partnership). A partner's right in specific partnership (real and personal) property is not inheritable.
11. *Rights and duties of partners upon expiration of the agreed duration of the partnership,* after which partners continue partnership business. Unless otherwise agreed, the terms of the previous partnership agreement become the terms governing the new partnership.

B. Duties of partners to each other. Each partner:
   1. Owes a *fiduciary duty* to every other partner, i.e., a duty of absolute and unconditional loyalty;
   2. Has a duty *to render financial accounting* for all partnership monies and properties within his or her control and possession;
   3. Must exercise *ordinary care* in conducting partnership business, i.e., refrain from negligence;
   4. Has a *contractual duty* to carry out the terms of the partnership agreement;
   5. Has a duty *to convey material information* regarding partnership business to other partners; and
   6. Owes a duty *not to disclose confidential information* to third parties.

LIABILITY OF PARTNERS TO THIRD PERSONS

XI. A partnership may be liable to third persons in contract or in tort for the acts of its partners.
   A. *Contractual liability.* Each partner is an agent for the partnership and for other partners for purposes of contracts entered into by the partner with third persons. If a contract is authorized, it is binding upon the partnership and the other partners. Authority of individual partners to act for and to bind other partners is very similar to that of an agent in an agency relationship.
      1. A partner's authority to bind other partners to third persons may be express, implied, or apparent. In addition, a partner can acquire liability by subsequently ratifying a previously unauthorized act by another partner.
         a. *Express authority* is authority actually granted to each partner to act in behalf of the partnership with third persons.
            (1) It may be found in the partnership agreement or in a collateral agreement.
            (2) It may be written or oral.
         b. *Implied in fact authority. Test:* What authority is reasonably proper and necessary for a partner in order to carry out the business of the partnership?
            (1) It is neither expressly granted nor expressly denied, but it is that authority which is reasonably deduced from:
               (*a*) Express authority;
               (*b*) The nature of the partnership, i.e., trading or nontrading; or
               (*c*) Custom or usage of the trade in which the partnership is engaged.
            (2) Examples of implied authority.
               (*a*) Contracts. A partner may make any contract necessary to the transaction of partnership business.
               (*b*) Sales. A partner may sell in the regular course of business any part or all of the inventory of the partnership, i.e., the goods kept for sale.
               (*c*) Purchases. A partner may purchase any kind of property within the scope of partnership business for cash or on credit.
               (*d*) Loans.
                  i. Trading partnership. A partner may borrow money for partnership purposes. Along with this authority the partner may also execute negotiable instruments in the name of the partnership, i.e., notes and drafts.
                  ii. Nontrading partnership. A partner does not ordinarily possess the power to borrow money for partnership purposes or to execute negotiable instruments in the name of the partnership.
               (*e*) Insurance. A partner has the implied authority to:
                  i. Insure firm property;

           ii. Cancel a policy of coverage; or

           iii. Make proof of claims and accept settlement for loss.

        (*f*) Contracts of employment. A partner may hire agents and employees to carry out the partnership purposes.

        (*g*) Debts of the partnership. A partner has authority to adjust, receive payment, and release debts and other claims of the partnership.

        (*h*) Claims against the partnership. A partner has authority to compromise, adjust, and pay bona fide claims against the partnership.

    c. *Apparent authority* (a given authority may be implied authority as well as apparent authority) exists when a partner is held out to third persons as having authority either by the nature of the partnership or by the words or conduct of the other partners.

      (1) Apparent authority is based on the theory of estoppel.

      (2) The third person must *not* have knowledge or notice of the lack of actual authority.

      (3) Secret limitations on a partner's authority are not effective against a third party where authority is "apparent."

    d. *Ratification* is the express or implied assent by the partnership to the entire unauthorized act of a partner previously done in behalf of the partnership.

    e. *Implied in law authority.* In an emergency, a partner has implied in law authority to enter into any contracts necessary to protect partnership business or property.

B. *Acts that require authorization from all partners.* The following acts *do not* bind the partnership to third persons unless performed by *all* the partners or by one partner with actual authority from all others:

  1. Assignment of partnership property for the benefit of creditors;

  2. Disposition of the goodwill of the business;

  3. An act which would make it impossible to carry on the ordinary business of the partnership;

  4. Confession of judgment against the partnership;

  5. Submission of a partnership claim or liability to arbitration;

  6. Execution of contracts of guaranty or suretyship in the firm name.

C. The *nature of liability of individual partners* to third persons for contracts, torts, and crimes (see Figure 14-5).

  1. *Contracts.* Partners are *jointly liable* on all debts and contract obligations of the partnership.

    a. A court judgment based on a joint obligation is not effective unless rendered against all partners.

    b. A release of one joint obligor releases all.

  2. *Torts.* Partners are *jointly and severally liable* in respondeat superior for torts committed by a partner or by an employee of the partnership in the course of partnership business. Whether a tort has been committed in the course of partnership business is determined in much the same manner as the liability of a principal for the torts of its agent. See Chapter 13.

    a. Joint and several obligors can all be sued in one lawsuit, or they may each be sued separately.

    b. A judgment upon a joint and several obligation against one of the obligors does not bind the others, nor does it bar a subsequent suit against them until it is satisfied.

    c. A release of one joint and several obligor does not release all.

  3. *Crimes.* A partner is not liable for a crime committed by other partners unless the partner personally participated or consented in its perpetration.

FIGURE 14-5   LIABILITY OF PARTNERS TO THIRD PERSONS

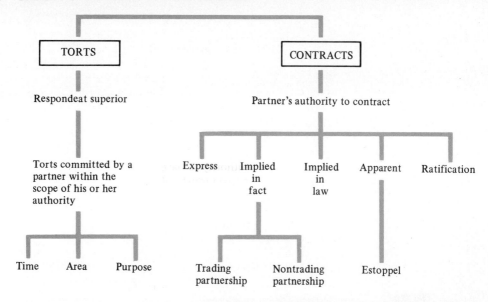

D. *Liability through estoppel (partner by estoppel).*
  1. A person is held liable as though he or she were a member of the partnership if that person holds himself or herself out as a partner to third parties and the latter justifiably rely upon that person's representations. Such a partner is estopped from asserting that he or she was not an actual partner. For example, X owns a store. In attempting to secure a loan from bank Z, X represents that Y, his girl friend and a wealthy socialite, is a partner in X's store. Y knows of X's misrepresentation but does nothing about it. Bank Z, relying on Y's credit, extends the loan to X. If X defaults, Y will be liable to bank Z and will be estopped from asserting that she is not a partner with X to the extent of the loan.
  2. By holding himself or herself out to be a partner, that person becomes an agent of those partners who consent expressly or impliedly to such representation.
    a. Partners who do not consent to the holding out of another person as a partner do not become liable for that person's actions.
    b. Consenting partners are liable to any third person who gives credit to the partnership in reliance upon such representation.
E. *Liability of new partners* to third persons (see Figure 14-6).
  1. A new partner who is admitted to an ongoing partnership is liable for all the partnership debts and obligations arising before the new partner's admission. *However*, the new partner's liability can be satisfied only out of the partnership property; i.e., the partner's liability is limited only to the extent of the partner's capital contribution to the partnership.
  2. A new partner has unlimited liability for all partnership debts and obligations arising after the new partner's entry into the new partnership.
F. *Effect of dissolution on a partner's liability* to third persons. A partner remains liable for existing partnership debts and obligations after dissolution *unless the creditors expressly release the partner* or until the claims against the firm are satisfied. This is true even though the remaining partners expressly agree to pay the ex-partner's share of the liabilities. For example, X, Y, and Z were partners. Z retired. X, Y, and Z agreed that in exchange for a reduction of the dollar amount of

FIGURE 14-6   LIABILITY OF A GENERAL PARTNER

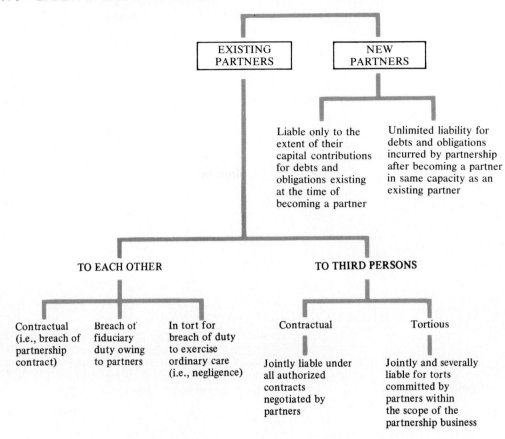

Z's partnership interest, X and Y would pay all outstanding partnership debts existing at the time of Z's retirement. The debts were not paid, and X and Y left the country. Z is liable for all partnership debts that were outstanding on the date of her retirement.

DISSOLUTION, LIQUIDATION, AND TERMINATION

XII. Final legal and physical termination of a partnership is caused by dissolution and liquidation (see Figure 14-7).

    A. Definitions.

        1. *Dissolution* is an event which terminates all authority of each partner to act in behalf of the firm except authority to wind up partnership affairs and complete pending transactions.

        2. *Liquidation* is the process of assembling (in some instances, "marshaling") assets, discharging partnership obligations, performing existing contracts, and accounting to partners for their respective financial interests.

            a. The *doctrine of marshaling of assets* arises only in courts of equity or in courts of bankruptcy.

                (1) *"Marshaling"* means segregating and considering separately the assets and liabilities of the partnership and the respective personal assets and liabilities of the individual partners.

(2) Priorities. Partnership creditors have first priority over partnership assets; individual creditors have first priority over individual assets of partners.

3. *Termination* finally ends a partnership's legal as well as actual existence.

B. Methods and causes of dissolution (see Figure 14-7).

    1. By acts of partners.

        a. *Express or implied agreement* whereby partners indicate by their words or conduct that they clearly do not intend to continue the partnership;

        b. *Withdrawal or addition of a new partner;* i.e., a partnership dissolves whenever its membership changes for any reason;

        c. *Expulsion* of a partner, rightful or wrongful;

        d. *Expiration by the terms of the partnership agreement:*

            (1) The duration of the partnership as established by the original partnership agreement expires; or

            (2) The purpose of which the partnership was formed is accomplished.

        e. *Note: Assignment of interest.* Neither a voluntary nor an involuntary sale of a partner's interest for the benefit of creditors works a dissolution of the partnership. The creditors do not become partners. They obtain the partner's right to profits, surplus, goodwill, repayment of loans, and return of capital upon dissolution.

    2. By operation of law.

        a. *Death*, even though the agreement provides for the continuation of the business, e.g., a buy and sell agreement (business continuation agreement);

        b. *Bankruptcy* of a partner or the partnership;

        c. *Subsequent illegality of the partnership;* e.g., a partnership is formed to sell DDT insecticide, and the sale of DDT is subsequently banned by statute.

FIGURE 14-7   DISSOLUTION, LIQUIDATION, AND TERMINATION OF A PARTNERSHIP

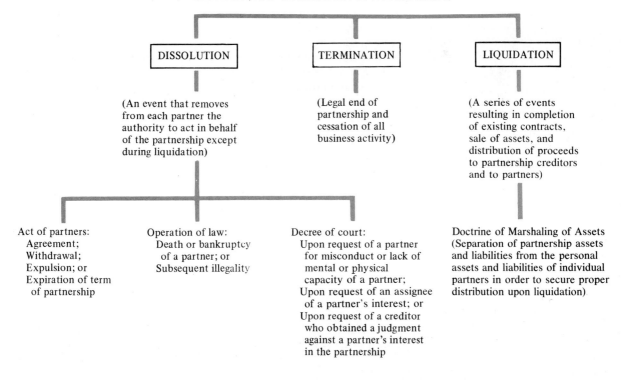

DISSOLUTION

(An event that removes from each partner the authority to act in behalf of the partnership except during liquidation)

Act of partners:
  Agreement;
  Withdrawal;
  Expulsion; or
  Expiration of term
  of partnership

Operation of law:
  Death or bankruptcy
  of a partner; or
  Subsequent illegality

TERMINATION

(Legal end of partnership and cessation of all business activity)

Decree of court:
  Upon request of a partner
  for misconduct or lack of
  mental or physical
  capacity of a partner;
  Upon request of an assignee
  of a partner's interest; or
  Upon request of a creditor
  who obtained a judgment
  against a partner's interest
  in the partnership

LIQUIDATION

(A series of events resulting in completion of existing contracts, sale of assets, and distribution of proceeds to partnership creditors and to partners)

Doctrine of Marshaling of Assets
(Separation of partnership assets and liabilities from the personal assets and liabilities of individual partners in order to secure proper distribution upon liquidation)

3. By court order or decree upon request by a partner. A partner may request a decree of dissolution under the following conditions:
    a. Where a partner is *judicially determined to be insane*;
    b. Where a partner shows *incapacity* other than adjudicated insanity, e.g., physical or mental;
    c. For *misconduct of a partner* which is prejudicial to the business, e.g., habitual drunkenness;
    d. Where the *business can be carried on only at loss*;
    e. For *wilful or continuous breach* of the partnership agreement; or
    f. For other equitable reasons.
4. Dissolution upon application of a third person.
    a. An assignee of a partner's interest may petition and obtain from a court a decree of dissolution:
       (1) After the end of the specified term or event designated in the partnership agreement to dissolve the partnership; or
       (2) At any time if the partnership was a "partnership at will" at the time of the assignment. A "partnership at will" is one in which there has been no agreement as to its duration.
    b. A creditor who has charged a partner's interest with a judgment that has not been paid may petition a court for a decree of dissolution.
C. Appointment of a *receiver* upon dissolution. Where no provision is made for winding up partnership affairs in the partnership agreement and the partners cannot agree on the management, control, and procedures during the winding-up period, any partner may petition the court to appoint a receiver. Grounds for appointment of a receiver are as follows:
1. Wasting of partnership assets;
2. Fraudulent conduct of partners;
3. Insolvency of the partnership;
4. Mental incompetency of a partner;
5. Refusal of a partner to render an accounting;
6. Exclusion of a partner from management of the business; or
7. Refusal of partners to allow a partner the right to inspect partnership books and records in their possession.
D. Effect of dissolution on rights and duties of partners.
1. Vested rights of partners at the time of dissolution remain enforceable.
2. Existing liabilities are not discharged.
3. Partners as between themselves lose all authority to enter into contracts in behalf of the firm, *except*:
    a. In winding up partnership affairs;
    b. In completing transactions begun during the life of the partnership;
    c. Where one partner does not have actual or constructive notice of dissolution by an act of a partner or an agreement by other partners.
4. A partner who *rightfully* withdraws (causes dissolution) from a partnership is entitled to the following:
    a. To have the value of the partnership's goodwill included in computation of the value of his or her interest; and
    b. To have the value of the interest paid within a reasonable time after that partner's withdrawal.
5. A partner who *wrongfully* withdraws (causes dissolution) from a partnership is entitled neither to the benefit of partnership goodwill in the computation of

interest nor to be paid the value of his or her interest in the partnership until the expiration of the term of the partnership. Such a partner is also liable to the partnership for any damages suffered by it because of the wrongful withdrawal.

E. Notice of dissolution eliminates the possibility of any liability by estoppel or apparent authority.

    1. Notice to partners.

        a. A withdrawing partner must give notice to the fellow partners that the withdrawing partner is no longer a member of the partnership in order to be relieved of liability for their actions after the withdrawal (other than in winding up).

        b. Where a firm is dissolved by an act of a partner, notice is not required to be given to other partners when the acts of the partner are known to the partners and the acts clearly show (constructive notice) an intent to withdraw from or dissolve the firm.

    2. Notice to third parties.

        a. Where dissolution is caused by the act of a partner or the agreement of the partners, notice must be given to third persons.

            (1) *Actual notice* must be given to those who had prior dealings with the partnership.

            (2) *Constructive notice* (notice by publication) is sufficient notice to persons who knew of the partnership's existence but have had no previous dealings with the partnership.

            (3) Failure to give notice continues the power (apparent authority) of any partner to bind the partnership in respect to third persons for contracts within the scope of the business.

        b. Where dissolution has been caused by operation of law, notice to third persons is generally not required.

F. *Winding up* partnership business.

    1. As a general rule, rights to wind up are vested in *all* the partners when the partnership is dissolved by agreement or by expiration of its agreed term. The right to wind up partnership affairs is denied to:

        a. Partners whose wrongful acts have caused the dissolution;

        b. A partner whose bankruptcy has caused the dissolution;

        c. The administrator or executor who is the legal representative of a deceased partner;

        d. All partners when a receiver is appointed by the court to wind up partnership affairs;

        e. Persons who are not partners.

    2. Rights of a partner in winding up of partnership affairs are to:

        a. Complete all unfinished partnership business;

        b. Inspect all partnership accounts;

        c. Sell the partnership property;

        d. Collect monies due; and

        e. Perform such acts and enter into any contracts as the nature of the business and circumstances demand in order to liquidate and distribute the partnership's assets.

    3. The partner in charge of winding up partnership affairs retains a fiduciary duty to other partners.

    4. A partner *is* entitled to reasonable compensation for winding-up activities and reimbursement for necessary expenses incurred.

G. Distribution of partnership assets.

    1. Partnership creditors have first priority to partnership assets, and creditors of individual partners share in any remaining assets.

        a. Secured creditors have priority over unsecured creditors in regard to property subject to the security interest.

        b. Unsecured creditors stand on an equal footing with each other.

    2. Individual (nonpartnership) creditors have first claim to the individually owned assets of their respective debtors (partners) and also a subordinate (to that of the partnership creditors) right to participate in partnership assets to the extent of the interest therein of the individual partners (debtors).

    3. After the firm liabilities to creditors other than partners have been paid, the remaining partnership assets are distributed according to the following priorities:

        a. Loans (advances) made by partners to the partnership and any interest due thereon;

        b. Capital contributions and any agreed-upon interest;

        c. Profits, if any, of the partnership; and

        d. If a deficit is present, the loss is shared in the same manner as profits.

H. Partnership liquidation problem. A, B, and C are partners. A contributed $10,000 to capital, B contributed $5,000 to capital, and C contributed her skill. Later B advanced $4,000 without interest. The partnership is terminated by the expiration of time specified in the articles of partnership. At that time, debts and liabilities to third parties total $6,000 and assets total $13,000. What distributions must be made upon liquidation?

    Solution: Computation of net liability of the partnership:

$10,000	Capital contribution by A
5,000	Capital contribution by B
4,000	Loan to partnership B
6,000	Debts owed to creditors
$25,000	Gross liability of the partnership
−13,000	Assets on hand
$12,000	Net liability of the partnership

Computation of each partner's share of the net liability of the partnership:

$\dfrac{\$\,4,000}{3)\,\$12,000}$ = each partner's share of net liability of the partnership

Computation of amounts owing to the partnership from partners and amounts owing to partners from the partnership:

	Partner A	Partner B	Partner C
Capital contributions	$10,000	$5,000	0
Loans to partnership by partners	0	4,000	0
Gross liability of partnership to partners	$10,000	$9,000	0
Partners' share of net liability of partnership	−4,000	−4,000	−4,000
	$ 6,000	$5,000	$ 4,000

Distribution upon liquidation:

$13,000	Assets on hand
4,000	C's payment to partnership of her share of net partnership liability
$17,000	Total assets available for distribution
−6,000	Paid to partnership creditors
$11,000	
−5,000	Paid to B
$ 6,000	
−6,000	Paid to A
$ 0	

LIMITED PARTNERSHIPS

XIII. A *limited partnership* must be authorized and formed pursuant to the provisions of a limited partnership statute and consist of *one or more general partners* by whom the business is conducted and *one or more limited partners* who contribute capital to the firm but do not take part in the management of the business and are not liable for debts of the partnership beyond the amount of their capital contribution. *Compare:* A general partnership can come into existence merely by the agreement to do so by two or more persons without any statutory authorization.

FORMATION OF LIMITED PARTNERSHIPS

XIV. The Uniform Limited Partnership Act (ULPA) prescribes the procedures for the creation of limited partnerships and defines the rights and duties of the partners.

 A. To create a limited partnership, a certificate of limited partnership signed by all general and limited partners must be filed with the state having jurisdiction and recorded in the proper county recorder's office. The certificate must also include:

 1. The name of the partnership and the address of its principal place of business;

 2. The character of the business and the duration of partnership;

 3. The names and residences of the general and limited partners;

 4. The amount, nature, and description of capital contributions of each limited partner; and

 5. The share of profits to which each limited partner is entitled.

 B. There must be at least one general partner in order to create a limited partnership.

 C. Capital contributions of limited partners can be in cash or property but cannot consist of services.

 D. The name of the business cannot contain the surname of a limited partner unless it is the same as that of a general partner.

 E. In the absence of statutory restriction, the limited partnership may conduct any business which a general partnership may carry on.

RIGHTS AND LIABILITIES OF GENERAL PARTNERS

XV. A general partner possesses all the rights and powers and is subject to all the liabilities of a partner in a general partnership.

 A. However, neither one nor all of the general partners have the authority, without written consent of all limited partners, to do any of the following:

 1. Do any act in contravention of the certificate of partnership;

 2. Do any act which makes it impossible to carry on the ordinary business of the partnership;

3. Confess a judgment against the partnership;
4. Admit a general partner, or a limited partner unless the right to admit limited partners is conferred by the certificate; or
5. Continue the business, utilizing partnership property, upon the death, retirement, or insanity of a general partner.

RIGHTS OF LIMITED PARTNERS

XVI. The rights of a limited partner (except in management) are:
   A. To receive profits and compensation as provided in the certificate of partnership;
   B. To have books kept at the principal place of business and to inspect and make copies of the books and formal accounts;
   C. To demand and receive complete information and accounting of partnership affairs;
   D. To receive his or her capital contribution upon withdrawal from the partnership (subject to creditor's rights);
   E. To obtain dissolution and liquidation by court decree under appropriate circumstances;
   F. To assign his or her interest to a third party.

LIABILITIES OF LIMITED PARTNERS

XVII. Liabilities of a limited partner are prescribed by the Uniform Limited Partnership Act.
   A. A limited partner is held liable as a general partner when:
      1. The limited partner takes an active part or interferes in the management of the partnership; or
      2. The limited partner allows his or her surname to be used in the name adopted for partnership itself.
   B. A limited partner is not personally liable to the firm's creditors and shares in partnership losses only to the extent of his or her capital contribution (i.e., capital investment).

DISTRIBUTION OF ASSETS UPON LIQUIDATION

XVIII. Order of distribution of assets upon dissolution and liquidation of the limited partnership is as follows:
   A. To creditors other than partners in order of priority as established by law. For example, secured creditors have priority over unsecured creditors. A limited partner is considered to have the same legal status as any other creditor with respect to money which the limited partner lent to the partnership.
   B. To limited partners in respect to their share of undistributed profits or income on their capital contributions;
   C. To limited partners in respect to their capital contributions;
   D. To general partners other than for capital and profits;
   E. To general partners in respect to profits of the partnership;
   F. To general partners in respect to capital contributions.

GENERAL AND LIMITED PARTNERSHIPS DISTINGUISHED

XIX. Table 14-2 illustrates the important distinctions between limited and general partnerships.

TABLE 14-2   GENERAL AND LIMITED PARTNERSHIPS DISTINGUISHED

	General	Limited
Formation	Agreement is required	Agreement plus compliance with statute is required
Formalities	Agreement may be oral or written	Written certificate of limited partnership and compliance with statute are required
Partnership name	Surnames of partners allowed in partnership name	Surname cannot be used without exposing limited partner to unlimited liability
Membership	All partners are general partners	At least one general and one limited partner is required
Nature of a partner's interest	Personal property	Personal property
Type of business activity	Any lawful business (trading or nontrading)	Any lawful business (trading or nontrading)
Capital contributions	Cash, property, or services	Cash or property but not services from limited partners
Management	All partners have absolute right to manage	Limited partners who take an active part in management acquire unlimited liability
Liability of partners	Unlimited, joint, and several liability	Limited partners are liable only to the extent of capital contribution; general partners have unlimited liability
Liability for torts	A general partner is liable for the torts committed within the scope of business by other partners, agents, or employees of the firm	Limited partners are not liable for torts committed by general partners, agents, or employees of the firm; general partners have tort liability
Authority to bind partnership to contracts	Partners have authority to bind other partners to contracts entered into in the regular course of the partnership's business	Usually, a limited partner does not have authority to bind the partnership to contracts
Sharing of profits and losses	Unless otherwise agreed upon, all partners share equally in profits and losses	Limited partners share in profits and losses only as specified in the statutory certificate of limited partnership; any excess belongs to the general partners
Assignment of a partner's interest	A partner's interest (share of profits, surplus, and capital) is assignable; the assignee does not automatically become a partner	A limited partner's interest (share of profits, surplus, and capital) is assignable in whole or part; the assignee does not automatically become a substitute limited partner
Dissolution	Death, total disability, or bankruptcy of a partner will cause dissolution	Death, total disability, or bankruptcy of a limited partner *does not* cause dissolution
Order of distribution of assets upon liquidation	1. To secured creditors other than partners 2. To unsecured creditors other than partners 3. To partners in respect to loans to the partnership 4. To partners in respect to capital contributions 5. To partners in respect to profits and losses	1. To secured creditors other than partners 2. To unsecured creditors other than partners (including loans from limited partners) 3. To limited partners in respect to profits 4. To limited partners in respect to capital contributions 5. To general partners in respect to loans to the partnership 6. To general partners in respect to profits 7. To general partners in respect to capital contributions

SELF-QUIZ

To check your understanding of the key words and concepts and the accuracy of your answers to the questions, refer to the text material as referenced by page number.

KEY WORDS AND CONCEPTS

General partnership   **405**
Limited partnership   **423**
Trading partnership   **409**
Nontrading partnership   **409**
Partnership by estoppel   **409**
Real partner   **410**
Ostensible partner   **410**
General partner   **410**
Silent partner   **410**
Secret partner   **410**
Dormant partner   **410**
Limited partner   **410**
Tenancy in partnership   **411**
Partner's interest   **411**
Partnership capital   **412**
Loan   **412**
Contribution   **414**
Indemnity   **414**
Right of an accounting   **414**
Express authority   **415**
Implied in fact authority   **415**
Apparent authority   **416**
Ratification   **416**
Implied in law authority   **416**
Joint liability   **416**
Joint and several liability   **416**
Partner by estoppel   **417**
Dissolution   **418**
Liquidation   **418**
Marshaling of assets   **418**
Termination   **419**
Receiver   **420**
Winding up   **421**

QUESTIONS

1. List the distinctive characteristics of a partnership. **(407)**
2. List the differences between partnerships and corporations. **(408)**
3. What persons have legal capacity to become partners? **(409)**
4. List and explain the basic distinction between a general and limited partnership. **(425)**
5. List and explain the different types of partners. **(410)**
6. Is all property used and possessed by a partnership owned in tenancy in partnership? **(411)**
7. Are partnership rights assignable? If so, what rights does an assignee receive? **(412)**
8. List and explain the rights of partners as owners of the partnership. **(412)**
9. What are the duties of partners with respect to each other? **(412)** In a general partnership? **(412)** In a limited partnership? **(423)**
10. What authority do partners possess which enables them to bind the partnership to third persons? **(415)** How is this authority derived? **(415)**
11. What are a partner's actual or potential liabilities in the following situations:
    a. Contracts, torts, or crimes committed by a partner **(416)**
    b. A person holds himself or herself out as a partner **(417)**
    c. An incoming new partner **(417)**
    d. When dissolution occurs **(421)**
12. What is the legal effect of dissolution upon the authority of partners? **(420)**
13. List and explain the methods and causes of dissolution. **(419)**
14. Under what circumstances may the partnership retain a withdrawing partner's interest? **(420)**
15. What is the effect upon the rights of partners and those of third persons in the event of failure to give notice of the dissolution of a partnership? **(421)**
16. What are the rights and duties of partners during the winding-up process? **(421)**
17. Describe the procedure and order of distribution of partnership assets upon final liquidation of the partnership. **(422, 425)**
18. How must a limited partnership be formed? **(423)**
19. What are the distinguishing characteristics between general partners and limited partners in regard to liabilities, rights of management, authority, investments, firm name, compensation, and distribution of assets upon liquidation? **(425)**

SELECTED QUESTIONS AND UNOFFICIAL ANSWERS

OBJECTIVE QUESTIONS

Select the best answer for each of the following items. Mark only one answer for each item. Answer all items.

NOVEMBER 1980

19. Perone was a member of Cass, Hack & Perone, a general trading partnership. He died on August 2, 1980. The partnership is insolvent, but Perone's estate is substantial. The creditors of the partnership are seeking to collect on their claims from Perone's estate. Which of the following statements is correct insofar as their claims are concerned?

a. The death of Perone caused a dissolution of the firm, thereby freeing his estate from personal liability.

b. If the existing obligations to Perone's personal creditors are all satisfied, then the remaining estate assets are available to satisfy partnership debts.

c. The creditors must first proceed against the remaining partners before Perone's estate can be held liable for the partnership's debts.

d. The liability of Perone's estate can *not* exceed his capital contribution plus that percentage of the deficit attributable to his capital contribution.

20. The partnership agreement of one of your clients provides that upon death or withdrawal, a partner shall be entitled to the book value of his or her partnership interest as of the close of the year preceding such death or withdrawal and nothing more. It also provides that the partnership shall continue. Regarding this partnership provision, which of the following is a correct statement?

a. It is unconscionable on its face.

b. It has the legal effect of preventing a dissolution upon the death or withdrawal of a partner.

c. It effectively eliminates the legal necessity of a winding up of the partnership upon the death or withdrawal of a partner.

d. It is *not* binding upon the spouse of a deceased partner if the book value figure is less than the fair market value at the date of death.

21. Watson decided to withdraw from the Sterling Enterprises Partnership. Watson found Holmes as a prospective purchaser and his successor as a partner in the partnership. The other partners agreed to admit Holmes as a general partner in Watson's place. As a part of the agreement between Watson and Holmes, Holmes promised to satisfy any prior partnership debts for which Watson might be liable. What potential liability does Holmes or Watson have to firm creditors?

a. Holmes has no liability for the obligations arising before he entered the partnership.

b. Holmes is liable for the obligations arising before he entered the partnership, but only to the extent of partnership property.

c. Holmes is fully liable to firm creditors for liabilities occurring before and after his entry into the partnership.

d. Watson's liability to firm creditors has been extinguished.

22. One of your audit clients, Major Supply, Inc., is seeking a judgment against Danforth on the basis of a representation made by one Coleman, in Danforth's presence, that they were in partnership together doing business as the D & C Trading Partnership. Major Supply received an order from Coleman on behalf of D & C and shipped $800 worth of goods to Coleman. Coleman has defaulted on payment of the bill and is insolvent. Danforth denies he is Coleman's partner and that he has any liability for the goods. Insofar as Danforth's liability is concerned, which of the following is correct?

a. Danforth is *not* liable if he is *not* in fact Coleman's partner.

b. Since Danforth did *not* make the statement about being Coleman's partner, he is *not* liable.

c. If Major Supply gave credit in reliance upon the misrepresentation made by Coleman, Danforth is a partner by estoppel.

d. Since the "partnership" is operating under a fictitious name (the D & C Partnership) a filing is required and Major Supply's failure to ascertain whether there was in fact such a partnership precludes it from recovering.

23. In the course of your audit of James Fine, doing business as Fine's Apparels, a sole proprietorship, you discovered that in the past year Fine had regularly joined with Charles Walters in the marketing of bathing suits and beach accessories. You are concerned whether Fine and Walters have created a partnership relationship. Which of the following factors is the *most* important in ascertaining this status?

a. The fact that a partnership agreement is *not* in existence.
b. The fact that each has a separate business of his own which he operates independently.
c. The fact that Fine and Walters divide the net profits equally on a quarterly basis.
d. The fact that Fine and Walters did *not* intend to be partners.

24. Ms. Walls is a limited partner of the Amalgamated Limited Partnership. She is insolvent and her debts exceed her assets by $28,000. Goldsmith, one of Walls' largest creditors, is resorting to legal process to obtain the payment of Walls' debt to him. Goldsmith has obtained a charging order against Walls' limited partnership interest for the unsatisfied amount of the debt. As a result of Goldsmith's action, which of the following will happen?

a. The partnership will be dissolved.
b. Walls' partnership interest must be redeemed with partnership property.
c. Goldsmith automatically becomes a substituted limited partner.
d. Goldsmith becomes in effect an assignee of Walls' partnership interest.

NOVEMBER 1979

14. Dowling is a promoter and has decided to use a limited partnership for conducting a securities investment venture. Which of the following is *unnecessary* in order to validly create such a limited partnership?

a. All limited partners' capital contributions must be paid in cash.
b. There must be a state statute which permits the creation of such a limited partnership.
c. A limited partnership certificate must be signed and sworn to by the participants and filed in the proper office in the state.
d. There must be one or more general partners and one or more limited partners.

15. Jon and Frank Clarke are equal partners in the partnership of Clarke & Clarke. Both Jon Clarke and the partnership are bankrupt. Jon Clarke personally has $150,000 of liabilities and $100,000 of assets. The partnership's liabilities are $450,000 and its as-

sets total $250,000. Frank Clarke, the other partner, is solvent with $800,000 of assets and $150,000 of liabilities. What are the rights of the various creditors of Jon Clarke, Frank Clarke, and the partnership?

a. Jon Clarke must divide his assets equally among his personal creditors and firm creditors.
b. Frank Clarke will be liable in full for the $200,000 partnership deficit.
c. Jon Clarke's personal creditors can recover the $50,000 deficit owed to them from Frank Clarke.
d. Frank Clarke is liable only for $100,000, his equal share of the partnership deficit.

16. King, Kline and Fox were partners in a wholesale business. Kline died and left to his wife his share of the business. Kline's wife is entitled to

a. The value of Kline's interest in the partnership.
b. Kline's share of specific property of the partnership.
c. Continue the partnership as a partner with King and Fox.
d. Kline's share of the partnership profits until her death.

17. Which of the following will *not* result in a dissolution of a partnership?

a. The bankruptcy of a partner as long as the partnership itself remains solvent.
b. The death of a partner as long as his will provides that his executor shall become a partner in his place.
c. The wrongful withdrawal of a partner in contravention of the agreement between the partners.
d. The assignment by a partner of his entire partnership interest.

Items 18 and 19 are based on the following information:

Teal and Olvera were partners of the T & O Real Estate Investment Company. They decided to seek more capital in order to expand their participation in the booming real estate business in the area. They obtained five individuals to invest $100,000 each in their venture as limited partners.

18. Assuming the limited partnership agreement is silent on the point, which of the following acts may Teal and Olvera engage in without the written consent of all limited partners?

a. Admit an additional person as a general partner.

b. Continue the partnership business upon the death or retirement of a general partner.

c. Invest the entire amount ($500,000) of contributions by the limited partners in a single venture.

d. Admit additional limited partners from time to time in order to obtain additional working capital.

19. Which of the following rights would the limited partners *not* have?

a. The right to have a dissolution and winding up by court decree where such is appropriate.

b. The right to remove a general partner by a majority vote if the limited partners determine that a general partner is not managing the partnership affairs properly.

c. The right upon dissolution to receive their share of profits and capital contributions before any payment is made to the general partners.

d. The right to have the partnership books kept at the principal place of business and to have access to them.

30. Which of the following is a correct statement concerning the similarities of a limited partnership and a corporation?

a. Shareholders and limited partners may both participate in the management of the business and retain limited liability.

b. Both are recognized for federal income tax purposes as taxable entities.

c. Both can only be created pursuant to a statute and each must file a copy of their respective certificates with the proper state authorities.

d. Both provide insulation from personal liability for all of the owners of the business.

NOVEMBER 1978

16. For which of the following purposes is a general partnership recognized as an entity by the Uniform Partnership Act?

a. Insulation of the partners from personal liability.

b. Taking of title and ownership of property.

c. Continuity of existence.

d. Recognition of the partnership as the employer of its members.

17. In the course of your audit of Harvey Fox, doing business as Harvey's Apparels, a sole proprietorship, you discovered that in the past year Fox had regularly joined with Leopold Morrison in the mar-

keting of bathing suits and beach accessories. You are concerned whether Fox and Morrison have created a partnership relationship. Which of the following factors is the *most* important in ascertaining this status?

a. The fact that a partnership agreement is *not* in existence.

b. The fact that each has a separate business of his own which he operates independently.

c. The fact that Fox and Morrison divide the net profits equally on a quarterly basis.

d. The fact that Fox and Morrison did *not* intend to be partners.

18. Which of the following is a correct statement concerning the similarities of a limited partnership and a corporation?

a. Both provide insulation from personal liability for all of the owners of the business.

b. Both can only be created pursuant to a statute and each must file a copy of their respective certificates with the proper state authorities.

c. Both are recognized for federal income tax purposes as taxable entities.

d. Shareholders and limited partners may both participate in the management of the business and retain limited liability.

23. In determining the liability of a partnership for the acts of a partner purporting to act for the partnership without the authorization of his fellow partners, which of the following actions will bind the partnership?

a. A written admission of liability in a lawsuit brought against the partnership.

b. Signing the partnership name as a surety on a note for the purchase of that partner's summer home.

c. An assignment of the partnership assets in trust for the benefit of creditors.

d. The renewal of an existing supply contract which the other partners had decided to terminate and which they had specifically voted against.

26. Which of the following is a correct statement with respect to the rights of a limited partner?

a. The limited partner will only have taxable income if the limited partnership makes a distribution in the tax year.

b. The partnership is required to purchase the limited partnership interest at the current book value if the limited partner demands this.

c. The limited partner may assign his partnership interest to whomsoever he wishes at any time.

d. The limited partner must first offer his interest to the partnership before he may sell to another party.

7. Marshall formed a limited partnership for the purpose of engaging in the export-import business. Marshall obtained additional working capital from Franklin and Lee by selling them each a limited partnership interest. Under these circumstances the limited partnership

a. Will generally be treated as a taxable entity for federal income tax purposes.

b. Will lose its status as a limited partnership if there is ever more than one general partner.

c. Can limit the liability of all partners.

d. Can only be availed of if the state in which it is created has adopted the Uniform Limited Partnership Act or a similar statute.

8. Concerning the order of distribution for satisfying firm debts upon the dissolution and winding up of a general partnership, which of the following is a correct statement?

a. General creditors, including partners, who are also general creditors, are ranked first.

b. Profits are distributed only after all prior parties, including partners, have had their various claims satisfied.

c. Secured obligations are disregarded entirely insofar as the order of distribution.

d. Capital contributions by the partners are distributed before unsecured loans by the partners.

Answers to Objective Questions

November 1980		November 1979	
19. b	**22.** c	**14.** a	**18.** c
20. c	**23.** c	**15.** b	**19.** b
21. c	**24.** d	**16.** a	**30.** c
		17. d	

November 1978		November 1977	
16. b	**23.** d	**7.** d	**8.** b
17. c	**26.** c		
18. b			

Explanation of Answers to Objective Questions

19. (b) In a partnership, a general partner has unlimited liability for the partnership debts. Upon the death of a partner this liability continues and is assumed by the deceased partner's estate. Under the doctrine of marshalling of assets personal creditors have first priority to Perone's personal assets, with any excess going to the partnership creditors. This makes answer (b) correct and answers (a) and (d) incorrect. Answer (c) is incorrect since each partner, including a deceased partner's estate, is individually liable for the entire amount of partnership debts. However, if a partner pays more than his share of the partnership debts, he can sue his co-partners to recover the excess.

20. (c) Such a partnership agreement does not prevent the dissolution of the partnership upon the death or withdrawal of a partner; it merely eliminates the necessity of the second step in the termination of the partnership which is the winding up process. Such an agreement is enforceable. Answer (c) is the correct answer.

21. (c) Normally, an incoming partner is liable for existing partnership obligations only to the extent of his/her capital contributions. However, a new partner can become personally liable for these debts through an assumption or a novation. The agreement that Watson and Holmes entered into would constitute an assumption of the prior partnership debts by Holmes. This makes answer (c) correct.

22. (c) A partnership can be created by estoppel. This occurs when a third party changes his position in reliance upon a misrepresentation of the fact that a partnership exists. Danforth is a partner by estoppel. Danforth does not need to make a statement to become a partner by estoppel; his silence would be sufficient considering he is present at the time Coleman represents that they are partners. Answer (c) is correct.

23. (c) Two or more persons sharing profits of a business is prima facie evidence (raises a presumption) that a partnership exists. This presumption is overcome if it can be shown that the sharing of profits are for: services rendered; interest on loans, payment of debts, rent; any other reasonable explanation. The lack of intent or lack of a partnership agreement will not necessarily determine whether a partnership exists. Answer (c) is the correct answer.

24. (d) Goldsmith's charging order would in effect make him assignee of Wall's partnership interest. A limited partner may assign his partnership interest to whomever he wishes at any time. However, the assignee will not become a partner without consent of the existing partners. Goldsmith's charging order would operate as an involuntary assignment of Wall's limited partnership interest. Goldsmith would have a right to Wall's share of the profits plus Wall's capital contributions if the partnership is dissolved. Answer (a) is incorrect because an assignment of any type of partnership interest (general or limited) does not dissolve a partnership.

NOVEMBER 1979

14. (a) It is not a necessary requirement that limited partners' capital contributions be paid in cash. Limited partners cannot make their contribution in services, but they frequently contribute property, which is permissible. Answers (b), (c), and (d) generally set out the requirements for forming a valid limited partnership, i.e., there must be a state statute authorizing limited partnerships (usually based on the Uniform Limited Partnership Act); the partnership certificate must be signed and sworn to by the participants and filed in the proper offices in the state; and there must be one or more general partners and one or more limited partners.

15. (b) Frank Clarke, as a partner, is fully liable for all of the partnership debts. Answer (a) is incorrect because Jon Clarke's personal creditors under the marshalling of assets rule have first priority over his personal assets to the exclusion of the firm creditors. Answer (c) is incorrect because a partner is not responsible for the personal obligations of his partners in the absence of highly unusual circumstances. Answer (d) is incorrect because as stated in (b) above, Frank Clarke is fully liable for all partnership debts and not merely his equal or pro rata share of the partnership deficit.

16. (a) When a partner dies, his heirs or those named in his will are entitled to the value of the deceased partner's interest in the partnership. The heirs do not become and are not entitled to become partners as in answer (c) and the survivors acquire

no interest in specific property of the partnership as in (b). The heirs are only entitled to the deceased partner's interest in the partnership. Answer (d) is incorrect because the surviving wife of a deceased partner is only entitled to her husband's rights at the time of his death.

17. (d) The assignment by a partner of his entire partnership interest does not dissolve a partnership. Answer (a) is incorrect because the bankruptcy of a partner or of the partnership itself results in dissolution. Answer (b) is incorrect because the death of a partner generally results in a court ordered dissolution even if there is a purported agreement which attempts to substitute an executor as a partner in place of the decedent. Answer (c) is incorrect because the wrongful withdrawal of a partner even though in contravention of the partnership agreement will result in a dissolution of the partnership.

18. (c) The investment decisions of the T & O Investment Limited Partnership are properly made by the general partners without consent of limited partners. The Uniform Limited Partnership Act specifically prohibits a limited partner from taking an active part in management decisions. Answers (a), (b), and (d) are each acts which are beyond the general partner's authorities: admitting another person as a general partner, continuing the partnership on the death, retirement, or insanity of a general partner, or admitting additional limited partners.

19. (b) Limited partners, in order to retain their limited liability, would not have the right to remove a general partner by majority vote for mismanagement or other reasons. Such action would be deemed to be taking an active role in management of the limited partnership, which is prohibited by the Uniform Limited Partnership Act. Limited partners are to remain passive. The limited partners, however, would have the right to seek a dissolution and winding up by court decree where such is appropriate as in answer (a), (e.g., includes situations of mismanagement by the general partners). Limited partners also have the rights, as in answers (c) and (d), to receive their share of profits and capital contributions before any payment is made to the general partners. The limited partners are also entitled to have the partnership books kept at the principal place of business and to have access to them.

30. (c) The clear similarity of a limited partnership and a corporation is that both can only be created pursuant to a statute and each must file a copy of their respective certificates with the proper state authorities. Answer (a) is incorrect because limited partners in a limited partnership may not participate in management of a business and retain their limited liability. Answer (b) is incorrect because the limited partnership is not generally recognized for federal income tax purposes as a taxable entity. Income and losses flow through the partnership to the partners. Answer (d) is incorrect because general partners which are required in each limited partnership are not insulated from personal liability.

NOVEMBER 1978

16. (b) While a partnership is not a legal entity, it is recognized as an entity for the purpose of taking title and ownership of property under the Uniform Partnership Act. Answer (a) is incorrect because partners are liable for most acts of other partners and debts of the partnership. Answer (c) is incorrect because there is no continuity of existence of partnerships as in the case of corporations. Partnerships are automatically dissolved by the death or withdrawal of a partner. Answer (d) is incorrect because a partnership is not recognized as an entity so as to give recognition to the partnership as the employer of its partners. The partners are considered self-employed.

17. (c) Sharing of profits is one of the most important factors in determining whether a partnership exists. This is evidenced by the fact that Fox and Morrison divide the profits from their business activity equally on a regular basis. Lack of a partnership agreement and the fact that each of the purported partners owns a separate independent business are relatively unimportant factors in ascertaining whether or not a partnership exists. Also, it is not necessary to intend to be partners for a partnership to exist.

18. (b) Corporations and limited partnerships are similar in that both can only be created by statute and must file copies of their certificates with the proper state authorities. Answer (a) is incorrect because a limited partnership does not provide insulation from personal liability for all owners of a limited partnership since the general partners have personal liability. Answer (c) is incorrect because the limited partnership is generally not recognized as a taxable entity under federal income tax laws. Answer (d) is incorrect because a limited partner may not participate in the management of a limited partnership. If a limited partner participates in the management of a limited partnership, he loses his limited liability.

23. (d) A partner has apparent authority to renew an existing supply contract which is apparently for the purpose of carrying on the partnership business in a usual way. In the absence of knowledge by a third party that such action was unauthorized by other partners, the contract renewal is binding on the partnership. The matters described in answers (a), (b), and (c) are actions requiring unanimous consent of the partners:

1. Written admission of liability of partnership in a lawsuit.
2. Committing partnership as surety on a partner's personal debt.
3. Assignment of partnership assets to creditors.

Therefore a partner does not have apparent authority to bind the partnership in these matters because third parties are supposed to be aware of the requirement of unanimity.

26. (c) In general, a limited partner may assign his partnership interest to whomever he wishes at any time. However, the assignee will not become a partner without agreement by the other partners. Answer (a) is incorrect because a limited partner's taxable income is based on the earnings of the limited partnership whether or not a distribution of such earnings is made. Answer (b) is incorrect as a general statement of limited partnership law, because the partnership is not required to purchase a limited partner's interest unless the partnership agreement specifically so provides. Answer (d) is incorrect because the right of first refusal by the partnership does not exist unless specifically stated in the limited partnership agreement.

NOVEMBER 1977

7. (d) Limited partnerships are special creations of the state and are only valid in states where they are authorized, e.g., by the Uniform Limited Partnership Act. Answer (a) is incorrect because limited partnerships, like general partnerships, are not treated as taxable entities. Profits and losses flow through to the partners. Answer (b) is incorrect because a limited partnership may have any number of general partners or limited partners. Answer (c) is incorrect because there must be at least one general partner and his liability cannot be limited.

8. (b) The order of distribution upon the dissolution of a general partnership is first to creditors (other than partners); second to partners for loans to the partnership; third to partners for capital contributions; fourth to partners for profits. Secured obligations are treated as other debt but still take priority in their class, i.e., secured loans come before unsecured loans.

ESSAY QUESTIONS AND ANSWERS

MAY 1981 (Estimated time: 15 to 20 minutes)

5. Part a. Davis and Clay are licensed real estate brokers. They entered into a contract with Wilkins, a licensed building contractor, to construct and market residential housing. Under the terms of the contract, Davis and Clay were to secure suitable building sites, furnish prospective purchasers with plans and specifications, pay for appliances and venetian blinds and drapes, obtain purchasers, and assist in arranging for financing. Wilkins was to furnish the labor, material, and supervision necessary to construct the houses. In accordance with the agreement, Davis and Clay were to be reimbursed for their expenditures. Net profits from the sale of each house were to be divided 80% to Wilkins, 10% to Davis, and 10% to Clay. The parties also agreed that each was to be free to carry on his own business simultaneously and that such action would not be considered a conflict of interest. In addition, the agreement provided that their relationship was as independent contractors, pooling their interests for the limited purposes described above.

Ace Lumber Company sold lumber to Wilkins on credit from mid-1980 until February 1981. Ace did not learn of the agreement between Davis, Clay and Wilkins until April 1981, when an involuntary bankruptcy petition was filed against Wilkins and an order for relief entered. Ace Lumber has demanded payment from Davis and Clay. The lumber was used in the construction of a house pursuant to the agreement between the parties.

Required: Answer the following, setting forth reasons for any conclusions stated.

In the event Ace sues Davis and Clay as well as Wilkins, will Ace prevail? Discuss the legal basis upon which Ace will rely in asserting liability.

Answer: Yes. Ace will prevail. A partnership did exist and the parties are jointly liable. The legal basis upon which Ace will seek recovery is that a partnership exists among Wilkins, Davis, and Clay. If the parties are deemed partners among themselves, then Ace can assert liability against such partnership and against the individual partners as members thereof, since they are jointly liable for such partnership obligations.

The Uniform Partnership Act, section 7, provides rules for determining the existence of a partnership. Although it is frequently stated that the intent of the parties is important in determining the existence of a partnership relationship, this statement must be significantly qualified: It is not the subjective intent of the parties that is important when they categorically state that they do not wish to be considered as partners. If much effect were given to such statements, partnership liability could easily be shed. Further, the party dealing with the partnership need not in fact rely upon the existence of a partnership. Thus, the fact that Ace did not learn of the Davis, Clay, Wilkins agreement until after he had extended credit does not preclude him from asserting partnership liability.

The bearing of section 7 of the Uniform Partnership Act on this case can be examined as follows. First, joint, common, or part ownership of property of any type does not of itself establish a partnership. It is only one factor to be considered and was present to a limited extent in this case. Second, the sharing in gross returns does not of itself establish a partnership, but its importance is rendered moot as a result of the profit-sharing arrangement between the parties. Finally, and the key factor in partnership determination, is the receipt of profits: The act states "the receipt by a person of a share of the profits of a business is prima facie evidence that he is a partner in the business. . . ."

Sharing in profits is prima facie evidence of the existence of a partnership. The defendants (Davis and Clay) must affirmatively rebut this prima facie case against them or lose. There do not appear to be facts sufficient to accomplish this.

5. Part b. Lawler is a retired film producer. She had a reputation in the film industry for aggressiveness and shrewdness; she was also considered somewhat overbearing. Cyclone Artistic Film Productions, a growing independent producer, obtained the film rights to "Claws," a recent best seller. Cyclone has decided to syndicate the production of "Claws." Therefore, it created a limited partnership, Claws Productions, with Harper, Von Hinden and Graham, the three ranking executives of Cyclone, serving as general partners. The three general partners each contributed $50,000 to the partnership capital. One hundred limited partnership interests were offered to the public at $50,000 each. Lawler was offered the opportunity to invest in the venture. Intrigued by the book and restless in her retirement, she decided to purchase 10 limited partnership interests for $500,000. She was the largest purchaser of the limited partnership interests of Claws Productions. All went well initially for the venture, but midway through production, some major problems arose. Lawler, having nothing else to do and having invested a considerable amount of money in the venture, began to take an increasingly active interest in the film's production.

She frequently began to appear on the set and made numerous suggestions on handling the various problems that were encountered. When the production still seemed to be proceeding with difficulty, Lawler volunteered her services to the general partners who as a result of her reputation and financial commitment to "Claws" decided to invite her to join them in their executive deliberations. This she did and her personality insured an active participation.

"Claws" turned out to be a box office disaster and its production costs were considered to be somewhat extraordinary even by Hollywood standards. The limited partnership is bankrupt and the creditors have sued Claws Productions, Harper, Von Hinden, Graham, and Lawler.

Required Answer the following, setting forth reasons for any conclusions stated.

What are the legal implications and liabilities of *each* of the above parties as a result of the above facts?

Answer: The limited partnership, the general partners, and Lawler are all jointly liable for the debts of Claws Productions.

Claws Productions limited partnership is liable and must satisfy the judgment to the extent it has assets. Harper, Von Hinden, and Graham are liable for the unpaid debts of the limited partnership. An

interesting problem posed by the fact situation is Lawler's liability. The general rule, in fact the very basis for the existence of the limited partnership, is that the limited partner is not liable beyond its capital contribution. However, a notable exception contained in section 7 of the Uniform Limited Partnership Act applies to the facts presented here:

> A limited partner shall not become liable as a general partner unless, in addition to the exercise of his rights and powers as a limited partner, he takes part in the control of the business.

The statutory language covers the facts stated. Lawler assumed a managerial role vis à vis the partnership and in the process became liable as a general partner.

MAY 1979 (Estimated time: 20 to 25 minutes)

4. Part a. Strom, Lane, and Grundig formed a partnership on July 1, 1974, and selected "Big M Associates" as their partnership name. The partnership agreement specified a fixed duration of ten years for the partnership. Business went well for the partnership for several years and it established an excellent reputation in the business community. In 1978, Strom, much to his amazement, learned that Grundig was padding his expense accounts by substantial amounts each month and taking secret kick-backs from certain customers for price concessions and favored service. Strom informed Lane of these facts and they decided to seek an accounting of Grundig, a dissolution of the firm by ousting Grundig, and the subsequent continuation of the firm by themselves under the name, "Big M Associates."

Required Answer the following, setting forth reasons for any conclusions stated.

1. Were there any filing requirements to be satisfied upon the initial creation of the partnership?
2. What will be the basis for the accounting and dissolution and should such actions be successful?
3. Can Strom and Lane obtain the right to continue to use the firm name if they prevail?

Answer

1. Yes. Although no filing of the partnership agreement is required, virtually all states have statutes that require registration of fictitious or assumed names used in trade or business. The purpose of such statutes is to disclose the real parties in interest to creditors and those doing business with the company. This is typically accomplished by filing in the proper office of public records the names and addresses of the parties doing business under an assumed name. The statutes vary greatly in detail (e.g., some states require newspaper publication).

2. The facts indicate a clear breach of fiduciary duty by Grundig. Section 21 of the Uniform Partnership Act holds every partner accountable as a fiduciary. It provides that "every partner must account to the partnership for any benefit, and hold as trustee for it any profits derived by him without the consent of other partners from any transactions connected with the . . . conduct . . . of the partnership or from any use by him of its property." Grundig's conduct is squarely within the act's language. Section 22 of the act gives any partner a right to a formal accounting of partnership affairs if there is a breach of fiduciary duty by a fellow partner.

Section 32(c) and (d) of the act provides for a dissolution by court decree upon application of a partner whenever—
• A partner has been guilty of conduct that tends to prejudicially affect the business.
• A partner willfully or persistently commits a breach of the partnership agreement or otherwise so conducts himself in matters relating to the partnership business that it is not reasonably practicable to carry on the business in partnership with him.

Certainly Grundig's conduct would appear to fall within one or both of the above categories. He breached his fiduciary duty, was dishonest with his fellow partners, was in fact stealing from his partners, and may have involved the partnership in illegal price discrimination. Thus, the grant of application for dissolution would be appropriate.

3. Probably yes. Section 38(2)(b) of the Uniform Partnership Act relating to the right to continue the business in the same firm name, under the circumstances described, is narrowly drawn. This provision was designed to cover situations where partnerships have fixed durations and one of the partners has caused a dissolution wrongfully "in contravention of the partnership agreement." The facts indicate that Big M Associates did have a fixed duration (10 years); consequently, this requirement is met. While the acts by Grundig are not in contravention of any specific express language of the partnership agreement, as would be the case where a partner wrongfully withdraws, the courts treat other types of wrongful conduct to be in contravention of the partnership agreement and, thus, to be the basis for dissolution. Strom and Lane could obtain the right to continue to use the firm name for the duration of the partnership agreement if Grundig's conduct was deemed both wrongful and in contravention of the agreement.

4. Part b. Palmer is a member of a partnership. His personal finances are in a state of disarray, although he is not bankrupt. He recently defaulted on a personal loan from the Aggressive Finance Company. Aggressive indicated that if he did not pay within one month, it would obtain a judgment against him and levy against all his property including his share of partnership property and any interest he had in the partnership. Both Palmer and the partnership are concerned about the effects of this unfortunate situation upon Palmer and the partnership.

Required Answer the following, setting forth reasons for any conclusions stated.

1. Has a dissolution of the partnership occurred?
2. What rights will Aggressive have against the partnership or Palmer concerning Palmer's share of partnership property or his interest in the partnership?
3. Could Palmer legally assign his interest in the partnership as security for a loan with which to pay off Aggressive?

Answer

1. No. Since the facts clearly indicate that Palmer is not bankrupt, his financial problems will not precipitate a dissolution of the partnership. However, if Palmer were bankrupt, the Uniform Partnership Act (Sec. 31(5)) specifically provides that the bankruptcy of one of the partners causes a dissolution. The fact that creditors take action against a delinquent partner's interest in the partnership, although annoying and inconvenient, does not result in a dissolution.

2. Aggressive will have no rights to the partnership property either directly or indirectly by asserting Palmer's rights. In fact, Palmer only has the right to the use of partnership property for partnership purposes. Since partnership property is insulated from attack by Aggressive, Aggressive will assert its rights against Palmer's partnership interest. The method used to reach this interest is to reduce its claim against Palmer to a judgment and then obtain from the court a "charging order" to enable Aggressive to collect on the judgment. In effect, Aggressive has obtained a right comparable to a lienholder against Palmer's interest in the partnership. The "charging order" would provide Aggressive with the right to payments (earnings or capital distributions) that would ordinarily go to Palmer, the partner-debtor.

3. Yes. There is nothing in the Uniform Partnership Act that prevents a partner from assigning all or part of his interest in a partnership. The assignment may be outright or for the more common purpose of securing a loan. If there is to be any such restriction on a partner's right to assign his partnership interest, the partnership agreement must so provide. Section 27 of the Uniform Partnership Act specifically provides that a partner's assignment of his partnership interest does not cause a dissolution. The act limits such an assignment to the partner's right to share in profits and capital distributions but does not make the assignee a partner.

CHAPTER

15

Corporations and Other Forms of Business Organizations

The following is a generalized listing of subjects to be tested through the May 1983 Uniform CPA Examination.

The third major area is corporate law with emphasis on traditional state law regulation of the corporation as contrasted with federal regulation of the corporation. Included in the subject matter are corporate characteristics; incorporation; corporate rights, powers, and liabilities; corporate financing; directors' and officers' duties and liabilities; and stockholder rights. The Model Business Corporation Act prevails in this area.[1]

The AICPA Board of Examiners has adopted a new content specification outline for the business law section of the Uniform CPA Examination, *to be effective with the November 1983 examination*. The outline lists the following topics to be tested under the titles "Corporations" and "Other Forms of Business Organizations."

C. Corporations
   1. Formation
   2. Purposes and Powers
   3. Stockholders, Directors, and Officers
   4. Financial Structure, Capital, and Dividends
   5. Merger, Consolidation, and Dissolution
D. Other Forms of Business Organizations
   1. Individual Proprietorships
   2. Trusts and Estates
   3. Joint Ventures
   4. Associations[2]

---

[1] AICPA, *Information for CPA Candidates*, Copyright © 1975, 1979, by the American Institute of Certified Public Accountants, Inc.
[2] AICPA, *Business Law—Content Specification Outline*, approved by the AICPA Board of Examiners on August 31, 1981.

CORPORATIONS

I. *Introduction.* A corporation must be formed pursuant to the provisions of an existing incorporation statute. It cannot come into existence merely by an agreement to do so on the part of its organizers. Each state has enacted an incorporation statute. These statutes vary in their provisions from state to state. The AICPA has indicated that its questions on the Uniform CPA Examinations shall be based on the provisions of the Model Business Corporation Act (hereinafter referred to as the Model Act), related statutes, and the common law. Unless otherwise indicated, the material presented in this chapter is based on the provisions of the Model Act.

    A. *Definition.* A *corporation* is an artificial being or legal entity created by or under the law, possessing only those powers which its articles of incorporation and law confer upon it, either expressly or as incidental to its express powers.

    B. *Legal entity.* A corporation exists as a legal entity separate and distinct from its shareholders.

        1. It has continuous existence during the period of time provided for in its articles of incorporation. The articles of incorporation may provide that its existence is to be perpetual or limited by a specified period of time or be determined by the occurrence of a specified event. Some examples are:

            a. A corporation organized for a period of ten years; or

            b. A corporation organized to subdivide a parcel of land into residential lots and sell them to prospective homeowners.

        2. The existence of a corporation is not affected by the death or incapacity of a shareholder, director, officer, or employee or by the transfer of its shares.

        3. However, a corporation can be terminated at any time if by proper action, its board of directors and shareholders voluntarily dissolve it or it is involuntarily dissolved by a court. See XVIII below.

TYPES OF CORPORATIONS

II. Corporations are classified as follows:

    A. *De jure corporation.* A de jure corporation exists when its incorporators comply with all of the mandatory provisions of an incorporation statute and fulfill all the prerequisites for its organization. No one, not even the state of incorporation, can question its legal existence.

    B. *De facto corporation.* Under the common law, a de facto corporation exists where the incorporators fail in some material respect to comply with the mandatory provisions of an incorporation statute. For example, the required signature of an incorporator was missing from the application for incorporation. As another example, the incorporators failed to file the articles and certificate of incorporation in the appropriate county recorder's office.

        1. A de facto corporation is formed when:

            a. There is a valid statute under which the corporation could be formed;

            b. The parties have made an honest effort to organize under the law; and

            c. They have conducted business thereafter in good faith as a corporation believing that it has complied fully with the incorporation statute.

        2. The Model Business Corporation Act has gone one step further. It provides that the *issuance of a certificate of incorporation* by the state is conclusive evidence against all persons *except the state* that all statutory conditions required for incorporation have been performed and that a corporation exists.

        3. The corporate existence of a de facto corporation or one that has been issued a certificate of incorporation by the state of incorporation cannot be collaterally questioned.

    a. That is, in a lawsuit by or against the corporation, neither the corporation nor the other party to the suit will be permitted to defend on the ground of defects in the corporation's organization.

    b. However, the state may attack the claim of corporate status in a direct suit brought for that purpose. The state may sue either to cancel or to revoke the certificate of incorporation on the basis that the corporation has not complied with the mandatory provisions of its incorporation law.

  4. Where a de facto corporation is found to exist or a certificate of incorporation has been issued, the shareholders have limited liability for the corporation's torts and contracts as if the corporation were de jure. They are liable only to the extent of their investment in the corporation.

  5. Where persons attempt to organize a corporation but no certificate of incorporation is issued and their efforts are so inadequate that not even a de facto corporation comes into existence, the courts usually hold such persons to be general partners and liable as such for their torts and contracts.

C. *Corporation by estoppel.* The words "corporation by estoppel" are used to describe a legal concept that operates to prevent a person from denying the existence of a corporation after that person has dealt with an association or organization as if it were a corporation. The concept "corporation by estoppel" does not cause a corporation to come into existence. It merely prevents a person from escaping contractual or other liability by asserting the nonexistence of a corporation. Corporation by estoppel is applicable when:

  1. An association of persons is held out in good faith as being a corporation by statements, business operations, or otherwise; and

  2. A person reasonably relies upon such representation and deals with the association in the good faith belief that it was legally a corporation. For example, X and others agreed to form a corporation to be named Pell City Farms Inc. They also agreed that once formed, the corporation would pay all of X's existing debts in exchange for title to X's farm. Prior to incorporation, X deeded her farm to Pell City Farms Inc. After incorporation, X actively participated as an officer, director, and shareholder. X later sued Pell City Farms Inc. and asserted that she was still the owner of the farm because Pell City Farms Inc. was not legally in existence at the time she executed and delivered the deed to it as grantee. The court held that X was estopped from denying the existence of the corporation at the time she executed the deed. As another example, Garson, Boyd, and Pat decided to incorporate their business. They did not know that compliance with statutory requirements was necessary to form a corporation and consequently took no steps to comply. They adopted a corporate name, held board of directors meetings, appointed corporate officers, and issued shares of stock. Subsequently, Garson, Boyd, and Pat negotiated and entered into a contract in the name of their "corporation" to sell $100,000 worth of goods to Davis. Davis never received the goods. After discovering that no corporation existed, Davis sued Garson, Boyd, and Pat, claiming that they were personally liable as partners for breach of contract. The concept of corporation by estoppel applies. Davis is estopped to deny the existence of the corporation.

D. A *public corporation* is one created by a state, federal, or other government for governmental purposes, e.g., Tennessee Valley Authority, Federal Deposit Insurance Corporation (FDIC), or an incorporated county sanitary district.

E. A *quasi-public corporation* is one that is privately organized for profit. Its activities so affect the public interest that they must be incorporated under special incorporation statutes, and they are subject to special state or federal regulation. Examples: public utilities, savings and loan associations, banks, and insurance companies.

F. A *private corporation* consists of private individuals who have incorporated to conduct business activities other than governmental.

G. A *domestic corporation* is a corporation doing business in the state where it was incorporated.

H. A *foreign corporation* is a corporation doing business in any state other than the state where it was incorporated.

I. A *closed (close) corporation* is one whose stock is closely held by a relatively small number of persons who are usually actively engaged in its management. Its stock is not available for purchase by the public.

J. A *profit corporation* is formed under a business corporation act such as the Model Act for the purpose of engaging in business for profit. It may or may not distribute profits to its shareholders.

K. A *nonprofit corporation* is one that is formed for charitable, religious, educational, or civic purposes.

L. *Subchapter S corporations.* The Internal Revenue Code allows shareholders of a closed corporation by unanimous agreement of all the shareholders to free the corporation from corporate income taxes on its profits. Shareholders as individuals are required to pay taxes on their pro rata share of the profits of a subchapter S corporation. They are also permitted to deduct on their returns their pro rata share of the corporation's net loss for each taxable year.

   1. Shareholders of a closed corporation may elect subchapter S status for the corporation if the following requirements are met:

      a. The corporation has only one class of stock;

      b. It has no more than twenty-five shareholders who are American citizens or resident aliens; and

      c. The corporation must derive most of its income from an active source rather than a passive source.

         (1) Active source. Eighty percent of its gross receipts must be derived from the sale of goods and services.

         (2) Passive source. No more than 20 percent of its gross receipts can be derived from royalties, rents, dividends, interest, annuities, and gains from sale or exchange of stock or securities.

M. *Qualified subchapter S trusts.* Under the Internal Revenue Code, a beneficiary of a qualified subchapter S trust can elect to free the trust from income taxes on its trust income and cause it to be taxed as ordinary income to the beneficiary. A qualified subchapter S trust is one that:

   1. Has only one beneficiary who is an American citizen or resident alien;

   2. Must distribute its income currently; and

   3. Its corpus may be distributed to such beneficiary only during the term of the trust.

ORGANIZATION AND FORMATION OF A CORPORATION

III. The following are the basic procedures required for the organization and formation of a legally existing corporation, i.e., a de jure corporation.

   A. *Statute of incorporation.* There must be a statute permitting the issuance of a charter (usually evidenced by a certificate of incorporation) upon compliance with its provisions.

   B. *Promotion of the corporation.* The prospective corporation must be promoted by its organizers (i.e., promoters). Promotion includes procurement of offers from subscribers to buy stock, preparation of an application for a certificate of incorporation, the articles of incorporation, and the negotiation of contracts for land, buildings, employees, and inventory needed to begin operations. (See Figure 15-1.)

1. *Incorporators* are those persons who sign and file the articles of incorporation and apply for the certificate of incorporation. Most states require at least one incorporator who is a natural person of at least eighteen or twenty-one years of age.

   a. The Model Act allows a domestic or foreign corporation to be an incorporator.

   b. The articles of incorporation and the application for incorporation must be signed by the requisite number of incorporators.

   c. Incorporators may also be subscribers and act as promotors for the corporation. A few states require each incorporator to be a subscriber.

2. *Promoters* are persons who associate together for the purpose of organizing a corporation, issuing the prospectus, procuring offers of stock subscriptions, and performing other necessary tasks to secure a charter and enter into necessary contracts in behalf of the yet nonexisting corporation. Promoters are personally bound to the terms of contracts they negotiate in behalf of the nonexistent corporation.

   a. Promoters have a *fiduciary relationship* toward the prospective corporation and have the following additional duties and liabilities:

      (1) A promoter has a duty to complete all necessary acts which precede and determine the formation, purpose, and structure of the corporation and determine the method by which shares and interests are to be issued and distributed.

      (2) The promoter is not an agent of the corporation since no agency relationship can exist where there is no existing principal. Nevertheless, the promoter owes a fiduciary duty to the subscribers, the shareholders, and the corporation once the latter comes into existence. The promoter's duty is to act with utmost loyalty. For example, a promoter who negotiates leases in his or her own behalf in order to sell them to the prospective corporation is liable to the corporation for any *secret* profits realized from the sale.

FIGURE 15-1   PROCESS OF INCORPORATION

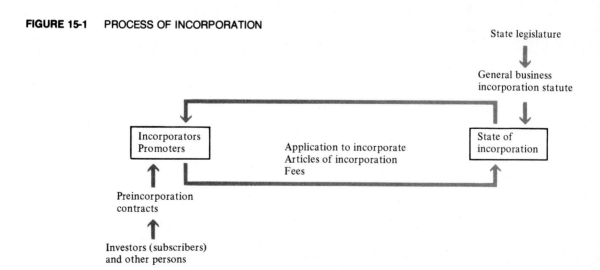

(*a*) Upon coming into existence, a corporation is not bound by any earlier contracts of the promoter even though these agreements were made in the name of the corporation and on its behalf.

(*b*) The corporation will become bound to the promoter's contracts with third persons only if it expressly or impliedly adopts them after it comes into existence.

   i. *Express adoption* is formal adoption by the board.

   ii. *Implied adoption* occurs where a corporation accepts the benefits of the contracts. For example, a promoter signed a research engineer to a five-year employment contract on behalf of the nonexistent corporation. Upon incorporation, the shareholders and the board of directors failed to expressly adopt the employment contract. However, the engineer was allowed to perform his duties under the contract. The corporation impliedly adopted the promoter's contract.

(3) Even though the new corporation expressly or impliedly adopts the promoter's contracts, the promoter remains personally liable until the preincorporation contracts are fully performed by the corporation or the promoter is released from liability by the parties to such contracts.

3. *Subscribers* are those persons, associations, or entities who offer to purchase shares of stock in a corporation. The offer to purchase is called a *stock subscription*. If it is an offer to purchase stock in a prospective corporation, it is referred to as a *pre-incorporation subscription*.

   a. Under the Model Act, a preincorporation subscription is irrevocable for six months unless:

   (1) The subscription agreement provides otherwise; or

   (2) All subscribers agree to its revocation.

   b. The offer in the preincorporation subscription is held to be automatically accepted by the corporation at the time it comes into legal existence. Under the Model Act, a corporation comes into existence at the time of the issuance of the certificate of incorporation by the state.

4. Some or all of the functions necessary for incorporation may be performed by the same or different person or persons. For example, an incorporator may at the same time also be a subscriber and a promoter, or the subscribers, incorporators, and promoters may all be different persons.

C. *Articles of incorporation.* The articles must be executed by the requisite number of incorporators and be approved by the state of incorporation. In most states, the articles of incorporation must include:

   1. An application (request) for issuance of a certificate of incorporation;

   2. The name of the corporation (the name must contain the word or abbreviation of the word "corporation," "company," "incorporated," or "limited");

   3. The name and address of the corporation's primary place of business and its registered office;

   4. The name of its registered agent;

   5. The duration or life of the corporation, which may be perpetual or for a limited time or purpose;

   6. The names and addresses of every incorporator;

   7. The purposes for which the corporation is to be formed. Under the Model Act, the purposes may be to accomplish any lawful business for profit except insurance and banking. Most states have enacted special statutes which allow incorporation by professionals (i.e., accounting, law, medicine, etc.) and those who engage in highly regulated activities such as insurance, banking, savings and

loans, and public utilities. Most states also have enacted special statutes to enable persons to incorporate for charitable, religious, educational, or civic purposes.

    8. The number of authorized shares and the par value of each unless no par stock is issued;

    9. If these shares of stock are to be divided into classes, the class designation, preferences, limitations, and relative rights of shares in each class;

    10. If there is to be any preferred stock, the preference must be stated.

    11. The number and identity of directors constituting the initial board of directors;

    12. A method of distribution of net assets upon dissolution of the corporation;

    13. Voting rights. At least one class of shares must have unrestricted voting rights. Unless provided otherwise in the articles, all shares have equal voting rights;

    14. If *preemptive rights* are to be either allowed or denied, the articles must so provide. The Model Act contains alternate provisions, section 26 and 26a, which permit the articles of incorporation to deny or allow such rights. See XIV, below;

    15. The signatures of the requisite number of incorporators. As previously stated, at least one incorporator is required in most states. Most states require that the signatures be acknowledged by a notary public.

D. *Certificate of incorporation.* After review and approval of the articles of incorporation, the secretary of state in the state of incorporation issues, files with the state, and forwards a certificate of incorporation to the incorporators. The Model Act, section 56, provides that the corporation begin its legal existence "upon the issuance of the certificate of incorporation."

E. *Initial shareholders' meeting.* An initial shareholders' meeting at which the members of the board are elected must be conducted. Subsequent to the initial postincorporation shareholders' meeting, the board of directors has the sole and ultimate responsibility for the management of the corporation.

F. *Initial directors' meeting.* The initial directors' or organizational meeting for purposes of adopting bylaws, electing officers, and transacting any other business which may rightfully be brought before the board must be held.

    1. The corporation's *bylaws* are the rules and regulations adopted by the corporation for its *internal* management.

    a. They are subject to, and must be consistent with, the constitution and statutes of the state of incorporation and the articles of incorporation.

    b. Unless reserved by the shareholders, the power to alter, amend, or repeal the bylaws or adopt new bylaws is vested in the board of directors.

G. *License to do business.* In some instances, a corporation may be required to obtain a permit or license to do business within the jurisdiction of a local governmental unit.

H. *Securities registration.* Unless exempt from state or federal securities regulation, the corporation must register its securities (i.e., bonds and stocks) pursuant to state and federal securities laws. See Chapter 19.

    1. The federal Securities Act of 1933 requires all nonexempt newly issued securities to be registered with the Securities Exchange Commission (SEC).

    2. State securities laws (*Blue Sky laws*) usually require additional registration with each state within which the securities are sold or offered to be sold.

I. *Issuance of shares.* Shares (i.e., common or preferred) are issued to preincorporation subscribers pursuant to authorization in the articles of incorporation in exchange for proper payment, i.e., cash, property, or prior services rendered in behalf of the corporation. See VII-E-2 below.

POWERS OF A CORPORATION

IV. A corporation has only those powers which its articles of incorporation and the state of incorporation have conferred upon it. Corporate powers are either express or implied.

A. *Express powers* are those powers which are specified in the statute of incorporation and those which are stated in the articles of incorporation. Section 4 of the Model Act grants the following powers to a corporation:

1. To have perpetual existence by its corporate name unless a limited period is stated in the articles;
2. To sue or be sued in its corporate name;
3. To have a corporate seal;
4. To buy, possess, own, lease, and sell real and personal property;
5. To sell, convey, mortgage, pledge, lease, exchange, transfer, or otherwise dispose of all or any part of its property and assets;
6. To lend money and use its credit to assist employees;
7. To buy, own, vote, pledge, sell, or otherwise deal in securities of other domestic or foreign corporations or governments;
8. To make contracts, borrow money, incur liabilities, issue notes and bonds, and mortgage or pledge its property;
9. To lend money for corporate purposes, invest and reinvest its funds, and possess property as security for loans;
10. To conduct its business, operate, have offices, and in doing so, exercise the powers granted under the act;
11. To elect or appoint officers and agents, define their duties, and fix their compensation;
12. To make or alter bylaws, not inconsistent with its articles of incorporation and the laws of the state of incorporation;
13. To make donations for public welfare or for charitable, scientific, or educational purposes;
14. To conduct any lawful business;
15. To pay pensions and to establish pension, profit-sharing, stock bonus, stock option, and other incentive plans;
15. To be a promoter, partner, member, associate, or manager of any enterprise;
17. To have and exercise all powers necessary and convenient to accomplish its purposes as stated in the articles of incorporation.

B. *Implied powers* are those powers, other than those expressly conferred, which are reasonably necessary to carry out the express powers of the corporation.

C. *Ultra vires acts of a corporation.* *Ultra vires* acts are those acts which are beyond the power of the corporation. For example, XYZ was incorporated with the expressed purpose to prepare, publish, and sell instructional tapes. These activities having become unprofitable, XYZ leased a manufacturing plant and entered into contracts for raw materials for the purpose of manufacturing energy-efficient motor scooters. The lease and other contracts are ultra vires.

1. A corporation cannot use ultra vires as a defense in any lawsuit to impose liability upon it for breach of contract or in a tort action brought against it on the basis of respondeat superior.
2. The attorney general in the state of incorporation or a shareholder can sue the corporation to enjoin (i.e., an injunction) it from committing ultra vires acts.
3. The corporation may sue officers or directors of corporations for damages or to enjoin them from committing ultra vires acts.
4. The attorney general of the state of incorporation may sue to dissolve the corporation for repeated and intentional ultra vires acts.

STOCK SUBSCRIPTIONS

V. A stock subscription is an offer made by a subscriber to purchase stock from an issuing corporation. Subscriptions are either preincorporation or postincorporation.

    A. *Preincorporation subscription.* Under section 17 of the Model Act, a subscription for the shares of a prospective corporation is irrevocable for six months *unless* the subscription agreement provides otherwise or unless all subscribers agree to a revocation.

        1. As a general rule, a preincorporation subscription (i.e., offer) is automatically accepted by the corporation without any action by the board of directors upon the issuance of the certificate of incorporation by the secretary of state.

        2. Subscribers automatically become shareholders even though certificates of stock have not been issued and paid for.

    B. *Postincorporation subscription.* A postincorporation subscription (i.e., offer) may be revoked by a subscriber at any time prior to its acceptance by the corporation. Its existence, duration, and acceptance are governed by the general rules of contract law.

NATURE OF CORPORATE SECURITIES

VI. A corporation may issue either debt (bonds) or equity (stock) securities when authorized to do so by its articles of incorporation or bylaws or by statute. A security may be "certificated" or "uncertificated" (UCC Sec. 8-101). A *certificated security* is one represented by an instrument (i.e., a writing) issued in bearer or registered form. An *uncertificated* security is one which is *not* represented by an instrument and the transfer of which is registered upon books maintained for that purpose by or on behalf of the issuer. Certificated securities are negotiable instruments. The transfer of ownership of a certificated security is accomplished by the proper transfer of the certificate itself. Ownership of an uncertificated security may be transferred by its owner's expression of intent to do so, with or without the delivery to the transferee of a written "instruction" ordering the issuer to register the security in the name of the transferee. See Chapter 4.

    A. *Bonds* (debt securities). A bond may be issued as a certificated or uncertificated security. The issuance of a bond creates a debtor-creditor relationship between the corporation and its bondholders. It is a binding promise to pay a stated amount of principal and interest to a bondholder on or before its maturity date.

        1. The Model Act allows a corporation to borrow money, mortgage any and all of its property, and issue bonds without shareholder approval, i.e., by action of the board of directors [4(h), 78]. However, corporate power in this regard may be limited by the corporate bylaws.

        2. When issued in bearer or registered form and dealt in as a medium of investment, a bond is a *negotiable security* [UCC 8-102(1), 8-105(1)].

        3. The contractual rights and duties of the corporation and its bondholders are specified in the bond agreement, i.e., the *indenture*.

        4. Bonds are classified as follows:

            a. *Registered.* These bonds are registered on the books of a corporation in the name of their owners. Payments of principal and interest are made only to owners of record.

            b. *Bearer.* These are not registered in the name of any person. They have interest coupons attached to them. Principal and interest are payable to the person in possession of the bond and its coupons.

    c. *Debenture.* A debenture is written evidence of any unsecured debt of a corporation.

    d. *Mortgage.* A mortgage bond is written evidence of a corporation's debt which is secured by a lien on the issuer's real property.

    e. *Redeemable.* A redeemable bond is one that evidences a debt which is subject to being paid before its maturity at the option of its issuer; i.e., it is callable.

    f. *Convertible.* This is a type of bond that may be exchanged for a specified amount of a different security, usually common stock.

B. *Shares of stock* (equity securities). Shares of stock, like bonds, may be issued certificated or uncertificated and are transferable accordingly. A share of stock is a proportionate ownership interest in the issuing corporation. As mentioned above, it may or may not be represented by a certificate of stock [UCC 8-102 (1)(c)(b)].

  1. *Authorized shares and classes of shares of stock.* A corporation cannot validly issue shares of stock unless such shares are issued pursuant to authority provided in the articles of incorporation. The articles of incorporation prescribe the authorized classes of shares as well as the authorized maximum amount of shares to be issued within each class of shares. The issuance of an unauthorized class of shares or an unauthorized number of shares within an authorized class of shares is void.

    a. The person who purchased the shares is not a shareholder.

    b. Subscribers have the right to rescind their subscription agreements and recover any consideration given to the issuing corporation in exchange for the void shares of stock.

  2. *Classes of stock.* Unless otherwise provided by the articles of incorporation, all shares have equal rights as to voting, dividends, and net assets. Shares of stock are usually classified in articles of incorporation as preferred or common.

    a. *Preferred shares* are shares having contractual preference over other classes of stock, normally with respect to dividends and distributions of assets upon dissolution but generally having no voting rights. (See Figure 15-2.)

      (1) Preferred stock may be classified as either *cumulative* or *noncumulative*.

        (*a*) If a preferred stock is cumulative and dividends have not been paid to it in one or more prior years, the shareholder is entitled to all dividends in arrears before any dividend can be paid to owners of common stock.

        (*b*) A provision in the articles of incorporation which guarantees dividends is interpreted to mean that the dividends are cumulative.

        (*c*) Unless expressly issued noncumulative, preferred stock is held to be cumulative.

      (2) Preferred shares may be classified as either *participating* or *nonparticipating*. If a share is participating, shareholders are entitled to receive

FIGURE 15-2   PREFERRED STOCK: TYPES OF PREFERENCES

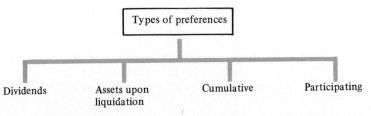

the stipulated dividend. In addition, they share excess profits declared as dividends proportionately with common shareholders.

    (3) Preferred shares are also those which have a preference as to distribution of corporate assets upon liquidation.

  b. *Common shares* are those shares which are issued without contractual preferences over other shares of the issuing corporation.

3. Shares of stock may be further classified as follows.

  a. *Par value* shares are shares issued with an arbitrary value printed on the face of the certificate.

  b. *No-par value* shares are shares having no fixed value.

  c. *Authorized shares* constitute a class of shares or the maximum number of shares within a class of shares that the corporation is authorized to issue by its articles of incorporation.

  d. *Issued* shares are stock certificates executed and delivered by the corporation to its shareholders.

  e. *Unissued* shares are stocks authorized but not yet issued.

  f. *Outstanding shares* are shares that are issued and held by shareholders other than the corporation itself.

  g. *Treasury stock* is stock that has been issued but has since been reacquired or returned to the corporation. It is authorized and issued but not outstanding.

    (1) A corporation may purchase its own shares from its shareholders if authorized to do so in its articles of incorporation (Model Act, Sec. 6).

      (*a*) Purchases may be made only from and to the extent of the corporation's unreserved and unrestricted surplus.

      (*b*) No purchase or payment can be made while the corporation is insolvent or when the purchase or payment would make it insolvent.

    (2) Treasury stock differs from other stock of a corporation as follows:

      (*a*) It cannot be voted;

      (*b*) It is not entitled to preemptive rights;

      (*c*) No dividends can be paid on it; and

      (*d*) A corporation may transfer ownership of treasury stock without receiving equal to par value or stated value in exchange. *Note*: Newly issued shares must be issued in exchange for value equal to par value or, if the shares have no par value, equal to stated value.

  h. *Redeemable* is stock of a corporation which is subject to recall at a fixed (callable) price at the option of the corporation. A *redemption* is in effect an involuntary sale of the shares to the corporation.

  i. *Convertible* is stock of a corporation which may be recalled in exchange for the issuance of a substitute security, for example, common stock in exchange for preferred stock.

  j. *Voting or nonvoting.* Shares of stock may be made voting or nonvoting by a provision in the articles of incorporation. If the articles are silent in this regard, each share of outstanding stock entitles its owner to one vote.

C. *Stock options and rights.* Section 20 of the Model Act allows a corporation to create and issue rights or options entitling their owners to purchase from the corporation shares or fractional shares of any class of authorized securities.

1. An *option* grants its owner the right to purchase a specified amount of shares of stock at a stated price within a specified period of time.

2. The writing that evidences the option is called a *warrant*. A warrant is a security under article 8 of the Uniform Commercial Code.

3. *Warrants* are issued by a corporation as a fringe benefit for its key executives or to its shareholders in recognition of their preemptive rights.

CORPORATE CAPITAL

VII. Corporate capital represents the monetary value of the combined ownerships (equities) of shareholders of a corporation (see Figure 15-3).

    A. *Stated capital* is the sum of the par value of all par value shares and the stated value of all no-par shares issued by a corporation.

    B. *Paid-in surplus* is the value received in excess of par value or stated value.

    C. *Surplus* means the excess of net assets of a corporation over its stated capital.

    D. *Earned surplus* (retained earnings) is that portion of the surplus of a corporation which is equal to the balance of its net profits, income, gains, and losses from the date of incorporation or from the last date on which a deficit was eliminated.

    E. *Watered stock.* In no event may a corporation issue a certificate of stock (or an "initial transaction statement" in the case of uncertificated shares) to a subscriber before it is fully paid. A corporation must receive at least a value (i.e., cash, property, or past services) equal to par value of par value shares and the stated value of no-par shares. If it fails to do so, the stock is said to be "watered" and its issuance is an ultra vires act.

        1. The shareholders are liable to the corporation for the extent of the "water," i.e., the difference between the value received by the corporation and the par value of the shares, or if they are no-par shares, the *stated value*.

        2. *Consideration for shares of stock.* A corporation can issue stock in exchange only for the following types of consideration:

            a. Cash;

            b. Property (real or personal); or

            c. Services performed prior to the issuance of the shares.

                (1) The directors establish the value of property or services received in exchange for shares of stock.

                (2) The value established by the directors cannot be successfully challenged if they acted in good faith.

                (3) If the directors acted in bad faith and the overvaluation of the property or services caused the corporation to receive inadequate consideration, the shares are watered.

                    (*a*) The corporation can sue the shareholders either for the amount of the water or to rescind the transaction.

                    (*b*) Directors are personally liable.

                    (*c*) Creditors who become creditors *subsequent* to the issuance of watered stock may recover the water from the shareholders. Creditors who become creditors before the issuance cannot recover.

        3. Shares of stock cannot be issued in exchange for promissory notes or for future services. If they are so issued, they are watered.

FIGURE 15-3   CORPORATE CAPITAL

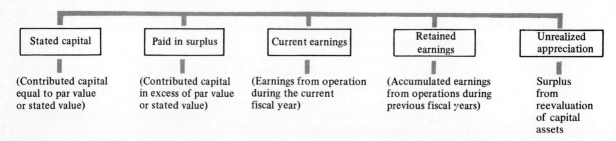

Stated capital	Paid in surplus	Current earnings	Retained earnings	Unrealized appreciation
(Contributed capital equal to par value or stated value)	(Contributed capital in excess of par value or stated value)	(Earnings from operation during the current fiscal year)	(Accumulated earnings from operations during previous fiscal years)	Surplus from reevaluation of capital assets

4. A bona fide purchaser for value is not liable either to the corporation or to creditors for the amount of water. A *bona fide purchaser* is one who pays value for shares of stock without knowledge that it is watered.

CORPORATE LIABILITY FOR CONTRACTS, TORTS, AND CRIMES

VIII. A corporation is liable as a legal entity for its contracts, torts, and crimes. Corporate liability is not the personal liability of the shareholders. They possess only limited liability; i.e., they stand to lose only the amount of their investment. The shareholders are also not personally liable for the actions of the corporate directors, officers, or employees, as the latter are agents of the corporation, not of the shareholders.

  A. *Liability for contracts.*

  1. *Ultra vires contracts.* Corporations are legally bound to the terms of their ultra vires contracts. See IV-C above.

  2. *Non-ultra vires contracts.* A corporation, as a legal entity, enters into contracts with third persons through its agents, i.e., those directors, officers, or employees who have received authority from the corporation to contract with third parties in its behalf. Even though an agent acts within the powers of the corporation, the corporation is not bound to the agent's contract with the third person unless the agent possessed express, implied in fact, apparent, and implied in law authority from the corporation or the agent's unauthorized contract is subsequently ratified by the corporation. See Chapter 13.

  B. *Liability for torts.* A corporation is liable for the torts committed by its agents, employees, officers, and directors while acting within the scope of their employment or authority. The liability is established under the concept of respondeat superior. Whether a tort has been committed in the scope of a corporation's business or authority is determined in much the same manner as the liability of a principal for the torts of its agent. See Chapter 13.

  C. *Liability for crimes.* A corporation is liable for its crimes. Although it obviously cannot be imprisoned, it can be fined. For example, corporations can be fined up to $1 million for a violation of the Foreign Corrupt Practices Act. As another example, a corporation can be fined for a violation of the Sherman Act, a federal antitrust law.

"PIERCING THE CORPORATE VEIL"

IX. In some circumstances, a court will refuse to recognize the existence of a de jure corporation in order to hold its shareholders, directors, and officers personally liable for crimes, contracts, or torts. When doing so, the court is said to be *"piercing the corporate veil."* This concept is most frequently applied to shareholders, directors, and officers of a closed corporation.

  A. The court will "pierce the corporate veil" whenever it finds that a corporation's shareholders, directors, or officers are wrongfully utilizing the corporate entity to escape personal liability for crimes, fraudulent practices, torts, or contracts. Such wrongful use is evidenced by:

  1. Failure to conduct business as a corporation. For example, failure to elect a board of directors or, if a board of directors is elected, failure to hold meetings; or failure to keep minutes for board of directors and shareholder meetings.

  2. Corporate property, assets, and cash are used for personal as well as corporate purposes; and

  3. The corporation is intentionally undercapitalized.

B. For example, X and Y formed Cab, Inc., for the purposes of conducting a taxicab business. X and Y constituted the membership of the board of directors, and each held an executive position. They then formed three other corporations. The stock of these corporations was owned by X and Y, and they also were organized for the purposes of conducting a taxicab business. Each of the three subsidiary corporations was undercapitalized. Each subsidiary owned two taxicabs. The liability insurance carried on each taxicab was the minimum allowed by law. One of the cabs struck a pedestrian, causing the latter to suffer severe personal injuries. The pedestrian sued X and Y personally. The court pierced the corporate veil, disregarded the corporation, and held X and Y personally liable for the injuries.

DIRECTORS

X. Section 35 of the Model Act bestows upon the board of directors the right and duty to manage the business of the corporation (see Figure 15-4).

  A. *Election of directors and term of office.*
   1. Directors are elected at the first shareholders' meeting and each annual meeting thereafter, and they hold office until their successors are chosen or until they resign or are removed.
   2. The Model Act requires a minimum of one director. Some states require a minimum of three.
   3. Any vacancy occurring on the board can be filled by a majority vote of the remaining directors even though such vote is less than a quorum of the board of directors.
   4. At a shareholders' meeting expressly called for that purpose, any director or the entire board can be removed with or without cause by a vote of the holders of a majority of the shares entitled to vote at that time.
   5. Existing directors whose terms have expired continue to hold office (i.e., "holdover" directors) until their successors are chosen by shareholders or until they resign or are removed.
   6. Directors can serve on the boards of two corporations even though they transact business with each other (i.e., an interlocking directorate).

FIGURE 15-4   CORPORATE RELATIONSHIPS

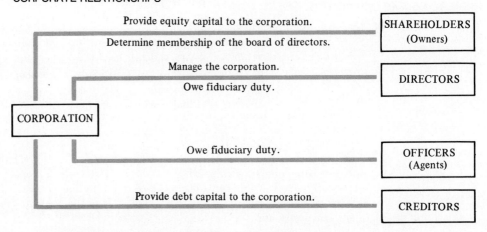

7. Under the Model Act, articles of incorporation may authorize directors to be elected to staggered terms whenever a board of directors consists of nine or more members.

B. *Powers of the board of directors.* Section 35 of the Model Act provides that the board of directors shall have the exclusive right and duty to manage the business and affairs of the corporation and in doing so shall exercise all corporate powers granted to the corporation by the state of incorporation, articles of incorporation, and bylaws.

1. Directors have implied powers to do whatever is reasonably necessary to carry out their express powers.

2. They have the right and power to manage the business and affairs of the corporation. They do not have the power to act alone to make fundamental changes in the character or financial structure of the corporation. Directors acting formally as a board have the power (not exclusive) to:

a. Appoint officers, agents, and employees; establish their salaries; invest them with authority; supervise their activities; and remove them from their office or position;

b. Establish corporate policies and ensure compliance;

c. Declare dividends from earned surplus (retained earnings);

d. Establish the stated value for newly issued no-par shares of stock;

e. Set the value of property or prior services received in exchange for newly issued shares of stock;

f. Purchase the corporation's shares of stock and cancel or retain such shares as treasury stock;

g. Alter, amend, or repeal bylaws or adopt new bylaws unless such power is reserved to shareholders in the articles of incorporation; and

h. *Initiate* proceedings by action of the board to affect articles of incorporation, corporate financial structure, all or substantially all of corporate assets, the corporate name, classes of stock, or the corporate duration. These types of actions require the additional approval of shareholders.

C. *Formal meetings of the directors* are required to be held either regularly at a time and place fixed in the bylaws or periodically as they may be called.

1. Regular meetings of the board or its executive committees can be held with or without notice as prescribed in the bylaws.

2. Special meetings of the board or its executive committees must be held with notice to directors as prescribed in the bylaws.

3. A *simple majority* (more than 50 percent) of the members of the board of directors present *at the beginning of a meeting* constitutes a *quorum.* A quorum is the minimum number of members required to transact valid business as a board.

4. A majority vote in favor of a resolution by directors present at a duly called and represented meeting constitutes valid action by the board.

5. Directors cannot vote by proxy.

6. A director acting individually without action of the board has no power to bind the corporation.

7. Directors must act formally as a board, not individually. *Exception:* Directors may take informal action (without a formal meeting) only by unanimous agreement, in writing and signed by all of the directors on the board.

8. Meetings of a board of directors can be held inside or outside the state of incorporation.

9. Cumulative voting by directors is not allowed. Each director is entitled to one vote on each matter presented to the board.

D. *Duties and liabilities of directors.* The duties and liabilities of directors are prescribed by state and federal statutes, the common law, articles of incorporation, and the bylaws. A director may be criminally or civilly liable for breach of duties.

1. *Criminal liability.*

    a. Section 36 of the Model Act imposes criminal liability on any director who knowingly signs false articles of incorporation, reports, or other documents filed with the secretary of state.

    b. A director is civilly and criminally liable for any wilful violation of any provision of the Securities Act of 1933 and the Securities Exchange Act of 1934 or any Securities Exchange Commission (SEC) rule promulgated thereunder. See Chapter 19.

    c. A director is criminally liable for the wilful nonpayments of taxes under the Internal Revenue Code.

    d. A director may violate state or federal criminal fraud statutes.

2. *Civil liability for damages.*

    a. *Fiduciary duty.* Directors owe a fiduciary duty to their corporation. The fiduciary duty obligates the director to act with utmost loyalty, good faith, and fair dealing in relationship with codirectors and the corporation and in the performance of corporate responsibilities.

        (1) *Corporate opportunities.* A director has a duty to disclose every business opportunity that would be of benefit to the corporation of which the director became aware in the course of performance of his or her duties. Any director (as well as any officer or employee) is allowed to take advantage of a corporate opportunity after disclosure when:

            (*a*) The corporation is financially unable to take advantage of it; or

            (*b*) Taking advantage of it would involve an illegal or ultra vires act; or

            (*c*) The board of directors, by a majority vote (excluding the vote of the interested director), refuses to accept it.

            (*d*) For an example of a breach of duty to disclose, a director of an oil development corporation failed to disclose the availability of certain oil leases and purchased them for herself. As another example; a director for a soft drink syrup manufacturer learned that the secret formula of a competitor was for sale. He secretly purchased the formula, organized his own corporation, and manufactured a competing soft drink. As a third example, a corporation sought a land site for a new motel. X, its director, located an excellent site, secretly negotiated its purchase, placed its title into a land trust, and then directed the trustee of the land to sell the land to a competitor at a large profit.

        (2) *Transactions with the corporation.* A director has a duty to make full disclosure of his or her personal financial interest in any transaction between the director (or a firm in which the director is a shareholder or a director) and the corporation. Such a transaction is voidable by the corporation and the director is liable for damages unless:

            (*a*) The transaction was fair and reasonable; or

            (*b*) After full disclosure (from the interested director or others), the board of directors approve or ratify the transaction and such approval or ratification is valid without counting the vote or consent of the interested director. *Note:* The interested director's presence and/or voting at the meeting does not invalidate the action of the board *unless* the interested director's vote was necessary to validate it; or

(c) After full disclosure, the transaction is approved by the shareholders.

(3) *Self-dealing and secret profits.* A director has a duty of utmost loyalty to the corporation. A director must refrain from self-dealing in any act or activity that is in conflict with the interests of the corporation. A director is not allowed to retain any salary, income, commission, or other profit that was received in connection with any act or activity in breach of the director's fiduciary duty. Some examples of self-dealing and secret profits of a director are:

(c) Being an owner of a competing company;

(b) Selling the corporation's customer lists or other secrets to other companies;

(c) Using corporate assets for the director's personal use;

(d) Selling property to the corporation through an intermediary;

(e) Being employed by a competitor; or

(f) Embezzling corporate funds and through their investment deriving income or capital gains.

(4) *Remedies for breach of fiduciary duty.* The remedy for breach of fiduciary duty is a lawsuit in equity by the corporation or, more often, a derivative lawsuit instituted by a shareholder in behalf of the corporation against the wrongdoing director for damages or to recover secret profits.

b. *Bad faith or negligence.* Directors have a duty to exercise good faith and ordinary care (due diligence) in the exercise of their power and authority. The standard of care required is that amount of care which a reasonably prudent person in the same or similar circumstances would exercise.

(1) A director is *not* liable for errors in judgment so long as the director exercised ordinary care. For example, X, a director for a major motel chain, learned from a reliable source that a state was to construct a major highway adjacent to a certain parcel of land. He purchased the land in behalf of the corporation for several hundred thousand dollars. The highway was never constructed. The director was held not to be liable.

(2) A director must use ordinary care to:

(a) Select and appoint honest and competent employees;

(b) Supervise officers and employees;

(c) Detect wrongs committed by codirectors, officers, or employees;

(d) Examine corporate books and records;

(e) Attend board meetings;

(f) Obtain sufficient knowledge in order to cast informed votes on matters presented to the board;

(g) Take an active part in management; and

(h) Keep advised of the financial condition of the corporation, i.e., its earned surplus and solvency.

   i. Directors are liable for declaration and payment of dividends which impair capital. However, they are not liable if their action in declaring and paying dividends was done in good faith in reliance upon incorrect financial statements furnished by corporate attorneys, accountants, or other experts (Model Act Sec. 35).

c. *Ultra vires acts.* Directors have a duty to refrain from engaging in ultra vires activities. Ultra vires activities are those which are beyond the powers of the corporation. "Ultra vires" does not mean illegal. As a general rule, the corporation is bound to ultra vires contracts with third persons.

(1) Ultra vires acts include:

   (*a*) Issuance of shares of the corporation at a discount.

   (*b*) Declaration and payment of a dividend when the corporation is insolvent or one which would cause corporate insolvency or at a time when corporate net assets are or would become less than stated capital.

   (*c*) Assent to any loan of corporate funds or assets to any director or officer not authorized by the shareholders.

   (*d*) An unauthorized purchase or sale of corporate real or personal property.

   (*e*) Acquisition of treasury stock that causes the corporation to become insolvent.

(2) Any director who votes for or assents to any ultra vires transaction is held to be liable if losses or damages occur.

   (*a*) If a director is present at a meeting of the board at which action on any corporate matter is taken, the director is conclusively presumed to have assented to such action unless in addition to dissenting, the director:

      i. Has his or her dissent entered on record in the minutes of the meeting;

      ii. Files a written dissent to such action before the meeting adjourns; or

      iii. Forwards a written dissent by registered mail to the secretary immediately after the adjournment of the meeting.

   (*b*) A director who has been held liable for assenting to an improper transaction is entitled to ratable contribution (indemnity) from other participating directors who are similarly liable.

(3) Remedies for ultra vires acts include:

   (*a*) A court injunction to prevent the performance of an executory ultra vires contract;

   (*b*) Damages against officers or directors responsible for the ultra vires act; or

   (*c*) Revocation of the certificate of incorporation upon petition to a court by the attorney general of the state of incorporation.

d. *Short-swing profits* (i.e., on purchases and sales of stock). Short-swing speculations are prohibited by the Securities and Exchange Act of 1934. See Chapter 19.

(1) The act applies to purchases and sales by *"insiders,"* that is, directors, officers, or any person owning 10 percent or more of the stock of the corporation, if the stock is listed on a national securities exchange or registered with the SEC.

(2) The act defines a *short-swing speculation* as a purchase or sale of the same shares of stock by one individual within any given six-month period.

(3) The act allows the corporation to recover any profits earned in a short-swing speculation by insiders.

E. *Delegation of duties by directors.* The board of directors cannot delegate its management (decision-making) responsibilities to nondirectors.

   1. *Executive committees.* The board can delegate some but not all of its managerial duties to one or more committees *composed only of directors.*

   2. *Ministerial duties.* A board may delegate its ministerial (i.e., routine and non-decision-making) duties to persons other than directors.

XI. Officers are agents and fiduciaries of the corporation. (See Figure 15-4.)

    A. *Election of officers and term of office.* Officers are elected or appointed by the board of directors at such time and in such manner as prescribed by the bylaws. (Model Act, Sec. 50.)

        1. The officers must consist of at least a president, one or more vice presidents, a secretary, and a treasurer.

        2. Any two or more offices may be held by the same person except the offices of secretary and president.

        3. An officer may also serve as a director.

        4. An officer may be removed by the board of directors when in its judgment the best interests of the corporation will be served.

            a. Election or appointment of an officer does not in itself create contract rights.

            b. However, contractual rights may be negotiated by an officer and the corporation. If contractual rights exist, an officer's wrongful removal constitutes a breach of contract.

    B. *Authority of officers as agents.* Officers, as agents of the corporation, have such express authority to manage the corporation as is provided to them in the bylaws and granted to them by the board of directors (Model Act, Sec. 50).

        1. In addition to an officer's express authority, the officer has the implied in fact, implied in law, and apparent authority to bind the corporation. The corporation may also ratify an officer's unauthorized act committed in its behalf. See Chapter 13.

    C. *Compensation of officers.* Salaries of officers are usually established by the board of directors.

        1. Where a director also occupies the position of an officer, the director may receive a salary but may not personally vote on the amount.

        2. In organizations in which the officers constitute a majority of the board of directors, the shareholders vote to resolve the salary issue.

        3. Unless otherwise agreed, officers are automatically entitled to salaries for services they actually perform. If the amount of the salary is not agreed upon, a reasonable salary is due to officers.

        4. Fringe benefit plans may be provided to compensate officers and key employees for the performance of their duties, for example, stock options, pension plans, and stock bonus plans.

    D. *Liabilities of officers to their corporation.* An officer's liability to the corporation is the same as the liability of an agent to the agent's principal. See Chapter 13.

    E. *Criminal and civil liability.* An officer's criminal and civil liability is the same as that of a director. See X-D above.

INDEMNIFICATION

XII. *Indemnification of directors, officers, employees, and agents.* Directors, officers, employees, and agents of a corporation are not liable to the corporation for errors in judgment when they act in good faith, with ordinary care (without negligence), and in the best interests of the corporation.

    A. Section 5 of the Model Act grants to a corporation power to indemnify the above-mentioned parties for expenses, attorney fees, judgments, fines, and amounts paid in settlement incurred by them in connection with any threatened or actual legal proceeding filed against them as a result of their good faith, nonnegligent actions in behalf of the best interest of the corporation, i.e., administrative, investigative, criminal, or civil legal proceedings.

    1. A judgment, settlement, conviction, or plea of nolo contendere in one of the legal proceedings does not create a presumption that the person acted in bad faith and not in the best interests of the corporation.

B. A corporation *must* indemnify such persons for all expenses, including attorney fees, *when they have been successful* on the merits or otherwise in the defense of any legal action, lawsuit, or administrative or investigative proceeding.

C. In lawsuits by a corporation against the above-mentioned persons, the corporation has the *power* to indemnify the latter for expenses including attorney fees that they incurred in connection with the defense or settlement of such lawsuits *unless* such persons have been adjudged to be liable for negligence or misconduct in the performance of their duties to the corporation.

CORPORATE DIVIDENDS

XIII. *Dividends* may take the form of distributions to shareholders in cash, property, or corporate stock.

    A. *Types of dividends.*

        1. *Cash dividends.*

        2. *Property dividends* are declared and paid out not in the form of cash but in some form of property, e.g., stock from another corporation or a bottle of wine.

        3. A *stock dividend* is a ratable distribution of equity in the corporation to its shareholders.

            a. The effect of a stock dividend is to reduce the value of the retained earnings account and increase the value of the capital account.

            b. No change in firm assets will occur.

            c. No change in stockholders' equity will occur unless the dividend is paid on only one of several classes of stock.

            d. The shareholders' total investment will remain the same.

            e. The total of outstanding and issued shares is increased.

        4. *Stock split* compared with stock dividend. Both a stock split and a stock dividend result in an increase in the number of shares outstanding, but the proportionate interest of the shareholder in the corporation remains the same.

            a. A stock split does not affect the accumulated earnings account or total sssets of the firm.

            b. A stock split increases the *number* of shares outstanding and reduces the par or stated value of the stock; e.g., 1,000 shares at $10 par value with a two-to-one stock split results in 2,000 shares at $5 par.

        5. A *liquidating dividend* is a distribution of capital as opposed to accumulated profits (retained earnings) or current earnings.

    B. *Sources of dividends.*

        1. Dividends may be payable out of the following sources:

            a. *Earned surplus* (retained earnings). Cash or stock dividends are allowed to be paid from earned surplus on common and preferred shares.

            b. *Paid-in surplus or stated capital.* A cash or stock dividend is payable to preferred or common shares if authorized by the board of directors *and* approved by the holders of at least two-thirds of the outstanding shares of stock of each class.

            c. *Unrealized surplus from revaluation of assets.* Only a stock dividend is payable from this source and only upon approval of the board of directors *and* the shareholders.

C. *Declaration and payment of dividends* are at the good faith discretion of the directors of the corporation.
  1. If a distribution is to be made, dividends must be paid to preferred shareholders before any distribution to common shareholders.
  2. There can be no discrimination in the declaration of dividends among shareholders of the same class.
  3. Even though the dividend is to be paid from a proper source, it is improper if:
     a. It is paid while the corporation is insolvent; or
     b. Its payment will render the corporation insolvent.
  4. Once properly declared, a *cash dividend* is considered a *legal debt* of the corporation on the date of its declaration or, if a date of record is established, on that date.
     a. In the event of failure to pay or insolvency, the shareholders may prosecute their claims to the dividend as unsecured creditors in a court of law or in bankruptcy court.
     b. Infrequently, a special fund is set up at the time of declaration out of which the dividends are to be paid. This fund has sometimes been regarded as a trust to which the shareholders have a preferred claim upon the corporation's solvency.
  5. A declaration of *stock dividends* (unlike cash dividends) may be revoked at any time prior to distribution. It does not create a debtor-creditor relationship between the corporation and the shareholder.

RIGHTS OF SHAREHOLDERS

XIV. Shareholders are the owners of a corporation. As shareholders they have the following rights:
  A. *Right to a certificate or an initial transaction statement* (issued for uncertificated shares). Each shareholder has the right to receive a certificate or an initial transaction statement evidencing the shareholder's ownership interest (class and number of shares) in the corporation.
  B. *Preemptive rights.* The Model Act, sections 26 and 26a, contains alternate provisions which permit the articles of incorporation to deny or allow preemptive rights. Under the common law, unless expressly denied in the articles of incorporation or in the provisions of an incorporation statute, each shareholder has preemptive rights. When preemptive rights exist, each shareholder has the right to purchase a pro rata share of every new offering of stock by the corporation in order to preserve his or her proportionate interest in the equity of the corporation. For example, X owns 100 shares of the 1,000 shares outstanding in ABC Corporation, which wants to increase its capital stock to 2,000 shares. X will have preemptive rights entitling him to purchase 10 percent of the 1,000 new shares or an aggregate of 200 shares of the 2,000 shares to be outstanding.
  C. *Voting rights.* The right to vote in most states entitles the shareholder to one vote for every share of stock which the shareholder owns unless limited or denied in the articles of incorporation.
    1. *Voting trust.* The shareholders may transfer their shares into a voting trust whereby the trustee holds legal title to the stock and possesses all voting rights (maximum duration is ten years).

2. *Proxy.* A shareholder may also transfer the right to vote by giving a proxy (a written power of attorney) to another. A proxy is revocable in writing, by the shareholder appearing at the shareholders' meeting and voting his or her own shares, or by the shareholder giving a second proxy to vote the same shares to another person.

3. *Cumulative voting* is a method of voting which allows a shareholder more than one vote for each share of stock he or she owns in electing members of the board of directors. Cumulative voting is not allowed for any other purpose.

    a. It is not allowed unless authorized by statute.

    b. Cumulative voting allows a shareholder to multiply the number of voting shares he or she owns against the number of *directors to be elected* (not the total number of directors on the board). The shareholder may cast all of his or her votes for one director or distribute them in any manner.

D. *Inspection of corporate records.* A shareholder has the right to inspect the books and records of the corporation, in person or by an attorney, agent, or accountant, and to make transcripts from them so long as the inspection is at a reasonable time and place and for a legitimate purpose.

    1. Refusal by an officer or director to allow a shareholder to properly inspect the books and records will subject the officer to liability for damages.

    2. The right may be denied to any shareholder who previously used the corporation for a wrongful purpose, to any shareholder whose purpose is to embarrass or cause loss to the corporation, or to any shareholder who demands an unreasonable inspection.

E. *Right to dividends.* The shareholder has the right to dividends only after the dividend has been formally declared by the board of directors.

    1. A court of equity will grant an injunction and require the directors to declare a dividend only when the following conditions exist:

        a. Corporate earnings or surplus are available out of which a dividend may be declared;

        b. The earnings or surplus must be in the form of available cash, not in accounts receivable or inventories; and

        c. The directors are acting so unreasonably in withholding dividends that their conduct clearly amounts to an abuse of their management discretion; i.e., they are acting in bad faith.

    2. It is the shareholder's duty to refund dividends, if any, where:

        a. The dividend was paid when the corporation is insolvent; or

        b. The shareholder received the dividend as a result of the shareholder's own fraud or with knowledge of illegal dealings.

    3. No duty exists to refund any illegal dividend from a *solvent* corporation where the dividend was received in good faith by the shareholder.

F. *Right to transfer ownership.* As a general rule, a shareholder has the right to freely transfer shares of stock to whosoever the shareholder chooses. *Restrictions on transfer* of corporate stock may be imposed by the articles of incorporation or bylaws and by agreement between the stockholders and the corporation.

    1. Any restriction that places an unreasonable burden on the transfer of stock or makes the stock nontransferable is against public policy and is void.

    2. Only *reasonable* restrictions are valid. If noted conspicuously on the certificate, a restriction is valid against *all* subsequent purchasers of the stock. Unreasonable restrictions are void and therefore are not binding on subsequent purchasers.

    3. A restriction which provides that the shareholder must first offer the certificate

of stock back to the corporation or to other shareholders at its market value at the time of transfer does not render the restriction unreasonable.
- **a.** The fact that the purpose of the restriction is to maintain control of a close corporation against outsiders does not render the restriction unreasonable.
- **b.** A restriction requiring the shares to be offered back to the corporation at book value or at a value to be set by the directors is unreasonable and void.

G. *Right to share in assets upon dissolution.* The shareholder has the right upon dissolution to share pro rata with other shareholders in the remaining assets after all the claims of creditors and preferred shareholders have been satisfied.

H. *Right to receivership and dissolution.* Shareholders have the right to receivership and dissolution upon application to a court of equity to liquidate the business when it appears that:
- **1.** The directors are deadlocked in the management and the shareholders can do nothing to prevent irreparable injury;
- **2.** Acts of directors are illegal, oppressive, or fraudulent; or
- **3.** The corporate assets are being misapplied or wasted by the officers or directors.

I. *Right to rescind a stock subscription.* A shareholder who is fraudulently induced to subscribe to a corporate issue of stock by its officers or directors is entitled to the remedy of either rescission or damages.
- **1.** If the shareholder obtains a judgment for damages, that shareholder stands on equal footing with general creditors.
- **2.** If the shareholder chooses to rescind the purchase of stock, the shareholder's rights are subordinate to those of general creditors; but the shareholder has priority over nonrescinding shareholders.

SHAREHOLDERS' MEETINGS

XVI. Shareholders' meetings are mandatory as well as discretionary.
- **A.** *Annual meetings.* Shareholders are required to meet annually.
- **B.** *Special meetings.* Special meetings may be called by the board or shareholders as authorized in the articles of incorporation or bylaws.
- **C.** *Notice of meetings.* Written notice of a special meeting must be given to each shareholder.
- **D.** *Voting.* A shareholder is entitled to one vote for each share on each matter submitted to a vote at a shareholders' meeting unless cumulative voting *for members of the board of directors* is authorized by statute. Cumulative voting entitles a shareholder to a total number of votes determined by multiplying the total number of the shareholder's shares by the number of *directors to be elected* (not the number of members on the board). The shareholder may then cast all of his or her votes for one candidate for director or divide the votes in any manner among some or all of the candidates.
- **E.** *Proxy.* A shareholder may vote in person or by written proxy.
- **F.** *Quorum.* A simple majority (i.e., more than 50 percent) of outstanding shares, represented in person or proxy *at the beginning* of the meeting, constitutes a *quorum.*
- **G.** *Valid action.* If a quorum is present, an affirmative vote of the majority of shares represented at the meeting is the act of the shareholders.
- **H.** *Formal and informal meetings.* As a general rule, shareholders may act only in a formal meeting. *Exception:* Shareholders may take informal action only by unanimous agreement in writing and signed by all the shareholders.

    XVII. Merger, consolidation, and purchase of assets of another corporation.

        A. Definitions.

            1. *Purchase or sale of assets.* The purchase of one or all of a corporation's assets by another corporation does not affect the legal existence of either corporation. Each corporation continues its separate existence.

            2. A *merger* of two or more corporations is the combination of all of their total assets, title to which is vested in the *surviving corporation.*

                a. Each of the merging corporations legally ceases to exist as an entity.

                b. All liabilities become the liabilities of the surviving corporation.

            3. A *consolidation* of two or more corporations is the combination of all their total assets, title to which is taken by a *newly created corporation.*

                a. Each of the consolidating corporations legally ceases to exist as an entity.

                b. All liabilities become the liabilities of the newly formed corporation.

        B. *Board of directors and shareholder approval.* The purchase or *lease* by one corporation of *all* assets of another, consolidation, and merger require approval by the board of directors *and* the affirmative vote of the holders of a majority of the shares entitled to vote.

            1. Dissenting shareholders may demand and be paid by the corporation the "fair value" of their stock, provided that they comply with statutory procedures.

            2. To protect the right to receive "fair value," a dissident shareholder is usually required to follow the following statutory procedures:

                a. File with the corporation a written objection prior to the shareholders' meeting at which the issue is to be presented;

                b. Abstain from voting in favor of the issue; and

                c. Make a written demand for payment of the fair value of his or her shares within ten days after the action by the shareholders.

            3. Fair value is *not* the same as market or book value. *Fair value* is determined by taking into consideration the following factors:

                a. Quality of management;

                b. Current financial position;

                c. Past earnings;

                d. Future projected earnings;

                e. Nature of the corporate business; and

                f. Goodwill.

DISSOLUTION AND LIQUIDATION

    XVIII. *Dissolution of a corporation* may occur by act of legislature, expiration of corporate life, voluntary act of all the outstanding shareholders, voluntary act by board of directors and the affirmative vote of the holders of a majority of shares entitled to vote, decree of a court of equity, or the surrender of corporate charter.

        A. The assets of the corporation are liquidated and used to pay secured and unsecured creditors according to their respective rights. Any remainder is distributed to the shareholders pro rata according to stock preferences, if any exist.

        B. Where corporate assets are not liquidated and distributed, title to them is vested in shareholders as tenants in common according to their proportionate ownership interests.

            1. These assets, however, are subject to the claims of creditors for a statutory period of time after dissolution. During such time, suit may be brought by any creditor against the corporation.

RIGHTS OF CREDITORS

XIX. Rights and remedies of corporate creditors are as follows:
  - **A.** As a general rule, creditors have no right to participate in management.
  - **B.** Secured creditors have priority over unsecured creditors as to property which is subject to their security interests.
  - **C.** Unsecured creditors stand on an equal footing with each other in respect to their rights against corporate assets.
  - **D.** Creditors' rights with respect to unpaid stock subscriptions:
    1. The unpaid balance is an asset of the corporation that passes to the trustee in bankruptcy, who has the authority to bring an action at law against the subscriber and obtain a judgment for any balance due.
    2. A creditor of a corporation may sue a shareholder directly after obtaining a judgment against the corporation if the judgment is not paid even though the corporation is not in bankruptcy.
  - **E.** Watered stock is a liability of shareholders and is enforced by a bill in equity by creditors who relied on the representation that the stock was fully paid, i.e., those persons who became creditors after the watered stock was issued.

FOREIGN CORPORATIONS

XX. A *foreign corporation*, before "doing business" within a state, must obtain a license or certificate of authority to do so.
  - **A.** *"Doing business"* means actively engaging in multiple transactions for the purpose of financial gain or profit. A single transaction or activity does not constitute doing business within a state.
  - **B.** Where a foreign corporation has been found to be doing business within a state, the state has authority to:
    1. Require qualification or registration of the foreign corporation;
    2. Impose taxes; and
    3. Provide for service of legal process to cause it to be subject to the jurisdiction of its courts.
  - **C.** A foreign corporation must designate a local registered agent, file annual reports with the state, and adhere to the restrictions upon the use of certain corporate names and types of businesses permitted in that state.
  - **D.** A foreign corporation doing business in a state without a license or certificate of authority is not allowed access to local courts to enforce contracts arising out of such business.

OTHER FORMS OF BUSINESS ORGANIZATIONS:[1] INDIVIDUAL (SOLE) PROPRIETORSHIP

XXI. The sole proprietorship is the simplest and oldest form of business organization.
  - **A.** *Definition.* A *sole proprietorship* is a form of organization in which one individual owns, manages, and assumes all losses and profits from the performance of a trade or the operation of a business.
  - **B.** *Formation.* No formal legal procedures are necessary to carry on a business as a sole proprietorship, but most states may require that a license be obtained prior to the start of business operations. If a fictitious name is used, most states require publication to that effect in a local newspaper that also reveals the owner's name.

---

[1] A new subject matter approved by the AICPA Board of Examiners on August 31, 1981, that can be included in the Uniform CPA Examination *beginning in November 1983.*

C. *Duration.* A sole proprietorship legally ceases to exist at the death of its owner unless the trade or business is operated by an executor or administrator of the owner's estate or the owner had in his or her lifetime entered into a business continuation agreement (i.e., a buy-out arrangement upon owner's death) with another person (usually a close relative or a key employee) to "take over" the business.

D. *Liability for torts and contracts.* A sole proprietor has unlimited liability for torts and contracts.

    1. *Torts.* Sole proprietors are personally liable for their own torts and for the torts of their agents or employees committed within the scope of agency or employment.

    2. *Contracts.* Sole proprietors are liable for their own contracts and for contracts entered into on their behalf by authorized agents.

E. *Tax liability.* A sole proprietor is taxed as an individual.

F. *Nonentity.* A sole proprietor's business is not a separate entity apart from its owner.

G. *Management.* The exclusive right to manage and control the trade or business is vested in the sole proprietor.

ASSOCIATION

XXII. *"Association"* is a generic term used to describe any group of persons who have joined together for a common purpose or business enterprise. An association can be incorporated or nonincorporated, profit or nonprofit. It may be organized for a specific and temporary purpose or for one which is general and intended to be permanent.

A. The liability of the parties to third persons, rights to profits, liability for losses, rights and duties as to each other, and the right to control or direct the business are determined from the legal form which the association has assumed, i.e., corporation, trust, partnership, joint venture, or Massachusetts (business) Trust.

B. A "pure" unincorporated association is managed by its designated officers. These officers or "managers" are personally liable for contracts they or their agents enter into on behalf of the association and also for the torts that they or their agents may commit during their supervision, control, and operation of the association's activities. Members of the association who have not participated in management, authorized a contract, or participated in the commission of a tort are not liable to third persons in contract or tort.

SYNDICATE

XXIII. A *syndicate* is an association of persons of mutual interest which is organized *for a specific and temporary purpose of carrying out a specific business objective or transaction.* A syndicate can take the form of a corporation, trust, general or limited partnership, or joint venture. For example, an organization formed as a trust with the specific purpose of subdividing a large parcel of farmland and selling off the lots for purposes of construction of residences, or an association of securities broker-dealers organized to assist a securities underwriter to market the investment securities of an issuer.

MASSACHUSETTS (BUSINESS) TRUST

XXIV. A *Massachusetts (business) Trust* is a common law trust created by the transfer of legal title and possession of property or a business to a trustee under an agreement whereby the trustee agrees to manage and operate the property or a business for the benefit of specific beneficiaries.

A. *Statute of Frauds*. The Statute of Frauds applies to the creation of the trust if a transfer of title to real estate is involved.

B. *Purpose*. A Massachusetts (business) Trust may be organized for any legal purpose, e.g., real estate investment (i.e., managing, improving, selling, or leasing real estate for profit), carrying on a commercial business, buying and selling investment securities, or operating manufacturing plants.

C. *Certificate of ownership*. Certificates, representing beneficial ownership of the trust, are issued to beneficiaries.

   1. The certificates are either negotiable or transferable by assignment. They are investment securities under article 8 of the UCC and the federal Securities Act of 1933.

   2. The beneficiaries are usually referred to as *certificate holders* or stockholders.

   3. As against third parties, the trust agreement may legally limit the personal liability of certificate holders to the amount of their investment, i.e., provide for limited liability.

D. *Beneficiaries*. The beneficiaries are entitled to the income from the trust during its existence and to its principal upon its termination in proportion to their respective ownership interests as set out in the trust agreement and their certificates.

   1. Death, disability, or bankruptcy of a certificate holder does not dissolve the trust.

   2. Certificate holders are not personally liable for the torts or contracts of the trust or trustee.

E. *Duration*. The duration of the trust may be perpetual or for a specified period of time.

F. *Trustee*. The trust is managed by a trustee or trustees.

   1. Trust and trustee powers, rights, and privileges are derived from the trust agreement subject to the laws governing contracts and trusts.

   2. Death, disability, bankruptcy, or incapacity to serve of a trustee does not dissolve the trust.

   3. The trustee owes a fiduciary duty to the certificate holders.

   4. A trustee is personally liable to third parties for torts and contracts arising out of trust business. However, the trustee is entitled to indemnity (reimbursement) for expenses and payments properly paid in behalf of the trust.

G. The trust is taxed as a legal entity.

REAL ESTATE INVESTMENT TRUST (REIT)

XXV. A *real estate investment trust (REIT)* is a trust organized and operated under the provisions of the Real Estate Investment Trust Act. It is created by a transfer of the legal title to real estate to a trustee (incorporated or unincorporated) under a trust agreement whereby the trustee is bound to manage the trust real property for the benefit and profit of specified beneficiaries.

A. *Purpose*. The purpose of the trust is to serve as a real estate investment vehicle and prevent double taxation of trust income.

B. *Statute of Frauds*. A REIT falls within the Statute of Frauds and therefore must be in writing to be enforceable.

C. *Trustee*. The trustee possesses legal title, and the beneficiaries are vested with equitable title (beneficial interest).

   1. The beneficiaries' interest is evidenced by certificates of beneficial ownership.

   2. The certificates are personal property and are purchased and sold (traded) in much the same manner as a stock in a corporation.

D. *Income tax consequences*. A real estate investment trust, properly organized and operated under the provisions of the Real Estate Investment Trust Act, is *not* treated as a legal entity for income tax purposes. Income distributed by the trust is taxable only to the beneficiaries. To qualify for this special tax treatment, the following requirements must be met:

1. The certificates of beneficial ownership must be freely transferable;
2. There must be a minimum number of beneficiaries; i.e., 100 or more and no fewer than 6 may own 50 percent of all outstanding certificates;
3. The trust's primary business *cannot* be to buy and sell real estate, i.e., be a dealer in real estate;
4. It must be a real estate investment vehicle; i.e., most of its gross income must be derived from rents, interest on mortgages, dividends, or other similar income (i.e., passive income) from real estate; and
5. The trust must distribute at least 95 percent of its earned income each year to its beneficiaries.

E. *Certificates as securities*. Certificates are considered securities for the purpose of the federal Securities Act of 1933, the Securities Exchange Act of 1934, and article 8 of the UCC.

F. *Beneficiaries*. Certificate holders (beneficiaries) are not personally liable for debts and other obligations of the trust. Their liability is limited to the amount of their investment.

JOINT VENTURE

XXV. A *joint venture* (joint adventure) is a special express or implied contract in which two or more persons, jointly and severally, bind themselves to carry out a *single business transaction* for their mutual profit or other benefit but not as a partnership.

A. *Partnership law applies*. Joint ventures are generally governed by the same rules of law as partnerships. See Chapter 14.

B. *Joint ventures and partnerships distinguished*. The following are some important distinctions between joint ventures and general partnerships.

1. A joint venture usually is formed to complete only one particular transaction, while a partnership, by definition, must be "to carry on . . . a business" (i.e., a series of continuing business transactions or activities). For example, oil companies 1, 2, and 3 enter into a contract to drill twelve exploration oil holes on the continental shelf, jointly and severally agree to be liable for all expenses incurred in doing so, and agree to divide any proceeds of their venture.
2. In a joint venture, the parties obligate themselves to be jointly and severally liable for all debts and obligations. In a partnership, unless otherwise agreed, partners are jointly liable for partnership debts and jointly and severally liable for torts committed by a partner.
3. A joint venture is never treated as an entity. A partnership is considered a legal entity for some purposes, e.g., to sue or be sued, file a partnership informational tax return, adopt a firm name, or hold title to real estate.
4. A joint venture can exist for a nonprofit purpose. To be a partnership, the association of the parties must be for a profit purpose.

C. *Joint venture-partnership similarities*. Some important similarities are:

1. Joint venturers owe a fiduciary duty to each other.
2. A joint venturer is entitled to the remedy of an accounting in equity.
3. All joint venturers are liable not only to the extent of their investment but also personally for torts, debts, and other obligations incurred while fulfilling the purposes of the joint venture.

SELF-QUIZ

To check your understanding of the key words and concepts and the accuracy of your answers to the questions, refer to the text material as referenced by page number.

KEY WORDS AND CONCEPTS

Corporation   **438**
De jure corporation   **438**
De facto corporation   **438**
Incorporator   **441**
Promoter   **441**
Stock subscription   **445**
Preemptive rights   **457**
Stock split   **456**
Cumulative voting   **458**
Liquidating dividend   **456**
Fiduciary duty   **452**
Insider   **454**
Blue Sky laws   **443**
Merger   **460**
Short-swing speculation   **454**
Consolidation   **460**
"Doing business"   **461**
Stated capital   **448**
Paid-in surplus   **448**
Corporation by estoppel   **439**
Closed corporation   **440**
Articles of incorporation   **442**
Bylaws   **443**
Corporate capital   **448**
Watered stock   **448**
Dividend   **456**
Stock dividend   **456**
Domestic corporation   **440**
Foreign corporation   **440**
Ultra vires   **453**
Par value   **447**
Stated value   **448**
Authorized shares   **447**
Outstanding shares   **447**
Issued shares   **447**
Treasury stock   **447**
Cumulative preferred stock   **446**
Participating preferred stock   **446**
Redemption   **447**
Joint venture   **464**
Association   **462**
Syndicate   **462**
Convertible security   **447**

Formal meeting   **451**
Massachusetts (business) Trust   **462**
Certificate holder   **457**
Real estate investment trust (REIT)   **463**

QUESTIONS

1. Define legal entity. **(438)**
2. List the advantages and disadvantages of the corporate form of doing business. **(408)**
3. Identify the sources of corporate powers. **(444)**
4. Explain the liability of the corporation or its shareholders for the actions of its directors, officers, agents, and employees. **(449)**
5. What is the source of the power to incorporate? **(438)** List the persons involved in the formation of a corporation. **(441)**
6. List the basic procedures necessary to incorporate and to begin corporate business. **(440)**
7. What are the liabilities of a promoter? **(441)**
8. Distinguish between common and preferred stock. **(446)**
9. Explain the difference between par value and no-par stock. **(447)**
10. List and explain the rights associated with ownership of shares of stock. **(457)**
11. Discuss the contractual and legal rights of shareholders concerning payment of dividends. **(458)**
12. Discuss the rights and duties of officers and directors of the corporation. **(455, 450)**
13. Explain fully the fiduciary duty owed by directors and officers to the corporation. **(452)**
14. What remedies are available when an ultra vires act is threatened? Performed? Who may assert these remedies? **(444)**
15. What is the tenure of directors and officers? **(450)** How and when may they be removed from office? **(450)**
16. What procedures are necessary to change the corporate structure? **(451)** To sell the corporate assets? **(451)** To merge or consolidate? **(460)**
17. What actions may cause a corporation to be dissolved? **(460)** Discuss the effect of dissolution on the rights of shareholders, creditors, and title to the corporate assets. **(460)**
18. What are the rights of creditors with regard to management, unpaid stock subscription, and watered stock? **(461)**
19. What legal consequences result from a corpora-

tion's failure to receive permission to do business in a state other than that of its incorporation? **(461)**

20. Compare a Massachusetts (business) Trust discussed in this chapter with trusts generally covered in Chapter 11 and V-G in Chapter 10. **(462, 343, 305)**

21. What are the similarities between a general partnership and a joint venture? **(464)** The dissimilarities? **(464)**

22. What are the important legal distinctions and similarities between a Massachusetts (business) Trust and a real estate investment trust (REIT)? **(462)**

23. How does a corporation qualify itself for subchapter S status under the Internal Revenue Code? **(440)**

SELECTED QUESTIONS AND UNOFFICIAL ANSWERS

OBJECTIVE QUESTIONS

Select the best answer for each of the following items. Mark only one answer for each item. Answer all items.

MAY 1981

21. Universal Joint Corporation has approached Minor Enterprises, Inc., about a tax-free statutory merger of Minor into Universal. The stock of both corporations is listed on the NYSE. Which of the following requirements or procedures need *not* be complied with in order to qualify as a statutory merger pursuant to state and federal law?
- **a.** The boards of directors of both corporations must approve the plan of merger.
- **b.** Universal, the surviving corporation, must apply for and obtain a favorable revenue ruling from the Treasury Department.
- **c.** The boards of both corporations must submit the plan of merger to their respective shareholders for approval.
- **d.** The securities issued and exchanged by Universal for the shares of Minor must be registered since they are considered to be "offered" and "sold" for purposes of the Securities Act of 1933.

22. The consideration for the issuance of shares by a corporation may *not* be paid in
- **a.** Tangible property.
- **b.** Intangible property.
- **c.** Services to be performed for the corporation.
- **d.** Services actually performed for the corporation.

23. Bixler obtained an option on a building he believed was suitable for use by a corporation he and two other men were organizing. After the corporation was successfully promoted, Bixler met with the Board of Directors who agreed to acquire the property for $200,000. Bixler deeded the building to the corporation and the corporation began business in it. Bixler's option contract called for the payment of only $155,000 for the building and he purchased it for that price. When the directors later learned that Bixler paid only $155,000, they demanded the return of Bixler's $45,000 profit. Bixler refused, claiming the building was worth far more than $200,000 both when he secured the option and when he deeded it to the corporation. Which of the following statements correctly applies to Bixler's conduct?
- **a.** It was improper for Bixler to contract for the option without first having secured the assent of the Board of Directors.
- **b.** If, as Bixler claimed, the building was fairly worth more than $200,000, Bixler is entitled to retain the entire price.
- **c.** Even if, as Bixler claimed, the building was fairly worth more than $200,000, Bixler nevertheless must return the $45,000 to the corporation.
- **d.** In order for Bixler to be obligated to return any amount to the corporation, the Board of Directors must establish that the building was worth less than $200,000.

24. Delta Corporation has decided to purchase $2,000,000 of its own outstanding shares. In connection with this acquisition, which of the following is a correct statement?
- **a.** The shares may *not* be acquired out of capital surplus.
- **b.** The shares in question must be classified as treasury shares if *not* cancelled.
- **c.** A subsequent offering of the acquired shares to the public in interstate commerce would be exempt from SEC registration.

d. If the shares are acquired at a price less than the original offering price, the corporation has realized a taxable capital gain.

25. The stock of Crandall Corporation is regularly traded over the counter. However, 75 percent is owned by the founding family and a few of the key executive officers. It has had a cash dividend record of paying out annually less than 5% of its earnings and profits over the past 10 years. It has, however, declared a 10% stock dividend during each of these years. Its accumulated earnings and profits are beyond the reasonable current and anticipated needs of the business. Which of the following is correct?
a. The shareholders can compel the declaration of a dividend only if the directors' dividend policy is fraudulent.
b. The Internal Revenue Service can *not* attack the accumulation of earnings and profits since the Code exempts publicly held corporations from the accumulations provisions.
c. The fact that the corporation was paying a 10% stock dividend, apparently in lieu of a cash distribution, is irrelevant insofar as the ability of the Internal Revenue Service to successfully attach the accumulation.
d. Either the Internal Revenue Service or the shareholders could successfully obtain a court order to compel the distribution of earnings and profits unreasonably accumulated.

26. Global Trucking Corporation has in its corporation treasury a substantial block of its own common stock, which it acquired several years previously. The stock had been publicly offered at $25 a share and had been reacquired at $15. The board is considering using it in the current year for various purposes. For which of the following purposes may it validly use the treasury stock?
a. To pay a stock dividend to its shareholders.
b. To sell it to the public without the necessity of a registration under the Securities Act of 1933, since it had been previously registered.
c. To vote it at the annual meeting of shareholders.
d. To acquire the shares of another publicly held company without the necessity of a registration under the Securities Act of 1933.

27. The Larkin Corporation is contemplating a two-for-one stock split of its common stock. Its $4 par value common stock will be reduced to $2 after the split. It has 2 million shares issued and out-

standing out of a total of 3 million authorized. In considering the legal or tax consequences of such action, which of the following is a correct statement?
a. The transaction will require both authorization by the Board of Directors and approval by the shareholders.
b. The distribution of the additional shares to the shareholders will be taxed as a dividend to the recipients.
c. Surplus equal to the par value of the existing number of shares issued and outstanding must be transferred to the stated capital account.
d. The trustees of trust recipients of the additional shares must allocate them ratably between income and corpus.

28. At their annual meeting, shareholders of the Laurelton Corporation approved several proposals made by the Board of Directors. Among them was the ratification of the salaries of the executives of the corporation. In this connection, which of the following is correct?
a. The shareholders can *not* legally ratify the compensation paid to director-officers.
b. The salaries ratified are automatically valid for federal income tax purposes.
c. Such ratification by the shareholders is required as a matter of law.
d. The action by the shareholders serves the purpose of confirming the board's action.

NOVEMBER 1980

10. Hargrove lost some stock certificates of the Apex Corporation which were registered in his name, but which he had indorsed in blank. Flagg found the securities and sold them through a brokerage house to Waldorf. Apex, unaware of Hargrove's problem, transferred them to Waldorf. Hargrove is seeking to recover the securities or damages for their value. Which of the following is correct?
a. The stock in question is transferable but Waldorf takes subject to Hargrove's claim of title.
b. Waldorf is a holder in due course of a negotiable instrument and therefore will prevail.
c. Apex is liable for wrongfully transferring Hargrove's stock to Waldorf.
d. Waldorf qualifies as a bona fide purchaser and acquires the stock free of Hargrove's adverse claim.

6. Barton Corporation and Clagg Corporation have decided to combine their separate companies pursuant to the provisions of their state corporation laws. After much discussion and negotiation, they decided that a consolidation was the appropriate procedure to be followed. Which of the following is an *incorrect* statement with respect to the contemplated statutory consolidation?

'a. A statutory consolidation pursuant to state law is recognized by the Internal Revenue Code as a type of tax-free reorganization.

b. The larger of the two corporations will emerge as the surviving corporation.

c. Creditors of Barton and Clagg will have their claims protected despite the consolidation.

d. The shareholders of both Barton and Clagg must approve the plan of consolidation.

7. Mark Corporation is a moderate-sized closely held corporation which is 80% owned by Joseph Mark. The remaining 20% of stock is owned by Mark's wife, sons, daughter, and parents. One son, David Mark, who recently graduated from business school, has been hired by the corporation as financial vice president at a salary of $60,000 per year. Other members of the family are either officers or directors of the corporation and are all generously compensated. Joseph Mark is paid $300,000 as Chairman of the Board and Chief Executive Officer. The corporation is profitable, solvent, and meeting all claims as they become due. Who of the following would have standing to attack the reasonableness of the salary payments?

a. The creditors of the corporation.

b. The attorney general of the state in which Mark is incorporated.

c. The Internal Revenue Service.

d. The Securities and Exchange Commission.

8. The Board of Directors of Wilcox Manufacturing Corporation, a publicly held corporation, has noted a significant drop in the stock market price of its 7% preferred stock and proposes to purchase some of the stock. The proposed purchase price is substantially below the redemption price of the stock. The Board has decided to acquire 100,000 shares of said preferred stock and either place it in the treasury or retire it. Under these circumstances, which of the following is a correct statement?

a. The corporation will realize a taxable gain as a result of the transaction.

b. The preferred stock so acquired must be retired and may *not* be held as treasury stock.

c. The corporation may *not* acquire its own shares unless the articles of incorporation so provide.

d. Such shares may be purchased by the corporation to the extent of unreserved and unrestricted earned surplus available therefor.

9. A major characteristic of the corporation is its recognition as a separate legal entity. As such it is capable of withstanding attacks upon its valid existence by various parties who would wish to disregard its existence or "pierce the corporate veil" for their own purposes. The corporation will normally be able to successfully resist such attempts *except* when

a. The corporation was created with tax savings in mind.

b. The corporation was created in order to insulate the assets of its owners from personal liability.

c. The corporation being attacked is a wholly owned subsidiary of its parent corporation.

d. The creation of and transfer of property to the corporation amounts to a fraud upon creditors.

12. Golden Enterprises, Inc., entered into a contract with Hidalgo Corporation for the sale of its mineral holdings. The transaction proved to be *ultra vires*. Which of the following parties, for the reason stated, may properly assert the *ultra vires* doctrine?

a. Golden Enterprises to avoid performance.

b. A shareholder of Golden Enterprises to enjoin the sale.

c. Hidalgo Corporation to avoid performance.

d. Golden Enterprises to rescind the consummated sale.

13. Grandiose secured an option to purchase a tract of land for $100,000. He then organized the Dunbar Corporation and subscribed to 51% of the shares of stock of the corporation for $100,000, which was issued to him in exchange for his three-month promissory note for $100,000. Controlling the board of directors through his share ownership, he had the corporation authorize the purchase of the land from him for $200,000. He made no disclosure to the board or to other shareholders that he was making a $100,000 profit. He promptly paid the corporation for his shares and redeemed his promissory note. A disgruntled shareholder subsequently learned the full details of the transaction and brought suit against Grandiose on the corporation's behalf. Which of the following is a correct statement?

a. Grandiose breached his fiduciary duty to the corporation and must account for the profit he made.

b. The judgment of the board of directors was conclusive under the circumstances.

c. Grandiose is entitled to retain the profit since he controlled the corporation as a result of his share ownership.

d. The giving of the promissory note in exchange for the stock constituted payment for the shares.

14. Destiny Manufacturing, Inc., is incorporated under the laws of Nevada. Its principal place of business is in California and it has permanent sales offices in several other states. Under the circumstances, which of the following is correct?

a. California may validly demand that Destiny incorporate under the laws of the state of California.

b. Destiny must obtain a certificate of authority to transact business in California and the other states in which it does business.

c. Destiny is a foreign corporation in California, but *not* in the other states.

d. California may prevent Destiny from operating as a corporation if the laws of California differ regarding the organization and conduct of the corporation's internal affairs.

16. Plimpton subscribed to 1,000 shares of $1 par value common stock of the Billiard Ball Corporation at $10 a share. Plimpton paid $1,000 upon the incorporation of Billiard and paid an additional $4,000 at a later time. The corporation subsequently became insolvent and is now in bankruptcy. The creditors of the corporation are seeking to hold Plimpton personally liable. Which of the following is a correct statement?

a. Plimpton has *no* liability directly or indirectly to the creditors of the corporation since he paid the corporation the full par value of the shares.

b. As a result of his failure to pay the full subscription price, Plimpton has unlimited joint and several liability for corporation debts.

c. Plimpton is liable for the remainder of the unpaid subscription price.

d. Had Plimpton transferred his shares to an innocent third party, neither he nor the third party would be liable.

49. A group of real estate dealers has decided to form a Real Estate Investment Trust (REIT) which will invest in diversified real estate holdings. A public offering of $10,000,000 of trust certificates is contemplated. Which of the following is an *incorrect* statement?

a. Those investing in the venture will *not* be insulated from personal liability?

b. The entity will be considered to be an "association" for tax purposes.

c. The offering must be registered under the Securities Act of 1933.

d. If the trust qualifies as a REIT and distributes all its income to the investors, it will *not* be subject to federal income tax.

Items 9 and 10 are based on the following information:

Dexter, Inc., was incorporated in its home state. It expanded substantially and now does 20% of its business in a neighboring state in which it maintains a permanent facility. It has *not* filed any papers in the neighboring state.

9. Which of the following statements is correct?

a. Since Dexter is a duly-incorporated domestic corporation in its own state, it can transact business anywhere in the United States without further authority as long as its corporate charter so provides.

b. As long as Dexter's business activities in the neighboring state do *not* exceed 25%, it need *not* obtain permission to do business in the neighboring state.

c. Dexter must create a subsidiary corporation in the neighboring state to continue to do business in that state.

d. Dexter is a foreign corporation in the neighboring state and as such must obtain a certificate of authority or it will *not* be permitted to maintain any action or suit in the state with respect to its intrastate business.

10. Which of the following statements is *incorrect*?

a. Dexter has automatically appointed the secretary of state of the neighboring state as its agent for the purpose of service of legal process if it failed to appoint or maintain a registered agent in that state.

b. Dexter will be able to maintain an action or suit

in the neighboring state if it subsequently obtains a certificate of authority.

c. Dexter can *not* defend against a suit brought against it in the neighboring state's courts.

d. The attorney general of the neighboring state can recover all back fees and franchise taxes which would have been imposed plus all penalties for failure to pay same.

Answers to Objective Questions

May 1981			May 1980		
21. b	25. c		6. b	12. b	49. a
22. c	26. a		7. c	13. a	
23. c	27. a		8. d	14. b	
24. b	28. d		9. d	16. c	

November 1980		November 1978	
10. d		9. d	10. c

Explanation of Answers to Objective Questions

MAY 1981

21. (b) There is no provision requiring the surviving corporation of a tax-free statutory merger to apply for and obtain a favorable revenue ruling from the Treasury Department. Answers (a) and (c) are incorrect because the board of directors and shareholders of both corporations must approve the merger. Answer (d) is incorrect since only securities issued in conjunction with a court supervised reorganization are exempt from the registration requirements of the Securities Act of 1933. For purposes of the act, the shares exchanged between Union and Universal would be "offered" and "sold".

22. (c) Consideration for the issuance of shares by a corporation may be paid in cash, property or prior services. The following items do not constitute consideration for common stock: promise to perform future services, promise to pay (e.g., a promissory note). Answer (c), services to be performed for the corporation, is the only one that would not act as consideration for the issuance of shares. Answers (a), (b) and (d) all qualify as proper consideration for shares.

23. (c) Promoters are persons who originate and organize the formation of a corporation. They have a fiduciary duty to act for the corporation and its

shareholders. For Bixler to retain the profits made from the sale of property to the corporation, he must make full disclosure to and receive approval from either the board of directors or existing shareholders. Since Bixler did not comply with these procedures, the $45,000 would be considered secret profits and must be returned to the corporation even though the building might have a market value of $200,000. Thus, answers (b) and (d) are incorrect. Answer (a) is incorrect since the promoter may enter into preincorporation contracts (e.g., employment contracts, options on property) on behalf of the corporation. The corporation is not liable on these contracts until it adopts such agreements or enters a novation (a second agreement whereby corporation replaces the promoter under the same terms as the preincorporation contract). The corporation cannot ratify the agreement since the corporate entity was not in existence when the promoter entered the contract.

24. (b) When a corporation purchases its own stock these shares are classified as treasury shares if not cancelled. Treasury shares are issued but not outstanding; these shares cannot be voted on and do not receive dividends. Answer (a) is incorrect because a corporation is required to purchase treasury stock with capital surplus. Capital surplus consists of earned surplus (retained earnings) and paid-in-surplus (the amount paid for stock over par or stated value). It is illegal for a corporation to buy treasury stock with legal capital (par value of issued stock). Answer (c) is untrue because the corporation would have to comply with SEC requirements when the treasury stock was resold. Answer (d) is incorrect since a corporation never recognizes gains or losses on transactions with its own stock.

25. (c) The fact that the corporation was paying a 10% stock dividend instead of a cash distribution would not hinder the IRS from attacking the accumulation of earnings. Answer (a) is incorrect because stockholders can compel the declaration of a dividend when withholding dividends would be a clear abuse of the board of directors' discretion, even when such a dividend policy is not fraudulent. The Code does not exempt publicly held corporations from the accumulation provisions, therefore, answer (b) is incorrect. Answer (d) is incorrect because the IRS cannot compel the corporation to distribute earnings and profits that have unreasonably accumulated. However, the corporation is subject to an additional tax on earnings retained in excess of $150,000 if such retention is unreasonable.

26. (a) Treasury stock may be disposed of at the discretion of the board of directors through a sale or through the declaration of dividends to shareholders. Answer (b) is incorrect since the original public offering was sufficiently long ago to require the filing of a new registration statement before selling these treasury shares. Answer (c) is incorrect because treasury shares cannot be voted. Answer (d) is incorrect because treasury shares exchanged for the stock of another publicly held corporation are considered to be "offered" and "sold" for the purposes of the Securities Act of 1933. Therefore, a registration statement would have to be filed and approved before the transaction could be completed.

27. (a) Both the board of directors and the shareholders of a corporation must approve a fundamental change in the corporate structure. Examples of fundamental corporate changes would be: dissolution of corporation, amendment of corporate charter, increase of capital stock, etc. Larkin would need to amend its corporate charter to increase the number of authorized shares before engaging in the stock split. Answer (b) is incorrect because stock splits are normally exempt from income tax because the shareholder-recipient maintains the same proportionate interest of ownership. Answer (c) is incorrect because a stock split decreases the par value in proportion to the increase in the number of shares. Therefore, total par value is unchanged. Answer (d) is incorrect because trustees are to include shares received through a stock split or stock dividend in the principal (corpus) of the trust. Cash dividends are considered income when allocating trust items between principal (corpus) and income beneficiaries.

28. (d) The compensation of corporate officers is fixed by a resolution of the board of directors. If none is fixed, the law implies that the officer is paid a reasonable sum for his services. Any action by the shareholders serves merely to confirm the board's action concerning the officers' salaries. It is not needed as a matter of law, therefore, answer (c) is incorrect. Answer (a) is incorrect because the directors can confirm the officers' salaries even though not legally needed. Answer (b) is incorrect because the IRS has the power to attack any officer's salary as unreasonable. If the compensation is deemed un-

reasonable, the IRS treats the excessive amount as a constructive dividend.

10. (d) If stock certificates endorsed in blank are lost and then later sold by the finder to a bona fide purchaser, the BFP will take the certificates free of any claims by the prior owner. Waldorf purchased for value, in good faith and without notice of any adverse claim, thus he qualifies as a BFP. Neither Apex nor Waldorf would have any liability to Hargrove. This makes answer (d) correct.

6. (b) A consolidation is the unifying of two or more corporations into one new corporation, extinguishing both existing corporations. Therefore, answer (b) is the correct answer since neither corporation will survive the consolidation. Answer (a) is incorrect because under the Internal Revenue Code reorganizations, including statutory mergers or consolidations, receive non-recognition treatment for tax purposes. Answer (c) is incorrect because the rights of the creditors of the consolidating corporations are in no way impaired by the consolidation. Before a corporation can engage in a consolidation or merger, shareholder approval must be obtained. Approval by a majority is normally sufficient but some states demand approval by two-thirds of the shareholders.

7. (c) The correct answer is (c) because the Internal Revenue Service has the right to attack the reasonableness of salary payments and not permit the deduction on the tax return. The attorney general and Securities and Exchange Commission have no authority to question the reasonableness of salary payments.

8. (d) Answer (d) is the correct choice because a corporation is limited to the amount of unappropriated retained earnings for purchases of treasury stock. Answer (a) is incorrect because no treasury stock transactions, either purchases or sales, result in taxable gains or losses. Answer (b) is incorrect because it is legal to hold preferred or common shares as treasury stock. Answer (c) is also incorrect because it is *not* required to be stated in the articles of incorporation that a corporation be allowed to reacquire outstanding shares of its own stock.

9. (d) A corporation is recognized as a separate legal entity except when the creation of or transfer of property to the corporation is used to perpetrate a fraud upon creditors. In these situations, the courts may disregard the entity and "pierce the corporate veil," leaving the shareholders with unlimited liability for corporate obligations. Therefore, the correct answer is (d). One advantage of a corporation is the limited liability of its owners, thus this is a proper motive for creating a corporation. Creating a corporation for tax savings is also a valid reason for forming a corporation. Answer (c) is incorrect because a wholly owned subsidiary is recognized as a separate legal entity unless it is merely an "agent" or instrumentality of its parent corporation.

12. (b) An *ultra vires* doctrine applies when a corporation enters a contract outside the scope of its express or implied authority granted by its articles of incorporation. Answer (b) is correct because since the state or shareholder has the right to object to an *ultra vires* act, a competitor could not object. A shareholder can institute a derivative action against directors and officers to recover damages for such acts. Answers (a) and (c) are incorrect because when an *ultra vires* contract has been executed on one side, most state courts hold the nonperforming party may not raise the defense of *ultra vires*. Answer (d) is incorrect because when both parties have performed, neither party may sue to rescind an *ultra vires* contract.

13. (a) Grandiose has a fiduciary duty to the corporation through his ability to control the board of directors. He is in effect a director since he has 51% control. A director may deal with the corporation only if he does so openly and in good faith, i.e., permitting the board to decide free from Grandiose's influence. If a profit is derived at the corporation's expense, the director must account for the profit made. Answer (b) is incorrect because the board is not independent of the interested party. Answer (c) is incorrect because Grandiose must account for the profit to the corporation. Answer (d) is incorrect because a promissory note is not valid to support the sale of stock. The purchase of shares requires the exchange of cash, property, or past services.

14. (b) A corporation "doing business" in a state other than that of incorporation must comply with that state's license requirements. This usually re-

quires filing a certificate of authority. The concept of doing business involves something more than isolated transactions. Answer (a) is incorrect because a corporation is not required to incorporate in a state in which it does business. Answer (c) is incorrect because Destiny is a foreign corporation in any state in which it does business other than that state in which it is incorporated. Answer (d) is incorrect because Destiny needs to comply only with the incorporation laws in its state of incorporation, in this case, Nevada.

16. (c) Plimpton has breached his subscription contract with the Billiard Ball Corporation, and is therefore liable for the remainder of the unpaid subscription price. Shares may be purchased for money, services already rendered, and property. Promissory notes are not proper consideration for the purchase of shares. Plimpton is liable to creditors for the balance due on the subscription price. This is true even if Plimpton transfers the shares to an innocent third party. The issuing corporation has a lien on those shares that have not been paid for fully. However, this lien would not be effective against an innocent third party purchaser unless the lien was conspicuously noted on the stock certificate. Plimpton's failure to pay the full purchase price of the shares would not change his limited liability concerning corporate debts.

49. (a) The investors in a Real Estate Investment Trust (REIT) have limited liability, similar to that of shareholders in a corporation. Therefore, answer (a) is an incorrect statement, making it the correct answer. The REIT is considered an association for tax purposes but its income will be subject to income tax only if it distributes less than 95% of its ordinary taxable income. Shares in a REIT would qualify as securities under the Securities Act of 1933, thus the offering must be registered.

NOVEMBER 1978

9. (d) Dexter Corporation is foreign to the neighboring state and if Dexter fails to register to do business as required by that state's laws, it commonly is not permitted to maintain an action or suit in the state. Answer (a) is incorrect because a corporation must comply with the laws of other jurisdictions in order to transact business there. Answer (b) is incorrect because there are generally no volume exceptions to the requirement of registering to do business in a foreign state. Answer (c) is incorrect because it is not necessary to form a separate or subsidiary corporation in the neighboring state; Dexter must merely comply with the registration laws of that state.

10. (c) Note the requirement is the statement which is incorrect; although Dexter may not bring an action in a state where it has not properly registered to do business, any corporation may defend itself if it is sued. Answers (a), (b), and (d) are not the correct choice because their statements are generally true. Answer (a) is incorrect because it is common for state laws to provide the secretary of state as an agent for purposes of legal service on corporations that have failed to appoint a registered agent in that state. Answer (b) is incorrect because it is generally true that a corporation can cure the failure to register properly and after so doing is permitted to maintain an action in that state's courts. Answer (d) is incorrect because the attorney general of each state can recover all back fees and franchise taxes plus penalties against corporations who failed to register.

ESSAY QUESTIONS AND ANSWERS

MAY 1979 (Estimated time: 25 to 30 minutes)

3. Part a. The Decimile Corporation is a well-established, conservatively-managed, major company. It has consistently maintained a $3 or more per share dividend since 1940 on its only class of stock, which has a $1 par value. Decimile's board of directors is determined to maintain a $3 per share annual dividend distribution to maintain the corporation's image in the financial community, to reassure its shareholders, and to prevent a decline in the price of the corporation's shares which would occur if there were a reduction in the dividend rate. Decimile's current financial position is not encouraging although the corporation is legally solvent. Its cash flow position is not good and the current year's earnings are only $0.87 per share. Retained earnings amount to $17 per share. Decimile owns a substantial block of Integrated Electronic Services stock which it purchased at $1 per share in 1950 and which has a current value of $6.50 per share. Decimile has paid dividends of $1 per share so far this year and contemplates distributing a sufficient number of shares of Integrated to provide an additional $2 per share.

Required Answer the following, setting forth reasons for any conclusions stated.

1. May Decimile legally pay the $2 per share dividend in the stock of Integrated?
2. As an alternative, could Decimile pay the $2 dividend in its own authorized but unissued shares of stock? What would be the *legal* effect of this action upon the corporation?

Answer

1. Yes. The Model Business Corporation Act authorizes the declaration and payment of dividends in cash, property, or the shares of the corporation as long as the corporation is not insolvent and would not be rendered insolvent by the dividend payment. The act limits the payment of dividends in cash or property to the unreserved and unrestricted earned surplus of the corporation. Decimile meets this requirement since it has retained earnings of $17 per share. Thus, payment of the dividend in the shares of Integrated is permitted.

2. Yes. The Model Business Corporation Act permits dividends to be declared and paid in the shares of the corporation. However, where the dividend is paid in its authorized but unissued shares, the payment must be out of unreserved and unrestricted surplus. Furthermore, when the shares paid as a dividend have a par value, they must be issued at not less than par value. Concurrent with the dividend payment, an amount of surplus equal to the aggregate par value of the share issued as a dividend must be transferred to stated capital.

3. Part b Clayborn is the president and a director of Marigold Corporation. He currently owns $1,000 shares of Marigold which he purchased several years ago upon joining the company and assuming the presidency. At that time, he received a stock option for 10,000 shares of Marigold at $10 per share. The option is about to expire but Clayborn does not have the money to exercise his option. Credit is very tight at present and most of his assets have already been used to obtain loans. Clayborn spoke to the chairman of Marigold's board about his plight and told the chairman that he is going to borrow $100,000 from Marigold in order to exercise his option. The chairman was responsible for Clayborn's being hired as the president of Marigold and is a close personal friend of Clayborn. Fearing that Clayborn will leave unless he is able to obtain a greater financial interest in Marigold, the chairman told Clayborn: "It is okay with me and you have a green light." Clayborn authorized the issuance of a $100,000 check payable to his order. He then negotiated the check to Marigold in payment for the shares of stock.

Required Answer the following, setting forth reasons for any conclusions stated.

What are the legal implications, problems, and issues raised by the above circumstances?

Answer The Model Business Corporation Act specifically deals with loans to employees and directors. If the loan is not for the benefit of the corporation, then such a loan must be authorized by the shareholders. However, the board of directors may authorize loans to employees when and if the board decides that such loan or assistance may benefit the corporation. It would appear that the loan was made for the benefit of the corporation so the latter rule applies. However, the chairman's individual authorization clearly does not meet these statutory requirements and could subject him to personal liability. Therefore, a meeting of the board should be called to consider the ratification or recall of the loan.

3. Part c. Towne is a prominent financier, the owner of 1% of the shares of Toy, Inc., and one of its directors. He is also the chairman of the board of Unlimited Holdings, Inc., an investment company in which he owns 80% of the stock. Toy needs land upon which to build additional warehouse facilities. Toy's president, Arthur, surveyed the land sites feasible for such a purpose. The best location in Arthur's opinion from all standpoints including location, availability, access to transportation, and price, is an eight-acre tract of land owned by Unlimited. Neither Arthur nor Towne wish to create any legal problems in connection with the possible purchase of the land.

Required Answer the following, setting forth reasons for any conclusions stated.

1. What are the legal parameters within which this transaction may be safely consummated?
2. What are the legal ramifications if there were to be a $50,000 payment "on the side" to Towne in order that he use his efforts to "smooth the way" for the proposed acquisition?

Answer

1. The Model Business Corporation Act allows such transactions between a corporation and one or more of its directors or another corporation in which the director has a financial interest. The transaction is neither void nor voidable even though the director is present at the board meeting which authorized the transaction or because his vote is counted for such purpose if—

- The fact of such relationship or interest is disclosed or known to the board of directors or committee that authorizes, approves, or ratifies the contract or transaction by a vote or consent sufficient for the purpose without counting the votes or consents of such interested directors; *or*
- The fact of such relationship or interest is disclosed or known to the shareholders entitled to vote and they authorize, approve, or ratify such contract or transaction by vote or written consent; *or*
- The contract or transaction is fair and reasonable to the corporation. Common or interested directors may be counted in determining the presence of a quorum at a meeting of the board of directors or a committee thereof that authorizes, approves, or ratifies such contract or transaction.

2. A $50,000 payment to Towne would be a violation of his fiduciary duty to the corporation. In addition, it might be illegal depending upon the criminal law of the jurisdiction. In any case he would be obligated to return the amount to the corporation. Furthermore, the payment would constitute grounds for permitting Toy to treat the transaction as voidable.

MAY 1978 (Estimated time: 25 to 30 minutes)

4. Part a. Grace Dawson was actively engaged in the promotion of a new corporation to be known as Multifashion Frocks, Inc. On January 3, 1978, she obtained written commitments for the purchase of shares totaling $600,000 from a group of 15 potential investors. She was also assured orally that she would be engaged as the president of the corporation upon the commencement of business. Helen Banks was the principal investor, having subscribed to $300,000 of the shares of Multifashion. Dawson immediately began work on the incorporation of Multifashion, made several contracts for and on its behalf, and made cash expenditures of $1,000 in accomplishing these goals. On February 15, 1978, Banks died and her estate has declined to honor the commitment to purchase the Multifashion shares. At the first shareholders' meeting on April 5, 1978, the day the corporation came into existence, the shareholders elected a board of directors. With shareholder approval, the board took the following actions:

1. Adopted some but not all of the contracts made by Dawson.
2. Authorized legal action, if necessary, against the Estate of Banks to enforce Banks' $300,000 commitment.
3. Declined to engage Dawson in any capacity (Banks had been her main supporter).
4. Agreed to pay Dawson $750 for those cash outlays which were deemed to be directly beneficial to the corporation and rejected the balance.

Required Answer the following, setting forth reasons for any conclusions stated.

Discuss the legal implications of each of the above actions taken by the board of directors of Multifashion.

Answer In general, pre-incorporation contracts are not binding upon a newly created corporation prior to their adoption by its board of directors. Overall, one would conclude that the board acted properly and legally with respect to the actions taken. Each item is discussed separately below.

1. The board's action was proper and within its discretion. Care, however, should be taken to avoid an implied adoption by having the corporation avail itself of some or all of the benefits of a contract while purporting to reject the contract. The corporation is not legally bound prior to adoption, because it was not in existence at the time the contract was made. Dawson, on the other hand, has liability on the contracts she made prior to incorporation. Moreover, with respect to the contracts adopted by the corporation, she assumes the status of a surety unless a novation was entered into, releasing Dawson of all liability. The nonexistent principal rule would apply to Dawson unless the contract she made was contingent upon the corporation's adopting it after coming into existence.

2. An exception is made to the general rule of pre-incorporation actions insofar as stock subscriptions are concerned. Due to necessity and practical considerations, the parties who agree to provide the capital vital to the corporation's creation are not permitted to withdraw their commitments for six months. The Model Business Corporation Act provides that "a subscription for shares of a corporation to be organized shall be irrevocable for a period of six months, unless provided by the terms of the subscription agreement or unless all of the subscribers consent to the revocation of such subscriptions." Hence, the subscription by Banks is valid and is a bona fide claim against the Estate of Banks.

3. The board of a newly created corporation is, at its inception, free to either adopt or reject pre-incorporation contracts made on behalf of the corporation. This general rule also applies to the employment contract of a promoter such as Dawson. The rationale for the rule is founded upon the belief that the corporation should not be shackled by commitments that it did not have an opportunity to adequately consider. In addition, promoters as a class have often abused their power and made what have proved to be self-serving contracts. Thus, the board acted properly, and it need not engage Dawson.

4. The only problem that arises is that Dawson was not paid in full. She might be entitled to the full $1,000 under two possible theories. The first is a contract implied in fact (an implied adoption) by the board accepting all the benefits of the $1,000 expenditure. The other theory would be a contract implied in law based upon unjust enrichment. Under this theory, if Dawson can prove that the corporation did receive benefits which were worth $1,000, she can recover the additional $250.

4. Part b. Duval is the chairman of the board and president of Monolith Industries, Inc. He is also the largest individual shareholder, owning 40 percent of the shares outstanding. The corporation is publicly held, and there is a dissenting minority. In addition to his position with Monolith, Duval owns 85 percent of Variance Enterprises, a corporation created under the laws of the Bahamas. During 1977 Carlton, the president of Apex Industries, Inc., approached Duval and suggested that a tax-free merger of Monolith and Apex made good sense to him and that he was prepared to recommend such a course of action to the Apex board and to the shareholders. Duval studied the proposal and decided that Apex was a most desirable candidate for acquisition. Duval informed the president of Variance about the overture, told him it was a real bargain, and suggested that Variance pick it up for cash and notes. Not hearing from Duval or Monolith, Carlton accepted an offer from Variance and the business was sold to Variance. Several dissenting shareholders of Monolith learned the facts surrounding the Variance acquisition and have engaged counsel to represent them. The Variance acquisition of Apex proved to be highly profitable.

Required Answer the following, setting forth reasons for any conclusions stated.

Discuss the rights of the dissenting Monolith shareholders and the probable outcome of a legal action by them.

Answer Directors and officers of a corporation are fiduciaries in their relationship to the corporation they serve. As such, they can neither directly nor indirectly benefit in their dealings with or for the corporation. They cannot engage in transactions that are in violation of their fiduciary duty to protect and further the best interests of their principal. Making a secret profit or acquiring a personal advantage out of their office is an act which the corporation may seek to have set aside as voidable.

Based upon this general statement of directors' and officers' fiduciary duty, it appears that the dissenting shareholders could sue derivatively on behalf of Monolith. That is, they could institute legal action on behalf of and in the name of Monolith to set aside the Variance-Apex transaction and have the business transferred to Monolith along with the profits earned during the interim. As an alternative, they could seek to recover directly from Duval damages that would be payable to Monolith.

The result seems clear in light of the facts. First, the opportunity came to Duval in his capacity as the chairman of the board and president of Monolith. Next, he did not pursue the matter but instead informed Variance's president of the opportunity to purchase Apex. Duval's conduct appears to be a case of self-dealing, duplicity, secrecy, and perhaps deceit. Taking the law and all the circumstances surrounding the purchase of Apex assets by Variance, Monolith's dissenting shareholders would probably be successful in a derivative shareholder action.

PART
SEVEN

Government Regulation of Business (15%)*

---

* This percentage allocation represents the relative weight to be given to this *area* of business law on the Uniform CPA Examinations beginning in November 1983. It also indicates the approximate percentage of the total achievable test score to be assigned to this *area* of business law for each Uniform CPA Examination beginning in November 1983.

CHAPTER

16

Administrative Law

Beginning with the November 1983 Uniform CPA Examination, the following business law subjects can be covered in the business law section of the examination.

A. Administrative Law
1. Activities Subject to Regulation
2. Functions of Regulatory Agencies
3. Judicial Review of Agency Decisions[1]

ACTIVITIES SUBJECT TO REGULATION AND TYPES OF ADMINISTRATIVE AGENCIES

I. Administrative agencies exist on all levels of government, i.e., federal, state, and local. Each agency has the authority to regulate only those activities that are within its jurisdiction. Several agencies may have jurisdiction over the same activity.

A. *Federal regulation.* A list (not exclusive) of activities subject to regulation and the agencies having authority to regulate such activities is provided below.

　　1. *Transportation:*

　　　　a. National Highway Traffic and Safety Administration (NHTSA)

　　　　b. Interstate Commerce Commission (ICC), regulates rates charged by interstate carriers.

　　　　c. Federal Aviation Administration (FAA), regulates in the area of safety during air travel.

---

[1] AICPA, *Business Law—Content Specification Outline*, approved by the AICPA Board of Examiners on August 31, 1981, to become effective with the November 1983 Uniform CPA Examination.

d. Civil Aeronautics Board (CAB), regulates in the areas of licensing new airlines, plus approving airline schedules and air fares.

2. *Environment*: Environmental Protection Agency (EPA), regulates activities that may adversely affect our air, water, land or other natural resources, i.e., pollution control.

3. *Agriculture*: Department of Agriculture (DOA), regulates in the areas of crop subsidies and the federal food stamp program.

4. *Finance and banking*:
   a. Federal Reserve System (FRS), regulates credit and banking institutions and activities.
   b. Federal Deposit Insurance Corporation (FDIC), regulates all activities of national bank and insures savings accounts.
   c. Securities and Exchange Commission (SEC), regulates the offer or sale of securities in interstate commerce, issuers of such securities, and stock exchanges or broker-dealers that deal in such securities.
   d. Federal Trade Commission (FTC), regulates "unfair or deceptive acts or practices" in the extension or denial of consumer credit and the collection of consumer debt.

5. *Employment*:
   a. National Labor Relations Board (NLRB), regulates labor-management relations.
   b. Occupational Safety and Health Administration (OSHA), regulates in the area of safety for employees.
   c. Department of Labor enforces labor laws and regulates pension plans.
   d. Equal Employment Opportunity Commission (EEOC), regulates employment practices that may discriminate on the basis of sex, religion, race, color, national origin, age, or marital status.

6. *Marketing of goods or services and consumer products*:
   a. Federal Trade Commission (FTC), regulates "unfair methods of competition" and "unfair or deceptive acts or practices" by firms in the areas of competition, credit, sales of goods, and advertising.
   b. Consumer Product Safety Commission (CPSC), regulates consumer product safety.
   c. Food and Drug Administration (FDA).

7. *Public utilities*:
   a. Federal Power Commission (FPC), regulates rates charged by public utilities for natural gas and electricity.
   b. Federal Communications Commission (FCC), regulates interstate telephone and telegraph services and the television and radio industries.
   c. Nuclear Regulatory Commission (NRC).

8. *Taxation*: Internal Revenue Service (IRS)

B. *State and local (i.e., counties, cities, or towns) regulation.* The number and type of state and local regulated activities and administrative agencies are almost too numerous to mention. Some common types of state and local agencies are:

   1. Alcohol control boards (state and local).
   2. Workers' compensation boards (state).
   3. Motor vehicle departments (state).
   4. Public utility boards (state).
   5. Zoning boards (local).
   6. Building code enforcement boards (local).
   7. Consumer protection agencies (state or local).
   8. Environmental protection agencies (state or local).

II. An *administrative agency* is any government official or body to which power is delegated by a legislature to affect private rights by making rules and rendering decisions, i.e., to regulate.

A. *Independent agency.* An administrative agency may either operate as part of or be totally independent of the legislative, judicial, or executive branches of government. An agency that possesses rule-making, adjudicatory, and supervisory power is usually an independent regulatory agency; e.g., the Federal Trade Commission (FTC). An independent agency exists and operates entirely separate and distinct from the legislative, judicial, and executive branches of government, even though it performs similar functions and possesses similar powers.

B. *Control of administrative agency power and actions.* An agency, even though independent, is not beyond control. A legislature can enact legislation that nullifies an agency's rules or limits the scope of its jurisdiction or power. A legislature may even take such drastic action as to abolish the agency. Administrative agency actions are also subject to review by the courts. Judicial review of administrative agency action is discussed later in this chapter.

C. *Delegation of legislative authority to administrative agencies.* The legislature may constitutionally create an administrative agency and delegate some of its legislative power to that agency, if it does so under a declared policy or a defined standard (guideline) and provides procedural due process safeguards to assure fairness.

    1. *Legislative policies and standards.* The policies or standards declared need not be detailed or specific, but may be stated in very broad and general terms. For example, the following standards have been upheld by the U.S. Supreme Court: "excessive profits," "just and reasonable," "public interest, convenience and necessity," and "unfair or deceptive acts or practices in commerce."

    2. *Procedural due process* (see III and IV below).

D. *Powers of administrative agencies.* An administrative agency may possess one or more of the following powers (see Figure 16-1):

    1. *Quasi-legislative power* (rulemaking):

        a. Investigate for the purpose of obtaining facts upon which to promulgate rules or regulations.

        b. Investigate alleged violations of its rules and orders and statutes over which it has jurisdiction.

        c. Promulgate rules and regulations that have the force of law.

        d. *Subpoena* witnesses.

    2. *Quasi-judicial power* (adjudicatory):

        a. Hold trial-type hearings on alleged violations of the rules, orders, and statutes over which it has jurisdiction.

        b. Subpoena witnesses to appear and testify at hearings.

        c. Issue cease and desist orders against a violator.

        d. Recommend criminal prosecution of alleged violators.

        e. Seek injunctions against violators.

FIGURE 16-1   ADMINISTRATIVE AGENCY POWER

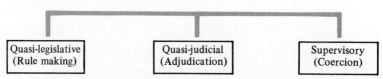

| Quasi-legislative (Rule making) | Quasi-judicial (Adjudication) | Supervisory (Coercion) |

3. *Supervisory power.* An administrative agency has the power to coerce a regulated party by methods other than rulemaking (quasi-legislative) and adjudication (quasi-judicial) to comply with regulatory statutes and its own rules and regulations. In the exercise of its supervisory power, administrative agencies may take the following civil actions, if appropriate and authorized:

    a. *Issue stop orders.* For example, the SEC issued a stop order to prevent trading of a security on a stock exchange;

    b. After informal hearings, *compromise disputes* with alleged violators and *issue consent orders;*

    c. *Issue advisory opinions;*

    d. *Levy civil fines,* impose civil penalties, or order forfeitures;

    e. *"Jawbone."* "Jawboning" involves the use of oral or written arguments designed to convince an alleged violator not to engage in a certain course of conduct or type of activity;

    f. *Administer prelicensing tests and examinations;*

    g. *Grant or deny licenses;*

    h. *Seize and destroy property in violation* of an order if it is an imminent threat to the public health or safety, e.g., impure foods;

    i. *Issue cease and desist orders;*

    j. *Close a business or factory* because its employees are being subjected to extremely hazardous working conditions in violation of a statute.

ADMINISTRATIVE AGENCY PROCEDURES

III. The emphasis in this chapter is placed on federal administrative agency law and procedure. With the exception of the detailed requirements of the *Federal Administrative Procedure Act (APA),* the general rules subsequently discussed in this chapter are also applicable to administrative agencies at the state and local levels. Federal administrative agencies are required to follow rules of procedure provided in the Federal Administrative Procedure Act (APA). The act prescribes procedures to be followed by an agency in both its quasi-legislative (rule-making) and quasi-judicial (adjudicative) functions.

    A. *Quasi-legislative (rule-making-type) procedures.* Procedures in a quasi-legislative (rule-making) type of hearing are as follows.

        1. *Notice and opportunity to comment requirements.* If a proposed rule *is general in its application and would have a "substantial impact"* on the regulated industry, a class of its members, or the products of that industry, the agency must comply with the following "notice and opportunity to comment" requirements of the act.

            a. *Notice.* General notice of the proposed rule must be published in the *Federal Register* at least thirty days prior to the effective date of the proposed rule. The notice must include:

                (1) The time, place, and nature of the rule-making proceedings; and

                (2) Either the terms of the proposed rule or a description of the subjects and issues involved.

            b. *Opportunity to comment and right to participate.* Opportunity to comment on a proposed rule must be given to "interested" persons (i.e., persons who may be affected by the existence or nonexistence of the proposed rule). The opportunity to comment includes the right to participate in the rule-making process.

                (1) *Written comment.* The right to participate includes only the right to submit *written* data, views, or argument.

(2) *Oral comment*. The right to participate does not include the right to oral presentation. Oral presentations (i.e., argument type) by an interested person is solely within the discretion of the administrative agency. An argument-type (oral) hearing involves oral presentation of data, views, and arguments in the presence of the members of the administrative agency. It is investigative, informational, and advisory rather than adjudicatory (decision making), as is true in *trial-type hearing*. *Compare*: An adjudicatory (trial-type) hearing involves a procedure whereby parties present oral and written evidence, engage in cross-examination and rebuttal, present arguments, and thereafter the presiding administrative law judge renders a decision based on the evidence presented of record (see III-B below).

c. *Exemptions from notice and opportunity to comment requirements*. The following actions of an administrative agency are exempt from notice and opportunity for comment requirements of the APA:

(1) Any rule that is narrow in its application and will *not* have a substantial impact on the regulated industry, its members, or the products of such industry;

(2) Rules governing internal administrative agency procedure, organization, or practice;

(3) Interpretive rules, i.e., rules that interpret the meaning of a statute; and

(4) General statements of administrative agency policy.

2. *Discretionary power of the administrative agency*. An administrative agency may, at its discretion, establish a rule without holding either a quasi-judicial hearing (trial-type) or non-quasi-judicial hearing (argument-type). As stated above, the Administrative Procedure Act (APA) provides only minimum requirements of "notice and opportunity to comment" and the right to participate *when* a proposed rule is "general in its application" and would have a "substantial impact" on the "regulated industry." Whether or not to hold a hearing at all or what type of hearing is to be held is left to the discretion of the administrative agency.

a. *The requirement of due process of law*. A rule issued without an appropriate prior hearing, whose effect is to deprive a person of life, liberty, or property without due process of law, is subject to challenge on constitutional grounds upon judicial review (see IV below).

3. *Publication of final rule*. After a final rule is established, it must be published in the *Federal Register*.

B. *Quasi-judicial (trial-type) procedures*. Procedures in a quasi-judicial (trial-type) hearing are as follows.

1. *Mandated by statute or due process of law*. A quasi-judicial hearing may be either:

a. Mandated by statute; or

b. Required by virtue of the constitutional right of persons to receive *"due process of law"* if an administrative agency's action affects them or their property. As a general rule, a party is entitled to a trial-type hearing under due process of law *whenever an agency rule, order, or decision will be based on the past or present acts, conduct, or activities of such party*. Conclusions drawn on these facts usually answer the questions of who, what, when, where, and why. *Compare*: "Pure" rulemaking may take into consideration past or present facts, but its intent is to produce rules or regulations that are to operate in the future. It does not involve a controversy and the rights of persons are not adjudicated.

2. *Formal hearing procedures*. These procedures are similar to those followed in a trial court during a trial of a legal controversy.
  a. *Complaint*. A trial-type hearing is initiated by the filing of a complaint with the administrative agency that has jurisdiction in the matter.
    (1) The complaint is a writing that provides *notice* to an alleged violator of the allegations, the particular statute, rule, or regulation that is alleged to have been violated, and the time and place of the hearing on these alleged violations.
    (2) A complaint against an alleged violator may be filed with the administrative agency by:
      (*a*) A person injured by the alleged violation;
      (*b*) A member of the public;
      (*c*) The administrative agency itself; or
      (*d*) The U.S. Attorney General.
  b. *Service of complaint and summons*. The complaint and summons must be served upon the alleged violator. The *summons* is notification to alleged violators that they must appear at the scheduled hearing to answer the complaint filed against them.
  c. *Answer*. An *answer* is the written response by an alleged violator to the allegations made in the complaint. The answer may set forth defenses to the allegations as well as attack the jurisdiction of the agency.
  d. *Investigation*. An informal investigation is conducted by the administrative agency staff and their findings are reported to an administrative law judge. If the findings do not provide a reasonable basis to support the allegations in the complaint, it will be dismissed. If the findings reveal such a reasonable basis, a hearing will be ordered.
  e. *Hearing* (trial-type). The hearing is a formal procedure held before an *administrative law judge*. The administrative law judge is independent from the administrative agency.
    (1) It is similar to a court trial in that the parties have the right to:
      (*a*) Legal counsel;
      (*b*) Proper notice of the time and place of the hearing;
      (*c*) Introduce oral and written evidence;
      (*d*) Examine and cross-examine witnesses;
      (*e*) Present objections to testimony;
      (*f*) Present motions in their own behalf;
      (*g*) Procure a copy of the transcript of the proceedings; and
      (*h*) Judicial review.
    (2) It differs from an actual court trial as follows:
      (*a*) The rules of evidence are not as strict. For example, hearsay evidence is admissable, leading questions of witnesses are permitted, and nonexpert opinions are allowed into evidence.
      (*b*) An alleged violator does not have the right to a jury trial.
      (*c*) The administrative law judge is usually an expert in the field regulated by the administrative agency.
      (*d*) The administrative law judge is allowed to use facts that are relevant and within their expert knowledge even though such facts were not presented during a hearing. A presiding judge at a court trial must base his or her decision solely on facts presented at a trial.
      (*e*) The administrative law judge is not required to be an attorney, whereas a presiding judge at a court trial must be.

f. *Decision of the administrative law judge.* Upon the conclusion of presentation of evidence and arguments, the administrative law judge renders a decision. The administrative law judge's decision is final unless it can be appealed to the membership of the administrative agency as a body.

g. *Appeal to membership of administrative agency as a whole.* Any "interested" party may appeal the administrative law judge's decision to the membership of the administrative agency as a whole. The membership as a body has the right to reverse, affirm, or modify the administrative law judge's decision and findings of fact or remand the case for rehearing.

h. *Final decision.* If no judicial review takes place, the decision of the administrative agency is final.

JUDICIAL REVIEW OF ADMINISTRATIVE AGENCY DECISIONS

IV. The Federal Administrative Procedure Act (APA) creates a statutory right of judicial review of all actions by federal administrative agencies with the following exceptions: (1) If judicial review is precluded by statute; or (2) if the discretionary action was committed to the sole discretion of the agency by law. The *judicial review* may take the form either of a lawsuit filed in a federal district court for an injunction against the agency or of a petition for review filed with a federal court of appeals or the U.S. Supreme Court.

A. *Conditions for review.* The following conditions must be met by complainants before they can exercise their right of review:

1. *"Standing" to obtain review.* Under the APA, "A person suffering legal wrong because of agency action, or adversely affected or aggrieved by agency action within the meaning of a relevant statute, is entitled to judicial review thereof." The U.S. Supreme Court has held this provision to mean that the party seeking judicial review must establish the existence of the following in order to have standing to obtain review:

   a. *Injury*, i.e., suffers "legal wrong," or is *"adversely affected" or "aggrieved."*

   (1) The parties seeking review must have a personal stake in the outcome of the controversy. This means that they must allege facts showing that *they themselves* were adversely affected or aggrieved or that they suffered a legal wrong as a result of agency action, i.e., that they were "injured."

   (2) The alleged "injury" may be either actual or threatened.

   (3) It may be monetary, economic, competitive, aesthetic, recreational, or any other type that results in a legal wrong.

   (4) An *"injured person"* is any individual, association, corporation, or business whose personal or property rights are threatened or adversely affected by an administrative agency decision.

   (5) The "injured person" need not have been a participant in the agency proceedings that gave rise to the agency action.

   b. Examples of "injured persons" are as follows:

   (1) A person denied a television broadcasting license by the Federal Communications Commission (FCC);

   (2) A firm ordered by the Federal Trade Commission (FTC) to spend money for corrective advertising;

   (3) A firm found guilty of an unfair labor practice by the National Labor Relations Board (NLRB);

   (4) A defeated candidate in a union election whose request to the secretary of

labor to bring a civil suit to set aside the election was denied after investigation; and

    (5) A competitor of a firm to whom the Federal Communications Commission (FCC) granted a radio broadcasting license.

2. *Exhaustion of administrative remedies.*

    a. Injured persons must have *exhausted* (i.e., taken advantage of) all of available administrative agency remedies before they are entitled to judicial review.

    b. Injured persons have "exhausted" all of their administrative remedies when they have unsuccessfully pursued all remedies available under the procedures of the administrative agency, including administrative appeal.

3. *Final order rule.* Agency decisions prior to a final action are not judicially reviewable.

    a. Preliminary, procedural, or intermediate agency action is not reviewable until after a final decision is rendered by the agency.

    b. Specific agency actions made reviewable by statute are not subject to the final order rule.

    c. Exception to the final order rule. When a preliminary agency action threatens irreparable injury, judicial review will be allowed. *Irreparable injury* is damage that could not be remedied by a favorable decision on judicial review of a final rule. For example, an administrative agency has issued a rule and made it effective prior to a trial-type hearing on the issues. A party who stands to suffer severe economic loss as a result of an agency's preliminary action can obtain judicial review as though the agency's preliminary action was a final order.

B. *Process of judicial review.* Judicial review of an administrative agency's ruling or order consists of the reviewing court's examination and analysis of the written transcript (i.e., the record) of the agency's hearing, written briefs (i.e., written legal arguments and precedents) submitted by the parties, and oral arguments by legal counsel.

C. *Scope of judicial review.* As a general rule, the reviewing court does *not* ordinarily conduct a trial *de novo* (i.e., a new trial). It does not hear or receive oral or written evidence for a second time and attempt to reach its own *conclusions of fact.* Its responsibility is to examine the evidence as it appears in the transcript (i.e., the record) of the agency's hearing and determine only questions of law.

1. *Review for errors of law.* As stated above, the reviewing court must review only alleged errors of law. In reviewing questions of law, the reviewing court has complete freedom to substitute its judgment for that of the administrative agency. Some examples of *questions of law* are as follows:

    a. Did the agency follow statutory, constitutional, and its own procedural requirements? (That is, did it afford the complainant procedural due process?)

    b. Did the agency have jurisdiction in the matter before it? (That is, did it act within the scope of its authority?)

    c. Was the agency action "arbitrary, capricious, or an abuse of its discretion"? That is, based on the record as a whole, was the agency's action "contrary to all reason" or "without a rational basis"? (The arbitrary and capricious test.)

    d. Was the power granted to the agency an unlawful delegation of legislative power?

    e. Did the agency action violate federal or state constitutional rights of the complainant (that is, rights protected by the due process and equal protection clauses of the federal constitution)?

f. Was the order, rule, or decision a result of prejudice, bribery, or other wrong-doing? That is, was it in bad faith or fraudulent?

g. Was the complainant entitled to but denied a trial-type hearing?

h. Did the agency properly interpret the legal meaning of the provisions of a regulatory statute? and

i. Was there "substantial evidence" in the trial-type or formal rulemaking record as a whole to support the agency's findings of fact? (The substantial evidence test.)

2. *Review of agency's findings of fact.* As a general rule, administrative agency findings of fact are binding on the reviewing court unless there is "no substantial evidence" in the record to support them. *Substantial evidence* is that quantity and quality of evidence that provides a sufficient basis for a reasonable person to reach the same findings and conclusions as those made by the administrative agency. The court will not substitute its judgment for that made by experts in the field (i.e., the members of the administrative agency), even though it feels that the agency decision is erroneous. The "substantial evidence test" is applied only when the review is of agency decisions made in a trial-type or formal rule-making hearing. Some examples of *findings of fact* are as follows:

a. That the construction of a jail and detention center will have a "significantly" adverse environmental impact;

b. The percentage share of a retail market possessed by a firm after a merger;

c. The value of a tract of land;

d. That a product does not perform as advertised;

e. That a product advertised as "free" was not actually free;

f. The existence and extent of a "relevant competitive market" for antitrust purposes;

g. That the snail darter is an endangered species of fish;

h. That an employer employed persons under the age of 16; and

i. That a power company generated electricity that was transmitted in interstate commerce.

D. *Decision on judicial review.* The reviewing court has power to reverse, remand, or modify an administrative action or decision.

SELF-QUIZ

To check your understanding of the key words and concepts and the accuracy of your answers to the questions, refer to the text material as referenced by page number.

KEY WORDS AND CONCEPTS

Administrative agency **480**
Delegation of legislative authority **480**
Quasi-legislative power (rulemaking) **480**
Quasi-judicial power (adjudicatory) **480**
Supervisory power **481**
Subpoena **480**
Federal Administrative Procedure Act **481**
Notice and opportunity to comment **481**
Federal Register **482**
Trial-type hearing **482**

Due process of law **482**
Complaint **483**
Summons **483**
Answer **483**
Discretionary power **482**
Administrative law judge **483**
Judicial review **484**
"Standing" to obtain judicial review **484**
"Adversely affected" or "aggrieved" **484**
"Injured person" **484**
Exhaustion of administrative remedies **485**
Final order rule **485**
Questions of law **485**
Conclusions of fact **485**
Substantial evidence **486**
Findings of fact **486**

1. From what source does Congress derive its power to establish administrative regulatory agencies? **(480)**
2. A federal administrative agency may exercise three types of broad powers. Name and explain them. **(480)**
3. Explain the "notice and opportunity for comment" requirements of the Administrative Procedure Act (APA). **(481)**
4. Under what circumstances must an administrative agency conduct a hearing? What type of hearing? **(482)**
5. Distinguish between quasi-judicial (trial-type) hearings and quasi-legislative hearings held by administrative agencies. **(481)**
6. Explain the administrative and judicial review procedures available to a person claiming to be "injured" by an administrative agency decision. **(484)**
7. Upon what grounds may a reviewing court reverse, modify, or remand an administrative agency decision? **(485)**

SELECTED QUESTIONS AND UNOFFICIAL ANSWERS

AUTHOR'S OBJECTIVE QUESTIONS

Select the best answer for each of the following items. Mark only one answer for each item. Answer all items.

1. A federal appellate court has decided to review a decision made by the Federal Trade Commission (FTC). As a general rule, the court during the course of its review, will:
a. Refuse to defer to the expertise of the administrative law judge in matters other than law;
b. Reexamine questions of law;
c. Question the credibility of witnesses who testified at the administrative hearing;
d. Reexamine questions of fact.

2. Magla, Inc., advertised on television that its product turns to a form of gasoline when added to water and that this mixture can be used to power automobiles. Silvo used the product without success. After receipt of a complaint from Silvo and many other persons, the Federal Trade Commission (FTC) ordered Magla to temporarily stop the advertisement and produce substantiating evidence for its product claims. Magla refused. It stated that results from extensive testing by an independent agency revealed that its claims were truthful. The FTC can institute a trial-type administrative proceeding by issuing one of the following:
a. Summons;
b. Notice and opportunity to comment;
c. Complaint;
d. Answer.

3. Which of the following statements concerning an administrative agency is correct?
a. It cannot accept hearsay evidence at an agency hearing.
b. It makes only findings of fact.
c. Its membership is composed of court-type law judges.
d. Its actions are reviewable by courts.

4. An administrative agency is said to possess three types of governmental powers. Which one of the following powers is *not* possessed by an administrative agency?
a. Power to enact legislation;
b. Power to decide legal controversies;
c. Power to create rules and regulations that have the force of law;
d. Supervisory power.

5. Damon, Inc., a manufacturer of crib mattresses, was charged with violating an administrative agency rule to the effect that crib mattresses had to comply with the same flammability standards as all other mattresses. A trial-type hearing was conducted before a federal administrative law judge. The judge found Damon, Inc., guilty and imposed a large fine. The agency's internal rules of procedure provided for automatic review of all of its decisions by the members of the agency as a whole. Before the automatic review could be commenced, Damon, Inc., filed a lawsuit in federal district court requesting the court to overturn the administrative law judge's decision and to issue an injunction ordering

the agency to halt any further agency proceedings. Which of the following statements is incorrect?

a. The administrative agency had the power to levy a fine against Damon, Inc.

b. Damon, Inc., does not have "standing" to obtain judicial review.

c. A finding by the agency that Damon, Inc., sold flammable crib mattresses is a "finding of fact."

d. The federal district court will dismiss the lawsuit filed by Damon, Inc.

6. Assume the same facts as stated in question 5 above, except that Damon, Inc., did submit to the review of the administrative law judge's decision in front of the members of the agency as a whole, the decision of the administrative law judge was affirmed, and Damon, Inc., filed a petition for review to a federal appellate court. Which of the following statements is correct?

a. The appellate court must hold a trial *de novo* and reach its own conclusions of fact and questions of law.

b. The court will use the "substantial evidence test" in reviewing the agency's findings of fact.

c. The court will reverse the agency's decision if it finds that hearsay evidence was admitted during the hearing.

d. The court will reverse the agency's decision if it finds that the administrative law judge did not complete his or her last year of law school.

7. Because of their quasi-judicial power, administrative agencies have been compared to courts. Which one of the following powers is possessed by both administrative agencies and trial courts?

a. To investigate;

b. To prosecute;

c. To hold informal hearings;

d. To adjudicate.

8. Some agency actions are exempt from the "notice and opportunity to comment" requirements of the Federal Administrative Procedure Act. One action that is *not* exempt is:

a. An agency rule issued to interpret the meaning of a statute.

b. A procedural rule that governs internal agency procedures or a party's access to the agency.

c. A general statement of administrative agency policy.

d. A rule that would apply to products of a specific industry.

9. Which one of the following procedures is *not* a part of a quasi-judicial hearing?

a. Answer;

b. Presentation of oral and written evidence;

c. Notice and opportunity to comment;

d. Complaint.

10. An administrative agency has power to compromise disputes within its jurisdiction with an alleged violator of a regulatory statute. If such compromise is reached, the agency will issue a:

a. Stop order;

b. Consent order;

c. License;

d. Cease and desist order.

Answers to Author's Objective Questions

1. b	**3.** d	**5.** b	**7.** d	**9.** c
2. c	**4.** a	**6.** b	**8.** d	**10.** b

Explanation of Author's Answers to Objective Questions

1. (b) The purpose of judicial review is to reexamine questions of law; i.e., to review administrative agency jurisdiction, procedures, and decisions for alleged errors of law. Answer (a) is incorrect because a reviewing court will defer to the expertise of the administrative law judge and accept his or her findings of fact unless they are not supported by substantial evidence. Courts do not wish to substitute their judgment for that of the members of the administrative agency. Answer (c) is incorrect because the appellate court will not question the credibility of such witnesses. The credibility of witnesses is a matter exclusively within the province of the administrative agency. Answer (d) is incorrect. Courts will not question an administrative agency's findings of fact. However, they can rule that agency findings of fact were not, as a matter of law, supported by substantial evidence. Substantial evidence exists if, from the evidence presented in the record of the agency hearing on the whole, a reasonable person could have reached the same conclusion as that reached by the administrative agency.

2. (c) An administrative agency, a member of the public, the U.S. Attorney General, or a person "injured" by an alleged violation can initiate a trial-type administrative hearing by filing a complaint. A complaint is a formal written allegation of a violation that is delivered to an alleged violator. It provides notice to alleged violators of allegations made against them and the time and place of the hearing. Answer (a) is incorrect. A summons is a court order delivered to an alleged violator, notifying that person of the complaint and of the requirement to answer. Answer (b) is incorrect because "notice and opportunity to comment" procedures are only required prior to a quasi-legislative (rule-making) type of administrative hearing. Answer (d) is incorrect because an "answer" is an alleged violator's written formal response to allegations made in a complaint.

3. (d) An administrative agency's jurisdiction, authority, procedures, decisions, rulings, regulations, and other actions are reviewable by the courts. Answer (a) is incorrect because, unlike a court, an administrative agency can accept hearsay evidence. Answer (b) is incorrect because it not only makes findings of fact but also findings of law. It can not only determine what an alleged violator did (i.e., a factual issue) but also decide whether such conduct was in violation of a statute or agency regulation or ruling (i.e., a legal issue). Answer (c) is incorrect because members of administrative agencies are not law judges or even lawyers. They are usually business executives, engineers, chemists, bankers, or other experts whose expertise and experience are required in order to develop sound regulatory policies and make proper decisions in areas that are beyond the expertise of Congress or some other legislature.

4. (a) An administrative agency does not have the power to enact legislation. That power is reserved to Congress and the legislature of each state of the United States. It does have quasi-legislative (i.e., rule-making) power, but only if such power was delegated to it by a legislature. An administrative agency has power to promulgate rules and regulations, which have the force of law, in order to carry out the purposes of statutes within its jurisdiction. Answer (b) is incorrect because, in the exercise of its quasi-judicial (adjudicatory) power, it does make decisions on questions of law. Answer (c) is incorrect for the reason stated above. Answer (d) is incorrect because an administrative agency does have supervisory power to coerce compliance with regulatory statutes and its rules or regulations. For example, it can levy fines, issue stop orders, impose

penalties, order forfeitures, seize and destroy property, issue consent or cease and desist orders, and investigate or prosecute violators.

5. (b) Damon, Inc., does have "standing" to obtain judicial review. To have standing to obtain review a party must allege facts showing that it was "injured" by agency action. A party is "injured" whenever its personal or property rights are threatened or adversely affected by agency action. The agency decision finding Damon, Inc., guilty of violating its rule and the imposition of a fine clearly had an adverse affect on its property rights. Answer (a) is incorrect because administrative agencies have the power to levy fines against violators of their rules. Answer (c) is incorrect. Whether or not a party did something is a question of fact. Whether or not the sales violated agency rules is a question of law. Answer (d) is incorrect. The court will dismiss the lawsuit filed by Damon, Inc. In addition to the requirement of standing to obtain review, a party must have exhausted all available administrative agency remedies. Damon, Inc., did not do so. Damon, Inc., must first submit to the automatic review of the administrative law judge's decision before it can have access to a court for judicial review.

6. (b) A reviewing court will not question an administrative agency's findings of fact. It reviews only questions of law. In doing so, it looks to the record of the hearing as a whole. A reviewing court may, however, reverse an administrative agency's findings of fact as a matter of law if, upon reviewing the record as a whole, it concludes that the agency's decision was "arbitrary, capricious, or an abuse of its discretion," i.e., it was "without a rational basis" or "contrary to all reason." An administrative action or decision is "without a rational basis" or "contrary to all reason" when there is "no substantial evidence" in the record to support it. Answer (a) is incorrect because a court will not hold a trial *de novo* (i.e., a new trial) on judicial review. Upon judicial review, a court may review the record of the administrative hearing, hear oral arguments, and receive and read written briefs filed by legal counsel for both parties. It will not substitute its judgment for that of the agency on questions of fact. However, it can freely do so on matters of law. Answer (c) is incorrect because hearsay evidence is admissible during an administrative agency hearing. Agency rules relating to the admissibility of evidence during a hearing are much more lenient than those applicable to a court trial. Answer (d) is incorrect because an administrative law judge or any other member of an administrative agency need not be a law judge, a lawyer, or have any formal legal training whatsoever.

7. (d) Administrative agencies and courts adjudicate, i.e., resolve questions of law. The agency power is said to be quasi- ("as if") judicial. It is called quasi-judicial because an administrative agency is not a court of law, yet it can and does adjudicate questions of law. Answers (a), (b), and (c) are incorrect. A trial court does not have the power to investigate alleged violations, prosecute alleged violators, or to hold informal hearings. A trial court always acts "after the fact." It adjudicates only legal controversies. If such controversy does not exist, it will not take jurisdiction. A court will never render an advisory decision. A court may not act as prosecutor and judge, but must be totally impartial in the controversy between the parties to the lawsuit. During the trial, the court is bound to follow strict rules of evidence and procedure. It cannot conduct an informal proceeding. On the other hand, an administrative agency can investigate an alleged violation, and subsequently act as a complainant, prosecutor, and judge in a trial-type administrative hearing.

8. (d) If a proposed rule is general in its application and would have a "substantial impact" on the regulated industry, a class of its members or the products of that industry, the agency must comply with the "notice and opportunity to comment" requirements of the APA. Compliance consists of a notice published in the *Federal Register* at least thirty days prior to the effective date of the proposed rule. The agency must provide opportunity to "interested" persons to participate in the rulemaking process by the submission of written comment. "Interested" persons are those who may be affected by the nonexistence or existence of the proposed rule. Answers (a), (b), and (c) are incorrect. These administrative actions are specifically exempt from its notice and opportunity for comment requirements by the APA.

9. (c) Notice and opportunity to comment is not a part of a quasi-judicial (i.e., trial-type) hearing. Notice and opportunity to comment is required whenever an administrative agency exercises its quasi-legislative (i.e., rule-making) power. Answers (a), (b), and (d) are incorrect because, in a trial type of hearing, due process of law requires, among other things, that a party be advised of the allegations, (i.e., the complaint), be allowed to respond to the allegations (i.e., answer), and be allowed to present oral and written evidence in his or her behalf. In addition, a party has the right to examine and cross-examine witnesses and be represented by legal counsel.

10. (b) A consent order is an agreement between an administrative agency and an alleged violator whereby the latter, without admission of guilt, agrees to subject itself to the action of the agency. It is for settlement purposes only. After it is issued by the agency on a final basis, a consent order carries the force of law with respect to future actions. A violation of such order may result in a civil penalty. Answer (a) is incorrect. A stop order is an order issued by the Securities Exchange Commission (SEC) to prevent trading of a security on a stock exchange. Answer (c) is incorrect because a license is a privilege and in some cases a right to conduct a business or other activity regulated by statute. Answer (d) is incorrect because a cease and desist order is issued against a person who has been found to be in violation of a statute or agency rule or regulation to prevent future violations.

AUTHOR'S ESSAY QUESTIONS AND ANSWERS

(Estimated time: 10 to 15 minutes)

1. The Food and Drug Administration (FDA) issued regulations that provided new standards for proving the effectiveness of drug products. The FDA regulation was applied retroactively, so that the continued sales of thousands of drug products sold with previous FDA approval was threatened. The FDA had not yet challenged the effectiveness of those drugs. The FDA adopted the new regulation without a public hearing. The regulations apply to more than 2,000 drug products marketed since 1938 with FDA approval. A pharmaceutical manufacturer's association (PMA), on behalf of its members, filed a lawsuit in federal district court for a preliminary injunction restraining the Commissioner of Food and Drugs from enforcing the FDA regulations. The PMA contended that the FDA regulations were invalid because they were issued without notice and opportunity for comment in violation of the requirements of the Federal Administrative Procedure Act. The FDA defended on the grounds that the PMA did not have standing to obtain judicial review of the FDA's action.

Required Should the preliminary injunction be granted?

Answer Yes. The PMA, as a representative of its members has standing for judicial review. PMA's contention is correct.

Standing to obtain judicial review. The Administrative Procedure Act (APA) provides that any person "adversely affected" or "aggrieved" by any action is entitled to judicial review thereof. "Adversely affected" or "aggrieved" has been interpreted by the courts to mean, among other things, economic injury that is either actual or threatened. An injured person can be an individual, association, corporation, or business. In this case, pharmaceutical manufacturers stand to have their right to market some 2,000 drug products summarily destroyed by order of the FDA under its new regulation.

Notice and opportunity requirement. The Administrative Procedure Act (APA) requires that an agency comply with its notice and opportunity to comment requirement prior to issuance of a rule whenever the proposed rule is general in its application and would have a substantial impact on the regulated industry, a class of its members, or the products of that industry. The regulations issued by the FDA have an immediate and substantial impact on the conduct of PMA members in their everyday business of manufacturing and marketing drug products. The regulations apply to more than 2,000 drug products previously marketed with FDA approval and place them in jeopardy. The substantial impact of the regulation also extends through the drug industry to prescribing physicians and their patients. Because the minimal notice and opportunity to comment requirements were not met, the FDA's regulation is invalid and the preliminary injunction should issue.

(Estimated time: 8 to 12 minutes)

2. X filed a complaint against Reva, Inc., with the National Labor Relations Board (NLRB) and alleged that Reva, Inc., discharged her from employment solely on the basis of her race. The NLRB held a trial-type hearing. It decided in favor of X and issued an order reinstating X to her job with back pay. The NLRB also ordered Reva, Inc., to cease and desist from future discriminatory employment practices. The employer filed a petition for review of the NLRB orders before the federal circuit court of appeals. After a review of the record of the proceedings before the NLRB, the circuit court of appeals reversed the NLRB and denied enforcement of its orders because of insufficient evidence. In its written opinion, it stated that its decision was based on its finding that the evidence in the record of the NLRB hearing was not "clearly convincing" or it did not "clearly show" that discrimination occurred. X appealed the reversal to the U.S. Supreme Court. X contended that the appellate court erred by requiring that the NLRB have "clearly convincing" evidence to support its decision.

Required Is X's contention correct? Explain.

Answer Yes. Whether or not the employer discriminated against X because of race is a question of fact. On judicial review, a court is not allowed to substitute its judgment for that of the administrative agency on questions of fact. The reviewing court must apply the "substantial evidence" test. Substantial evidence is all that is required to support an administrative agency's findings of fact. "Substantial evidence" is that quantity and quality of evidence that is sufficient for a reasonable person to reach the same findings and conclusions of fact as those made by the administrative agency. If substantial evidence exists on review of the record as a whole, the court must affirm the decision of the administrative agency even though the court is convinced that it is erroneous.

CHAPTER

17

Antitrust

The following is a generalized listing of subjects to be tested through the May 1983 Uniform CPA Examination.

Questions are based upon the basic provisions of federal antitrust laws which concern the preservation of competition—and their application in situations requiring accounting disclosure. The Sherman, Clayton, Robinson-Patman, and Federal Trade Commission Acts are the major sources of law in this area.[1]

The AICPA Board of Examiners has adopted a new content specification outline for the business law section of the Uniform CPA Examination, *to be effective with the November 1983 examination.* The outline lists the following topics to be tested under the title "Antitrust."

B. Antitrust Law
   1. Price-Fixing and Other Concerted Activities
   2. Mergers and Acquisitions
   3. Unfair Methods of Competition
   4. Price Discrimination
   5. Sanctions[2]

---

[1] AICPA, *Information for CPA Candidates*, Copyright © 1975, 1979, by the American Institute of Certified Public Accountants, Inc.
[2] AICPA, *Business Law—Content Specification Outline*, approved by the AICPA Board of Examiners on August 31, 1981.

ANTITRUST CONCEPTS AND TERMS

I. The following terms and concepts are important to the mastery of antitrust law.

A. *"In interstate commerce."* Activity or conduct is "in interstate commerce" if it takes place between or among states in the United States; e.g., a tractor manufacturer sells its product throughout the United States.

B. *"Affects interstate commerce."* All activity or conduct "in interstate commerce" also "affects interstate commerce." Intrastate (local) activity or conduct "affects interstate commerce" if it has a "substantial" effect on interstate commerce; e.g., real estate brokers in Louisiana maintained a commission schedule for fees to be charged by local real estate brokers for services rendered in behalf of sellers of local real estate. A court ruled that the real estate brokerage (trade or commerce) had a "substantial effect" on interstate commerce in that the mortgage purchase money for the real estate had its origin from out-of-state-lenders under federal mortgage insurance programs (FHA financing).

C. *"Persons covered."* All individuals, associations, and entities, domestic or foreign, that engage in "interstate" business activity or conduct are covered by the antitrust laws. This definition includes trade and professional associations and corporations, profit and nonprofit associations and corporations, partnerships, sole proprietorships, and individuals employed by the latter. It does not include certain limited exemptions specified in the antitrust laws.

D. *Agreement (contract, combination, or conspiracy).* The terms "contract," "combination," and "conspiracy" are synonymous with "agreement." An "agreement" by definition must involve two or more "persons." It includes oral or written (express) contracts or other agreements, implied in fact (evidenced by conduct) contracts, or any other types of agreements, understandings, and "gentlemen's agreements."

E. *Exemptions.* As a general rule, persons, property, or economic activity currently regulated by the federal or state government are exempt from federal antitrust regulation to the extent that they are regulated; e.g., communications, securities, electricity and natural gas, air carriers, and transportation. In addition, certain businesses, industries, and organizations have received special and limited statutory immunity from federal antitrust law during the conduct of certain activities; e.g., organized labor, agricultural cooperatives and associations, exporters and importers in foreign trade, insurance, and other industries "affected with a public interest" (see also III below).

F. *Horizontal agreement or conduct.* This type of agreement or conduct always involves associations, entities, or individuals that compete on the same level in a marketing channel of distribution; e.g., manufacturers, wholesalers, retailers, franchisors, franchisees, consignors, consignees, licensors, licensees, or distributors.

G. *Vertical agreement or conduct.* This type of agreement or conduct always involves associations, entities, or individuals on different levels in a marketing channel of distribution; e.g., a resale price maintenance agreement between a manufacturer and a retailer, termination of a franchise by the franchisor, or reciprocity (i.e., "I'll buy from you if you'll buy from me").

H. *Per se violation.* A type of agreement or conduct ruled by the U.S. Supreme Court to be an automatic antitrust violation without any inquiry into its need, justification, or explanation; e.g., price fixing, horizontal allocation of market territories, group boycotts, production control, tying arrangements, or reciprocity.

I. *Rule-of-reason violation.* It is not a per se violation, but is determined from the application of the "rule-of-reason test." This test may be stated as follows: *Does the agreement or conduct impose an "unreasonable" restraint (restriction) upon competition? That is, does it promote competition or does it suppress or destroy competition? This test is used to determine a violation under the provisions of the Sherman Act. A similar test is used to determine violations under the Clayton Act. That is, *could* the agreement or conduct have a substantial adverse affect on competition (i.e., "may substantially lessen competition") or tend to create a monopoly?

    J. *"Conscious parallelism."* Conscious parallelism is a specific type of conduct by one competitor that is similar or identical to the conduct of other competitors, all of whom are aware of each other's conduct; e.g., identical or similar credit terms, discounts, or advertising allowances allowed by competitors within a relevant competitive market.

    K. *Revelant competitive market.* The relevant competitive market is the product-line and the geographic location in which "persons" are in competition with each other (see V below).

    L. *Monopoly power.* Monopoly power is the power to control prices or exclude competition in a relevant competitive market; e.g., a manufacturer's share of the market for designer jeans is 90 percent.

FEDERAL JURISDICTION

II. Federal antitrust laws regulate "persons" and their business or professional activities and conduct "in interstate commerce," in "foreign" commerce, as well as in some types of "intrastate" activities and conduct.

    A. Business activities or conduct are "in interstate commerce" when they occur between and among states in the United States (see I-A above).

    B. Intrastate (purely local) business and professional activities or conduct are within the jurisdiction of the federal antitrust laws when they substantially "affect interstate commerce" (see I-B above).

    C. Federal antitrust laws also apply to foreign companies doing business in the United States as well as American "persons" doing business in foreign countries, if their activities or conduct affect interstate or foreign commerce, e.g., imports and exports.

    D. Individuals, associations, and entities (i.e., "persons"), domestic or foreign, that engage in "interstate" business or professional activity or conduct are within the jurisdiction of the federal antitrust laws (see I-C above).

    E. The right of Congress to regulate trade or business is derived from its constitutional power to regulate interstate and foreign commerce under article I, section 8 of the U.S. Constitution.

EXEMPTIONS FROM ANTITRUST LAWS

III. Exemptions from federal antitrust laws include the following:

    A. *Organized labor* is exempt in its conduct of ordinary union activities, strikes, and boycotts, but not if it engaged in conspiracies to fix prices, allocate markets, or boycott other employers.

    B. *Agricultural cooperatives and associations* are exempt when engaged in handling, processing, and marketing products, but not if involved in activities or conduct that restrain competition, such as a conspiracy to fix prices, limit production, or monopolize or attempt to monopolize.

    C. *Exporters and importers* are exempt so long as their activities or conduct do not affect U.S. interstate or foreign commerce, i.e., have an anticompetitive effect.

    D. *Industries "affected by a public interest"* to the extent regulated under other federal or state laws are exempt; e.g., electric power, banking, investments, insurance, radio, and television.

THE SHERMAN ACT (1890)

Section 1 "Every contract, combination in the form of trust or otherwise, or conspiracy, in restraint of trade or commerce among the several states, or with foreign nations is declared to be illegal."

Section 2 "Every person who shall monopolize, or attempt to monopolize, or combine or conspire with another person or persons to monopolize any part of the trade or commerce among the several states, or with foreign nations shall be deemed guilty of a felony . . ."

JOINT AND UNREASONABLE RESTRAINTS

IV. Under section 1 of the Sherman Act, *joint and unreasonable restraints* on competition in interstate commerce or with foreign nations are illegal. To be a "joint" restraint two or more "persons" must enter into an "agreement" (i.e., contract, combination, or conspiracy). See I-D above for a more comprehensive definition and explanation of an "agreement." "Persons" include any individual, association, or entity that engages in interstate business activity (see I-C above). Joint and unreasonable restraints are either illegal per se or are subject to the rule-of-reason test. (See Figure 17-1.)

A. *Illegal per se restraints.* Certain joint (by "agreement" between two or more "persons") restraints are so inherently inconsistent with a free competitive economic system and have such a detrimental effect on competition that they are unreasonable (unjustifiable) and consequently illegal. That is, they are illegal by (or in) themselves (per se), and *no* defense is available for this type of conduct.

FIGURE 17-1 THE SHERMAN ACT

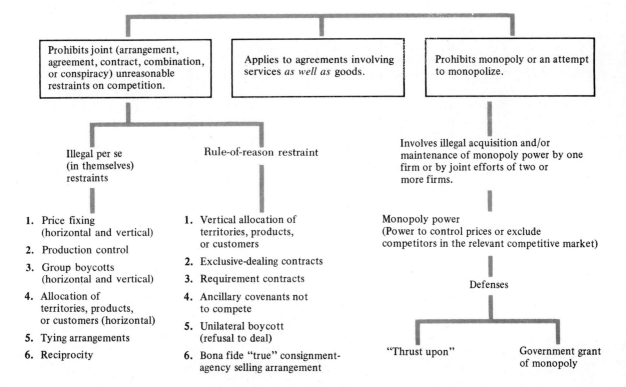

These restraints are conclusively presumed to be illegal, and consequently a court will not inquire into lack of injury to competition or the business excuse or reason for engaging in them. The following restraints are illegal per se:

1. *Price fixing.* Any agreement to "raise, depress, fix, peg, or stabilize" prices is illegal per se. It is no defense that the prices fixed are reasonable, that they were established to meet "cutthroat" competition, or that competitors are also engaging in illegal price fixing. Both horizontal and vertical fixing are illegal per se. Review I-F, G, above, for an explanation of horizontal and vertical agreements and conduct.

   a. *Horizontal price fixing* occurs when individuals, associations, or entities that compete on the same level in a marketing channel of distribution jointly enter into an agreement that directly or indirectly affects prices.

      (1) The following agreements between competitors are examples of horizontal price fixing:
          (*a*) On minimum prices;
          (*b*) On maximum prices (i.e., ceiling prices);
          (*c*) On amounts of discounts or markups;
          (*d*) On amounts of rebates;
          (*e*) On amounts of advertising, trade-in, or other allowances;
          (*f*) On credit terms;
          (*g*) To follow a distributed price list;
          (*h*) To eliminate discounts, markups, rebates, or allowances;
          (*i*) To rotate bids (i.e., rig bids);
          (*j*) On a uniform fee schedule for services rendered;
          (*k*) On standard costs; and
          (*l*) On a basing-point system to compute shipping costs. A *basing-point system* is one in which shipping costs are calculated from a designated city regardless of where the goods are actually shipped from and regardless of the actual shipping costs incurred.

   b. *Vertical price fixing* occurs when individuals, associations, or entities on different levels of a marketing channel of distribution jointly enter into an agreement that directly or indirectly affects prices; i.e., between manufacturers and retailers, franchisors and franchisees, licensors and licensees, manufacturers and distributors, manufacturers and wholesalers, or wholesalers and retailers. Any agreement between a seller and a buyer to establish the resale price of a specified product is illegal per se (i.e., resale price maintenance). This type of agreement is illegal regardless of whether the resale price is established directly or indirectly or whether it is sold under the trademark, name, or brand name of the supplier. Patented as well as unpatented goods are also subject to this rule.

      (1) The following are examples of vertical price-fixing agreements:
          (*a*) On minimum or maximum prices;
          (*b*) To establish or eliminate rebates, markups, discounts, or allowances;
          (*c*) On amounts of rebates, markups, discounts, or allowances;
          (*d*) On credit terms;
          (*e*) To follow price lists distributed by the seller; and
          (*f*) On any other term of the resale that may influence the resale price.

      (2) *"Suggested" resale prices.* A seller is not prohibited from suggesting a resale price. However, if the suggested resale price is accompanied by a *resale price maintenance* agreement, the suggested resale price is illegal per se price fixing.

(a) A seller (supplier) has the right to sell or refuse to sell to anyone. Under the Colgate doctrine established by the U.S. Supreme Court, a seller (supplier) *that acts alone* can refuse to sell or discontinue selling to any buyer that will not or does not follow the seller's suggested resale price. A seller (supplier) acts alone when it does not act under any understanding or agreement with a third party that the latter is to implement or coerce a distributor to comply with a "suggested" resale price. For example, a manufacturer uses some of its other buyers to inform on a disobedient retailer or to exert pressure upon the retailer to follow the seller's suggested resale price.

(3) *Sham "consignment" or "agency."* In a *"true" consignment* or agency, title to the goods is retained by the supplier. The consignee or agent is given possession of the goods and authority to sell on behalf of the supplier. The "resale" by the consignee or agent is in reality a sale by the supplier (owner of the goods) to the buyer. The supplier, as owner of the goods, has the right to dictate the price at which the goods are to be "sold" by its distributor. A *sham transaction* occurs when the supplier actually transfers title to the goods to a distributor for resale at an agreed-upon resale price under the disguise of a "consignment" or "agency." This type of arrangement is an illegal per se price-fixing scheme. For example, a manufacturer and retailer entered in a "consignment" relationship by which the retailer obtained title and agreed to resell the goods at a specified resale price. The manufacturer retained the risk of loss to the goods, agreed to insure the goods at its own expense, and reserved the right to take back the goods if they were not resold by the retailer. This agreement is a sham "consignment."

c. There need be no proof of an outright agreement to establish the existence of illegal pricing arrangements. Circumstantial evidence is sufficient to establish price fixing. However, accidental or incidental price uniformity among competitors ("conscious parallelism") alone is not conclusive evidence of an illegal agreement or conspiracy. Substantiating circumstantial evidence of a price-fixing scheme must be present in order to establish a conspiracy. For example, a manufacturer discontinued certain allowances to its retailers that would cause a serious loss of business unless all manufacturers in the line of business discontinued the same allowances. Shortly thereafter, other manufacturers discontinued the same allowances.

2. *Production control.* Concerted (jointly agreed-upon) actions in restricting production or supply of a product are per se violations. The public is entitled to receive the benefit of optimal production of goods and services at the lowest possible prices. For example, manufacturers A, B, C, realizing that prices were depressed because of an oversupply of their product, agreed to create a shortage by drastically reducing production.

3. *Allocation of markets or customers:*

   a. *Horizontal market allocation.* Any joint action to assign markets geographically or to allocate customers between competitors at the same level of distribution is illegal per se. For example, several steel pipe manufacturers divide their total geographic market into smaller regions and each consents to sell only in its specific geographic area. As another example, three bubble-gum machine competitors agree to allocate their customers and not to solicit each other's customers. As a third example, retailers X, Y, Z, and C each enjoy a reasonable volume of sales of toothpaste within a relevant competitive market, and each is content with its share of the product market. They have frequently discussed the market among themselves and have stated repeatedly that they would be foolish to "rock the boat" and "disturb the status quo." As a last example, a group of cement manufacturing companies agreed that some of the members of the group would bid only on road construction projects in 1981, while other members would bid on road construction projects that are to take place in 1982.

b. *Vertical market allocation.* This type of agreement is not illegal per se. It is illegal only if it imposes an unreasonable restraint on competition (i.e., rule-of-reason restraint). Rule-of-reason restraints are discussed below.

(1) A vertical market allocation is an agreement between a supplier (manufacturer or wholesaler) and its distributor or between a franchisor and franchisee wherein the distributor or franchisee is given the exclusive right to sell a product in a designated territory. For example, GTE Sylvania granted franchises to dealers that restricted each franchisee to the sale of Sylvania products in a specified territory. The court refused to hold that the franchising system was a per se violation of the act and applied the "rule of reason" test to the territorial restrictions to determine the extent of the restraint on competition.

(2) Courts may consider these factors to determine whether or not vertical territorial restrictions impose unreasonable restraint on competition:

(*a*) The strength of the competition between and among brands (i.e., interbrand competition);

(*b*) The size of the market possessed by the supplier;

(*c*) The amount of increase in a supplier's market, if any, as a result of the territorial restrictions; and

(*d*) Whether or not the territorial restrictions are tied to an illegal resale price maintenance agreement between the supplier and distributor or franchisee.

4. *Boycotts* (i.e., refusals to deal):

a. *Horizontal group boycott* (concerted refusal to deal). Any concerted activities or agreements designed to prevent other competitors from access to a market or to a source of supply, or to gain any other competitive advantage are illegal per se. The primary purpose of any horizontal group boycott is to stifle competition; therefore, this type of group activity or agreement is illegal under section 1 of the Sherman Act.

(1) Concerted threats of refusal or refusals by manufacturers, dealers, or trade associations to deal with customers (buyers) or suppliers are illegal; for example:

(*a*) Several manufacturers boycott certain retailers because the latter dealt with competing dress manufacturers who were copying (i.e., design or style pirates) the boycotters' patterns

(*b*) A trade association of manufacturers and retailers adopted a rule forbidding its members to buy from or sell to nonmembers.

(*c*) Arco, Marco, and Trox are retailers who refuse to sell discounted goods. Saxon, a competing retailer, discounts the same or identical goods on a regular basis with great success. Arco, Marco, and Trox notify Tram, a supplier, that they will not purchase from Tram unless it ceases to supply to Saxon.

b. *Unilateral vertical boycotts* (i.e., unilateral refusal to deal). As a general rule, a unilateral vertical boycott is not illegal per se. This type of boycott is subject to the rule-of-reason test (see "suggested" resale prices in IV-A-1-b above and unilateral boycotts in IV-B-5-b below).

5. *Tying arrangements* involving patented, copyrighted, or trademarked products. These are types of arrangements whereby a seller agrees to sell one product (i.e., the tying product) upon the condition that the buyer agrees to purchase the seller's other product or products (i.e., the tied product(s)). Tying arrangements may come within the provisions of section 3 of the Clayton Act (i.e., they "substantially lessen competition"), section 5 of the Federal Trade Commission Act (i.e., "unfair methods of competition"), as well as those of section 1 of the Sherman Act (i.e., "a contract, combination or conspiracy").

   a. As a general rule, tying arrangements involving patents, trademarks, or copyrights are considered to be illegal per se restraints.

   b. Elements of an illegal per se tying arrangement are:

      (1) The sales of two separate and different products being tied together;

      (2) The seller possesses dominant market power. Ownership of a patent, copyright, or trademark automatically establishes sufficient economic power. *Note:* Dominant market power of a seller is not an essential element for a Clayton Act violation if the tying arrangement "tends to substantially lessen competition"; and

      (3) A "not insubstantial amount of commerce" in the tied product is affected; i.e., a significant amount of commerce must be affected.

   c. The following are examples of some illegal tying arrangements:

      (1) International Salt leased patented salt machines on the condition that the lessee purchase all of its salt requirements from International.

      (2) A manufacturer of metal cans leased its patented can sealing machines to canners on the condition that the latter would agree to buy cans from the manufacturer.

      (3) Movie producing companies leased high-demand films to theaters only if the theaters agreed to lease and show low-demand films.

6. *Reciprocity.* As a general rule, reciprocity ("I'll buy from you if you'll buy from me") is illegal per se if:

   a. It results from an understanding or an express or implied agreement; or

   b. It was obtained by coercion (i.e., threats, implications, or innuendos made by a dominant firm to its supplier). For example, General Motors Corporation used its market strength (i.e., the large volume of shipping business given to railroads) to exert pressure on the railroads to get them to agree to buy only locomotives manufactured by a G.M. subsidiary in exchange for G.M.'s continued use of the railroad's services.

7. *Other per se joint restraints* include the following concerted (joint) conduct by competitors:

   a. Pooling of profits, losses, patents, or licenses. For example, Zebra Corporation and Logan Company agree to pool their patents and withhold them from competitors;

   b. Refraining from advertising certain allowances that are available only to preferred retailers;

   c. Refraining from advertising prices; and

   d. Refraining from bidding against each other.

B. *Common law rule-of-reason restraints.* Section 1 of the Sherman Act does not prohibit all agreements and concerted (joint) activities or conduct in restraint of trade or commerce. Because not all restraints on competition are illegal per se, a common law *rule-of-reason test* has been evolved by the courts. Agreements or concerted activities (other than those illegal per se) are found to be illegal *only if their purpose or effect* is found to be an *unreasonable restriction on competition* after the court has taken into consideration all of the relevant economic factors and circumstances. Some of the agreements and concerted activities to which the rule-of-reason test is applied are as follows:

1. *Ancillary covenants not to compete.* These covenants are commonly found in employment contracts and in contracts for the purchase (sale) of an existing business. For example, Jones in a contract to sell his hardware store and business to Rodriquez, promised (covenanted) not to compete with Rodriquez in the hardware business within the entire state of Illinois for a period of fifty years. This covenant is illegal and void. Both the territorial and time restriction on competition are unreasonable, plus the restrictions are far in excess of those needed to protect the goodwill of the business purchased by Rodriquez. As another example, an accountant entered into a written contract of employment with a large Chicago accounting firm. The contract contained a covenant not to compete. The accountant promised that upon termination of her employment, she would not practice accounting in Chicago for a period of five years. Both restrictions are excessive (i.e., unreasonable) and consequently are illegal and void.

2. *Patent licensing agreement.* In this type of agreement a licensor grants to its licensee a right to use its patent, but restricts the licensee's use of the patent in a way that competition is unreasonably restricted. For example, a license between a manufacturer of a patented machine and a retailer prohibits the latter from selling competing machines. This restriction would be illegal under the rule-of-reason test. *Note:* A patent owner *can* lawfully impose territorial restrictions on the use of its patent in the licensing agreement as well as limit the number of its licensees. These types of restrictions are valid under the provisions of a federal statute that allow a patent owner to limit its exclusive right to use its patent in " . . . the whole or any part of the United States."

3. *Bona fide "true" consignee-agency selling arrangements.* These may impose price, customer, or territorial restrictions. As a general rule, the owner of goods, *by itself or an agent*, can sell its products at any price it establishes, to whomever it chooses, and wherever it desires, so long as there is no evidence of any anticompetitive purpose. *Note*: A "true" consignment is not a sale for the purpose of resale to a customer of a consignee. It is a sale (i.e., transfer of title in exchange for a consideration) from the consignor (owner) "through" the consignee-agent to a customer (see "suggested" resale prices and sham "consignments" or "agency" in IV-A-1 above).

4. *Exclusive-dealing and requirements contracts.* These types of contracts are subject to attack under section 3 of the Clayton Act (as a contract that may substantially lessen competition in a relevant competitive market), under section 5 of the Federal Trade Commission Act (as an unfair method of competition), as well as under section 1 of the Sherman Act (as an unreasonable joint restraint of trade).

   a. *Exclusive-dealing contracts* are contracts or agreements between a supplier and a purchaser that obligate the purchaser to purchase the supplier's product and forbid the purchaser from handling competitive products.

   b. A *requirements contract* involves an agreement between a supplier and a purchaser wherein the purchaser binds itself to buy all or substantially all of its "requirements" of a certain product from the supplier during a specified period of time.

   c. Both the *quantitative test* and the *qualitative test* are used by the courts to determine whether or not the restraints imposed by these types of contracts are reasonable.

(1) *Quantitative test.* Is a substantial share of the market foreclosed to competition as a result of the arrangement? For example, Standard Oil of California required that its dealers stock only its tires, oil, and gasoline. Standard sold 23 percent of the gasoline marketed in the relevant market. It had exclusive-dealing contracts with 16 percent of the retail outlets within this market. The latter accounted for about 7 percent of the gasoline sales. The court held that the foreclosed competition equal to about 7 percent imposed an unreasonable restraint on competition. Application of the quantitative test will therefore reveal an illegal exclusive-dealing arrangement, when:

(a) The supplier controls a substantial share of the market; and/or

(b) The distributor has a large (dominant) share (position) in the market.

(2) *Qualitative test.* This test is used to determine whether or not an unreasonable restraint has been imposed on competition by examining the following factors or circumstances:

(a) Duration of the arrangement;

(b) Percent of the market controlled by the arrangement. For example, a manufacturer of paper clothing patterns maintained exclusive-dealing contracts with 40 percent of the pattern dealers in the United States. *Note*: These facts alone would be sufficient to satisfy the quantitative test and support a ruling that the restraint imposed on competition was unreasonable;

(c) Ease by which competitors are able to enter the market; and

(d) Existence of competitors in the relevant market.

5. *Group and unilateral boycotts:*

a. *Group boycotts* (concerted refusals to deal) are illegal per se and consequently the rule-of-reason test is not applicable to them (see IV-A-4 above).

b. *Unilateral boycotts* are individual refusals to deal or to continue to deal with a customer. Unilateral boycotts are subject to review under the rule-of-reason test.

(1) As a general rule, a supplier (owner-seller of goods) has the right to *unilaterally* refuse to deal or discontinue dealing with any customer. Customers include distributors, franchisees, licensees, or any other customers.

(2) However, if the unilateral refusal to deal or discontinuance of dealing is in *concert (jointly)* with or under some understanding with a customer's competitors, the conduct will be either illegal per se or in violation of the rule-of-reason test.

(a) Refusal to deal coupled with the aid of a third party to coerce resale price maintenance is illegal per se (see "suggested" resale prices in IV-A-1 above).

(b) Refusal to deal, coupled with a conspiracy involving a customer's competitors or a plan (scheme) to restrain competition or attempt to monopolize, is illegal per se.

(3) A unilateral boycott *does not violate* the rule-of-reason test (absent evidence of involvement of a customer's competitors) if it was imposed to improve or protect the supplier's business or economic interests; for example:

(a) A franchisor terminated a franchisee because the latter failed to abide by the provisions of a franchise agreement;

(*b*) The refusal to continue dealing was based on a contract provision allowing termination without cause;

(*c*) A refusal to deal because of the customer's poor credit ratings;

(*d*) A refusal to continue dealing because of the incompetence of a customer's management or sales force; or

(*e*) A refusal to deal because of the supplier's policy not to deal with non-franchised customers.

RELEVANT COMPETITIVE MARKET

V. To violate the provisions of either section 2 of the Sherman Act or those of the Clayton Act (including its amendments) the prohibited activity or conduct must occur or threaten to occur within a "relevant competitive market." The *relevant competitive market* is determined by:

A. The *product market*. The product market is determined by identifying and including the products of others that are competitive substitutes for the products of the alleged violator, taking into consideration quality, function, use, and price. For example, men's, women's, and children's shoes; fabricated steel; dehydrated spices (onions and garlic); or laundry soaps and detergents.

B. The *geographic market* for the product line. The geographic market is the location (area) where products within a product market are in competition with each other. The geographic market area can be local (city), regional, national, or international. For example, a local market involving taxi service or sales of unimproved residential lots; a market defined as the largest cities in the United States, or the state of Michigan and along the borders of Ohio and Pennsylvania; a national market involving auto parts, or a three-state region including Wisconsin, Illinois, and Michigan.

MONOPOLY OR ATTEMPT TO MONOPOLIZE

VI. Section 2 of the Sherman Act makes it a violation for a single firm or for two or more firms acting in concert (i.e., jointly by agreement or conspiracy) to "*monopolize or attempt to monopolize*" in interstate or foreign commerce. The violation occurs whenever a firm or two or more firms (jointly) acquire or maintain *monopoly* power with the intent to use it.

A. *Monopoly power* is the power to control prices or exclude competitors in a relevant competitive market.

B. "*Monopolize*" means to exercise monopoly power in a relevant competitive market. "Attempt, combine, or conspire to monopolize" means to unilaterally or by concerted activities or conduct attempt to acquire monopoly power through means other than reasonable business practices.

1. Mere size of a firm or combination of firms does not of itself constitute monopoly power. However, if a firm or combination of firms controls an "unreasonably" large percentage of the relevant competitive market, that control may alone be held to be existence of monopoly power. For example, one court held that 90 percent would be sufficient but 33 percent would not.

2. The mere attempt to obtain monopoly power or its existence is not in itself illegal. The acquisition or maintenance of monopoly power must be accompanied by the intent to use it. The intent may be inferred from the activities or conduct of an alleged violator; for example:

a. Joint conduct such as price fixing, group boycotts of competitors, or horizontal market or customer allocation is conduct evidencing concerted monopoly or attempt to monopolize.

b. Unilateral conduct, such as coercive refusals to deal (unilateral boycott), below-cost pricing, discontinuance of allowances, control of the supply of critical raw materials, or the insistence on tying the sale of several products, is conduct evidencing unilateral monopoly or an attempt to monopolize.

3. *Defenses to monopoly.* A firm does have several defenses to a charge of monopoly or the attempt to monopolize.

a. *"Thrust-upon" defense.* A firm has a defense when its monopoly was acquired and is maintained for a legitimate business reason. For example, a firm has a monopoly because of its superior skills and foresight; it alone has survived because it was the only firm that could absorb extremely high production costs in a low-demand market; or all of the firm's competitors decided to leave the market.

b. *Government grant of monopoly.* For example, patents, copyrights, or a monopoly status granted to a utility by a state or the federal government.

SANCTIONS AND REMEDIES UNDER THE SHERMAN ACT

VII. The Sherman Act provides both criminal and civil sanctions against persons found guilty of violating either section 1 or 2. The *Department of Justice* has exclusive responsibility to enforce the provisions of the Sherman Act. (See Figure 17-2.)

A. The Department of Justice, Antitrust Division, can institute criminal proceedings against a violator.

1. Violations under sections 1 and 2 are felonies and carry a maximum sentence of up to three years in prison.

2. Violators are also subject to fines.

a. The maximum fine that can be imposed against an individual is $100,000.

b. The maximum fine that can be imposed against a "firm" is $1,000,000.

B. Violators may also be subjected to civil sanctions. For example:

1. The Department of Justice, Antitrust Division, may institute civil proceedings to obtain an *injunction* restraining conduct in violation of the act.

2. Any person or business injured by a violation of the act may sue for treble damages individually or as a class action. In a *class action* the individual or business not only sues in its own behalf but also in behalf of all other individuals or businesses that may have incurred similar damages as a result of an antitrust violation. *Treble damages* are equal to three times the amount of damages actually incurred as a result of a violation.

3. The Department of Justice, Antitrust Division, may institute legal proceedings to obtain a court order of dissolution, divorcement, or divestiture.

a. *Dissolution* involves the legal termination of a business combination; e.g., an illegal merger is ordered dissolved.

b. *Divorcement* involves the termination of a certain business activity by a violator; e.g., meatpackers were ordered to cease engaging in the sale of meat at retail.

c. *Divestiture* involves the relinquishment of specified ownership interests. For example, DuPont was ordered to divest itself of General Motors stock; Sunkist Growers, Inc., was ordered to divest itself of all of its interest in its Arizona Products Division, which included a citrus processing plant and a cold storage facility.

FIGURE 17-2 SANCTIONS AND REMEDIES UNDER THE SHERMAN ACT

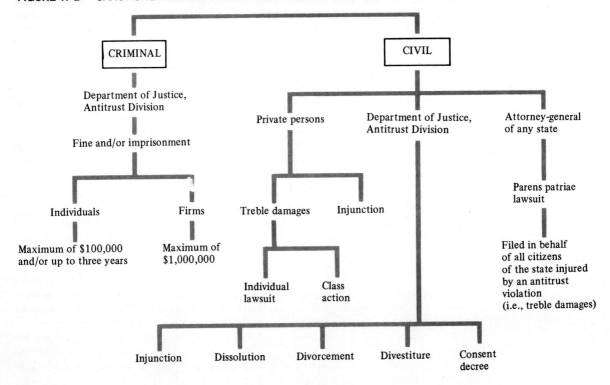

4. *Goods* that are subject to an illegal pricing arrangement may be *seized during shipment* in interstate commerce.
5. Under the Antitrust Improvement Act (1976), an amendment to section 7 of the Clayton Act, any state attorney general has the right to bring a *parens patriae lawsuit* for damages against violators of the Sherman Act in behalf of injured citizens (consumers) of his or her state.
6. *Corrective affirmative action.* A violator may be compelled to take action to eliminate the monopoly; i.e., to cease refusing to deal and sell to all customers in a relevant competitive market, or to share specialized knowledge or trade secrets with competitors.

THE CLAYTON ACT (1914): ANTICOMPETITIVE PRACTICES THAT MAY SUBSTANTIALLY LESSEN COMPETITION OR TEND TO CREATE A MONOPOLY

    VIII. The Clayton Act was enacted to supplement and strengthen the Sherman Act. It is designed to halt specific anticompetitive practices before they actually cause harm to competition. (See Figure 17-3.)

EXCLUSIVE-DEALING AND REQUIREMENTS CONTRACTS, TYING ARRANGEMENTS, AND RECIPROCITY

    IX. Section 3 of the Clayton Act prohibits exclusive-dealing and requirements contracts, tying arrangements, or reciprocity if there is *a reasonable probability that they will substantially lessen competition or tend to create a monopoly in a relevant competitive market.*

Section 3 "It shall be unlawful for any person engaged in commerce . . . to lease or make a sale or contract for sale of goods, . . . or other commodities, whether patented or unpatented . . . on the condition, agreement, or understanding that the lessee or purchaser thereof shall not use or deal in the goods . . . or other commodities of a competitor or competitors of the lessor or seller, where the effect of such lease, sale, or contract for sale or such condition, agreement, or understanding *may be* to substantially lessen competition or tend to create a monopoly in any line of commerce. . . ." [That is, a relevant competitive market.]

A. *Sale or lease of commodities.* This section applies only to the sale or lease of goods or other commodities, *but not to* the sale or lease of services. *Note:* If these types of arrangements involve services, they cannot be in violation of section 3 of the Clayton Act, but they may be found to be in violation of section 1 of the Sherman Act (i.e., a contract, combination, or conspiracy) and/or section 5 of the Federal Trade Commission Act (i.e., "an unfair method of competition"). If they involve goods, they are subject to attack under the provisions of all three acts.

B. *Exclusive dealing, tying contracts, requirements contracts, and reciprocity. Exclusive dealing* refers to a contract or an agreement between a supplier and a distributor wherein the latter commits itself to sell only the supplier's product line and no other. For example, Wilson contacts the school bookstore and agrees to supply them with sporting equipment under the condition that they do not sell or handle any other sporting goods. *Tying contracts* or agreements are those where a seller agrees to sell one product only on the condition that the buyer also purchases a different ("tied") product from the seller. Examples would be the ABC Company leasing patented tabulating machines on the condition that the lessees use only ABC punch cards in the machines; and X company leasing its salt-dispensing machines only if the lessees agree to buy all of the salt to be used in the machines from X company. A *requirements contract* binds a buyer or lessee to buy or lease all or part of its goods or other commodities from one seller or lessor during a specified period of time. *Reciprocity* occurs whenever a buyer agrees to purchase a seller's good or other commodity and the seller reciprocates by agreeing to purchase a

FIGURE 17-3   THE CLAYTON ACT

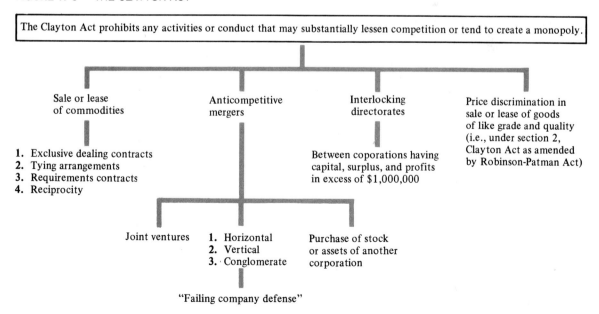

The Clayton Act prohibits any activities or conduct that may substantially lessen competition or tend to create a monopoly.

Sale or lease of commodities

1. Exclusive dealing contracts
2. Tying arrangements
3. Requirements contracts
4. Reciprocity

Anticompetitive mergers

Joint ventures

1. Horizontal
2. Vertical
3. Conglomerate

Purchase of stock or assets of another corporation

"Failing company defense"

Interlocking directorates

Between coporations having capital, surplus, and profits in excess of $1,000,000

Price discrimination in sale or lease of goods of like grade and quality (i.e., under section 2, Clayton Act as amended by Robinson-Patman Act) specified good or other commodity from the buyer; i.e., "I'll buy from you if you'll buy from me."

C. *"Substantially lessen competition" or "tend to create a monopoly"*. Violation of the provisions of section 3 of the Clayton Act occurs when these arrangements involve the sale or lease of goods or other commodities and raise a reasonable probability that they will either "substantially lessen competition" or "tend to create a monopoly." The tests used by the courts to determine a violation under this section are essentially the same as the rule-of-reason tests applied to determine a violation under section 1 of the Sherman Act (see IV-B-4 above for a detailed discussion of the rule-of-reason test).

   1. Such arrangements will have a reasonable probability of *"substantially lessening competition"* whenever:

      a. The supplier controls a substantial share (dominant market power) of the market. For example, a supplier sold 30 percent of the products in a relevant product market and had arrangements with 20 percent of the distributors in that market; and/or

      b. The distributor possesses a large (dominant) share in the relevant market; e.g., 10 percent of the total sales within the relevant market.

   2. These types of arrangements *"tend to create a monopoly"* whenever their effect is to establish monopoly power; i.e., the power to control prices or eliminate or preclude competitors from a relevant competitive market (see VI above for a discussion of activities and conduct that provide evidence of monopoly power).

D. *"Sale or lease."* An actual sale or lease arrangement must have been made. Goods shipped for resale to a consignee-agent under a "true" consignment-agency would not come within the provisions of section 3 of the Clayton Act because no sale or lease would be involved (see IV-B-3 above). However, a "true" consignment can be attacked under section 1 of the Sherman Act as a rule-of-reason restraint on trade or commerce.

PREMERGER NOTIFICATION

X. The Antitrust Improvement Act of 1976, an amendment to section 7 of the Clayton Act, requires that a *"target company"* (a firm with annual sales of $10 million or more) being acquired by a firm with annual sales of $100 million or more must notify the Antitrust Division of the Justice Department and the Federal Trade Commission (FTC) thirty days prior to the consummation of the acquisition. (See Figure 17-3.)

ANTICOMPETITIVE CORPORATE ACQUISITIONS AND MERGERS

XI. Under section 7 of the Clayton Act, a merger, whether horizontal, vertical, or conglomerate, is not illegal unless the effect of it may be "substantially to lessen competition" or "tend to create a monopoly." There need only be a reasonable probability that the merger will have anticompetitive effects on the relevant competitive market. A merger may also be found to violate the provisions of sections 1 and 2 of the Sherman Act. (See Figure 17-3.)

Section 7 "No corporation engaged in commerce shall acquire, . . . the whole or any part of the *stock . . . or assets* of another corporation engaged also in commerce, where in any line of commerce in any section of the country, the effect of such acquisition may be substantially to lessen competition, or to tend to create a monopoly.

This section shall not apply to corporations purchasing such stock solely for investment . . ."

Note: This section was amended in 1950 by the Celler-Kefauver Act to include the assets of another company, not just the stock. (See Figure 17-3.)

A. A merger is the acquisition by one corporation of the *assets or stock* of another, independent corporation where the acquired corporation becomes controlled by the acquirer. A merger may be horizontal, vertical, or conglomerate.

    1. A *horizontal merger* combines two or more competing firms that are at the same level of economic activity (sell the same product line) and compete in the same geographic area, e.g., a combination of two competing clothing manufacturers.

    2. A *vertical merger* is a combination of two or more firms that are engaged at different levels of economic activity, that is, two companies that have a buyer-seller relationship. Examples include an automobile manufacturer that acquires control of a fabric manufacturer and a shoe manufacturer that acquires a retail shoe chain.

    3. A *conglomerate merger* combines two or more firms that are neither competitive nor vertically related, that is, they sell in different product markets. For example, a cigarette manufacturer acquires a food distributor.

B. When the legality of a *horizontal merger* is questioned, the court will look at the following factors to determine whether or not the merger is in violation of section 7 of the Clayton Act. *Note:* The Justice Department, Antitrust Division, considers a market "highly concentrated" whenever shares of the four largest firms in that market equal 75 percent or more.

    1. *Largeness of the size of the resulting market share* caused by the merger. For example, a merger of two or more firms that possess significant existing market shares results in dominance of the relevant competitive market.

    2. If a *merger results in a strong trend toward industry concentration*, it will most likely be held to be illegal, even though the resulting market share is not large. For example, Von's Grocery, the third largest grocery chain in Los Angeles, California, merged with Shopping Bag Food Stores, the sixth largest retail grocery chain. The market share resulting from the merger was approximately 7 percent. The court noted that the number of grocery chains was increasing, while the number of small, independent grocery stores was decreasing in the relevant competitive market, indicating a trend toward concentration and ordered divestiture.

    3. If a *merger takes place in an already too concentrated industry and has the effect of eliminating a competitor*, the merger will probably be held to be illegal even though the merger added only an insignificant market share to the larger company. For example, Alcoa Aluminum, a large company merged with Rome Corporation, a relatively small company. The resulting increase of market share to Alcoa would have been approximately 1.3 percent. The court held the merger to be illegal because it would have the effect of eliminating a potential competitor (Rome Corporation) in an already concentrated market.

C. In a *vertical merger*, if the effect is that it may reduce (i.e., foreclose or may foreclose) or does reduce the available markets or supplies for others in the industry, the merger will be unlawful. If one company acquires another for the sole purpose of forcing it to buy its products from the parent company, the merger will be deemed illegal. Consolidated Foods sought to merge with Gentry, a processor of onion and garlic food products. The courts prohibited the merger on the grounds that all Consolidated Food stores would sell only Gentry's onion and garlic food products, thus eliminating an outlet for other onion and garlic food processors. In addition to foreclosure or the possibility of *foreclosure of competitors* from the relevant market, the following factors are also considered by the courts:

1. Trend toward industry concentration;
2. Percentage of the relevant market involved; and
3. Motive of the acquirer; i.e., was it predatory or for a bona fide business motive?

D. With respect to *conglomerate mergers*, a large firm will not be permitted to acquire a firm in a highly concentrated industry if the effect would be to provide already existing firms with a larger, more powerful competitor. When Procter & Gamble tried to acquire the Clorox Company (which controlled 50 percent of the bleach sales), the court ruled it illegal. It warned that a merger of this type would transform the liquid bleach industry into an arena of big business competition, that Procter & Gamble would use its name and power to strengthen Clorox, thereby creating a barrier for entry by new competitors, and that existing bleach producers in the relevant competitive market would possibly be put out of business.

E. *Joint ventures* are also subject to the provisions of section 7 of the Clayton Act. A joint venture will be held illegal if there is reasonable probability that it will lessen competition or tend to create a monopoly in a relevant competitive market. A joint venture may also be in violation of the Sherman Act.

F. *The "failing company" defense.* A merger of large companies may be held to be legal even if it will substantially lessen competition, if its purpose is to save a company from business failure. The company acquired must be in imminent danger of financial failure and have no other prospective purchaser of its shares of stock.

INTERLOCKING DIRECTORATES

XII. Section 8 prohibits *interlocking directorates* between ". . . two or more corporations, any one of which has capital, surplus, and undivided profits aggregating more than $1,000,000 engaged in whole or part in commerce. . ." where ". . . the elimination of competition by agreement between them would constitute a violation of any of the provisions of any of the antitrust laws." For example, the FTC adopted a consent order barring an individual from serving on the board of directors of Chrysler Corporation and General Electric Company, which were competing manufacturers of air conditioners. (See Figure 17-3.)

THE ROBINSON-PATMAN ACT (1936)
(An amendment to Section 2 of the Clayton Act)

XIII. *Price discrimination.* Section 2 of the Clayton Act as amended by the Robinson-Patman Act provides that it is a violation for any seller engaged in commerce to discriminate directly or indirectly in price between different buyers of commodities (tangible personal property, i.e., goods or "products") of like grade and quality where the effect may be to substantially lessen competition or tend to create a monopoly in a relevant competitive market. The act *does not* apply to the sale of services or intangible personal property. (See Figure 17-4.)

A. *Primary-line and secondary-line price discrimination.* Price discrimination most frequently occurs at two levels of competition; that is, the "primary-line" (i.e., seller's level) or the "secondary-line" (i.e., buyer's level).

1. *Primary-line* (seller's level) (supplier and its competitors) price discrimination occurs when a seller, who competes in several marketing areas, sells at a lower price in only one of the market areas; i.e., the price of the same commodity charged by the same seller is higher in one relevant competitive market than it is in another. For example, seller 1 sells its product in two market areas, Detroit and Chicago. Seller 2 sells a like grade and quality product in Chicago. Seller 1 reduced the price of its product sold in Chicago but did not reduce the price of its product sold in Detroit.

2. *Secondary-line* (buyer's level) (buyer and its competitors) price discrimination occurs when a seller sells a product of like grade and quality at different prices to competing buyers in the same relevant competitive market. For example, a supplier charges a different price for the same product to a small independent than to a large chain within the same market.

B. *Persons covered.* Sellers as well as buyers are covered by the act.

    1. Sellers (suppliers) may not sell at unjustified discriminatory prices.

    2. Buyers may not knowingly induce or coerce unjustified discriminatory prices from the seller (supplier). For example, a retailer induced a manufacturer to offer a discriminatory price by falsely representing that it was necessary to meet a competitor's low price.

C. *Subject matter covered.* "Commodities of like grade and quality."

    1. *Commodities* includes tangible personal property, such as goods or products. It does not include services or intangible personal property; e.g., TV advertising time is not a commodity.

    2. *Like grade and quality* means two or more commodities that are either physically (form as well as chemistry) *or* commercially identical.

FIGURE 17-4   ROBINSON-PATMAN ACT (AN AMENDMENT TO THE CLAYTON ACT)

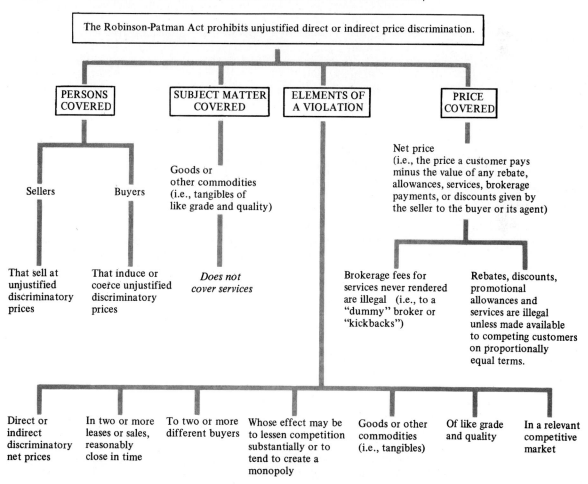

a. Labels, brands, or advertisements will not differentiate physically identical products. For example, Borden Company sold its milk nationally under its own label. It also sold the same milk to chain stores to be sold under their private labels, at a cheaper price. The court held that all of the milk sold was of "like grade and quality."

b. If the products are made from different materials or require different processes, they are not of "like kind and quality." For example, specially manufactured automobiles sold with customer-designated equipment, parts, or sizes.

D. *Price.* The price to be compared is the *net price* charged to the buyer (customer). It is the actual price paid by the buyer less the value of any rebates, allowances, services, discounts, and brokerage payments received by the buyer or its agent.

1. Brokerage fee payments for services never rendered are illegal under the act. For example, payments to a "dummy" broker or "kickbacks" to the buyer or its agent (see XV-A below).

2. Promotional rebates, allowances, discounts, or services are also illegal if they are not made available to competing buyers on proportionately equal terms (see XV-B below).

E. *"Direct price discrimination"* occurs when the seller unjustifiably charges a different price for the "same" product in separate sales reasonably close in time to two or more buyers.

F. *"Indirect price discrimination"* occurs when a seller unjustifiably grants rebates, discounts, allowances, or services to a buyer, but does not make them available to competing buyers on proportionately equal terms; e.g., free goods, favorable credit terms, or free delivery.

G. *Elements of illegal price discrimination:*

1. Unjustified direct or indirect discriminatory prices;

2. Charged in two or more different sales reasonably close in time;

3. Of commodities;

4. Of like grade and quality;

5. To two or more buyers;

6. In a relevant competitive market;

7. The effect of which may be to lessen competition, tend to create a monopoly, or injure, destroy, or prevent competition;

8. In "any line of commerce;" i.e., "in interstate commerce."

Note: The intent (illegal) to discriminate is not an essential element. It need only be established that a seller *unjustifiably* charged one or more buyers a different price.

JUSTIFICATIONS FOR PRICE DISCRIMINATION

XIV. Not all price discriminations under the Robinson-Patman Act are illegal. A seller may successfully assert any one of the following *justifications (i.e., defenses) for a price differential* between different buyers. (See Figure 17-5.)

A. *Nonexistence of price discrimination.* Proof of the nonexistence (absence) of any one of the elements of a prohibited price discrimination is a justification.

B. *Cost justification.* Price differentials based on differences in the cost of manufacture, sale, or delivery is justified if the differences in cost result from differences in methods or quantities.

1. The burden of proving the defense is upon the seller.

2. This defense is not available to a *criminal* charge of illegal brokerage payments, promotional services, or discrimination in advertising (see XVI-A below).

Nonexistence of any one of the elements of price discrimination	Cost justification (Price differential is due to a difference in the seller's cost of manufacture, sale or delivery resulting from different methods or quantities.)	Made in good faith to meet equally low price of a competitor	Distress sales (Price differential is due to adverse market conditions, inherent nature of the goods, or an adverse change in the marketability of the goods involved, or sale pursuant to court order.)

C. *Good faith meeting of equally low prices of competitors.*

   1. It is not a defense for a firm to follow a competitor's clearly unlawful pricing scheme.

   2. The defense applies only to meeting the price of the competitor, not to lowering the price below that charged by the competitor.

   3. The defense is good whether the seller is trying to avoid losing a customer or attempting to gain customers away from a competitor.

D. *Change in the market for or marketability of commodities.* A seller may in good faith change its prices in response to changing market conditions. Some of these changing market conditions are as follows:

   1. Actual or threatened deterioration of perishable commodities.

   2. Obsolescence of seasonal commodities.

   3. Distress (mandatory) sales under court order.

   4. Sales in good faith in discontinuance of business in goods concerned, e.g., a bulk sale.

BROKER'S FEES AND PROMOTIONAL ALLOWANCES AND SERVICES

XV. In addition to actual price discrimination, the Robinson-Patman Act prohibits specified activities or conduct that do not appear to be discriminatory on their face but do result in price discrimination (i.e., indirect price discrimination).

   A. *Brokerage payments.* Section 2(c) of the act prohibits any person to pay or receive any compensation, allowance, or discount unless the latter was paid or received for services actually rendered in connection with the sale or purchase of goods.

   1. These types of payments, allowances, or discounts are prohibited when they are paid to the buyer or to any person controlled directly or indirectly by the buyer, regardless of whether or not the payment does, in fact, ever reach the buyer. For example, *dummy brokerage*. A "dummy" broker is one controlled by the buyer that receives payments from a seller for fictitious services, and subsequently passes these payments on to the buyer. As another example, a seller received the full purchase price from the buyer, but subsequently returned ("kickbacks") a portion of that price to the buyer or a person under its control.

   2. True *functional discounts* are not prohibited. These are discounts granted to the buyer in exchange for the buyer's performance of one or more *of the seller's marketing functions*, e.g., warehousing, packaging, or transportation.

   3. Brokerage payments to third-party *independent* brokers for services rendered are not prohibited.

   4. No effect on competition need be shown to establish a violation. This is in effect a per se violation.

B. *Promotional (i.e., advertising) allowances and services:*

    1. It is unlawful for any seller (supplier) to:

        a. Make any payment to a buyer or its agent for services or facilities provided by the buyer (customer) in promoting the sale of goods; or

        b. To provide promotional services and facilities to a buyer (customer); *unless*

        c. Such payments, services, and facilities are "made available" to all other buyers (customers) on "proportionately equal terms."

    2. This is also, in effect, a per se violation because no effect on competition need be proved.

    3. *"Services"* and *"facilities"* include the following:

        a. Books of coupons that offer one-third price discounts;

        b. Catalogs, display equipment, or product demonstrators;

        c. Advertising; e.g., clocks that prominently display the name of a beer and its manufacturer;

        d. Contests and prizes.

    4. *"Payments"* include rebates and discounts.

    5. *"Made available"* on *"proportionately equal terms."*

        a. "Made available" means uniformly communicated and offered to buyers (customers).

        b. Payments, services, or facilities determined by relative volume of sales are on a proportional basis. For example, a co-op advertising plan wherein the seller (supplier) agrees to reimburse its buyers (customers) at a differing rate based on the amount of product sold by the customer and the type of advertising used is held to be proportionately equal. As another example, quantity discounts based on the size of each individual sale rather than the cumulative total of sales over a specified period of time would also be "proportionately equal."

SANCTIONS AND REMEDIES UNDER THE CLAYTON ACT AND ITS AMENDMENTS

  XVI. The Clayton Act as amended by the Robinson-Patman Act provides both criminal and civil sanctions and remedies. (See Figure 17-6.)

    A. *Criminal sanctions.* The only criminal violations under the Clayton Act as amended are imposed by the Robinson-Patman Act. All other violations of the Clayton Act as amended are civil in nature. Under section 3 of the Robinson-Patman Act a violator may be fined a maximum of $5,000 and/or be imprisoned for up to one year for the following criminal conduct:

        1. *Knowingly* take part in a price discrimination against a competitor;

        2. To *intentionally* take part or assist in territorial price discrimination *for the purpose of* destroying competition or eliminating a competitor; or

        3. To sell at unreasonably low prices, i.e., *"predatory" prices for the purpose of* destroying competition or eliminating a competitor.

    B. *Civil remedies.* With the following exception, the same civil remedies available to private persons, the Department of Justice, Antitrust Division, or the Federal Trade Commission (FTC) under the Sherman Act are also available for violations under the Clayton Act:

        1. Seizure of goods shipped in interstate commerce.

THE FEDERAL TRADE COMMISSION ACT (1914)

  XVII. *Creation and jurisdiction of the Federal Trade Commission (FTC).* The Federal Trade Commission Act, as amended, created the Federal Trade Commission (FTC) and gave

FIGURE 17-6   SANCTIONS AND REMEDIES UNDER THE CLAYTON ACT

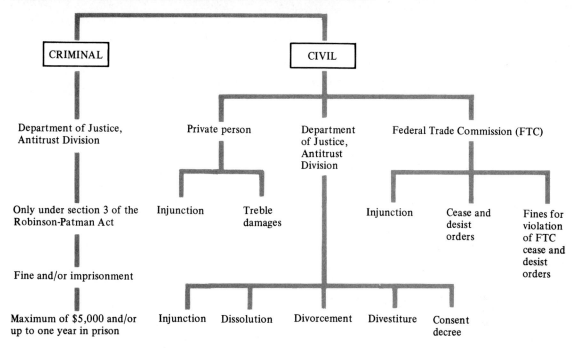

it broad investigative, rule-making, and regulatory power. The FTC's primary responsibility is to aid the Department of Justice, Antitrust Division, in its enforcement of the policies set forth in the Clayton Act, as amended, and the Federal Trade Commission Act, as amended. The FTC *does not* have criminal enforcement authority. Its authority is entirely civil in nature (see also XVIII-B below).

A. *Powers of the Federal Trade Commission (FTC).* The Federal Trade Commission Act, as amended, gave the FTC *exclusive* power to act against "unfair methods of competition" and "unfair or deceptive acts or practices" in or affecting interstate commerce. The FTC has sole enforcement authority of the provisions of the Federal Trade Commission Act. (See Figure 17-7.)

FIGURE 17-7   SANCTIONS AND REMEDIES UNDER THE FEDERAL TRADE COMMISSION ACT

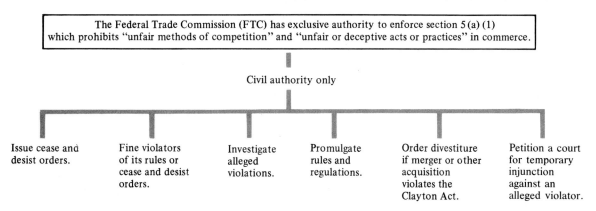

1. *Unfair methods of competition.* Unfair methods of competition include any activities or conduct that would be in violation of the Sherman Act and the Clayton Act, as amended. Unfair methods of competition include the following: A firm or group of firms steals a competitor's business secrets, spreads false rumors about its credit, or induces or coerces its customers to breach their contracts with competitors.
2. *Unfair or deceptive acts or practices.* This standard relates primarily to the FTC's civil authority in the area of consumer protection enforcement. The FTC's role in the area of consumer protection was discussed in Chapter 9.

B. For remedies for violation of the Federal Trade Commission Act, see XVIII-B below.

ENFORCEMENT OF ANTITRUST LAWS

XVIII. Enforcement of federal antitrust laws may be initiated either by the Antitrust Division of the Department of Justice or by the Federal Trade Commission (FTC). (See Figure 17-8.)

A. The *Antitrust Division of the Department of Justice* can institute either civil or criminal proceedings (file lawsuits) against alleged violators of any federal antitrust law.
1. *Civil proceedings* are filed for the purposes of obtaining either an injunction or a consent decree. (A *consent decree* is a court's acceptance of a legal settlement between an alleged violator and the Justice Department wherein the alleged violator does not plead guilty but promises to refrain from specified activities.)
2. *Criminal proceedings* are filed to obtain a court's imposition of a monetary fine and/or imprisonment of a violator.
3. The Department of Justice has *exclusive* responsibility to enforce the provisions of the Sherman Act *and concurrent* responsibility with the Federal Trade Commission (FTC) to enforce the Clayton Act, as amended.

B. *The Federal Trade Commission (FTC)*, a federal administrative agency, has civil enforcement authority under the provisions of the Clayton Act, as amended, Federal Trade Commission Act, as amended, and numerous other regulatory statutes relating to businesses and consumers. It does *not* have criminal enforcement au-

FIGURE 17-8   ENFORCEMENT OF FEDERAL ANTITRUST LAWS

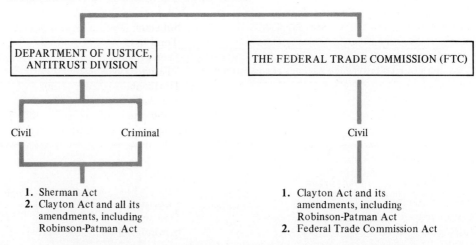

DEPARTMENT OF JUSTICE, ANTITRUST DIVISION

THE FEDERAL TRADE COMMISSION (FTC)

Civil   Criminal   Civil

1. Sherman Act
2. Clayton Act and all its amendments, including Robinson-Patman Act

1. Clayton Act and its amendments, including Robinson-Patman Act
2. Federal Trade Commission Act

thority. The FTC has the *exclusive* jurisdiction to enforce the provisions of the Federal Trade Commission Act, as amended. In the exercise of its duties to enforce the antitrust policies set forth in the Clayton Act and the Federal Trade Commission Act, the FTC can exercise the powers listed below:

1. *Investigate* alleged violations;
2. *Issue cease and desist orders* against violators of FTC trade regulations (rules);
3. *Promulgate rules* (trade regulations);
4. *Fine persons or entities* that violate its cease and desist orders or a FTC trade regulation (rule);
5. *Order divestiture;*
6. *Petition a court for a temporary injunction* against an alleged violator.

C. *A private citizen* who has been financially injured as a result of a violation may file a lawsuit individually or by a class action to recover treble damages from a violator of the Sherman Act or the Clayton Act, as amended.

D. Any *state attorney general* under the Antitrust Improvement Act of 1976, has the right to file a parens patriae (a form of class action) lawsuit, in behalf of citizens of his or her state, against persons, entities, or associations alleged to be in violation of the provisions of the Sherman Act.

SELF-QUIZ

To check your understanding of the key words and concepts and the accuracy of your answers to the questions, refer to the text material as referenced by page number.

KEY WORDS AND CONCEPTS

QUESTIONS

1. Describe different types of price fixing. **(496)**
2. The presidents of four leading manufacturing companies have decided to eliminate "senseless price cutting." They have established, through verbal agreement, price leadership rotation. What are the legal implications of this agreement? **(496)**
3. Southdown wishes to acquire a controlling share of Custer Company, one of its leading competitors. Detail the legal complications that may arise with this merger. What would the situation have to be for this merger to be deemed legal? **(506)**
4. Are interlocking directorates between corporations illegal per se? **(508)**
5. Boyle Manufacturing Company sells its products at different prices all over the country. Dis-

cuss situations in which price discrimination may be deemed legal or illegal. **(508)**
6. Define "unfair methods of competition" under the Federal Trade Commission Act and give several examples of each. **(514)**
7. What remedies are available to government and to a private person against a person or entity found in violation of:
   a. Sherman Act **(503)**
   b. Clayton Act **(512)**
   c. Robinson-Patman Act **(512)**
   d. Federal Trade Commission Act **(513)**
8. Which two agencies have been charged with the enforcement of federal antitrust laws? **(514)**
9. What types of arrangements or agreements may be subject to attack under the Sherman Act, Clayton Act, and the Federal Trade Commission Act? Identify the grounds upon which these contracts could be attacked under each of the three statutes. **(499, 505)**
10. Explain the merger prenotification provision of the Antitrust Improvement Act of 1976. **(506)**
11. Are joint ventures subject to the merger provision of the Clayton Act? Why? **(506)**; Sherman Act? **(495)**
12. List the defenses a seller legally may assert to justify discriminatory price differentials in the sale of goods. **(510)**
13. Identify the parties or agencies who may initiate civil or criminal enforcement of federal antitrust laws. **(514)**
14. List and explain each of the enforcement powers of the FTC. **(515)**

SELECTED QUESTIONS AND UNOFFICIAL ANSWERS

OBJECTIVE QUESTIONS

Select the best answer for each of the following items. Mark only one answer for each item. Answer all items.

MAY 1981

55. The Aden Corporation entered into its standard dealership contract with the Downtown Corporation. The contract provided Downtown with an exclusive right to sell Aden's products in Columbia County. Which of the following provisions, if included as a part of the contract, will *not* create a potential antitrust problem?

a. Aden retains all rights, title, and interest to the goods shipped to Downtown.
b. Downtown agrees to certain resale price ranges stipulated by Aden.
c. Downtown may *not* sell any product which Aden Corporation designates as being competitive with its products.
d. Downtown agrees *not* to sell to certain retailers designated by Aden as price cutters.

56. The Radiant Furnace Company entered into agreements with retail merchants whereby they agreed not to sell beneath Radiant's minimum "suggested" retail price of $850 in exchange for

Radiant's agreeing not to sell its furnaces at retail in their respective territories. The agreement does not preclude the retail merchants from selling competing furnaces. What is the legal status of the agreement?

a. It is illegal even though the price fixed is reasonable.

b. It is legal if the product is a trade name or trademarked item.

c. It is legal if the power to fix maximum prices is *not* relinquished.

d. It is illegal unless it can be shown that the parties to the agreement were preventing cutthroat competition.

57. Global Reproductions, Inc., makes and sells high quality, expensive lithographs of the works of famous artists. It sells to art wholesalers throughout the United States. It requires that its wholesalers not purchase lithographs of competing companies during the three-year duration of the contract. They may sell all other types of pictures, including oil, watercolor and charcoal. The Federal Trade Commission has attacked the legality of this exclusive dealing arrangement. This exclusive dealing arrangement

a. Is legal *per se* since its duration is less than five years.

b. Could be found to be illegal under the Sherman, Clayton, and Federal Trade Commission Acts.

c. Will be tested under the rule of reason, and only if found to be unreasonable, will be declared illegal.

d. Is legal since the wholesalers are permitted to sell all other types of pictures.

NOVEMBER 1980

18. Divco Corporation manufactured and sold a high quality line of distinctive calculators. In order to fully realize the potential of the products, it decided to engage in a franchising arrangement with selected outlets throughout the country. Its basic arrangement was to grant to each dealer the exclusive right to sell in a designated area and each dealer agreed not to sell outside its allotted geographic area. Which of the following *best* describes the status of the law?

a. Such arrangements are *per se* illegal.

b. Divco *must* sell on consignment, thereby retaining title, in order to avoid illegality.

c. Such franchising arrangements will be tested

under the rule of reason and as long as they are found to be reasonable they are legal.

d. Such arrangements are specifically declared to be illegal under existing antitrust statutes.

MAY 1980

1. Jay Manufacturing Company sells high quality, high-priced lawn mowers to retailers throughout the United States. Jay unilaterally announced suggested retail prices in its advertisements. Jay also informed retailers that its products would not be sold to them if the retailers used them as "loss leaders" or "come-ons." There was no requirement that any retailer agree to sell at the suggested prices or refrain from selling at whatever price they wished. Monroe Sales, Inc., a large home supply discounter, persistently engaged in loss-leader selling of the Jay mower. Jay has terminated sales to Monroe and declined to do any further business with it. Monroe claims that Jay has violated the antitrust laws. Under the circumstances, which is a correct statement?

a. The arrangement in question is an illegal joint boycott.

b. The arrangement in question amounts to price-fixing and is illegal per se.

c. The mere unilateral refusal to deal with Monroe is *not* illegal under antitrust laws.

d. Even if it were found that in fact the overwhelming preponderance of retailers had willingly agreed to follow the suggested prices, Jay would *not* have violated antitrust laws.

2. Congress recently amended the antitrust laws to provide stiffer penalties and increased sanctions for violation of the various acts' provisions. Which of the following represents an *incorrect* statement of the changed provisions?

a. The maximum fine for corporations was increased to one million dollars.

b. Violations of the Sherman Act are now classified as felonies with a maximum prison term of 3 years.

c. Punitive damages obtainable in private antitrust actions have been increased from 3 times to 5 times actual damages.

d. The maximum fine for individuals has been increased to $100,000.

4. Marble Manufacturing, Inc., produces a high quality, trademarked line of distinctive clocks which it sells to selected wholesalers and retailers. The clocks are sold in free and open competition with the clocks of many other manufacturers. The selection of the wholesalers and retailers is dependent upon their agreeing to the pricing policies of Marble. Several other manufacturers also have similar marketing arrangements. The above-described marketing arrangement is

a. Legal, in that Marble is merely "meeting the competition" of other clock manufacturers.

b. Legal, since it is a permissible resale price maintenance agreement.

c. Fully subject to the general antitrust prohibitions against price fixing.

d. To be tested under the rule of reason, since the agreement is not among competitors but rather between a supplier and its customers.

5. The Duplex Corporation has been charged by the United States Justice Department with an "attempt to monopolize" the duplex industry. In defending itself against such a charge, Duplex will prevail if it can establish

a. It had *no* intent to monopolize the duplex industry.

b. Its percentage share of the relevant market was less than 50%.

c. Its activities do *not* constitute an unreasonable restraint of trade.

d. It does *not* have monopoly power.

NOVEMBER 1979

6. The Flick Corporation sold various interrelated products that it manufactured. One of the items was manufactured almost exclusively by Flick and sold throughout the United States. Flick realized the importance of this product to its purchasers and decided to capitalize on the situation by requiring all purchasers to take at least two other products in order to obtain the item over which it has almost complete market control. At Flick's spring sales meeting, its president informed the entire sales force that they were to henceforth sell only to those customers who agreed to take the additional products. As a result of this plan, gross sales of the additional items increased by more than $1 million. Which of the following *best* describes the legality of the above situation?

a. It is illegal only if the products are patented products.

b. It is an illegal tying arrangement.

c. It is legal as long as the price charged to retailers for the other products is competitive.

d. It is legal if the retailers do *not* complain about purchasing the other products.

21. Wanton Corporation, its president, and several other officers of the corporation are found guilty of conspiring with its major competitor to fix prices. Which of the following sanctions would *not* be applicable under federal antitrust laws?

a. Suspension of corporate right to engage in interstate commerce for *not* more than one year.

b. Treble damages.

c. Seizure of Wanton's property illegally shipped in interstate commerce.

d. Fines against Wanton and fines and imprisonment of its president and officers.

34. Which of the following activities engaged in by a corporation will *not* be deemed illegal under the antitrust law?

a. A price-fixing agreement with competitors aimed at lowering prices to a reasonable level.

b. The charging of a price aimed at maximizing its profits based upon economic analysis of supply and demand for its products.

c. Participating in a plan suggested by the trade association aimed at territorial allocations of markets to cut costs.

d. The payment of brokerage commissions to the purchasers of goods.

35. The Donner Corporation has obtained a patent on a revolutionary coin-operated washing machine. It is far superior to the existing machines currently in use. Which of the following actions taken by Donner will *not* result in a violation of federal antitrust law?

a. Maintaining the resale price for machines it sells to distributors.

b. Obtaining a near total monopolization of the market as a result of the patent.

c. Requiring the purchasers of the machines to buy from Donner all their other commonplace supplies connected with the use of the machine.

d. Joining in a boycott with other appliance manufacturers to eliminate a troublesome discount distributor.

36. Expansion Corporation is an aggressive, large-sized conglomerate. It is seeking to obtain control of several additional corporations including Resistance Corporation. Expansion does *not* currently buy from, sell to, or compete with Resistance. Which of the following statements applies to this proposed takeover?

a. Since Expansion does *not* buy from, sell to, or compete with Resistance, antitrust laws do *not* apply.

b. If Expansion can consummate the acquisition before there is an objection to it, the acquisition can *not* subsequently be set aside.

c. The acquisition is likely to be declared illegal if there will be reciprocal buying and there is a likelihood that other entrants into the market would be precluded.

d. The acquisition is legal on its face if there will be cost efficiency resulting from combined marketing and advertising.

37. The Justice Department is contemplating commencing an action against Lion Corporation for monopolizing the off-shore drilling business in violation of Section 2 of the Sherman Act. Which of the following would be Lion's *best* defense against such an action?

a. Since the drilling is off-shore, interstate commerce is not involved.

b. The monopoly was originally the result of a long since expired patent.

c. Lion had *no* specific wrongful intent to monopolize.

d. Lion's market share is such that it does *not* have the power to fix prices or to exclude competitors.

42. Nicks is a troublesome chain store furniture dealer. He constantly engaged in price cutting on widely advertised name products in order to lure customers to his store so that he could sell them other products. The "big three" manufacturers agreed that Nicks could no longer sell their products unless he ceased and desisted from such practices. Nicks refused and the three manufacturers promptly cut off his supply of their branded products. Which of the following is a correct statement?

a. Since a businessman has the freedom to choose with whom he will deal, the conduct in question is *not* illegal under the antitrust laws.

b. If the harm to the public was minor, and the products were readily available from other appliance dealers in a market marked by free and open competition, there would be *no* violation of the law.

c. The conduct described is a joint boycott, and as such is illegal per se.

d. Since the conduct described was unilateral, and Nicks did *not* agree to stop his price cutting, the manufacturers' conduct is legal.

Answers to Objective Questions

May 1981		November 1979	
55. a	**57.** b	**6.** b	**36.** c
56. a		**21.** a	**37.** d
		34. b	**42.** c
November 1980		**35.** b	
18. c			
May 1980			
1. c	**4.** c		
2. c	**5.** a		

Explanation of Answers to Objective Questions

MAY 1981

55. (a) This agreement is an example of vertical territorial allocation which is judged under the rule of reason. The fact Aden retains title to the goods would not create a potential antitrust problem but serve to substantiate the fact that the rule of reason (i.e., the agreement can be legally justified) should be applied. Answer (b) is incorrect because the provision would qualify as vertical price fixing which is illegal per se (i.e., no legal justification). Answer (c) is incorrect because the provision would create an exclusive dealing contract which could result in an antitrust violation. Answer (d) is incorrect because the provision would result in the creation of a joint boycott which is illegal per se.

56. (a) The agreement is an example of vertical price fixing which is illegal per se under the Sherman Act. This means there is no legal justification for entering into this type of agreement. Proof of engaging in this type of activity is sufficient to constitute a violation, even though the price charged is reasonable. Such activity had been allowed under the Fair Trade laws but these laws were recently repealed. Answers (b), (c) and (d) are all incorrect because they do not state legal justification for entering a vertical price fixing agreement.

57. (b) The contract provision described in the question is an exclusive dealing arrangement. While the Clayton Act is usually referred to in determining the legality of such arrangements, both the Sherman and Federal Trade Commission Acts contain provisions governing exclusive dealings contracts. Basically, the criterion used to judge the legality of this type of contract is one of quantitative substantiality, i.e., the contract provision will be judged according to objective standards such as the percentage of market control gained through such restrictions of the dollar amount of transactions involved (e.g., contracts involving $500,000 are normally considered to be illegal automatically). Since these standards are objective in nature, use of the rule of reason answer (c) is normally not accepted as justification once the dollar or percentage limits are exceeded. Answer (a) is incorrect as exclusive dealings contracts are not illegal per se under the various Acts, and the duration of a contract provision will not determine whether or not an agreement is illegal per se. Answer (d) is incorrect because whether the wholesalers are allowed to sell other pictures would be irrelevant in deciding whether this exclusive dealing contract restricts competition in lithographs.

NOVEMBER 1980

18. (c) Under a secret change in antitrust law an agreement between a manufacturer (franchiser) and a dealer (franchisee) which gives the dealer an exclusive right to sell in a designated area and each dealer agrees not to sell outside this area is tested under the rule of reason. In the past, such franchising agreements creating vertical territorial limitations were illegal per se unless the franchiser retained title to the goods involved. However, that has been changed by a recent supreme court ruling, making answer (c) correct.

MAY 1980

1. (c) A joint boycott requires that two or more parties agree not to deal with a third party. The mere unilateral refusal to deal with Monroe would not be a joint boycott under the provisions of the Sherman Antitrust Act. Since there is no agreement to fix prices between Monroe and Jay this activity is not a per se violation. However, if an overwhelming preponderance of the retailers had agreed to follow the price, then there would be an agreement that constituted price fixing, which is illegal per se.

2. (c) Answer (c) is the correct answer because

treble damages is still an appropriate sanction under the antitrust laws. Answers (a), (b), and (d) are incorrect because these state sanctions presently existing under the antitrust laws.

4. (c) Marble's refusal to sell to retailers who do not follow Marble's pricing policy is sufficient activity to constitute price fixing, an illegal per se violation of the Sherman Antitrust Act. Answer (a) is incorrect because price fixing is an illegal per se violation meaning that there is no justification (meeting the competition) for engaging in such activity. Answers (b) and (d) are incorrect because vertical price fixing (resale price maintenance agreement) is also illegal per se since the repeal of the Miller-Tydings Act no longer allows fair trade laws. Thus the rule of reason does not apply to this type of violation.

5. (a) The charge is "an attempt to monopolize," not to create a monopoly. Therefore, the government will need to show such intent on the part of Duplex. The fact that Duplex has a small percentage of the relevant market (answer (b)) or that the corporation cannot control prices or exclude competition (monopolistic powers) (answer (d)) would not be valid defenses. The charge pertains to Section 2, not Section 1, of the Sherman Antitrust Act; therefore the fact that Duplex's activities do not constitute an unreasonable restraint of trade would not be a proper defense.

NOVEMBER 1979

6. (b) The requirement by the Flick Corporation that its customers buy at least 2 products in order to obtain the item they want is an illegal tying arrangement. Answer (a) is incorrect because illegal tying arrangements are determined on the basis of economic policy and are not affected by whether the products are patented or not. Answer (c) is incorrect because under the antitrust laws, it is immaterial that prices are competitive under an otherwise illegal tying arrangement. Generally, the courts treat tying arrangements as illegal per se so long as the dollar volume is not insignificant, i.e., where the seller has sufficient economic power to impose an appreciable restraint on free competition in the tied product. Answer (d) is incorrect because the illegality is based on the above explanation and not on whether the retailers complain about the tying arrangement.

21. (a) The suspension of a corporation's right to engage in interstate commerce as a result of violations of the antitrust act is not one of the authorized sanctions under federal antitrust laws. Treble damages as in answer (b) are available to injured parties. Answer (c), seizure of property being illegally shipped in interstate commerce in violation of the antitrust laws, is also an authorized sanction. Likewise, fine and imprisonment of the corporation's officers, as in answer (d), are also authorized sanctions.

34. (b) It is permissible under the antitrust laws for a corporation to charge a price aimed at maximizing profits based upon economic analysis of supply and demand. Answer (a) is illegal: price fixing is a per se violation of the antitrust laws, even if it results in lower prices. Answer (c) also is a violation of the antitrust laws: participation in a plan of allocating sales market. The fact that it was actually offered by a trade association is immaterial. Answer (d), the payment of brokerage commissions to purchasers of goods, is generally deemed to be a violation of the Robinson-Patman Act. The effect of such rebates constitutes price discrimination between purchasers.

35. (b) The obtaining of a near total monopoly of a market for a particular product as a result of a patent does not generally result in violation of the federal antitrust laws. The issuance of the patent, which is an exception to the antitrust laws, results in the monopoly being "thrust upon" the patent holder. Answer (a) is incorrect because an attempt by a seller to maintain the resale price for his product is a violation of the antitrust laws. Answer (c) is incorrect because it is an illegal tying arrangement to require the purchasers to buy all their commonplace supplies as a condition for obtaining the desired machines. Answer (d) is incorrect because joint boycotts aimed at excluding certain troublesome buyers from the market restrain trade and are per se illegal activities.

36. (c) Even though Expansion Corporation does not currently buy from, sell to, or compete with Resistance Corporation, the acquisition is likely to be declared illegal if there will be reciprocal buying and other entrants into the market may be precluded. The antimerger section of the Clayton Act prohibits mergers which will substantially lessen competition or tend to create a monopoly. Answer (a) is incorrect because the fact that Expansion and

Reliance do not do business with each other does not mean that the antitrust laws do not apply. Section 7 of the Clayton Act is intended to cope with monopolistic trends in their incipiency stage before Sherman Act violations occur. Answer (b) is incorrect because the government may proceed against a merger at any time if the merger threatens to restrain commerce. A government proceeding after the merger is accomplished seeks divestiture. Answer (d) is incorrect because mergers or acquisitions are not legal just because there may appear to be cost efficiencies resulting from combined marketing, advertising, and other activities. Acquisitions are considered to be legal if it is apparent that competition has not or will not be lessened.

37. (d) The best defense against an allegation of monopolizing under Section 2 of the Sherman Act is to demonstrate that the defendant's market share is not large enough to permit price fixing or exclusion of competitors. In making such a determination, the court looks primarily to the percentage share of the relevant market. Answer (a) is incorrect because the antitrust laws apply to all U.S. companies wherever they operate. Furthermore, the acts prescribe activity which has an effect on interstate commerce, i.e., the activity does not have to be in interstate commerce. Answer (b) is not the best defense since the monopoly was a result of an expired rather than a current, patent. Answer (c) is incorrect because no specific wrongful intent to monopolize need be proven by the Justice Department.

42. (c) Conduct aimed at maintaining prices by excluding a certain troublesome buyer from the market is a restraint of trade and a per se illegal violation of the antitrust laws. Answer (a) is incorrect because a businessman can only individually choose not to deal with a certain customer. A joint action or conspiracy as described above, however, is an illegal boycott. Answer (b) is incorrect because a joint boycott is per se illegal. Joint boycotts are without legal justification, and mere proof of having engaged in this type of activity is sufficient to constitute a violation. There is no additional necessity to show that the specific boycott activity represented an unreasonable or harmful effect on competition. Answer (d) is incorrect because the joint boycott activity is not unilateral as there was an agreement between 3 manufacturers. Furthermore, as a general rule, all control of the resale price by the seller ends at the time of sale. Thus, Nick's conduct is legal. Finally, just because defendants are unsuccessful in their anticompetitive attempts does not lessen their liability for the violations.

ESSAY QUESTIONS AND ANSWERS

NOVEMBER 1980 (Estimated time: 8 to 10 minutes)

2. Part b. In 1979 Banner was one of 38 retail Marco gasoline stations in greater Fort Wayne, Massachusetts, and one of 8 such stations in its particular sales territory. The nearest competing Marco station was 11 blocks away. Banner's supplier, Marvel Company, was a major integrated refiner and distributor of petroleum products. Like other Marco stations in Fort Wayne, Banner purchased gasoline from Marvel at 94.1 cents per gallon and resold it at 98.9 cents per gallon.

In September 1979 Best by Test Oil Company, operator of a chain of 65 retail gasoline stations, opened its only Best by Test station in Fort Wayne diagonally across the street from Banner and began selling its gasoline at 96.9 cents per gallon. Best by Test was exclusively a retailer and did not compete with Marvel. This differential of 2 cents per gallon between Banner's and Best by Test's retail prices was the normal differential between "major" and "non-major" brands of gasoline. Subsequently however, beginning in December, Best by Test from time to time reduced its price, sometimes to 91.9 cents or 90.9 cents per gallon, and on each occasion Banner's sales suffered. Banner sought assistance from Marvel to meet Best by Test's competition. After four months of watchful waiting, Marvel gave Banner a discount of 1.7 cents per gallon in April 1980 to permit the latter to reduce its retail price to 95.9 cents per gallon to counter a Best by Test retail price of 94.9 cents per gallon, later lowered to 93.9 cents per gallon. At this point, other Marco dealers, located within a three and one-half mile radius of Banner, suffered substantial declines in sales; they had not received any discount from Marvel and had not reduced their retail prices. They observed some of their former customers buying gasoline from Banner. Those Marco retail stations which suffered losses as a result of Marvel's pricing policies have claimed a violation of federal antitrust law by Marvel and have brought legal action against it to recover damages.

Required Answer the following, setting forth reasons for any conclusions stated.

1. Will the Marco retail stations which suffered losses prevail?
2. What probable defense will Marvel assert in order to avoid liability?

Answer

1. Yes. Marvel's price discrimination is a violation of the Robinson-Patman Act, and the defense of "meeting competition" is not available. The price discrimination involved is at the buyer level, a secondary-line price discrimination. That is, it was a price discrimination among various customers (the retail gas stations) of the manufacturer or producer (Marvel) that enables the customer receiving the lower price to undersell its competitors. Marvel's selling to Banner at 1.7¢ less than it sold to its other service stations is squarely within the proscribed conduct. Where there is such a secondary-line price discrimination, the requirement of "injury to competition" is met if there is a reasonable possibility that competition will be adversely affected. Here, the decreased sales and loss of customers by the other stations would satisfy such a requirement, and thus, there is a prima facie Robinson-Patman violation.

2. Marvel's chief defense would be that it had reduced its prices to meet the lower prices of a competitor. However, the facts indicate that Marvel and Best by Test did not compete since Best was not a supplier. The price reduction being met must be that of a competitor of the firm cutting its price, not a competitor of a purchaser of that firm. Thus, the good faith "meeting competition" defense is not available.

MAY 1977 (Estimated time: 20 to 25 minutes)

6. Part a. During the audit of the accounts receivable of the Flint Charcoal Company, it was learned that one of the customers, Cranston, refused to pay for the charcoal purchased over the past six months. An analysis of the correspondence revealed the following facts.

Flint is a large manufacturer and distributor of charcoal briquettes. It sells the briquettes in interstate commerce to wholesalers, jobbers, and directly to retail outlets. Several of the wholesalers have recently opened up their own retail outlets in the area in which Cranston's store is located. Six months ago, Better Buy Charcoal, one of Flint's major competitors, uniformly reduced the price of charcoal briquettes to its wholesalers. Better Buy sells exclusively to wholesalers. When Flint's wholesale customers learned of the cheaper prices offered by Better Buy, they told Flint "it had better lower its prices or they would switch to Better Buy." Flint promptly matched Better Buy's price reduction in order to retain its wholesale customers. Flint could not totally justify on a cost basis the difference in price at which it sold to wholesalers as compared with retailers. Cranston, upon discovering the unfavorable price differential, refused to pay on the orders he received and notified Flint that he would not pay more than the price charged to the wholesalers. Cranston warned Flint that if legal action were taken by Flint, he would counterclaim for damages based upon Flint's "illegal pricing policies."

Required Answer the following, setting forth reasons for any conclusions stated.

What are the legal problems and implications of the above facts?

Answer The problem Flint Charcoal Company faces is a possible violation of the Robinson-Patman Act. The act sharply proscribes price differentials where they "may tend to lessen competition or create a monopoly" in interstate commerce. Here we have a so-called secondary line price discrimination between competing buyers. The wholesalers, who also sell at retail, have an obvious price advantage over competing retailers. In such a case, injury to competition is presumed. The Robinson-Patman Act contains several defenses. First, cost savings resulting from sales in larger quantities are permitted to be passed on to the buyer. In the case of Flint, however, the price differential is not entirely due to cost savings attributable to quantity orders. Therefore, the quantity discount defense would fail.

The Robinson-Patman Act also permits a price discrimination if it is made in good faith to meet a legal price charged by a competitor. Since Better Buy sells only to wholesalers at the same price, Better Buy is not engaging in illegal price discrimination. The facts also indicate that Flint's price reduction was made in good faith to meet Better Buy's price, and thereby retain its wholesale customers. Flint's price reduction was not a violation of the Robinson-Patman Act.

6. Part b. The CPA firm of Christopher and Diana was engaged to audit the books of Starr Antenna Company. An examination of Starr's files revealed the threat of a lawsuit by Charles Grimm, the owner of Grimm's TV Sales and Service Company. An analysis of the pertinent facts revealed the following.

Grimm's complaint arose because Grimm could not obtain the quantity of television antennas ordered from Starr. The three other antenna manufacturers, who supplied the tri-state area in which Starr did business, would not sell antennas to Grimm. Grimm knows that several other retailers are encountering similar problems with Starr and the three major competitors. Diana, the partner in charge of the audit, found this to be a strange situation and talked with Baxter, Starr's Vice President of Marketing. Baxter explained that about a year ago there had been a period of "cutthroat" competition among the four major antenna manufacturers involved. In order to avoid a repetition of this disastrous situation, they had entered into an unwritten gentlemen's agreement to "limit output per manufacturer to the amount produced in the year immediately preceeding that in which the cutthroat competition had occurred." They also agreed that each manufacturer would not sell to the acknowledged customers of the others. Baxter said there was still plenty of competition for new customers in the tri-state area and that they were contemplating raising the production limitation by 25%. He said that "this arrangement had made life a lot easier and profitable for all concerned." He also indicated that the prices charged were "reasonable" to the purchasers.

Required Answer the following, setting forth reasons for any conclusions stated.

What are the legal problems and implications of the above facts?

Answer The fact situation described poses obvious violations of the Sherman Act. First, the four competing antenna manufacturers entered into an illegal "contract, combination, or conspiracy" in restraint of interstate commerce when they agreed to limit their output. This is akin to price fixing and is, per se, illegal. The fact that the understanding was oral does not matter, nor does it matter that their goal was to eliminate destructive price cutting or charge reasonable prices. Additionally, the agreement among the four antenna manufacturers to allocate customers among themselves is another clearly anticompetitive device which has been placed in the, per se, illegal category. The anticompetitive effects are so obvious that this kind of conduct has been held to be without legal justification.

6. Part c.

The General Pen Company is one of the largest manufacturers of fountain pens and does business in every state in the United States. General developed a new line of prestige pens called the "Diamond Line" which it sold at a very high price. In order to uphold its prestige and quality appeal, General decided to maintain a high resale price. Consequently, it obtained agreements from department stores, jewelers, and other outlets not to sell the pen below the $15 suggested retail price. The Double Discount Department Store refused to sign the agreement and used the pen as a sales gimmick to attract customers. Double advertised and sold Diamond Line pens for $12, to which General objected. Double threatened General with a treble damage action for price-fixing if it did not withdraw its objections.

Required Answer the following, setting forth reasons for any conclusions stated.

What are the legal problems and implications of the above facts?

Answer The problem raised by the facts is whether the price-fixing arrangement engaged in by General Pen Company is illegal. Normally, price fixing is, per se, illegal. However, Congress originally permitted an exception to this blanket prohibition. In effect, the price-fixing agreement was legal if there was (1) a state law permitting resale price maintenance (a manufacturer fixing the minimum price at which purchasers could sell); (2) free and open competition among other makers of the product; and (3) one or more retail sellers agreeing to retail price maintenance. The facts of the case indicate that General Pen comes within the scope of the prior "fair trade" laws. However, in 1975, Congress amended the law concerning resale price maintenance and removed the exception previously permitted under the Sherman Act. Consequently, resale price maintenance (vertical price fixing) is now illegal. Thus, Double Discount has a valid cause of action against General Pen based upon the amended statute.

CHAPTER
18
Regulation of Employment

The following is a generalized listing of subjects to be tested through the May 1983 Uniform CPA Examination.

Questions on this topic are based upon the Fair Labor Standards Act, the Social Security Act, and typical state workmen's compensation laws. The emphasis of these questions is on the impact that these laws have on employer-employee relationships.[1]

The AICPA Board of Examiners has adopted a new content specification outline for the business law section of the Uniform CPA Examination, *to be effective with the November 1983 examination*. The outline lists the following topics to be tested under the title "Regulation of Employment."

C. Regulation of Employment
1. Equal Employment Opportunity Laws
2. Federal Unemployment Tax Act
3. Workmen's Compensation
4. Federal Insurance Contributions Act
5. Fair Labor Standards Act[2]

FEDERAL INSURANCE CONTRIBUTIONS ACT (FICA): SOCIAL SECURITY ACT

I. *Purpose.* To provide old-age, survivor, and disability insurance and health insurance benefits to wage earners, self-employed persons, and their dependents.

II. *Types of work covered.* Almost all kinds of employment and self-employment are covered by Social Security. However, some types of work are covered only if certain conditions are met.

---

[1] AICPA, *Information for CPA Candidates*, Copyright © 1975, 1979, by the American Institute of Certified Public Accountants, Inc.

[2] AICPA, *Business Law—Content Specification Outline*, approved by the AICPA Board of Examiners on August 31, 1981.

A. *Farm employees:*
 1. Farm employees' work is covered by the act if they are paid at least $150 each in wages in cash from one employer in one year; or
 2. If the farm employee works for one employer for twenty or more days during one year, regardless of the amount of pay.
B. *Household workers.* A domestic worker's cash wages are covered by the act if they amount to $50 or more from one employer in any one calendar quarter.
C. *Family employment.* As a general rule, work done by one family member as an employee of another is covered by the act only if the work is done in the course of trade or business.
D. *Employees of nonprofit organizations* (charitable, religious, scientific, educational, etc.) are not automatically covered. To be covered, the organization must file a waiver of exemption.
E. *Government employees:*
 1. Federal employees are exempt from Social Security tax if covered by a retirement system already established by Congress.
 2. All wages for active duty with U.S. armed forces are covered under the act.
 3. Employees of state and local government are not automatically covered. They may be covered under a voluntary agreement between the state and the federal government.
F. *Railroad workers* are exempt from the Social Security Act.
G. *Employees receiving tips.* Cash tips of $20 or more in any month while working with one employer are covered by the act.
H. *Clergymen, Christian Science practitioners, and members of religious orders* are automatically covered unless they file an application for exclusion from the provisions of the act.
 I. *Farm operators or ranchers* are covered if their net earnings from self-employment are $400 or more during a year.
III. *Financing the program* through taxation of wages and self-employment income.
 A. All benefits available under the Social Security Act are financed by a tax on earnings (wages and self-employed income) covered under the act. General revenues are *not* used to fund Social Security benefits.
 B. *Taxation on wages of an employee:*
  1. Both the employer and employee are taxed an equal amount. The tax is computed by multiplying a fixed percentage times the employee's wages up to a specified maximum amount. (The percentage and the maximum amount limitation are subject to change as the Social Security Act is amended by Congress.)
  2. The employee's tax is deducted from the employee's pay at the end of each pay period.
  3. The employer is required to forward the employee's tax with an equal amount to the Internal Revenue Service.
  4. The employer is liable for the full amount of the tax, regardless of whether or not the employer withheld the employee's share.
  5. The employer who fails to collect and deposit taxes, file tax returns, or commits fraud is subject to penalties and is liable for interest on the amount due.
 C. *Taxation of income from self-employment:*
  1. Self-employed persons are required to report their own taxable earnings and pay the Social Security tax.
  2. Their duty to pay the tax arises when they have net earnings of $400 or more in one year.
  3. The computation of a self-employed person's tax is also based on a percentage multiplied by earnings up to a specified maximum amount.

D. Federal unemployment tax under the *Federal Unemployment Tax Act:*

  1. This tax is imposed on all industrial and commercial employers who employ one or more individuals for some portion of a day in each of twenty weeks in a current or preceding calendar year or who pay $1,500 or more in wages in any calendar quarter. *This tax is paid only by employers.*

  2. The tax is used to provide unemployment compensation benefits to workers in industrial and commercial employments who lost their jobs and cannot find replacement work.

  3. The tax is based upon a percentage multiplied by the first wages paid to an employee up to a specified maximum amount.

  4. An employer is entitled to a credit against its federal tax for state unemployment compensation taxes paid.

  5. *Eligibility for unemployment compensation benefits.* Unemployed people are eligible for federal unemployment compensation benefits if they are qualified to receive benefits under the applicable state unemployment compensation law. A typical state unemployment compensation law prescribes eligibility for benefits if a person:

     a. Was employed by a covered employer but subsequently became unemployed;

     b. Filed a claim for benefits; and

     c. Is able, willing, and available for work but is unable to find any.

E. *Income not taxed.* The following income is excluded from Social Security taxation:

  1. Payment in any medium other than cash;

  2. Reimbursement for travel or other expenses;

  3. Payments to employee on account of retirement;

  4. Capital gains;

  5. Dividend income.

IV. *Acquisition of "quarters of coverage" and types of insured status* under Social Security.

  A. Acquisition of "quarters of coverage":

  1. Beginning in 1983, employees and self-employed persons will receive one-quarter of coverage for each $370 of covered annual earnings. *Note:* The amount of covered and taxed earnings needed to obtain a quarter of coverage will increase automatically in the future on an annual basis to keep pace with the increase in average wages and earnings.

  2. No more than four quarters can be earned for any year, regardless of a person's total annual earnings.

  3. Self-employed persons cannot receive credit for any quarters in any one calendar year unless their net earnings during that year amounted to at least $400.

  B. *Fully insured.* To be fully insured a person must have been credited with forty quarters of coverage before a claim for benefits accrues, i.e., death or eligibility for retirement.

  C. *Currently insured.* To be currently insured, a person must have been credited with at least six quarters of coverage during the three years before a claim for benefits accrues, i.e., before death or eligibility for retirement.

  D. *Disability insured:*

  1. To be eligible for disability benefits, a person age 31 or over must be fully insured and have a Social Security credit of five years' work in the ten years (disability insured) immediately prior to disability.

  2. Persons between the ages of 24 and 31 must have received Social Security credits during 50 percent of the time between age 21 and the date they become disabled.

3. A person under 24 years of age must have received Social Security credit for one and one-half years' work in the three years immediately prior to disability.

V. *Types of benefits* and eligibility.

   A. *Retirement* (fully insured). Benefits are payable to the retired worker and dependent spouse and children.

   B. *Survivorship* (fully insured or currently insured). Widow or widower and dependents are entitled to benefits.

   C. *Disability* (fully insured and/or disability insured; see IV-D above):

      1. A six-month *waiting period* during disability must be fulfilled before benefits begin being paid.

      2. The person disabled and any dependents are entitled to disability benefits.

   D. *Medicare* (hospital-surgical-medical insurance):

      1. *Automatic coverage* (hospital insurance):

         a. Any person age 65 or over who is entitled to Social Security or railroad retirement benefits is automatically eligible for hospital insurance.

         b. Hospital insurance coverage is financed in the same manner as are retirement, survivorship, disability, and death benefits.

      2. *Voluntary coverage* (surgical-medical insurance):

         a. This coverage is not automatic. A person eligible for Social Security or railroad retirement benefits must apply for coverage within a specified period of time after eligible retirement.

         b. This insurance is paid for by eligible retirees in the form of monthly premiums deducted from their retirement benefits.

   E. *Lump-sum death benefits* (fully insured or currently insured). The benefit is payable to the surviving widow, widower, or dependents.

VI. *Reduction, increase, or loss of benefits.* Benefits may be reduced, increased, or lost in the following ways:

   A. Termination of dependency (benefits are lost).

   B. Dependent child not enrolled in school attains age 18 (benefits are lost).

   C. Dependent child enrolled in school attains age 22 (benefits are lost).

   D. Widowed spouse receiving benefits remarries (benefits are lost).

   E. Divorce (benefits are lost).

   F. Early retirement (results in reduced benefits).

   G. Excess earnings after retirement results in reduced benefits of $1 in benefits for each $2 of earnings above a specified amount of annual earnings. Beginning in 1983, a person age 70 or older will not suffer a reduction in retirement benefits because of earned income.

   H. Dependent child marries (benefits are lost).

   I. Automatic cost-of-living increases in benefits:

      1. Social security benefits are subject to annual automatic increases based on annual increases in cost of living.

      2. If living costs increase 3 percent or more in any one year, benefits will be increased by the same percentage and paid beginning the following July unless Congress has already acted to increase benefits.

WORKERS' COMPENSATION

VII. *Purposes* of state workers' compensation laws.

   A. To provide *employees* (not independent contractors) compensation for injuries or death occurring in the course of employment, whether or not the injury or death is caused by the fault of the employer (i.e., a type of no-fault liability).

B. To require the cost of injuries to employees to be borne by employers (industry).

C. To eliminate the following *common law defenses* available to employers against employees in a common law action in tort:

    1. *Contributory negligence* by the injured employee;

    2. *Assumption of the risk* by the injured employee;

    3. *Fellow servant doctrine* (the injury is caused by a coemployee).

VIII. *Enterprises and businesses covered* by the workers' compensation laws.

    A. The law automatically applies to the following enterprises or businesses:

        1. Those deemed to be *extrahazardous*; for example:

            a. Erecting, maintaining, removing, remodeling, altering, or demolishing of any structure;

            b. Transportation by land, water, or air;

            c. Construction, excavating, or electrical work;

            d. Operation of a warehouse;

            e. Mining or quarrying;

            f. Enterprises in which explosives are manufactured or used;

            g. Enterprises in which chemicals are used;

            h. Enterprises in which cutting tools, grinders, or implements are used;

            i. Establishments open to the public where alcoholic beverages are sold.

            j. Business or enterprise serving food to the public for consumption on the premises.

        2. Any state or federal corporations or businesses.

    B. Any *business not automatically covered may elect* to come under the workers' compensation laws.

    C. *Commonly excluded from coverage* are:

        1. Employers who employ less than a specified number of employees (e.g., three);

        2. Domestic employees, e.g., maids, valets, etc.;

        3. Government employees, e.g., state university professors;

        4. Agricultural workers; and

        5. Part-time employees.

    D. *Employee's remedy for a covered* employer's noncompliance with the law. If a *covered employer* does not comply with the funding provisions of a workers' compensation law, the injured employee has the right to sue the employer under the common law in tort for damages (see X-A, B below). As a further result of the noncompliance:

        1. The employer *is denied* defenses ordinarily available under the common law to employers against employees (see VII-C above);

        2. The workers' compensation law is not applicable; and

        3. There is no limit on the amount of damages that can be awarded by the court to the employee under the common law action in tort.

IX. *Injuries and death covered by workers' compensation laws.* To be covered, an injury or death must have been *caused by* an *accident that arose out of and in the course of the employment.*

    A. The following circumstances *will not* preclude recovery by an employee under a workers' compensation law:

        1. The injury or death was caused by the employee's own ordinary negligence or even gross negligence.

        2. The injury or death was caused by the negligent or even intentional act of a fellow employee.

        3. The injured or deceased employee assumed the risk of injury or death on the job.

     4. The injury or death occurred outside of the employer's premises.

     5. The injury or death was caused by a third person unrelated to the employer or the employer's business.

  B. *Accidental injuries and death.* Workers' compensation laws provide benefits only for injury or death *caused by accident.* Any employee who intentionally self-inflicts an injury or death is precluded from recovery.

  C. *"Arising out of and in the course of employment."* As a general rule, an injury or death of an employee is held to have arisen "out of and in the course of the employment" if it happened to the employee:

     1. During an authorized time;

     2. In an authorized geographical area; and

     3. While acting in furtherance of the employer's purpose.

X. *Funding.*

  A. Any enterprise or business covered under workers' compensation laws must qualify as a self-insurer, certify that it has insured its obligations with an insurance, or contribute to a state workers' compensation insurance fund.

  B. If a firm chooses to be a *self-insurer*, it must furnish such security as an indemnity bond or other financial security.

XI. *Employee's exclusive remedy.* In most states where the employee is covered by a workers' compensation law, the sole remedy against the employer is that applicable under the act.

XII. *Benefits payable* under workers' compensation laws.

  A. *Disability benefits:*

     1. The disability may be total or partial, permanent or temporary.

     2. Payments are based on wages lost, usually a percentage of weekly earnings subject to a minimum and a maximum amount for a maximum period of time.

  B. *Death benefits.* Schedules are used to determine maximum and minimum benefits payable. The benefits are usually required to be paid to a surviving spouse and minor children.

  C. *Burial expenses* are compensated.

  D. *Hospital, medical, and surgical expenses* are payable.

  E. In some states, injured employees whose injuries have resulted in permanent disability must submit to a program of *rehabilitation.*

XIII. *To whom benefits are payable.* Compensation is paid to either the employee or his or her dependents.

XIV. *Subrogation* right of the employer.

  A. An employer or its insurance carrier, upon payment of worker's compensation benefits, is subrogated to the rights of an employee against a third person who caused the injury.

  B. Any recovery in excess of workers' compensation benefits belongs to the employee.

  C. An injured employee may also sue the third party for damages. If the employee has been paid workers' compensation benefits, a part of the recovery (equal to workers' compensation benefits received) belongs to the employer or the employer's insurance carrier; i.e., the employer or its insurance carrier has a right of indemnity under these circumstances against the employee.

XV. *Steps in administration* of workers' compensation claims.

  A. *Notice* of the accident must be given to the employer by the employee within a specified time.

  B. An *application for claim* must be filed with the Industrial Commission. The application must include time, place, manner, and character of the accident.

  C. Once application is filed, the commission establishes a date and place for a *hearing before an arbitrator.*

D. If a party feels aggrieved by the arbitrator's decision, it can file a *petition for review* before the Industrial Commission.

E. An *appeal* from a decision of the Industrial Commission may be taken to the courts.

THE FAIR LABOR STANDARDS ACT OF 1938 (FLSA) AND AMENDMENTS _delete_

XVI. *Purpose.* The purpose of the Fair Labor Standards Act (FLSA) of 1938 is to regulate wages, hours of employment, overtime, use of child labor, discrimination in pay between employees, in businesses engaged in interstate commerce.

XVII. *Automatically excluded* from all coverages under the act *are persons not employed in private businesses*; for example:

A. Members of the armed forces;

B. Certain government employees at local, state, or federal levels;

C. Self-employed persons;

D. Unpaid family workers.

XVIII. *Jurisdiction of the act.*

A. The legal basis of the FLSA is the power of Congress to regulate interstate commerce.

B. *Interstate commerce* is any business activity that falls into any of the following four categories:

1. "Production for interstate commerce." Production of goods intended for shipment across state lines, e.g., manufacturing, mining, agriculture.

2. "Interstate commerce itself." The actual shipment or transaction of business across state lines; e.g., shipping, transportation, telephones, telegraphs, other forms of communication, banking, finance, and wholesaling.

3. "Sale of goods that have been moved in interstate commerce." The resale of goods that have been produced in or shipped from another state before reaching the ultimate seller, e.g., retail and service businesses.

4. Businesses that "affect interstate commerce." These are businesses that are not in direct interstate transactions, production for interstate commerce, or distribution of interstate goods. This category encompasses any business that has activity and impact upon interstate commerce. The classic example is a purely local (i.e., intrastate) service business that competes in its locality with an interstate firm.

XIX. *Enforcement.* The FLSA is under the direction of the secretary of labor, U.S. Department of Labor, Employment Standards Administration, Wage and Hour Division.

XX. *Businesses covered by the FLSA.*

A. Industries in which the annual *gross dollar sales volume test* applies. *Test:* Greater than or equal to a specific dollar amount constitutes inclusion within the FLSA. Examples include:

1. Construction industry;

2. Reconstruction industry;

3. Local transit; and

4. Service stations.

B. Industries covered that are not influenced by any particular dollar volume test (not exclusive):

1. Retail or service businesses;

2. Laundry and dry cleaning enterprises;

3. Clothing and factory repairs;

4. Hospitals;

5. Nursing homes;

6. Preschools, schools, and colleges (both private and public);

7. Hotels;

8. Motels;
9. Restaurants;
10. Retail service establishments;
11. Taxi cab companies;
12. Certain farm workers;
13. Cotton ginning employees;
14. Certain fruit and vegetable transporters; and
15. Domestic services workers.

XXI. *Areas regulated* by the act.

    A. *Minimum wages.* The act provides that a minimum hourly wage be paid to each covered employee.

    B. *Overtime pay.* The act requires that a wage rate of not less than *one and one-half times the regular rate* be paid for hours worked *beyond forty hours* in any given *work week* except for those employed in agriculture, seasonal employment in recreation, or engaged in the delivery of health care services for the sick.

    C. *Minimum age* [*child (oppressed) labor provision*]:

        1. Sixteen years of age is the minimum age for employment of persons in particular hazardous occupations or those that may be detrimental to health or well-being.

        2. Employment of a person who has not attained the age of 16 is considered oppressive and in violation of the act.

        3. There are *special exemption provisions* for employment in agriculture, child actors, employment by a parent, nonhazardous work, and newspaper delivery.

    D. *Equal pay for equal work.* Discrimination in wages on the basis of sex is a violation. The same wages must be paid for the same work whether performed by a male or female (see XXVI below).

XXII. Some *exemptions* to the act are as follows.

    A. Minimum wage and maximum hour (overtime) provisions of the act do not apply to the following employees:

        1. Executives and administrators (i.e., supervisory personnel);

        2. Certain agricultural employees;

        3. Professionals;

        4. Outside salespersons;

        5. Employees of an employer engaged in commercial fishing or forestry;

        6. Handicapped workers;

        7. Employees of farms and businesses whose operations are solely intrastate; and

        8. Learners, apprentices, and messengers.

FIGURE 18-1   EQUAL EMPLOYMENT OPPORTUNITY LAWS

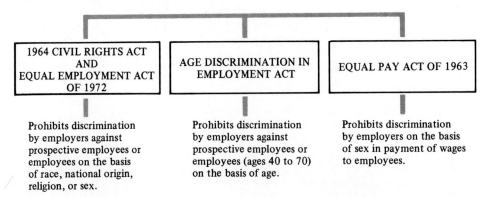

1964 CIVIL RIGHTS ACT AND EQUAL EMPLOYMENT ACT OF 1972	AGE DISCRIMINATION IN EMPLOYMENT ACT	EQUAL PAY ACT OF 1963
Prohibits discrimination by employers against prospective employees or employees on the basis of race, national origin, religion, or sex.	Prohibits discrimination by employers against prospective employees or employees (ages 40 to 70) on the basis of age.	Prohibits discrimination by employers on the basis of sex in payment of wages to employees.

XXIII. *Sanctions* for violation. Violators of any provisions of the act can be subjected to civil as well as criminal sanctions.

    A. *Criminal*:

        1. Fine or imprisonment.

    B. *Civil*:

        1. Injunction against future violations may be obtained by the secretary of labor.

        2. Civil lawsuit by an employee for unpaid wages due, overtime pay, and attorney fees and court costs.

        3. Secretary of labor may sue an employer on behalf of an employee for unpaid wages.

EQUAL EMPLOYMENT OPPORTUNITY LAWS[1]
1964 CIVIL RIGHTS ACT AND EQUAL EMPLOYMENT ACT OF 1972

XXIV. The 1964 Civil Rights Act, Title VII, and the Equal Employment Act of 1972 establish the legal foundations to provide *equal employment opportunity*. (See Figure 18-1.)

    A. *Discrimination prohibited*. The law makes it illegal for a covered employer or other "person" to discriminate against a prospective employee or an employee in the area of employment or job status on the basis of race, color, national origin, religion, or sex.

        1. *Employers and "persons" covered* are:

            a. Public or private employers having at least fifteen employees;

            b. Unions;

            c. Employment agencies; and

            d. Federal contractors who receive more than $10,000 from the U.S. government.

        2. *Affirmative action* is required of employers to ensure that persons who are hired and employees on the job are accorded equal opportunity under the law.

        3. *Defenses* available under the law. A covered employer or "person" is allowed to discriminate on the basis of sex, national origin, or religion of any individual if such action is reasonably necessary for the normal conduct of its business.

    B. The *Equal Employment Opportunity Commission (EEOC)* was created to administer and enforce the law.

        1. *Powers*. The EEOC has the following powers:

            a. Receive and investigate complaints;

            b. Instigate and sustain informal conciliation proceedings;

            c. Sue an alleged violator; and

            d. Issue and publish interpretations of Title VII of the act.

        2. *Remedies*. The EEOC has the following statutory remedies at its disposal:

            a. Reinstate employees to their prior employment;

            b. Award *back pay* to employees;

            c. Obtain an injunction to refrain future violations of the law; and

            d. Exercise any other relief for a person "injured" as a result of a violation of the law.

THE AGE DISCRIMINATION IN EMPLOYMENT ACT

XXV. The Age Discrimination in Employment Act (1967), as amended, prohibits employers from discriminating against employees (ages 40 to 70) on the basis of age. (See Figure 18-1.)

---

[1] A new subject matter approved by the AICPA Board of Examiners on August 31, 1981, that *can be included in the Uniform CPA Examination beginning in November of 1983.*

A. *Employers covered.* Essentially the same employers that are covered under Title VII of the 1964 Civil Rights Act are covered under this law.

B. *Types of discrimination allowed.* The law allows (available defenses) an employer to discriminate on the basis of age in any of the following circumstances:

    1. A certain age is a bona fide occupational requirement reasonably necessary for the usual conduct of the employer's business.

    2. The classification or differentiation made by the employer is based on reasonable criteria other than age.

    3. The person is not hired, is discharged, is disciplined, or his or her change in job status is for good cause.

    4. The treatment accorded the employee is pursuant to the terms of a bona fide *seniority system* or employee benefit plan; e.g., a layoff, pension, promotion, or insurance plan.

C. *Administrative agency.* The law is administered by the Department of Labor.

EQUAL PAY ACT OF 1963 (An Amendment to the FLSA)

XXVI. The Equal Pay Act of 1963, an amendment to the Fair Labor Standards Act (FLSA), prohibits *discrimination in wages on the basis of sex.* (See Figure 18-1.)

A. *Jurisdiction.* The act applies to every employer subject to the minimum wage provisions of the FLSA (see XX above).

B. *Equal pay for equal work.* An employer cannot discriminate by paying some employees lower wages than those paid to employees of the opposite sex where equal work is performed by such employees and such work requires equal skill, effort, and responsibility to be performed under similar working conditions.

C. *Justifications for unequal pay.* The act provides four types of justification for payment of different wages to employees of opposite sexes. Justification exists when the different wages are paid according to a:

    1. Seniority system;

    2. Merit system;

    3. System that measures earnings by quantity or quality of production, e.g., piece work; or

    4. Differential based on any other factor other than sex.

D. *Criminal and civil sanctions.* Violators of any provision of the act are subject to the following criminal and civil sanctions:

    1. Fine or imprisonment;

    2. Injunction against future violations; and

    3. Recovery of back pay by the discriminated-against employee plus fees and court costs.

SELF-QUIZ

Note: To check your understanding of the key words and concepts and the accuracy of your answers to the questions, refer to the text material as referenced by page number.

KEY WORDS AND CONCEPTS

QUESTIONS

1. What are the purposes of the Social Security Act and the workers' compensation laws? **(525)**
2. What kinds of employment are automatically covered by the Social Security Act? **(525)**
3. How is the Social Security program financed? **(526)**
4. Does the Social Security Act establish a federal unemployment tax? **(527)** For what purpose is the tax levied? **(527)** Who must pay the tax? **(527)**
5. What types of insured status are possible under the Social Security Act? **(527)**
6. List the benefits payable under the following acts:
   a. Social Security. **(528)**
   b. Workers' Compensation **(530)**
7. Explain how Social Security benefits may be reduced, increased, and totally lost. **(528)**
8. What common law remedies were eliminated by workers' compensation laws? **(529)**
9. What types of injuries are covered under workers' compensation laws? **(529)**
10. List the benefits available under workers' compensation laws. **(530)**
11. Explain the employer's right of subrogation under workers' compensation laws. **(530)**
12. List the four areas of employment regulated by the FLSA. **(532)**
13. What types of employees are exempt from the provisions of the FLSA? **(532)**
14. What are the consequences of a covered employer's noncompliance with the funding provisions of a workers' compensation law? **(529)**
15. Who are covered "employers and persons" under the following laws?
    a. 1964 Civil Rights Act **(533)**
    b. Equal Employment Act of 1972 **(533)**
    c. Age Discrimination in Employment Act **(534)**
    d. Equal Pay Act of 1963 **(534)**
16. What administrative agency has been charged with the responsibility of ensuring compliance with the provisions of the 1964 Civil Rights Act and the Equal Employment Act of 1972? **(533)**
17. Under what circumstances can an employer discriminate against employees on the basis of age? **(534)** On the basis of sex in regard to wages? **(534)**
18. List the remedies available to an employee and to the government against a violator of the equal opportunity laws. **(533)**

SELECTED QUESTIONS AND UNOFFICIAL ANSWERS

OBJECTIVE QUESTIONS

Select the best answer for each of the following items. Mark only one answer for each item. Answer all items.

MAY 1981

59. The Social Security Act provides for the imposition of taxes and the disbursement of benefits. Which of the following is a correct statement regarding these taxes and disbursements?
a. Only those who have contributed to Social Security are eligible for benefits.
b. As between an employer and its employee, the tax rates are the same.
c. A deduction for federal income tax purposes is allowed the employee for Social Security taxes paid.
d. Social Security payments are includable in gross income for federal income tax purposes unless they are paid for disability.

60. Musgrove Manufacturing Enterprises is subject to compulsory worker's compensation laws in the state in which it does business. It has complied with the state's worker's compensation provisions. State law provides that where there has been compliance, worker's compensation is normally an exclusive remedy. However, the remedy will *not* be exclusive if

a. The employee has been intentionally injured by the employer personally.
b. The employee dies as a result of his injuries.
c. The accident was entirely the fault of a fellow-servant of the employee.
d. The employer was only slightly negligent and the employee's conduct was grossly negligent.

MAY 1980

18. At age 66, Jonstone retired as a general partner of Gordon & Co. He no longer participates in the affairs of the partnership but does receive a distributive share of the partnership profits as a result of becoming a limited partner upon retirement. Jonstone has accepted a part-time consulting position with a corporation near his retirement home. Which of the following is correct regarding Jonstone's Social Security situation?

a. Jonstone's limited partner distributive share will be considered self-employment income for Social Security purposes up to a maximum of $10,000.
b. There is *no* limitation on the amount Jonstone may earn in the first year of retirement.
c. Jonstone will lose $1 of Social Security benefits for each $1 of earnings in excess of a statutorily permitted amount.
d. Jonstone will be subject to an annual earnings limitation until he attains a stated age which, if exceeded, will reduce the amount of Social Security benefits.

NOVEMBER 1979

48. Yeats Manufacturing is engaged in the manufacture and sale of convertible furniture in interstate commerce. Yeats' manufacturing facilities are located in a jurisdiction which has a compulsory workmen's compensation act. Hardwood, Yeats' president, decided that the company should, in light of its safety record, choose to ignore the requirement of providing workmen's compensation insurance. Instead, Hardwood indicated that a special account should be created to provide for such contingencies. Basset was severely injured as a result of his negligent operation of a lathe which accelerated and cut off his right arm. In assessing the potential liability of Yeats, which of the following is a correct answer?

a. Federal law applies since Yeats is engaged in interstate commerce.
b. Yeats has *no* liability, since Basset negligently operated the lathe.
c. Since Yeats did *not* provide workmen's compensation insurance, it can be sued by Basset and cannot resort to the usual common law defenses.
d. Yeats is a self-insurer, hence it has *no* liability beyond the amount of the money in the insurance fund.

MAY 1978

47. Barnaby is an employee of the Excelsior Manufacturing Company, a multi-state manufacturer of toys. The plant in which he works is unionized and Barnaby is a dues paying member. Which statement is correct insofar as the Federal Fair Labor Standards Act is concerned?.

a. Excelsior is permitted to pay less than the minimum wage to employees since they are represented by a bona fide union.
b. The act allows a piece-rate method to be employed in lieu of the hourly rate method where appropriate.
c. The act excludes from its coverage the employees of a labor union.
d. The act sets the maximum number of hours that an employee can work in a given day or week.

48. Jones has filed a claim with the appropriate Workmen's Compensation Board against the Atlas Metal & Magnet Company. Atlas denies liability under the State Workmen's Compensation Act. In which of the following situations will Jones recover from Atlas or its insurer?

a. Jones intentionally caused an injury to himself.
b. Jones is an independent contractor.
c. Jones is basing the claim upon a disease unrelated to the employment.
d. Jones and another employee of Atlas were grossly negligent in connection with their employment resulting in injury to Jones.

NOVEMBER 1977

13. During the 1976 examination of the financial statements of Viscount Manufacturing Corporation, the CPAs noted that although Viscount had 860 full-time and part-time employees, it had completely overlooked its responsibilities under the Federal Insurance Contributions Act (FICA).

Under these circumstances, which of the following is true?

a. *No* liability under the act will attach if the employees voluntarily relinquish their rights under the act in exchange for a cash equivalent paid directly to them.

b. If the union which represents the employees has a vested pension plan covering the employees which is equal to or exceeds the benefits available under the act, Viscount has *no* liability.

c. Since employers and employees owe FICA taxes at the same rate and since the employer must withhold the employees' tax from their wages as paid, Viscount must remit to the government a tax double the amount assessed directly against the employer.

d. The act does *not* apply to the part-time employees.

14. Fashion Industries, Inc., manufactures dresses which it sells throughout the United States and South America. Among its 5,000 employees in 1976 were 165 youngsters aged 14 and 15 who worked in a wide range of jobs and were paid at a rate less than the minimum wage. Which statement is correct in accordance with the general rules of the Fair Labor Standards Act?

a. Fashion was exempt from regulation because less than 5% of its employees were children.

b. Fashion did *not* violate the law since both male and female youngsters were paid at the same rate and only worked on Saturdays.

c. Fashion violated the law by employing children under 16 years of age.

d. Fashion was exempt from regulation if more than 10% of its sales were in direct competition with foreign goods.

15. The theatrical agency of Power & Tyrone employs two people full time. Which of the following is true with regard to federal unemployment insurance?

a. In terms of industry and number of employees, Power & Tyrone is within the class of employers covered by the federal unemployment tax.

b. Service agencies are exempt.

c. Since the number of employees is small, an exemption can be obtained from coverage if a request is filed with the appropriate federal agency.

d. If the employees all reside in one state and do *not* travel interstate on company business,

Power & Tyrone is exempt from compliance with the act.

13. Which of the following classes of employees is *exempt* from both the minimum wage and maximum hours provisions of the Federal Fair Labor Standards Act?

a. Members of a labor union.

b. Administrative personnel.

c. Hospital workers.

d. *No* class of employees is exempt.

Answers to Objective Questions

May 1981		November 1977	
59. b	60. a	13. c	15. a
		14. c	

May 1980	
18. d	May 1977
	13. b

November 1979
48. c

May 1978
47. b   48. d

Explanation of Answers to Objective Questions

MAY 1981

59. (b) An employer is required to match contributions of employees to the Social Security System on a dollar-for-dollar basis. Answer (a) is incorrect since benefits may be paid to the surviving spouse or other dependents of a deceased individual who was covered under the Social Security System. Answer (c) is incorrect since the amount of Social Security taxes paid is not an allowable deduction on an individual's tax return. Payments to the system are taxed in full when made, and are recovered on a tax-free basis when received by the individual in the form of benefits. Answer (d) is incorrect because Social Security payments are not included in the gross income of a taxpayer.

60. (a) If the employer intentionally injures the employee, the employee would not only have a right to proceed under worker's compensation, but could sue the employer in a civil court of law on the basis of an intentional tort. Answers (b), (c) and (d) are incorrect because they do not state grounds that would allow the injured employee to sue in a civil court of law if covered by a proper worker's compensation plan. Even though the injury was caused by contributory negligence of the employee or the act of a fellow servant, the injured employee could still recover, but recovery under worker's compensation would be the exclusive remedy.

MAY 1980

18. (d) Answer (d) is correct because there is no limit on earnings after age 72 under the Social Security laws. Answer (a) is incorrect because under Social Security law an individual's wages normally shall be computed without regard to any maximum limitations and a partner's distributive share will be excluded entirely if certain requirements are met. Answer (b) is incorrect because the limitation on Jonstone's earnings may occur in the first year if he had excess earnings above the statutorily permitted amount. Answer (c) is incorrect because Social Security law does reduce benefits on the basis of a complicated statutory formula that would not result in a loss of $1 of Social Security benefits for each $1 of earnings in excess of a statutorily permitted amount.

NOVEMBER 1979

48. (c) The usual result when the employer fails to provide workmen's compensation insurance is that the injured employee may sue in a common law action, and the employer cannot resort to the usual common law defenses (such as contributory negligence, assumption of risk, or fellow servant rule). Answer (a) is incorrect because there is no federal law applying to workmen's compensation. Workmen's compensation is regulated by state statutes, which are only affected by federal guidelines. Answer (b) is incorrect because the employer does have liability for job-related injuries even if the injured employee was negligent. Answer (d) is incorrect in that Yeats is not a self-insuror because the problem indicates that he is doing business in a state that has a compulsory workmen's compensation act, i.e., does not recognize self-insurance plans.

MAY 1978

47. (b) The Fair Labor Standards Act (FLSA) prescribes the minimum wages which may be paid to employees. The FLSA allows methods of payment other than an hourly rate, including the piece-rate method, if it at least equals the hourly minimum. Answers (a) and (c) are incorrect because union employees are covered by the FLSA as are non-union employees and they may not be paid less than the minimum wage. Answer (d) is incorrect because the FLSA does not set the maximum number of hours that employees can work, but instead provides for minimum wages and payment for overtime.

48. (d) Workmen's compensation provides benefits to employees who are injured on the job even though the employee may have been negligent, or even grossly negligent. Answer (a) is incorrect, because workmen's compensation does not provide benefits for injuries which the worker intentionally inflicts. Answer (b) is incorrect also because an independent contractor is not an employee and therefore is not entitled to workmen's compensation coverage. Answer (c) is incorrect because an injury must be job-related to obtain workmen's compensation benefits.

NOVEMBER 1977

13. (c) It is the employer's duty to withhold FICA taxes from the employee and remit both these and the employer share to the government. If the employer neglects to withhold, the employer is liable for both the employer and employee taxes, i.e., to pay double. Answer (a) is incorrect because FICA is mandatory and employees may not relinquish their rights. Answer (b) is incorrect because pension plans and other benefits are no substitute for FICA. Answer (d) is incorrect because FICA applies to all employees whether part-time or full-time.

14. (c) It is a violation of the FLSA to employ children under the age of 16 except in very limited circumstances. Answer (a) is incorrect because there are no exemptions based on the number of children employed. Answer (b) is incorrect because equal pay and weekend work do not excuse employing children under 16. Answer (d) is incorrect because competition with foreign or any other goods is also not an excuse. Child labor exceptions are agriculture, child actors, employment by a parent, and newspaper delivery.

15. (a) Federal unemployment tax must be paid if there are one or more employees being paid wages. Answer (a) is incorrect because service agencies are included as is any other business. Answer (c) is incorrect because there is no exemption for few employees. Answer (d) is incorrect even if the employees do not leave the state, as long as some part of the business concerns interstate commerce or the mails are used, the business is included.

MAY 1977

13 (b) Administrators, executives, professional employees, and "outside" salespersons are exempt from both the minimum and maximum hours provisions of the FLSA. Answer (a) is incorrect because members of a labor union as wage earners are covered. Answer (c) is incorrect because hospital workers are specifically covered by the FLSA. Answer (d) is incorrect for the reasons stated above.

ESSAY QUESTIONS AND ANSWERS

NOVEMBER 1978 (Estimated time: 7 to 9 minutes)

3. Part c. Eureka Enterprises, Inc., started doing business in July 1977. It manufactures electronic components and currently employs 35 individuals. In anticipation of future financing needs, Eureka has engaged a CPA firm to audit its financial statements. During the course of the examination, the CPA firm discovers that Eureka has no workmen's compensation insurance, which is in violation of state law, and so informs the president of Eureka.

Required Answer the following, setting forth reasons for any conclusions stated.

1. What is the purpose of a state workmen's compensation law?
2. What are the legal implications of not having workmen's compensation insurance?

Answer

1. Workmen's compensation laws provide a system of compensation for employees who are injured, disabled, or killed as a result of accidents, or occupational diseases in the course of their employment. Benefits also extend to survivors or dependents of these employees.

2. In all but a distinct minority of jurisdictions, workmen's compensation coverage is mandatory. In those few jurisdictions that have elective workmen's compensation, employers who reject workmen's compensation coverage are subject to common law actions by injured employees and are precluded from asserting the defenses of fellow-servant, assumption of risk, and contributory negligence. The number of such jurisdictions having elective compensation coverage has been constantly diminishing. The penalty in these jurisdictions is the loss of the foregoing defenses.

The more common problem occurs in connection with the failure of an employer to secure compensation coverage even though he is obligated to do so in the majority of jurisdictions. The one uniform effect of such unwise conduct on the part of the employer is to deny him the use of the common law defenses mentioned above.

In addition to the foregoing, an increasing number of states have provided for the payment of workmen's compensation by the state to the injured employee of the uninsured employer. The state in turn proceeds against the employer to recover the compensation cost and to impose penalties that include fines and imprisonment. Other jurisdictions provide for a penalty in the form of additional compensation payments over and above the basic amounts, or they require an immediate lump-sum payment.

CHAPTER

19

Federal Securities Regulation

The following is a generalized listing of subjects to be tested through the May 1983 Uniform CPA Examination.

Knowledge of the Securities Act of 1933 and the Securities Exchange Act of 1934 (including the Foreign Corrupt Practices Act of 1977) and related federal disclosure requirements is tested under this topic. Included are the scope of the 1933 Act's registration requirements, exempt securities, exempt transactions and the liability of the various parties involved in making a public offering of securities. Included within the coverage of the 1934 Act are the application of the Act's rules to both listed and unlisted corporations, corporate reporting requirements, antifraud provisions, disclosure of insider information, short-swing profits, proxies, and tender offers.[1]

The AICPA Board of Examiners has adopted a new content specification outline for the business law section of the Uniform CPA Examination, *to be effective with the November 1983 examination*. The outline lists the following topics to be tested under the title "Federal Securities Acts."

  D. Federal Securities Acts
    1. Securities Registration and Reporting Requirements
    2. Exempt Securities and Transactions
    3. Insider Information and Antifraud Provisions
    4. Short-Swing Profits
    5. Civil and Criminal Liabilities
    6. Corrupt Practices
    7. Proxy Solicitations and Tender Offers[2]

---

[1] AICPA, *Information for CPA Candidates*, Copyright © 1975, 1979, by the American Institute of Certified Public Accountants, Inc.
[2] AICPA, *Business Law—Content Specification Outline*, approved by the AICPA Board of Examiners on August 31, 1981.

INTRODUCTION TO SECURITIES REGULATION

I. Both federal and state statutes regulate the sales of securities. The state statutes are called "Blue Sky" laws and they are designed to protect investors in the sale of securities in "intrastate commerce." Federal statutes regulate the sale of securities "in interstate commerce" and the activities of national securities exchanges. The jurisdiction of the federal statutes is extremely broad. It includes the use of any means or instruments of communication in interstate commerce or the use of the mails, directly or indirectly, as well as a sale between citizens of different states.

The *Securities Exchange Commission (SEC)* was created by the federal Securities Exchange Act of 1934. The act gave the SEC the mandate and authority to enforce the provisions of all federal securities laws. The SEC was given rule-making (quasi-legislative) and adjudicatory (quasi-judicial) power to carry out its mandate (see Chapter 16, II).

Both criminal and civil liabilities are prescribed by the federal and state securities laws.

SECURITIES ACT OF 1933

II. *Introduction.* The Securities Act of 1933 (the 1933 act) regulates *"primary offerings"*; that is, securities being sold to the public for the first time (i.e., *going public*). It makes it unlawful for any "person" to use the mails or any means or instruments of transportation or communication in interstate commerce in violation of its provisions. The purpose of the act is to protect investors from fraud as well as innocent misrepresentations by issuers of securities, controlling persons, underwriters, or dealers. The act is not designed to guaranty the sale of valuable or even valid securities. It is a disclosure law that is designed to ensure that the potential securities investor is supplied with enough information to make a prudent investment. The act does not prohibit the sale of value-less securities. To carry out its purpose, the act requires that new issues (i.e., those being offered for sale to the public for the first time) subject to its jurisdiction be registered with the SEC prior to any sale. It also requires that a prospectus be furnished to each buyer (investor) before or at the time a sale of nonexempt securities takes place.

PRIMARY OFFERINGS (NEW ISSUES) OF SECURITIES IN INTERSTATE COMMERCE

III. *Registration statement and prospectus requirements.* Under section 5a of the 1933 act, *newly issued* nonexempt "securities" cannot be lawfully "offered for sale" or "sold" to the public "in interstate commerce" unless a registration statement is filed with the SEC and is in effect and a prospectus is delivered to the purchaser prior to or at the time of the "offer" or "sale." The registration statement must contain a large amount of detailed information about the issuer, such as its assets and business, management, and financial status (see IV-A below). Any "person" who violates the provisions of section 5a may be criminally and civilly liable, as well as be subject to SEC-imposed sanctions (see IX below).

A. *Security defined.* The term *security* has a broad definition, which includes the instruments usually associated with the word securities (stock and bonds), along with any other instrument or evidence of an arrangement whereby people invest money in some business or financial endeavor with the right to earn a return from that money (profit) through the efforts of someone other than themselves (i.e., an investment contract). Limited partnership interests, promissory notes, interests in a cattle feeding lot, a right to profit from a citrus grove, interests in oil wells, beaver raising schemes, whiskey warehouse receipts, savings and loan certificates of deposit, and some types of variable life annuity contracts have been held to be "securities" under the federal securities laws.

    1. It is immaterial whether or not the ownership interest in the business enterprise is evidenced by a formal certificate. It is only necessary that there exist an oral or written arrangement whereby investors provide money to a common enterprise and are led to expect profits from significant efforts of someone other than themselves (i.e., the investment contract test).

    2. The 1933 act does exempt from its definition of "security" any note that has a maturity at the time of issuance of not more than nine months.

B. *Offered for sale or sale in interstate commerce.* Securities that are *"offered for sale"* or are *"sold"* by mail or *"by any means* or instruments of communications in interstate commerce" are regulated by the 1933 act.

    1. *"Offered for sale"* includes any oral or written solicitation, by advertisement or otherwise, of an offer to buy securities or any other attempt to dispose of a security for value.

    2. A *"sale"* includes every contract for sale or disposition of a security for value. Mergers or consolidations are considered to involve a "sale." However, a sale does not include the preliminary negotiations between an issuer and a potential underwriter.

    3. The term *"by any means, instrument, or communication in interstate commerce"* includes the telephone, telegraph, or mail, even though the solicitation or advertisement was purely intrastate in nature. For example, all events concerning a stock sale took place in Illinois. The court found jurisdiction because a telephone call was made from one station in Illinois to another. It is the interstate nature of the means, instrument, or communication that is regulated by the act. It also includes oral offers to sell or sales between citizens of different states or territories.

C. *"Persons" regulated.* The following "persons" are regulated under the act. "Persons" include individuals, corporations, partnerships, Massachusetts (business) trusts, and unincorporated associations. (See Figure 19-1.)

    1. An *issuer* is any person who proposes to issue or issues new (never-before-issued) securities. *Issuer includes a controlling person.*

    2. A *controlling person* is any person who is directly or indirectly in control of an issuer, or is in common control with an issuer. For example, a person who owns a controlling majority (i.e., more than 50 percent) stock interest in an issuer; or a person who owns only 15 percent of an issuer's stock but also is a member of its board of directors. A parent company is in control of its subsidiary. *Note:* Ownership or power to vote securities or actual participation in management with other owning voting securities is strong evidence of control.

    3. An *underwriter* is a person who has purchased securities from an issuer with the intent to distribute the security, one who offers to sell the security for the issuer, or one who has guaranteed its sale.

    4. A *dealer* is a person who is engaged, whether full- or part-time, directly or indirectly, as an agent or principal, to offer, buy, sell, deal with, or trade securities issued by another person.

REGISTRATION, REGISTRATION STATEMENT, AND PROSPECTUS REQUIREMENTS

IV. *Filing and registration.* As previously discussed, section 5 prohibits any offer for sale of newly issued (nonexempt) securities prior to the filing of a "registration statement" with the SEC. No written materials other than the "red herring" prospectus (i.e., a preliminary prospectus) may be used, and no written offers or sales may be made prior

FIGURE 19-1   SECURITIES ACT OF 1933

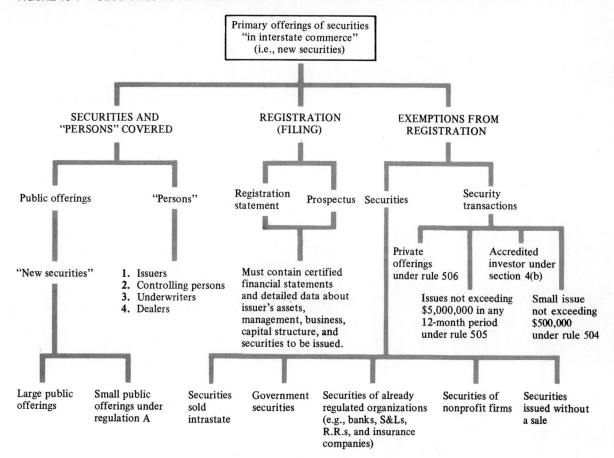

to the effective date of the registration statement. *"Registration"* occurs on the date that the registration statement becomes effective. (See Table 19-1.)

A. *Contents of a registration statement.* A properly completed *registration statement* must be signed by authorized representatives of the issuer and contain the following information. This list is not exclusive.

1. Historical and current information about the nature of the issuer's business.
2. Description of the securities to be issued.
3. Capital structure of the issuer.
4. An estimate of the amount of proceeds and their anticipated use.
5. Underwriting arrangements involved in the distribution and sale of the securities.
6. Certified financial statements.
7. *Signatures.* All registration statements and each subsequent amendment must be signed by the issuer's duly authorized officer, one or more of its executive officers, its comptroller, or principal accounting officer, and by at least a majority of its directors.

B. *Place of filing.* The registration statement (except one filed under Regulation A) is filed at the national office of the SEC in Washington, D.C.

TABLE 19-1 COMPARISON OF THE PROVISIONS OF THE SECURITIES ACT OF 1933 WITH THOSE OF THE SECURITIES EXCHANGE ACT OF 1934

Subject	Securities Act of 1933	Securities Exchange Act of 1934
1. Securities regulated	Primary offerings (i.e., issue of securities to the public for the first time).	Secondary offerings (i.e., securities already issued).
2. Requirement of prospectus	Required to be given to prospective buyer prior to or at time of sale of security.	None required.
3. Identity and amount of securities registered	Registration of a specified total number of shares of identified securities. Any shares in excess of the amount specified must be subsequently registered.	Registration of a class or classes of securities. Securities within a class can be sold in the future without being reregistered.
4. Reporting requirements	One-time report; i.e., the submission of registration statement and prospectus to the SEC.	Continuous reporting by the filing of required periodic reports; e.g., forms 8-K, 10-K, and 10-Q reports.
5. "Persons" regulated	*Narrow coverage:* Covers issuers, controlling persons, and underwriters, accountants, directors or attorneys, appraisers, and other experts involved with statements in registration statement or prospectus.	*Broad coverage:* Covers issuers, insiders, "beneficial owners," stock exchanges, brokers, dealers, and *any* other person whose conduct or activity violates any provision of the act.
6. Activities or conduct regulated	1. Offering to sell and sales of securities. 2. Preparation, contents, and filing of a registration statement. 3. Preparation, contents, and delivery of prospectus to an investor.	1. Registration of national stock exchanges, corporations, dealers, and brokers. 2. Insider trading and reporting of security holdings. 3. Periodic reporting to the SEC. 4. Proxy solicitation. 5. Tender offers. 6. Recordkeeping, accounting procedures, and internal auditing control. 7. Margin requirements.

7. Sanctions and remedies	1. Criminal sanctions:
	  a. Fine up to $5,000 and/or
	  b. Imprisonment up to five years
	
	2. Civil:
	  a. SEC sanctions and remedies:
	   (1) Suspension of registration
	   (2) Stop order
	   (3) File lawsuit for injunction
	   (4) Refer matter to U.S. Attorney General
	  b. Remedies for "injured" persons:
	   (1) Rescission and restitution, or
	   (2) Damages (out-of-pocket losses)
		1. Criminal sanctions:
		  a. Fine up to $10,000 for misstatements and omissions and/or
		  b. Imprisonment up to two years
		  c. $100 per day penalty for failure to file required documents
		
		2. Civil:
		  a. SEC sanctions and remedies:
		   (1) File lawsuit for injunction
		   (2) Suspend trading of a security
		   (3) Revoke registration
		   (4) Delist a security from an exchange
		   (5) Investigate suspected violators
		   (6) Promulgate rules
		  b. Remedies for "injured" persons:
		   (1) For violations under filing requirements—none.
		   (2) For violations of SEC section 10b and Rule 10b-5, "out-of-pocket" loss, consequential damages, and increased value of securities held by the violator
		   (3) For violations of other sections, "out-of-pocket" losses

C. *Twenty-day waiting period: Review and response by the SEC.*

   1. The SEC can require amendment or revision (i.e., by use of a *"deficiency letter"* or *"letter of comment"*) of the registration statement if it believes it to be incomplete, inaccurate, or misleading. If an amendment or revision is filed, a new twenty-day period is established.

   2. Upon the refusal of an issuer to file an amendment, the SEC may either issue a stop order or allow the deficient registration statement to become effective automatically on the twentieth day of the waiting period. If the latter occurs, the issuer may be subject to criminal sanctions and civil remedies for false or misleading statements or omissions as discussed below.

   3. The issuer is prohibited from making written offers for sale or sales during the waiting period. For a violation, the SEC can issue a stop order terminating any further consideration of the registration statement.

   4. Although issuers are not allowed to make written offers to sell or sales during the twenty-day waiting period, they can make or solicit oral offers and publish "announcements" advertising the sale of securities in the future. The *"announcement"* may take the following forms:

     a. *Oral communications* to investors, dealers, or underwriters.

     b. *"Red herring" prospectus* (i.e., a preliminary prospectus), which:

       (1) Contains essentially the same investment information as a final prospectus.

       (2) Derives its name from a somewhat lengthy statement in red ink on its front page that is required to be at least as conspicuous or prominent as the print in the remainder of the prospectus. The statement indicates that the prospectus is "preliminary"; the registration statement has been filed but is not yet effective; and the securities may not yet be sold nor can offers to buy be accepted lawfully.

       (3) A *"final"* prospectus must be provided to every purchaser prior to or at the time of the consummation of a sale of securities, i.e., at the time the security is delivered.

     c. *"Tombstone ad."* A *tombstone ad* is a written advertisement whose purpose is to locate potential purchasers of the securities and to inform them of the availability of a preliminary prospectus. Only a limited amount of information is allowed to be disclosed. For example, the name and business of the issuer, the identity of the security to be sold, where a preliminary prospectus may be obtained, the price of the securities, and the identity of the underwriters.

D. *Effective date of registration.* A registration statement, whether deficient or nondeficient, becomes effective automatically on the twentieth day after it is filed, unless:

   1. An amendment to the registration statement is filed by an issuer whether on its own initiative or because of the receipt of a "deficiency letter" (or a letter of comment) from the SEC. (The filing of any amendment prior to the effective date of a registration statement automatically reestablishes a new twenty-day waiting period);

   2. The SEC moves up the effective date; or

   3. The SEC stops further consideration of the statement by issuing a stop order.

E. *Prospectus requirements.* The prospectus must contain essentially the same information as that required for the registration statement.

   1. A *prospectus* includes any written notice, circular, advertisement, and letter, as well as any radio or TV communication that offers for sale or consists of an acceptance of an offer to buy (i.e., a confirmation of sale) any security.

2. A prospectus *must* be tendered (offered to be given) to every purchaser of a security, either prior to or concurrently with the consummation of the transaction i.e., delivery of the security to the purchaser.

REGULATION A: SMALL PUBLIC OFFERINGS

V. Small public offerings of new issues under Regulation A. Technically, *Regulation A* does not establish an exemption. It merely provides a more simplified and less expensive method of the registration of small public offerings of new issues with the SEC.

  A. *Qualifying offering* is one in which the aggregate offering price does not exceed $1,500,000 for an issuer during any twelve-month period.

    1. The aggregate offering price is determined by the lower of the actual offering price to the public or the market value of the securities on a specified date within fifteen days prior to the filing of the offering statement with the SEC.

  B. *Offering statement.* The offering statement required by Regulation A must consist of the following parts:

    1. Part I. *Notification* to the SEC as to intent to issue securities under Regulation A.

    2. Part II. *Offering circular*, which must be furnished to a purchaser prior to or at the time of any written offer to sell or actual sale of the securities. An offering circular differs substantially from a regular registration statement or prospectus used in a regular filing in that:

      a. Certified financial statements are not usually required in the circular.

      b. The required disclosures are not as extensive as those required in a registration statement in a regular registration.

    3. Part III. *Exhibits.*

  C. *Filing of the offering statement.* The offering statement must be filed with the SEC at least ten days (Saturdays, Sundays, and holidays excluded) prior to the date that the securities are first offered for sale or are sold.

    1. *Signatures.* The statement must be signed by the issuer and every other person for whose account any of the securities are to be offered.

    2. *Local filing.* The statement is filed with the SEC Regional Office for the region in which the issuer's principal business operations are conducted, rather than in the SEC's national office in Washington, D.C., as is required in a regular filing (i.e., registration).

  D. *Ten-day waiting period: Review and response by the SEC*:

    1. A filing automatically becomes effective on the tenth day of the waiting period unless the SEC issues a stop order, which suspends consideration of the offering statement.

    2. The SEC can demand amendment or revision of the offering statement if it believes it to be incomplete, inaccurate, or misleading. Such a demand is made in a deficiency letter (i.e., letter of comment) sent to the issuer by the SEC. If an amendment or revision is filed, a new ten-day waiting period is established.

    3. If the issuer refuses to file an amendment or revision, the SEC can either issue a stop order or allow the deficient offering statement to become effective automatically on the tenth day of the waiting period.

  E. *Ten-day waiting period: Written offer to sell or sales.* No written offers to sell or sales of securities are allowed prior to the time that an offering circular becomes effective, i.e., during the ten-day waiting period.

  F. *Ten-day waiting period: Preliminary offering circular.* A preliminary offering circular accompanied or followed by oral offers to sell securities may be distributed during the ten-day waiting period if the following requirements are met:

1. It must contain substantially the same information contained in the offering circular filed with the SEC;
2. It must bear the caption "Preliminary Offering Circular" on the outside front cover page and a statement containing the following information located along the left-hand margin of the page, printed perpendicular to the text, and in boldface type at least as large as that used in the body of the circular:
   a. An offering circular pursuant to Regulation A has been filed with the SEC;
   b. The information in the preliminary offering circular is subject to completion or amendment;
   c. The securities cannot be sold and offers to buy cannot be accepted prior to the delivery of an offering circular that is not designated as a preliminary offering circular,
   d. The preliminary offering circular *is not* an offer to sell or a solicitation of an offer to buy;
   e. There can be no sales of the securities in any state in which an offer, solicitation, or sale would be unlawful prior to registration or qualification under its Blue Sky laws.
3. It must relate to a proposed public offering of securities to be sold by or through one or more underwriters who are broker-dealers registered with the SEC under section 15 of the Securities Exchange Act of 1934;
4. A complete and accurate offering circular that is not designated as a preliminary offering circular must be furnished with or prior to delivery of the confirmation of sale to all persons who were furnished with a preliminary offering circular.

G. *After the ten-day waiting period: Commencement of the offering:*
   1. Informational advertisements in writing and on radio or television are allowed prior to sending or giving copies of the offering circular to prospective purchasers. The advertisements cannot contain offers to sell. The information in the advertisement is limited to the identity of the issuer and the character of its business, the name of the security, amount being offered, its price, and the sources from which an offering circular may be obtained.
   2. No security can be offered for sale or sold unless an offering circular is furnished to the purchaser before or at the time of the consummation of the sale, i.e., the delivery of the security to the purchaser.

H. *Filing notice of sales.* Interim and final reports are required.
   1. An *interim report* must be filed reporting sales during each six-month period after the date of the offering circular.
   2. A *final report* must be filed upon completion or termination of the offering.

I. *"Stale" offering circular.* If an offering is not complete within nine months from the date of the offering circular, the issuer must prepare, file, and use the revised offering circular according to the rules under Regulation A as if it were an original offering circular.

EXEMPTIONS FROM REGISTRATION

VI. The Securities Act of 1933 exempts specified securities as well as certain security transactions from its registration requirements. (See Figure 19-1.)

A. *Exempt securities.* The following securities are exempt from registration:
   1. Securities of federal, state, and local governments.

2. Securities issued by organizations already regulated by governmental agencies other than the SEC. For example, national and state banks, federal and state savings and loan associations, and railroads.
3. Securities issued by nonprofit organizations, such as charitable, religious, educational, or civil organizations.
4. Securities issued by life insurance companies other than variable annuities.
5. Securities issued without a sale, as when an issuer simply exchanges its securities for securities currently owned by shareholders, e.g., stock split.
6. Securities issued pursuant to court order in a bankruptcy reorganization case.
7. Commercial paper not exceeding a maturity of nine months, i.e., notes and drafts.
8. *Intrastate exemption under Rule 147.* This rule exempts any security that is part of single issue from registration and prospectus requirements, if the following requirements are met.
   a. The issuer must be organized and doing business within the same state as the state of residence of all offerees and purchasers. An issuer is "doing business" in a particular state if 80 percent of its gross revenue is derived from operations in the state.
   b. All offers as well as sales of the entire issue must be limited to residents of the state in which the issuer is organized and doing business. A sale of a single security to an out-of-state resident would destroy the exemption for the entire issue. Residence is defined by the SEC as follows:
      (1) Corporation. State in which it was organized.
      (2) Limited partnerships, trust, or other business organizations organized under special state statutes. State in which it was organized.
      (3) General partnerships or other business organizations organized under the common law. State where its principal office is located.
      (4) Individuals. State where their principal residence is located.
   c. Since the word intrastate under the rule applies only to the residence of the issuer, offerees, and purchasers, there is no prohibition against the use of the mails, or any means or instrument of interstate commerce in the offer and sale of the securities.
   d. SEC Rule 147 prohibits any resales of any part of an intrastate issue to nonresidents while the issue is being offered and for a period of nine months after the last sale thereof by the issuer.
      Note: If a specific type of *security* is exempt from registration, any transaction involving the sale of that security is also exempt. However, if only a specified type of securities *transaction* is exempt, the security itself is not exempt and any subsequent sale of the security must be registered or sold in another exempt transaction.
B. *Exempt securities transactions.* The following specific securities transactions are exempt under the Securities Act of 1933.
   1. *Transactions by persons other than an issuer, controlling person, or underwriter.* All persons other than an issuer, controlling persons, or underwriters need not file a registration statement with the SEC or provide a prospectus to a purchaser of their securities; e.g., resale of securities by investors with respect to securities previously issued.
   2. *Accredited investor exemption under the section 4(6) of the 1933 act.* Section 4(6) was added to the 1933 act by the Small Business Investment Incentive Act of 1980 (the "Incentive Act").
      a. *Issuer qualifications.* All issuers qualify.
      b. *Aggregate offering price* of an issue of securities cannot exceed $5,000,000.

c. *Number of investors.* The securities may be offered and sold to an *unlimited* number of "accredited investors."

d. *Qualifications of investors.* The offers and sales of securities can *only* be made *to one or more accredited investor.* An *"accredited investor"* for the purposes of this section is defined as follows.

  (1) *Institutional investors.* For example, banks, insurance companies, trusts, registered investment advisors, and any employee benefit plan (ERISA) with total assets of $5,000,000.

  (2) *Private business development companies.* This category includes companies organized for the purpose of making investments and that also provide "significant managerial assistance" to issuers of the securities involved.

  (3) *Tax exempt organizations with total assets in excess of $5,000,000.* For example, religious, charitable, literary, or educational organizations.

  (4) *Directors, executive officers, or general partners of the issuer of the securities being offered or sold.* This category also includes directors, executive officers, and general partners of general partners of that issuer.

  (5) *Purchasers of $150,000 or more of the securities if the total purchase price does not exceed 20 percent of the investor's net worth at the time of the purchase.*

   (a) The joint net worth of the investor and the investor's spouse can be used to measure the ratio of the purchase price to net worth.

   (b) The purchase price may be paid in cash, marketable securities, an unconditional debt to pay cash or marketable securities within five years of purchase, or by cancellation of an indebtedness.

  (6) *Purchasers (i.e., natural persons) whose net worth or joint worth with that person's spouse is in excess of $1,000,000 at the time of the purchase.*

  (7) *Purchasers (i.e., natural persons) who had an income in excess of $200,000 in each of the last two years and who reasonably expect an income in excess of $200,000 in the current year.*

  (8) *Entities in which all of the equity owners are accredited investors.*

e. *Commissions* are allowed to be paid to persons who solicit the sale of the securities on behalf of the issuer.

f. *Limitations on resale.* The issuer must control the purchasers' right to resell the securities. The following methods are used to control resales:

  (1) The *investment letter* signed by the purchaser. In this letter, the purchaser states that he or she knows that the securities purchased are exempt and that the purpose of the purchase is for investment and not for resale;

  (2) A *conspicuous warning* on the stock certificates evidences that the securities have not been registered under the act and that they cannot be sold in the absence of an effective registration; and

  (3) The issuer places a *"stop transfer order"* with its stock transfer agent. The transfer agent is obligated to refuse to transfer and reregister on the books of the corporation any stock certificate subject to the stop transfer order.

g. *Disclosure requirements.* No disclosure is required.

h. *Limitation on public offering. No* general public advertising or solicitation can be used to promote the sale of the securities.

i. *Notice of sales.* The issuer must file an initial, interim, and final report of the sales of the securities with the SEC as a condition of maintaining the exemption.

3. *Private offerings. SEC Rule 506 under Regulation D:*

  a. *Issuer qualifications.* All issuers qualify.

   b. *Aggregate offering price.* There is *no* limit on the aggregate offering price of securities.

   c. *Number of investors.* Issuers may sell the securities without registration to thirty-five nonaccredited persons and an unlimited number of "accredited investors." (See "Qualifications of investors," VI-B-2-d, above.)

   d. *Qualification of investors.* The purchasers or their "offeree representatives" must be sophisticated investors; e.g., financial institutions, trusts, insurance companies, or wealthy and well-advised business executives. Accredited investors are presumed to qualify as sophisticated investors.

   e. *Commissions* are allowed to be paid.

   f. *Limitations on resale.* The issuer must use essentially the same methods to control resales of the securities as are required of issuers under section 4(b) of the 1933 act. (See "Limitations on resale," VI-B-2-f, above.)

   g. *Disclosure requirements:*
     (1) If the securities are sold only to accredited investors, no information need be provided to them.
     (2) If the securities are sold to both accredited investors and nonaccredited persons, the issuer must provide to such investors, prior to the sale, detailed information about its management, capital structure, salaries of officers and directors, and financial affairs.

   h. *Limitations on public offering. No* general public advertising or solicitation can be used to promote the sale of the securities.

   i. *Notice of sales.* The issuer must file an initial, interim, and final report with the SEC as a condition of maintaining the exemption.

4. *"Small issue exemption": offers and sales of an issue of securities not exceeding $500,000. SEC Rule 504 under Regulation D:*

   a. *Issuer qualifications.* Only issuers who are *not* subject to the reporting requirements of the Securities Exchange Act of 1934 can use this exemption; i.e., issuers who have not voluntarily registered a class of securities with the SEC, or those who do not meet the $1,000,000 total asset and 500 shareholder test for mandatory registration (see XIII-A, B below). Investment companies and companies reporting to the SEC are not allowed to use this exemption.

   b. *Aggregate offering price* cannot exceed $500,000.

   c. *Number of investors.* There is *no* limitation.

   d. *Qualifications of investors.* Investors may be accredited or unaccredited.

   e. *Commissions* are allowed to be paid.

   f. *Limitations on resale.* The issuer must use essentially the same methods to control resales as those required of issuers under section 4(b) of the 1933 act *unless* the securities are registered and a disclosure document is delivered to a purchaser pursuant to the provisions of a state Blue Sky law. (See "Limitations on resale," VI-B-2-f, above.)

   g. *Disclosure requirements.* No disclosure is required.

   h. *Limitations on public offering. No* general public advertising or solicitation is permitted to promote the sale of the securities by the issuer or any person on its behalf *except* in those states where the security is registered pursuant to a state Blue Sky law that requires delivery of a disclosure document to a purchaser.

   i. *Notice of sales.* The issuer must file an initial, interim, and final report of sales of the securities with the SEC as a condition of maintaining the exemption.

5. *Offers and sales of an issue of securities not exceeding $5,000,000 during any twelve-month period. SEC Rule 505 under Regulation D:*

a. *Issuer qualifications.* All issuers qualify except investment companies.

b. *Aggregate offering price* cannot exceed $5,000,0000 during any twelve-month period.

c. *Number of investors.* The issue may be sold to not more than thirty-five unaccredited persons and an unlimited number of accredited investors. (See "Qualifications of investors," VI-B-2, above.)

d. *Qualifications of investors.* Investors may be accredited or unaccredited.

e. *Commissions* are allowed to be paid.

f. *Limitations on resale.* The issuer must use essentially the same methods to control resales of the securities as are required of issuers under section 4(6) of the 1933 act. (See "Limitations on resale," VI-B-2-f, above.)

g. *Disclosure requirements.* Disclosure is required. The type of information required to be disclosed and the persons to whom disclosure must be made are essentially the same as are required pursuant to a "private offering" under SEC Rule 506, Regulation D. (See "Disclosure requirements," VI-B-3-g, above.)

h. *Limitations on public offering.* General public solicitation or advertising is prohibited.

i. *Notice of sales.* The issuer must file an initial, interim, and final report with the SEC as a condition of maintaining the exemption.

C. *Dealer-exempt transactions.* The primary purpose of the 1933 act is to regulate public distributions of newly issued securities by or on behalf of issuers, controlling persons, and underwriters (as defined in III-C-3 above). Its purpose is not to regulate public trading (i.e., buying and selling) of seasoned securities by ordinary investors or their brokers and dealers on the over-the-counter markets or the securities exchanges.

1. A dealer (including an underwriter no longer acting as an underwriter in respect to the securities sold in such transaction) need not deliver a prospectus (or in the case of a Regulation A registration, an offering circular) to a purchaser of securities in the following securities transactions.

a. *Regular public offering:*

(1) A sale of securities by a dealer that took place either *forty or ninety days or more after the first date upon which there was a bona fide offer of the securities to the public* by an issuer or underwriter.

(a) Forty days or more if the issuer had sold a previous issue under an effective registration statement; or

(b) Ninety days or more if the securities were a part of an issuer's first public offering.

(2) A dealer is also exempt if the sale of securities took place either *forty or ninety days or more after the effective date of a registration statement* that covered the securities sold.

(a) Forty days or more if the issuer had sold a previous issue under an effective registration statement; or

(b) Ninety days or more if the securities are a part of the issuer's first public issue.

b. *Regulation A public offering.* A sale of securities by a dealer is exempt if it took place ninety days or more after the first date upon which there was a bona fide offer of the securities to the public by an issuer or underwriter. *Note*: The words "bona fide" are used to enable dealers to begin trading securities a specified number of days after a genuine public offering, even though there may have been one or more unlawful previous offers to the public.

VII. *Special Note:* The exemption of specific securities or specific securities transactions from registration *does not* eliminate or preclude criminal or civil liability of any person, entity, or association that violates the antifraud or other provisions of the Securities Act of 1933 and the Securities Exchange Act of 1934.

BLUE SKY LAWS: STATE SECURITIES REGULATION

VIII. Securities registered with the Securities and Exchange Commission must also be qualified under any *Blue Sky laws* (disclosure laws) in any state where they are offered for sale. Securities exempt from registration under the 1933 act are *not* automatically exempt from state securities regulation.

SANCTIONS AND REMEDIES UNDER THE 1933 ACT

IX. The 1933 act imposes criminal penalties, SEC sanctions, and civil liability for damages upon violators of its registration, prospectus, antifraud, and other provisions. (See Figure 19-2 and Table 19-1.)

A. *Criminal penalties of a fine* of up to $5,000 *and/or imprisonment* up to five years may be imposed upon any "person" who willfully violates any provision of the 1933 act or any rule or regulation promulgated by the SEC under the 1933 act.

B. *Civil Sanctions and remedies. Securities Exchange Commission (SEC) sanctions.* The following civil sanctions and remedies are available to the SEC.

1. *Injunction.* The SEC can petition a court for an injunction to stop the following violations:

a. Offers to sell or sales of securities without registration with the SEC.

b. Offers to sell or sales of securities prior to the effective date of registration.

FIGURE 19-2   SANCTIONS AND REMEDIES UNDER THE SECURITIES ACT OF 1933

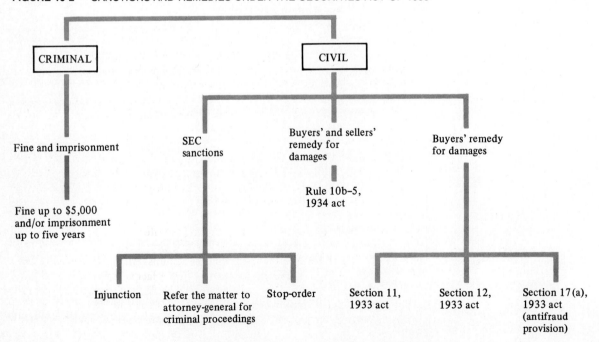

    c. Offers to sell or sales of securities after the effective date of registration without tendering a prospectus to prospective buyers before or in conjunction with the sale.

  2. *Stop order.* The SEC has the power to issue a stop order during or after the registration process is completed.

    a. Issue it before the effective date of registration to stop further consideration of the registration statement by the SEC.

    b. Issue it after the effective date of registration to stop further offers to sell or sales.

    c. A stop order lasts for an indefinite duration of time.

  3. *Referral for criminal proceedings.* The SEC has the authority to refer the matter to the U.S. Attorney General for criminal proceedings against a violator.

C. *Civil liabilities for damages to private persons.* In addition to criminal penalties and SEC sanctions, the 1933 act also imposes civil liability upon violators. Persons "injured" as a result of a violation can recover damages (i.e., out-of-pocket losses). Sections 11 and 12 prescribe the types of statements, omissions, conduct, and activities that are in violation.

  1. *Section 11: Liability for misstatements and omissions in registration statements.* This section gives purchasers of securities (i.e., the original purchaser and subsequent purchasers) the right to recover damages (i.e., out-of-pocket losses) from specified persons for their *false or misleading statements or omissions of material fact* made in any part of an effective registration statement, including a prospectus.

    a. *Liability without fault.* The liability imposed is a form of liability without fault (i.e., absolute or strict liability) for false or misleading statements or omissions of material fact, subject only to the defenses explained below. An injured party need not prove that the violator committed negligence or fraud. All that need be proved is the existence of the false or misleading statements or omissions of material fact. The violator then has the burden of establishing a defense in order to escape liability.

    b. *"Persons" liable.* The following persons may incur liability under section 11:

      (1) *Signers of the registration statement.* These include the issuer, principle executive, financial or accounting officers, and others (see IV-A-7 above). *Note:* The "due diligence" defense discussed below is not available to an issuer. "Issuer" includes a controlling person.

      (2) *Directors, partners, or other persons.* Directors, partners, or other persons who gave their consent to be named as such or are named as about to become directors or partners are liable.

      (3) *Experts* such as accountants, attorneys, appraisers, engineers, or geologists who are named as having prepared or certified a part of the registration statement. See also Chapter 20. *Note:* The liability of these persons only extends to false or misleading misstatements or omissions in statements, reports, documents, or other material prepared or certified by them.

      (4) *Underwriters of the securities.* All underwriters of securities under a registration statement are liable under this provision.

    c. *Materiality.* The false statement or misleading omission must be of a *material fact* in an effective registration statement. *Test:* A fact is material if a "reasonable person," acting in the securities market, would likely attach importance to its statement or its omission and thereby be influenced.

    d. *Privity, scienter, or reliance.* Neither privity, scienter, nor reliance is required for liability.

(1) Original purchasers as well as a subsequent purchaser (i.e., those not in privity of contract) can recover damages.

(2) The purchaser need not prove that the person being sued (defendant) possessed *"scienter"* at the time the false or misleading statement or omission was made, i.e., the intent to deceive, manipulate, or defraud.

(3) The purchaser need not have relied on the false or misleading statement or omission. The purchaser may recover even though he or she did not even see them.

e. *Causation.* The false or misleading statements or omissions must have been the cause of the purchaser's loss.

f. *Defenses.* The absolute liability under this section has been eroded by the defenses discussed below.

(1) *"Due diligence" defense* is available to all persons except the issuer (including a controlling person). The burden of proving "due diligence" is on the "person" being sued.

(a) As a general rule, "due diligence" is established by proof that, after the defendant (i.e., party being sued) made a reasonable investigation, he or she had no *reasonable* grounds to believe and did not believe that the statements made in the registration statement were false and that there were omissions. Due diligence is, in effect, the lack of negligence or fraud. This requirement of reasonableness is commonly referred to as the *"prudent man" standard.* It requires that a person exert the same amount of care that is required of prudent people in the management of their own property.

(b) *Issuers.* As stated above, the issuer cannot avail itself of the "due diligence" defense.

(c) *Signers of the registration statement, existing directors and partners and consenting future directors, and partners or underwriters* (to the extent of their underwriting commitment).

    i. *"Nonexperts'" statements or omissions.* In regard to this type of statement or omission, these defendants must prove that their belief was formed and based upon their reasonable investigation.

    ii. *"Experts'" statements or omissions.* In regard to this type of statement or omission, these defendants are not required to investigate. They *need only prove* that they had no reasonable grounds to believe and they did not believe that there were untrue statements or misleading omissions in the experts' statements, reports, or evaluations. In other words, they are not liable when they reasonably rely upon statements, certifications, reports, documents, or evaluations made by experts and that are included in the registration statement.

(d) *Experts* (i.e., accountants, attorneys, appraisers, engineers, geologists, etc.):

    i. The existence of false or misleading statements or omissions made by experts is determined at the time registration becomes effective, not at the time that they provided their statements, certifications, reports, documents, or evaluations to the issuer.

    ii. To be relieved of liability, experts must prove that as regards any part of the registration statement that consists of or is derived from their statements, certifications, reports, documents, or evaluations that they had after a reasonable investigation no reasonable grounds to believe, at the time the registration statement became effective, that the statements made therein were untrue and that there were misleading omissions of material facts. All knowledge that a "prudent person" with similar qualifications and under similar circumstances would have discovered is imputed to the "expert."

    (2) *Prior knowledge of purchaser.* A defense is established by proof that the purchaser had actual knowledge of the falsity of the statement or the misleading nature of the omission prior to or at the time of the purchase of the securities.

    (3) *Lack of materiality.* If the fact misstated or omitted was not material to the decision to purchase, a defense exists.

    (4) *Statute of limitations.* The cause of action for damages is lost if the purchaser does not file a lawsuit for damages against the alleged violator within one year after the false statement or misleading omission was or should have been discovered but no more than three years after the security was offered to the public.

g. *Out-of-pocket losses* (i.e., damages). A violator is liable to a purchaser for out-of-pocket losses.

    (1) If the purchaser is still the owner of the securities involved in the violation, that purchaser may recover the difference between the amount paid and the market value of the security at the time of the lawsuit.

    (2) If the purchaser no longer owns the security, the amount recoverable is the difference between the amount paid for the security and the amount received when it was sold.

2. *Section 12(1): Liability for sales without an effective registration statement.* Section 12(1) of the 1933 act prohibits offers to sell or sales of securities in violation of section 5a. As previously discussed in this chapter, section 5a of the 1933 act provides that newly issued nonexempt securities cannot be lawfully offered for sale or sold in interstate commerce or through the mails unless a registration statement is effective and a prospectus relating to the securities is delivered before or at the time of the sale to the purchaser (see IV above). *Note:* Section 11 liability is based on false or misleading statements or omissions of material facts *in an existing effective registration statement,* while liability under section 12(1) is based on the *nonexistence of an effective registration statement.*

a. *Liability without fault.* The liability is absolute, and does not depend on fault (i.e., negligence or fraud).

b. *"Persons" liable.* Any "person" who offers or sells an unregistered security in violation of section 5 is liable.

    (1) The words "offers" or "sells" have the same meaning here as they did under section 5.

    (2) "Persons" include issuers, controlling persons, underwriters, and dealers (review III-C above).

c. *Privity is not generally required for recovery:*

    (1) Privity is not required to recover out-of-pocket damages from a violator.

    (2) Privity is required in order to assert the remedies of rescission and restitution.

    (3) See 2-e below.

d. *Scienter or reliance.* Neither scienter nor reliance is required for recovery of damages.

e. *Remedies of the purchaser:*

    (1) *Damages.* A purchaser who no longer owns the security may recover damages from a violator of section 12(1).

    (2) *Rescission and restitution.* A purchaser who is still the owner of the security may rescind the purchase, obtaining a refund (i.e., restitution) of the purchase price paid plus the statutory rate of interest, less any income received thereon, i.e., dividends, profits, or interest.

3. *Section 17a, the antifraud provision.* A seller is liable to a purchaser for damages caused by the seller's fraudulent conduct or activity in respect to any offer or sale of *any* securities to such purchaser.

    a. *Introduction.* As noted previously, liability under section 11 (for false or misleading statements and omissions in an effective registration statement and prospectus) and under section 12(1) (for sales of nonexempt securities without an effective registration statement) is extremely narrow in its scope and application. Section 17a is intended to prohibit all types of schemes and devices to defraud utilized by a seller of any securities.

    b. *Fraudulent statements, conduct, or activities.* Section 17a makes it unlawful for any person in the offer or sale of any security "by the use of any means or instruments of transportation or communication in interstate commerce or by the use of the mails, directly or indirectly":

        (1) To make oral or written fraudulent misrepresentations of material facts;

        (2) To fraudulently conceal material facts;

        (3) "To employ any device, scheme, or artifice to defraud"; or

        (4) "To engage in any transaction, practice, or course of business that operates or would operate as fraud or deceit."

    c. *Persons liable.* Any seller of securities can be liable for a violation of this section.

    d. *Persons entitled to recover.* This section provides a remedy for damages to a purchaser of securities. A seller who has been defrauded by a purchaser has no remedy under this section. *Note:* Section 10b and SEC Rule 10b-5 under the 1934 act provide a remedy to both sellers and purchasers for similar fraudulent statements, omissions, conduct, or activities (see g below).

    e. *Scope of coverage.* The section applies to all securities; listed or unlisted, registered or unregistered, and exempt or nonexempt.

    f. *Elements of a violation* are:

        (1) *Scienter* (i.e., the intent to deceive, manipulate, or defraud).

        (2) *Materiality* of facts fraudulently misrepresented or concealed.

        (3) *Causation.* The fraudulent conduct must have been the cause of the purchaser's out-of-pocket loss.

        (4) *Reliance.* The purchaser must have relied upon the fraudulent misrepresentation or concealment; i.e., it must have induced the purchaser to make the purchase.

    g. *Civil liability for damages.* This section does not expressly provide a remedy for damages to a purchaser. A few lower federal courts have allowed a private cause of action for damages to a purchaser under this section. Other courts have refused to do so. The U.S. Supreme Court has not yet ruled that such cause of action exists.

    Note: If a court would deny a purchaser a private cause of action for damages under this section, that purchaser would be able to recover under section 10b and Rule 10b-5 under the 1934 act (see XIX-C-2 below).

STATUTE OF LIMITATIONS

X. *Statute of limitations.* Neither a criminal action nor a private lawsuit for damages can be filed against a violator more than one year after the false statement or misleading omission was or should have been discovered, or more than three years after the security was first offered to the public. If the time limitation has expired, a purchaser is without a civil remedy and the violator is not subject to criminal prosecution.

SECURITIES EXCHANGE ACT OF 1934 (As Amended)

XI. The Securities Exchange Act of 1934 (the 1934 act) adds to the disclosure requirements of the Securities Act of 1933 (the 1933 act). The objective of the 1934 act is basically the same as that for the 1933 act; that is, the protection of investors by requiring full and fair disclosure. The 1933 act regulates the distribution and marketing of new issues of securities (i.e., "going public") by requiring the disclosure of material information pertaining to the issuer, the securities to be issued, and the issuing transaction. The 1934 act is primarily concerned with the regulation of trading in classes of securities after their initial issue (i.e., seasoned securities). It continues the requirement of disclosure of material information and regulates all aspects of securities trading activities. (See Figure 19-3 and Table 19-1.) Some of the persons and activities regulated by the 1934 act are as follows:

A. Issuers of listed and unlisted securities;

B. Reporting by issuers, officers, directors, "insiders," and brokers and dealers;

C. Tender offers;

D. Stock exchanges and stock exchange activity;

E. Over-the-counter securities and trading;

F. Proxy solicitations and statements;

G. Foreign corrupt practices;

H. Fraudulent manipulations and schemes;

I. Fraudulent statements and misleading omissions of material fact in filings with the SEC;

J. Margin requirements and borrowing by broker-dealers;

K. Registration of classes of securities;

PERSONS, ASSOCIATIONS, AND ENTITIES REGULATED

XII. Issuers, officers and directors of an issuer and other "insiders," national securities exchanges, broker and dealer members of national security exchanges, and brokers and dealers who are not members of a national security exchange, if they buy or sell securities "in interstate commerce," and certain other persons and entities are regulated by the 1934 act. They may be criminally or civilly liable for a violation of its registration, reporting (i.e., disclosure), antifraud, or other provisions.

A. *Issuer* includes an individual, association, or entity that issues or proposes to issue a security "in interstate commerce."

    1. *Listed issuer* is one with any class of its securities listed and traded on a national securities exchange approved by the SEC. Equity as well as debt securities can be listed.

    2. *Unlisted issuer* is one whose securities are not listed but are traded on the *over-the-counter securities market.*

B. *Officers and directors of an issuer.* "Officers" include a president, vice president, treasurer, secretary, comptroller, and any other person who performs the duties of the foregoing officers. For example, a general manager of a business would be an "officer."

FIGURE 19-3   SECURITIES EXCHANGE ACT OF 1934

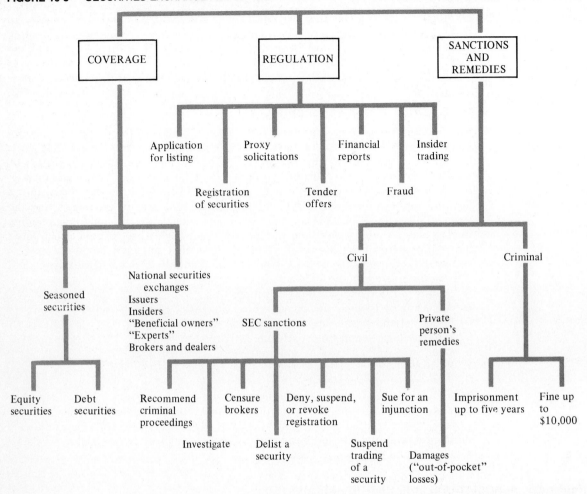

C. *Insider.* The term "insider" has different meanings depending on the nature of the transaction and the applicable provision of the 1934 act.
  1. *Reporting and short-swing trading provisions.* Under these provisions, an insider includes any officer and director of the issuer and any person (shareholder) who directly or indirectly (i.e., the beneficial owner) owns 10 percent or more of any class of an issuer's equity securities (see XV-B-1 below for a more detailed definition of an "insider").
  2. *Civil liability for damages under SEC Rule 10b-5.* Under Rule 10b-5, an "insider" includes controlling persons, officers, directors, and employees of an issuer, beneficial owners of 10 percent or more of any class of an issuer's registered securities, *or any person* to whom the issuer or its officers and directors entrust material inside (nonpublic) information, *and any person* who knowingly acquired inside (nonpublic) material information (see XVI below).
D. *National securities exchanges.* A national securities exchange is an association of stockbrokers approved (registered) by the SEC that engage in buying and selling securities and related activities.

E. *Members of national securities exchanges* are brokers who possess the right to use exchange facilities for the purpose of dealing in securities.

F. *Brokers and dealers.* A *"broker"* is any person or entity (other than a bank) that is in the business of effecting purchases or sales of securities for others. A *"dealer"* is one that is in the business of buying and selling securities for its own account. A *"broker-dealer"* is one that is in the business of effecting purchases and sales of securities for its own account as well as for the accounts of others. Banks, trustees, and persons who do not buy or sell stock as a part of a regular business are not dealers. An issuer is not a broker or dealer because it is not in the business of effecting purchases or sales of securities for others, or in the business of buying and selling securities for its own account. Brokers, dealers, or broker-dealers become subject to regulation under sections 15 and 15b of the 1934 act in one of the following ways:

   1. By dealing in securities as members of a national securities exchange; or
   2. As nonmembers of a national securities exchange, they deal in securities "in interstate commerce."

G. *Beneficial owner for purposes of reporting acquisitions and public tender offers to acquire 5 percent of any class of equity security.* "Beneficial owner" of equity securities for these purposes includes any person who, directly or indirectly, possesses or shares in:

   1. *Voting power.* Voting power includes the power to vote, or to direct voting of an equity security.
   2. *Investment power.* Investment power includes the power to dispose of, or to direct the disposition of an equity security.

   Note: The definition of "beneficial owner" for the purposes of the 1934 act is much different than that used to determine whether any particular shareholder is an "insider" (see "Insider" XV-B-1 below).

H. *Other individuals, associations, and entities.* These may include any person, association, or entity that knowingly receives inside (nonpublic) information, or accountants, attorneys, engineers, appraisers, geologists, and others who may violate the provisions of the 1934 act.

SECTION 12: REGISTRATION REQUIREMENTS

XIII. Certain issuers, national securities exchanges, certain brokers and dealers, and insiders are subject to the registration provisions of the 1934 act. The act provides for both mandatory and voluntary registration. (See Figure 19-4 and Table 19-1.)

A. *Mandatory registration.* An issuer, insider, broker, or dealer who does not comply with the mandatory registration requirements of the act may be subject to SEC sanctions, civil liabilities, and criminal penalties.

   1. *Issuers of unlisted equity securities* (i.e., equity securities *traded on the over-the-counter securities market*). Registration is required of all issuers of unlisted (nonexempt) equity securities if the following three conditions exist (Section 12g).

      a. *Interstate Commerce.* This condition is met whenever any issuer engages in interstate commerce or in a business affecting interstate commerce. It also is satisfied when the issuer's securities are traded in interstate or intrastate commerce by the use of the mails, any facility of a national securities exchange, the telephone, or any other interstate instrumentality or means of communication;

      b. The issuer owns *total (i.e., gross, not net) assets exceeding $1,000,000;* and

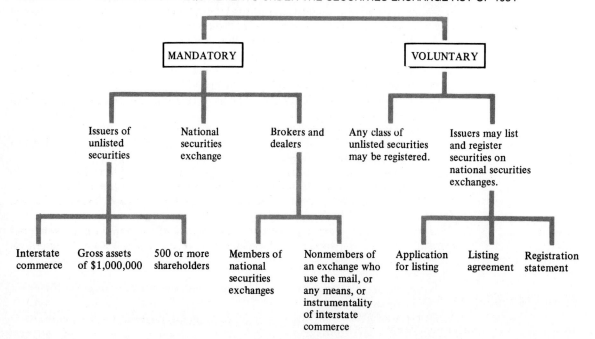

c. *Any class of the issuer's equity securities* (i.e., nonexempted) is *"held of record" by 500 or more persons.*

(1) A *class of securities* includes all of an issuer's securities with substantially similar characteristics and in which its owners possess substantially similar rights; e.g., "Class A" common stock, or cumulative participating preferred stock.

(2) *Equity securities* include stock (i.e., common or preferred), or similar securities, and any security convertible into or exchangeable for stock of a similar security, e.g., convertible bonds and stock warrants.

(3) *Exempt securities.* This provision exempts from registration any securities that are:

(*a*) Issued by state or federal savings and loan associations;

(*b*) Issued by religious, educational, or charitable not-for-profit organizations;

(*c*) Listed on and registered with a national securities exchange;

(*d*) In the form of mortgage notes with principal and interest guaranteed by the U.S. government, e.g., FHA mortgages;

(*e*) Issued by agricultural cooperatives; and

(*f*) Issued by a state-regulated insurance company.

2. *National securities exchanges* must register with the SEC.

3. *Brokers and dealers* must register with the SEC if they either deal in listed securities as members of a national securities exchange, or as nonmembers of a national securities exchange, they use the mails or any means or instrumentality of interstate commerce to effect any transaction in, or induce or attempt to induce the purchase or sale of *any* security other than an exempted security. A broker or dealer that deals exclusively in intrastate commerce and does not use the facilities of a national securities exchange is not required to register.

B. *Voluntary registration:*

    1. *Unlisted securities.* Section 12(g)(1) allows voluntary registration of any class of securities by its issuer. For example, issuers of unlisted securities (i.e., traded over-the-counter) who do not meet the $1,000,000 total asset and 500 shareholder tests for mandatory registration.

    2. *Listed securities.* Section 12b allows issuers to list and register any class of their securities on a national securities exchange.

        a. To list and register a class of securities on a national securities exchange the issuer is required to:

            (1) Submit an *application for listing* to the exchange;

            (2) Enter into a *listing agreement* with the exchange that binds the issuer to a specified code of conduct; and

            (3) File a *registration statement* with the exchange and the SEC.

        b. Section 12(a) makes it unlawful for any member of a national securities exchange or any broker to deal with an unlisted (unregistered) security on the exchange.

C. *Content of the registration statement.* The registration statement must contain a large amount of detailed information about the issuer, such as its assets, business, management, and financial status.

EFFECT OF REGISTRATION

XIV. An issuer's registration of any class of its securities subjects itself and its "insiders" to regulation under the provisions of the 1934 act. Brokers, dealers, and national securities exchanges registered in compliance with the registration requirements of the 1934 act are also regulated. *Note:* The listings of the types of regulation below are provided to give the reader an overview of the types and scope of regulation imposed upon persons upon registration with the SEC. These types of regulation and others are discussed in detail later in this chapter.

    A. *Issuers* are subject to the following types of regulation:

        1. The periodic reporting requirements under section 13; i.e., annual (10-K), quarterly (10-Q), current (8-K), and other required reports;

        2. The accounting, recordkeeping, and internal control requirements under the "corrupt practices" amendment to the 1934 act;

        3. Proxy solicitation requirements under section 14 and SEC rules and regulations;

        4. Potential civil and criminal liability.

    B. *Insiders* are automatically subject to regulation upon registration of any class of equity securities by an issuer. Insider activities and conduct regulated include the following:

        1. Reporting requirements of section 16(a). This section requires insiders to file an initial statement of equity security holdings and thereafter file reports of their purchases or sales of equity securities registered by the issuer in which they are insiders.

        2. Short-swing profits reporting requirements and liability under section 16(b);

        3. The beneficial ownership reporting requirements under section 13(d)(1); i.e., acquisition of 5 percent or more of a class of the equity securities of a company other than the one in which a person is an insider;

        4. Potential civil and criminal liability.

    C. *Brokers, dealers, or broker-dealers.* Their conduct and activities are subject to the following regulation:

        1. Margin requirements and restrictions on borrowing under sections 7 and 8;

        2. Specialized reporting requirements under sections 15 and 17;

3. Records and books of accountkeeping requirements under sections 11 and 17;
4. Rules of conduct for broker-members of national securities exchanges under section 6;
5. Financial responsibility requirements under SEC rules and section 15(c); and
6. Potential civil and criminal liability.

D. *National securities exchanges.* Upon registration, a national securities exchange and its members are subject to the following provisions of the 1934 act and regulation by the SEC:
1. Reporting requirements;
2. A registered exchange must adopt disciplinary rules that control the conduct of its members under section 6(b);
3. Its disciplinary rules must provide for expulsion, suspension, or other disciplinary measures for members who fail to follow such rules;
4. Provisions for civil and criminal liability.

REPORTING (DISCLOSURE) REQUIREMENTS

XV. *In general.* The reporting (disclosure) requirements of the 1934 act apply to registered issuers, insiders, certain brokers and dealers, any persons acquiring or holding 5 percent or more of a registered class of equity securities of another company, and to any persons who intend to make a public cash tender offer to buy registered equity securities if such purchase will result in that person becoming the owner or beneficial owner of more than 5 percent of a class of registered equity securities.

A. *Section 13: Issuers.* Subsequent to mandatory or voluntary registration under section 12, issuers are required, under section 13, to continue reporting to the SEC on an annual, quarterly, and current basis. These reports continue to update the information previously provided by the issuer in its registration statement.
1. *Annual reports.* Form 10-K is commonly used for filing annual reports. Some of the information required to be included in the annual report is as follows:
   a. Certified financial statements. *Note:* Certified financial statements are not usually required for quarterly or current reports;
   b. List of directors and officers;
   c. Summary of earnings and its analysis by management;
   d. Description of the issuer's business and its product lines;
   e. Information about its securities, such as their principal trading market, market prices, and dividends paid.
2. *Quarterly reports.* Form 10-Q is used for quarterly reports. Its purpose is to disclose quarterly and year-to-date information. It reveals changes in an issuer's operations, management, and financial condition or structure that may occur in the interim between annual reports. Certification of unconsolidated financial statements is not required in the quarterly reports.
3. *"Current reports."* Form 8-K is used to report important events, circumstances, or changes that may affect the issuer in a material way. The current report must be filed with the SEC within fifteen days of the happening of the important event, circumstance, or change. Financial statements are not usually required to be included in a current report. Examples of important matters to be reported are:
   a. Initiation or termination of important lawsuits by or against the issuer;
   b. Change in controlling interests in the issuer;
   c. Substantial acquisitions or dispositions of an issuer's assets outside of the regular course of business;

d. Change in the issuer's certifying accountants; or

e. A repurchase by an issuer of 10 percent of its outstanding stock.

4. *Suspension of reporting requirements.* In any fiscal year other than that in which an issuer's registration became effective, the reporting requirements of section 13 are suspended if at the beginning of that fiscal year securities of the class registered are held of record by less than 300 persons.

B. *Insiders and insider trading.* Persons who are "insiders" at the time an issuer registers any class of its equity securities with the SEC, persons who become "insiders" subsequent to a registration of securities, and "insiders" who engage in trading of any registered equity security are required to file disclosure reports with the SEC. (See Figure 19-5.)

1. *Insider.* For purposes of reporting and insider trading under section 16(a) and Rule 16a-1, an "insider" includes the following persons:

    a. *Officers and directors of a registered issuer.* "Officer" includes a president, vice president, treasurer, secretary, comptroller, and any other person who performs the duties of the foregoing officers (Rule 3b-2). For example, a general manager of a business would be an "officer." "Directors" include directors of corporations or persons who perform similar functions with respect to an incorporated or unincorporated organization [section 3(a)(7)].

    b. *Any legal owner or beneficial owner of more than 10 percent of any class of nonexempt registered and outstanding equity securities.* Treasury stock is excluded from computation of the 10 percent (Rule 16a-2). Equity securities are "beneficially owned" if they are owned by:

        (1) An officer's, director's, or legal owner's spouse, minor children, or other relative who shares the same home;

        (2) A trust in which its settlor (i.e., its creator) has the right to either revoke the trust, to obtain the income from it, or to direct the sale of equity securities in the trust (Rule 16a-8). For example, the beneficiaries (i.e., the trust certificate holders) of a Real Estate Investments Trust (REIT) or a Massachusetts (business) Trust (see Chapter 15, XXIV and XXV, for a detailed discussion of these types of trusts); or

FIGURE 19-5 DISCLOSURE (FILING) REQUIREMENTS FOR ISSUERS AND INSIDERS UNDER THE SECURITIES EXCHANGE ACT OF 1934

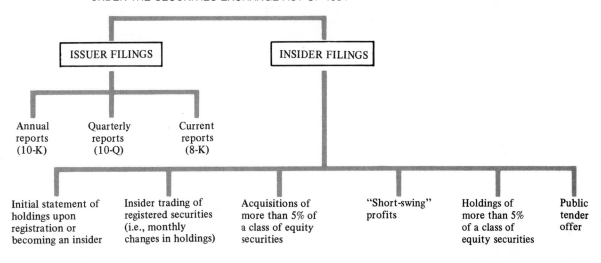

(3) A trustee if either the trustee or a member of the trustee's immediate family possesses an unconditional and absolute right to the income from the trust or to withdraw its principal (i.e., its corpus);

(4) All partners are beneficial owners of their individual pro rata share of equity securities owned by the partnership (Rule 16a-8).

2. *"Equity security."* An equity security is any written evidence of any ownership interest in a business endeavor. It includes stock, any security convertible to stock, and any warrant or right to subscribe to or purchase stock [section 3(a)(11) and Rule 3a 11-1]. Written evidences of debt are not equity securities.

3. *Reporting requirements of insiders.* Insiders may be required to report because they are insiders of an issuer that has registered either any class of its securities or because they hold or seek to acquire privately or publicly more than 5 percent of any class of equity securities registered by an issuer, (i.e., other than the one to whom they stand in relationship to as insiders).

   a. *Upon registration* of any one class of equity securities by an issuer, its insiders must file an initial statement of holdings with the SEC that discloses the extent of their ownership of any class of that issuer's equity securities [section 16(a) and Rule 16a-1].

   b. *Upon becoming an insider* of a registered issuer, a person must file an initial statement with the SEC disclosing the extent of personal ownership in any class of that issuer's equity securities (Rule 16a-1).

   c. *Insider trading.* Insiders must report to the SEC any changes in their ownership of equity securities in any month in which such changes occur (Rule 16a-1).

   d. *Acquisitions of more than 5 percent of any class of registered equity securities.* Section 13(d) and SEC rules thereunder. All persons *acquiring* (i.e., by private purchases or on the open market) direct or indirect beneficial ownership of more than 5 percent of any class of registered equity securities of *any* issuer must report such acquisition to the SEC. (See XV-C below for a detailed discussion of this reporting requirement.)

   e. *Holdings of more than 5 percent of any class of registered equity securities.* Section 13b and SEC rules thereunder. Persons *holding* directly or indirectly beneficial ownership of more than 5 percent of any class of registered securities of *any* issuer must report their holdings to the SEC.

   f. *Public cash tender offers.* Section 14(d)(1). An insider or any other person must file a report to the SEC prior to making, inviting, or soliciting a public cash tender offer to purchase any securities of a registered class of securities if after such purchase the insider or other person would be the beneficial owner of more than 5 percent of that class of equity securities (see XV-D below).

4. *Insider trading: Short-swing profits* under section 16(b). Any *short-swing profit* that an insider derives from any purchase of the issuer's securities within any one six-month period (i.e., less than six months) must be paid over to the company.

   a. *Automatic liability.* Liability automatically attaches if there is any way that profit can be determined matching *any* sale with *any* purchase or vice versa. For example, an officer of Y corporation made the following purchases and sales of Y corporation's stock. A purchase at $20 per share on April 10, 1981, a sale at $19 per share on June 10, 1981, and a purchase at $18 a share on July 10, 1981. These transactions amount to a $1 per share profit even though the officer incurred an actual monetary *net* loss of $2 per share. The sale at $19 a share is matched against the purchase at $18 a share to derive the $1 per share profit.

b. *"Sale" and "purchase."* These terms have a broad meaning. For example, the exercise of a stock option is considered to be a purchase under section 16(b). As another example, "sales" or "purchases" include certain mergers, conversions of convertible stocks or bonds, or the exercise of stock warrants.

c. *No defenses.* Good faith, lack of inside (nonpublic) information, or lack of intent to profit will not relieve an insider from liability. Liability is automatic.

d. *Derivative lawsuit.* If the insider does not pay over short-swing profits to the issuer, any shareholder of the issuer has a right to file a lawsuit in the name of and in behalf of the issuer and recover the profits. An issuer can also sue in its own name to recover. Exceptions:

(1) Transactions involving securities with a market value of less than $3,000;

(2) Securities that have not been purchased or sold within a period of six months; and

(3) Securities transactions by executors, administrators, guardians, receivers, and trustees in bankruptcy.

C. *Private or open-market acquisitions of more than 5 percent of any class of registered equity securities.* Section 13(d)(1) and SEC Rule 13d-1(a) require filing (disclosure) of an *"information statement"* with the SEC within ten days after any person acquires, directly or indirectly, the beneficial ownership of more than 5 percent of any class of registered equity securities; i.e., those securities registered under the mandatory or voluntary registration provisions of section 12 (see XIII-A and XIII-B above).

1. *Parties to whom disclosure is required.* The information statement must be:

a. Filed with the SEC;

b. Sent to the issuer of the class of equity securities;

c. Sent to each securities exchange where the securities are traded.

2. *Time of disclosure.* The information statement must be filed and sent as indicated above within ten days after the acquisition.

3. *Contents of the information statement.* At a minimum, the information statement must reveal the purpose of the acquisition, the class of equity securities and their issuer, the name of the acquirer and its management, and the source and amount of funds to be used to carry out the acquisition.

4. *Multiple filing requirement.* The information statement is not a substitute for the reports required to be filed by "insiders" under any other section of the 1934 act (see XV-B-3 above). In other words, an insider of one issuer may become a "beneficial owner" of a class of equity securities of another issuer, and thereby be subject to the additional reporting requirements of section 13(d)(1) and Rule 13d-(a).

5. *Beneficial ownership.* "Beneficial ownership" for the purposes of this section is defined as having or sharing the power, directly or indirectly, to vote or direct voting of an equity security, or to dispose, or to direct the disposition of, an equity security. The following are examples of beneficial owners of equity securities:

a. A holder of an option to purchase equity securities that is exercisable at any time or within a sixty-day period of time (Rule 13d-3).

b. A holder of warrants or stock rights evidencing the right to acquire securities within sixty days (Rule 13d-3).

c. A holder of bonds convertible to equity securities within sixty days (Rule 13d-3).

d. A person who has a right to acquire securities pursuant to a right to revoke a trust, a securities account, or other arrangement at any time within a period of sixty days (Rule 13d-3).

6. *Class of equity security.* The term "class of equity securities" was previously defined in this chapter (review XIII-A-1 and XV-B-2 above).

7. *Exemptions.* Section 13(d)(6) provides the following exemptions:
   a. Acquisitions by the issuer of the securities, i.e., treasury stock;
   b. Acquisitions exempted by the SEC; for example, the SEC has exempted persons who acquire more than 5 percent of a class of securities pursuant to preemptive rights;
   c. Acquisitions by a person if that person's total acquisitions of the same class of securities during the preceding twelve months do not exceed 2 percent of that class.

D. *Public cash tender offers.* Section 14(d)(1) makes it unlawful for any "person" without first complying with its reporting and disclosure requirements to make, request, or invite a tender offer for the purchase of any class of registered equity securities if after such purchase the "person" would be the beneficial owner of more than 5 percent of such class of equity securities.

1. *Purpose.* The purpose of this section is to give issuers and shareholders of issuers prior notice of acquisitions of large blocks of equity securities of any one issuer and to alert such issuer to a possible take-over.

2. *Parties to whom disclosure is required.* A *"tender offer statement"* must be:
   a. Filed with the SEC;
   b. Sent to the issuer of the class of equity securities involved in the tender offer; and
   c. Sent to each securities exchange where the equity securities are traded.

3. *Time of disclosure.* The "tender offer statement" must be filed and sent prior to the making, requesting, or inviting of a tender offer.

4. The following terms have been previously defined in this chapter:
   a. "Class of equity security" (review XIII-A-1 and XV-B-2 above).
   b. "Beneficial ownership" (review XV-C-5 above).

5. *Tender offer statement.* The tender offer statement must disclose essentially the same information as that required to be disclosed in the information statement for private or open-market acquisitions (see XV-C-3 above).

6. *Solicitations or recommendations to security holders to accept or reject a tender offer.* A *"target"* company (i.e., the issuer of the securities sought to be acquired), its management, or a competing tender offeror who solicits or recommends acceptance or rejection of a filed tender offer must also file a similar disclosure statement with the SEC and send copies to the issuer of the class of equity securities involved as well as to each securities exchange on which the securities are traded [section 14d-4(a)].

7. *Exemptions.* Section 14(d)(8) exempts the following persons and transactions from compliance with the tender offer disclosure requirements:
   a. Acquisitions by the issuer, i.e., treasury stock;
   b. If the acquisition or securities proposed in the tender offer, together with all other acquisitions by the same person of securities of the same class during the preceding twelve months, would not exceed 2 percent of that class; and
   c. SEC exemptions by rules, regulations, or orders:
      (1) Call and redemption of equity securities; and
      (2) Offers to purchase fractional interests in equity securities.

E. *Proxy solicitations.* Section 14(a) of the 1934 act makes it unlawful for any person, by use of the mails or any means or instrumentality of interstate commerce or any facility of a national securities exchange or otherwise, in violation of SEC Rules 14a-1 through 14a-12, to solicit, or to permit the use of his or her name to solicit, any proxy or consent of authorization in respect to any security registered pursuant to section 12 of the act (see XIII-A and XIII-B above).

1. *Purpose.* The purpose of section 14(a) and SEC Rules 14a-1 through 14a-12 is to ensure reliable and fair disclosure of information to equity security holders so that they can act in an informed manner in regard to the proxy solicitation.

2. *Definitions.* Some important definitions follow:

   a. *Proxy.* The term includes every proxy, consent, or authorization. The consent or authorization may take the form of failure to object or to dissent.

   b. *Solicitation.* The terms "solicit" and "solicitation" include:

   (1) Any request for a proxy in any form;

   (2) Any request to execute or not to execute, or to revoke a proxy; or

   (3) Any other communication to shareholders reasonably calculated to result in obtaining, withholding, or revoking a proxy.

3. *Solicitations regulated.* All solicitations of a proxy with respect to equity securities registered under section 12 are regulated.

4. *Disclosure requirement.* No solicitation is lawful unless each shareholder solicited is provided a copy of a written *proxy statement*, either before or at the time of the solicitation. If the solicitation is made on behalf of the management of the issuer and it relates to an annual meeting of shareholders at which directors are to be elected, an annual report must also be furnished to the shareholders no later than the proxy statement.

   a. *Proxy statement.* Some of the important information required to be included in a proxy statement is as follows:

   (1) Revocability of the proxy;

   (2) Rights of dissenting shareholders;

   (3) Identity of the solicitors;

   (4) Voting securities and owners of record entitled to vote;

   (5) Identity of directors and principal executive officers and their remuneration either in the form of money or fringe benefits;

   (6) Identity and information about the issuer's past and present independent public accountants;

   (7) Stock options, warrants, or rights;

   (8) Contemplated mergers or acquisitions;

   (9) Contemplated modification, authorization, or issuance of securities;

   (10) Certified financial statements, if the actions indicated in (8) and (9) above are to be taken; and

   (11) Any other information material to the action to be taken and for which the proxy will be utilized.

5. *Proxy.* The proxy must be written and contain the following material:

   a. Whether or not it is being solicited on behalf of the management of the issuer;

   b. A clear and impartial statement of each matter to be acted upon;

   c. A means by which the person solicited can make a choice between approval and disapproval of each matter to be acted upon;

   d. A statement that the shares represented by the proxy shall be voted pursuant to the choice specified by the person solicited.

6. *Parties to whom disclosure is required.* The proxy, the proxy statement, and all other solicitation material must be:

   a. Filed with the SEC; and

   b. Sent to each securities exchange on which *any* class of the issuer's equity securities is listed.

7. *Time of disclosure.* The proxy, proxy statement, and all other solicitation materials must be filed and sent prior to or on the date that the same materials are first sent or delivered to any shareholder.
8. *False or misleading statements or omissions.* SEC Rule 14a-9 prohibits false or misleading material statements or omissions, oral or written, made in conjunction with a proxy solicitation.
   a. Filing with or the examination of the solicitation material by the SEC does not constitute a finding that the statements made therein are accurate, complete, truthful or not misleading.
   b. The SEC rule lists the following facts and circumstances that may be misleading:
      (1) Claims regarding the results of a proxy solicitation made prior to a shareholders' meeting;
      (2) Unsubstantiated material that impugns the integrity, character, or personal reputation of any person; and
      (3) The failure to distinguish clearly one person's solicitation material from that of others.
   c. *Sanctions and remedies.* Violators are subject to civil sanctions by the SEC, criminal sanctions, and remedies by private persons for damages under the antifraud and other provisions of the act.
F. *Brokers and dealers.* The student should review XII-F and XIV-C above.

MATERIAL INSIDE (NONPUBLIC) INFORMATION

XVI. It is unlawful for *any* "person" who has knowingly received *material inside (nonpublic) information* pertaining to an issuer to buy from or sell to a person any of the issuer's securities without first disclosing such information to that person.
A. The purchase or sale is voidable by the person lacking the material inside information.
B. Damages may also be recovered from the nondisclosing party under section 10b and Rule 10b-5, the antifraud provisions of the 1934 act. Violations of section 10b and Rule 10b-5 are discussed under XIX-C-2 below.
C. Some examples of material inside information are:
   1. A significant oil and natural gas discovery by an issuer;
   2. The trading of a security on a securities exchange was suspended by the SEC;
   3. The existence of a substantial embezzlement by an issuer's officers and directors; and
   4. A merger or substantial acquisition by the issuer is being finalized.

FOREIGN CORRUPT PRACTICES ACT

XVII. The Foreign Corrupt Practices Act (the act) was enacted by Congress in 1977 as an amendment to section 13(b) of the Securities Exchange Act of 1934. (See Figure 19-6.)
A. *Purpose.* The purpose of the act is to prevent a U.S. corporation from using its money or property to bribe a foreign official as a means of securing a contract, increasing business, or otherwise promoting business interests.
B. *Regulation under the act.* The act contains two important provisions: (1) accounting, recordkeeping, and internal control and (2) antibribery.
   1. *Accounting, recordkeeping, and internal control provision:*
      a. *"Covered" corporations.* All corporations (whether or not engaged in foreign operations) that are under the jurisdiction of the Securities Exchange Commission (SEC) are subject to this provision of the act. These include:

FIGURE 19-6   FOREIGN CORRUPT PRACTICES ACT

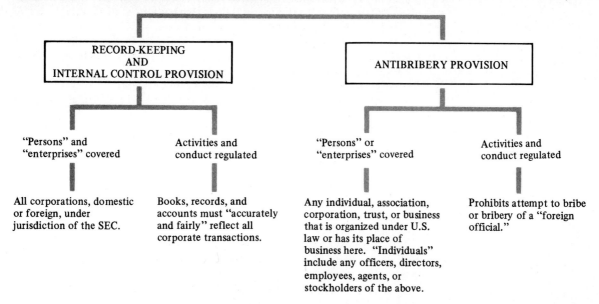

(1) Corporations that have securities registered on a national securities exchange; and

(2) Corporations that trade on the over-the-counter markets and have $1,000,000 in assets and 500 or more shareholders.

b. *Accurate books, records, and accounts.* The act imposes affirmative duties on "covered" corporations to establish and maintain accurate books, records, accounts, and a system of internal controls.

(1) The books, records, and accounts must *"accurately and fairly"* reflect the transactions and disposition of assets of the corporation.

(2) The system of internal accounting controls must be such that it is *"sufficient to provide reasonable assurances"* that transactions are authorized and recorded and that corporate assets are accounted for.

(3) The act does not change existing disclosure requirements of the SEC. A corporate payment or practice that is not unlawful under this act may still be material to investors and be required to be disclosed under the Securities Act of 1933 or the Securities Exchange Act of 1934.

(4) The words "accurately and fairly" and "sufficient to provide reasonable assurances" are not defined in the act. However, a minimum standard would seem to be that the corporate records and system of internal control should reflect, at a minimum, generally accepted accounting principles.

c. The SEC is charged with the enforcement of the accounting, record-keeping, and internal control provision. Pursuant to its regulatory authority, the SEC has adopted Rules 13b 2-1 and 13b 2-2.

(1) Rule 13b 2-1, "Falsification of Accounting Records," prohibits any person from directly or indirectly falsifying or causing to be falsified any book, record, or account.

(2) Rule 13b 2-2, "Issuer's Representations in Connection with the Preparation of Required Reports and Documents," prohibits a director and officer of an issuer from, directly or indirectly, making or causing another person to make false or misleading statements or omissions of

material facts to an accountant in connection with any required audit or any preparation of a required document or report.

    (3) The SEC intends to apply these rules to audits of financial statements by independent accountants, as well as the preparation of required periodic and special reports by independent or internal accountants, e.g., forms 10-K, 10-Q, 8-K, and other reports or documents filed with the SEC.

d. *Criminal sanctions and civil remedies.* Corporate officers, directors, accountants, insiders, and any other person can be held liable if their wilful (fraudulent) conduct would constitute either a violation of the rules stated above or any antifraud provision of the Securities Act of 1933, the Securities Exchange Act of 1934, and SEC Rule 10b-5 (see XIX below).

2. *Antibribery provision:*

  a. *"Covered enterprises."* Covered enterprises include any corporation, partnership, association, joint stock company, business trust, unincorporated organization, or sole proprietorship which has either:

    (1) Its place of business in the United States; or

    (2) Is organized under the laws of a state of the United States or a territory, possession, or commonwealth of the United States.

  b. *"Persons covered."* Persons covered include any officer, director, employee, agent, or any stockholder acting in behalf of any covered enterprise.

  c. *Foreign bribery.* This provision makes it a crime for a covered enterprise or person to commit "foreign bribery." *Foreign bribery* consists of:

    (1) The use of the mails or any means or instrumentality of interstate commerce;

    (2) To "corruptly" influence (i.e., with intent to wrongfully influence). *Note:* If a foreign official's duties are primarily ministerial or clerical in nature (nondiscretionary), a payment made to facilitate a transaction would not be a "corrupt" practice;

    (3) Make a gift, promise to give payment, promise to pay, or an authorization to pay or give anything of value to a "foreign official." The term "foreign official" includes:

      (*a*) Any officer or employee of a foreign government;

      (*b*) Any officer or employee of any department, agency, or instrumentality of a foreign government; or

      (*c*) Any person acting in an official capacity for or on behalf of such foreign government, or department, agency, or instrumentality.

    (4) With the intent to obtain or retain business for or with, or direct business to, any person.

  d. *Criminal sanctions.* The criminal penalties for violation of the antibribery provision are as follows:

    (1) "Covered" enterprises: Fines up to $1,000,000;

    (2) "Covered" persons: Fines up to $10,000, imprisonment up to five years, or both;

    (3) The act prohibits a "covered enterprise" to pay, directly or indirectly, any fine imposed under the act upon its officers, directors, agents, employees, or shareholders.

  e. *Civil remedies.* Civil remedies are available to the SEC against any violator of this provision (see XIX-B below). A violator may also be liable for damages to a private person caused by a violation of the antifraud provisions of section 10b and Rule 10b-5 (see XIX-C-2 below).

OTHER IMPORTANT SECTIONS OF THE 1934 ACT

XVIII. Other important sections that impose criminal penalties as well as civil sanctions and remedies upon violators are listed below.

   A. Section 17(a) and Rule 17(a)-5: Failure of exchange members or broker-dealers to keep appropriate books and records.

   B. Section 6(b): Violation of national securities exchange rules by exchanges or their members.

   C. Section 7(c): Violation of *margin requirements* set by Federal Reserve Board regulations.

   D. Section 11(d)(2): Failure of a member of a national securities exchange or broker-dealer to inform a customer in writing (in connection with a securities order from a customer) whether it is acting for its own account, for the account of a customer, or as a broker for some other person.

   E. Section 16(c): Insider short trading ("short sales"). The sale by an insider of any equity security of an issuer that the insider does not own.

   F. Section 9(a)(1): "*Wash sales.*" Sale and purchase of the same securities by the same parties so as to give an appearance of an active market.

   G. Section 15(c)(1), Rule 15(c)-1-7: "*Churning.*" Under discretionary authority to buy and sell securities for the account of a customer, the broker engages in excessive trading in order to generate increased commissions.

   H. Section 9(a)(1): "*Matched transactions.*" Purchasing or selling securities, knowing that others are taking the other side of the transaction with the intent to affect market prices.

   I. Section 9(a)(3): False statements made by broker-dealers to affect prices on a securities exchange.

   J. Section 9(a)(5): "*Touting.*" Being paid by a broker-dealer, a securities purchaser, or a securities seller to influence the price of securities listed on a securities exchange.

SANCTIONS AND REMEDIES UNDER THE 1934 ACT

XIX. A violator of the 1934 act or of any SEC rule or regulation is subject to criminal sanctions, SEC-imposed civil remedies, and civil lawsuits for damages by private persons. (See Table 19-1.)

   A. *Criminal penalties* of fine and/or imprisonment are provided for (1) any *wilful* violation of any provision of the 1934 act or any SEC rule or regulation, and for (2) any *wilful* falsification or omission of material fact in a registration statement, application, report, or other required document (section 32a).

   1. A securities exchange that commits a violation is subject to a fine of up to $500,000.

   2. Other violators are subject to a fine of up to $10,000 and/or imprisonment up to five years.

   B. *SEC-imposed sanctions or remedies.* The SEC has the power to take the following action against violators:

   1. *Injunction.* File a lawsuit to enjoin future violations;

   2. *Suspension of trading.* Suspend temporarily or permanently trading of a security over-the-counter or on exchanges;

   3. *Denial, suspension, or revocation of registration.* Deny, suspend, or revoke registration of an issuer, securities exchange, broker, or broker-dealer;

   4. *Delist a security.* Delist a security from a securities exchange;

5. *Censure.* Censure a broker or broker-dealer for unlawful conduct;

   6. File a lawsuit to temporarily or permanently enjoin a broker or broker-dealer from engaging in securities brokerage;

   7. *Limit broker operations.* Place limitations on operations, activities, or functions of brokers or broker-dealers;

   8. *Investigate.* Initiate investigations to determine violations of any provision of the 1934 act or SEC rules and regulations; and

   9. *Recommend criminal proceedings.* Recommend to the Department of Justice that criminal proceedings be instituted against a violator.

C. *Remedies of private persons.* Civil remedies are available under section 18 or section 10(b) and SEC Rule 10b-5 to persons who suffered a financial loss as a result of a violation. *Exception:* No private person can recover damages on the basis that the violator failed to comply with the *registration requirements* under the 1934 act. The act does, however, subject this type of violator to criminal liability and SEC-imposed sanctions.

   1. *Antifraud provisions: Civil liability in damages for fraudulent misstatements in filed applications, reports, registrations, or documents.* Section 18 of the 1934 act imposes civil liability for damages upon *any* person *who made or caused to be made* any fraudulent, false, or misleading statement of material fact in any application, registration, report, or document filed with the SEC. This remedy is available only to sellers or buyers of securities whose prices were affected by the false or misleading statement. Because of the strict requirements of proof required to establish a violation of section 18, the remedy thereunder is rarely sought and obtained. *Note:* Most lawsuits for damages under the 1934 act are brought under the antifraud provisions of section 10b and SEC Rule 10b-5 to be discussed later in this chapter. The elements of a section 18 violation are as follows:

   a. *Purchase or sale.* To recover damages under this section, a complainant must prove that it purchased or sold a security.

   b. *False or misleading statement* of material fact in any application, registration, report, or document required under the 1934 act, i.e., a false, incomplete, or deficient disclosure.

   c. *Reliance.* The sellers or buyers of the security must prove that they relied upon the misstatement; i.e., that they would not have sold or purchased the security had the truth been known to them.

   d. *Materiality.* A fact is material if it is so relevant or important to the transaction that it would have influenced the decision of a reasonable investor. (See also the definition of materiality in XIX-C-2 below.)

   e. *Scienter.* Scienter is the mental state of a person who intends to deceive, manipulate, or defraud. Reckless conduct is held to satisfy the requirement of scienter; i.e., actual knowledge of the truth or of the material facts without disclosure satisfies the requirement of scienter. Negligent or innocent misrepresentations do not establish scienter.

   f. *Causation.* The buyer or seller must prove that, at the time the security was purchased or sold, its price was affected because of the fraudulent misstatement.

   g. *Privity.* Privity *is not* a requisite for recovery.

   h. *Good faith defense.* Liability may be avoided by proving that one "acted in good faith and had no knowledge that such statement was false."

   i. *Statute of limitations.* A lawsuit for damages must be filed within one year after the discovery of the false or misleading statement but not later than three years after the false or misleading statement was made.

2. *Civil liability in damages for fraud under section 10b and SEC Rule 10b-5.* The provisions of section 10b and Rule 10b-5 cover an extremely wide range of fraudulent conduct and activities *in connection with the purchase or sale of a security*. They make unlawful *all types of fraudulent conduct and activities* of *all persons* engaged in *all buy and sell transactions* and *all other "persons"* who are under the jurisdiction of the Securities Act of 1934 when these transactions, conduct, or activities involve the mails, the use of any means, instrumentality, or communication in interstate commerce, or the facility of any national security exchange.

a. *Damages.* Violators are liable for actual out-of-pocket losses incurred by any person as a result of a violation of section 10b or Rule 10b-5.

b. *Conduct prohibited.* Section 10b and *Rule 10b-5* make the following conduct or activity unlawful when such conduct or activity occurs in connection with the purchase or sale of any security:

(1) To use or employ *any manipulative or deceptive device or contrivance* in violation of SEC rules and regulations;

(2) To make any oral or written false or misleading statement or omission of a material fact;

(3) To employ *any device, scheme, or artifice to defraud*; or

(4) To engage in any act, practice, or course of business that operates or would operate as a fraud.

c. *Potential violators.* Section 10b applies only to sellers and buyers. Rule 10b-5 extends liability to *any* "person" who violates its antifraud provisions. The following persons are potential violators of Rule 10b-5.

(1) Sellers;

(2) Buyers;

(3) Issuers;

(4) Insiders, i.e., officers or directors of an issuer or a person owning more than 10 percent of any class of an issuer's equity security;

(5) Beneficial owners of more than 5 percent of a registered equity security;

(6) Stock exchanges;

(7) Members of a national stock exchange;

(8) Brokers;

(9) Broker-dealers;

(10) Dealers;

(11) Tender offerors;

(12) Underwriters;

(13) Persons who *"aid and abet"* securities fraud violations;

(14) Controlling persons of issuers;

(15) Signers of registration statements, applications, reports, and documents filed with the SEC;

(16) "Experts" such as accountants, attorneys, appraisers, engineers, or geologists who prepare or certify required statements, reports, or other material;

(17) Any person who possesses inside information and trades in a security;

(18) Any person who solicits proxies; and

(19) Any person who violates the antifraud provisions.

d. *Securities and securities transactions covered.* The antifraud provision applies to all securities and securities transactions under the jurisdiction of the 1933 and 1934 acts.

(1) Exempt and nonexempt, listed and unlisted, and registered and unregistered securities; and

(2) All buy-sell securities transactions. A buy-sell transaction includes the following:

    (*a*) Direct trading between persons;

    (*b*) Transactions involving brokers, dealers, or broker-dealers:

    (*c*) Mergers or consolidations;

    (*d*) Tender offers;

    (*e*) Contracts to sell or buy securities; and

    (*f*) Conversion of convertible bonds or convertible preferred stock into common stock.

e. *Elements of a violation.* A seller or purchaser of securities must prove the following elements of an antifraud violation in order to recover any loss.

(1) *Scienter.* Scienter is the intent to deceive, manipulate, or defraud. Reckless conduct (gross negligence) satisfies the scienter requirement.

(2) *Reliance.* The seller or purchaser must have relied upon the fraudulent statement, omission, conduct, or activity.

(3) *Materiality.* The U.S. Supreme Court in *TSC Industries, Inc. v. Northway, Inc. (1976)* stated that a fact is material if there is "a substantial likelihood that the disclosure of the omitted fact would have been viewed by the reasonable investor as having significantly altered the total mix of information made available."

(4) *Causation.* The fraudulent conduct or activity must have caused the losses of the "injured" person.

(5) *Loss.* The "injured" person must prove an out-of-pocket loss that resulted from the reliance upon the faudulent statement, omission, conduct, or activity.

    (*a*) *Buyers.* The out-of-pocket loss to a buyer is the difference between the price paid by the buyer and the true value of the security at the time of the purchase.

    (*b*) *Sellers.* Sellers are allowed to recover:

        i. Their out-of-pocket loss; i.e., the difference between the price received and the true value of the securities at the time of the sale; and

        ii. The amount of increase in the value of the securities while they were possessed by the violator.

    (*c*) *Consequential damages* (i.e., losses). Persons entitled to recover out-of-pocket losses are also entitled to recover consequential damages such as brokerage fees, transaction taxes, and unreceived dividends. Attorney fees are generally not recoverable.

(6) *Privity.* Privity is not required for recovery; i.e., the person "injured" need not have purchased a security from or sold a security to the violator. Lack of privity is not a defense to the violator.

f. *Contribution.* A violator who is required to pay a loss suffered by an "injured" party is entitled to *contributions from coviolators* (sections 9 and 18). Each violator's contribution is equal to the total amount required to be paid by one violator divided by the total number of violators that caused the loss.

g. *Examples of violations.* The following types of fraudulent statements, omissions, conduct, or activities may be held to be in violation of Rule 10b-5:

(1) An employee of a printing company, who obtained material inside information by reading a corporation's tender offer being printed by her employer, subsequently traded in the stock of the "target" corporation.

(2) Nondisclosure of material facts in a proxy solicitation.

(3) A corporation published a misleading press release regarding discovery of minerals in Canada.

(4) A broker or group of brokers predicted to potential investors future performance of corporations or market prices without having any justified basis to do so.

(5) A parent corporation used its subsidiary to manipulate the market price of its stock.

(6) Excessive trading for the purposes of giving investors the appearance of active trading in order to drive the market value of a security upward.

(7) A broker or dealer failed to disclose material information to a customer.

(8) Insiders "leaked" their "tips," based on inside information, to friends and relatives, who later traded in the securities.

(9) A corporation repurchased its stock from shareholders without disclosing to them its merger plans.

(10) An accountant made false and misleading statements and omissions in an annual financial report filed with the SEC.

(11) An appraiser, in exchange for stock in a corporation, intentionally overvalued assets, and such overvaluation was reflected in reports filed with the SEC.

(12) A president of a corporation helped prepare a false press release. He was held liable as an aider and abettor.

(13) A dealer engaged in *"wash sales"*; i.e., the sale and purchase of securities of an issuer by the same person so as to give investors the appearance of an active market.

(14) A broker falsely represented a security as registered.

(15) *"Matched transactions"* by brokers; i.e., a broker buys or sells securities knowing that other brokers are buying and selling the same securities with the intent to affect market prices.

(16) A broker-dealer gave out fictitious stock quotations on over-the-counter market securities to generate increased sales and thereby earn more commissions.

(17) A broker-dealer made false statements to affect prices of a security on a national securities exchange.

(18) A tender offeror made false or misleading material statements or omissions in the tender statement filed with the SEC.

(19) A broker-dealer engaged in *"churning,"* i.e., the buying and selling of securities by a broker-dealer from its customer's account on a large scale solely to increase the amounts of its commissions.

h. Statute of limitations: Section 10b and Rule 10b-5. Federal securities law does not expressly provide a statute of limitations to bar actions for damages under section 10b and Rule 10b-5. The federal courts have applied various state statutes of limitations. There is no uniformity between state statutes as to prescribed time periods within which lawsuits must be filed.

SELF-QUIZ

To check your understanding of the key words and concepts and the accuracy of your answers to the questions, refer to the text material as referenced by page number.

KEY WORDS AND CONCEPTS

Securities Exchange Commission (SEC)   **541**
Primary offering   **541**

QUESTIONS

1. Name the persons who are under a duty to comply with the registration requirements of the Securities Act of 1933. **(542)**

2. What information must be provided in a registration statement? **(543)**

3. When does a registration become effective? **(545)**

4. List and explain the specific securities exempted under the provisions of the Securities Act of 1933. **(547)**

5. List and explain the specific securities *transactions* exempted under the provisions of the Securities Act of 1933. **(548)**

6. Explain the antifraud provision of both the Securities Act of 1933 and the Securities Exchange Act of 1934. **(556, 572)**

7. Name the "persons" whose practices and activities are regulated by the Security Exchange Act of 1934. **(557)**

8. Explain the liability of insiders for short-swing trading in corporate securities. **(564)**

9. Under what circumstances must an officer, director, employee of a corporation, or other person reveal material inside information? **(568)**

10. What criminal and civil remedies are available under both the Securities Act of 1933 and the Securities Exchange Act of 1934? **(552, 571)**

11. In what circumstances would a certified public accountant be liable for damages under the Securities Act of 1933 and the Securities Exchange Act of 1934? **(553, 573)**

12. Identify and explain the functions and powers of the Securities and Exchange Commission. **(541, 553, 561, 569, 571)**

13. Which corporations are regulated by the Foreign Corrupt Practices Act? **(568)** Which persons? **(570)**

14. Identify and explain the two most important provisions of the Foreign Corrupt Practices Act. **(568, 570)**

15. What sanctions can be imposed against a violator of the Foreign Corrupt Practices Act by the SEC? **(571)** By the courts? **(570)** By others? **(572)**

16. Compare the provisions of the Securities Act of 1933 with those of the Securities Exchange Act of 1934 in the following areas of regulation:
   a. Securities regulated **(544)**
   b. Prospectus **(544)**
   c. Identity and types of securities **(544)**
   d. Reporting requirements **(544)**
   e. Persons regulated **(544)**
   f. Conduct and activities regulated **(544)**
   g. Sanctions and remedies for violations **(544)**

SELECTED QUESTIONS AND UNOFFICIAL ANSWERS

OBJECTIVE QUESTIONS

Select the best answer for each of the following items. Mark only one answer for each item. Answer all items.

NOVEMBER 1980

39. The Securities Exchange Act of 1934 requires that certain persons register and that the securities of certain issuers be registered. In respect to such registration under the 1934 Act, which of the following statements is *incorrect*?
   a. All securities offered under the Securities Act of 1933 also must be registered under the 1934 Act.
   b. National securities exchanges must register.
   c. The equity securities of issuers, which are traded on a national securities exchange, must be registered.
   d. The equity securities of issuers having in excess of $1 million in assets and 500 or more stockholders which are traded in interstate commerce must be registered.

40. Theobold Construction Company, Inc., is considering a public stock offering for the first time. It wishes to raise $1.2 million by a common stock offering and do this in the least expensive manner. In this connection, it is considering making an offering pursuant to Regulation A. Which of the following statements is correct regarding such an offering?
   a. Such an offering can *not* be made to more than 250 people.
   b. The maximum amount of securities permitted to be offered under Regulation A is $1 million.
   c. Only those corporations which have had an initial registration under the Securities Act of 1933 are eligible.
   d. Even if Regulation A applies, Theobold is required to distribute an offering circular.

41. Shariff is a citizen of a foreign country. He has just purchased six percent (6%) of the outstanding common shares of Stratosphere Metals, Inc., a company listed on a national stock exchange. He has instructed the brokerage firm that quietly and efficiently handled the execution of the purchase order

that he wants the securities to be held in street name. What are the legal implications of the above transactions? Shariff must

a. Immediately have the securities registered in his own name and take delivery of them.

b. Sell the securities because he has violated the anti-fraud provisions of the Securities Exchange Act of 1934.

c. Notify Stratosphere Metals, Inc., of his acquisition and file certain information as to his identity and backbround with the SEC.

d. Notify the SEC and Stratosphere Metals, Inc., only if he acquires ten percent (10%) or more of Stratosphere's common shares.

42. Which of the following statements concerning the scope of Section 10(b) of the Securities Exchange Act of 1934 is correct?

a. In order to come within its scope, a transaction must have taken place on a national stock exchange.

b. It applies exclusively to securities of corporations registered under the Securities Exchange Act of 1934.

c. There is an exemption from its application for securities registered under the Securities Act of 1933.

d. It applies to purchases as well as sales of securities in interstate commerce.

43. Which of the following statements is correct regarding qualification for the private placement exemption from registration under the Securities Act of 1933?

a. The instrumentalities of interstate commerce must *not* be used.

b. The securities must be offered to *not* more than 35 persons.

c. The minimum amount of securities purchased by each offeree must *not* be less than $100,000.

d. The offerees *must* have access to or be furnished with the kind of information that would be available in a registration statement.

44. The Foreign Corrupt Practices Act of 1977 prohibits bribery of foreign officials. Which of the following statements correctly describes the Act's application to corporations engaging in such practices?

a. It only applies to multinational corporations.

b. It applies to all domestic corporations engaged in interstate commerce.

c. It only applies to corporations whose securities are registered under the Securities Exchange Act of 1934.

d. It applies only to corporations engaged in foreign commerce.

27. Taylor is the executive Vice President for Marketing of Reflex Corporation and a member of the Board of Directors. Based on information obtained during the course of his duties, Taylor concluded that Reflex's profits would fall by 50% for the quarter and 30% for the year. He quietly contacted his broker and disposed of 10,000 shares of his Reflex stock at a profit, some of which he had acquired within 6 months of the sale. In fact, Reflex's profits did *not* fall, but its stock price declined for unrelated reasons. Taylor had also advised a friend to sell her shares and repurchase the stock later. She followed Taylor's advice, sold for $21, and subsequently repurchased an equal number of shares at $11. A shareholder has commenced a shareholder derivative action against Taylor and the friend for violation of the Securities Exchange Act of 1934. Under these circumstances, which of the following is correct?

a. Taylor is *not* an insider in relation to Reflex.

b. Taylor must account to the corporation for his short-swing profit.

c. Taylor and the friend must both account to the corporation for their short-swing profits.

d. Neither Taylor nor the friend has incurred any liability under the 1934 act.

28. Which of the following is exempt from registration under the Securities Act of 1933?

a. First mortgage bonds.

b. The usual annuity contract issued by an insurer.

c. Convertible preferred stock.

d. Limited partnership interests.

29. Under the Securities Act of 1933, an accountant may be held liable for any materially false or misleading financial statements, including an omission of a material fact therefrom, provided the purchaser

a. Proves reliance on the registration statement or prospectus.

b. Proves negligence or fraud on the part of the accountant.

c. Brings suit within four years after the security is offered to the public.

d. Proves a false statement or omission existed *and* the specific securities were the ones offered through the registration statement.

32. Whitworth has been charged by Bonanza Corporation with violating the Securities Exchange Act of 1934. Whitworth was formerly the president of Bonanza, but he was ousted as a result of a proxy battle. Bonanza seeks to recover from Whitworth any and all of his short-swing profits. Which of the following would be a valid defense to the charges?

a. Whitworth is a New York resident, Bonanza was incorporated in New York, and the transactions were all made through the New York Stock Exchange; therefore, interstate commerce was *not* involved.

b. Whitworth did *not* actually make use of any insider information in connection with the various stock transactions in question.

c. All the transactions alleged to be in violation of the 1934 act were purchases made during February 1979 with the corresponding sales made in September 1979.

d. Whitworth's motivation in selling the stock was solely a result of the likelihood that he would be ousted as president of Bonanza.

MAY 1979

43. Tweed Manufacturing, Inc., plans to issue $5 million of common stock to the public in interstate commerce after its registration statement with the SEC becomes effective. What, if anything, must Tweed do in respect to those states in which the securities are to be sold?

a. Nothing, since approval by the SEC automatically constitutes satisfaction of any state requirements.

b. Make a filing in those states which have laws governing such offerings and obtain their approval.

c. Simultaneously apply to the SEC for permission to market the securities in the various states without further clearance.

d. File in the appropriate state office of the state in which it maintains its principal office of business, obtain clearance, and forward a certified copy of that state's clearance to all other states.

48. Harvey Wilson is a senior vice president, 15% shareholder and a member of the Board of Directors of Winslow, Inc. Wilson has decided to sell 10% of his stock in the company. Which of the following methods of disposition would subject him to SEC registration requirements?

a. A redemption of the stock by the corporation.

b. The sale by several brokerage houses of the stock in the ordinary course of business.

c. The sale of the stock to an insurance company which will hold the stock for long-term investment purposes.

d. The sale to a corporate officer who currently owns 5% of the stock of Winslow and who will hold the purchased stock for long-term investment.

49. The Securities Exchange Act of 1934 holds certain insiders liable for short-swing profits under section 16(b) of the act. Which of the following classes of people would *not* be insiders in relation to the corporation in which they own securities?

a. An executive vice president.

b. A major debenture holder.

c. An 11% owner, 8% of which he owns in his or her own name and 3% in an irrevocable trust for his or her benefit for life.

d. A director who owns less than 10% of the shares of stock of the corporation.

NOVEMBER 1978

33. Young owns 200 shares of stock of Victory Manufacturing Company. Victory is listed on a national stock exchange and has in excess of one million shares outstanding. Young claims that Truegood, a Victory director, has purchased and sold shares in violation of the insider trading provisions of the Securities Exchange Act of 1934. Young has threatened legal action. Which of the following statements is correct?

a. Truegood will have a valid defense if he can show he did *not* have any insider information which influenced his purchases or sales.

b. Young can sue Truegood personally, but his recovery will be limited to his proportionate share of Truegood's profits plus legal expenses.

c. In order to prevail, Young must sue for and on behalf of the corporation and establish that the transactions in question occurred within less than six months of each other and at a profit to Truegood.

d. Since Young's stock ownership is less than 1%, his only recourse is to file a complaint with the SEC or obtain a sufficient number of other shareholders to join him so that the 1% requirement is met.

6. Mr. Jackson owns approximately 40% of the shares of common stock of Triad Corporation. The rest of the shares are widely distributed among 2,000 shareholders. Jackson needs funds for other business ventures and would like to raise about $8,000,000 through the sale of some of his Triad shares. He accordingly approached Underwood & Sons, an investment banking house in which he knew one of the principals, to purchase his Triad shares and distribute the shares to the public at a reasonable price through its offices in the United States. Any profit on the sales could be retained by Underwood pursuant to an agreement reached between Jackson and Underwood. In this situation

a. The securities to be sold probably do *not* need to be registered with the Securities and Exchange Commission.

b. Underwood & Sons probably is *not* an underwriter as defined in the federal securities law.

c. Jackson probably is considered an issuer under federal securities law.

d. Under federal securities law, *no* prospectus is required to be filed in connection with this contemplated transaction.

Answers to Objective Questions

November 1980

39. a	**42.** d	
40. d	**43.** d	
41. c	**44.** b	

May 1979

43. b	**49.** b
48. b	

November 1978

33. c

November 1979

27. b	**29.** d
28. b	**32.** c

May 1978

6. c

Explanation of Answers to Objective Questions

NOVEMBER 1980

39. (a) The correct answer is (a). The Securities Act of 1933 applies to the initial issuance of securities and has the purpose of providing investors with full and fair disclosure concerning these securities. The Securities Exchange Act of 1934 generally applies to the subsequent trading of securities but not necessarily all securities required to register

under the 1933 Act. Each of the following are required to register under the 1934 Act: (1) national securities exchange, (2) brokers and dealers, (3) dealers in municipal securities, (4) securities that are traded on any national exchange, (5) equity securities traded in interstate commerce having in excess of $1 million in assets and 500 or more shareholders.

40. (d) The correct answer is (d). Small issues (up to $1,500,000) may be exempt from the full registration requirements of the SEC Act of 1933 if there is a notification filing with the SEC and an offering circular under Regulation A. A Regulation A offering can be made to any number of people as long as issuance does not exceed $1,500,000. A corporate issuer need not show an initial registration under the Securities Act of 1933 before being eligible to make a Regulation A offering.

41. (c) According to the tender offer provisions of the Securities Exchange Act of 1934, anyone who acquired more than 5% of a company's equity securities must notify the issuer and disclose his/her identity and other relevant facts to SEC. If a tender offer is involved (in this question it was not present) the purchaser must give this information to SEC and shareholders before making the offer. Thus answer (c) is correct.

42. (d) Answer (d) is correct because under Rule 10b-5 (Securities Exchange Act of 1934) it is unlawful to use any manipulative or deceptive devices in the purchase or sale of securities if the mail, interstate commerce, or a national stock exchange is used. Answer (a) is incorrect because it is unlawful to use the mail or any instrumentality of interstate commerce in addition to a national stock exchange. The rule is not limited to securities subject to the 1934 Act but applies to any sale of a security if interstate commerce is used. Therefore, answers (b) and (c) are incorrect.

43. (d) The correct statement is (d). Answer (b) is wrong since it is SEC practice, not law, to limit the number of offerees to 35. Answer (c) is false because there is no minimum dollar amount requirement to comply with concerning the private placement exemption. Answer (a) is not one of the qualifications for the private placement exemption.

44. (b) Answer (b) is correct. The Foreign Corrupt

Practices Act of 1977 applies to any U.S. business enterprise engaged in interstate commerce including companies required to register with the SEC under the 1934 Act and domestic business organizations. Answers (a), (c), and (d), therefore, are incorrect.

NOVEMBER 1979

27. (b) Taylor, as executive Vice President and a member of the Board of Directors, is classified by the 1934 Securities Act as an insider and therefore must account to the corporation for short-swing profit on stock which he acquired within 6 months of sale, or profits that he acquired from unfairly using inside information about the company for his personal gain. Answer (a) is incorrect because an officer and director is an insider. Answer (c) is incorrect because there is no provision requiring the friend who acquired information from an insider to account to the corporation for his/her short-swing profits. Answer (d) is incorrect because as stated above, Taylor is liable under the 1934 Securities Act for the short-swing profits.

28. (b) Usual insurance and annuity contracts (including variable annuities) issued by an insurance company are exempt from the Securities Act of 1933. Answers (a), (c), and (d) are incorrect because each is regulated first mortgage bonds, convertible preferred stock, and limited partnership interests.

29. (d) Under the Securities Act of 1933, an accountant is liable to a purchaser of securities if the purchaser proves a false financial statement (including statements with a material omission), and the specific securities were ones offered through a registration statement. Answer (a) is incorrect because the purchaser need not prove reliance on the registration statement or prospectus. Instead, the burden is shifted from the plaintiff to the defendant accountant to show that he is not responsible for the investment loss by the purchaser, i.e., accountant must prove due diligence. Answer (b) is incorrect because the purchaser need not prove negligence or fraud on the part of the accountant. Again, all that need be proven is the misstatement or omission. Answer (c) is incorrect because the maximum time limitation for bringing such an action is 3 years after the security is offered to the public.

32. (c) Transactions in excess of 6 months are not short-swing profits since the statute defines short-swing as 6 months or less. Purchase of the stock in February and sale in September is more than 6 months. Answer (a) is incorrect because the securities were traded on the New York Stock Exchange. Thus, Bonanza stock was offered, if not sold, to persons in very many states. Answer (b) is not a good defense because the 1934 statute provides that all short-swing profits by an insider belong to the corporation, i.e., proving that insider information was used is not necessary. Answer (d) is not a good defense because the motivation in selling the stock is not relevant. The issue is whether or not the stock was sold in less than a 6 month period. The insider's motive and intent are irrelevant.

MAY 1979

43. (b) Anyone planning to issue common stock must make a filing in those states that have laws governing such offerings and obtain their approval in addition to meeting the registration requirements of the SEC. Answer (a) is incorrect since approval by the SEC does not automatically constitute satisfaction of state "blue-sky" laws. Answer (c) is incorrect because the issuer must apply to each state for permission to market the securities in addition to the SEC. Answer (d) is incorrect because each state makes its own approval of the stock issue; it cannot be done by one state for the other states.

48. (b) Wilson, the officer and stockholder of Winslow, Inc., will be required to comply with SEC registration requirements if he chooses to dispose of his 15% stock in the corporation by having it sold by several brokerage houses in the ordinary course of business. Wilson is deemed to be a controlling person, i.e., one who has the power to influence management and policies of the issuer, and thus his stock would be considered to be restricted stock. Sale by a controlling person through a broker is not exempted from SEC registration if more than 1% of the outstanding stock is sold. Answer (a) is incorrect because a redemption of stock is not an offering to the public and therefore not covered by the 1933 Act. Answers (c) and (d) are not subject to the SEC registration requirements because they are private placements of securities to sophisticated investors.

49. (b) A major debenture holder is not considered an insider. Insiders are defined as officers, directors, and owners of greater than 10% of any class of the issuer's securities. Therefore answers (a) and (d) are incorrect. Answer (c) is incorrect because beneficial ownership will satisfy the over 10% ownership requirement. Stock held by an irrevocable trust is beneficially owned by the beneficiary.

NOVEMBER 1978

33. (c) A stockholder of a corporation whose stock is traded on an exchange may sue for and on behalf of the corporation for profits on insider purchases and sales of company stock occurring within less than six months of each other. Insiders are corporate directors and officers; also stockholders owning more than 10% of any class of stock are insiders. Answer (a) is incorrect because insiders are liable for any profit from the purchase and sale of securities held for less than six months whether or not they have insider information. Answer (b) is incorrect because Young cannot sue Trueblood personally, but instead must do so for and on behalf of the corporation. Answer (d) is incorrect because no rule requires a stockholder to own 1% or more of the stock of the corporation if the stockholder is seeking enforcement of the insider trading provisions of the Securities Act of 1934.

MAY 1978

6. (c) Jackson is considered to be an issuer under the Securities Act of 1933. The definition of issuer includes a controlling person. Jackson is a controlling person because as substantial holder (40%), he has the power to influence the management and policies of the corporation. This transaction does not come within any exception and therefore is required to be registered with the SEC. Thus answer (a) is incorrect since a registration is required. Answer (b) is incorrect because Underwood & Sons is an underwriter. It has purchased securities from an issuer for public distribution. Answer (d) is incorrect since this is a public sale of securities under the provisions of the Securities Act of 1933, i.e., all registration requirements including the filing of a prospectus are necessary.

ESSAY QUESTIONS AND ANSWERS

MAY 1981 (Estimated time: 15 to 20 minutes)

4. Part a. Delwood is the Central American representative of Massive Manufacturing, Inc., a large diversified conglomerate listed on the New York Stock Exchange. Certain key foreign government and large foreign manufacturing company contracts were in the crucial stages of bidding and negotiation. During this crucial time, Feldspar, the CEO of Massive, summoned Delwood to the company's home office for an urgent consultation. At the meeting, Feldspar told Delwood that corporate sales and profits were lagging and something definitely had to be done. He told Delwood that his job was on the line and that unless major contracts were obtained, he would have to reluctantly accept his resignation. Feldspar indicated he was aware of both the competition and the legal problems that were involved. Nevertheless, he told Delwood "do what is necessary in order to obtain the business." Delwood flew back to Central America the next day and began to implement what he believed to be the instructions he had received from Feldspar. He first contacted influential members of the ruling parties of the various countries and indicated that large discretionary contributions to their re-election campaign funds would be forthcoming if Massive's bids for foreign government contracts were approved. Next, he contacted the large foreign manufacturers and indicated that loans were available to them on a nonrepayment basis if they placed their business with Massive. These payments were to be accounted for by charging certain nebulous accounts or by listing the payments as legitimate loans to purchasers. In any event, the true nature of the expenditures were not to be shown on the books. All this was accomplished, and Massive's sales improved markedly in Central America.

Two years later the Securities and Exchange Commission discovered the facts described above.

Required Answer the following, setting forth reasons for any conclusions stated.

What are the legal implications of the above to Delwood, Feldspar, and Massive Manufacturing?

Answer The legal implications of the conduct described can be best described as grave. Massive Manufacturing, Delwood, and its CEO, Feldspar, will all undoubtedly face criminal prosecution as a result of their conduct. Massive Manufacturing also has potential civil liability. The facts reveal clearcut criminal violations of the Foreign Corrupt Practices Act of 1977.

The Foreign Corrupt Practices Act of 1977 prohibits payments to any foreign official or foreign political party or official thereof to influence the act or decision of that person or party acting in an official capacity. Any issuer convicted of engaging in such illegal conduct is subject to fines not exceeding $1 million. The act also requires that adequate accounting books and records must be maintained. This broad and somewhat nebulous provision applies to any securities issuer that is subject to registration under section 12 of the Securities Exchange Act of 1934 and that must file reports thereunder. This provision applies to Massive in that its stock is listed on a national exchange. Massive has obviously violated the part of the act stating that an issuer must "make and keep books, records and accounts which in reasonable detail accurately and fairly reflect the transactions and dispositions of the assets of the issuer." This separate violation is subject to the omnibus criminal and civil sanctions applicable to activities proscribed by the Securities Exchange Act of 1934.

Feldspar and Delwood, acting in their capacities as officers, agents, and/or directors of Massive, are personally subject to the provisions of the Foreign Corrupt Practices Act. If they are convicted of willfully violating the act, each is subject to a fine of not more than $10,000 or to imprisonment for not more than five years or both.

In addition the SEC may take administrative action against Massive by seeking injunctive relief, which could result in the suspension of trading of Massive's shares.

MAY 1980 (Estimated time: 10 to 13 minutes)

2. Part b. The directors of Clarion Corporation, their accountants, and their attorneys met to discuss the desirability of this highly successful corporation going public. In this connection, the discussion turned to the potential liability of the corporation and the parties involved in the preparation and signing of the registration statement under the Securities Act of 1933. Craft, Watkins, and Glenn are the largest shareholders. Craft is the Chairman of the Board; Watkins is the Vice Chairman; and Glenn is the Chief Executive Officer. It has been decided that they will sign the registration statement. There are two other directors who are also executives and shareholders of the corporation. All of the board members are going to have a percentage of their shares included in the offering. The firm of Witherspoon & Friendly, CPAs, will issue an opinion as to the financial statements of the corporation which will accompany the filing of the registra-

tion statement, and Blackstone & Abernathy, Attorneys-at-Law, will render legal services and provide any necessary opinion letters.

Required Answer the following, setting forth reasons for any conclusions stated.

Discuss the types of potential liability and defenses pursuant to the Securities Act of 1933 that each of the above parties or classes of parties may be subject to as a result of going public.

Answer The Securities Act of 1933 permits an aggrieved party to sue various parties connected with the registration statement for an untrue statement of a material fact in the registration statement or the omission of a material fact required to be stated therein or necessary to make the statements therein not misleading. Those having potential liability include issuers of the security, those who signed the registration statement, every director, underwriter, and expert.

Any acquirer of the security may sue unless it is proved that at the time of such acquisition he knew of such untruth or omission.

Since all the directors and signers are also issuers along with the corporation, they may be sued in that capacity, since with the one exception mentioned above, issuers may not avoid liability for untrue statements or omissions. They are insurers of the truth contained in the registration statement; that is, they are liable without fault.

Contrast their liability with that of the accountants and lawyers who are both experts. As such, they are not liable for parts of the registration statement on which they did not render an expert opinion. Moreover, as experts, they have the benefit of the "due diligence" defense. That is, liability can be avoided if it can be shown by the expert that he had, after reasonable investigation, reasonable ground to believe and did believe at the time such part of the registration statement became effective that the parts for which he gave expert opinion were true and that there was no omission to state a material fact required to be stated.

The act also provides certain defenses based on the amount of damages and their relationship to the misstatements or omissions.

NOVEMBER 1976 (Estimated time: 20 to 25 minutes)

7. Darius Corporation has 1,000,000 shares of common stock outstanding of which 450,000 shares are publicly traded over-the-counter and 550,000 are owned by Lynn, its president. The market price of the stock has ranged from $3 to $4 per share over the past year. Lynn obtained his Darius shares on August 10, 1976, when Darius acquired a company wholly owned by Lynn pursuant to an exchange of 550,000 Darius shares for all of the shares of Lynn's company. The Darius shares received by Lynn were unregistered and contained a legend which restricted transfer except on the opinion of counsel that the shares were transferable. The number of Darius shares held by the public was 450,000 both before and after the August 10 exchange.

On September 22, 1976, Archer & Co., Lynn's broker, purchased from Lynn, for its own account and in ten separate transactions, a total of 10,000 shares of Darius at $4.50 per share. The next day Archer purchased from Lynn in eight separate transactions an additional 8,000 shares in total at $5.50 per share, again for its own account. These were the only transactions on September 22 and 23, and trading in Darius shares over-the-counter had otherwise been light in recent months. On September 24, 1976, Archer circulated a story that there was an active demand for Darius shares. Within a few days, Darius stock was quoted over-the-counter at $9 per share.

On September 30, 1976, Archer sold, as agent for Lynn, 50,000 of Lynn's Darius shares for $9 a share to buyers in several states which Archer had solicited in the open market. Archer also sold for $9 per share the 18,000 Darius shares purchased the prior week for its own account. Soon thereafter, trading activity in Darius stock subsided to its normally light volume which was reflected in the market price retreat to $3 per share.

Required Answer the following, setting forth reasons for any conclusions stated.

a. What is the general statutory rule requiring registration under the Securities Act of 1933, and would the Darius shares sold by Archer be exempt as a so-called "transactions by any person other than an issuer, underwriter or dealer" or as a so-called "brokers' transaction"?

b. Did Archer violate the Securities Exchange Act of 1934 when buying and selling the 18,000 shares of Darius?

c. Is Lynn liable to Darius under the Securities Exchange Act of 1934 because he sold 68,000 shares of Darius?

Answer

a. The Securities Act of 1933 provides that it is unlawful for any persons, directly or indirectly, to sell a security in interstate commerce unless a registration statement for such security is in effect. Here, there was no registration statement in effect with respect to Darius shares sold by Archer; thus, these shares appear to have been sold in contravention of the registration requirement of the 1933 act.

It might be argued, however, that these unregistered shares were sold pursuant to an exemption from the registration requirements of the 1933 act. One exemption is that accorded "transactions by any person other than an issuer, underwriter or dealer." The term "underwriter" generally means any person who has purchased from an issuer with a view toward, or offers or sells for an issuer in connection with, the distribution of any security. For purposes of determining whether a person is an underwriter, an "issuer" includes, in addition to the corporation issuer-in-fact, any person directly or indirectly controlling the corporate issuer. Here, Lynn owns 55% of the shares of Darius Corporation and is, thus, a person in control of the issuer. Archer, having purchased for its own account 8,000 shares from Lynn and having resold the shares within a week, most likely would be an underwriter under the 1933 act. The reason is that Archer appears to have purchased Darius Securities from an issuer with a view to distributing them to the public. Lynn is deemed to be an issuer of Darius securities because he is a controlling shareholder. Similarly the sale of 50,000 shares by Archer as agent for Lynn would appear not to come within this exemption because Archer has made a sale for an issuer in connection with the distribution of the Darius shares to the public.

Another exemption from registration under the 1933 act is the one granted for "brokers' transactions." Generally, this exemption applies to ordinary brokers' transactions, that is, where neither the seller nor his broker solicits orders to buy the security involved, where the broker does no more than execute the order to sell as agent, and where the broker receives no more than the customary broker's commission. Here, in connection with the sale of Lynn's 50,000 shares, Archer solicited buyers for Darius shares. And regarding the 18,000 shares, Archer purchased them as principal for its own account rather than as agent on behalf of Lynn. For these reasons, the brokers' transactions exemption would not appear to be available in the given circumstances.

b. Yes, Under the Securities Exchange Act of 1934, it is unlawful for any person, directly or indirectly, by the use of any means of interstate commerce or the mails, in connection with the purchase or sale of any security, to employ any manipulative or deceptive device or fraudulent scheme or practice, or to misstate, or omit to state, any material fact. The purchases by Archer from Lynn in multiple transactions and the subsequent circulation of a story that there was active demand for Darius shares would be considered a manipulative or deceptive device to raise the price of the stock for personal gain at the public's expense.

c. Yes, To prevent the unfair use of inside information that may have been obtained by a beneficial owner of more than 10% of any class of equity security of the issuer, the 1934 act provides that any profit realized by the beneficial owner from the purchase and sale of that security within any period of less than six months shall be recoverable by the issuer. Here, Lynn has purchased and sold 68,000 Darius common shares within a six-month period, while owning up to 55% of Darius common stock. Thus, Lynn would be liable under this provision to pay Darius the profits he realized on these transactions.

PART
EIGHT

The CPA and the Law (10%)*

---

* This percentage allocation represents the relative weight to be given to this *area* of business law on the Uniform CPA Examinations beginning in November 1983. It also indicates the approximate percentage of the total achievable test score to be assigned to this *area* of business law for each Uniform CPA Examination beginning in November 1983.

CHAPTER
20

Accountants' Legal Responsibility

The following is a generalized listing of subjects to be tested through the May 1983 Uniform CPA Examination.

Knowledge of the accountant's common law civil liability to clients and third parties is tested under this topic. The common law civil liability is based either upon contract or tort (negligence or fraud). Also included is the accountant's civil and criminal liability imposed by federal statutes, such as the Federal Securities Acts of 1933 and 1934 and the Internal Revenue Code. Finally, the accountant's rights regarding his working papers and privileged communication are included.[1]

The AICPA Board of Examiners has adopted a new content specification outline for the business law section of the Uniform CPA Examination, *to be effective with the November 1983 examination*. The outline lists the following groups and topics to be tested under the area of "The CPA and the Law."

A. Common Law Liability to Clients and Third Persons
B. Federal Statutory Liability
   1. Securities Acts
   2. Internal Revenue Code
C. Workpapers, Privileged Communication, and Confidentiality[2]

I. *Liability in General.* Accountants are required to conform to standards of conduct established by their profession, by legislation, and by judicial decisions. An accountant may be civilly liable for damages to the client or to third persons for violation of common law or statutory duties. Accountants may also be subject to criminal liability under provisions of various state and federal laws. (See Figure 20-1.)

---

[1] AICPA, *Information for CPA Candidates*, Copyright © 1975, 1979, by the American Institute of Certified Public Accountants, Inc.
[2] AICPA, *Business Law—Content Specification Outline*, approved by the AICPA Board of Examiners on August 31, 1981.

II. *Civil liability.* The question of legal liability of an accountant for damages usually arises when a loss is sustained by the client or third parties. The loss may have been the result of the accountant's breach of the engagement contract with the client or caused by the accountant's negligent or fraudulent conduct in the preparation of financial statements, reports, documents, or otherwise.

A. *Liability to client.* The accountant has a duty to the client not only to perform the engagement exactly as promised but also to do so in a nonnegligent manner.

    1. *Breach of the engagement contract.* The accountant must perform according to the terms of the engagement (i.e., contract) with the client. If the accountant's performance is not exactly as agreed upon in the engagement, a breach of contract results. The client has the right to recover all monetary losses it suffered that were reasonably foreseeable from the breach. The law of contracts as discussed in Chapter 2 applies to all aspects of the engagement.

        a. It is no defense to the accountant that the services rendered conformed to the highest professional standards. Liability is *not* based on fault.

        b. The specific legal question is whether or not the accountant performed according to the contract with the client. It is not necessary for the client to

FIGURE 20-1   ACCOUNTANTS' LEGAL RESPONSIBILITIES

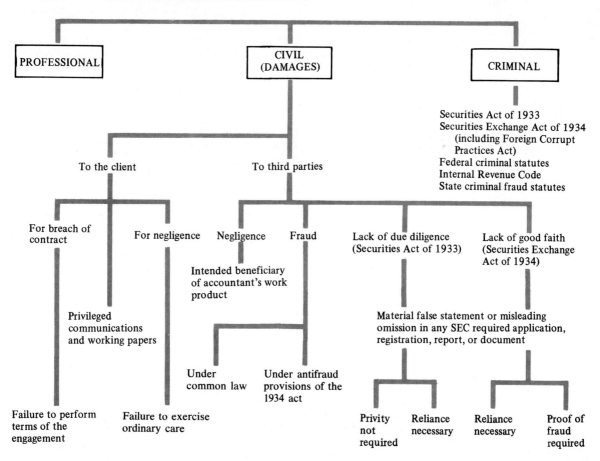

prove that the accountant's failure to perform was due to the accountant's negligence. For this reason, contributory negligence on the part of the client is not available as a defense to the accountant in a lawsuit for breach of contract.

   c. The accountant is liable for the out-of-pocket losses caused by the breach of contract.

   d. The remedy for breach of contract is only available to the client. It is not available to third persons unless they qualify as assignees or intended third-party beneficiaries of the contract between the client and the accountant (see "Intended beneficiary," II-B-1 below).

2. *Liability for negligence.* The accountant must be free from *negligence*; that is, the accountant must exercise reasonable care in the performance of the contract.

   a. *Duty to exercise reasonable care. Reasonable care* is defined as that amount of skill or care in the performance of the contractual duties to the client that a reasonably prudent and skillful accountant would be expected to exercise while practicing in the particular locality and under the same or similar circumstances.

      (1) *Duty to discover fraud or defalcation (i.e., embezzlement).* As a general rule, accountants are *not* under a duty to look for fraud or defalcation. Accountants are not liable for the failure to discover fraud *unless* they were negligent, failed to perform any duty expressed or implied from the engagement, or failed to disclose suspicious facts and circumstances to the client.

         (*a*) If the auditors' negligence prevents discovery of fraud, they are liable for all losses that could have been prevented from the discovery.

         (*b*) Failure of the auditors to perform any duty expressed or implied in the engagement is negligence.

            i. The duties implied from an audit engagement are to confirm accounts receivable, observe physical inventories, verify cash, and adhere to accepted professional standards.

            ii. Auditors must also strictly adhere to the express duties or procedures agreed to in the engagement.

         (*c*) A lesser standard of care is required of accountants who are engaged to perform "write up" work or to prepare unaudited financial statements. However, accountants were held liable in the following write-up situations.

            i. The accountant personally allowed state insurance examiners to examine his working papers and rely on entries the accountant made in the books. Consequently, the examiners did not discover that the client was insolvent and that its management was involved in embezzlement. The evidence revealed that the accountant did not use reasonable care to investigate and discover the nature, meaning, and substance of transactions during the write-up work. He failed to learn that management had embezzled a large sum of money over a period of time and that his client was insolvent. His working papers consequently misrepresented the financial status of his client. The court allowed the court appointed receiver of the insolvent client to recover from the accountant.

            ii. An accountant was held liable for her failure to disclose the responsibility assumed in preparation of a financial statement. The accountant issued an erroneous statement without qualification under her own letterhead, i.e., she did not write "unaudited" on a balance sheet in breach of existing and accepted accounting standards.

    iii. An accountant during write-up work acquired a reason to believe that fraud had been committed by the management of the client. He failed to fulfill his duty to disclose to the client the facts or circumstances that gave rise to his belief and was held liable.

    iv. As another example, an accountant was held liable for failure to inform the client that she discovered that certain invoices allegedly paid by the client's managing agent were unaccounted for and missing.

b. *Respondeat superior.* The negligence (i.e., tort) of a junior accountant or any other employee committed in the course of employment is legally attributable to the employer under the concept of *respondeat superior.*

c. *Defenses.* An accountant has the following defenses to a cause of action for damages based on negligence:

    (1) The accountant was not negligent;

    (2) If the accountant was negligent, the negligence was not the cause of the client's losses; or

    (3) The client was *contributorily negligent*; i.e., the client's negligence combined with the accountant's negligence to cause the loss.

d. *Accountants are not guarantors* of the accuracy of their work product. In absence of negligence or breach of the engagement contract, they are not liable for mere errors in judgment.

e. *Measure of damages.* The client can recover money damages from the accountant equal to the actual out-of-pocket losses caused by the accountant's negligence (i.e., tort).

3. *Breach of fiduciary duty.* The accountant who is not totally independent owes a duty of utmost loyalty to the client. The accountant may not disclose any confidential information acquired during the engagement to third parties without the consent of the client. If a wrongful disclosure is made, the accountant is subject to dismissal from the engagement, is liable for any damages caused by the disclosure, and a court, at its discretion, may impose punitive damages. *Note:* An accountant is not ordinarily liable for punitive damages for negligence or breach of the engagement contract (see also II-A above). A totally independent auditor would not be in a fiduciary relationship with its client.

B. *Liability to third persons* (those persons other than the client). Ordinarily, the accountant does not owe any duty to persons not in privity of contract. However, there are very important exceptions to this general rule that have been established by common law and legislation.

1. *Liability for negligence.* The accountant is liable for ordinary negligence (tort) to any party who is the "intended beneficiary" of the accountant's work product.

a. *Intended beneficiary.* A third person is an *intended beneficiary* if the accountant knows or should have known (should have foreseen) the identity of the third person and that the latter intended to rely upon the accountant's work product. For example, when the intended beneficiary is identified in the accountant's engagement contract with the client. As a second example, an accountant knew that the financial statements were to be used to acquire a loan from a financial institution, but was unaware of the specific institution

FIGURE 20-2   INTENDED BENEFICIARY OF ACCOUNTANT'S WORK PRODUCT

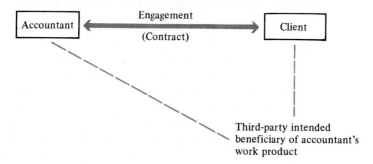

involved. As a third example, an accountant who prepares tax returns for a limited partnership should know that its limited partners would rely upon those returns. (See Figure 20-2.)

b. The intended beneficiary is entitled to recover any "out-of-pocket" monetary losses it suffered as a result of the accountant's negligence.

2. *Liability for misstatements and omissions of material facts in registration statements under section 11 of the Securities Act of 1933.* The federal Securities Act of 1933 imposes upon the accountant the duty to use due diligence in the preparation of the financial statements included in the registration statement required to be filed with the SEC prior to an offering of securities. The due diligence defense satisfies the burden of proving that the accountant was neither negligent nor fraudulent in certifying the financial statements. The accountant may satisfy this burden by showing that a reasonable investigation was made, that there was a reasonable basis for belief, and that there was good reason to believe that certified financial statements were true, complete, and accurate.

a. *Duty to use due diligence in preparation of registration statement.* If the accountant fails to use due diligence in the preparation of this statement and such failure results in a false statement or a misleading omission of a material fact on the date when the registration statement becomes effective, then the accountant is liable to all persons who purchased the securities and suffered losses.

(1) *Accuracy of the registration statement.* The financial statement must be accurate on the effective date of the registration statement. Therefore, the accountant has a duty to make a reasonable investigation during the time between certification of the financial statement and the date of effective registration so as to assure the truth of the previously certified financial statement.

(2) *Reliance is not an element.* The person injured need not prove that there was reliance upon the materially false statement or misleading omission.

(3) *Privity not required.* There is no requirement of privity between the accountant and the security purchasers.

(4) Liability is imposed upon the accountant even though the purchaser was not an intended third-party beneficiary.

(5) *Material fact must have been misrepresented or omitted.* Something is material if it would have influenced a reasonably prudent investor's (includes a speculator) decision had the truth of the matter been known. The volume of sales, profits earned, and the amount of receivables have been held to be material under the provisions of this act.

b. *Due diligence defense.* The accountant has the burden of proving *due diligence*; i.e., the freedom from negligence or fraud.

    (1) The fact that the accountant performed according to generally accepted auditing standards and accounting principles or practices does not necessarily or automatically constitute due diligence.

    (2) The failure to follow generally accepted accounting principles or auditing standards is proof of a lack of due diligence.

    (3) To establish the due diligence defense, accountants must prove that, as regards the certified financial statement that they prepared, they had, after a reasonable investigation, reasonable ground to believe, and that they did believe at the time the registration statement became effective, it did not contain any false or misleading statements or omissions of material facts.

    (4) An accountant was held not to have exercised due diligence when sole reliance was placed upon information furnished by a corporation's officers and directors in preparation of the registration statement. The accountant must resort to other sources and verify such information.

    (5) It is not due diligence when an accountant, after the preparation and filing of a registration statement with the SEC, discovers an omitted material fact and does not amend the registration statement prior to the time that it becomes effective.

c. Fault of any other coviolator of this provision that helped cause or contributed to the false or misleading statements or omissions of material fact is not a defense available to the accountant.

3. *Liability for fraud.* An accountant may be liable on the basis of fraud for damages to third persons under the common law and sections 18, 10b, or Rule 10b-5 of the Securities Exchange Act of 1934. (See Figure 20-1.)

a. *Liability under the common law.* The accountant is liable to all third persons who suffer a monetary loss as a result of their reliance upon an accountant's actual or constructive fraud. These third persons may include lenders to the accountant's client, purchasers and sellers of securities, or any other person.

    (1) *Actual fraud* is present whenever the accountant intentionally misrepresents a material fact upon which a third person or persons relied to their financial detriment.

    (2) *Constructive fraud* is present whenever the accountant's conduct in the performance of the engagement is so grossly negligent that the law will infer fraud.

b. *Liability for fraudulent misstatements or omissions in material filed with the SEC.* Section 18 of the 1934 act imposes civil liability for damages on the accountant if he or she makes or causes to be made any *fraudulent false and misleading statements or omissions* of material fact in any application, registration, report, or document filed with the SEC.

    (1) *Scope of liability.* The scope of section 18 liability is narrow in that it applies only to false and misleading statements of material facts in applications, registrations, reports, and documents *filed with the SEC.* It does not apply to oral statements made in connection with the purchase or sale of securities, to annual corporate reports sent to shareholders, or to other matters.

    (2) *Remedy for sellers or buyers of securities.* This remedy is *available only to sellers or purchasers.*

    (3) *Reliance.* The accountant's liability is only to a person who purchased or sold a security in reliance upon the fraudulent false and misleading mate-

rial statement. *Note:* Reliance is a required element under this provision of the 1934 act, but it is not required for liability for false or misleading statements or omission in a registration statement under section 11 of the 1933 act.

   (4) *Good faith defense.* The accountant can be exonerated of liability upon proof that the action was made in "good faith" and that there was no knowledge that the financial statement was false and misleading. *Note:* The 1934 act is less stringent than the 1933 act, which requires the accountant to prove "due diligence" in order to escape liability.

   (a) *Good faith* involves an honest intention to abstain from taking an unconscionable advantage of another person. In other words, the accountant must prove lack of scienter (i.e., the lack of the intent to deceive, manipulate, or defraud). Reckless conduct or gross negligence will negate good faith.

   (5) *Knowledge of the falsity on the part of the seller or the buyer* of securities is also a defense available to the accountant.

c. *Antifraud provisions of the 1934 act.* The antifraud provisions of the 1934 act are found in section 10b and SEC Rule 10b-5. The scope of application of these provisions is extremely wide. They apply not only to an accountant's fraudulent misstatements of material facts in written material filed with the SEC but also to any fraudulent oral statements or omissions and any other type of fraudulent conduct or activities in *connection with the purchase or sale of any security* within the jurisdiction of the SEC.

   (1) *Section 10b.* Section 10b of the Securities Exchange Act of 1934 makes it:

   "... unlawful for any person, directly or indirectly, by the use of any means or instrumentality of interstate commerce or of the mails, or of any facility of any national securities exchange to use or employ, in connection with the purchase or sale of any security registered on a national securities exchange or any security not so registered on a national securities exchange, any manipulative or deceptive device or contrivance in contravention of such rules and regulations as the Commission may prescribe as necessary or appropriate in the public interest or for the protection of investors."

   (2) *Rule 10b-5.* Securities and Exchange Commission Rule 10b-5 provides:

   "It shall be unlawful for any person, directly or indirectly, by the use of any means or instrumentality of interstate commerce, or of the mails, or of any facility of national securities exchange,
   (a) To employ any device, scheme, or artifice to defraud,
   (b) To make any untrue statement of a material fact or to omit to state a material fact necessary in order to make the statements made, in light of the circumstances under which they were made, not misleading, or
   (c) To engage in any act, practice or course of business which operates or would operate as a fraud or deceit upon any person, in connection with the purchase or sale of any security."

   (3) *Remedy for sellers or purchasers of securities.* Only sellers and purchasers are entitled to recover damages under these provisions.

   (4) *Elements of a violation.* A seller or purchaser must prove the following elements of an antifraud violation in order to recover a monetary loss from an accountant:

   (a) *Scienter.* The accountant must have had the intent to deceive, manipulate, or defraud. Proof of reckless conduct (gross negligence) satisfies the scienter requirement. Proof of negligence alone is not sufficient to recover under these provisions of the act. For example, the negligent "failure" to conduct proper audits of a firm, thereby failing to discover irregular internal practices of a firm utilized by its president and owner of 92 percent of its stock to perpetuate a fraudulent securities scheme, did not subject an accountant to liability under Rule 10b-5.

(b) *Reliance.* The seller or purchaser must have relied upon the fraudulent statement, omission, conduct, or activity.

(c) *Materiality.* Materiality is a requirement. Something is material if it is so relevant or important to the securities transaction that it would have influenced the decision of a reasonable investor (i.e., the prudent investor test) (see also "Materiality," XIX-C-2, covered in Chapter 19).

(d) *Causation.* The fraudulent statement, omission, conduct, or activity must have caused the loss to the seller or purchaser. The presence of materiality also establishes causation.

(e) *"In connection with the purchase or sale of a security".* The violation must occur in connection with the purchase or sale of a security.

    i. "A security" includes those that are exempt and nonexempt, listed and unlisted, and registered and unregistered.

    ii. All buy-sell securities transactions are covered (see also "All buy-sell securities transactions," XIX-C-2 in Chapter 19).

    iii. All conduct and activities related to buy-sell securities transactions are covered. For example, an accountant's preparation of reports, auditing, and certification activities are "in connection with the purchase or sale of a security." This is so even though the reports, documents, and certified or noncertified financial statements are not filed with the SEC but are prepared for other purposes; e.g., financial statements prepared for purposes of negotiating and completing a merger, or financial statements prepared for use by broker-dealers. As another example, the acceptance of payoffs by an accountant from a securities broker for purposes of influencing investors to use the broker's services was also held to be within the provisions of Rule 10b-5.

    iv. Conduct and activities of internal as well as independent public accountants are regulated.

(f) *Privity.* Proof of privity is not required for recovery.

(5) *Contribution among coviolators.* An accountant who is required to pay a loss suffered by a seller or purchaser of securities is entitled to a *contribution* from the coviolators (sections 9 and 18). Each violator's contribution is equal to the total amount required to be paid by one violator divided by the total number of violators that caused the loss.

(6) *Measure of damages.* The seller or purchaser must prove an out-of-pocket loss that resulted from reliance upon the accountant's fraudulent statement, omission, conduct, or activity.

(a) *Sellers.* Sellers are allowed to recover:

    i. Their *"out-of-pocket" loss*, i.e., the difference between the price received and the true value of the securities at the time of the sale; and

    ii. The amount of increase in the value of the securities while they were possessed by the violator.

(b) *Buyers.* The out-of-pocket loss to a buyer is the difference between the price paid by the buyer and the true value of the security at the time of the purchase.

(c) *Consequential damages* (i.e., losses). Persons entitled to recover out-of-pocket losses are also entitled to recover *consequential damages*, such as brokerage fees, transaction taxes, and unreceived dividends. Attorney fees are generally not recoverable.

C. Review IX-C and XIX-C in Chapter 19.

D. *Statutes of Limitation for civil liability.* State and federal statutes prescribe the time within which a lawsuit must be filed against the accountant in order to preserve an "injured" person's cause of action for damages.

    1. *Breach of contract (the engagement) including breach of fiduciary duty.* Causes of action for breach of contract are governed by the *Statute of Limitations* of the state that has jurisdiction over the transaction. Although the time limitations for filing a lawsuit are not the same in all states, most states provide the limitations specified below.

        a. *Oral engagement contract.* Under an oral engagement the client must file a lawsuit against the accountant within five years after the date that the breach occurred.

        b. *Written engagement contract.* The client must file a lawsuit against the client within ten years after the date of the breach.

    2. *Negligence (tort).* Causes of action based on the tort of negligence are also governed by the Statute of Limitations of the state that has jurisdiction over the dispute. Although the time period within which the lawsuit must be filed varies throughout the United States, the most common period ranges between two to five years after the negligence occurred.

    3. *Liability under the 1933 act.* A lawsuit for damages cannot be filed by an "injured" person against an accountant after more than one year after the false statement or misleading omission was or should have been discovered, but never more than three years after the security was first offered to the public.

    4. *Liability under the 1934 act.*

        a. *For violations of all provisions other than the antifraud provision under Rule 10b-5.* The statute of limitations here is identical to that provided under the 1933 act (see 3 above).

        b. *For Rule 10b-5.* There is no limitation period expressly provided for lawsuits under Rule 10b-5 by federal securities laws. Federal courts have applied state statutes of limitations where appropriate. The state statutes are not uniform as to time periods within which lawsuits must be filed. The time periods vary from two to five years.

CRIMINAL LIABILITY

III. *In general.* The accountant may be criminally liable (i.e., fine and/or imprisonment) under state and federal criminal codes, the Securities Act of 1933, the Securities Exchange Act of 1934 and its Foreign Corrupt Practices amendment, and the Internal Revenue Code. (See Figure 20-1.)

A. *Securities Act of 1933.* The 1933 act prescribes criminal penalties for *willfully* making materially false statements or misleading omissions in a registration statement and for violation of its antifraud provisions.

B. *Securities Exchange Act of 1934.* The 1934 act prescribes criminal penalties for *willfully* making materially false statements or misleading omissions in reports, applications, registrations, and documents filed with the SEC or for violations of its antifraud provisions.

C. *Internal Revenue Code.* The code prescribes criminal penalties for the following *wilful* acts of tax evasion by an accountant:

1. Aiding or assisting filing false tax returns; e.g., inflating a client's tax deductions;
2. Failure to pay over to the IRS tax received from the client;
3. Attempting to evade or defeat tax, e.g., illegal payoffs to IRS agents;
4. Delivery or disclosure to the IRS of any list, return, account, statement or other document known to be false;
5. *Aid or assist* in preparing false documents in connection with *any tax evasion*;
6. Wrongfully disclosing or using confidential information provided by a taxpayer-client for the purpose of tax return preparation.

D. *State criminal statutes.* Criminal penalties for criminal fraud, embezzlement, bribery, and other criminal conduct or activities are prescribed by state statutes.

LIABILITIES OF COMPENSATED INCOME TAX RETURN PREPARERS

IV. *In general.* A compensated income tax return preparer may be subject to criminal as well as civil penalties. A *compensated income tax return preparer* is any person who prepares for compensation, or who employs one or more persons to prepare any income tax return or tax refund for compensation.

A. *Criminal penalties.* See III-C above.

B. *Civil liabilities or sanctions.* Compensated income tax return preparers may be liable for damages suffered by their clients. They may also be subject to IRS-imposed civil fines and sanctions.

1. *Damages to the client.* The accountant who undertakes to prepare and file tax returns must comply with the exact terms of the engagement and must do so in a nonnegligent manner. To fail to do so will result in the following liabilities:
   a. Tax penalties and interest assessed against the accountant's client for failure to file returns correctly or on time.
   b. Punitive damages if the client's losses resulted from the accountant's gross negligence or fraudulent conduct with respect to the engagement.
   c. Income taxes paid by a client because it followed the erroneous advice of its accountant. For example, a principal shareholder in several corporations was incorrectly advised that it could sell securities of one corporation to the other without incurring any tax liability.
   d. Losses caused by the accountant's wrongful disclosure or use of confidential information.

2. *IRS-imposed civil penalties.* Civil penalties (i.e., fines) may be imposed upon the income tax preparer in amounts ranging from $25 to $500 for the following acts or omissions:
   a. The negligent or intentional disregard of income tax rules or regulations resulting in an understatement of the taxpayer's federal income tax liability;
   b. The negotiation or other transfer of the taxpayer's tax refund check;
   c. Failure to:
      (1) Provide a copy of the complete income tax return to the taxpayer;
      (2) Sign the return;
      (3) Record the preparer's identification number on the taxpayer's return;
      (4) Retain a copy of all returns prepared or a list of all taxpayers for whom returns had been prepared for a period of three years; or
      (5) File an annual report with the IRS.

3. *Injunction.* The Internal Revenue Service (IRS) is empowered to sue for injunctive relief to prevent a preparer from engaging in the following prohibited practices:
   a. Disclosure or use of confidential information provided by taxpayers for purposes other than preparation of the return;

b. Negligent or intentional disregard of income tax rules or regulations that result in understatement of taxpayer liability;

c. Misrepresentation of eligibility to practice before the IRS, experience, or educational qualifications as an income tax return preparer;

d. Guarantee of payment of a tax refund or of allowance of a tax credit;

e. Conduct subject to criminal penalties under the Internal Revenue Code. See III-C above for a list of the criminal acts of an accountant; or

f. Other fraudulent or deceptive conduct that substantially interferes with proper administration of the internal revenue laws.

Note: If a compensated income tax preparer has repeatedly engaged in wrongful conduct, the IRS may obtain an injunction restraining the preparer from practicing as an income tax preparer in the future.

DISCLOSURE OF ACCOUNTANT-CLIENT COMMUNICATIONS

V. *Introduction.* There are two aspects in respect to disclosure of *confidential accountant-client communications.* The first is whether or not an accountant has the right to voluntarily disclose confidential information about a client to third parties. The second is whether or not the accountant may be forced to disclose such information by legal process.

A. *Voluntary disclosure.* It is clearly established that the accountant is liable for voluntarily disclosing any confidential information without the client's consent. To do so, is a breach of the accountant's fiduciary duty to the client (see II-A-3 above and VI-B below).

1. AICPA ethics rules also prohibit disclosure of confidential information, except in the following circumstances:

a. To comply with a valid court order, i.e., a subpoena or summons;

b. To respond to an ethics inquiry by the AICPA, a CPA society, or state regulatory agency;

c. To avoid violating auditing standards and accounting principles.

B. *Involuntary disclosure.* There is no accountant–client legal privilege for an accountant to refuse disclosure of confidential information about the client. Such privilege does not exist unless it is specially provided for in a state or federal statute.

1. *State statutes.* Less than one-half of the states have statutes that create some form of the accountant-client privilege. Even in states where the privilege exists, it may be waived by the client, thereby allowing the accountant to disclose the confidential information as a witness in court or under a subpoena.

2. *Federal statutes.* There is no federal accountant-client privilege in federal tax cases and federal criminal proceedings. The accountant must testify in regard to confidential oral or written information under a subpoena.

ACCOUNTANTS' WORKING PAPERS

VI. An *accountant's working papers* are usually considered to consist of reviews of systems of internal control, methods and results of testing accounts, work programs, memoranda that contain explanations of handling exceptions or extraordinary situations, and abstracts of company documents and records prepared by the auditor to indicate conclusions reached on important and significant matters.

A. *Ownership of working papers.* Under the common law, an accountant *employed as an independent contractor* is the sole and absolute owner of his or her working papers. The accountant is entitled to possession and control of them even as against the client. As many as twenty-five states have enacted statutes that specifically provide that working papers are owned by the independent accountant.

- B. *Confidential nature of working papers.* Because of the confidential relationship between the accountant and the client, the accountant may not voluntarily disclose information found in working papers without the client's consent (see II-A-3 and V-A above).

- C. *Judicial access to working papers.* Working papers are subject to summons by the Internal Revenue Service (IRS), to subpoena by a grand jury in a federal criminal case, to subpoena by a regulatory agency such as the SEC, and to search warrants issued for probable cause by a federal court. A state accountant–client confidential information privilege does not apply to federal tax cases, federal regulatory investigations, and federal criminal cases.

CPA FIRM MANUALS

VII. Internal accounting and auditing manuals and procedures are confidential and legally protected as trade secrets. They are subject to court-ordered disclosure in any judicial proceeding only upon a showing of actual need and direct relevance to the legal matters in issue. For example, a federal court case allowed a restrictive order to be issued requiring a CPA firm to produce its internal accounting and auditing manuals for use by a plaintiff to question accountants on the issue of whether or not they followed generally accepted accounting practices and procedures during an audit.

SELF-QUIZ

To check your understanding of the key words and concepts and the accuracy of your answers to the questions, refer to the text material as referenced by page number.

KEY WORDS AND CONCEPTS

QUESTIONS

1. What three duties does the accountant owe to a client? **(589)**
2. Can third parties recover damages for the accountant's breach of contract with the client? Under what circumstances? **(591)**
3. Are all accountants required to possess superior knowledge or skill in performing their contractual duties? If not, what is the amount of skill or care necessary to avoid liability? **(590)**

4. Under what circumstances is an accountant liable to an "intended beneficiary" but not to other third parties? **(591)**

5. To whom is an accountant liable for fraud or constructive fraud in the preparation of reports? **(593)** Is contributory negligence a defense available to the accountant for these acts? **(591)**

6. What duty is imposed upon an accountant under the Securities Act of 1933? **(592)**

7. Does the accountant's liability under the 1933 act end with the certification of the registration statement, or does it extend to the effective date of the registration statement? **(592)** To which persons is the accountant liable for materially false statements or misleading omissions in the registration statement? **(592)**

8. In order to recover damages under the 1933 act, is it necessary for a third party to prove reliance upon the materially false statement or misleading omission contained in the registration statement? **(592)**

9. When is a fact considered material? **(592)** Give examples of facts that have been held to be material under the provisions of the Securities Act of 1933. **(592)**

10. Under the provisions of the Securities Act of 1933, the injured party does not have to prove reliance on the financial statements. Is this also true of the Securities Exchange Act of 1934? **(593)** What requirements are necessary for the third party to recover from a financial loss suffered under the act of 1934? **(593)**

11. What must the accountant prove to attain exoneration of liability for damages from false and misleading statements under the Securities Exchange Act of 1934? **(594)**

12. Does the accountant have exposure to criminal liability? What statutes provide criminal liability for the accountant for wilful falsification of financial statements or reports? **(596)**

13. Who is the owner of the accountant's working papers? **(598)** Describe the nature of the legal relationship between the accountant and the client. **(591, 598)**

14. Can the accountant disclose information compiled in his or her working papers without the client's consent? To whom? Under what circumstances? **(599)**

15. Are the communications between the accountant and the client privileged under the law? In federal cases? In state courts? **(598)**

16. What are the potential liabilities of an accountant who prepares income tax returns? **(597)**

SELECTED QUESTIONS AND UNOFFICIAL ANSWERS

OBJECTIVE QUESTIONS

Select the best answer for each of the following items. Mark only one answer for each item. Answer all items.

MAY 1981

1. DMO Enterprises, Inc., engaged the accounting firm of Martin, Seals & Anderson to perform its annual audit. The firm performed the audit in a competent, nonnegligent manner and billed DMO for $16,000, the agreed fee. Shortly after delivery of the audited financial statements, Hightower, the assistant controller, disappeared, taking with him $28,000 of DMO's funds. It was then discovered that Hightower had been engaged in a highly sophisticated, novel defalcation scheme during the past year. He had previously embezzled $35,000 of DMO funds. DMO has refused to pay the accounting firm's fee and is seeking to recover the $63,000 that was stolen by Hightower. Which of the following is correct?

a. The accountants can *not* recover their fee and are liable for $63,000.

b. The accountants are entitled to collect their fee and are *not* liable for $63,000.

c. DMO is entitled to rescind the audit contract and thus is *not* liable for the $16,000 fee, but it can *not* recover damages.

d. DMO is entitled to recover the $28,000 defalcation, and is *not* liable for the $16,000 fee.

2. The CPA firm of Knox & Knox has been subpoenaed to testify and produce its correspondence and workpapers in connection with a lawsuit brought by a third party against one of their clients. Knox considers the subpoenaed documents to be privileged communication and therefore seeks to

avoid admission of such evidence in the lawsuit. Which of the following is correct?

a. Federal law recognizes such a privilege if the accountant is a Certified Public Accountant.

b. The privilege is available regarding the working papers since the CPA is deemed to own them.

c. The privileged communication rule as it applies to the CPA-client relationship is the same as that of attorney-client.

d. In the absence of a specific statutory provision, the law does *not* recognize the existence of the privileged communication rule between a CPA and his client.

3. Major, Major & Sharpe, CPAs, are the auditors of MacLain Industries. In connection with the public offering of $10 million of MacLain securities, Major expressed an unqualified opinion as to the financial statements. Subsequent to the offering, certain misstatements and omissions were revealed. Major has been sued by the purchasers of the stock offered pursuant to the registration statement which included the financial statements audited by Major. In the ensuing lawsuit by the MacLain investors, Major will be able to avoid liability if

a. The errors and omissions were caused primarily by MacLain.

b. It can be shown that at least some of the investors did *not* actually read the audited financial statements.

c. It can prove due diligence in the audit of the financial statements of MacLain.

d. MacLain had expressly assumed any liability in connection with the public offering.

4. Donalds & Company, CPAs, audited the financial statements included in the annual report submitted by Markum Securities, Inc., to the Securities and Exchange Commission. The audit was improper in several respects. Markum is now insolvent and unable to satisfy the claims of its customers. The customers have instituted legal action against Donalds based upon section 10b and rule 10b-5 of the Securities Exchange Act of 1934. Which of the following is likely to be Donalds' best defense?

a. They did *not* intentionally certify false financial statements.

b. Section 10b does *not* apply to them.

c. They were *not* in privity of contract with the creditors.

d. Their engagement letter specifically disclaimed

any liability to any party which resulted from Markum's fraudulent conduct.

5. The 1976 Tax Reform Act substantially changed the regulation of tax return preparers by

a. Granting the Internal Revenue Service the power to seek injunctive relief against a wrongdoing preparer.

b. Providing criminal sanctions.

c. Imposing civil liability regardless of whether the preparer does the preparation for compensation.

d. Expanding the legal remedies of the client for whom the return was prepared.

6. If a CPA firm is being sued for common law fraud by a third party based upon materially false financial statements, which of the following is the best defense which the accountants could assert?

a. Lack of privity.

b. Lack of reliance.

c. A disclaimer contained in the engagement letter.

d. Contributory negligence on the part of the client.

NOVEMBER 1978

2. Magnus Enterprises engaged a CPA firm to perform the annual examination of its financial statements. Which of the following is a correct statement with respect to the CPA firm's liability to Magnus for negligence?

a. Such liability can *not* be varied by agreement of the parties.

b. The CPA firm will be liable for any fraudulent scheme it does *not* detect.

c. The CPA firm will *not* be liable if it can show that it exercised the ordinary care and skill of a reasonable man in the conduct of his own affairs.

d. The CPA firm must *not* only exercise reasonable care in what it does, but also must possess at least that degree of accounting knowledge and skill expected of a CPA.

11. A CPA firm is being sued by a third party purchaser of securities sold in interstate commerce to the public. The third party is relying upon the Securities Act of 1933. The CPA firm had issued an unqualified opinion on incorrect financial statements. Which of the following represents the best defense available to the CPA firm?

a. The securities sold had *not* been registered with the SEC.

b. The CPA firm had returned the entire fee it charged for the engagement to the corporation.

c. The third party was *not* in privity of contract with the CPA firm.

d. The action had *not* been commenced within one year after the discovery of the material misrepresentation.

32. On July 25, 1978, Archer, the president of Post Corporation, with the approval of the board of directors, engaged Biggs, a CPA, to examine Post's July 31, 1978, financial statements and to issue a report in time for the annual stockholders' meeting to be held on September 5, 1978. Notwithstanding Biggs' reasonable efforts, the report was not ready until September 7 because of delays by Post's staff. Archer, acting on behalf of Post, refused to accept or to pay for the report since it no longer served its intended purpose. In the event Biggs brings a legal action against Post, what is the probable outcome?

a. The case would be dismissed because it is unethical for a CPA to sue for his fee.

b. Biggs will be entitled to recover only in quasi contract for the value of the services to the client.

c. Biggs will *not* recover since the completion by September 5th was a condition precedent to his recovery.

d. Biggs will recover because the delay by Post's staff prevented Biggs from performing on time and thereby eliminated the timely performance condition.

NOVEMBER 1977

1. A CPA is subject to *criminal* liability if the CPA

a. Refuses to turn over the working papers to the client.

b. Performs an audit in a negligent manner.

c. Willfully omits a material fact required to be stated in a registration statement.

d. Willfully breaches the contract with the client.

3. A CPA was engaged by Jackson & Wilcox, a small retail partnership, to examine its financial statements. The CPA discovered that due to other commitments, the engagement could *not* be completed on time. The CPA, therefore, unilaterally delegated the duty to Vincent, an equally competent CPA. Under these circumstances, which of the following is true?

a. The duty to perform the audit engagement is delegable in that it is determined by an objective standard.

b. If Jackson & Wilcox refuses to accept Vincent because of a personal dislike of Vincent by one of the partners, Jackson & Wilcox will be liable for breach of contract.

c. Jackson & Wilcox must accept the delegation in that Vincent is equally competent.

d. The duty to perform the audit engagement is nondelegable and Jackson & Wilcox need *not* accept Vincent as a substitute if they do *not* wish to do so.

4. Gaspard & Devlin, a medium-sized CPA firm, employed Marshall as a staff accountant. Marshall was negligent in auditing several of the firm's clients. Under these circumstances which of the following statements is true?

a. Gaspard & Devlin is *not* liable for Marshall's negligence because CPAs are generally considered to be independent contractors.

b. Gaspard and Devlin would *not* be liable for Marshall's negligence if Marshall disobeyed specific instructions in the performance of the audits.

c. Gaspard & Devlin can recover against its insurer on its malpractice policy even if one of the partners was also negligent in reviewing Marshall's work.

d. Marshall would have *no* personal liability for negligence.

5. Sharp, CPA, was engaged by Peters & Sons, a partnership, to give an opinion on the financial statements which were to be submitted to several prospective partners as part of a planned expansion of the firm. Sharp's fee was fixed on a per diem basis. After a period of intensive work, Sharp completed about half of the necessary field work. Then due to unanticipated demands upon his time by other clients, Sharp was forced to abandon the work. The planned expansion of the firm failed to materialize because the prospective partners lost interest when the audit report was *not* promptly available. Sharp offers to complete the task at a later date. This offer was refused. Peters & Sons suffered damages of $4,000 as a result. Under the circumstances, what is the probable outcome of a lawsuit between Sharp and Peters & Sons?

a. Sharp will be compensated for the reasonable value of the services actually performed.

b. Peters & Sons will recover damages for breach of contract.

c. Peters & Sons will recover both punitive damages and damages for breach of contract.

d. Neither Sharp nor Peters & Sons will recover against the other.

42. If a CPA firm is engaged by a law firm to aid it in the administration of a decedent's estate, its duties will invariably *not* include

a. Preparation of the federal estate tax return.

b. Preparation of the estate's fiduciary income tax returns.

c. Presentation of the necessary schedules and summations to be used in rendering an accounting to interested parties.

d. Consideration of the validity of the surviving spouse's right to take against the will.

Answers to Objective Questions

May 1981		November 1977	
1. b	**4.** a	**1.** c	**5.** b
2. d	**5.** a	**3.** d	**42.** d
3. c	**6.** b	**4.** c	

November 1978

2. d	**32.** d
11. d	

Explanation of Answers to Objective Questions

MAY 1981

1. (b) In this case, a client is seeking to sue its auditor because defalcations perpetrated by management were not discovered during an annual audit. A client may sue its auditor under common law for breach of fiduciary duty, negligence, gross negligence or fraud. The auditor is obligated to plan the audit, to search for such irregularities, and to investigate matters coming to the auditor's attention that might indicate the existence of irregularities, but the auditor does not guarantee that these activities will be discovered. If the auditor is not negligent in the performance of his duties (e.g., he does not violate GAAS), he will not be liable for irregularities not discovered during the audit. In addition, the absence of negligence also precludes the client from withholding the auditor's fee. Thus, answer (b) is correct since the question specifically indicates that the auditor performed the audit in a "competent, nonnegligent manner." Answers (a), (c), and (d) are incorrect since they all indicate some degree of liability on the part of the auditor.

2. (d) Under common law, no provision exists which grants privileged communication status to CPA-client relationships. Under the Code of Ethics, a CPA is generally prohibited from revealing client information without the client's permission except in situations involving a CPA firm's peer review evaluation, AICPA trial board inquiries, and information subpoenaed by a court of law. In the preceding situation, the CPA has no right to withhold client information from the requesting authorities. However, some state statutes do grant privileged communication status to confidential communications between a client and his accountant. But, unless such a state statute exists, no law will permit a CPA to avoid testifying in a lawsuit brought against his client. Answer (a) is incorrect because no federal law recognizes a privileged status of CPA-client relations. Answer (b) is incorrect because the fact that a CPA owns the workpapers has no effect on a CPA's duty to disclose information contained therein in the situations described above. Answer (c) is incorrect because the law does recognize the privileged nature of an attorney-client relationship; thus, this type of relationship is not the same as a CPA-client relationship.

3. (c) The SEC Act of 1933 concerns the regulation of initial public offerings of stock. The Act requires the filing of a registration statement including a certified financial statement. Any person acquiring a security covered by the registration can sue the accountant, if the certified financial statements contained false statements or omitted material facts. The presence of such misstatements and omissions is prima facie evidence that the accountant is liable. This means that plaintiff-purchaser does not have the burden of proving the accountant's negligence; the accountant must prove he was not negligent and that he acted with due diligence (skill and care of the average accountant). Answer (a) is incorrect since the auditor's certification of the financial statements covers management's representations. The fact that the errors were caused by MacLain's actions will not relieve the auditor of liability. Answer (b) is also incorrect since the plaintiff does not have to prove reliance on the financial statements or that the loss was suffered from the misstatement. Answer (d) is incorrect since Mac-Lain's express assumption of liability will not relieve the auditor.

4. (a) The SEC Act of 1934 has antifraud provisions. These provisions apply to all transactions involving interstate commerce, mail, or transactions on the national exchange involving the purchase *or* sale of securities. Rule 10B5 makes it unlawful for any person to defraud, make untrue statements of material facts or omit material facts on the financial statements or engage in a business which operates as a fraud on persons involved in the purchase or sale of the securities. The correct answer is (a) since this would be the best defense. Scienter by the auditor must be established to hold them liable. This means that the defendant had knowledge of false statements or that the statement was made with a reckless disregard of the truth. Answer (b) is incorrect because Rule 10B5 applies to the accountants. Answer (c) is incorrect because privity (a contract between the creditors and the accountants) is not required to hold accountants liable. Answer (d) is incorrect since the auditor cannot disclaim liability in this manner.

5. (a) This question deals with the substantial changes enacted by the Tax Reform Act of 1976. The principal effect of this act was to allow the IRS to seek an injunction against tax preparers who engage in the following activities: conduct subject to civil or criminal penalties under the Internal Revenue Code, misrepresentation of a preparer's qualifications to practice, guarantees that clients will receive refunds or tax credits on returns, or any other fraudulent or deceptive conduct. The only answer which reflects the above changes is answer (a). Answers (b) and (d) are incorrect because the 1976 Act did not substantially change either the criminal sanctions already available under previous acts (b) or the legal remedies available for clients (d). Answer (c) is incorrect because a preparer is always liable whether or not he prepares a return for compensation; in either case he must sign the tax return without modifying the liability clause contained therein.

6. (b) Under common law, a plaintiff must typically prove that: 1) there was negligence or fraud on the part of the preparer, 2) that misleading statements were prepared or distributed, 3) that the plaintiff relied on those misleading statements, and 4) that a loss resulted from this reliance. If a plaintiff is unable to prove, or if the auditor is able to disprove, any of these four requirements, the auditor will not be held liable. Thus, answer (b) in which the auditor attacks the validity of one of the above

four conditions (reliance on the misleading statements) is correct in that this is the best defense of those listed in the possible answers. Answer (a) is incorrect because in cases of actual or constructive fraud, privity of third parties is not necessary in order to bring suit. Answer (c) is incorrect because a disclaimer contained in an engagement letter is not effective in relieving an accountant's liability for certified statements. Answer (d) is incorrect in that a client's negligence will not absolve the auditor of his responsibilities to third parties in any situation.

2. (d) A CPA firm must exercise reasonable care and also must possess that degree of accounting knowledge and skill expected of an average CPA. Answer (a) is incorrect because a CPA's liability can be varied by agreement between the CPA and the client. Answer (b) is incorrect because a CPA firm is not liable for failing to detect fraudulent schemes provided their negligence did not prevent discovery. Answer (c) is incorrect because a CPA firm must exercise the care and skill of an average CPA rather than that of a reasonable person who is not trained as a CPA.

11. (d) The best defense for the CPA firm is that the third-party purchaser failed to commence his action within one year after discovery of the untrue statement or omission, or after such discovery should have been made by the exercise of reasonable diligence. This is the statute of limitations under the Securities Act of 1933. Answer (a) is not the best defense, because these securities should have been registered with the SEC and therefore the CPA firm can be held liable under the 1933 Act whether or not the securities were registered. Answer (b) is not the best defense because an accountant can be held liable whether or not he was paid. Answer (c) is not the best defense because the Securities Act of 1933 eliminates the necessity for privity of contract.

32. (d) Accountants are responsible for performing contracts with their clients in accordance with the contractual terms. Additionally the rules of contracts also apply, and since Biggs was prevented from performing timely due to the client's delays, Biggs will recover his fees. Answer (a) is incorrect because a suit by an accountant to collect his fee would be handled as would any other contract for personal services. Similarly, answer (b) is incorrect because Biggs may recover in full under the contract. Answer (c) is incorrect because the client prevented Biggs from meeting the deadline.

NOVEMBER 1977

1. (c) Criminal liability is only incurred by violating a statute. A CPA who willfully omits a material fact required to be stated in a registration statement is in violation of the Securities Acts and is subject to criminal liability. Civil liability is incurred by violating a legal duty owed to another. Answers (b) and (c) are incorrect because performing an audit in a negligent manner and willfully breaching a contract are violations of a legal duty owed to another and give rise to a civil liability. Answer (a) is incorrect because a CPA owns his workpapers and has no duty to turn them over to a client.

3. (d) The duty to perform the audit is not delegable, because the audit is a contract for personal services based on personal trust or character. Only in certain cases, i.e., where services are mechanical and only the end result is desired, can personal services be delegated, e.g., moving goods, but never an audit. Jackson and Wilcox need not accept Vincent as a substitute, but they may if they wish. Thus answers (a) and (c) are incorrect. Answer (b) is incorrect because since Jackson and Wilcox have no duty to accept Vincent, they may refuse him for any reason, even personal dislike.

4. (c) Gaspard & Devlin can recover on its malpractice insurance no matter who in the firm was negligent, i.e., a malpractice policy insures negligence. Although CPA firms and individual practitioners are independent contractors, the firm independently contracted with the client. Answer (a) is incorrect because the firm as employer is liable for the negligence of its employees acting within the course and scope of their employment. Answer (b) is incorrect because Marshall's disobeyance of instructions would not matter because the firm is responsible for the actions of its employees. Answer (d) is incorrect because Marshall may be held personally liable either by the client, or by the firm if it is held liable by the client.

5. (b) The probable outcome is that Peters & Sons will recover their damages, because Sharp knew the purpose of the audit and it was Sharp's fault that the audit was not finished. Answer (a) is incorrect because Sharp will not be compensated, since he breached the contract and Peters & Sons realized no value from his work. Answer (c) is incorrect because punitive damages are not usually allowed for breach of contract. Punitive damages are allowed for fraud, gross negligence, and intentionally inflicted wrongs.

42. (d) Consideration of the validity of the surviving spouse's right to take against the will is a legal question and not within the competency of a CPA. Therefore this will not be a duty of a CPA firm. Preparation of tax returns and schedules (answers (a), (b), and (c)) used in rendering an accounting is within a CPA's expertise and is routinely done by CPA firms.

ESSAY QUESTIONS AND ANSWERS

NOVEMBER 1980 (Estimated time: 15 to 20 minutes)

4. Part a. Whitlow & Company is a brokerage firm registered under the Securities Exchange Act of 1934. The Act requires such a brokerage firm to file audited financial statements with the SEC annually. Mitchell & Moss, Whitlow's CPAs, performed the annual audit for the year ended December 31, 1979, and rendered an unqualified opinion, which was filed with the SEC along with Whitlow's financial statements. During 1979 Charles, the president of Whitlow & Company, engaged in a huge embezzlement scheme that eventually bankrupted the firm. As a result substantial losses were suffered by customers and shareholders of Whitlow & Company, including Thaxton who had recently purchased several shares of stock of Whitlow & Company after reviewing the company's 1979 audit report. Mitchell & Moss' audit was deficient; if they had complied with generally accepted auditing standards, the embezzlement would have been discovered. However, Mitchell & Moss had no knowledge of the embezzlement nor could their conduct be categorized as reckless.

Required Answer the following, setting forth reasons for any conclusions stated.

1. What liability to Thaxton, if any, does Mitchell & Moss have under the Securities Exchange Act of 1934?
2. What theory or theories of liability, if any, are

available to Whitlow & Company's customers and shareholders under the common law?

Answer

1. In order for Thaxton to hold Mitchell & Moss liable for his losses under the Securities Exchange Act of 1934, he must rely upon the antifraud provisions of section 10(b) of the act. In order to prevail Thaxton must establish that:

- There was an omission or misstatement of a material fact in the financial statements used in connection with his purchase of the Whitlow & Company shares of stock.
- He sustained a loss as a result of his purchase of the shares of stock.
- His loss was caused by reliance on the misleading financial statements.
- Mitchell & Moss acted with scienter.

Based on the stated facts, Thaxton can probably prove the first three requirements cited above. To prove the fourth requirement, Thaxton must show that Mitchell & Moss had knowledge (scienter) of the fraud or recklessly disregarded the truth. The facts clearly indicate that Mitchell & Moss did not have knowledge of the fraud and did not recklessly disregard the truth.

2. The customers and shareholders of Whitlow & Company would attempt to recover on a negligence theory based on Mitchell & Moss' failure to comply with GAAS. Even if Mitchell & Moss were negligent, Whitlow & Company's customers and shareholders must also establish either that:

- They were third party beneficiaries of Mitchell & Moss' contract to audit Whitlow & Company, or
- Mitchell & Moss owed the customers and shareholders a legal duty to act without negligence.

Although recent cases have expanded a CPA's legal responsibilities to a third party for negligence, the facts of this case may fall within the traditional rationale limiting a CPA's liability for negligence; that is, the unfairness of imputing an indeterminate amount of liability to unknown or unforeseen parties as a result of mere negligence on the auditor's part. Accordingly, Whitlow & Company's customers and shareholders will prevail only if (1) the courts rule that they are either third-party beneficiaries or are owed a legal duty and (2) they establish that Mitchell & Moss was negligent in failing to comply with generally accepted auditing standards.

4. Part b. Jackson is a sophisticated investor. As such, she was initially a member of a small group who was going to participate in a private placement of $1 million of common stock of Clarion Corporation. Numerous meetings were held among management and the investor group. Detailed financial and other information was supplied to the participants. Upon the eve of completion of the placement, it was aborted when one major investor withdrew. Clarion then decided to offer $2.5 million of Clarion common stock to the public pursuant to the registration requirements of the Securities Act of 1933. Jackson subscribed to $300,000 of the Clarion public stock offering. Nine months later, Clarion's earnings dropped significantly and as a result the stock dropped 20% beneath the offering price. In addition, the Dow Jones Industrial Average was down 10% from the time of the offering.

Jackson has sold her shares at a loss of $60,000 and seeks to hold all parties liable who participated in the public offering including Allen, Dunn, and Rose, Clarion's CPA firm. Although the audit was performed in conformity with generally accepted auditing standards, there were some relatively minor irregularities. The financial statements of Clarion Corporation, which were part of the registration statement, contained minor misleading facts. It is believed by Clarion and Allen, Dunn and Rose, that Jackson's asserted claim is without merit.

Required Answer the following, setting forth reasons for any conclusions stated.

1. Assuming Jackson sues under the Securities Act of 1933, what will be the basis of her claim?
2. What are the probable defenses which might be asserted by Allen, Dunn, and Rose in light of these facts?

Answer

1. The basis of Jackson's claim will be that she sustained a loss based upon misleading financial statements. Specifically, she will rely upon section 11(a) of the Securities Act of 1933, which provides the following:

In case any part of the registration statement, when such part became effective, contained an untrue statement of a material fact or omitted to state a material fact required to be stated therein or necessary to make the statements therein not misleading, any person acquiring such security (unless it is proved that at the time of such acquisition he knew of such untruth or omission) may, either at law or in equity, in any court of competent jurisdiction, sue . . . every accountant . . . who has with his consent been named as having prepared or certified any part of the registration statement . . .

To the extent that the relatively minor irregularities resulted in the certification of materially false or misleading financial statements, there is potential liability. Jackson's case is based on the assertion of such an untrue statement or omission coupled with an allegation of damages. Jackson does not have to prove reliance on the statements nor the company's or auditor's negligence in order to recover the damages. The burden is placed on the defendant to provide defenses that will enable it to avoid liability.

2. The first defense that could be asserted is that Jackson knew of the untruth or omission in audited financial statements included in the registration statement. The act provides that the plaintiff may not recover if it can be proved at the time of such acquisition she knew of such "untruth or omission."

Since Jackson was a member of the private placement group and presumably privy to the type of information that would be contained in a registration statement, plus any other information requested by the group, she may have had sufficient knowledge of the facts claimed to be untrue or omitted. If this be the case, then she would not be relying on the certified financial statements but upon her own knowledge.

The next defense assertable would be that the untrue statement or omission was not material. The SEC has defined the term as meaning matters about which an average prudent investor ought to be reasonably informed before purchasing the registered security. For section 11 purposes, this has been construed as meaning a fact that, had it been correctly stated or disclosed, would have deterred or tended to deter the average prudent investor from purchasing the security in question.

Allen, Dunn, and Rose would also assert that the loss in question was not due to the false statement or omission; that is, that the false statement was not the cause of the price drop. It would appear that the general decline in the stock market would account for at least a part of the loss. Additionally, if the decline in earnings was not factually connected with the false statement or omission, the defendants have another basis for refuting the causal connection between their wrongdoing and the resultant drop in the stock's price.

Finally, the accountants will claim that their departure from generally accepted auditing standards was too minor to be considered a violation of the standard of due diligence required by the act.

NOVEMBER 1979 (Estimated time: 20 to 25 minutes)

5. Part a. Marcall is a limited partner of Guarcross, a limited partnership, and is suing a CPA firm which was retained by the limited partnership to perform auditing and tax return preparation services. Guarcross was formed for the purpose of investing in a diversified portfolio of risk capital securities. The partnership agreement included the following provisions:

> The initial capital contribution of each limited partner shall not be less than $250,000; no partner may withdraw any part of his interest in the partnership, except at the end of any fiscal year upon giving written notice of such intention not less than 30 days prior to the end of such year; the books and records of the partnership shall be audited as of the end of the fiscal year by a certified public accountant designated by the general partners; and proper and complete books of account shall be kept and shall be open to inspection by any of the partners or his or her accredited representative.

Marcall's claim of malpractice against the CPA firm centers on the firm's alleged failure to comment, in its audit report, on the withdrawal by the general partners of $2,000,000 of their $2,600,000 capital investment based on back-dated notices, and the lumping together of the $2,000,000 withdrawals with $49,000 in withdrawals by limited partners so that a reader of the financial statement would not be likely to realize that the two general partners had withdrawn a major portion of their investments.

The CPA firm's contention is that its contract was made with the limited partnership, not its partners. It further contends that since the CPA firm had no privity of contract with the third-party limited partners, the limited partners have no right of action for negligence.

Required Answer the following, setting forth reasons for any conclusions stated.

Discuss the various theories Marcall would rely upon in order to prevail in a lawsuit against the CPA firm.

Answer The issue of privity is clearly raised by the CPA firm's contention that the duty of care is to the limited partnership with which it had contracted and not to third-party limited partners, such as Marcall.

The common law privity limitation, as it applies to CPAs, is currently in a state of change. However, recent cases indicate a gradual erosion of this limitation of the recovery rights of third parties. Because the basis of Marcall's claim is clearly negligence and not fraud, the traditional fraud exception to the privity rule is not available. The following theories undoubtedly would be asserted by Marcall:

- The third-party beneficiary doctrine would be asserted based upon the fact that it was clear that the audit was intended to benefit the limited partners. Therefore, although not directly parties to the contract, they may sue as its intended beneficiaries.
- The services of the accountants clearly did not extend beyond a class of persons actually known and limited at the time of the engagement. The privity barrier is essentially based upon a reluctance to impose liability against CPAs to the extensive and indeterminable investing public-at-large. However, where the audit was expected to be relied upon by a fixed, definable, and contemplated group whose conduct was to be governed by the audit, the duty of care extends to this class of people. It is not necessary to state the duty in terms of contract or privity.
- Although the facts indicate ordinary negligence, it is possible that gross negligence might be present. The dividing line between ordinary and gross negligence is such that liability to third parties could be found on this basis.
- Although the audit was performed pursuant to a contract with the limited partnership, the real parties-in-interest were the partners. The partnership is not a separate and distinct entity for this purpose. The general partners signing the engagement letter were doing so as agents for each of the members of the limited partnership.

5. Part b. Farr & Madison, CPAs, audited Glamour, Inc. Their audit was deficient in several respects:

- Farr and Madison failed to verify properly certain receivables which later proved to be fictitious.
- With respect to other receivables, although they made a cursory check, they did not detect many accounts which were long overdue and obviously uncollectible.
- No physical inventory was taken of the securities claimed to be in Glamour's possession, which in fact had been sold. Both the securities and cash received from the sales were listed on the balance sheet as assets.

There is no indication that Farr & Madison actually believed that the financial statements were false. Subsequent creditors, not known to Farr & Madison, are now suing based upon the deficiencies in the audit described above. Farr and Madison moved to dismiss the lawsuit against it on the basis that the firm did not have actual knowledge of falsity and therefore did not commit fraud.

Required Answer the following, setting forth reasons for any conclusions stated.

May the creditors recover without demonstrating Farr & Madison had actual knowledge of falsity?

Answer Ordinarily, users of financial statements, other than those who contracted for the audit and those known in advance to the auditor, may not recover for ordinary negligence by the auditor in the performance of an audit. Usually, recovery of damages by third parties must be based on fraud. Actual knowledge of falsity (scienter) is generally required for an action based upon fraud; however, the scienter requirement for an action based upon fraud may be satisfied by either

- Showing a reckless disregard for the truth.
- Demonstrating that the auditor was grossly negligent.

It appears that the three deficiencies in the audit by Farr & Madison might be sufficient to satisfy either approach. The deficiencies of failure to check the existence of certain receivables, collectibility of other receivables, and existence of security investments, taken collectively, if not individually, appear to show a reckless disregard for the truth by the auditor. In fact, the audit probably lacks sufficient competent evidential matter as a reasonable basis for an opinion regarding the financial statements under examination.

The audit appears to have been conducted in a woefully inadequate fashion, without regard to the usual auditing standards and procedures necessary to exercise due professional care. Therefore, the auditors were grossly negligent in the performance of their duties.

5. Part c. The Bigelow Corporation decided to liquidate. A board member suggested the possibility of electing a one calendar month liquidation pursuant to section 333 of the Internal Revenue Code. In order to determine whether this type of liquidation was desirable, Bigelow engaged Fanslow & Angelo, CPAs, to perform a tax analysis of the corporation's data and figures to ascertain the amount of dividend per share that would be taxable as dividend income to the shareholders if this method of liquidation were elected. Such a determination is largely dependent on the amount of earnings and profits present, both current and historical.

In making the computation, Fanslow and Angelo treated retained earnings as stated in the financial statements as earnings and profits for tax purposes. However, on two prior occasions transfers were made from retained earnings to stated capital upon the issuance of stock dividends. The result of failure to adjust earnings and profits to reflect these transfers was to understate the amount of taxable dividend income per share by some $20 per share.

Required Answer the following, setting forth reasons for any conclusions stated.

Do Fanslow & Angelo have any liability under the above-stated facts?

Answer Yes. Fanslow & Angelo were negligent in the performance of the task undertaken. The concept of retained earnings resembles earnings and profits for tax purposes, but it is clear they are not identical. Several adjustments are normally required to be made to reconcile one with the other. To assume retained earnings are equivalent to earnings and profits without a careful analysis of all prior years, after 1913, is to proceed at one's peril. Any competent tax accountant would be aware of the distinction. Furthermore, stock dividends have no impact on earnings and profits, but they may affect retained earnings as was the case here.

The facts are not sufficient to determine the exact amount of damages. Fanslow & Angelo would be held liable for any interest and penalties imposed upon the shareholders, and they might also be held liable for additional taxes incurred by the shareholders as a result of their erroneous advice.

MAY 1978 (Estimated time: 20 to 25 minutes)

3. Part a. A CPA firm was engaged to examine the financial statements of Martin Manufacturing Corporation for the year ending December 31, 1977. The facts revealed that Martin was in need of cash to continue its operations and agreed to sell its common stock investment in a subsidiary through a private placement. The buyers insisted that the proceeds be placed in escrow because of the possibility of a major contingent tax liability that might result from a pending government claim. The payment in escrow was completed in late November 1977. The president of Martin told the audit partner that the proceeds from the sale of the subsidiary's common stock, held in escrow, should be shown on the balance sheet as an unrestricted current account receivable. The president was of the opinion that the government's claim was groundless and that Martin needed an "uncluttered" balance sheet and a "clean" auditor's opinion to obtain additional working capital from lenders. The audit partner agreed with the president and issued an unqualified opinion on the Martin financial statements which did not refer to the contingent liability and did not properly describe the escrow arrangement.

The government's claim proved to be valid, and pursuant to the agreement with the buyers, the purchase price of the subsidiary was reduced by $450,000. This adverse development forced Martin into bankruptcy. The CPA firm is being sued for deceit (fraud) by several of Martin's unpaid creditors who extended credit in reliance upon the CPA firm's unqualified opinion on Martin's financial statements.

Required Answer the following, setting forth reasons for any conclusions stated.

Based on these facts, can Martin's unpaid creditors recover from the CPA firm?

Answer Yes. The CPA firm is guilty of a common law *deceit*, commonly referred to as "fraud." The CPA firm was associated with financial statements that were not in conformity with generally accepted accounting principles because of the failure to disclose the restriction on the cash received, as well as the contingent liability. This association constitutes the commission of an actionable tort (deceit) upon the creditors. The fact that there was no privity of contract between the creditors and the accountants is immaterial in relation to an action based on deceit. Where *deceit* is involved, the defense of lack of privity is not available. Deceit is an intentional tort, and those who engage in it must bear the burden of their wrongdoing, even though they may not have intended harm to those affected.

The common law elements of deceit in general are—

1. A false representation of a material fact made by the defendant.
2. Knowledge or belief of falsity, technically described as "scienter."
3. An intent that the plaintiff rely upon the false representation.
4. Justifiable reliance on the false representation.
5. Damage as a result of the reliance.

Clearly, the elements of deceit are present. The only element that needs further elaboration is the "scienter" requirement. About the only defense available to the CPA firm would be that it honestly believed that the government's claim was groundless based upon the president's statement. However, even if this were true, the CPA firm did not have a sufficient basis to express an unqualified opinion that the financial statements were fairly presented. The law includes not only representations made with actual knowledge or belief of falsity but also those made with a reckless disregard for the truth. The fact that the CPA firm did not intend to harm anyone is irrelevant. The CPA firm must be considered liable in light of its training, qualifications, and responsibility and its duty to those who would read, and might act upon, financial statements with which the firm is associated.

3. Part b. A CPA firm has been named as a defendant in a class action by purchasers of the shares of stock of the Newly Corporation. The offering was a public offering of securities within the meaning of the Securities Act of 1933. The plaintiffs alleged that the firm was either negligent or fraudulent in connection with the preparation of the audited financial statements which accompanied the registra-

tion statement filed with the SEC. Specifically, they allege that the CPA firm either intentionally disregarded, or failed to exercise reasonable care to discover, material facts which occurred subsequent to January 31, 1978, the date of the auditor's report. The securities were sold to the public on March 16, 1978. The plaintiffs have subpoenaed copies of the CPA firm's working papers. The CPA firm is considering refusing to relinquish the papers, asserting that they contain privileged communication between the CPA firm and its client. The CPA firm will, of course, defend on the merits irrespective of the questions regarding the working papers.

Required Answer the following, setting forth reasons for any conclusions stated.

1. Can the CPA firm rightfully refuse to surrender its working papers?
2. Discuss the liability of the CPA firm in respect to events which occur in the period between the date of the auditor's report and the effective date of the public offering of the securities.

Answer

1. No. Neither federal nor common law recognizes the validity of the privilege rule insofar as accountants are concerned. Furthermore, even where the privilege rule is applicable, it can only be claimed by the client. Only a limited number of jurisdictions recognize the rule, and these jurisdictions have by statute overridden the common law rule which does not consider such communications to be within the privilege rule. The privilege rule applies principally to the attorney-client and doctor-patient relationships.

2. The Securities Act of 1933 requires a review by the auditor who reported on the financial statements accompanying the registration statement of events in the period between the date of the auditor's report and the date of the public sale of the securities. The auditors must show that they made a reasonable investigation, had a reasonable basis for their belief, and they did believe the financial statements were true as of the time the registration statement became effective. The auditor defendants have the burden of proving that the requisite standard was met. Therefore, unless the auditors can satisfy the foregoing tests, they will be liable.

INDEX